George Tyrrell

IN SEARCH OF CATHOLICISM

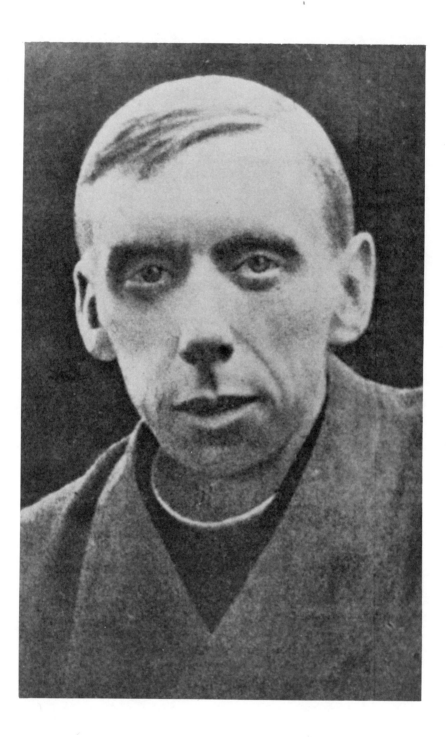

George Tyrrell

IN SEARCH OF CATHOLICISM

by David G. Schultenover, S.J.

THE PATMOS PRESS SHEPHERDSTOWN

1981

To those who have given me life
and clues to its meaning:

my mother and father
my brothers and sisters
my brother Jesuits

Imprimi Potest
Joseph J. Labaj, S.J., Provincial
Wisconsin Province of the Society of Jesus

Library of Congress Cataloging in Publication Data

Schultenover, David G., 1938–
    George Tyrrell: in search of Catholicism.

    Bibliography: p.
    Includes index.
    1. Tyrrell, George, 1861–1909. 2. Modernism—
Catholic Church—History. I. Title.
BX4705.T9S38   230'.2'0924   81-38406
ISBN 0-915762-13-7   AACR2

Manufactured in the United States of America

Preface

On 3 July 1907 the Holy Roman Office of the Inquisition issued the decree *Lamentabili sane exitu* condemning sixty-five propositions culled from the writings of unnamed persons soon to be known as modernists. Two months later, on 8 September, Pope Pius X promulgated the encyclical *Pascendi dominici gregis*, outlining and condemning the modernist doctrines. Three weeks later George Tyrrell, the foremost English "modernist,"[1] responded with a trenchant critique of the encyclical in the *Giornale d'Italia* of 26 September and the *Times* for 30 September and 1 October. For this affront, on 22 October 1907 he was excommunicated.

Three years later, to eliminate the last remnants of resistance and extend the effects of *Lamentabili* and *Pascendi*, Pius X issued the *motu proprio, Sacrorum antistitum*. It provided that an antimodernist oath be sworn by all clerics as a condition for ordination, by priests as a condition for appointment to various offices and dignities, and, at the beginning of every school year, by the rectors and professors of all canonically erected seminaries, universities, and faculties. The oath required the swearer to affirm five positive propositions, repudiate five specific errors, and give interior and unconditional assent to all the condemnations, declarations, and prescripts of *Pascendi* and *Lamentabili*.

On 31 May 1967 the Congregation for the Doctrine of the Faith quietly withdrew this oath and substituted a brief and general affirmation of faith.

What had occurred between 1907, when modernism was condemned as the "compendium of all heresies," and 1967, when the antimodernist oath was lifted, was a widespread conversion of mentality. Pope John XXIII was among the first to recognize it, though perhaps not in these terms.[2] On 25 January 1959, when he announced his intention to convoke the twenty-first ecumenical council, he caught the church completely by surprise. It was imperative that the church admit and face the consequences of a profound development: the majority of Roman Catholics had passed out of a classicist world view to an existential-historical world view; they had moved away from categories that were deductive, static, abstract, universal, and unchanging to categories that were concrete, dynamic, personal, communal, and historical—precisely those categories that the "modernists" found operative in the biblical world view and whose centuries-long neglect in Roman Catholicism they had decried.

Since the third century the Western church governed and worshipped in Latin; since the thirteenth century the church formulated its teaching in scholastic categories, and in its preaching tended to indoctrinate rather than educate. Thus clerics were trained in seminaries by hearing lectures in scholastic philosophy and theology often delivered in Latin, which they ill understood. The assumption was that nothing would or could change. Thomas's method of faith seeking understanding had degenerated into a method that was defensive, didactic, dogmatic, and—in the neo-scholastic era—enforced by Rome's coercive power. It is little wonder that the modernist effort, described by Baron Friedrich von Hügel as an ongoing attempt to express and interpret the "Old Faith" according to the best and most abiding elements of contemporary thought,[3] ran full tilt into the neo-scholastic monolith and was ground under.

Though smitten, the modernist effort was not slain. It remained vital underground and continued to operate there until, with the pontificate of Pius XII—who himself, as a young seminarian in Rome, had consorted with "modernists"—it received official, if anonymous, recognition as a legitimate and necessary aspiration. His encyclicals, *Divino afflante Spiritu* (1943) and *Humani generis* (1950), exonorated and approved the historical critical method as applied to biblical studies and gave exegetes a determinative role in church teaching. In 1964 the Pontifical Biblical Commission under Pope John XXIII issued the instruction, *Sancta Mater Ecclesia*, acknowledging the major findings of historical criticism.

Biblical studies was not the only area where rethinking and reformulation were proceeding. Certainly it was the most foundational because there one found the normative categories for interpretation called for since the Renaissance and now demanded by the modern world. Yet seminal work was progressing in all areas of the church's life—spiritual, intellectual, and pastoral—and in the decrees of Vatican II one can read the results.

I do not mean to suggest that Vatican II simply exonorated. modernism. Even the experts in modernist studies have not adequately enough sorted out and evaluated the controverted issues to be able to make such a claim; and certainly the church's magisterium will be slow to admit that in 1907 Pius X and his advisers erred by indiscriminately grouping and condemning the "modernists." I do suggest that "modernists" had asked many of the same questions addressed by Vatican II and had given tentative answers that find close parallels in the council's decrees. If one would seek a deeper appreciation of that council and its implications, one could study the history of "modernism" and the issues raised therein with rich results.

Unfortunately no comprehensive history of that period is yet available—for two reasons: first, because "modernism" is an enormously complex and far-reaching phenomenon, involving a wholesale reviewing of incarnational revelation and its institutional expression from a converted world view; second, because the antimodernist campaign set back *aggiornamento* by more than two generations. It is only now becoming possible to study the modernist era and publish findings without provoking widespread reaction. To be sure, scholars are working toward a comprehensive history, but as Lawrence Barmann observed in the preface to his study on von Hügel, what is needed first is a series of analytical monographs on the principal figures of the "modernist movement."

The present volume is a contribution to that end. Its genre is intellectual history as distinguished from institutional history, and it arises out of the conviction that it is in the former rather than the latter that the abiding interest in Roman Catholic modernism lies. As intellectual history, it aims to describe not the "modernist movement" but the intellectual development of a major contributor to the "movement" by focusing on the man as the key to his thought.

George Tyrrell's thought has a public and private aspect. His public thought is available in his published writings and can be conveniently considered under the categories of philosophy of religion and apologetics. The method used in this study was designed to lay open the foundations and genesis of these two lines of thought not only from the public perspective of published writings but especially from the private perspective of unpublished manuscripts and correspondence. The former sources allow the composition of the topography of Tyrrell's mind, the latter an inside understanding and interpretation of that topography.

It is regrettable that the sources for Tyrrell's formative years are so limited. There is only the two-volume *Autobiography and Life of George Tyrrell,* in which Tyrrell tells his own story up to 1884, the year his mother died, and Maude Petre, Tyrrell's close friend and associate of nearly ten years, completes the story. Invaluable as these volumes are, they suffer from the myopia of a self-portrait. Their view needs a complement, a full and objective biography that takes account of all manuscript as well as published sources and treats the subject with aesthetic distance as well as sympathy. That kind of biography, however, will not be possible until Rome opens its archives for the years of Pius X's pontificate.

Tyrrell's manuscript correspondence proved most valuable for the present study. The earliest extant letter, however, dates from late 1891 when Tyrrell was already thirty years old, and from that year until 1900 only a handful of correspondence remains. Not that there ever was very much. From 1891 to 1896 Tyrrell lived a secluded life in houses of study and a small mission church, and for four years following his emergence into the public eye as a writer for the *Month,* most of his communication consisted of published essays, preaching, and counseling, rather than letters. But in 1900 the scene changed, and Tyrrell's correspondence mushroomed. Alarmed by the gossip about Tyrrell's unusual prescriptions for unusual cases, ecclesiastical officials moved to mitigate the danger. Tyrrell was forthwith relieved of his position in London and ensconced in a remote Jesuit church in Richmond-in-Swaledale. There, away from the multitude who claimed his attention in London—some of them sent by the cardinal archbishop himself—he had time to answer in writing the appeals that continued to arrive daily by post. This move was a boon to historians, because as Tyrrell emerged into public life, his private life became accessible through the store of a full and remarkable correspondence.

The nature of the sources changes, therefore, as Tyrrell's life changed, and my method attempts to keep pace. Thus the reader will observe a gradual shift from dependence on published works to dependence on correspondence. There, from 1900 on, one finds a side of Tyrrell that remains largely hidden in the public works. One sees, for example, the backstage problems that drew on his energies and affected his writings; his mind and emotional state as he composed a work and reflected on it; his friends, his correspondents, the authors whose works he now had time to study and their influence on him. Also revealed in a sentence or two is the intended thrust of a work, the real points of emphasis that had been lost or obscured because he had to edit for censors. Most important, through it all one comes to know the man.

The present study, therefore, proposes to be not another description of Tyrrell's philosophy of religion and apologetic, but a description of their foundations and genesis as seen from Tyrrell's own perspective. His story is told in great detail up to and including the year 1903, whence the epilogue completes it in broad outline. That year is a convenient end point for the principal purpose of this study, because with the appearance of *Lex Orandi* and *The Church and the Future*, Tyrrell's philosophy of religion and apologetic for Roman Catholicism reached their zeniths. From 1904 on, his attention turned to polemical issues of religious and ecclesiastical polity, and his contribution to the world of religious thought declined. The full story of those troubled years remains to be told.

Acknowledgments

With profound gratitude, I wish to acknowledge my indebtedness to all who have contributed to the production of this work: To Professor Lawrence F. Barmann, who first introduced me to Tyrrell and advised and encouraged me throughout nearly a decade of research and composition; to Professor Thomas Michael Loome, who generously made available to me the results of his own enormous research. To all who facilitated my archival labors: Mrs. Katherine Pirenne, niece of Maude Petre; Sr. Teresa of the Holy Child, prioress of the Carmelite Monastery, St. Charles Square, London; Fr. Francis Edwards, archivist of the English Province of the Society of Jesus; Mr. Ronald K. Browne, former librarian at the Farm Street Jesuit Community, London; Mr. D. MacArthur, former librarian, Mr. A. Graham Mackenzie, librarian, Mr. Robert N. Smart, keeper of manuscripts, and their staff at University Library, St. Andrews; Fr. Osmund Lewry of the Blackfriars, Oxford; Mr. Peter Hebblethwaite, former editor of the *Month,* and Mme. Anne Louis-David, through whose efforts I received from the late Père André Blanchet copies of Tyrrell's letters to Bremond; Padre Antonio Gentili, who provided copies from the Semeria Papers; the earl of Halifax and his archivist, Major Thomas Ingram; Miss Elizabeth Poyser, archivist of the archdiocese of Westminster; Dr. Arthur W. Adams, dean of divinity at Magdalen College, Oxford, and keeper of the Katherine Clutton Papers; Ms. Margaret Clarke, assistant keeper of manuscripts, Fitzwilliam Museum, Cambridge; Miss Bridget Hanbury, former literary editor of the *Month;* Mr. D. Steven Corey, special collections librarian at the University of San Francisco; Fr. Leo J. Tibesar, librarian and archivist at the St. Paul Seminary, St. Paul, Minnesota; and the staffs of the British Library, the University Library, Cambridge, the Bodleian Library, Oxford, and the Bibliothèque nationale, Paris. Quotations from the Petre Papers and the Waller Papers are reproduced by permission of the British Library. I am grateful to the staff of the Donohue Rare Book Room, Gleeson Library, University of San Francisco, for permission to reproduce the illustrations used in this book. To the many who assisted in the production of the final draft: Fr. John F. X. Sheehan, S. J., and Professor Mary Jo Weaver, who offered numerous helpful criticisms; to Miss Camille Slowinski, Mrs. Ellie LaValla, and Mrs. Juanita Hoelle for their careful preparation of the typescript; and to the novices at Jesuit College, St. Paul, Minnesota, who humored me during the final revisions and assisted in the proofreading; and Sr. Mary Paton Ryan of Marquette University who read the final galleys. To Fr. Joseph J. Labaj, provincial of the Wisconsin Province of the Society of Jesus, his assistant, Fr. Patrick J. Burns, and his consultors; to Frs. Richard C. Harrington and Walter J. Stohrer, past and present rectors of Marquette University Jesuit Community, and to the Department of Theology at Marquette University, who so graciously provided me both temporal and spiritual support. To my colleagues in the Roman Catholic Modernism Working Group of the American Academy of Religion for their enduring interest and encouragement. Finally to my copyeditor, Dr. Ann Hofstra Grogg, and to the codirectors of The Patmos Press, Drs. James C. and Mary G. Holland, who insisted with care and sympathy on that elusive extra. To all, my esteem and heartfelt thanks.

Contents

Preface   v

Acknowledgments   xi

CHAPTER 1. *The Hidden Years*   3

CHAPTER 2. *The Orthodox Years (1882-96):*
Mounting an Offensive   28

CHAPTER 3. *Mediating Liberalism (1896-1900):*
Uneasy Detente   48

CHAPTER 4. *The Parting of Ways*   113

CHAPTER 5. *Drawing the Lines of Conflict*   166

CHAPTER 6. *Tyrrell's Philosophy of Religion*   188

CHAPTER 7. *The Church and the Future*   246

Epilogue   319

List of Abbreviations   361

Notes   362

Selected Bibliography   434

Index   487

George Tyrrell

IN SEARCH OF CATHOLICISM

CHAPTER 1

The Hidden Years

A TRAGIC INTERPLAY: HISTORY AND PERSONALITY

George Tyrrell was inclined by nature to a life of study and prayer, quiet reflection broken only by the cure of souls and occasional essays on spiritual matters. Instead, for a complex of reasons, some apparent, others obscure, he chose a life of scholarship and polemics, thereby squandering his inheritance and in the process incurring dismissal from his religious order and excommunication from his church. His personal suffering aside, the real tragedy for some was the waste of his gift as a spiritual master, and they lamented this greater work he left undone and the higher place he might have won.[1] But that is hypothetical and mere conjecture. Tyrrell's importance to history pertains to what in fact he did accomplish, what place he did establish in the church, and the reasons why.

These concerns are caught within the maze of Tyrrell's complex personality, or rather in the interplay of his personality with historical exigencies.[2] One must seek there the factors that determined him to the path he in fact chose over the path he might have chosen. Some of these factors are monumentally obvious; others are subtle but nonetheless compelling. A personality such as Tyrrell's, composed of competing elements, exists in a state of unsteady equilibrium that can be upset or propelled in a certain direction by pressures which would go undetected in a less sensitive personality. Tyrrell was extraordinarily alive to pressures of all sorts and felt keenly the interdependence and interaction of all components of life. He readily saw worlds of meaning in faint movements that most men pass by unseeing.

3

All we can say is that our fate is determined by straws, one way or the other; and that the greatest events in history—let alone the little events of a little life—can all be shown to depend, in some part of their course, on some microscopic vibration of air or ether. The truth is that everything great and small, without exception, depends on everything else; and if there be not a God over all, it is hardly worth labouring to adapt ourselves to conditions so incalculable and complex, and we must turn to the East for light to be tranquil and indifferent.[3]

In the absence of other sources, the succeeding pages will draw heavily on Tyrrell's self-portrait, with a dependence that could yield an excessively subjective and therefore inaccurate picture. But Gabriel Daly, an acute observer of Tyrrell's character, lays to rest undue concern. "Tyrrell's more personal writings contain a continuous and rich vein of self-analysis. He was a deeply introspective person, quietly fascinated by what he discovered in himself, yet in no way narcissistic; capable of describing his findings, yet curiously innocent of vanity. Few men have made their conscious minds so available to others as he; and fewer still have been less concerned to preserve a facade." Still, a caution must be observed. Tyrrell's passion for truth, especially about himself, led him at times to overstate his case, so that, as Daly advised, the reader "must simply learn to dilute to taste."[4]

UNTIMELY BORN . . .

George Tyrrell was the last of four children born to William Henry Tyrrell and his wife Mary Chamney. Melinda, born about 1849 or 1850, died in infancy. Willie was born in November 1851, then Louisa, affectionately called "Louy," in February 1859. Finally, George was born on 6 February 1861, at 91 Dorset Street, Dublin.

Probably the most significant influence on young George's personality was a negative one: the absence of his father, who died two months before George was born. What George learned of his father he got almost entirely through the not-unbiased eyes of his mother. William Henry Tyrrell was a talented journalist. For years he subedited the Dublin *Evening Mail,* one of the earliest Protestant Tory organs in Ireland, and earned the respect and admiration of the public. Unfortunately that is all he seems to have earned from his wife, too. She respected and admired him, but she also feared rather than loved him. They were a fine match for wit and satire, and they enjoyed moments of high mutual entertainment. But those same gifts could become weapons. Apparently William had a violent temper. He had managed to contain it during courtship, but it burst upon the marriage scene with increasing frequency, and ill temper carried the day.[5]

Doubtless one reason for William's short temper was that he worked extraordinarily long hours for meager wages, and when he died in December 1860, he left his wife and children practically penniless. "I don't know how it can be done, darling," he lamented to his wife the morning he died, "but if anyone can do it, you can."[6]

So she did, with help from relatives and by the talents of her children. Willie, now age nine, was sent off to be educated in the care of Rev. James Bell, husband to cousin Lizza Tyrrell. For Willie it was the beginning of a scholarly career that was promising but brief, as he died at age twenty-seven. The cause of death was laid to a fall he had suffered as a child that had left him physically deformed and sickly, and consequently embittered.

George and Louy went with their mother to live with her brother Robert Chamney who was himself not well off. When he ran into financial trouble, the children were entrusted to a Mrs. Meyers, a kindly old Methodist lady, while their mother went to seek employment. This move was only the first of many changes of residence for the Tyrrells. Indeed George recalled that his mother seemed to court change for its own sake, as she uprooted the family sometimes two and three times in a single year. There were eighteen moves in the eighteen years that George spent at home.

The constant changing of residences was probably the second most significant factor in young George's development. Vagabondage sowed in him an insecurity and restlessness that could not but affect his later behavior and perhaps even determined the course of his life in the liberal rather than the conservative direction. Cast adrift with neither home nor father and often without supervision of any kind, George was to develop that bent of character that relentlessly searches. Never secure in the present, he cast a line either to the past or to the future, imagining that things had been or were going to be better. With a pervasive sense of drifting, he naturally and constantly sought footing. He was sure that footing could be found, but he was never quite sure that his foot had found it.[7]

It is important to note that, on the one hand, Tyrrell's goal was a resting place. On the other hand, since he never was nor ever could be satisfied with what he found, his life must be characterized as a search. Caught between the conservative's security and the liberal's questing, Tyrrell was curiously detached from and critical of both poles, a paradoxical position he felt to be in some degree a misfortune, as it was impossible to maintain with equanimity. He was simultaneously two classes of men: the conservative who cannot bear to wrench himself free from the comfort of his collectivity long enough to realize his need to stretch out, and the liberal who is too attached to his individualism to benefit from the natural restraints of the collectivity. For Tyrrell it was as if each of the two classes in him craved in the other what it lacked in itself, but neither was uncomfortable enough to risk changing. So Tyrrell fluctuated between the two poles. Neither a conservative nor a liberal, he was a hybrid at disequilibrium. Discomfort with his current position was his only position, and that position, formed from childhood, was to dominate all his later interactions, both private and public, personal and theological.

. . . REARED WITHOUT SHAM . . .

Terrors were the earliest recollections of George Tyrrell's childhood, "the speechless terrors of infancy, that could not be explained or alleviated."[8] George woke to consciousness in the arms not of his mother but of Mrs. Meyers, to whom he and Louy had been entrusted. She was wonderfully warm and inviting. His mother, with whom he was at length reunited, seemed pale and unattractive by comparison. Still, he recalled that it was not long before he found great pleasure in her company. She became companion and playmate as well as mother. She could transport herself into her children's world without pretense or condescension but with a sympathetic sense of reality and authenticity that George was quick to perceive and appreciate. It was she who etched his character with an egalitarian spirit and practiced his discrimination between reality and unreality, authenticity and sham.

Dangens Farm, not far from Portarlington and Mountmellick, was the family's first home after being reunited. Here terror passed to pleasure as George "woke to the joy of sunshine and flowers and groves and fields." "It was the first sip of life's cup, and surely it was the sweetest, the best, and the purest." Here, too, began his "artificial education, religious and secular."[9] This, however, was less than sweet, engaged in mostly out of envy and competition with Louy, who would repeat her lessons before her sibling with an inflammatory air of sophistication. Not to be bested, George demanded and received, at the age of three, the rudiments of reading, writing, and numbers.

His first religious recollections were some of his happiest. The family would sit evenings before a great fire, while the mother would draw out of her great Evangelical store endless tales and hymns to the enraptured delight of the children.[10] But George's first conceptions of God and divine righteousness were considerably less wholesome. They fell out of a kind of moral picture book

> in which was portrayed a certain *Ugly Jane*, with her hair in a net, who was addicted to the evil habit of making grimaces before the glass; upon which a justly enraged heaven caught her *flagrante delicto* in the act of putting out her tongue, and there fixed her for ever to the consequences of her wilful choice—surely an apt illustration of the irreparable and eternal consequences of mortal sin! Well—He alone knows why—but that young lady, dreeing her sad doom, served as my phantasm of God for years and years; and even now, if the word is pronounced as we were taught to pronounce it—*Gaud* (as distinct from the short-vowelled gods of the heathen) that grotesque image is the first thing that starts into my imagination. "Jesus" was a somewhat insipid, long-haired female, derived very possibly from a religious picture. But, for some reason or other, I personified heaven as an old woman after the image and likeness of Mrs. Meyers, with a huge cap tied under her chin and a red plaid shawl folded across her capacious bosom.[11]

Sometime in 1864 and for seven years thereafter, the free-spirited and quite un-Calvinistic upbringing that George was enjoying at the hands of his mother received some straightening at the hands of his childless Aunt Melinda, who joined the Tyrrell household on the death of her husband. Whereas George's mother had not pressured the children, they now heard a great deal more about religion than they cared to, and regular attendance at unintelligible services became a strict injunction. Sundays became "a day of dreariness and funereal solemnity. . . . Above all, the sitting still and keeping silent and general repression, made churchgoing an agony all the years of my childhood."[12]

Aunt Melinda's redoubtable efforts, however, were rendered largely futile through the countereffect of George's irreverent and irreligious brother Willie, who rejoined the family for that same period. Severe pain in his back and general ill health forced him home from boarding school. The importance of Willie cannot be overestimated. He was the principal male figure during seven critical years of George's development, including adolescence. George and Louy regarded Willie with religious awe. "He was the director and inspirer of our games from his throne on the sofa; our oracle on a thousand matters, not reached by formal instructions; and also our assiduous tormentor and tease."[13] Predisposed by the need for a father figure, George identified with Willie in all ways, but in none more significant than in his religious attitude.

Moral imperative never worked with George, and nowhere less than in formal education. As long as learning could be made to seem a game, an adventure, or even tinkering—a proclivity awakened early in his life by his favorite uncle Robert Chamney—George eagerly threw himself into it. But "as soon as lessons ceased to be a privilege and became an obligation I took the attitude of a minimiser and did as little as I could."[14] He learned to control that attitude, but he never lost it.

George's first year of school was no challenge whatsoever. For one thing, he had already learned at home what was being taught in school, so he was able to devote his powers of inventiveness not to lessons but to scheming, and still carry off, week after week, the blue ribbon for highest honors.

> Thanks to my mother's teaching I easily passed as a "good boy," and was only once in jeopardy of Miss Ball's cane, owing to my holding my pen as I hold it at this moment, close to the point, between index and thumb. Do writing masters never reflect that hands are constructed differently? When I held it in the orthodox fashion my hand shook and large blobs of ink defiled the virgin page, for which I got scolded. Hence I learned to keep my eye on Miss Ball, and when she looked at me I held my pen correctly and affected abstraction, as it were pausing in my labour; when she looked away I produced satisfactory results in my own unorthodox way. My God! how like my present methods![15]

For another thing, formal learning did not begin to engage his powers of imagination. What others considered exciting competition and high achievement, he considered mere routine and the deadliest of virtues.

This same attitude is evident in George's approach to games, where one can see foreshadowed his later comportment with religious and ecclesiastical superiors. From the beginning he regarded himself, and was regarded, as an outsider. His interest lasted only long enough for him to analyze the game and understand its nature.

> It was the improvised novelty that ever appealed to me. . . . Extemporised games and plays, that involved invention, were part of my idleness, but rule-governed games I never cared for. . . .
>   I also disliked and resented the discipline of those games, being compelled to obey arbitrary rules and being ordered about by my equals, robed in an authority as brief and imaginary as the Emperor's invisible clothes. . . . I liked other forms of exercise like gymnastics and fighting and tearing about, and climbing and courting danger; provided it was informal, and not obligatory or according to rule.

To his classmates games were serious business. To George they were occasions to be suffered through by private bantering and gossip. "Thus I made myself odious to the heads of teams and elevens, and fell into disgrace very early in my career."[16] Still, he was a gregarious youth and well liked by his peers, but surely more for his satire and wit than for his athletic skills.

It was not simply lack of challenge that led to George's idleness in school. Changing schools nearly as often as changing residences must share the blame. His attitude of detachment and humbug was already set before he found himself in one school long enough to form any semblance of a stable relationship with his associates. He played *his* games, but being a clever and solitary child, classmates and teachers never caught on to his scheming quickly enough to force him to play *theirs*.

Then too, George's immoderate love of liberty and egalitarianism worked against traditional scholastic achievement. He resented moral coercion of any kind, but none so intensely as the reproach of Willie's brilliance and success, which was constantly flung in his face. To these goads George reacted simply by resisting. For Willie schooling was a self-chosen way. Had their roles been reversed, George felt, Willie would have responded in a similar manner. Neither could tolerate domination by another will.

Willie had been attending Rathmines School in Dublin. His kind and gentle headmaster, Dr. Charles W. Benson, was so impressed with him that he offered to take charge of his younger brother's education without payment. Accordingly, in November 1869 George enrolled in Rathmines School and for a year matched expectations all round. The matter for study was still close enough to what he had learned at home not to tax him in the least, and he swept all the prizes at the examination. But by the ease of ill-gotten gains he fell prey to not one but two evils: "first, a confirmed habit of idleness; secondly, an overweening conceit of my own powers."[17]

In the six years he spent under Dr. Benson, George learned surprisingly little from books. But in his teacher, who spent endless informal hours with his boys, George read the greater lessons of life about openheartedness, generosity, and compassion. "Dearest and best of men! it is impossible to do justice to his character or to estimate the influence of his personality on my own. . . . There was too much of the Gospel, too little of the Law, in Dr. Benson's dispensation."[18]

It was from Dr. Benson that Tyrrell acquired his first taste for religion—High Church religion at that, as the headmaster, although Evangelical at heart, loved liturgical observance. He would open school each morning with an abbreviated choral matins and seize the occasion critically to expose some passage of scripture. To these services, George confessed, "I owe my acquaintance, not only with the text, but with the sense of the Scriptures, and also my liturgical taste, which, later, helped me on towards Catholicism."[19]

. . . UNGODLY BECOME

In the matter of behavior, George described himself as having been, at least until about age fourteen, essentially godless and amoral. If he shrank from sin, it was because sin offended his natural sensibilities, not because sin offended God. "Otherwise I had now, reflexly and deliberately, given up all attempt at self-restraint, and was, for moral scepticism, an unconscious disciple of Nietzsche."[20] Fear of hell or the desire of heaven never swayed him in the least. Nor were they ever a motive for him in later life.

This natural godlessness amidst generally pious surroundings is quite anomalous, and Tyrrell was hard pressed to explain it. He pointed first to himself, then to his brother Willie. For his part, until the age of nine or ten, he was no different from other children who mechanically imitate the motions of religious convention. But surprisingly early he began to require reasons. "The fact is I began to think long before I was capable of thinking, and became a monstrosity in consequence."[21] The blind repetition of formulas with no appreciation of their underlying significance became insufferable. It was mere playacting. But no one was on hand to show him the difference between symbols and the realities symbolized. Even had someone advanced appropriate images of that unseen world, George was not yet capable of comprehending them. At first he identified religious truth with absurd anthropomorphisms and assigned them to the realm of fairy tales, so when he came to debunk fairy tales, he debunked religious truth as well.

With advancing age he was allowed more self-determination in the practice of religion. But as he found prayer and the intangible world of God, heaven, hell, and sin increasingly less attractive, he simply dropped them. It was not a matter of ideology. "It was simply my first self-chosen attitude in regard to religion; I did not cease to be a believer, but, from a non-believer, I became an unbeliever at about the age of ten."[22]

Incapable at this time of inference, George's only real guide in the matter was authority. Enter brother Willie. In all intellectual matters (where George then placed religion) it was Willie's views, not his mother's, that counted. And it was at this time that Willie fell under the irreligious influence of his master at the university and completely and definitively abandoned belief. Willie generally reserved his argument for his mother, since George was too young, but George was a sharper listener than they realized, and from the controversies between the two he precociously became aware of the process and reasons for passing from belief to unbelief.

Willie's unintended tutoring did not last long at this juncture. Frustrations and bitterness over his affliction led to increasingly frequent paroxysms of rage and made it advisable that he should board entirely at school. Since Louy, too, was now boarding at school, Willie's departure left George at the age of eleven bereaved of his spiritual adviser and alone with his mother as sole confidant and companion. These events conspired to turn a carefree child prematurely gray and seasoned on matters about which most children care not a whit. From an already independent child was born an even more independent young man. That was not all to the good. The premature awareness and assumption of responsibilities carried over into adult life and led Tyrrell to feel the problems of others as his own and to grow increasingly irritated with the increasing burden. ACоА

TOWARD ROME À *REBOURS*

In 1872 George Tyrrell received his first sympathetic introduction to Roman Catholicism. It came in the person of Anne Kelly, the maid-of-all-work at Peter Place, where the reduced family of two was now living. Her bright and cheery ways instantly captured George's affection, and her kitchen became his frequent haunt, as she would delight him with songs and stories. Her charm aside, George inclined to take indiscriminately to whomever he met of whatever status—his was a thoroughly democratic society. An early need to love and be loved, or at least accepted, seemed to develop in him an "unconscious *finesse*" for differences among people that allowed him to speak to each in his or her own language. It also fostered in him a tendency to dignify all his relations. "In my early days, far more than now, all my geese were swans, and if I admired anything I admired everything." Anne Kelly was one of his early swans, so much so that when his mother, who was also fond of Anne, would slip into controversy over religious differences, George found himself rejoicing "when it seemed to me that the weaker party had triumphed, and my sympathies were all with Rome, or, rather, with Anne Kelly."[23]

George also had a surprisingly advanced appreciation of paradox and irony and a fascination for the forbidden, which played straight into the hands of Romanism. He found himself with an "anxiety to say something in favour of so preposterous a religion as Popery; while my secret unbelief made me find little objection to the gnats of Romanism after the camels of Christianity" to which Willie had introduced him. He began surreptitiously to examine Roman prayer books and manuals and found to his surprise much the same sort of Christianity he had previously assumed to be an exclusively Protestant preserve. He also found much that was silly. Still, "there was so much more to know about it than about bald, Low-Church Protestantism; it was so much more complex and mysterious, and had moreover . . . the spell of being not only novel and paradoxical, but even dangerous, wicked and forbidden."[24] He claimed, however, that his interest was not in religion as such, but simply in paradox and novelty, and it fell dormant as soon as he and his mother abandoned Peter Place and Anne Kelly.

About this same time George was moving into adolescence, and his behavior, particularly toward his mother, assumed the pattern of Willie's and his father's. When his mother could no longer manage his tantrums, she resorted to the tactic she had used on Willie and in 1873 packed him off to Middleton College, County Cork, a school with a reputation for severity. George felt that this reputation, especially in his case, was richly deserved, but in retrospect he considered his time there a healthy experience. Unfortunately it lasted only one term. Ill health put his mother out of work and out of income, so the boy returned to Rathmines School and the easier gospel of Dr. Benson.

The following year a series of those straws that George later saw as fate-determining fell across his path and turned him unwittingly toward Rome. First, his Aunt Melinda died and left an inheritance that allowed him to board with one of Dr. Benson's masters. This move put him near Willie, so he was now able regularly to visit his elder, though still on bended knee. Shortly, however, George's capacity for abstraction awakened, and with that his relationship with Willie moved toward intimacy.

One day, while browsing in his master's library, George lit upon Joseph Butler's *Analogy,* a book he had seen in Willie's room.[25] Out of a desire to peer into Willie's world and spurred by his master's taunt that he would not understand a word of it, George plowed through the book. Later, back at Willie's, he was careful to allude to it. Willie, at first amused, probed his brother to expose his pretense, but amusement passed to amazement at what this fourteen-year-old had grasped. Willie then darkened and proceeded methodically to annihilate Butler's arguments. Still, the seed of apologetics was sown in George's mind, and the long germination began.

Also about this time a chance remark during a scoffing match with a classmate over the "ritualistic extravagances" of certain other classmates stirred George's earlier fascination with the paradoxical and mysterious complexities of Romanism. St. Bartholomew's, George remarked, was regarded in Dublin as "mildly High Church" and "a nest of Jesuitry." Whereupon his companion, who had introduced him to more than one vice, countered that "it was nothing like so bad as Grangegorman Church." Grangegorman— the music of the sound and the suggestion of perversity caused the name to stick "in my ear as a mote might have stuck in my eye."[26]

On Easter Day 1875 that name came echoing back. George had returned home for vacation, and, as his mother's authority still counted for something, he had to announce where he would attend services that day: "the name 'Grangegorman' rose chancewise to my memory; and, learning that it was not very far . . . , I announced my intention of going there." It was a church shot through with popery, even to birettas and cassocks, with as advanced a case of sacramentalism as could be found in the Church of Ireland. What struck Tyrrell most was the altar in place of a communion table. By some undifferentiated instinct he sensed that the difference was infinite,

> that it meant a totally different religion, another order of things altogether, of which I had no experience. Naturally my fundamental assumption was that the religion I was brought up in was the only authorised and tenable form of Christianity; that popery was utterly indefensible except as a paradox, and for the sake of shocking Protestant propriety. But here now was something more piquant; popery in a Protestant Church and using the Book of Common Prayer. I cannot doubt that it was the wrongness, the soupcon of wickedness or at least of paradox, that faintly fascinated me. . . . I had almost discovered a new sin, and found the sensation novel and agreeable.[27]

The following summer George returned again and again to Grangegorman and found his first impression deepened. But he knew that opposition would mount, particularly from his mother, so he began to prepare a case as he always did for his first loves. At first it was not a matter of religious fervor but of having chosen a side in an argument for which he would fight as for his very life. He trained all his powers on the reasons for his choice in much the same way that, as a child, he would dissect a toy to see how it worked and maybe improve on it, always with a view to denying mystery as long as possible. But here was undeniable mystery.

Further study and discussion with another companion, an epicure of High Churchism, revealed that there was far more to Grange-gormanism than George at first dreamed possible. It pointed to an eonian rootedness and stability that could not be shaken by some sixteenth-century squabble with Rome, and he sensed that he could not rest until he got to the very bottom of it.

True to his own instincts and patterns of character, Tyrrell configured himself to a method that would direct him through Anglo-Catholicism to Roman Catholicism. His religious evolution might more accurately be described as a *de*volution. Driven by the need for consistency and coherence, he began at the fringes of confessional practices and worked his way backward, through externals, to the heart and center. It was in some sense, he said,

> the story of Newman *à rebours*. In that pure soul the presence of God in the voice of conscience was from the first . . . as self-evident as the fact of his own existence; although the outward evidence of the world's condition seemed to him to make for atheism, and to stand as a cumulative difficulty against this luminous interior intuition. . . . To me this conception came at the end, and not at the beginning. Not merely was my earliest reason in revolt against the external, fetichistic God of the popular imagination, but when I came to hear of sacramental and supernatural indwelling I conceived it in the literal terms in which it was expressed, as the ingress of the external Deity into the soul—a notion, if possible, more unreal and more make-believe than the other—but of the natural union of the soul with God, as with the very ground of her being, I was too inquisitive, too eager for clearness, to accept the popular materialism; and of the spiritual truth I had learned nothing beyond words: *Foris Te quaerebam et intus eras*.[28]

Personal needs required that Tyrrell identify with his cause not merely on the level of idea but on the experiential level of worship and morals as well, else it would be mere playacting and sham, behavior he found utterly revolting in others. But he had to begin where he was—on the outside. He found it excruciating to begin again to parrot prayers and don the trappings of religion, as this was playacting at its most shameful. But he would neither admit his indirection nor even consider it, so determined was he to make the experience real.

Added to the pain of living with himself in this state of impersonation—he had gone so far as to conceal crucifixes and images in his room and to indulge in even more distinctively papish mischief such as sleeping on boards and using iron girdles and disciplines—was the pain of moral reform. It was not reform in the sense of a converted sinner, since at this time Tyrrell still had no sense of sin.

Rather it was a clinical or philosophical reform, in the sense of self-mastery, and it did violence to his spirit, as it lacked the humanizing motives of faith, love, and sorrow. These did not enter his life until the spring of 1876.

George was in just the wrong frame of mind for making a vocational choice. Nonetheless, in late 1875 he determined to go the distance. He would enter the clerical state and give his life to the service of the church and the cause of religion. His course was set. Now almost any straw crossing his path in whatever direction would shift him ineluctably toward Rome.

One such straw fell in March 1876 when he and his mother were on the move again. They had an option on two furnished apartments. As his mother could not make up her mind, George came down on the side of the one belonging to a Miss Lynch for the sole reason that she was Roman Catholic, although for his mother he invented other reasons. The implication of that choice, he admitted, was that he harbored a deep-down wish "that even Romanism should be defensible. . . . There was no religion or faith in the wish, no love of truth as such, but only a desire that the truth might lie in a certain direction." Miss Lynch was for Tyrrell a symbol of that as yet-unreached center toward which he gravitated. She happened along, or rather George and his mother happened on her, just when he was passing through the most sensitive and tangled stage of his odyssey. "This quiet, holy, unselfish little woman," he once confessed, "had more to do with my destiny than any other," not by overt prosyletizing—that was not her way—but simply by being who she was.[29] She provided the atmosphere, but not the precise occasion for conversion. That was still to come.

For several months yet Tyrrell existed in a painful state of fakery. He wore the wedding garment, but was not allowed into the feast. Something was still lacking, he knew not what. He longed for some breakthrough that would authenticate his being. He was close to despair when, ironically, tragedy renewed his will. On 19 August 1876, after a brief but virulent illness, his brother Willie died. It was a severe blow. The two previous months had kindled a great hope in George for Willie and their relationship. Willie had been home on holiday, and the two spent endless hours in intimate conversation on the deepest issues of life. George thought he detected in Willie a wish to believe, and, perhaps more significantly, he began at last to feel real affection for him. Now all that was ended. Willie's death was a necessary, if cruel, lesson. Willie could not now repay George's affection with affection, but he gave him something more precious. He was the altar of sacrifice for his brother's reason. "[Willie's death] brought me rudely face to face with the problem of life's meaning and value, and made me *feel* what my rationalism had taught me for so many years, that what most men lived and fought for was mere vapour and illusion; that there was no logical or defensible resting-place between the ark of God and the carrion that floated on the surrounding waters—between divinity and piggery."[30]

Now more contemptuous than ever of ordinary life and increasingly anxious to experience as true "the fair dreams of Catholicism," George plunged, like Augustine, into the lives of the saints, men and women who like himself contemned mediocrity. Montalembert's *Monks of the West (1861-70)* inflamed him with the need to be "not merely respectably moral" but enthusiastic and "wholly God-possessed."[31] His prayer suddenly became real, and at last he began to care for Catholicism rather as a life than as a truth.

On 21 March 1877—he remembered few dates so precisely—feeling unusually hopeless about the state of his reform, Tyrrell paused in his reading of compline and "straight in the teeth of [his] Protestant conscience" prayed to Saint Benedict, whose portrait by Montalembert was still spinning in his head. He resumed reading at the words: *Quoniam in me speravit, liberabo eum; protegam eum quoniam cognovit nomen meum; clamabit ad me et ego exaudiam eum; cum ipso sum in tribulatione, eripiam eum et glorificabo eum.* "I have lived on that and two or three similar coincidences ever since."[32]

BREACH WITH ANGLICANISM

Another straw to cross Tyrrell's path at this time and shift him from a perilous course was the influence of Robert Dolling, the later famous and sometimes infamous Father Dolling, Anglican churchman, social reformer, scourge of politicians, and bane of bishops. Dolling was still a layman at this juncture, but he had an insider's knowledge of Anglo-Catholicism from his association at Trinity College, Cambridge. Ophthalmia forced him to quit the university, and upon his mother's death he rejoined his father's household in Mountjoy Square, Dublin. There he devoted his free time to aiding the poor and counseling young workingmen.

Exactly how Dolling and Tyrrell met is not known, but Tyrrell reported that Dolling's first notice of him was due to some skeptical remark Tyrrell dropped as the two walked from church early one Sunday morning. Upon questioning, Dolling learned that Tyrrell had been indulging in Catholic practices under the influence of Dr. William Maturin of Grangegorman—receiving communion, even confessing his sins, and generally finding himself "in danger of becoming a narrow precisionist in ascetical theory." Dolling was totally out of sympathy with the "Jansenistic narrowness and Tory High Churchism" of Dr. Maturin, so he then and there instructed Tyrrell on his excesses and began to shore up his "desultory knowledge of the Christian religion" with the "more *tout-ensemble* and harmonious conception" of Samuel Wilberforce, Henry Liddon, and the like. "Thus I seemed to leave the narrow lanes and byways of controversy for the royal highroad of Catholic truth."[33]

Dolling was very sympathetic to Roman Catholicism. He saw it as a religion of the people and for the poor, but a religion fettered by Vaticanism with its niggling dogmatic subtleties. His way was to sweep aside all pettiness and compulsive ritualism in the interest of the people. Whether to hold a prayer meeting or a high mass depended not on church doctrine but on the needs of those in attendance. "'The Sabbath for man, and not man for the Sabbath,' was the key-note of his broad, human-hearted religion—something of which I had, as yet, no experience at all." But Tyrrell learned well and passed it on. "All my love of the *benignitas et humanitas Dei Salvatoris nostri;* all that people care for in 'Nova et Vetera'; all my evangelical sympathies; all my revolt against the Pharisee and the canon-lawyer, is the outgrowth of the seeds of his influence."[34]

In rectifying Tyrrell's course, however, Dolling had not allowed for the former's rationalism. While the mystical and philosophical Christianity of Liddon and Wilberforce appealed to Tyrrell, he found its ecclesiastical incarnation jejune and incoherent. He needed a religious system that was consistent, historically as well as intellectually. Thus his rationalism carried him further than Dolling was himself prepared to go.

Disabused of Grangegormanism, Tyrrell was left without sacramental consolations, an aching void he sought to fill by the only other means at hand—the Roman Catholic Church. True to Dolling's spirit, he began now to steal into Roman churches for mass and benediction and even confession, but he refrained from communicating because communion under one kind was intolerably papish. Instead he continued to communicate at Grangegorman. He did not tell Dolling of his duplicity but kept his own counsel, arguing that "the ignorant intolerance of the Romish priests ought not to stand in the way of availing myself of their services, since we were all Catholics alike."[35]

At this point it seemed that Rome and even the priesthood

would claim Tyrrell. Dolling himself had predicted it. Several times he had told Tyrrell that Rome would be his only resting place because he needed a position of finality, a dogmatic religion. Only years later did Tyrrell understand Dolling's meaning—that he had to accede to the experimental method and see beliefs not as products of inquiry and rational discourse but as laws growing out of life itself. His chance to experiment free from the censure of family and friends was close at hand.

In October 1878, under Dolling's encouragement, Tyrrell matriculated at Trinity College, Dublin, with ordination as a vague possibility. That goal was quickly vitiated, however, when Grangegorman initiated proceedings quietly to excommunicate Tyrrell for giving scandal by attending Roman Catholic services. Dolling, who was seen as Tyrrell's principal seducer, had a stormy interview with the Grangegormanites but effected nothing. Exasperated, he decided to shake the dust from his feet and invited Tyrrell to join him. Nothing more was keeping him in Dublin, as his father had died the previous September, so he arranged to move to London and there direct a guild and semireligious club for postal workers. He hoped to show Tyrrell a sane Anglo-Catholicism in action and thereby prevent his terminal step to Rome.

Tyrrell accepted the offer, but with ulterior motives. He was even then looking for a way to test out his desires to become not only a Roman Catholic but a priest and even—finality of finalities—a Jesuit. The latter for two reasons: "first, because I wanted to live wholly for the Catholic cause, and I believed the Society worked for it *per fas et nefas;* secondly, because I thought that no other religious Order would have me, whereas the Society was lax and unscrupulous."[36]

Tyrrell had a number of misconceptions about the Society of Jesus that would later yield to his own experience. He never thought of it as a religious order but merely as some loosely federated organization for propaganda. Nor did he realize that his spiritual bent toward monasticism would not be satisfied in the Jesuit order. Indeed, had he sorted out early enough his confusions over the several styles of religious life, he might never have become a Jesuit.[37]

CROSSING THE THRESHOLD OF ROME . . .

There were other and deeper questions raised by his decision to fly to London. He would be abandoning his mother and sister, whom he loved and who loved him as life itself. Was it right? Was it loving? Was it even just? Tyrrell did not then face those questions, but years later, when he was left as sole survivor of his father's line, they fell on him with sickening force.

> Looking back on this crooked, selfish, untruthful past, is it more antecedently likely that my motive was interested or disinterested; pure or impure; truth or illusion? Can evil be the path of good? Had I been faithful to duty all along; had I worked hard at school and after; had I left aside problems that really did not concern me; had I stayed at home and supported my mother and sister, and made their sad narrow lives a little wider and brighter, would not God have given me light had it been needful for my salvation? Would not my chances of salvation have been better than they are now? Have I done so much good to others, who had no claim on me, as to atone for my neglect of those who had every claim? What have I given up or forsaken for the service of God, as I suppose some would call it, except my plain duty?

But his duty was not all that plain. He countered:

> Had I lived at home, instead of going on this wild-goose chase after abstractions and ideals, I might have made common what has remained sacred; I might have broken those hearts whose love was everything to me, and to which my love was everything. That is my faint hope, and the salve of my conscience, when I think, with bitterness, how I abandoned the life of affection for the service of so barren a mistress as truth, and let the substance of life escape me in the pursuit of shadows.

Nonetheless, with the abandon of youth he bade farewell and sailed for London where, he remarked with black humor, "I landed . . . and opened this new era of my life on the Feast of All Fools, 1879."[38]

Failure of the experiment with Anglo-Catholicism was a foregone conclusion, and making for England was like making for Rome. As Dolling had disabused Tyrrell of Grangegormanism, Anglicanism of any form was suspect. It was easy for him to conclude that High Church worship in England made no more historical sense than it did in Ireland. It was not the "utterance of the great communion of the faithful, past and present, of all ages and nations" but "merely of a few irresponsible agents acting in defiance of the community to which they belonged." The Roman services, on the other hand, however perfunctory and graceless, impressed him more than ever with their sense of reality, their "continuity that took one back to the catacombs; here was no need of, and therefore no suspicion of, pose or theatrical parade; its aesthetic blemishes were its very beauties for me in that mood." It was the sense, the feeling, the mood that in the end settled matters, and Tyrrell admitted as much. "When I came to London my mind was not free and impartial; I felt it would be Rome or nothing."[39]

Just then another straw crossed Tyrrell's path. One day as he walked past a Catholic publishing company, Paul Féval's *Jesuits* (1877), a "perfervid eulogium" of the Society of Jesus, caught his eye. He recalled his former curiosity about that order and the parting advice of Miss Lynch that if he should become a priest he should be a Jesuit, as "they are very learned and very holy men."[40] Then and there he bought the book and consumed it with ardor. It confirmed his fondest imaginings of that order as a militant energy marshaled in the cause of Catholicism and the Faith. Subsequently Tyrrell would learn how uncritical Féval was, but for the moment his vision of the zeal and courage of Ignatius and companions, who bore calumny and outrage solely for others and the glory of God, played into Tyrrell's not entirely healthy self-image and swept him off his feet.

> I had been much more anxious about my personal sanctification during the past year; more for the sake of others and as a condition of the priesthood than for any really solid conviction of the worth of my own soul. Then, as now, I felt myself a sort of Balaam, forced . . . to slave in the cause of Christ; . . . nor have I ever seriously considered my own salvation as more than a slight probability. . . . I have always inverted Kant's ethical rule, which bids us so to act that our conduct may be a guide for all to follow, in so far as my interest has been primarily in the conduct of others, and dependently in my own. This grave moral defect I ascribe to the practical destruction of my own character and personality in early life, and a consequent pessimism and despair in my own regard. I am like one who has lost his own fortune through imprudence, and devotes his life to warning others off the same shoals.[41]

Hardly two weeks after setting foot in London, Tyrrell was knocking on the Jesuits' door at Farm Street to seek instructions. He was put in the care of Fr. Albany Christie who, though kindness itself, was distressingly simple. He gave Tyrrell a penny catechism and told him to return when he had mastered its profundities. It was an insult to Tyrrell's intelligence. Nonetheless his trenchant mind fell before a wholly questionable syllogism from James Mumford's anti-Protestant apologetic, *The Catholic Scripturist* (1662), which Father Christie had also loaned him: "Given that there must be a Church on earth claiming infallibility, no body that disclaims it can be that Church; and if only one body claims it, that must be the Church."[42] Tyrrell's loathing of insincerity was at war with his passion for faith. Rebellion was crushed and his rigorous intellect straightened to conform to his will to believe. On 18 May 1879 he was received into the Roman Catholic Church.

. . . AND OF JESUITISM

Immediately upon the ceremony of reception, Father Christie inquired about Tyrrell's plans for the future. Tyrrell hesitated to admit what seemed outrageous presumption—that he was thinking of becoming a priest and even a Jesuit—because he feared that his past moral and scholastic excesses would be viewed with impassable displeasure. But Father Christie took the re-creation of even conditional baptism quite literally. Without further ado, he sent Tyrrell off to Fr. George Porter, who not only made light of the assumed obstacles but urged Tyrrell to join, if not at once, then no later than September. Thus, on the very day of his reception, Tyrrell emerged not only a papist but half a Jesuit as well.

Tyrrell was astounded at the accessibility of that exalted order, but his elation at having found yet another swan hardly concealed the half-suspected truth that the standard had been lowered, not that he had been elevated. An interview with the provincial superior, Fr. James Jones, however, somewhat restored the Févallian portrait. He took a stricter view and advised that Tyrrell first serve a year's apprenticeship in Catholic and Jesuit ways at the new Jesuit college in Cyprus. Disappointed, yet secretly approving this decision, Tyrrell set out and reached Cyprus at the beginning of November 1879.

He did not remain there long, however. The political indiscretions of one Fr. Francesco Paolo Riotta of the Sicilian Province, who could not resist apprising his largely Orthodox students of the errors to which Photius had left them heir, succeeded in closing the college just three months after its opening. So Tyrrell finished his year's probation at the English College in Malta. Although his stay in Cyprus was brief, he took with him a cherished and lasting remembrance. He had come to know and love Fr. Henry Kerr, his first real Jesuit acquaintance and ever after the one he regarded as his true novice master.

Malta was another matter. There he came face to face with undeniable blemishes, and he reluctantly concluded that a great man like Henry Kerr happens along now and then not because of but in spite of the system. More important, beyond the glaring humanity of the Malta community, Tyrrell learned that the Society of Jesus had departed from what he thought was its original purpose. He believed that the early Jesuit lived to extend the faith to outsiders like himself by learning their minds and meeting them on their own ground. Now its mission included born-and-bred Catholics and above all the education of youth, works to which he had no attraction whatever. Indeed the apathy and ignorance with which he found his own class of convert regarded by members of the Society—"not as one who had courageously embraced a more difficult and somewhat paradoxical position, in lieu of an easier and more obvious one; but rather as a drunkard who had come to his senses—a repentant fool, if not a repentant rake"—made him suspect that he had bought into a losing proposition.[43]

The thought weighed heavily on him. "I sank down under the sense of the gulf I had fixed between myself and my old friends and lovers—all for what? for what? Had I found what I wanted? Truth whispered *No!* Hope shouted *Yes!*" Yet was it real hope? Or merely euphoria from his great success in the classroom and popularity among the students that bouyed him above total disenchantment? At any rate, when the date of departure for the novitiate arrived, Tyrrell's personal apprehensions were so indefinite and ambivalent that he simply yielded to the prearranged plan. "It seemed best to give the thing a chance, and to believe that my experience had been quite exceptional and unfortunate, and that Father Kerr was really the normal Jesuit."[44]

The original spark gone, George Tyrrell entered the Jesuit novitiate of Manresa outside London on 7 September 1880. Almost at once the misgivings of Malta returned in full force as he saw that the "normal" recruit was not the strong fiery convert willing to risk everything in the cause of Christ but rather a young schoolboy who merely changed headmaster for novice master. Of the eighteen men joining with Tyrrell, sixteen were from Jesuit secondary schools, "insiders" to each other and the system. They regarded Tyrrell as one of the odd few "from the world."

When one looks only at the practical, rational side of George Tyrrell, one wonders why or how he survived Jesuit life beyond the six weeks Dolling had given him. But Tyrrell explained that during those two years of novitiate his reason was held in abeyance by equally powerful nonrational influences that had worked on him since early childhood: the urge to love and be loved, the impulse instantly to like any and every person, the need to exalt his relationships, a certain simplicity and trustfulness and an affection and reverence for individuals that so often led to beguilement by the self-assured and dogmatic, and the search for rooting and stability that led him to adopt Catholicism along with any system serviceable to its ends.[45]

Tyrrell never grew to love or revere the Society of Jesus—not since his Maltese experience—but he did get interested in it as a system to be comprehended rather than questioned. And even though his powers of questioning were now fixed on comprehending, he did not sell himself wholesale but retained sufficient independence of thought to start a round of trouble with authorities that would multiply with his years in the Society.

Tyrrell's first conflict was, naturally enough, with the master of novices, Fr. John Morris. In general Tyrrell bowed to the master's judgment—he was one of those nonrational influences, a strong, self-assured personality "with an unwavering belief in the opinions and the cause he had embraced, and an absolute incapacity of seeing the other side." But from his Maltese experience, Tyrrell saw that the training given by Father Morris left the novices as unprepared for future life "as if they were for the first time cast into the surf to swim, with no other preparation than a rhapsody on the use and pleasures of swimming."[46] He could not accept the tried and true ascetical practices that for the past three hundred years had been indiscriminately and ineffectually forced upon novices of every culture without adaptation. He struggled to make sense of the system and to get it into some workable form for himself, but far from being assisted in this, he was only lectured on the virtue of obedience and the vice of independent judgment.

More serious and lasting difficulties arose from ideas Tyrrell gathered from Father Morris's own presentations on the poverty and simplicity of Christ. These, followed by a reading of Henri-Marie Boudon's *Hidden Life of Jesus* (1676), in which those evangelical counsels are contrasted with the pomp and parade of episcopal and papal courts, awakened in Tyrrell all the socialistic and democratic sympathies that Dolling had fostered and confirmed. Shocked and disillusioned, Tyrrell mentioned the discrepancy to Father Morris, only to receive a stern admonition to submit his judgment and above all not to speak of these matters to the other novices. Further, and unaware of the irony, Father Morris urged Tyrrell to greater devotion to the Sacred Humanity, the very devotion that begot Tyrrell's difficulty in the first place.

Tyrrell did in fact follow Father Morris's counsel, and in time he became freer and more fearless—witness numerous later essays critical of pride of place in ecclesiastical authorities. But for the moment and for several years hence Father Morris's sentence had to be served if Tyrrell was to avoid what seemed a greater indignity—being told to leave the Society. But it was not simply a matter of bending his will to avoid an indignity. He was still convinced that God had directed him to this life and to depart from it would be to depart from God. Moreover, at that age Tyrrell was not sure enough of his own powers of discrimination to stand up against a "man of such evident sincerity and such dogmatic certainty" and to separate his elements of truth and illusion.[47]

Both Father Morris and the new provincial superior Fr. Edward Purbrick had in fact advised Tyrrell to abandon the idea of becoming a Jesuit. They thought that the problems that manifested themselves now would in time resurface in a more virulent form. How right they were. Years later Tyrrell himself admitted it: "If I had a vocation to follow St. Ignatius, and to that Society which exists in the pages of Paul Féval, I had none whatever to the Society that exists here and now; and Father Morris was right instinctively, though wrong in his reasons."[48] But Tyrrell pleaded his case, submitted to the yoke, and received an eleventh-hour nod to pronounce his vows and pass out of the novitiate.

What little of positive value Tyrrell appropriated from his noviceship was due more to accident than to purpose. Aside from the "personal elevation of Father Morris's character," he singled out one book that salved his tortured spirit and left him with the only lasting good he received—Lacordaire's *Conferences on God* (1848).

> It was like meeting a cool spring in the arid waste of scholastic asceticism in which I had been wandering. Had he known its speculative trend, and the secret of its fascination for me, Father Morris would not have allowed me to read it; but he was not personally familiar with it. . . .
>
> Here I found the theism of Aquinas set forth with all the elegance and fire of Lacordaire's imagination. Here I realised that devotion and personal religion could find food and an object in the pure deity, released from the figures and idols of the imagination. Truly, it was an external God still, not the God Who is the centre and light of the heart and mind; still it set my confused conceptions in some sort of order, and quieted my mind, which had been dulled, but never satisfied, as to the difficulties of my earliest childhood. I had learned, in my own vague way, that though the God of the imagination was absurd, yet there was an unimaginable but conceivable God; and now this conception was first given a definite shape, and shown, moreover, to be harmonious with reason. It was an immense relief to me, and broke open the door into a new world of thought. . . . Nor was it merely speculative, but an appeal through the intellect to the heart; and it did more to give me a personal love of the Pure Divinity than any other book I have ever read, except St. Augustine's "Confessions."[49]

After pronouncing vows the fledgling Jesuit usually remained for two more years at Manresa to go through the London University course of humanities, but the day after vow day Tyrrell was sent directly to Stonyhurst near London to begin studies in scholastic philosophy. He was not given a reason for this exception, but he recalled that Father Morris had "said something vague about my needing philosophy to steady my mind."[50]

The scholastic system of philosophy and theology was one of the most important influences on George Tyrrell, and to that influence the entire next chapter will be devoted. Here it will suffice to notice only the bare bones of that influence as it affected Tyrrell in his earliest years in the Society.

The trouble that began at Manresa followed him to Stonyhurst. No sooner had he crossed the threshold than he found himself in a difficult and tenuous relationship from which he would never gracefully extricate himself. Again the nonrational influences were decisive. A certain Father M,[51] professor of logic and metaphysics, was acting superior in the absence of Fr. Walter Sidgreaves and was, moreover, an adherent of strict Thomism, a decidedly minority position among Jesuits of that era. Charm of manner, boyish freshness and brightness—qualities uncommon in Jesuits of professorial standing—predisposed Tyrrell immediately to adopt Father M's views. Tyrrell was grateful at finding himself in the school of Thomas rather than that of Francisco Suárez and the pseudo-scholastics, but he was duly embarrassed that it was by such shameless serendipity. Nonetheless he felt absolved and fortified by the fact that the pope himself had recently urged a return to Thomas.[52]

Tyrrell came to his new studies with high expectations and a mind readied by two fallow years. Father Morris had proposed to Tyrrell that scholasticism would prove a cure for his "ignorant questionings and dissatisfactions." But he had not anticipated that, following Father M's lead, Tyrrell would go straight to the texts of Thomas himself instead of to his third-rate commentators. This activity was a deviation that marked Tyrrell from the outset as a meddler and placed him beyond the pale. Years later he reflected that his having been "enlisted on the side of Thomism and the Pope and against the dominant and domestic tradition of the Society, gave birth to those first feelings of disaffection and distrust towards the Order which have since ripened into a profound dislike of its sectarian egotism."[53] Nonetheless he won great respect as perhaps the finest mind in his class.[54]

Tyrrell learned that scholasticism was regarded as Catholic philosophy and all other systems as therefore un-Catholic if not heretical. This persuasion played into his already strong bias for a system and his single-mindedness toward Rome. It was next to impossible for him to resist the conclusion that scholasticism was virtually incorporated into the Roman creed and that to profess one was to profess the other. "So now, almost by an extension of that same impulse, I threw myself wholly into the task of mastering and defending the scholastic—or rather Thomistic—system of philosophy and theology."[55]

On another side, Tyrrell was to learn that the spiritual mansion he had constructed under the direction of Father Morris was little more than a house of cards. When he revealed to his new spiritual director, a Father T,[56] all that he had learned from Father Morris of his spiritual dangers—his independence of judgment, his heretical leanings regarding ecclesiastical riches and worldly display, his rationalistic bias and overconfidence in natural means and natural virtues—Father T began, one by one, to reverse Father Morris's verdicts and to reinterpret all these horrors as blessings. His rector, Fr. William Eyre, concurred.

One might have expected Tyrrell to rejoice in this affirmation and the freer way now opened to him, but he felt, on the contrary, quite shaken. At Manresa he had learned painfully but well to question his own judgment and to submit to the system of Father Morris as *the* system of the Society if not of the universal church. Now he learned that Father Morris's was merely *a* system, and a highly questionable one at that. Again he was quite destroyed, and again he had to rebuild confidence in his own judgment as well as construct another ascetical system. Tyrrell threw himself into the project with an urgency and feeling that was, however, not for his own soul but for the system he was constructing, and not even for the system in itself but in its potential utility for all and everyone. So when he began to build anew, it was as if he himself were the *corpus vile* of an experiment for the sake of others, and he went at it with the same passion for discovery and invention that, as a child, set him to tinkering when he should have been at his lessons.

Deep within, however, still rumbled the moral judgment pressed on Tyrrell in the novitiate—that self-guidance was the broad road to depravity. Hence he felt himself, in his process of reconstruction, forced into a kind of bad faith in his relations with God. Still, he regarded all of his scholastic and spiritual difficulties of those years as "lesser troubles" compared with "the memories of one that had nothing to do with these self-induced, artificial interests, but with those which spring from our God-given natural affections, and which even Jesuit asceticism can never wholly uproot." Tyrrell left no further record of what this greater trouble was, but his biographer Maude Dominica Petre said that it had to do with the death of his mother in 1884. Apparently reflection thereon raised in him feelings that he found "too harrowing" to face, and so with 1884, the year of his mother's death, Tyrrell cut off his story and gave to his fragment the disparaging title, "History of a Mean or Medium Life."[57]

In 1885, his philosophical studies completed, Tyrrell returned to Malta to teach for three years. The extroversion of that experience was welcome relief from the excessive introspection of his seminary years, and he regarded those three years as the purest and best of his young religious life. They were succeeded by four years of theological studies at St. Beuno's College in North Wales. The scant record of those years will be reviewed in the following chapter. On 20 September 1891 Bishop Edmund Knight of Shrewsbury ordained George Tyrrell priest. After his fourth year of theology, he returned to Manresa, his first home in the Society, to complete his final year of formation, a year of "supplementary novitiate" designed to review the young priest's life and prepare him for the active apostolate to follow.

Now fully formed, Tyrrell was sent in 1893 for a very brief time to a mission house in Oxford, then for a year to St. Helen's mission in the poor coal country of Lancashire. No assignment could have been further from his original aims. Instead of calling unbelievers like himself to faith and conversion, he was spending his first enthusiasm on the intellectually and financially depressed believer. But if it was not what he himself would have chosen, neither was it inconsistent with that uncommon spirit of love and compassion for the poor fostered in him by Dolling. Tyrrell threw himself wholeheartedly into their lives, and they, though intellectually undeveloped, were quick to recognize his authenticity and goodness, and responded in kind. This happy, effective relationship between priest and people made Tyrrell's stay seem all too brief and his departure after only one year too sad. St. Helen's was burned forever into his affections. Of all his years as a Jesuit, that year of 1893–94 was perhaps the happiest.

Before Tyrrell emerged into the flaming critic of his public image, he passed through a phase of rigorous orthodoxy. At the heart of that phase lay the scholastic system of philosophy and theology, and with that system Tyrrell ever after contended. To it and its effect attention must now be given.

CHAPTER 2

The Orthodox Years (1882–96): Mounting an Offensive

TYRRELL'S PROTESTANT-CATHOLIC COMPLEX

Roman Catholic apologetics from the Counter-Reformation down to Tyrrell's day and beyond was more anti-Protestant than pro-Catholic. Its aim was to refute and even ridicule Protestant positions rather than to expose positively the intrinsic and extrinsic soundness of Catholic teaching. The unyielding framework for this heavily negative apologetic was the scholastic system of philosophy and theology, a system often erroneously arrogated to Roman Catholicism, for it was equally a Protestant stronghold.

In the early phase of his public life, George Tyrrell fell into the orthodox step. His Catholic apologetic could be as negative and anti-Protestant as any. At the same time, he stood out even from the beginning in a positive line, probably because he had to convince himself of the intrinsic soundness of the Catholic position. He could be at one time vigorously anti-Protestant and at another time intelligently pro-Catholic in a way that won him admirers and enemies from both camps. Within his own person he carried both the questions and the answers, the proposals and counterproposals of the eternal issues that eventually fell out of solution and, seeded by various strains of scholasticism, crystalized separately into Protestantism and Roman Catholicism.

To show the roots of this split in the various strains of scholasticism would take us beyond the scope of the present study. Suffice it to say that those roots were strongly embedded in Tyrrell's be-ing: his thought demonstrates both the tendency to parlay reason into the religious dimension, a characteristic of scholasticism whether Protestant or Catholic, and the tendency to distrust reason, to set great store by religious feeling, and to pit feeling against ec-clesiastical authority and the sacramental system. These positions were characteristic of an evangelical pietism rooted in Augustine, Scotus, Ockham, and the *devotio moderna* of the Brethren of the Common Life.

The genesis both of Tyrrell's apologetic for Roman Catholicism and of his philosophy of religion is linked from the very beginning with an unstable Protestant-Catholic composite within Tyrrell him-self. This unstable mix of traditions made for ambivalent feelings that led in turn to some equivocation and even inconsistencies in his writings, which critics were happy to point out. But given the tangle of traditions he was trying to hold in tension, all his inconsis-tencies can be understood if not forgiven. Beyond that and to his credit, he was one of a mere handful of theologians in his day who were capable of understanding and describing the convoluted strains clearly enough for inconsistencies to be spotted, let alone forgiven or condemned.

ENCOUNTER WITH NEO-SCHOLASTICISM: STONYHURST AND BEYOND (1882-94)

When Tyrrell began his study of philosophy in 1882, the church was confidently riding the crest of a philosophical-theological syn-ergism known as neo-scholasticism, a revival of Thomistic studies occasioned by a reaction to the liberal philosophies and theologies coming out of the Enlightenment. Scholasticism had been largely abandoned by the eighteenth century, except in certain centers of Suarezianism in Spain and Italy. Thus when the scare of German idealism swept the Western world, scholars retreated to tradition for answers and brought out Thomas with a new look. The turn to tradition took hold in Italy, where some of the older generation had maintained ties with it—men like Taparelli d'Azeglio, Serafino Sordi, Matteo Liberatore, Dominico Palmieri, and Josef Kleutgen.

A major problem with this neo-scholastic revival was that its advocates approached the Thomistic synthesis and its facsimiles with the ardor of converts and clung to their discovery as to the final word. Another problem was that the ardor of the now-voyagers turned not only toward Thomas himself but also toward his inter-preters and imitators. The latter focus led to an intramural controversy that split the scholastic front: Dominicans hailed Thomas as interpreted by himself; Jesuits hailed Thomas as interpreted by the Spanish Jesuit Francisco Suárez, who, they claimed, improved on the original.

Papal commendation of Thomistic philosophy and theology in Leo XIII's encyclical *Aeterni Patris* of 4 August 1879 not only heightened the fervor of the revivalists but also fanned the flames of the Thomist-Suarezian controversy. Each camp worked its own hermeneutic on the encyclical to bring it into accord with its prepossessions. The Thomists greeted the encyclical as a declaration for Thomas exclusively. The Suarezians rejoined that it only required that the mind of Thomas be preserved, which of course their system did and in a superior way.

Not all Jesuits, however, were Suarezian. The Italians, led by Liberatore, tended to be pure Thomists. Through study of the long-buried texts of Thomas, Liberatore concluded that Suárez had completely missed some of the subtler points of distinction in Thomas's all-pervading principles—or as Tyrrell put it, "that he had conceived in a gross and imaginary form distinctions of a purely intellectual character, and had thereby materialised the entire system." These Italian Jesuits had the pope's ear, and his encyclical reflected their leanings. Also on their side was the tradition of the Jesuit constitutions, which claimed Thomas for its philosopher and theologian *par excellence*. Nevertheless, Leo's encyclical flew in the teeth of the main body of the Society of Jesus because in the course of time the Society's own teachers had gained the ascendancy—and this, said Tyrrell, "for obvious reasons," meaning the anti-Dominican animus.[1]

Through constant pressure from Rome, the principles of *Aeterni Patris* were gradually forced on the Society. Recalcitrant professors were removed from the Roman College and other colleges under the immediate purview of Rome and replaced by orthodox Thomists. But beyond Rome's immediate influence, and particularly in Jesuit scholasticates and universities, resistance remained so strong that on 30 December 1892 Leo XIII addressed a sharp rebuke to the whole Society of Jesus to be incorporated into its constitutions.[2] But this directive, too, was rationalized away, and the status quo prevailed. *They take correction well, not seriously.*

So the battle raged, with Tyrrell in a familiar role of siding with the underdog. When he entered Stonyhurst in 1882, the first professor he met was a "traitor within the ranks," a pure Thomist, whom he identified in his autobiography as "Father M" but who could only have been Fr. Thomas Rigby.[3] Always susceptible to strong first impressions and to manly, enthusiastic types, Tyrrell immediately fell under Rigby's influence and espoused his cause. Then, too, the only student he knew on entering Stonyhurst—a friend from his Malta days whom he called "Brother D"—was also a confirmed disciple of Rigby and Thomas. In addition, Tyrrell felt compelled to go to sources, so that sooner or later one would find him poring over the texts of Thomas himself rather than the reflections of lesser luminaries. He had, in fact, several years prior read the *Summa*, apparently a copy he borrowed from Dolling shortly after arriving in London in 1879. Years later, in a letter to Canon Alfred Leslie Lillie, Tyrrell recalled how that first reading had made such a profound impression and given him such hope for the Thomistic synthesis that now to criticize his lifelong categories was to drink bitter gall.[4]

At the end of 1884, however, Tyrrell's side lost its most valuable advocate and patron. Father Rigby was shipped off to Demerara, ostensibly because of the trouble he caused by suggesting at a conference on the program of studies that there was room for improvement. But the real reason for the transfer, according to Tyrrell, was to satisfy the "complaints of Suarezian professors and the indignation of those who knew nothing whatever about the controversy and were of course vehement in proportion to their ignorance."[5]

Nonetheless, Tyrrell's facile and penetrating mind quickly grasped the scholastic system, so that by the end of his first year at Stonyhurst he was at the head of his class and regarded as one to be reckoned with. He drank deeply but not uncritically; he was far too independent for that. Almost at once he began to sense scholasticism's inadequacies, a sense profoundly reinforced by his reading in 1885 of John Henry Newman's *Grammar of Assent* (1870).[6] By 1901 he was convinced that the categories of scholasticism were too mechanical and material for philosophy, let alone theology, and that therefore it faltered badly when it attempted to explain in terms of lower realities the higher realities of thought, will, love, and action.[7] Tyrrell did, of course, realize that men can speak of the transcendent only in terms of lower realities, and he conceded that Thomism, as distinguished from scholasticism, was as flexible and serviceable a system as could be devised, provided only that one recognize the limitations inherent in speaking analogously and not absolutize it as the only possible system.

To absolutize Thomism would have been sinful enough, but to absolutize scholasticism was unforgivable. Yet this was the prevailing tide that Tyrrell found as he entered theological studies at St. Beuno's, and he set about at once to counter it. Unfortunately most of what he wrote during that period—occasional essays for the amusement of his classmates and all his personal notes—he sent up in flames.[8] But several published essays survive to provide a clue to his offensive.

The first, read on 22 February 1889 before St. Beuno's Essay Society, for which Tyrrell was then secretary, appraised and applauded the effort to revive Thomistic studies. Tyrrell later rewrote the essay for the *Month*, but the editor, Fr. Richard Clarke, found it unsuitable for his readers and sent it on to the *American Catholic Quarterly Review*. There it appeared anonymously in October 1891 as "Aquinas Resuscitatus."[9] On 3 December Tyrrell announced the essay's publication to his friend Fr. Herbert Thurston, who had recently left St. Beuno's for literary work at Farm Street, and explained that he did not know why his name had been deleted but that it was an unsought favor, as he had over the past two years modified his views considerably and to a great extent lost interest in the cause.[10] But at the time of its writing, Tyrrell saw Aquinas's system as the truest and most flexible for Catholic apologetics, and he aimed to give it its place according to the mind of Leo XIII and *Aeterni Patris*.

Tyrrell's article first dispatched two extreme interpretations: the divinization of tradition and Aquinas as the ultimate oracle on all questions, and the relegation of Aquinas to the dustbin of history, irrelevant to modern man. Then on the basis of a long-neglected distinction between positive and scientific or scholastic theology, Tyrrell argued that Leo XIII did not intend scholastic theology for every priest but only for those preparing to teach it. All that most priests have time and talent for, he contended, is positive theology— the facts, the conclusions, and maybe some of the arguments, enough for intelligent preaching and catechizing. And for that the manuals would do.

But more is required of the teacher. He must learn scholastic or scientific theology deeply, not only its arguments but the principles on which the arguments are based, so that he can adapt them and even develop new arguments for new circumstances. To succeed at his training, Tyrrell argued, the teacher must return to Thomas as the starting point and master his system. The point is not to produce slaves to a single system but merely to guarantee a uniformity of method and terminology, thereby eliminating useless confusion; to create a context of clear communication for the critical assessment of all other systems; to learn not merely what Thomas said but what he would say now. In other words, Thomism is to be studied as a method, not as a compendium of doctrines requiring the assent of faith.

Tyrrell's second article, "Cramming and Other Causes of Mental Dyspepsia," appeared in the *Month* for November 1889.[11] It was even more negative and critical of the state of seminary training. Here Tyrrell aimed by satire and wit to display as counterproductive the method he called "cramming," by which "boys are forced to apply themselves to abstract studies quite above their capacity" and thereby are led to assume as fact much that is mere conjecture and opinion. Such prejudicial ingestion, Tyrrell said, is ultimately harmful to both scientific and religious interests, for on the one hand it renders impossible an unbiased approach to scientific or historical investigation, and on the other it induces the formulation of often baseless and inadequate "scientific" arguments in support of religious beliefs, ultimately "to the discredit of religion and its defenders, and the great satisfaction of its enemies."[12]

Educators must recognize this danger and seek to render young minds apt instruments for the gradual attainment of truth rather than to force-feed them a system wholesale and unmasticated. The aim should be to teach the immature nothing so much as how to teach themselves, to show them not what to think but how to think. Educators must beware especially of the undue influence of authority, for it can so easily lead young minds to enshrine the creation of an author's mind and regard as eternal what is "only the petrifaction of one brief stage of his thought."[13]

Behind Tyrrell's criticism lay the vexing problem of knowledge: how and what one knows by faith, how and what one knows by reason, and how to put those two together. It was a problem that exercised his earliest scholastic mind and would haunt his later writings. In fact, it was the subject of Tyrrell's very first publication, "A Symposium on Immortality," a review of a collection of essays representing widely different views, written sometime during his first year of teaching in Malta.[14] Fresh from the studied unity and coherence of scholasticism as learned at Stonyhurst, Tyrrell descended on the argument of Prebendary Charles Adolphus Row, who apparently expected *a priori* that the Creator would have made a truth of such practical import as man's immortality one of the primary certainties of man's intellect. Even considering the bearing of such knowledge on human conduct, Tyrrell countered, no one should wonder that God has not made immortality a primary certainty of the mind. To do so is to forget how man knows anything at all, that all his knowledge comes to him through the senses and concerns primarily the intelligibilities of things sensible. Spiritual and immaterial objects such as the immortality of the soul "are only grasped inadequately and after long and tedious processes of negation and analogy, which as longer, are more liable to inexactitude."[15]

Three years later, when Tyrrell was locked in the hills of North Wales for his theological studies, he found time to return to the topic of reason versus faith and the analogy of being in a pastiche of four Swiftian essays that prefigure more deliberate treatments like *The Civilizing of the Matafanus* written eleven years later.[16] The first essay, "The Contents of a Pre-Adamite Skull," is representative. It introduces the Pre-Adamites, a race of creatures above man, who, though possessed of extraordinary powers of perception, are fully sensitive to their limits. They automatically understand that God willed to manifest himself only through nature as good, wise, and powerful. But since no finite intelligence can fully appreciate the eminence of these qualities except as set off against their contraries, the Pre-Adamites are not scandalized to find evil, disorder, and infirmity in creatures. In fact, they honor God because out of evil he draws good; out of disorder, harmony; and out of infirmity, strength. Steadily maintaining that God's excellence is immeasurably greater than they can conceive, anything that appears contrary to his wisdom, power, or goodness they at once ascribe to the error that must arise from their own partial estimation of the facts or their own feeble notions of wisdom, power, and goodness. As to God's existence and unity, these are taken as easy conclusions from reason, and any doubts on this score are regarded as symptoms of softening of the brain. With their heightened perceptions, the Pre-Adamites recognize God as pervading nature most intimately and yet transcending it. He is the first cause of everything positive, yet in nearly all things he uses the instrumentality of a hierarchy of secondary causes, chief among which are intelligences credited with all rational effects in the irrational world.

During these years, as well as subsequently, Tyrrell wrote on a wide range of topics: biblical criticism, Anglicanism, materialism, rationalism, zoophilism, socialism, and doctrinal development, all from a trenchantly orthodox point of view. He generally wrote quickly, out of his own experiences, and usually in reaction to something he had just read. Nor did deficiency of background give him pause. For instance, that he could not read German (until after 1901) and thus was deprived of the most recent scientific work in biblical scholarship did not prevent him from making an occasional foray into that wilderness.[17] His saving grace was that he was quite aware of his deficiencies and, as he confessed to Thurston, found himself "terribly handicapped in not knowing German and having almost completely forgotten Greek." He regretted his "somewhat

Quixotic devotion to philosophy and theology which induced me to water that dry stick with heroic assiduity for seven years in the vain hope that like Aaron's rod it might one day blossom forth and even bear fruit."[18]

But deficiences and all, Tyrrell felt compelled by circumstances to pour himself out on paper. As he confided to Thurston, he would often write from morning to night "regardless of the price of stationery," as though it were the only narcotic strong enough to make him forget himself and his imaginary woes. "Reading has lost all its efficacy. When writing fails I shall try prussic acid probably."[19]

Most of his essays Tyrrell simply roughed out and floated among his peers for their amusement. Occasionally he would send one to Thurston. Once when Thurston returned an essay with criticism and some exhortation to get the essay into proper form for publication, Tyrrell replied:

> I have no ideas of the art of composition, but am guided by my ear and my own taste and by a principle of writing down straight what I think, in the first form in which it occurs to me. I am afraid I am too far gone now to reform. Besides I am very lazy and fail to see any reason for exerting myself in the matter. My essays are designed to amuse the monks—albeit at my own expense—for a few moments. If they also help to fill a page or two in *The Month*, I don't object, but I really don't care.

Then, apparently to an appeal to use his God-given talents to their fullest, Tyrrell responded:

> Let me go on to say that from my earliest days I had the gospel of brains preached to me till I got to loathe it. I had my brother and my cousins flung at my head so often that I conceived a detestation of learned and brainy people that I have never got over. I like idiots and feel at home with them; and it is as, in some true sense, an idiot-asylum that the Catholic Church attracts me. Cleverness is in my mind an attribute of monkeys.[20]

From 1892 to 1894 Tyrrell's pen lay quiet as he found himself happily occupied with the spiritual and pastoral pursuits of tertianship and priestly work at St. Helen's. He published only two articles, both reviews of books by Wilfrid Ward on Newman and the Oxford Movement. In these reviews he tried to reconcile Newmanism with Scholasticism, a topic to be pursued in the next chapter.

RETURN TO STONYHURST: A SECOND OFFENSIVE (1894-96)

In the summer of 1894, much against his wishes, Tyrrell was up-rooted from St. Helen's and given a chair of philosophy at Stony-hurst, where he had studied nine years before. Maude Petre re-marked that this move seemed hardly more than incidental, since he was allowed to stay at Stonyhurst for only two years.[21] How-ever, from this period one can date the beginning of Tyrrell's posi-tive disaffection from the Society as it was then administered, his distrust of authorities, and his first efforts as a solemnly vowed Jesuit to assert himself against the prevailing tide.

As one might predict, Tyrrell was an outstanding and popular teacher. His nimble mind and warmth of character, his wit and sat-ire, and his democratic sense that would not allow him to patronize his students, quickly won him widespread allegiance. But this alle-giance also won Tyrrell trouble. He was promoting pure Thomism over against the Suarezianism of his faculty peers, and his students, most of whom could not appreciate the contested subtleties, simply flocked to his side. Having captured their imaginations, Tyrrell unwittingly evinced from his students a premature assent and thus violated one of his own precepts.

Maude Petre, from an interview with "one who possessed direct information," reported that by the end of his second year Tyrrell "had all the best minds among the young men enthusiastically loyal to him and . . . strongly opposed to the theses of the other two professors" who suffered "constant attacks from G.T.'s clever pu-pils" in consequence.[22] Tyrrell himself confirmed this. But others who had "direct information" challenged this version and claimed that some of the best minds were positively "repelled by Tyrrell's apparent willingness to challenge everything."[23] Whatever the facts, the truth was that Tyrrell troubled the waters and, as Petre put it, "It was obvious that he or they must go. The line of least re-sistance was taken, and G.T. went."[24]

What especially irked Tyrrell's philosophic sensibilities was the materiality of the Suarezian explanation of divine transcendencies. To the superficial, Tyrrell said, the difference between the Suarez-ian and Thomistic systems seems trivial enough, but in truth it is radical and all-pervading, since it affects the understanding of the categories of matter and form by which scholasticism is governed. Thomas himself did not escape indictment on charges of crudity, particularly in his psychology and cosmology. In these disciplines that are so closely related to the physical sciences, Tyrrell was dis-tressed to find that Thomas had committed himself so deeply to

Aristotelian physics. "It is said too hastily that we can separate the physics and the metaphysics of St. Thomas; but one might as well try to separate a man's body from his soul."[25]

Nonetheless, Tyrrell looked to Thomas not only as a great teacher of the past but as a great hope for future light and freedom. It did not hurt that Thomas's teaching was supported by the highest ecclesiastical authority, so that here Tyrrell found the causes of liberty and authority joined, a fact of considerable import to one still young in the Faith.[26] All things considered, Tyrrell concluded, it made little difference what system was taught, but all the difference as to how it was taught. Dogmatism enslaves young minds and renders them unsympathetic and narrow instead of flexible and comprehensive. Thomism, approached with the liberality of the author and taught coherently and critically as a system and not dogmatically as *the* system, could set ecclesiastics at a very great advantage in the work of philosophic criticism, instead of at a great disadvantage, as things then stood.

Under present circumstances Tyrrell figured that dogmatism was likely to reign regardless of the system, but he also figured that it would do less harm in the interests of pure Thomism than in the interests of Suarezianism. So he decided to enlist authority on his side and see if he could not force the Society in England to heave to as it had in Italy and elsewhere.

Accordingly Tyrrell wrote to the Jesuit Cardinal Camillo Mazzella, Pope Leo's prefect of studies and principal author of *Aeterni Patris*, about what was happening among English Jesuits. Mazzella replied that the pope wished Tyrrell's leaning to prevail in schools of Catholic philosophy, as it was more in line with the true doctrine of Saint Thomas. He added that this recommendation came from the pope himself.[27] What Tyrrell had done was not known to many, but word got around to his superiors. Petre reported that Cardinal Herbert Alfred Vaughan of London mentioned to her in a chance conversation that Fr. Luis Martin, superior general of the Society of Jesus, had complained to him that Tyrrell thought he knew more of Saint Thomas than all the rest of the Society. Petre remarked, "It is curious to find Leo XIII and Tyrrell opposed to the Society on this occasion, as Pius X and the Society were opposed to Tyrrell in later days."[28]

Mustering Rome and a sizable troop of students was seen as grievous disloyalty and not to be tolerated. Accordingly, at the end of August 1896, Tyrrell was removed from Stonyhurst and assigned to the scriptorium at Farm Street in the heart of London.

So much for the biographical aspect of Tyrrell's orthodox period. Still to be considered are his publications during his brief tenure at Stonyhurst. They may be considered in two sets: first, those concerning Thomism and the intellectual preparation of candidates for the priesthood; and second, those that are more apologetic and vigorously anti-Protestant.

Tyrrell's thought on the former issue has already been touched on. The first article of that set, "The 'Tabula Aurea' of Peter de Bergamo," appeared in Tyrrell's own script in the February 1896 issue of the *Blandyke Papers*, an informal monthly produced by the students of Stonyhurst.[29] Here Tyrrell urged students to boycott Thomas's interpreters, who invariably distort him through intramural biases and party prejudices, and to let Thomas interpret himself via Peter de Bergamo's concordance. Furthermore, he argued, the most a student can hope to do in three years is learn one system of philosophy *as a system;* only secondarily might he learn the truth of that system. It is more important that students be lifted out of their own mental grooves into intellectual sympathy with a superior intellect than that they determine the truth of the system. One must first learn *how* to think, only then learn *what to think*. Premature concentration on the latter to the neglect of the former results in assent without personal conviction, and thus in narrowness and insincerity. Theoretically any system would do. But, Tyrrell concluded, the church and the constitutions of the Society of Jesus were wise to require the study of Thomas, because not only is Thomas one of the world's greatest minds, but his teaching is in strict accord with the Catholic faith. The latter qualification, Tyrrell added, while distinctly advantageous, is less important during the triennium. Cries of heresy undoubtedly followed this last remark down the corridors of Stonyhurst.

Tyrrell took up the cause again in an unsigned review of J. B. Terrien's treatment of Thomas's teaching on the hypostatic union of Christ's two natures.[30] After complimenting Terrien on a compelling presentation, Tyrrell came to his point. Here was another happy sign of progress in the Holy Father's campaign to bring about greater harmony and understanding among Catholic theologians by requiring them to adopt a common method and terminology and critically study a common master. Tyrrell was convinced, as he wrote to Thurston sometime in the summer of 1895, that in this requirement as well as elsewhere "the Pope has struck a blow against sectarian narrowness and in favour of a Catholic and liberal uniformity."[31]

In the arena of Catholic apologetics Tyrrell devoted himself to the problem that brought him to Catholicism and exercised his zeal ever after: the problem of faith and reason. This problem was his overriding concern, but in addressing it he followed no grand

scheme. His method was entirely occasional. Thus in his first published apologetic, he used the occasion of reviewing Arthur James
Balfour's _Foundations of Belief_ to refute the British school of naturalism or empiricism.[32] In this review, Tyrrell welcomed the eminent Anglican statesman and intellectual into a holy alliance, a
move that might seem anomalous for Tyrrell's orthodox period except that he had earlier read a review in which the unsympathetic
author charged that Balfour's principles should land him squarely
in the Roman communion. This remark, intended as a _reductio ad
absurdum_, gave Tyrrell the opening to point out that if Balfour or
anyone else could spend the time it takes for an outsider to comprehend Roman Catholicism in its totality, he would find in it the
only and fullest satisfaction of his intellectual requirements. However, such a comprehension, Tyrrell noted with Balfour, could not
cause belief. For that something more is needed, some influence,
some kind of authority to offset the baleful psychological climate
of the modern world.

Balfour had pressed this point in the battle between science and
religion and tried to show that both are based on the same foundation, namely, authority. Regardless of the independence claimed
by science, he argued, if scientists are pushed enough to question
their own presuppositions and to supply reasons why phenomena
behave as they do, if they are forced to see that the only principle
they allow, namely, causality, can only imprison them within a system of observable and rationally explainable phenomena, they will
have to admit that they hold their premises on the basis of some
kind of external influence, in most cases what it is fashionable to
believe.

The review was sympathetic. On the one hand, Tyrrell appreciated Balfour's analysis of the futile attempts of empiricism (or
naturalism, in T. H. Huxley's language) to account for ethical behavior or for man's search for and instinctive appreciation of
beauty and truth. These appetites, Balfour had insisted, can be explained only by positing the existence of a standard of the Good,
True, and Beautiful, which man knows instinctively, though inadequately, by intuition.[33] On the other hand, Tyrrell applauded
Balfour's argument that the principles on which science rests are no
more defensible philosophically than those on which religion rests.
The reason why some people see an either/or choice between
science and religion or faith and reason, said Tyrrell, is not philosophical but psychological; that is, it has to do with the operations
of man's mental and spiritual faculties, a point on which Tyrrell
was critical of Thomas and did not himself come to much clarity
until he produced _Religion as a Factor of Life_ in 1902.[34] For the

moment Tyrrell saw that one transcends the self, whether in science or in religion, only by trusting one's senses to reveal the being that caused the sensations. "Faith in the Kantian sense—that is, a reasonable submission to quasi-instinctive beliefs and sentiments, philosophically unjustified—is as necessary for science as for ethics or theology."[35] In religion, this trust takes the form of believing what is revealed on the authority of those we trust, first our parents, then our teachers. As we mature and learn to think and judge for ourselves, we can find supporting reasons for our beliefs, but ultimately these supports are merely supportive and inadequate as proofs.

In saying this Tyrrell was saying no more than Thomas had said in his *Summa contra gentiles*—that natural theology alone is inadequate as a defence of belief.[36] It is invaluable, Tyrrell asserted, as an after-test and justification of conclusions gained by other means, namely, through authority, and for this purpose the scholastics developed a legitimate rationalism. The fact that this rationalism was abused and led to naturalism "does not necessarily throw any discredit upon it, so long as it does not pretend to an all-sufficiency which it cannot justify."[37]

If adversaries were looking for evidence against Tyrrell, they certainly had it in these words. Whether he was with Thomas or not, Tyrrell was here treading dangerously close to anathema. Vatican I had recently execrated all who said that God cannot be known with certainty by the natural light of human reason.[38]

Tyrrell engaged the faith-reason problem again in a long and incisive review of Benjamin Kidd's *Social Evolution*, a sociological statement on the function of religion in society.[39] Kidd attempted to establish the thesis that progress is impossible without religion or what he called "ultra-rational" beliefs, because religion provides an "ultra-rational" sanction for conduct in the individual. Thus where the individual's interests and those of the social organism are antagonistic, religion renders the former subordinate to the latter in the greater interest of the evolution of the race.

While Tyrrell found much of interest in the book, he also found much to criticize, particularly Kidd's basic assumption that human progress is an end in itself and that religion should serve that end. It was a criticism that Tyrrell would continue to level against liberal Protestantism to his dying day.[40] Catholics, he pointed out, regard earthly progress as natural and divinely sanctioned but by no means the sole end of religion. For them the present life is but the preface to the life to come, but for Kidd and most Protestant sects, the present life is the body of the book and the life to come merely its useful explanatory preface, wherein heaven and hell serve as ultrarational sanctions to guarantee such conduct as will promote the prosperity of the nation and race. "We promise children sugar-plums to induce them to take a disagreeable medicine, but we do not give them medicine as a necessary natural condition to giving them sugar-plums."[41]

Thus, in the matter of almsgiving, the truly Christian capitalist sees wealth as a means to his own salvation by using it in the best interests of the poor. In this charity he feels bound primarily to provide for their spiritual welfare and only secondarily and as a necessary means to that end to provide for their physical and mental welfare. Motives for almsgiving get distorted in the industrial countries when, Tyrrell asserted, religion gets pressed into the service of commerce as a stimulus to trade: lift up the poor, not to save them from insufficiency but to give them an equal opportunity. The result is materialism, and one by one the religious dogmas found inappropriate to that end are discarded, till at last even ultrarational sanctions are weakened and finally extinguished.

Tyrrell also found Kidd's terminology objectionable and self-contradictory in that it identified rational with empirical, reason with experience, ultrarational with metempirical, and that it relegated to faith whatever transcends experience, including all metaphysical truths. Natural theology would therefore be ultrarational and apprehended by "faith," rendering superfluous a supernatural religion, revealed and confirmed by miracle.

Finally Tyrrell deplored the fact that Kidd and many of his ilk were working in a climate isolated from Catholicism, so they continually hailed as new what Catholics had long taken for granted. For example, evolutionists suddenly discovered what the Catholic Church had affirmed centuries ago on the basis of an Aristotelian model—that society is organic rather than mechanical. Nor was it news that man, apart from the stimulus of want, is naturally inactive and retrograde. Aquinas had used precisely the same argument against socialism that Kidd so painfully elaborated as if for the first time. Nonetheless, Tyrrell found Kidd's arguments valuable as a support of ancient truisms, in that Kidd reached them by a different path. To those who would accuse Tyrrell of narrowness in recognizing Kidd's merits only where he agreed with Catholic teaching and condemning him where he departed, Tyrrell replied, "This . . . is precisely our position; we wish to judge Mr. Kidd by the rule of the Catholic Church, and by no means to judge the Catholic Church by the verdict of even the most popular and successful speculators of the passing hour."[42]

In a kindred two-part review of three works by Samuel Laing, Tyrrell's militancy warmed to vituperation.[43] He dismissed Laing's mass of archeological data against the Genesis accounts of creation as a "farrago of nonsense" and confessed that he would not waste time on Laing except that his books were historically, though not philosophically, interesting and if unanswered could lead young minds astray. As for Laing's appreciation of Christianity, it was "perfectly childish"—"a fault no doubt due to Protestantism, which repudiates the notion of a scientific body of doctrine, and reduces Christianity to the Bible in its surface sense."[44]

Of particular significance is not the fact that Tyrrell was here outrageously militant, but that in answering Laing he espoused a broader theory of biblical interpretation than most Catholics of the period would allow. Historical criticism, he admitted, was forcing Christians to try to accommodate the doctrine of inspiration and the literal record of scripture to historical facts. Not that one gives them up but that one determines gradually what inspiration and the record mean. For example, disproving the universality of the flood does not negate the doctrine of biblical inerrancy, for the latter covers not the literal but the prophetic meaning: "As far as the prophetic import of the Deluge is concerned, a very small local affair might be mystically large with foreshadowings, as we see with regard to the enacted prophecies of the later prophets."[45]

Tyrrell's conclusion leaves no doubt that he was not interested in gaining a sympathetic hearing from Laing and the naturalists but only in warning Catholic readers away.

> Here, then, we have a very fair specimen of the pseudophilosophy which is so admirably adapted to captivate the half-informed, wholly unformed minds of the undiscriminating multitudes whom Protestantism has defrauded of their right, duty, and ability to judge for themselves in matters for which a life-time of specialization is barely sufficient. A congeries of dogmatic assertions and negations raked together from the chief writers of a decadent school, discredited twenty years ago by all men of thought, Christian or otherwise; a show of logical order and reasoning which evades our grasp the instant we try to lay critical hands on it; a profuse expression of disinterested devotion to abstract truth, an occasional bow to conventional morality, a racy, irreverent style, an elaborate display of miscellaneous information, good paper, large type, cheap wood-cuts, and the work is done.[46]

This was one of the articles that Tyrrell deleted from the third edition of *The Faith of the Millions,* a collection of his early *Month* articles, and one can hardly regret his decision. "I was so sensible of its inadequacy and many ignorances," he explained to his friend André Raffalovich, "for indeed it is seriously fallacious in many points."[47] But that realization came only in 1904. To Abbé Ernest Dimnet, a professor at the Collège Stanislas in Paris, Tyrrell wrote:

> I quite agree with you that the essay on Samuel Laing is cheap and feeble—a sort of smart controversy which is much approved and encouraged in certain ecclesiastical circles, but which I have since absolutely repudiated. But it was, perhaps, the one essay about which my censors were enthusiastic, and I could not afford to deny Cerberus his sop. It was, perhaps, a little more *ad hominem* than you allow for—an attempt simply to discredit the witness; though at the time I could have defended many positions that I have since ceased to defend.[48]

In the same derisive spirit, Tyrrell wrote a spate of articles on Anglicanism and some of its quarrels, such as the meaning and place of the mass as a sacrifice and the validity of Anglican orders. At the same time he was working on the publication of two collections of devotional essays: *Nova et Vetera* and *Hard Sayings.*[49] These were singularly nonapologetic, as they were meant for the spiritual enrichment of serious Catholics. Soberly conceived and intelligently written, they were welcomed as solid meat compared to the truck of most spiritual writers of the day and made Tyrrell's reputation as a spiritual master among a certain circle of Catholics. But they are not the fare for which he is historically important and remembered.

Nonetheless, the appearance of *Nova et Vetera* in 1897 was significant as it was the occasion for a life-determining relationship. The book so impressed Baron Friedrich von Hügel that he immediately determined to meet its author. Their first meeting, on 9 October 1897, was the beginning of not only a lifelong friendship but also a critical influence that was to thrust Tyrrell into increasingly wider circles and realms of theological endeavor that guaranteed his remembrance.

TRANSITION TO MEDIATING LIBERALISM: "A CHANGE OF TACTICS"

Had Tyrrell remained locked in the unaccommodating orthodoxy of his early career, he probably never would have attracted ecclesiastical notice. The fact is that his chameleonic character precluded fixture in any position very long. Subsequent chapters will explore Tyrrell's increasing accommodation to the modern world in general and to liberal Protestant thought in particular. But first a careful review is in order of an early article that Tyrrell regarded as pivotal in his career. It bore the telling title "A Change of Tactics" and appeared in the *Month* for February 1896.[50] So significant did Tyrrell regard it that he placed it as the leading essay in *The Faith of the Millions* and gave it the new title, "A More Excellent Way." Still a shibboleth of orthodoxy in that it paraded the ideal that brought Tyrrell to Roman Catholicism, the Jesuits, and the priesthood, it also signaled a mellowing toward the religious world beyond Rome. It is Tyrrell's first broadly conceived manifesto on ecclesiology and apologetics.

The essay was occasioned by Wilfrid Ward's suggestion in his article, "The Rigidity of Rome," in the *Nineteenth Century* for November 1895, that the Catholic Church's attitude since the Reformation had been that of a bristling hedgehog. But now that the age of defensive assault has passed, the church must unbend and display her attractive side.[51] Tyrrell concurred. The time was right, he thought, because the modern mind was restless and searching for direction. Protestantism could not help, for as a dogmatic system it was disintegrating and groping in the dark. But Catholicism could help, because after the Reformation it alone among Christian religions retained a staunchly dogmatic character and continues to know exactly what it means and wants. Taken in its entirety, Tyrrell asserted, Catholicism is "the Heaven-sent answer to the problem of human life." It "provides a revealed First Philosophy" that harmonizes faith with reason and so can meet the needs of the wider world of unbelievers on a common ground.[52]

Unfortunately the Protestant-Catholic controversy brought the natural development of doctrine to a standstill. Instead of spreading the Gospel to unbelievers, Christians expended their energies on intramural controversies that gave birth to such unsymmetrical doctrines as justification by faith alone and the all-sufficiency of scripture as a guide to truth, as well as to Catholic counterclaims. But the Vatican Council has ended the conflict, and now the church must turn again to her old task of evangelizing the Gentiles. In this she must abandon aggressive and defensive polemics, and like her Master who came to state, proclaim, and reveal, she must invite, not compel. She must speak to hearts and present Catholicism "in its ethical and intellectual beauty; not as *a* religion, but as eminently *the* religion of mankind; as the complement of human nature, the 'desire of the nations.'"[53]

But for this, the Catholic Church must learn to know hearts, and so she must come out of her intellectual and social isolation and converse with the world. She must find interpreters, go-betweens who know and sympathize with both worlds, their strengths and their weaknesses, and who can interpret the age to the church and the church to the age.[54]

Here was the first clear statement of the program of "mediating liberalism" in Tyrrell's writings: to interpret the age to the church and the church to the age. A difficult task in the best of circumstances, because it requires interpreters who understand not only the age and church but also Protestantism and Catholicism and how these relate to the underlying issue of faith and reason. But it is especially difficult in view of the isolation and concomitant prejudices under which Protestantism and Catholicism developed.

For her part, Tyrrell said, the Roman Catholic Church needs to correct false impressions on two issues: the end for which the church exists and the exercise of authority in faith and discipline for the sake of that end. On the first point Tyrrell allied himself with Protestant liberalism against the Calvinist charge that Catholicism concerned itself only with man's supernatural and not his temporal welfare. In fact he turned the charge back on Calvinism, calling it a "pseudo-Christianity" that, contrary to the implications of the Incarnation, believes in "the irredeemable badness of human nature, and accordingly divorces the natural and supernatural orders altogether." The Catholic Church, Tyrrell retorted, contrives neither to join nor disjoin them but sees them working in concert, the lower serving the higher and the higher bringing the lower to perfection. Accordingly she does not identify culture with sanctification, nor does she see any opposition between them. Neither may be promoted for its own sake, but both are required for the full development of man's capabilities, and each in proper balance safeguards the other. Contrary to the Calvinist charge of egocentrism, "the Church exists, not for her own sake, but for the perfection of human nature, present no less than future, natural no less than supernatural, social no less than individual."[55]

On the issue of authority, Tyrrell urged that caricatures created by controversy be dispelled: Protestantism absolutizing private judgment and self-guidance, Roman Catholicism elevating authority to the essence of religion. In truth, Tyrrell explained, Catholicism sees authority merely as a means to an end, and then primarily as a directive power and only secondarily, in case of default, as a coercive power. When unjustly coercive, of course, authority is justly odious and inimical to true liberty. But when used justly and as a last resort, "it is no more hurtful to spiritual liberty than civil authority is to civil liberty."[56]

Another point of misunderstanding related to authority, which Tyrrell wanted to clarify, concerned the church's catholicity, her independence of national or racial boundaries. False charges can arise from the fact that different races and ages appropriate different points of doctrine and discipline in different ways. A given race might mistakenly identify its particular appropriation with the true faith and therefore cast aspersions on others. For example, a rationalistic and unimaginative people will be ready not only to defend but to exaggerate and distort the role of authority as truly Catholic while disparaging the mystical tradition as smelling of Protestantism. Another race may exaggerate the mystical element to the detriment of authority. The truth is that the church is not forced to choose one or the other, but embraces both. It would be narrow to conclude that Catholicism is peculiarly congenial to the Latins and Celts but uncongenial to the Teutons. Authority may be a greater problem to the Teutons, but authority is not the whole of Catholicism, and in other matters the tables may be turned.[57]

The critical task for apologetics, Tyrrell concluded, is to present the Catholic faith to the restless modern mind as a harmoniously articulated body of truth, not as disfigured and ill-proportioned by internecine strife. This task was begun by certain of the fathers and furthered by the scholastics. With the passing of the polemical centuries, the time has come to turn to that work again and carry it out in the broad and sympathetic spirit of Aquinas. Without that spirit one may silence or exasperate an adversary, but one will never win him or resolve a dispute. "Here then is a task that lies before the theologians and thinkers in this age and country; and it is those who, in obedience to His Holiness, imbue themselves with the spirit and method of Aquinas, that will be found equal to it."[58]

Despite the occasional bursts of militant orthodoxy in this essay, it was not considered orthodox by the faculty of theology at St. Beuno's. Its suggestion that Catholics mollify their attitudes toward "outsiders," its connecting this suggestion with the cause of Thomism, and its implication that herewith obedience to Rome was at stake simply created a furor. On 7 August 1896 Tyrrell sought solace in a letter to Thurston.

> It is a relief to address myself to an inane sheet of paper which at least if not sympathetic, is silent. The reception accorded to my last menstruation (of Febr.) by the faculty at St. Beuno's made me throw up my hands in despair. In spirit I have retired from all identification with any human cause or interest, esp. ecclesiastical; and from my private lodgings in the Jesuits' establishment at Stonyhurst look on at the progress of events as a faintly amused, wholly indifferent spectator of a farcical tragedy and tragical farce.[59]

It is hard to imagine that Tyrrell did not anticipate a hostile reaction from St. Beuno's faculty. His implications were clear and damning: that their theology was stunted and distorted; that as polemical it was diversionary from the normal course and thus interfered with the work of synthesizing faith and reason; that to this extent they were not carrying on the task of Saint Thomas and so were disobedient to the Holy Father; and that to the extent that they did not see their defects, they were narrow, unsympathetic, uncomprehending, and agitated. All these accusations may well have been true, but Tyrrell should at least have expected a protest that was not to be resisted, especially now that his intramural campaign at Stonyhurst had erupted into the public forum. Clearly he had to go.

Tyrrell's removal from Stonyhurst and assignment to the scriptorium at Farm Street effected a change of place but no change of tactics. His boldness of criticism and accommodation rose to a peak with his essay of December 1899, "A Perverted Devotion," and provoked further reprisals.[60] Delated to Rome, that essay was found "offensive to pious ears," and Tyrrell was in consequence dismissed from the staff of the *Month* and barred from publishing outside its pages. On 18 January 1900 Tyrrell sent his confrere Henri Bremond the following summary explanation:

> Since Ward's article on the "Elasticity of Rome" I began (with my article "A Change of Tactics") a practical refutation of his assertion that there was no place in the Society for kindlier views, and that the Ignatian principles of accomodation were practically obsolete among us. I hardly believed my own thesis; and more than half believed his. Still I would go on till I should be stopped; and I confess I never expected to get so far; for this is my first real check; and it is not yet final. All along, Ward & Co. have predicted my extinction; and, if there is no reprieve, they will be triumphantly right.[61]

What Tyrrell meant by a "practical refutation" of Ward was simply that he tried to make himself a proof-case against one reading of Ward, that the Jesuits had providentially come along in a time of crisis and by their exaltation of the virtue of obedience developed into "the antithesis of a thorough Protestant."[62] They were useful for fighting a war, but now that peace was declared, they have outlived their usefulness. Tyrrell wanted to emphasize that he, at least, was not "the antithesis of a thorough Protestant" but that, having been a Protestant, he was now capable of understanding and sympathizing with both sides and therefore of providing in his own person a symbol and pattern of reconciliation.[63]

In carrying out this reconciliation, it was Ward's program of "mediating liberalism" that Tyrrell first adopted and then took beyond its limits with such painful consequences. That program and Tyrrell's relationship to Ward are the subjects of the following chapter.

CHAPTER 3

Mediating Liberalism (1896–1900): Uneasy Detente

PIVOTAL YEARS: AN OVERVIEW

In the autumn of 1896, George Tyrrell, unseated from his chair of philosophy at Stonyhurst, joined the staff of writers for the *Month* at Farm Street, the Jesuit headquarters in the heart of London. Four years later he departed to a country parish in Yorkshire because he could no longer be tolerated on the staff of a journal that spoke for the Society of Jesus in England and that was subject to the censorship of the archbishop of Westminster. These were transitional years both for Tyrrell's apologetic and for his relationship to ecclesiastical authority. In this four-year span he passed from an avowedly orthodox apologetic to a liberal one, from a defensive stance over against Protestant claims to an increasingly accommodating posture. In the process he passed from a troubled and clouded relationship to authorities to a relationship that was still troubled but subjectively clear as to the reasons for the trouble. It was becoming obvious that his conflict was not simply with authorities but with an interpretation of ecclesiastical authority that stemmed from what he came to see as unacceptable presuppositions. The transition, therefore, had nothing to do with a moral or intellectual conversion but merely with acknowledging two conflicting sets of values and two behaviors operating out of those values. Tyrrell's change of direction from orthodox to liberal involved no change of character; it was simply a change of tactics

48

dictated by the encounter of his character with everyday pastoral needs. To an outsider the change may seem astonishingly sudden, perhaps even a bit bizarre, but to one who knows Tyrrell's character and the opposing ideologies that he was trying to hold in tension, the change is consistent and understandable.

When Tyrrell joined the scriptorium at Farm Street he was still suffering from the severe blow of expulsion from Stonyhurst. Consequently one finds in his first efforts for the *Month* some retrenchment from the program announced in "A Change of Tactics."[1] Indeed Tyrrell had to write with an eye constantly on the censors, and thus came those digressions and excursions for which he was sometimes criticized.[2] But he hoped that the discerning, at least, would find that program between the lines. To make this point firmly, when he gathered his *Month* articles into two volumes in 1901, he gave "A Change of Tactics" the lead position with the suggestive title, "A More Excellent Way." In fact, he wanted to call the whole work "Essays towards a More Excellent Way," but the editor of the *Month* demurred. On 11 July 1901 Tyrrell wrote to Maude Petre, "After great fuss and worry I have had to change the title of my essays to 'The Faith of the Millions'—a stupid and witless name enough. . . . But the truth is Gerard is afraid of the smack of Liberalism in that title."[3]

The first essay of note from Tyrrell's transitional period was a character sketch of Félicité de Lamennais inspired by William Gibson's *The Abbé de Lamennais and the Liberal Catholic Movement in France*.[4] It was also a striking self-portrait and an astute prophecy of the issue of Tyrrell's own life. Tyrrell saw Lamennais as a tragic figure, a man of enormous talent and fierce energy who, diverted from the path of his true vocation, ended in confusion and misery. It is hardly too bold to say that Tyrrell already knew within himself how such promise could fall so sadly short.

A creature of temperament, Lamennais rejected the pattern of his dutiful brother Jean and became by contrast unmanageable, lawless, and violent. Instead of following the prescribed lessons, he inflamed his tender mind on the likes of Diderot, Montaigne, Pascal, Voltaire, and Rousseau and in consequence "at twelve exhibited such infidel tendencies as made it prudent to defer his first Communion for some ten years."[5] Without self-restraint and the discipline that comes from a careful education, without that peace and tranquility of soul required for profound and free reflection, Lamennais's power of deliberation was crippled, and his new apologetic against Gallicanism and anti-Christian philosophy foundered on narrowness. He became simply a reactor. Some had turned metaphysics against the church, so Lamennais countered with traditionalism on the prepossession that "because there is a truth in Traditionalism, therefore, it is the whole and only truth; because metaphysics alone can do little, it is therefore unnecessary and worthless."[6]

Seeing Lamennais's genius frustrated by impetuosity, Tyrrell seemed to plead with himself. Had the man only exercised restraint and waited for the growth of subjective truth, he would have seen that Gregory XVI's condemnation of ultramontanism was not an implicit approval of Gallicanism, and he would have welcomed the papacy of Leo XIII as the dawn of fuller truth. On the other hand, had Gregory met Lamennais with an explanation instead of silence, he might have won an ally instead of a foe.

The prescription of patience and restraint that Tyrrell recommended for Lamennais became the very prescription recommended to Tyrrell by friends and enemies alike a few years hence. He concluded his essay with thoughts that came from and seem directed to his own heart: "There is indeed some kind of double personality in us all which is perhaps more observable in strongly-marked characters like De Lamennais, where, so to say, the bifurcating lines are produced further. Proud men have occasional moods of genuine humility; and habitual bitterness is allayed by intervals of sweetness; and conversely, there are ugly streaks in the fairest marble."[7]

Tyrrell followed his sketch of Lamennais with a trenchantly orthodox series on Anglican questions. "Keeping up Appearances" appeared in February 1897 and derided the archbishop of York's New Year's pastoral. This article, along with "Socialism and Catholicism," and "Round *versus* Russell" on Anglican orders and the sacrificial aspect of the Eucharist, was rejected for republication.[8]

"The Prospects of Reunion," however, was significantly different from the other articles of this series and merited a rebirth.[9] It appeared first in July 1897 and took up the question of reunion with Rome and the merits of the Anglo-Catholic movement. Its significance was twofold: it represented an incursion of the new liberal spirit into the old orthodoxy, and it caught Baron von Hügel's eye and drew him into correspondence and friendship with Tyrrell. It remained a perennial favorite of the baron and requires consideration here.

Tyrrell set the Anglican question within the broader question of reunion of all Protestant denominations with Rome. The latter he saw as virtually impossible at present because the gulf between Protestants and Rome was too wide even for hostility, let alone for affection. As to Anglicanism, he thought the time was not yet ripe for attempting corporate reunion. But for the moment the Anglican communion might serve as a buffer and bridge of communication between Catholics and the more remote Evangelicals, who might look benignly on the position of a moderate High Churchman but not waste a thought on Romanism. Similarly the High Churchman, though protesting the Romanizing extremes of Anglo-Catholicism, might be ready to see God working in it sufficiently to make rapprochement between the Church of England and Rome less unthinkable.

Thus Tyrrell adopted the unorthodox view that God is actually working within the Anglican communion and that it is his will that Anglicanism be not hindered, because whatever strengthens Anglicanism can only hasten reunion. If Catholics were as crafty and unprincipled as they are popularly supposed, Tyrrell concluded, they would never sacrifice eventual gain to some petty present triumph by unduly and prematurely proselytizing. They would wait for the roots of a future harvest to spread underground rather than secure an immediate but feeble crop of conversions day by day. This article echoes the program of mediating liberalism proposed in "A Change of Tactics," and for Friedrich von Hügel it represented the soul of what Tyrrell would later develop.[10]

BARON FRIEDRICH VON HÜGEL

Three months after "The Prospects of Reunion" appeared, von Hügel wrote to Tyrrell to say how much he enjoyed the article and admired "the rare power and finish of your style."[11] That was the second of hundreds of letters these two men would exchange over the next twelve years, so much did their lives become intertwined.

One month earlier the baron, impressed by Tyrrell's devotional work, *Nova et Vetera*, had introduced himself by letter and invited the author for a luncheon and a talk afterwards.[12] They met for the first time at the baron's home in Hampstead on 9 October 1897.[13] Many more meetings would follow, during which the two men shared their deepest hopes and fears. One wishes that a record of those meetings had been kept, as much passed between them that can be only surmised from their correspondence and from the baron's cryptic diary. Still, few men have left such a full correspondence in which the letters of both partners are extant. They allow a privileged view of a remarkable relationship.

Friedrich von Hügel was a virile and forceful character and exercised great influence on George Tyrrell. Thomas Loome argues convincingly that the key to understanding von Hügel rests in two figures: François Fénelon de Salignac de la Mothe, from 1695 archbishop of Cambrai, and Jean Mabillon, a Benedictine monk and the most distinguished ecclesiastical historian of the late seventeenth-century Maurists.[14] Doubtless it was Abbé Henri Huvelin, von Hügel's spiritual director and a Fénelon scholar, who first pointed the baron to Fénelon at a time when the baron was struggling to find his spiritual and intellectual identity within a deeply divided Catholicism. Fénelon had found in the late seventeenth century what von Hügel saw he and the church needed in the late nineteenth century: a centrist position based on deeply spiritual and intellectual motives that rejected the extremes of ultramontanism and liberalism and yet embraced both traditions on the conviction that they had once been one. The struggle for a deeply spiritual and intellectual centrist position within the Roman Catholic tradition became von Hügel's lifelong ambition and passion. What he required was, in Loome's words, "ecclesiastical loyalty joined with a critical spirit, a distinctly Roman Catholic temper wedded to love for truth."[15] It was around this ambition that he gathered his friends and associates and against this idea that he judged them.

Two such friends who influenced the baron in very different ways were William George ("Ideal") Ward and John Henry Newman, both principals of the Oxford Movement. Von Hügel and Ward were poles apart on matters of historical interpretation and ecclesiastical authority, but Ward's spirit was freewheeling and expansive and stimulated the baron's mind to consider areas and problems that he might otherwise have neglected. As to distinctly positive ideas, Newman was far more significant. At the age of seventeen von Hügel read Newman's *Loss and Gain* (1848) and told his friend H. I. D. Ryder that it was the first book that impressed on him "the intellectual might and grandeur of the Catholic position."[16] Over the next five years von Hügel read all of Newman's major writings and on 17 December 1874 wrote to Newman that his works had each "at different times and in different ways formed distinct epochs in my young intellectual and religious life. Such intellectual discipline as I have had, I owe it to your books."[17] Through several meetings and letters, the baron discussed with Newman a broad spectrum of religious problems, but his overriding interest was in Newman's philosophical principles, particularly as elaborated in *The Grammar of Assent*, a work that also profoundly influenced Tyrrell.

Philosophy of religion was not the baron's sole concern. He was equally interested in the scientific and critical study of scripture and the fathers. He learned to read them all in their original language and acquainted himself with the leading biblical and historical scholars of the day. He recognized, as few Catholic theologians then did, that to remain isolated from the findings of critical scholarship was to invite conflict and precipitate crises of faith such as those that would rock the church at the turn of the century. But for the most part von Hügel's deepest intellectual sympathies and interests were satisfied by Protestant theologians. In autumn 1902 he remarked to one of his few Catholic sympathizers, the Belgian Bollandist Père Charles de Smedt, that only in Protestantism did there now seem to exist that liberty of investigation so essential to critical scholarship, a liberty that until the sixteenth century had been part of the Catholic heritage, too.[18]

Besides the Bollandists, von Hügel exchanged ideas with a few other liberal-minded Catholics: Louis Duchesne of Paris, Gustav Bickell of Innsbruck, and Herman Schell of Würzburg. But they were all on the Continent. There was scarcely a like-minded Catholic in England with whom he could share his deepest feelings and concerns on a regular and intimate basis.

Von Hügel was ever on the lookout for such a person, and it is not surprising that in George Tyrrell he found a ready heart and mind. Tyrrell, too, suffered from an uncongenial atmosphere, and the two men, finding in each other mutual support and complementing personalities, struck a deep and lasting friendship and partnership in a common cause.

In that cause the baron enlisted two zeals intimately related and interacting—one for the intellectual, the other for the mystical element of religion within the Catholic tradition. Indeed, the deeper his contact with the scientific and philosophical movements of the modern world, the firmer his grasp of the ultimate realities of his Catholic faith. Although related, the two zeals were also separable, at least in the sense that he was able to discern which to emphasize and which to play down at any given period of his life.

But for many of his friends and associates in the "modernist movement," the two zeals were not separable, and they ultimately led to a parting of ways. In the final confrontation with authority, where the baron was able to deemphasize his intellectual zeal without strictly compromising his principles—because he could fall back on his spiritual zeal in whose service he really pursued the other—most of his friends clung tenaciously to what must ever be a secondary zeal. So, where the baron avoided condemnation, many of his friends either were excommunicated or left the church on their own. Even his relationship with Tyrrell, although it remained firm to the end, was sometimes strained over precisely this issue.

At the end of October 1897 von Hügel was preparing to migrate to Rome for the winter. On Wednesday, 27 October, he and Tyrrell had a long talk. Three days later the baron departed.[19]

Throughout that winter he and Tyrrell continued their separate studies and writings, but they kept in touch by letter.

WARDIAN LIBERALISM

Whether by occasion or cause, Tyrrell's first literary effort following his introduction to von Hügel was a manifesto of unmitigated mediating liberalism. It appeared in the *Month* for February 1898 as "Wiseman: His Aims and Methods."[20] Ostensibly a review of Wilfrid Ward's biography of Cardinal Wiseman, it was in fact a forum for expressing agreement with Ward on the principles of a liberal apologetic as found in Wiseman and Newman. Ward's epilogue especially interested Tyrrell, as it dealt with issues he himself had treated in "A Change of Tactics" and "The Prospects of Reunion."[21]

The main principle of Catholic apologetic, Tyrrell agreed, should be an equal insistence on the exclusive or dogmatic character of Catholicism and its all-embracing sympathy with every human interest. Against latitudinarianism, which makes reason the touchstone of beliefs, Tyrrell applauded the attempt of Newman and Wiseman to vindicate the need for dogma by showing that it is intimately bound up with faith and revelation and was characteristic not only of post-Tridentine Romanism but of the Christian church from its inception. If Christianity was to be a religion of the many and not a philosophy for the sophisticated, Tyrrell argued, it had to rely on faith and not on analytical reasoning, of which the multitudes are incapable. Not that the church eschews or distrusts reason. Indeed she has always used reason as a negative test for truth while denying its claim to be a positive guide to truth. She uses reason to support dogmatic propositions of faith and to show that if her propositions are nonrational they are at least not irrational. But she recognizes that faith is never the conclusion of a rational argument; it is an act of the will motivated by obedience.

Most of what people believe, Tyrrell observed, comes not from premises or direct experience but from tradition, which, though a nonrational source, is on the whole reliable—"a mirror of objective reality, whose error we can determine and allow for." But since the data of tradition are not based on reason, to force them to pass the bar of reason "is to risk rooting up the wheat with the tares."[22]

It is this risk that rationalism runs when it confounds reason with logic, and it is against this confusion that the church guards. Her wariness of reason is particularly evident around the fundamental religious truths concerning the ultimate end and use of life.

Especially in moments of crisis, when reason is most enfeebled and victimized by passion and temptation, "if the necessary laws of logic are the only road to truth, then, indeed, no man is responsible for his opinions and beliefs, religious or otherwise, and they are a matter of pure indifference; and again, if nothing is to be affirmed but what is forced upon us by those laws, then even the first principles of reason and morality, private and public, are imperilled."[23]

Wiseman's clear comprehension of this truth led him to assert that Rome alone had preserved the principles required for the healing of nations. Thus he worked for the Catholicizing of England and against the latitudinarianism of the established religion, with its consequent inability to respond to the religious needs of the age. His task was intrinsically difficult because it required making a dogmatic and exclusive religion appealing to a latitudinarian society. But it was also rendered extrinsically difficult by the fact that the Roman Catholic Church had, in protest against modern culture, methodically severed lines of communication with that society.

The first step, Wiseman saw, was to renew acquaintance by engaging in more neutral common interests, such as secular learning and civic projects. Catholics had to penetrate the intellectual life of the country and converse with society if they were ever to exert an influence for good. Prejudices had to be broken down and a "wish to believe"[24] created by drawing attention to the human and attractive side of Catholicism, its social utility, its sympathy with every cause of truth, justice, and charity. Or at least false impressions to the contrary had to be removed. Only then would suspicions be allayed and minds be disposed to believe that the church is always more willing to loose than to bind, that she binds only when forced by necessity, "that though final, so far as they exclude some definite error, her dogmas are never final in the sense of stating exhaustively truths that, being supernatural, are inexhaustible."[25] If she steps into a historical or scientific discussion, it is merely in the interest of truth, lest some greater truth be lost for the sake of a lesser, or to prevent the needless and harmful confusion of the multitudes in matters of supreme importance merely for the sake of a true but relatively inconsequential detail.

Certainly, Tyrrell conceded, a dogmatic religion lends itself to abuse, as the "dogmatizing instinct" is present in everyone so far as one is unregenerate. So it is no surprise to find that some in the church gratify this instinct either by imposing on others orthodox beliefs in an intolerant and narrow spirit or by trying to cloak purely private opinions under the mantle of ecclesiastical infallibility. Such abuses are inevitable, but it is a mistake to impute the dogmatism of individuals to the Catholic Church as a whole. A few years hence, Tyrrell would level precisely this charge of heretical dogmatism against the highest authorities of the Catholic Church.

Tyrrell's acquaintance with Ward actually began in December 1893 with a review of the latter's biographical study of his father, William George Ward, and the Catholic Revival.[26] This precipitated a protracted correspondence and a friendship that waned with the years.

In one exchange over Tyrrell's review of *Cardinal Wiseman*, Ward expressed surprise at the general coincidence of their views. Tyrrell replied that the coincidence did not surprise him as he had thoroughly studied Ward's epilogue as well as his volume on the Catholic Revival and moreover had always been "a devout disciple of Newman."[27]

Philosophically and theologically, Ward took his cue from his father and Newman, leading lights of the Oxford Movement and the Catholic Revival. Two core principles of Newman's Tractarian group, Ward maintained, were of contemporary apologetic value: anti-Erastianism and the insistence on authority and dogma. These anticipated and counteracted two current assaults on religion—one arising out of biblical criticism, the other out of naturalist rationalism.

On the relationship between scientific knowledge and religious doctrine, Ward contended that changes do indeed occur in the practical beliefs of Catholics due to scientific discoveries. For example, hell is no longer thought to be in the center of the earth, nor is the Resurrection any longer explained in terms of Aristotelian physics. But these changes do not affect the dogma properly speaking (in theological jargon, what is *de fide*). In other words, dogmas do not change, although their explication changes to keep pace with the consciousness of the age.

Ward was very concerned that Catholicism and science not be at odds, and yet that the continuity of Catholic truth be preserved. What guarantees these goals, he maintained, is the confident insistence on a strong centralized authority, which allows the church to tolerate free discussion without the danger that exists in non-Catholic groups of excessively broad views becoming stereotyped as tenable before being clearly proved. At the same time the church is able provisionally to tolerate enough of the new to satisfy those who feel that a narrow and uncandid theology makes faith appear to be merely a faculty for believing what one knows to be untrue.

In his essay, "New Wine in Old Bottles," Ward projected doctrinal authority as the protective coating for the individual's faith during crises induced by the confrontation of traditional beliefs with apparently incompatible scientific hypotheses. Doctrinal authority allows the believer to rest secure that the church's wisdom will in due time resolve the conflict. Meanwhile "he may simply be told . . . that the Church has not contemplated what is new, and has not pronounced on it; and he may be reminded that neither has science pronounced fully and finally. The lesson appropriate to the situation is that of prudence and patience."[28] The believer is therefore delivered from the tyranny of both scientific fads and individual theologians who attempt to impose their personal synthesis as if it were defined dogma.

On the one hand, then, Ward's liberalism advocated a circumspect *aggiornamento* of theological formulation in the light of historical and scientific knowledge, a process that had to be anchored in a firm but calm acceptance of the principle of authority if the faith of individuals was to be protected against a too-precipitous acceptance of untested but popular scientific hypothesis. In this process both an excessively authoritarian approach and the alternative of Protestant individualism were to be rejected. On the other hand, Ward's liberalism could scarcely conceal a triumphal gratitude that Roman Catholicism, as a strongly dogmatic religion, did not suffer from Protestant individualism with its correlative espousal of Erastian banalities. In his work on the Catholic Revival, Ward pointed out that both his father and Newman recognized from their own conversion experiences the need for an authoritative church, that religion without authority and dogma is reduced to what can be demonstrated by reason. A necessary antidote to that limitation and to the sorry individualism of Protestantism was the Vatican Council's definition of infallibility. *Pace* Ignaz von Döllinger, Ward asserted, the decree was neither a triumph for extremists nor a tragedy for scholarship. The truth of this assertion was obvious from the conciliar proceedings themselves as well as from postconciliar developments, as witness the resurgence of research in theology, church history, and scripture, endorsed and encouraged by Rome under the papacy of Leo XIII.

Ward's understanding of the position of Rome and papal authority was a paradoxical one that few could appreciate, especially few non-Catholics. Most would take it as highly quaint that he regarded the Catholic Revival of the nineteenth century, particularly as expressed in the decrees of Vatican I, as a sign that the siege mentality of the Counter Reformation had ended and that the time had come for laying down arms and replacing the principles and language of religious controversy with those of peaceful reconciliation.

TYRRELL'S LIBERALISM

For the time being, Tyrrell's mediating liberalism accorded with Ward's. Evidence of this agreement has already been seen in "A Change of Tactics" and the review of *Cardinal Wiseman*. Further evidence can be found in most of Tyrrell's other writings of this period.

In "'Liberal' Catholicism," appearing in the *Month* for May 1898, Tyrrell attempted to define the precise relationship of Catholic Christianity to the cause of civilization and progress and to vindicate the church against the charges of neglecting temporal interests for the sake of eternal.[29] He hit hard the Erastian view that the church's aim and purpose is to moralize the state and procure obedience to social law by supernatural sanctions. Some, he said, identify the cause of Christianity with the cause of progress and regard their interests as identical. But the church and the world have their own separate ideals of civilization that will always be more or less incompatible.

By "world" Tyrrell did not mean the state or secular society, but a certain nefarious tendency in everyone, which true Christian civilization must labor to counteract and transform into the Kingdom of God and his Christ. It was Luther's heresy to assert the identity between the state and the "world" of the Gospel and thus the incompatibility between church and state. He saw the church and the world, the spirit and the flesh, as antagonistic, not merely *de facto* but of necessity. Catholicism, on the contrary, acknowledges a *de facto* antagonism while denying a necessary one, and strives by every possible means to eliminate the opposition. Catholicism quarrels not with civilization but with counterfeit civilization, not with the world but with worldliness, with all principles hostile to the world's best interests, and this according to its own ageless principle that grace builds on nature and faith perfects science. The church's function is not to destroy but to fulfill.

Thus civilization, though it is not the direct aim of Christianity, is its indirect effect. It is the natural environment that Christianity strives to secure for the proper growth of the higher gifts of the spiritual life. The relation of the church to modern progress and civilization is in nearly every way parallel to that between grace and nature in the individual. "The Church may neither identify herself with 'progress' nor isolate herself from it. Her attitude must always be the difficult and uncomfortable one of partial agreement and partial dissent" before the paradox that must be faced, namely, that science is both always wrong and not wholly wrong, that it mingles "so much extravagance and excess with its reason, so much dross with its gold, as to make it invariably safe to hold back and wait."[30]

But the "liberal" will not abide such prudence. Not that his faith in the church is necessarily weak, but his faith in the world and progress is crude and strong. There is, however, a true liberalism, which, combined with a right proportion of conservation, is a necessary ingredient in the life of every society and therefore in the life of the church. It is the cutting edge of true progress in the church and in the world. But, as with a razor's edge, it is exceedingly difficult to traverse without slicing to one side or the other. It is not for everyone to try, only for the few who have "the leisure, capacity, and education for thinking widely, deeply, and temperately."[31]

His instruction on true and false liberalism in Catholicism completed, Tyrrell turned to the same task in Protestantism. In his review of Auguste Sabatier's *The Vitality of Christian Dogmas*, he tried to correct a liberal notion of development of dogma.[32] Sabatier espoused the liberal Protestant position that the Catholic Church has encrusted the revelation of the Gospel within tradition by committing herself irretrievably to various forms of pagan philosophies, including scholasticism, exalting philosophical ideas and principles into dogmas, and "failing to distinguish the emotional substance of religion from its intellectual involucre, which is as the husk to the kernel."[33] For Sabatier, Christian dogma is but the hypothetical theory and imagery in which the religious emotion of Christ—the essence of religion—clothed itself. Therefore, in different ages and cultures that same religious emotion, which Sabatier confounded with faith, stirs up new images to clothe that emotion.

But Sabatier's understanding of dogmatic development, Tyrrell charged, was false, and he proceeded to explain how and why the church came to adopt and guarantee free from error certain formulations and not others, and how this adoption is not a freezing of the Spirit's power but a divinely guided development of continuing revelation.

God's Spirit, when it instructs the mind of prophet or apostle by revelation, does not begin by teaching him a new language or a new philosophy. It takes whatever medium of expression is at hand and expresses the truth or mystery as adequately as that medium will allow. So it was with the deposit of faith handed on by the apostles. The language, imagery, philosophy, and science were their own, but the revelation and its translation into the language and philosophy of that time and place were from God. So, too, with the subsequent expression of the church's mind. If heterodoxy used the language and philosophy of Aristotle or the schools to advance false teachings, the church answered in kind. And so today, "if we would understand her mind, or the mind of the apostles and prophets, even of Christ himself, we must know how to speak and to think with them. We must study the language they spoke and the philosophy it involved."[34] But by expressing dogmas in Platonic or Aristotelian concepts, the church in no way implies that those philosophies are the only or even necessarily the best ones for that purpose, no more than does her use of Latin endorse that language as the best.

Indeed the church does not deny that, were the deposit of faith given today, its language and form might be different. But she retains the form in which it was first given because that form alone has been divinely guaranteed as the "form of sound words." Over the centuries she pondered these forms and in time recast them in the forms and phrases of scholasticism, wisely adopting a philosophy "little removed from the first spontaneous efforts of the mind towards unity."[35] And in using Latin, she imparts a certain catholicity, eternality, and immutability that befits the utterance of a universal religion. She does not forbid the translation of dogmas into the forms and phrases of other philosophies and languages to make them live for other cultures and ages, but she will not guarantee such translations.

PORTENTS OF DEPARTURE

In subsequent writings of this period Tyrrell reiterated the themes of his Sabatier article, but between the lines one can detect the elements of departure not only from his earlier orthodox stance but also from the Wardian mediating position toward greater accommodation to the most recent pressure from historical and scientific findings. Tyrrell's departure is signaled by increasingly trenchant criticism of the official apologetic. There is little doubt that the occasion of this shift was his association primarily with Baron Friedrich von Hügel and secondarily with Henri Bremond, with whom Tyrrell now began to correspond. Their influences will be considered shortly, but first a brief exposition of the evidence.

"The Church and Scholasticism" appeared in July 1898.[36] It began innocuously enough with the argument that the church has not committed herself to scholasticism and Latin as the only or even best philosophy and language, but simply the ones she happens to guarantee. That commitment came at a time when the need for analysis, ordering, and systematizing of the data of revelation within the thought system of the day was urgent, and so it resulted in a rapid growth and vitality of theological thought. That was all to the good.

Then suddenly Tyrrell changed tack and launched into a strong critique of scholastic philosophy and theology as inadequate for the modern era. Scholasticism's growth, he charged, for all its burgeoning vitality, was one-sided. It brought no new facts to light, and it neglected the historical and inductive methods that were then undreamed of. Its achieved harmonization, once painfully wrought, was regarded by scholastics as final and perpetual. They clung to that synthesis like Magdalens and consequently either ignored the radical shifting of modern thought or else labored—albeit in vain— to return the world to that philosophy which their synthesis supposed and for which alone it was suited.

To cultivate an analytical habit of mind, Tyrrell conceded a preference for Aristotelian philosophy, as it was coherent, systematic, and unsophisticated. But he warned that the cultivation of analytical habits to the exclusion of historical and positive methods can only lead to the narrowest rationalism and eventually to skepticism. This one-sidedness is what led from scholasticism to Protestantism and ultimately to the widespread skepticism of the world outside the church. Yet it is no less plain that a retreat to traditionalism would have given much the same result. The only proper response to shifting patterns of thought is accommodation, "for it is only in the right adjustment and tempering of all methods that truth is safeguarded."[37]

Tyrrell was convinced that scholasticism's overweening confidence in the power of analytical demonstration was a departure from Thomas. In a letter of 3 July 1898 to von Hügel, he underscored this conviction and pointed out that Thomas "never thought that demonstration advanced knowledge . . . but simply evolved what was involved; and made ideas, previously confused, distinct & articulate."[38]

A kindred article, "Rationalism in Religion," provoked by a plea in the *Westminster Gazette* of 19 November 1898 for optional use of the Athanasian Creed, defended dogma against the latitudinarian supposition that doctrines must justify themselves to our mental framework and that until they do we cannot really be said to believe them or have insight into them.[39] This supposition, Tyrrell charged, is a false position based on the premise that faith lies not in the submission of reason to belief in realities only partially disclosed and imperfectly apprehended but in the readiness of the *mind* to enter into *intelligent agreement* with what is revealed, to find therein not merely a speculative truth, but a practical "inspiration of life"—a pragmatic approach to be facilitated by juggling dogmatic formulations into forms that make sense.[40]

This approach sounds attractive, but a second look reveals how extremely problematic is the recasting of "sound words" to fit our understanding. If we know the object conveyed through metaphor and the exact point of parity, we can safely interchange metaphors. But if, as in the case of revelations, we know the object only in and through the metaphor, we do not know where correspondence begins or ends, so we cannot afford to meddle. Here Tyrrell appealed to Newman: "Thus revelation, being on the whole an inadequate and analogous presentment of other-world truth, no man might trust himself to depart from the 'form of words and the ordinances under which it comes to us, through which it is revealed to us, and *apart from which revelation does not exist*, there being nothing else given to us by which to ascertain or enter into it.'"[41]

Certainly reason plays a legitimate role in explicating truths of faith and morals. It may in some rare cases start from revealed premises to draw conclusions of theological certainty, for God does not gratuitously intervene where natural causes suffice. But it is precisely because the language of scripture and dogma, with its natural and concrete images, is "not adequate to what they image, but defective and ill-fitting, that we need a providential determination of points of development which reason alone cannot determine."[42]

Here is where a teaching church is needed. Reasoning from metaphors in matters of faith and morals can be carried out safely only when the precise point of similarity is otherwise determined, that is, by a divinely guided authority. Conclusions drawn even with faultless logic from ideas under which God has presented truths need to be confirmed by testing against the living sense of the church insofar as those ideas are analogous and not "proper."

Tyrrell later established the philosophical-psychological foundation for this assertion in *Religion as a Factor of Life* and *Lex Orandi*.[43] How he was able to publish such advanced notions of the inadequacy of the language of revelation and dogma with the blessing of ecclesiastical authorities remains to be seen.

The following May, in a review article titled, "Authority and Evolution: The Life of Catholic Dogma," Tyrrell drew his argument for a teaching church into the social dimension of man and in the process presented his clearest distinction to date between doctrine and dogma with regard to the theory of development.[44] He contended that the sense of the church as a test for doctrinal utterances is the touchstone of the Catholic conception of religion as a social and collective reality, in contrast to the individualist conception of Protestantism. What the individualist philosophy fails to see is that the power and therefore the duty of independent thought is relatively rare, and that the vast majority of people do, and indeed ought to, rule their minds by a certain floating body of public doctrine that comes to them out of the accumulated labors of the few independent thinkers. Thus even in the natural order the multitide is provided with a norm of belief that, though fallible, is practically sufficient for each age and country. The notion that each person can and ought to think independently on every matter has no basis in reality and leads in practice to anarchy. Man is a social being in the formation of his mind as well as in every other aspect of his existence.

In the growth of society, as in every vital organism, two principles are involved: a principle of permanence and sameness and a principle of movement and diversity. The first is founded in authority, which controls and guides the movements of the organism into concert with the fundamental idea by which its growth develops. Thus unity of end and design prevails together with extension and diversity of parts. In Roman Catholicism it is the pope who embodies the principle of authority, who gathers up and expresses the collective sentiment of the faithful in matters of faith and morals. But in the church, because it is also a supernatural religious society, a factor enters in of which philosophy takes no account. The church has received its deposit of truth or revelation not by merely human investigation and reflection. It uses human means to preserve and interpret that deposit, but divine assistance supplements it and ensures ultimate infallibility. Auguste Comte's idea of a diverse society unified toward a common goal by an authoritative principle was a good one, but Christ alone effected it.

To the Protestant rationalist, who denies the church's divine authority and regards it as an extrinsic force repressing the individual believer rather than as the faithful's own collective mind uttered from them, dogma and creeds drawn from scripture are but a human product to be altered with the times. To some even scripture is but a provisional attempt to give symbolic utterance to the felt but unknown object of the religious instinct. But to the Catholic every letter of the deposit of faith is treasured as divinely chosen. Words and symbolisms change, and therefore the original deposit needs to be explained in the language of the day. But this does not argue to changing the deposit itself. The deposit must remain unaltered as a source to which each age returns to have *its* mind and spirit altered, not *vice versa*.

Granted that most of the church's dogma arose as contradictions of heretical teachings and so is conservative rather than progressive. As a consequence, when the heresies are forgotten, so, too, may their dogmatic counterparts be forgotten. Still, the Catholic always regards dogma, whether conservative or progressive, as of divine authority and differing from scriptural expression only in this, "that in revelation the language, though human, is divinely chosen and inspired; in dogma it is chosen by human labour and only guaranteed from error through the intervention of Providence acting, not miraculously, but according to established laws."[45]

Development concerns neither scripture nor dogma (that is, those truths that the church solemnly defines as *de fide*). It concerns only the *understanding* of dogma and scripture, which the church in each age ponders and reexpresses in the form of doctrines. The latter may develop as subject to cultures and man's developing world view, but the revelation about which doctrines are formulated is given once and for all in the unchangeable form of sound words, and it is for us constantly to return to that form to seek for our own time its clearer, deeper, and fuller meaning.

External Religion: Its Use and Abuse, the last work and only book of Tyrrell's mediating period, was composed as a series of lectures for Catholic undergraduates at Oxford during the Lenten term of 1899.[46] It is an entirely apologetic statement of Tyrrell's ecclesiology and seems aimed beyond his hearers to the non-Catholic world. As such, and in accord with Wardian liberalism, Tyrrell aimed to present an honest picture of the Catholic Church and so to remove many misconceptions that had cropped up during centuries of fortification. With an eye to Protestantism as a point of comparison, and particularly liberal Protestantism of the Sabatier variety, Tyrrell insisted again on the principle of dogmatic authority. But totally absent now is the tone of arrogance and contempt that marked his militant period.

Tyrrell began by presenting Catholicism as an external servant-society molded in the image of the Incarnate Lord as healer of wounded nature. That image, Tyrrell submitted, does not set well with a certain false mysticism prevalent in Protestantism, which sees weakness as evil and so seeks to redeem the spirit by condemning the body.[47] But Christ redeemed humankind by becoming body and used the weaker elements to redeem the stronger— the spirit through the flesh, the invisible through the visible, the internal through the external. Thus God shows by the Incarnation that the seeming evil of the senses and material things is not in themselves but in the perverse will of whoever misuses them. Let the will be healed and rectified, and at once the material world returns to its original obedience. What before were stumbling blocks—the body with its senses, the imagination, the feelings and passions—are now through Christ's redemption instruments for sanctification.

The Catholic Church with its visible hierarchy and membership, its tangible rites and sacraments, its preaching and teaching expressed in human thought and language, is but an extension of that incarnational economy whereby flesh, the "visible word," once made opaque by sin, again becomes the transparent medium of intercourse between God and man. Now there is no dichotomy between the outward and the inward, the external and internal, the spirit and the body. Man is religious through and through and must outwardly express his inward religious meaning, just as the soul must have a body to express itself.

Not that the Incarnation and incarnational church are the only and necessary means to salvation. From the dawn of creation the Eternal Word was and remains the true light that enlightens every man that comes into the world. But from the very beginning the divine Will under the name of conscience has been struggling against the self-centered will of every child of Adam so constantly and persistently that men mistook it as their own natural spring of action. Here and there a Socrates or a Marcus Aurelius perceived the truth. But most men were too gross and self-ignorant to discern a presence so subtly intertwined with their own souls. Thus it was necessary, if not precisely for men's salvation, certainly for their full development, that their conscience, "this indwelling Will of God, this Power within making for justice, should go outside them, should become Incarnate and face them, and speak to them, as man to man: that God should live visibly and outwardly upon earth that life of humiliation which He lives millions of times over in human souls; that thus our slow minds might apprehend, at least in figure, that tragedy which is realized daily in the very core of our being."[48]

The Incarnation brings man himself to his own senses. It shows him what he does when he perpetrates evil against himself and against whatever is of God. "The Crucifix is the collective sin of the world made visible. It shows us our sins preying upon God, and God meekly submitting to our violence, lest it would react upon us to our destruction." And the Resurrection is "the outward counterpart of that inward resurrection of Christ in the soul when conscience, quickened from the dead by grace, reasserts itself once more and reigns victorious in the penitent heart."[49]

The sacraments merely continue that incarnational economy. They are external symbols of that internal Christ of conscience who could himself instruct us were not our hearts so closed. In the sacraments the external Christ faces us and calls aloud to our buried conscience to rise up to a new and supernatural life. "By this union of the outward and inward rule of Christ—the inward supplemented, corrected, and elevated by the outward—our nature is lifted up to companionship with God."[50]

The Reformers failed to appreciate the nature of the Incarnation when they depreciated an outward objective religion and substituted a false mysticism in which private inspiration and judgment prevailed. At the other extreme, however, and perhaps in reaction to the Reformers, Roman Catholicism tended toward a formalism that enshrined the elements of authority, obedience, and church membership as though external means were ends in themselves and the essence of Christian life rather than merely its condition. Formalism forgets that "our Catholic religion is principally, though not exclusively, interior, and does not *consist* in professions and observations, although it does not exist without them."[51]

Furthermore, does not the fact that there are many good people among those who practice no external religion at all, and many bad people among those who do, indicate much good in a purely internal religion and some seeming evil in an external religion? To this question Tyrrell answered that the good in a purely internal religion exists more fully in the Catholic religion, and that what seems evil in the Catholic religion is either in the eye of the beholder or not really a part of Catholicism and should be rejected by Catholic and Protestant alike.

There is, for example, the mistaken notion that sacramental grace, infallible teaching, and the promise of indefectibility are means to make life easier, to make Catholics suffer less. Some have charged—and not without foundation—that the Catholic doctrine of grace promotes indolence and softness, that the Church says equivalently, "Come to me, you that labour and are burdened, and I will make goodness cheap and easy for you."[52] Indeed many Catholics give credence to this charge by their frequent reception of sacraments without any consequent indication of growth in love for their neighbor, merely using sacraments as substitutes for the virtues they are meant to strengthen.

Similarly, the abuse of infallible teaching authority can lead to intellectual indolence and lack of independent thought even in secular and profane matters. But in fact authority was given so that Catholics might think and act with greater freedom and confidence and assume an even greater degree of responsibility for preaching the Gospel. The same with the promise of indefectibility. It was given not so that Catholics might be smug in their assurance of ultimate triumph but that they should exert themselves more for the

spread of the Gospel, so that they may have confidence and courage to struggle in many a crisis where common sense would tell
them to give up and surrender to the inevitable. It tells them not
that victory is gained without fighting, but precisely through fighting. The assurance of victory is encouragement not to quit but to
continue fighting. The promised perpetuity of the church is the result not of miraculous intervention but of divine assistance and
special providence within the workings of natural laws.

Still, Tyrrell pointed out, no matter how closely the church follows the natural laws of societies, there remains one crucial exception that the philosopher of history cannot explain. The initial impact of Christ and his disciples does not gradually die away like
ripples on a pond but is renewed again and again throughout history. Tyrrell's implication here is that what is largely responsible
for the persistence of that initial impact is its contemporaneous
availability in the externals of religion.

In his final lecture Tyrrell defined that foundational reality
which both expresses itself in the externals of religion and is, in
turn, fostered by them, namely faith. For Tyrrell faith means holding on blindly by the will to realities unseen but revealed by God.
It is essentially an act of obedience, a conformity of man's will to
God's, not an act of understanding or reason. Were it the latter,
only the faith of the few who are clever enough to stand toe to toe
with scientific knowledge would survive. (And indeed the clever
should strive to meet scientific objections and reconcile faith with
secular knowledge, realizing meanwhile that all such reconcilia-
tions are as tentative as secular knowledge itself.) But faith does
not rest on any defence of it, for "faith is produced not by the
power of arguments over the mind; but by the power and authority of God's will felt and obeyed by the human will—very much as
a dog feels and obeys the will of his master made known in a look
or a word."[53] Faith depends on hearing and obeying conscience,
the interior voice of God, "for in point of fact it is by *doing,* and
not by *thinking* or reasoning that we apprehend God and His truth
in this life."[54] Mind or imagination reaches not God but only one's
idea of God, a crude representation constructed out of the fragments of one's experience. If this is what we place before our
mind's eye when we pray and confess our love for God, it is no
wonder that God seems so distant, uncertain, and intangible.

But God wills to give himself to the multitude, not just to those
capable of an intellectualized religion. The poor and the simple
find God not in their minds and imaginings but in acts of obedience to God's will as expressed in scripture and interpreted by
legitimate ecclesiastical authority. His will works through con-

science and mingles his activity with man's, so that every good action becomes a joint enterprise, a common offspring that, as in married love, cements more firmly than ever the union of love between God and man. Out of this action comes an experimental knowledge of God, a firsthand sense that can never be got from the most elaborate philosophical or theological notions of the divine nature, nor even from meditation on God's self-revelation in Christ.

Tyrrell composed these lectures with great thought and care, as he drew numerous finely balanced distinctions. Nonetheless, he caught the baleful glance of Bishop Rafael Merry del Val, who later as Pius X's secretary of state would execute the campaign against the "modernists" and excommunicate Tyrrell. Originally ordained for the Westminster archdiocese but in the Vatican's employ since his student days in Rome, Merry del Val retained a special interest and close ties with family and friends in England. In fact in 1896 he was named secretary of the papal commission to investigate the question of the validity of Anglican orders (two years later declared null and void by the encyclical *Apostolicae curae*). In addition, the fact that at the time of Tyrrell's lectures Merry del Val was a consultor of the Sacred Congregation of the Index gave him further reason to watch England.

By June 1899 *External Religion* was in the bookshops. In September Merry del Val was visiting relatives in England,[55] and in October he wrote back to England from Rome that his attention had been called to lecture 5 of Tyrrell's book and that he had been "very unfavourably impressed." He confessed that he had not read the whole series. Nonetheless it was clear to him that "even if not pronounced to be explicitly unsound theology . . . the teaching is so confusedly and incompletely expressed as to leave an unsound impression upon the reader's mind," so much so that the majority of readers would draw conclusions that "must surely be in opposition with the teaching of all the Saints and masters of the Spiritual Life."[56]

Indeed some of Tyrrell's statements, if not read carefully against others, sound semi-Pelagian—like his suggestion that the purpose of prayer and the sacraments was to make people more responsible for moral living and exert themselves more on behalf of the Gospel and not less. The correlative was that the regular reception of the sacraments without a concomitant increase of charity—at least in one's heart if not in one's actions—would indicate an abuse of external means. To reinforce his point, Tyrrell suggested that perhaps, in cases of abuse, if external helps were suddenly withdrawn, abusers might for the first time in their lives "use the strength that was within them all along" and "make that painful exertion for which they secretly, almost unconsciously, hoped the frequentation of the sacraments might serve as a substitute."[57] Tyrrell made numerous related claims with a degree of seeming gratuity and force common to prophetic literature—and doubtless this attitude contributed to their disturbing quality—such as: "God does not give a people a rich and luxuriant soil in order to make them idle or to save them exertion, yet more often than not they so misuse His liberality that it makes for decadence rather than progress."[58] History could hardly prove Tyrrell right, but it could argue a strong case.

Merry del Val was worried that those among Tyrrell's readers who felt themselves making little or no progress in virtue despite sacramental helps would conclude that they should cease frequenting the sacraments and start operating out of their own strength. But Tyrrell was careful in this lecture and elsewhere to meet that charge and to cut a slender path between Pelagianism and Quietism. Obviously he was not careful enough.

Whether Tyrrell was aware of Merry del Val's displeasure with *External Religion* is unknown, but it is quite probable that he was. Certainly he received criticism, and precisely of lecture 5, because in the edition of 1900 and all subsequent editions he included a lengthy note to this lecture that began (petulantly?), "It might seem, on superficial consideration, that the view here set forth is barely consonant with that not uncommonly held . . . ."[59] In a letter of 2 January 1901 Tyrrell told Maude Petre that his note "attempted a return to S. Thomas' doctrine . . . & barely escaped the Index in consequence."[60] *External Religion* may have escaped the Index, but Tyrrell himself henceforth never escaped Merry del Val's eye.

IN SUM: TYRRELL *VIS-À-VIS* WARD

The foregoing exposition of Tyrrell's liberalism in action may now be clarified by enumerating its chief characteristics and then indicating some emphases that in time created an ideological rift between Tyrrell and Ward.

Although Tyrrell announced in "A Change of Tactics" that his aim was to interpret the age to the church and the church to the age, in practice, during his mediating period he did little of the former and much of the latter. Most of his writings aimed to present an honest and true picture of Catholicism to the non-Catholic world in order to remove Protestant misunderstandings of the Catholic position. But he also had in mind Catholic readers who through exaggerated counterreactions likewise developed incorrect notions of their own religion.

First, Tyrrell insisted with Ward on the exclusive and dogmatic character of Catholicism and vindicated this principle against the latitudinarian claim that would make reason the touchstone of what is to be held by all. At the same time, Tyrrell insisted on Catholicism's all-embracing sympathy with every human interest and advocated that Catholics quickly enter the neutral ground of secular learning and national interests on which acquaintances with Protestants might be renewed and dialogue and reeducation on controversial topics be developed.

Second, on matters of state and secular interests, Tyrrell pointed out that the principal aim of Catholicism—contrary to Erastian claims—is not to moralize the state but to sanctify the church's own members, although moralization of the state would follow as a necessary corollary, for faith perfects science and grace complements nature. The church's office is not to destroy but to fulfill. In pursuing her office, she "may neither identify with 'progress' nor isolate herself from it. Her attitude must always be the difficult and uncomfortable one of partial agreement and partial dissent."[61] She must proceed with caution and prudence in her assimilation of the latest scientific discoveries. Individuals who are well read and think deeply may run on ahead and coax and persuade authorities to hasten, but authorities must never be opposed or affronted by extremist assertions lest they react with equally extreme counterassertions. True liberalism, which is a fine blend of conservative with liberal elements, is only for the few. The multitude must take their thought ready-made from others.

Third, on the question of development of dogma, Tyrrell joined Newman and Ward in their contention that the deposit of faith—scripture and tradition as formulated in solemnly ratified dogmatic propositions—does not develop. Man's mind, his language, and his milieu develop, and as these change so does the church's *interpretation* of the deposit. It is the interpretation or church doctrine that can properly be said to develop.

Fourth, the church chose scholastic (Aristotelian) philosophy and Latin as the vehicle of her dogmatic formulations because they were and remain the most universal media for the expression of thought. By so choosing, the church neither claimed them to be the best philosophy and language, nor did she forbid dogmatic propositions to be retranslated into other philosophies and languages. Indeed they must be retranslated to communicate them to other ages and cultures. Only she will not guarantee retranslations as possessing the same degree of infallibility as the original statements. So every age must return again and again to the original deposit to be properly measured and fitted.

Finally, the Catholic religion is an external religion, and in this its conception is social and collective compared with the individualist conception of Protestantism. The externals of religion—the sacraments, the hierarchical structure, dogma, and scripture—were given by God as sacraments of that external Christ who stands outside as a standard of excellence and calls forth that interior Christ and our internal religion to reach for and grasp the external standard. The Catholic religion is a religion of the Incarnation, of the Word-made-flesh, a religion of the *Fiat*, a religion of obedience. It is principally and essentially a religion of conformity of man's will to God's as mediated through scripture, tradition, and those legitimately appointed to interpret the deposit of faith. Only secondarily and quite contingently is it a religion of conformity of intellect to some understanding of the deposit of faith.

In all these principles Tyrrell and Ward agreed. Where one can see divergence at this time is not so much in their ideas as in their expressions and emphases. With Ward, one can detect a note of triumphalism and a generous hint of his father's ultramontane spirit, whereas Tyrrell gloried in proving Protestants wrong rather than in proving Rome right. Concomitantly he was never touched with the ultramontane spirit, although he insisted with Ward on the legitimate and needful role of papal authority. Since joining Ward, Tyrrell lost his earlier vindictive and aggressive posture against Protestantism, because now he was the mediating liberal, interested in conciliation and peace, not war.

The two agreed in the aim to create a "wish to believe" in non-Catholics by the witness of good lives, but on the question of how to improve the witness of good lives there is a critical emphasis in Tyrrell that is not present in Ward. To influence the multitude, said Tyrrell, the church must win back the leaders, the clergy. She must raise the standards of clerical education and motivate pastors to focus attention on their own flocks and not on proselytizing. In this way the church will improve the lives of the multitude, who in turn will make the Gospel attractive by the example of their lives.

The note of criticism is most evident in *External Religion*, where Tyrrell disapproved of the tendency to seek salvation in externals and to make these an end rather than a means to calling forth the interior religious instincts that are more fundamental and anterior to the externals. Tyrrell also frowned on the church's abuse of scholasticism, her clinging to the scholastic synthesis as if it were absolute and final. Its synthesis, Tyrrell pointed out, was one-sided. It achieved the harmonization of church teaching with current scientific data, but it brought no few facts to light, neglected the historical and inductive methods, and so failed to change with the mentality of the secular world.

Finally, Tyrrell's emphasis in *External Religion* on experience as the point of departure for religion, his emphasis on the internal Christ and on conscience as that which ties men to God, are emphases to be found in liberal Protestantism. However, his definition of religious experience differs. For him it is a realized conformity of will with the will of God as experienced in Christian moral living and communicated through the externals of an essentially communitarian religion, rather than as experienced through a *Gefühl* stirred up by the direct action of God on the individual soul.[62] Nevertheless Tyrrell emphasized the priority of *personal obedience to conscience*. At the same time, he recognized that overemphasis on personal obedience could readily translate into the individualism of Protestantism, and that he wanted carefully to avoid.

TOWARD A NEW APOLOGETIC

To return to an earlier point, the occasion of Tyrrell's shift from Wardian liberalism toward a new apologetic was the influence of Baron Friedrich von Hügel and Henri Bremond. The former provided the intellectual stimulus, the latter the emotional.

In December 1897, two months after their first meeting, von Hügel introduced Tyrrell to the then-exploding scene of French Catholic apologetics and specifically the writings of Maurice Blondel and his disciple and elucidator Lucien Laberthonnière. Bremond, a sympathetic fellow Jesuit, furnished Tyrrell with the only truly ready ear that could fully understand the frustrations they both experienced in seeing the dwindling of their hopes that the Society of Jesus could ever recapture its original vitality and elasticity and once again assume its place as the church's apologist to the modern world. All of these personal influences—Bremond and von Hügel with his countless friends and ideas—entered Tyrrell's life at a critical point and were decisive in leading him, certainly not against his will, toward admitting into his Catholic apologetic more and more of the Protestantizing influences.

It is difficult at this point to be very specific about these influences without undue digression. Suffice it to say that they were all that curently interested von Hügel and might go under the broad heading of the "mystical element" of religion—that contact with Augustine's doctrine on the will that had been more actively preserved in the Protestant than in the Catholic tradition. Catholicism had saved reason in the Thomistic synthesis, but it subsequently elevated reason to a status never intended by Thomas. Protestantism, too, was guilty of exaggerated rationalism and in fact carried it to such extremes that by the end of the eighteenth century Friedrich Schleiermacher consolidated a counterreaction which tried to reconnect intellect with feeling or the will-element in a new synthesis of faith and reason in the mind-language of the day.

To Tyrrell, Schleiermacher was little more than a name. But the dialogue on faith and reason that he unleashed hit Tyrrell full force in the writings of Blondel and Laberthonnière. The admitted background for the synthesis Blondel achieved in his monumental thesis *L'Action* was the German idealist tradition, specifically the line of Spinoza-Kant-Fichte-Schelling-Hegel-(the later) Schelling.[63]

Newman and the French Apologists

That Tyrrell was in sympathy with liberal thought is not surprising, as a link connecting him with von Hügel, Bremond, Blondel, and Laberthonnière can be seen in the figure of John Henry Newman. It was Newman's *Grammar of Assent* that back in 1885 effected "a profound revolution" in Tyrrell's way of thinking.[64] Newman's impact on von Hügel was equally profound.[65]

Blondel was introduced to Newman by his director of studies at the École Normale in Paris, Léon Ollé-Laprune, to whom Blondel dedicated his dissertation. Ollé-Laprune's own dissertation, inspired by Newman, attempted to show the free and voluntary character of faith and Catholicism's harmony with the deepest aspirations of the human heart.[66] Ferdinand Brunetière, another of Blondel's teachers at the École Normale, wrote the preface to the French translation of Balfour's *Foundations of Belief*. Here and elsewhere Brunetière stressed the "bankruptcy of science" and its incapacity to furnish guidance for life or to demonstrate matters of faith—some of Newman's favorite themes.[67]

Laberthonnière's "Le Dogmatisme moral," an essay in elucidation of Blondel, followed the lines laid down by Newman in its emphasis on the part played by the will in achieving religious certitude.[68] Such certitude, he said, "is moral in the sense that it is our own work—a work which we accomplish with the help of God and of others, but for which our own action is indispensable."[69]

Henri Bremond entered the Society of Jesus in 1882 and spent the first ten years of his training in England. Already in the novitiate he was captivated by the Oxford Movement and its key figure, J. H. Newman. Bremond wrote his first article on Newman in 1896. Five other articles and four books followed.[70] When in 1896 Blondel was appointed professor at the University of Aix-en-Provence, Bremond was there completing his final year of Jesuit training. Here the two met and became friends. They subsequently engaged in an extraordinarily full correspondence over the years of the modernist crisis.[71] Newman was a frequent topic of discussion.

Newman's *Grammar of Assent* is the key to the shift in apologetics advanced by this cluster of associates. Newman was dissatisfied with traditional apologetics, particularly with the extravagant claims for what reason can prove about God. We have certitude about things unseen that cannot be accounted for by reason alone, he insisted. We have assents based not on inference, which can lead only to conditional assent, but on the total response of the whole person to a concrete fact, and this response alone can account for certitude. Newman's thesis of notional and real assent sent waves to the shores of France and back again.[72]

Blondel: L'Action *and "On Apologetics"*

Blondel's response to the German idealists in *L'Action* shows a marked similarity to Newman's ideas in *Grammar of Assent*.[73] A sketch of Blondel's principles is in order, because they were foundational for Tyrrell's philosophy of religion and apologetic.

Blondel's main thesis is that philosophy must take its impetus from "action" rather than from pure thought, "action" here referring to the whole of our life—thinking, feeling, and willing.[74] In its quest for truth, philosophy must turn from abstract thought and look to the whole person and to concrete experience, for it is concrete experience that motivates philosophical inquiry. Man by nature must act. Even to choose not to act is already to act. And having acted, man cannot help questioning the meaning of his action.

By an ingenious argument borrowed from Thomistic psychology, Blondel rejected any nihilistic attempt to skirt the question of the meaning of action. To affirm nothing, he argued, is really to affirm being, for the very idea of nothing can be formed only by conceiving something positive and then denying it. The nihilist's denials are supported by something affirmative, as shown in the satisfaction he derives from his pessimism. The extent of his denials reveals the greatness of what he wishes. Therefore, Blondel concluded, the problem of action and its meaning must have a positive solution.

The solution is to be found in a phenomenology of action, but one that demonstrates the necessity of passing beyond mere phenomena to the "supraphenomenal" by reason of a dialectic immanent in action itself, or by reason of what Blondel called "the logic of action."[75] That "logic" rests on the hiatus experienced between man's action and what he demands. His reach always exceeds his grasp, so a permanent dissatisfaction sets in and impels man to further action in an ever-widening search to close the gap. Man begins with self-regarding action, but soon felt limitations make him discontented enough to move to various forms of other-regarding action. These in turn reach their limit in the summit of moral action, promoting the good of all humankind.

Although the logic of action impels man to try to bridge the gap between action and its realization, at each stage the gap reopens. There is no immanent solution to the requirements of action. Yet an affirmative solution is demanded. The logic of action therefore points one from the immanent to the transcendent. Yet this quest for realization would be frustrated did not God in turn move from his transcendence toward man and support and supplement human action by divine grace.[76]

Action is concrete, and it is in action that man apprehends God. Therefore the beliefs that arise out of man's experience of acting cannot be merely abstract formulations. If one tries to capture the divine reality in a proposition or tries to prove God's existence by a logical demonstration, God escapes.[77]

L'Action was greeted with hostility.[78] To meet the criticism, Blondel serialized in *Annales de philosophie chrétienne* his "Letter on Apologetics." But this received even rougher treatment. In his opening paragraph he asserted, "Science is incompetent, and metaphysics, at least in its traditional form, is inefficacious when we are trying to bring back the men of our time to Christianity."[79] Taken as a criticism of traditional apologetics and scholastic philosophy in service thereof (which indeed it was), the "Letter on Apologetics" was delated to the Holy Office but later vindicated by Leo XIII at the request of Cardinal Adolphe Louis Perraud.[80]

The method of apologetics that Blondel advocated in the "Letter on Apologetics" was essentially that of the "logic of action" of *L'Action*, only he changed the name to the "method of immanence."[81] It was a method that was completely to redirect the trend of Catholic apologetics. Gregory Baum calls the new trend "The Blondellian Shift"—that is, a shift away from nineteenth-century extrinsicist apologetics, which, in wrestling with issues raised by the extremes of rationalism and fideism and yet trying to work between them, had introduced a radical distinction between faith and the rational credibility of faith.[82] Against the rationalists and with the fideists, the extrinsicists asserted that faith is a free gift from God and hence not demonstrable. But against the fideists and with the rationalists, they claimed that what can be demonstrated—ultimately by reference to miracles—is that church dogma is not a human but a divine message. Hence, however startling to reason, it is worthy of belief or is credible. This distinction that severed faith and credibility paid a stiff price: the exclusion of divine revelation from the process by which man comes to know what is for his salvation. The official theology allowed no inner continuity between the rational discernment of credibility and the Spirit-created acknowledgment of the divine Word. The credibility of faith remained totally extrinsic to faith itself.

What counted in traditional apologetics was not so much the content of revelation as its divine authorship. The content had little to do with the genesis of faith in the mind of the believer. Any message at all, whatever its content, so long as its divine origin is certified by miracles, can be the object of faith and a way of salvation. Faith in this context is viewed simply as a grace-created act of obedience to divine authority, with little regard of its intrinsic meaning for men and its effect on human life.

Blondel rejected this extrinsicist view and raised what became the preoccupying issue of twentieth-century apologetics, the issue of relevance. He realized that the irrelevant is also unbelievable and therefore that to continue to regard revelation as information about heavenly realities stuck onto human life from the outside without at the same time showing an *attrait* arising out of man's very nature is to jeopardize the chances of the Gospel's being heard at all. The God of the old apologetic—the outsider-God who dwells in a realm apart and intervenes from time to time—does not exist. But does not the Gospel attest to the existence rather of an insider-God? That is the question for twentieth-century apologetics. Its task is to urge an affirmative answer, to show how the Gospel not only offers a critique of human life and thus demonstrates its transcendence but also has power to transform human life and thus demonstrates its relevance.

This task can be best accomplished by the "method of immanence," which, based on man's experience, asserts that no truth can be acknowledged by the human mind unless it in some way proceeds from it. Man cannot accept an idea as true unless it corresponds to a question already present within his mind, unless it in some way arises out of his experience of reality. Truth cannot be pinned onto life; it is available within life itself.

Does this method lock man within his own finite framework of existence and thus suffer the very pitfall that Blondel saw in Kant? Not if the transcendent is present in the finite. Then man's own experience of reality and reflection thereon will eventually disclose it. Truth is present in man's own action, in his own willing, choosing, and doing, in the process of self-affirmation by which man becomes what he is by nature and determines his own history. Man only knows who he is, and he only envisions what he is to become through the incarnation of his conception of reality in action. The evaluation of life and the discernment of meaning take place in human action before they become concepts in the human mind. Living is prior to philosophizing. The formulation of truth in conceptual categories is only consequent to reflection on man's history. If there is present in human history a meaningful reality that transcends man and his universe, it will manifest itself within the structure of human action. Action itself possesses the proper synthesis between faith and reason, and reflection thereon will yield an apologetic suited to the natural structure of the human person whom the old apologetic no longer touches.[83]

As indicated earlier, from about mid-summer 1898 there is a shift in Tyrrell's tone toward greater accommodation to recent historico-critical discoveries. This shift is not nearly as noticeable in his publications, which had to satisfy censors, as in his correspondence, where he could vent himself freely over the inadequacy of traditional apologetics, the church's laggardly adaptation to the modern mind, and the incapacity of his religious order to advance the needed reforms.

Direct cause and effect is generally difficult to prove in the history of ideas, but coincident with Tyrrell's expressed impatience was his reading of Blondel's "Letter on Apologetics" and Laberthonnière's defense and elucidation thereof in "Le Dogmatisme moral" and "Le Problème religieux."[84]

Early Correspondence with von Hügel: New Friends, New Ideas

On Tuesday, 19 October 1897, von Hügel wrote Tyrrell to arrange a meeting prior to his winter migration to Rome.[85] The meeting occurred the following Wednesday, 27 October, and concerned two issues: the health of the baron's daughter Gertrud and several impressions and proposals connected with Tyrrell's writings.[86] It must have been at that meeting that von Hügel introduced Tyrrell to Blondel's work and left with him a "little brochure," because in Tyrrell's first letter to the baron in Rome he wrote, "I have read several times Blondel's little brochure and am much impressed with it, though I do not pretend to enter into all of his ideas owing to my unclearness as to much of his meaning." Tyrrell went on to explain his own sympathy with Blondel—wherever he understood him—especially Blondel's criticism of the current forms of apologetic and his wider view of faith. "It has driven me back to reconsider views of my own which I have always felt were censurable theologically as rash, but which would not always be rash. Now Blondel has gone far beyond me."[87]

Still, Tyrrell pointed out, Blondel's advance was not so much in his sense as in his sound. He had departed from scholastic terminology and assumed the current language of idealism and pragmatism and thus was bound to be a stumbling block to traditional Catholic scholars. "Put the penny catechism into idealist language and tho' the thing said is the same, yet it will be anathematised as *piis auribus offensiva*." But put Blondel into scholastic language, and none would recognize "an advance of thought save those fit and ready to receive it." Dissembling with language, Tyrrell confided, was the secret of his own Thomism, "which much puzzles many who know something of the lie in my mind. With that weapon I can out-Herod Herod, and be more orthodox than the pope."[88]

Tyrrell then outlined his undercover scheme and in the process exposed wounds still smarting from the battle of Stonyhurst—an important factor among those that nudged Tyrrell away from a mediating position. Tyrrell's plan was to use the neo-scholastic movement against itself by invoking Thomas himself as being "essentially liberal-minded and synthetic; with a strong infusion of Platonism through Augustine & the Victorines" and "as unlike as possible in tone and temper to the scholastics." Tyrrell would study Aquinas "not as an authority, but critically and historically as a genius," as one would study Dante, "in order that knowing the mind of another age we might know the mind of our own more intelligently." However, Tyrrell complained, his past efforts in this direction only succeeded in creating a vague impression of disloyalty to the anti-Dominican traditions of the Society of Jesus. He had hoped "that under cover of Aquinas, much might have been quietly introduced and assimilated unconsciously, that will be opposed if presented in an alien and hostile garb."[89]

Most of Tyrrell's correspondence with von Hügel during the

winter months of 1897-98 concerned the baron's daughter Gertrud, whom Tyrrell was guiding back to health after an interlude with spiritual distress induced by overexposure to her father's ideas. However, a few exchanges bear on the present discussion.

From the Hotel Germania the baron wrote on 26 January 1898 to tempt Tyrrell to become acquainted with "my good friend Prof. Eucken of Jena" and to learn German so as to read him. "How deeply *creaturely* his tone is; in moral disposition and view of life he is a Christian, tho' clearly stating and illustrating his nonacceptance of all dogma."[90] This is the first mention of Rudolf Eucken and von Hügel's first suggestion that Tyrrell learn German. Three years hence Tyrrell would begin German so as to read not only Eucken but a host of other German scholars familiar to von Hügel, many in the field of critical biblical studies of which Tyrrell at this time was quite innocent. Von Hügel, incidentally, also urged Eucken on Blondel and Bremond.[91]

At the University of Jena, Eucken operated in the tradition of Fichte, Hegel, and Schelling, the same tradition out of which Blondel worked. Perhaps that is why Eucken was one of the few scholars whose initial reaction to *L'Action* was favorable. In fact, he brought the book to von Hügel's attention, who then gave it to Tyrrell, who in turn pointed out to von Hügel its similarity to Eucken's *Der Wahrheitsgehalt der Religion*.[92] How Tyrrell incorporated Eucken's thought will be seen in a later chapter.[93]

On 26 April von Hügel began a four-week tour back to England, but before departing Rome he sent Tyrrell Laberthonnière's "Le Problème religieux"—"a beautiful and still and deep piece of thinking," which he hoped Tyrrell would like "at least as much as Blondel himself."[94] On his return the baron read works by Fichte, Ernst Troeltsch, Eucken, and Hermann Lotze, all in due time to be relayed to and have strong effect on Tyrrell.[95] He stopped over in Würzburg for visits with Albert Ehrhard and Herman Schell, then went on to Jena for six days of philosophical discussions with Eucken.[96] He arrived at Hampstead on 20 May and three days later invited Tyrrell for a weekend visit.

Von Hügel and Tyrrell did not actually meet until 6 June and then very briefly,[97] but the baron kept Tyrrell well supplied with agenda. On 20 and 28 June he sent packets of papers for Tyrrell to read,[98] among them another copy of "Le Problème religieux." Tyrrell replied on 29 June with all due gratitude that he already had a copy, "to lend about to the elect." Blondel, he remarked, requires simplification and recasting in "the form of sound words"; otherwise theologians of the ascendancy would appreciate him only as an adversary. "One can say & do so much good provided one does not shock the ear with unwonted sounds. Few care about the sense."[99]

One of the papers von Hügel sent was his own "The Historical Method and the Documents of the Hexateuch," delivered at the fourth International Scientific Congress for Catholics, 16 to 20 August 1897 at Freiburg in Switzerland.[100] The paper attempted a tenable accommodation of historical criticism to Catholic teaching. As such it was regarded as momentous and occasioned some significant comment. Alfred Loisy, who attended the congress—as did Ward and Blondel—heard the paper and described von Hügel as "Catholic to the marrow of his bones."[101] Bishop Eudoxe-Irénée Mignot of Fréjus, friend of the baron and supporter of his interests, assessed the paper as "something more than a learned study; you have performed a most courageous act. You have been brave enough to say aloud what all the specialists think silently; that the conclusions of sane criticism, however bold they may seem, are not in opposition with the Faith. . . . Your study will advance by twenty years the progress of true criticism among Catholics."[102]

Tyrrell's reaction was equally fervent. In fact, he told the baron, he was now sorely tempted to leap into that formidable sea that years ago, for lack of ability and leisure, he had resolved to leave to those more expert than himself. Seminary studies, he complained, virtually excluded priests from being at the forefront of biblical studies. "Seven years go to scholasticism which might all be fitted into two or three with gain. However I trust that events will be too strong for the old-world system, and that it will fall before the law of survival of the fittest."[103] It would take sixty years for this prophecy to be fulfilled, but only a few years hence more personal events provided Tyrrell the opportunity and incentive to plunge into the biblical question.

Meanwhile, encouraged by von Hügel, Tyrrell continued his Blondellian excursion. The baron's very long letter of 26 September 1898 was surely one of the most influential in drawing Tyrrell to affirm that God and meaning are to be sought through action and the concrete rather than by abstracting from life or fleeing from the "world."[104] Catherine of Genoa was on the baron's mind. The article he was writing on her was now two-thirds complete, and in this letter he outlined his views on mysticism as contrasted with the teaching of ecclesiastically approved mystics. It is an important statement, as it enunciates themes that one finds subsequently in Tyrrell's works.

The primary function of religion, said von Hügel, is to purify, not to console man. But the mystics generally teach that purification is gained by "turning away from the particular, by abstraction, and absorption more and more in the general, as leading away from the particularity of the creature to the simplicity of the Creator."[105] Logically, then, they would exclude the sciences from the mystical process as being so much of the world. Von Hügel therefore had to take exception.

His view was that the soul's processes parallel those of the body and mind and so require immersion in the concrete as well as in abstraction; that just as the body lives only by inhalation-exhalation, consumption-evacuation, and the mind only by sensible perception-spiritual elaboration, so the soul lives only by the double process of occupation with the concrete and abstraction from it. Ideally the process is perfectly balanced, and humanity is under strict obligation to seek this balance. But in fact at different periods one activity exceeds the other and requires a correction in the opposite direction. The multitude of humankind necessarily exceeds in occupation with the concrete, so that it falls to the few to compensate by an excess of abstraction. Still, in the individual, "the most difficult and yet most complete and most fruitful condition . . . would be the plunging into the concrete and coming back enriched to the abstract, and then returning, purified and simplified, from the abstract to transform and elevate the concrete."[106]

For von Hügel, science requires a large place in the mystical process, because occupation with the object of scientific investigation, the concrete stuff of the universe with its apparent fatefulness and determinism, was "mentally and emotionally costing" and therefore tremendously purifying. Von Hügel concurred with Blondel "that the true Absolute and Universal springs for us from the true concrete and particular," and with Lotze that "God . . . is the supremely concrete, supremely individual and particular," so that "mental and practical occupation with the particular must ever remain an integral part of my way to Him." Further, he noted how these ideas accorded with the church's sacramental teaching and practice, and how otherwise one falls into "a Neo-Platonic depersonalising of the soul."[107]

Tyrrell got the baron's point and produced *External Religion* as a practical application. There he argued with von Hügel that the many will incline toward the concrete and particular—thus the need for external religion, and thus, too, its abuses—while the few must compensate with abstraction and reflection. He concurred that the time was perhaps right for an emphasis on internal religion and its mystical elements.

But authenic abstraction, Tyrrell observed to von Hügel on 28 September, is not that of neo-Platonic mysticism. There the soul moves from the particular to God as the *Ens abstractissimum* or "Pure Being," the "barrenest of all ideas because the most general," and incomprehensible for its very emptiness. But in authentic abstraction the mind so contemplates the particular that for very fullness of interest it is drawn out of itself into a state that is properly *ecstasis* and in which God is apprehended in the particular as the *Ens concretissimum.* He

> is apprehended (*as every personality is apprehended*) rather by a certain *sense* or *gustus*, than by any reasoning process; and the sensitiveness of this sense (which I take it is simply our whole moral and spiritual being regarded as attracting and attracted by its like, as repelling and repelled by its unlike) depends on the purification of the heart and affections whereby they are brought into sympathy with God; and this again, is the chief end of life and experience and education of every kind. And as the heart is capable of indefinite purification, so God is indefinitely apprehensible, always infinitely exceeding the greatest apprehension of even the purest heart.[108]

Throughout October the exchange on mysticism continued as von Hügel brought his Saint Catherine article to birth. Generally, on this issue it was von Hügel who was seeking advice from Tyrrell as one well acquainted with both the theory and practice of mysticism. Nonetheless, in the asking, von Hügel was drawing a not unwilling Tyrrell more and more into the arena of his own interests, an arena that diverged, certainly not from authentic Catholic tradition but from the current rationalistic and mechanical approach of Roman Catholicism to knowledge of God. For the sake of identifying trends, the divergence can be characterized as leaning toward an authentic tradition not lost to Catholicism but existentially preserved in liberal Protestantism, which reacted both to the rationalism of neo-orthodoxy and to the intellectualism of the idealist school. The liberalism of appeal to von Hügel, therefore, moved along the Schleiermacher-Schopenhauer-Lotze-Eucken line and emphasized the will and action over the intellect as the more authentic organs of religious experience.

At this time Tyrrell was only beginning to investigate liberal Protestantism. It interested him greatly, but he found its development convoluted and had to struggle to make sense of it. By late October he had sorted through the jumble enough to express an opinion to Bremond, who had stimulated Tyrrell's thinking by remarking a coldness in modern Catholic piety compared to a certain strain of mysticism in Protestants. The two features were relatively new on both sides, Tyrrell suspected. In Protestants mystical piety was a reaction against "the dryness of the rationalistic spirit which is the soul of Protestantism," and in Catholics the coldness was a reaction to "Protestant 'fluency,' indefiniteness, sentimentality, etc. . . . to an extreme that has killed mysticism for the time being." He added that his publisher friend, C. Kegan Paul, who had recently converted to Roman Catholicism and "who knows the English mind well, says that it is only through a revival of mysticism that Protestants will be recovered to the church. . . . The Protestants have put on our mysticism and we have put on their rationalism."[109]

Meanwhile von Hügel continued to advise Tyrrell along these lines. In early November, while in the hospital with intestinal complications, the baron had Tyrrell help him touch up his essay on Saint Catherine. A week after returning home, on 21 November, he announced plans to write "a little book" on her and invited Tyrrell to write the introduction. He sent Tyrrell an outline of five chapters, the fourth of which—"Exterior Work and Interior Recollection"— was distinctly Blondellian.[110]

Sometime in October Tyrrell had sent the baron a copy of his new book *Hard Sayings*. Two months later the baron returned a detailed and largely positive criticism, encouraging Tyrrell in his emphasis on "the immanence of God, Heaven and Hell in each individual soul," which "in various forms, runs throughout all the book" and "is a point which I have so long cared for."[111] He again recommended Lotze—his *Microcosmus* (1856-64) and *Outlines of the Philosophy of Religion* (1875-79)—as very helpful in reconciling man's free will and moral evil with the goodness of an immanent God, but there is no positive evidence that Tyrrell ever read Lotze.

A week prior to this letter von Hügel had sent Tyrrell Blondel's article, "L'Illusion idéaliste," which he had already received from Bremond, and Laberthonnière's "Le Dogmatisme moral."[112] On the last day of 1898 Tyrrell wrote to thank the baron and commented that he had already read Blondel's article but without much profit because of the obscure style. "Le Dogmatisme moral," however, was delightful, "as giving a clearer insight into the 'Philosophy of action' or rather the Philosophy of the heart and of concrete human nature," and Tyrrell was already absorbing it into his own system. But he "noticed several places where the idea might have been expressed in a way less likely to give offence to the philistines—an evil to be avoided out of deference not to their opinion, but to their power of making mischief."[113]

Tyrrell was excited by Blondel's thought and was itching to become his English interpreter. On 11 January 1899 he wrote to Bremond: "Were I *sure* that I had caught his mind I should like to write an 'Appreciation & a Criticism' in order to prepare the way before him; but 'hominem non habeo'," and "the dear Baron is too deaf & too transcendental to understand my questions on the subject."[114] If Tyrrell was not secure enough of Blondel's mind to credit him explicitly, he was secure enough to weave his interpretation of Blondel into his Lenten lectures of 1899, and the baron was astute enough to recognize the mark of his own tutelage.

External Religion was off the press in early June 1899 and was in the baron's hands by the 18th. But not until his late autumn trip to Rome did he find time to study it. On 4 December he posted Tyrrell a long and exuberant critique. He singled out "certain crucial passages" in which he took "deep delight": the treatment of earthly paradise (pp. 9, 84), the doctrine of the Fall given "an exclusively human and spiritual application" (pp. 13, 14); miracles seen as "a stretching of the physical under the pressure of the spiritual" (p. 15); "the truly splendid teaching" about the functions and interrelationships of the immanental and the historical-external Christ (pp. 30–36); the "deep truth" that no two minds conceive God or Christ identically, and the "capital passage" about the possibility and conditions of individuality in the use of external forms (pp. 70–72); rules for helping one toward religious maturity (pp. 81–84); "watch and pray" interpreted better as *orate ut vigiletis* (pp. 88–89); the "noble protest" against eliminating mystery and splendor from religion (pp. 119–20); the insistence on "conceiving grace as *mingling* with nature" (p. 146); and "above all, as practically clenching the whole argument, the sentences on pp. 149, 150":

> Can you explain to another how you recognize some one by his tread, or by his voice or his expression? No, and yet you do not doubt it. And so though we may not be able to explain why the voice of conscience and of Christ and of the Church is to our ears all one, yet we who have once felt can never doubt it. . . .
>
> It is vitally important to realize that our faith does not and should not rest on the defence we can make of our faith—on any thread of syllogisms or arguments however skilfully spun. . . .
>
> Faith is produced not by the power of arguments over the mind; but by the power and authority of God's will felt and obeyed by the human will—very much as a dog feels and obeys the will of his master made known in a look or a word.

Finally, the baron baptized it all in Blondel's name:

> I think that in what strikes me as its two main doctrines,—the unconscious or variously obscure, but more real and, when favoured, powerful presence within us of an inward Christ pushing us upwards and outwards with a view to join hands with the outward Christ Who is pressing inwards, these two as necessary conditions for the apprehensions of Faith and Love; and the illuminative character of action, which makes the Christianity of the individual soul continually to re-begin with an experiment, and re-conclude by an experience,—that in these two main points it is entirely Blondel—and Laberthonnièrian, but, of course, with all the sound and sane mystics generally. How nobly and rightly modern these doctrines are—modern only, after all, in the sense of being *also* modern, for they are at bottom of and for all times, indestructible as Life and Love themselves.[115]

Correspondence with Bremond: On the Society of Jesus and the Church

Coincident with the ingredients of intellectual ferment supplied by von Hügel, Blondel, and Laberthonnière was the moral reinforcement of Tyrrell's Jesuit confrere Henri Bremond. Tyrrell's letters to Bremond show clearly that it was Bremond's support as much as any other factor that led Tyrrell to move in the direction of criticism indicated in *External Religion*, a direction that eventuated in a confrontation with authority.[116]

At the inception of their correspondence, both men were suffering deep emotional distress. Tyrrell's disillusionment with authority, both of the church and of the Society of Jesus, began almost from his first contact and continued with ups and downs on a line that would end in divorce. Most recently his effort to nudge the Society in the direction he thought intended by its founder was answered by expulsion from Stonyhurst. That experience wounded him deeply, and the conditions under which he worked at Farm Street never let him forgive or forget.

Bremond was temperamentally unlike Tyrrell, though their sympathies and frustrations were similar. As Jesuit authors, both suffered under censorship. But their approaches to their subjects were quite different. Whereas Tyrrell was intellectually involved in all the modernist questions from the inside, Bremond was, according to his good friend Maude Petre, a devout humanist, "a man of letters, with a strong religious bent . . . but with no theological or philosophical system to defend."[117] He was sympathetic with modernist interests, but he was involved with the people rather than with their ideas.[118]

The root of Bremond's distress was his strong aversion for the monasticism of nineteenth-century Jesuit life and for certain ascetical accretions of which he was severely critical. By his own account he had made a premature decision. He was still a boy of seventeen when he entered the French Jesuit novitiate in England, and it was the beauty of Sidmouth rather than any mature appreciation of what he was in for that led him to pronounce his vows. Petre testified that Bremond never realized the full significance of religious profession,[119] and his anxieties increased as the date of his final profession drew near.

Bremond found in Tyrrell a ready ear, and, *vice versa*, Tyrrell found in Bremond one whom he could trust with views and feelings that could not be trusted even to von Hügel—for example, the torment he felt over having made a tragic vocational choice. Since his expulsion from Stonyhurst, Tyrrell could no longer escape the conviction that the Society of Jesus, due to a wholesale embracing of conservative and reactionary ways, would and perhaps could no longer play the mediating role intended by its founder.

This conviction is the dominant theme of their correspondence even from Tyrrell's first letter of 6 July 1898:

> MY DEAR F. BREMOND . . .
>
> Thank you very much for your kind and encouraging letter. I suppose we have neither of us any right to expect to find a majority in agreement with our hopes and aspirations after a wider spirit. Indeed I feel it would be bad for me and I should only move too fast and speak too hastily were it not that I have to retard my pace so as to keep more or less in line with the very conservative body to which I belong. Irksome as the check has often been yet I thankfully acknowledge it has saved me from spoiling good ideas by giving them crude and impetuous expression. All this however makes an exhibition of sympathy from one of ours all the more refreshing.[120]

At this juncture Tyrrell fancied himself rather prudent, even more prudent than Baron von Hügel, a point he alluded to in his second letter, written in October. He had just learned that von Hügel also knew Bremond and would visit him in early February of the next year on his way to Rome.[121] So Tyrrell wrote to say how delighted he was that they had a mutual friend in the baron, "a dear good enthusiast though not sufficiently prudent to escape hostile reports which limit his influence for good." Bremond at the time was in Lyons, and Tyrrell wondered whether he had "fallen into the hands of the Philistines"—that is, sent there for disciplinary reasons. "If so, you have only to wait, the spirit is stronger than the letter, and will most surely assert itself even if not through us & in our time." Along with patience Tyrrell counseled elasticity in saving all that was good in the old order while admitting all that was good in the new, and avoiding rigidity on either side lest "the bottles burst & the wine is spilt." It was exactly the elasticity of the spirit of Ignatius of Loyola that was now needed to mediate between the old and the new and to interpret them one to another. So far as the Society of Jesus is true to her founding spirit, she will be able to accomplish this task. "It is a curious crisis in her history. Von Hügel & many others despair of us. I still cherish a hope that the stiffness of our limbs may be rheumatism and not old age—'not unto death, but that the glory of God may be revealed.'" But even should the Society fail, Tyrrell was prepared. "The Church, rather than any particular clique, has always been my 'donna gentile'—my Beatrice; so that my peace does not depend on her handmaids. Pray for me dear Father."[122]

Not that Tyrrell needed any help in assessing the Society of Jesus, but von Hügel's pessimistic assessment should be noted in view of his determining influence on Tyrrell. Tyrrell acknowledged this influence several times, but never more pointedly than in his confession to the baron of 20 November 1899, when he admitted with gratitude "the strong developing influence your friendship has exerted upon my mind; in how many cases it has determined me at points of bifurcation . . . and all with the happy result of making my mind more of a . . . city 'at unity with itself.'"[123]

But in the matter of mysticism and all that can be classed broadly under "protestantizing elements," it was now not only von Hügel but also Bremond who was tugging at Tyrrell. One of Bremond's complaints was the Society's mechanistic approach to man's relationship with God. To one such complaint Tyrrell replied that Jesuits had lost touch with the thoroughgoing mysticism of Ignatius, and Protestants had usurped the patrimony. The "systematizings" of meditation and "methods" of loving God found in Jan Roothaan's analysis of meditation and Antoine le Gaudier's "terrible machinery of sanctity . . . have created a fashion which the Contemplative Orders have not been strong enough to counteract. Of course all this applies far more to the English S.J. whose national defect of feeling is emphasized by such a system."[124]

Bremond was so impressed with Tyrrell's interpretation not only of the woes but also of the authentic spirit of the Society that he urged Tyrrell to write a commentary on Ignatius's *Spiritual Exercises* to get a saner and more critical view before the public. Such a commentary, Tyrrell replied, had been his dream for years, and in fact it was already completed in rough draft. He always thought that the only way to create "not a new spirit but the old spirit of the SJ . . . when flexibility & accommodation were the secret of a greatness on whose name & shadow we are now subsisting" was to begin at the root. But he confessed that in recent years he had grown "more fastidious, more reluctant to put out at once anything that might improve by keeping & pondering."[125]

Unfortunately the world never saw Tyrrell's commentary. His censure and removal from the scriptorium over "A Perverted Devotion" was a blow that broke his already tenuous affection for the Society of Jesus, and his manuscript went up in flames.[126] Thereafter, his doubts that the Society would fulfill its promise matched the baron's pessimism, and he would never again exert himself on behalf of Jesuit ideals. In fact, in one of his moods Tyrrell wished that the Society, since it was dead, were also buried. On that occasion Maude Petre had suggested temporary religious life for individuals. Tyrrell replied that he would propose the same for religious orders, that they should continue as long as the founder was alive but thereafter should die out ruthlessly. "All the misery comes from a mistaken loyalty to the letter of the founder's rule, which at last slays the spirit. Where more than with us? The most 'liberalising' order ever conceived has become the one block in the way of the Church's expansion."[127]

From this point of unmistakable disaffection up to his dismissal from the Jesuits in February 1906, Tyrrell adopted a *modus vivendi* that allowed him to exist in a twilight zone without grave violence to his conscience. He based that *modus* on the distinction between the existing Society and church and his idea of them, his *donna gentile*, his Beatrice. As long as he was convinced that he was being faithful to her, he could live with his conscience. This double existence he saw as necessary for the sake of those he had counseled and helped to remain in the church and who would now be shaken if he were to leave his order. The real Society of Jesus and the real church he saw as victims of a cancer that had to run its course and do itself in by its own poison. His task henceforth was not to impede that process but perhaps discreetly to hasten it along where he could.

In early May 1899 Baron von Hügel began his return from Rome. On the way he visited Bremond, and when back in England he reported his impressions to Tyrrell.[128] The tensions and anxieties of an ambiguous life were seriously affecting Bremond's health, and Tyrrell was deeply concerned. On 13 June he wrote to try to lift Bremond's spirits. The situation, he admitted, as reflected in the attitudes of the *Civiltà* and even of the *Month* and *Études*, was distressing, and there was no denying that "a powerful opposition to us is gathering force every day." But he saw it as "just a crisis where hope can shine most brightly." To meet that crisis and see it through for gain, one had to assume that greathearted indifference of Ignatius who asserted that he would need only a quarter hour of prayer to reconcile himself to the extinction of the Society of Jesus if the church's interest required it. In that spirit, then, one had to avoid "all attempts at premature & crude solutions of difficulties which are profound & immense" and particularly the "reckless pessimism" of those who lose heart when results are not instant. It only strengthens the opposition and excuses their undeniable extravagances to react to them with "an illiberal blind hostility" that cannot accord them a measure of justice and good faith.[129]

Bremond's reply troubled Tyrrell, as it betrayed "a state of mental perplexity altogether similar to my own."[130] Evidently Bremond asked Tyrrell how he suffered such contrarieties and still remained in the church and the Society. Tyrrell answered with an impressive profession of faith and described his *modus vivendi* in hopes that Bremond would find it suggestive for himself. It bears the stamp of Blondel throughout, which is not surprising, as it followed by one month the publication of *External Religion*.

Tyrrell moved progressively from his theism to his Christianism, Catholicism, and Jesuitism, explaining the basis for each in turn. The first was for him rooted not in propositions or hearsay but in his own experience of a Power in himself and all others "'making for righteousness' in spite of all our downward tendencies." His Christianism was founded on the concrete and intuitive recognition of the full manifestation of that Power in the man Jesus Christ as known historically. As for adherence to the Roman Church, Tyrrell did not elaborate on "all the concrete impressions" that led him to affirm her as the "only authorised representative of Christ on earth" and as holding revealed truth in her general teaching "like gold in the matrix." He confessed that "in the present crisis of transition" there was "much obscurity as to the Church's real mind on many questions—the retrogressives & the progressives each desiring to cover their own views with the mantle of infallibility." But when the sloughing season was over, the church would settle down comfortably in her bright new skin.[131]

Then the more poignant question: Would the Society have any

part in the new order? That, Tyrrell answered, depends on whether she could recapture the "vital flexible principles of Ignatius." The *Civiltà* apparently had recently pinned a new motto on her, one directly opposed to Ignatius's spirit: *Frangar, non flectar.* Tyrrell saw no escape from *Frangar,* and as evidence he cited the fact that those chosen to attend general congregations and set policy were "the oldest & most out-of-date men that can be chosen; men with no knowledge of, or sympathy with what is good in the modern world." Change could therefore not come from above, nor would it come from below since presently every effort was being made to resist democratic forces. Anyway, Tyrrell thought the democratic method too slow for such rapidly changing times. The only solution he looked for was a *reductio ad absurdum* and a reconstruction from the ruins.[132]

Meanwhile, Tyrrell would stand firmly in the Society, even though he saw it as "the deck of a sinking ship" and felt himself "totally out of sympathy with all but a mere handful of the body." He had made a decision early in life according to the imperfect light then at his command, and he would stick by the consequences so long as conscience was not violated. "A man takes a wife 'for better or for worse'—if it prove *for worse* he may not on that score divorce her. The Society is my wife; and though affection is impossible yet duty is possible." But Tyrrell also acknowledged that religious vows are not as irrevocable as marriage vows, and that "an occasion might arise where conscience would require severance; but that is not yet in sight." Till then, he would go on writing quietly until told to stop, which, he thought, might be sooner rather than later. But he had to confess that on the whole he had been dealt with liberally. And even if policy became more repressive, that would not be all to the bad. The fittest and strongest are irrepressible and would survive. Their number may be few, but to the few is due the fame and greatness of the Society, whose body consists of "average unoriginal minds." "Certainly all the men who have made their mark in this province are just the men who would *not* be sat upon. I think this is a sound principle of social progress."[133]

Six months later Bremond found himself increasingly distressed as the day of his final profession, 2 February 1900, approached. On the previous 22 December Tyrrell had sent him the benefit of his most recent second thoughts on religious profession, the upshot of further troubles in his own life.[134] He had just published "The Relation of Theology to Devotion" in the *Month* for November and "A Perverted Devotion" in the *Weekly Register* for 16 December, and was in consequence entering on the most painful phase of his career to date.[135] As if by premonition of shoddy treatment, Tyrrell urged Bremond to fidelity to choices in the face of every obstacle, even to bearing the consequences of what is later seen to be objective error. Tyrrell was decidedly despondent yet fiercely determined in the face of a hopeless prognosis.

For one thing, he told Bremond, very few people are able to choose their own lot in life. Most are set by circumstances on a particular path, regardless of aptitudes and inclinations. "Hence if my life is anyway irksome I am like the great majority." Second, even if one does decide one's own lot, it is usually at an early age, before the onset of wisdom so that the choice is usually unwise. Thus at the age of forty most look back and see objective error in their choice, though perhaps not subjective error. But at that age, even if the choice were revocable, it is often better to live with it than to waste life by attempting other perhaps equally mistaken courses. Surely acquiescence is the better course where the choice is irrevocable, as in marriage, because if it were acceptable to rescind such contracts when life becomes irksome, human society would become impossible. As Christ made plain, the critical thing is not vocational success but doing God's will, regardless of the chances for success. So one should not be unduly disturbed if only a small fraction of one's energies is actually used, for that is virtually a law of life.[136]

Thus, Tyrrell concluded, vocation was to him simply "the position in which a man finds himself by the ordinary course of providence," whether apt and inclined to it or not. "It was on these principles I took my last vows recognising them as contained in the contract I had already made when, as a boy in my credulity, I thought the S.J. was as Paul Féval painted it." Tyrrell's credulity was later disappointed, but he thought the disappointment no greater than is common in every vocation. Besides, it was to Ignatius's long-forgotten principles that he had bound himself, and not to the views of any individual Jesuits. "Hence I can live not only *in* the Society but in a certain sense *for* the Society. . . . I will do all I can (knowing the effort to be mainly futile) to make ours a little less narrow, a little more human & catholic-minded."[137]

IMPLICATING ESSAYS

By now the picture of Tyrrell's disposition as he composed those two life-determining essays, "The Relation of Theology to

Devotion" and "A Perverted Devotion," is quite full. But if the picture is full, it is not clear, because the background is crowded with a snarl of ideas and feelings. As to ideas, Tyrrell was reacting principally to those of Newman, von Hügel, Blondel, Laberthonnière, and their progenitors. As to feelings, along with Bremond, Tyrrell was becoming more and more disaffected from the existing Society of Jesus, while being very devoted to his conception of its ideal. Consequently he suffered the strain of an increasingly ambiguous position, which gradually took its toll on both body and spirit.

Essentially "The Relation of Theology to Devotion" was the philosophical and theological point of departure for the genuinely modernist phase of Tyrrell's career. But at the time of its composition Tyrrell was unaware of just how radical was his departure from the liberalism of Newman and Ward. He did not fully realize that he was advocating death to the development of dogma theory and resurrection to a life in which devotion and theology, while not to be wedded, might lie side by side in peace. In effect, he was giving up on the possibility of synthesizing faith and reason, but he was convinced that he had at least found a symbiotic formula: diversity does not have to mean hostility.

"The Relation of Theology to Devotion" was first published in the *Month* for November 1899 and was reprinted in volume one of *The Faith of the Millions* (1901) and in *Through Scylla and Charybdis* (1907). In 1902 it was expanded into a small book, *Religion as a Factor of Life*, and published under the pseudonym "Dr. Ernest Engels." This book, in turn, was incorporated into *Lex Orandi*, published in 1903 under Tyrrell's name and with *imprimatur*. It received practical application in his most famous (or infamous) work, *The Church and the Future*, published first pseudonymously in 1903 under the name "Hilaire Bourdon" and posthumously reprinted in 1910 under his own name, with a preface by Maude Petre.[138]

As years and ideas flowed, Tyrrell grew in awareness of the significance of that article. In 1907, when he reprinted it in *Through Scylla and Charybdis*, he explained that he was doing so "because it is fundamental to all the essays that follow, and to the whole point of view developed in the volumes *Lex Orandi* and *Lex Credendi*"—and thus its new, more cosmic title, "Lex Orandi, Lex Credendi." He confessed amazement on rereading the essay that he had advanced so little beyond it. "It is all here—all that follows—not in germ but in explicit statement—as it were in a brief compendium or analytical index." Moreover, he now recognized it as "a turning-point in my own theological experience." That is, previously he had accepted the scholastic view that the deposit of faith is foundational to but not distinct from Catholic theology, and he pointed to his early essays in *The Faith of the Millions* as attempts "to evade the obvious difficulties of that supposition by a liberal use of the theory of doctrinal development." Later he felt compelled to move away from the transitional notion of the deposit as a "form of sound words" to viewing it rather as "a Spirit, or a Principle, or an Idea—a view which would liberate theology and all the sciences with which it is necessarily entangled from bondage to the categories of a past age consecrated by Divine Authority." But in 1907 he saw that both ways of viewing the deposit could be reconciled by appealing to the distinction he made in 1899 between revelation and theology as "generically different orders of Truth and Knowledge" and by denying development to revelation and dogma but giving it to theology.[139]

The express purpose of the essay was not to exalt devotion over theology or theology over devotion but to point out their necessary correlation and mutual inadequacy as *separate* ways of expressing religious truth. Its underlying thesis is entirely Blondel and Laberthonnière over again: The traditional scholastic apologetic has become lifeless by too long neglecting the mystical conception and expression of religious experience. It has attempted to substitute an abstraction for a living belief and to present the mysteries of God, the universe, and the soul as rigidly ascertained facts of completed knowledge, not as the increasingly ascertainable certainties of a knowledge that grows as life grows.

By "theology" here Tyrrell meant scholastic theology, "the essay to translate the teachings of Catholic revelation into the terms and forms of Aristotelian philosophy; and thereby to give them a scientific unity."[140] By "devotion" he meant the very ordinary human way of conceiving and speaking about things. Where theology is abstract, orderly, and artificial, devotion is concrete, disorderly, and natural. Each needs and benefits by the other. Theology needs devotion just as science needs the data of experience. Isolated from experience, the abstract and ordered conceptions of theology are as true to life as butterflies impaled in a glass display. On the other hand, devotion without theology's power of abstraction grows wild and uncultivated and becomes susceptible to superstitious anthropomorphisms. The test for the validity of a theology is its fruitfulness for devotion: if it makes people pray, watch, and struggle more, it is true; if it makes them struggle less, it is false.

The interrelationship between theology, devotion, and creed on the one hand and revelation on the other is critical, but Tyrrell did not clearly delineate it. From all that he said about it, however, one may attempt his meaning. Devotion and creed stand to each other as the feet of a triangle whose apex is revelation. Devotion is more directly in contact with revelation than is creed. The latter is rather an abstraction from devotion and creed. But all three stand under revelation, which is the *lex orandi* and the *lex credendi*, the rule simultaneously of devotion, beliefs, and theology. But of the two rules, *lex orandi* enjoys a priority over *lex credendi*, just as devotion, as being more directly in contact with revelation, enjoys a priority over theology and creed but can never do without them.

Although Tyrrell did not want to minimize theology's importance, he did want to give it its proper place, and in so doing, he could scarcely avoid placing it lower than devotion. He put it where he did for two reasons: first, revelation is given in the concrete, colored, imaginative language of the *vulgus* and thus is available to the multitudes as well as to the theologians; second, Tyrrell saw church officials abusing theological language and philosophy by placing too much confidence in scholastic dialectics and thereby imposing dry rationalism on the multitudes and robbing them of their most important way of knowing God.

The more abstract and general the terms under which a thing is known, Tyrrell argued, the less we know about it. Thus he asserted, "On the whole the backwoods-man has a truer knowledge of Nature than a mere acquaintance with a science-manual could ever impart," and "the rudest clown knows better what man is than does some anatomist who knows nothing but the articulation of the human skeleton," however true this knowledge is as far as it goes.[141]

Tyrrell went further. Abstract knowledge, he said, is unreal compared to knowledge of the particular. This position borders on nominalism, which is tied in its roots to radical Evangelicalism and therefore belongs to Tyrrell's own roots. But Tyrrell buttressed his argument with an appeal to a scholastic tenet which holds that the connatural object of the human mind is the material world as presented to the senses. Everything else—that is, all supraworldly realities—must be seen analogously and therefore inadequately in terms of material realities. The chief benefit of metaphysical or natural theology is that it reminds us of this fact, not that it gives us a more comprehensible idea of God. Neither the metaphysical nor the vulgar idea of God is adequate taken alone. But if taken alone, the vulgar idea is less unreal. "The use of philosophy lies in its insisting on the inadequacy of the vulgar statement; its abuse, in forgetting

the inadequacy of its own, and thereby falling into a far more grievous error than that which it would correct." As Andrew Seth rightly
argued, "Both religion and the higher poetry—just because they
give up the pretence of an impossible exactitude—carry us . . .
nearer to the meaning of the world, than the formulas of an abstract metaphysics."[142]

The ravages of theological abuse were painfully evident to
Tyrrell in the nearly hopeless evacuation of the heart of revealed
mysteries. A glaring example was the church's doctrine of the Incarnation and its many implications. Through abstract and rationalist conceptualizations, Tyrrell lamented, the church explains
Christ's kenosis, or self-emptying, "in a minimising way almost
fatal to devotion, and calculated to rob the Incarnation of all its
helpfulness by leaving the ordinary mind with something perilously
near the phantasmal Christ of the Docetans."[143]

Christ did not reveal himself and his Father in the language of
philosophy but in human language that appeals to the imagination
and feelings, because it was in human terms that he wanted us to
think and speak of God. God revealed himself not to theologians
and philosophers, but to babes, fishermen, and peasants, "leaving it
to the others to translate it (at their own risk) into forms more acceptable to their taste."[144]

The church's task, Tyrrell argued—and here was his first, albeit
implicit, rejection of Newman's theory of development—is to preserve, not to develop, the exact ideas which that simple language
conveyed to its first hearers, despite its indefinite inadequacy to
the eternal realities it shadows forth.[145] "This is My Body" is the
revelational-dogmatic formula that is to be preserved and does not
develop. The metaphysics of transubstantiation adds nothing to the
dogma; it merely puts the matter to metaphysicians in their own
language and on their own assumptions. "If [the church] says the
soul is the 'form' of the body, it is not that she has a revelation of
philosophy to communicate, but because the question is asked by a
hylomorphist; and it is the nearest way the truth can be put to
him."[146]

The crux of the matter, which Tyrrell only hinted at in this article, is the church's authority and one's attitude toward it. The issue
is not that the church has a *revelation* to communicate, but that *she*
has a revelation to communicate. Thus, although theology, devotion, and creed all stand judged by revelation, it is revelation as
held and interpreted by the church. And all three—devotion,
theology, and creed—are inextricably bound up with the church's
interpretation. The decisive factor is trust in the church's authority

to interpret in whatever language and philosophy she chooses. This factor led Tyrrell to the further question, which again he only hinted at here: Exactly who in the church exercises this authority? Who is to be trusted?

The answer for Tyrrell was the saints, not the theologians, unless they happened also to be saints. For the theologians in aiding the formulation of the creed out of devotion are once removed from revelation. The saints are in closer contact with the *lex orandi*. They have always led the church away from superstition because purity of heart has been their safeguard. "It is the desire to 'exploit' religion, to bribe the Almighty, to climb up by some other way, rather than go through the one door of self-denial, that is the source of all corruption."[147]

In saying this, Tyrrell stressed a favorite theme: the saints are the real teachers of the church. They are the "consistent professors" of the deposit of faith, that "concrete religion left by Christ to His Church" and that is "in some sense more directly a *lex orandi* than a *lex credendi*."[148] The creed arises from the experience of the saints. It expresses and formulates their "facts." A wise and temperate theology may aid in extricating and formulating the creed from devotion, but theology is often not wise and temperate. It operates at a level once removed from the *lex orandi* and so in its work must yield to the saints. "I wish," Tyrrell wrote Ward several months later, "you wouldn't make the theologians an essential factor in the Church's life. I think it is rather in the subconsciousness of the faithful at large that God's spirit works; whereas theology is almost professed a human and artificial instrument."[149]

Before Tyrrell returned the page proofs of this article to the publisher, he sent them to von Hügel for a critical reading. On 8 October 1899 the baron returned them with a standing ovation: "The finest thing you have yet done. . . . It is really *splendid*." He was delighted at how Tyrrell used the scholastics' own position to prove that their "explanations" of the phenomena of the mind are inadequate and analogous. But there were two reasons in particular for the baron's enthusiasm. First, he found the essay intimately harmonious with his own life's work—"giving such crystal-clear expression to my dearest certainties, to the line of thought and living which alone can and does bring me light and strength." Second, he was encouraged to see "that you are let say these things, in your Order, and by your Order." Finally, he requested six copies, one each for Blondel, Laberthonnière, Giovanni Semeria, Eucken, Loisy, and Basil Champneys.[150]

Perhaps it was the baron's vigorous praise, perhaps Tyrrell was growing weary of self-repression, perhaps the slow or backward pace of his order's accommodation to the times got the better of him—it is difficult to put a finger on any one factor as decisive. The fact is, in December 1899 Tyrrell published "A Perverted Devotion" and brought the powers on high crashing down upon his head.[151]

The occasion of the article was an attack by two Redemptorists on an attempt by the Belgian Jesuit André Castelein to mitigate the severe interpretation of hell. It was a chance for Tyrrell to make concrete the distinctions he drew in "The Relation of Theology to Devotion." With satirical twist, Tyrrell sided with the hell-preachers against Castelein, whose liberal rationalizations he also opposed.

Now Tyrrell used "devotion" in a more restricted and ironical sense to mean a "special *attrait* towards some particular point of Catholic teaching" that suits some subjective and peculiar need of an individual, rather than the general and confused view of a mystery.[152] Every devotion, he said, is liable to perversion and excess if clung to in isolation from every other part and principle of Catholic truth, because feeling, which is always implied in devotion, is of its nature blind and tends to assert itself over mind and reason.

The idea of a devotion to the doctrine on hell, Tyrrell allowed, may seem strange. Yet when that doctrine is seen as an expression of the attribute of divine justice, "the strangeness must at once vanish." Tongue in cheek, Tyrrell went on: "There can be no adequate love of the divine goodness that leaves out any factor of that goodness; and justice no less than mercy, majesty no less than meekness, strength no less than gentleness, go to the building up of our conception of God's moral excellence." For every true and just person who has ever walked this earth, the power of divine love must be matched by the power of divine indignation. "You have loved justice and hated iniquity," says the Psalmist, and on these inseparable correlatives is based the hope of the saints and prophets that every wrong will be righted, every crooked thing straightened, every seemingly triumphant lie vanquished, and every seemingly strangled truth confirmed. But the decline of belief in human responsibility has, by weakening the impulse to love justice, also weakened the impulse to hate iniquity, "and canonised this emasculated morality, this flaccid indifferentism, under the name of benevolence."[153]

But one must be careful with this devotion, because as with Tertullian who heralded it, what may begin as a love of God's justice can quickly degenerate into an egoistic vindictiveness against adversaries. Then theology can be summoned in support, because in its own abstract line it is constrained by logic to say, "The blessed in Heaven rejoice in the will of God: but the torments of the reprobate are the will of God; therefore the blessed in Heaven rejoice in the torments of the reprobate." Now this notion may be tolerated from theologians "so long as it is clearly understood that the *minor* is not an obvious truth of common-sense, but a very profound mystery, and a very grievous burden to our faith." But when this harsh mystery is "explained" by an analogy from reason and the latter is put forth as a satisfactory and adequate explanation, "we at once resent this intrusion of pert rationalism into the *arcana fidei*, and send the would-be theologian about his business."[154]

Still more offensive is a heartlessness and lack of moral sense that disguises itself as a vigorous faith and zealous devotion to the justice of God. But more offensive still is the one who finds in the doctrine of hell "no perplexity for his reason, no shock to his affections, no violation of his sentiments." This passive submission Tyrrell saw as "mental and moral obliquity," because although faith sometimes requires one to believe that to be white which seems black, never does it require one to believe that what seems black also seems white. And so, if the doctrine of hell requires one to believe that what seems cruelty and injustice is only an illusion due to imperfect comprehension of the dogma that further revelation will banish, still the doctrine does not demand one to believe that it does not *seem* cruel and unjust, or that reason can justify and defend it.[155]

Reconciliation of these difficulties is possible neither by devotion nor by theology, but by faith alone. "When God appears to us in blood-stained garments and terrifying aspect, doubtless He intends that we should be terrified," but that we should at the same time be able to transcend or get behind appearances "by a faith which . . . is only the very perfection of reasonableness." Theology, as Tyrrell said in the previous article, is supposed to check and balance devotion, but in the case of this devotion it has actually reinforced the perversion particularly by its rationalism about the number of the damned and the nature and duration of their torment.[156]

Some devotées, Tyrrell observed, have taken more extreme views than others, depending on the ardor of their devotion. But he took exception to all "solutions" to what is essentially a faith problem. The appalling mystery is that God, foreseeing that even one person would be lost eternally, should permit the tragedy when he could have prevented it. This mystery is the camel that devout rationalists swallow while straining at gnats. It is strange that they seem unable to approach that side of God's mystery with the same intellectual humility and unshakable trust that lets them affirm the inconceivability and unsearchable depth of God's mercy and loving-kindness. Should not faith be as easy in one case as in the other? Yes, except where reason dares to elucidate.

Tyrrell's conclusion in particular was bound to raise snarls from Rome. Having excoriated the lucubrations of reason, Tyrrell proceeded to advocate a "temperate agnosticism" as an essential prerequisite of intelligent faith. He even went so far as to suggest that God's spirit sometimes works outside the church for the sanctification of those within. It was a providential mechanism that worked through rationalism like a fever working its own cure. Rationalism occasioned the defection of the sixteenth century and thereby demonstrated experimentally both the insufficiency of reason alone and the need of a saner spiritual philosophy that definitively abandons the attempt to establish higher realities by lower and that accepts as inevitable the "natural necessity of seeming contradictions and perplexities in our estimate of God's thoughts and ways." But admission of mental insufficiency neither excuses a naive credulity nor relieves the apologist of his burden to establish revelation to be as much an exigency of human nature as religion itself. Thus, Tyrrell concluded, as God's spirit goes outside the church to prepare an acceptable people, "we within must co-operate and go forward to meet this movement, by purging out of our midst any remnant of the leaven of rationalism that we may have carried with us from earlier and cruder days, when faith needed the rein more than the spur."[157]

AFTERMATH: THE STORM

The Mivart Affair: Complicity with the Devil

If "The Relation of Theology to Devotion" was the philosophical-theological point of departure for Tyrrell's modernist phase, "A Perverted Devotion" supplied the emotional charge, because it was the latter article that was delated to Rome and there found "offensive to pious ears." The delation must have occurred directly on publication, because by 18 January 1900 Rome had sent preliminary instructions for dealing with Father Tyrrell. On that date Tyrrell wrote to Bremond, "The 'Perverted Devotion' . . . has the unfortunate honour of being delated to Fr. General who has in consequence silenced me, *pendente lite*."[158] Further instructions would follow.

The scenario went something like this. Because of both the essay's title and its subject matter, Tyrrell could not help but be implicated in Roman minds with the notorious Dr. St. George Mivart, who had provoked a bitter controversy in 1893 with his essays, "Happiness in Hell" and its sequels, which ended up on the Index.[159] Then recently Mivart had refreshed Rome's memory of him by a broadside in the 17 October 1899 issue of the *Times* against the Catholic hierarchy and press in France for their fanatical attacks on Alfred Dreyfus and against the pope for his failure to speak out against this travesty of justice.[160] To compound matters, in early January 1900 Mivart published two articles that even von Hügel and Tyrrell considered extremist: "Some Recent Catholic Apologists," in which he attacked Wilfrid Ward among many others, and "The Continuity of Catholicism," in which he tried to reconcile dogma with the findings of modern science.[161]

Bishop Merry del Val, who was keeping an eye on things for the Sacred Congregation of the Index, intoned Rome's judgment in a letter to Cardinal Vaughan of 11 January: "evident heresy" and "blasphemies." Then, without naming names: "One can only be sorry for Mivart and pray for him. But his errors with which some liberal Catholics sympathize in a greater or less degree must be met."[162]

Vaughan immediately sent Mivart some rather ironic pastoral advice along with a document for his signature, excepting which he would be excommunicated. The document declared baldly that the scriptures contain no error and have God as their author. Mivart refused to sign and was excommunicated. The advice was that Mivart should consult Cardinal Johannes Baptist Franzelin's treatises and Leo XIII's *Providentissimus Deus*, "but perhaps more useful to you than this would be a conversation with Rev. Dr. Clarke, or with Father Tyrrell, S.J., both of whom would be able to understand your state of mind and to give you counsel and assistance. I refer you to them."[163] Evidently Vaughan was as yet unaware of Merry del Val's suspicions of Tyrrell.

Simultaneously, the Jesuit general in Rome registered some strong views with Tyrrell's superiors in London. One complaint, Tyrrell told von Hügel, was that all the English Jesuit writers and Tyrrell in particular were "too anxious to conciliate the enemies of religion" and were not "speaking strongly & boldly enough in condemnation of heretics & unbelievers." Rather, the general exhorted, the English writers were to remember their best traditions and walk worthy of the vocation to which they were called. "That is, of course, an order to emulate the violent and mendacious tone of the *Civiltà*." The general also forbade Tyrrell to publish outside the *Month* until his articles on hell had been resubmitted to censorship.[164]

Tyrrell told Ward that he replied to the general immediately and with a show of force, saying that he would "contest the matter to the very last" and was "prepared to face any scandal of ill-consequence rather than say the thing which is not. They always modify their terms if they think one will fight; and when I get the price down to its lowest I will see if I can afford it."[165]

Meanwhile Fr. Alexander Charnley, Tyrrell's vice-provincial acting in place of the absent Fr. John Gerard, gave the article to Frs. William Humphrey, Sydney Smith, and Herbert Thurston among others, to be reviewed again. All pronounced it clean and calculated to do good. This opinion Charnley forwarded to Rome. But Rome had its mind made up. "Quidquid sentiat Reverentia Vestra et consultores, hic Romae longe aliter sentitur," replied the general.[166] He enclosed the verdicts of two Italian censors and demanded that Tyrrell write another article in conformity with their criticisms. The second censor sounded the knell: "Post: *Happiness in Hell*, ab Ecclesia damnatam, jam habemus: *Devotion to Hell*, quae non minus damnabilis est."[167]

Tyrrell was exasperated. For whom was he to write? His English censors were all satisfied, but father general in Rome, he complained to Bremond, "finds it 'offensive to pious ears.' I wish Rome would either define pious ears, or give a list of them so that one might know." That the "popular unauthorized presentation of Hell offends really pious people & either drives or keeps them from the faith" seems of no concern to Rome "so long as superstitions are not disturbed."[168]

Then there was the explosion over Mivart's articles. Tyrrell called them "vulgar," "ill-judged," and "quite indefensible" and told Bremond that they simply "played into the hands of the narrowest party" and seemed to justify a raid on people like himself whom Rome supposed to be of Mivart's school.[169] To Ward and von Hügel, Tyrrell expressed fear that the Mivart affair had thrown everything back at least a decade "and left the Philistines in undisputed possession of the ark. . . . There is a sort of savage ferocity & shameless untruthfulness about these Ultramontanes that makes it impossible to say where their arrogance or tyranny will stop."[170]

What worried Tyrrell most was that the temporary restraint imposed on him would be made permanent and thus seriously hurt the Jesuit attempt in England to accommodate modern difficulties. If he did escape "inquisitorial lightenings," he told Bremond, he might silence himself for several years to avoid provoking any sort of condemnation that would undo much of his past work among pious Catholics "who else will quietly imbibe a freer spirit & be prepared for truths which 'they cannot bear now.'" Meantime he could busy himself with "innocuous pursuits," such as his work on the *Spiritual Exercises* of Ignatius or on Juliana of Norwich, whom he had recently discovered.[171]

Actually Tyrrell longed to wash his hands of the whole affair and simply stand aside as a curious but unconcerned spectator. He even considered the option of going into schism.[172] But, he told von Hügel, "there is that strange man on his cross who drives one back again & again," so that he could not but yield to his dominant conviction "that what Christ had to say to man is embedded in the Roman system as gold in the ore; and so as I cannot sever them I take them in the lump."[173]

With much reluctance Tyrrell set to work on a reply to his Roman censors that would tell. His best hope, he told Ward, was to play on the insult they gave to the English censors and to the whole English Province by demanding that his retraction go to Rome for censorship, as though none in England could be trusted.[174] Tyrrell had to exercise heroic restraint because, as he reported to von Hügel, the censors' objections were "founded throughout on the most glaring ignorance of English and a total failure to grasp the motive & totality of the article." Moreover he found himself identified with Mivart, Huxley, and Herbert Spencer; loaded with every epithet of theological billingsgate from "scandalous" to "proximately if not all together heretical"; and his "good faith" questioned and denied. Hence upon completing his task he took special pleasure in admitting that he was able to show up "these gentlemen . . . with much justice & little mercy."[175]

Gerard studied the reply along with Tyrrell's original article and was delighted with both. He then took them to his consultors, secured their approval, and finally, excising the sarcasms "which super-abounded through hardly avoidable irritation," he adopted the reply as his own and backed it with a letter saying that "if we are to take the *Civiltà* tone we may as well put up the shutters at once in England." The whole sad incident, Tyrrell lamented, "reduces this Roman centralisation to an absurdity. We are not even allowed to know England & English as well as Italians and Spaniards do."[176] The upshot of this issue will be seen shortly.

Meanwhile Tyrrell set to work on another requirement from Rome—that he draft a retraction or declaration of orthodoxy on the doctrine of hell in accord with the criticisms of the Roman censors. Tyrrell's letter to Ward of 24 February 1900 seems to indicate that Ward offered Tyrrell the use of his name in drawing up a position on the matter.[177] This step Tyrrell declined because he did not want any stand that he might have to take interpreted as coming from Ward. But he does seem to have accepted Ward's anonymous assistance, for, as he told Ward, "one needs to have the word of another in support of one's own better judgment at such times; and one's best Jesuit friends can hardly advise with perfect freedom, having one eye on the order and only the other on me."[178]

It was no simple task. Complicating factors kept arising. First, there was the posture to assume toward Mivart. Ward, von Hügel, and Tyrrell all agreed that Mivart was presently a menace to the mediating liberal cause and that they had to find a way to distance themselves from him without simply cutting him off—that was the ultramontane tactic. Then there was the question of who should answer Mivart. Tyrrell could not publish except in the *Month* and really had to explain himself on the Mivart question first of all to Rome. And as von Hügel was not on the scene, that left Ward. Certainly Ward had an entrée as one attacked by Mivart. But one gets the distinct impression that von Hügel was not happy with this alternative. Whatever Ward said, the baron wanted to be sure that his own view was represented.

Accordingly, on 18 February, von Hügel wrote Ward to say that given Mivart's attitude—"painfully unspiritual" and close in tone and method to his antagonists'—neither he nor Ward could say anything to satisfy it.[179] He agreed that Cardinal Vaughan had to act, but he might have offered Mivart a simpler, more general formulary to sign, and above all he might not have baited Mivart with Franzelin's treatises and *Providentissimus Deus*.

On the other hand—and here von Hügel moved in on Ward—were not Mivart's passion, earnestness, and enthusiasm in some sense admirable, along with his "keen sense of the defectiveness of an existing position" and "deep instinct or intuition of further or new truth," for from these necessarily spring the progress of all science and philosophy?[180] That sort of passion, the baron complained, was precisely what he found wanting in Ward's last *Quarterly* article.

Clearly irritated, Ward defended himself on the score of limitations of space and policy of the *Quarterly*. Furthermore, had he not already written in *Cardinal Wiseman* something close to what von Hügel wanted? He then moved in on von Hügel and impugned his powers of discernment:

> As to Mivart, do you remember how utterly wrongheaded I thought his letter to the *Times* which you thought serviceable though exaggerated? I do not say this as merely an "I told you so," but because I am quite sure that, in the difficult time I see coming on us, we must look very sharp to distinguish friend from foe if we are to hold our own. . . . That liberty of expression, even of saying what is useful and good, should be practically possible must depend on toleration not being abused by *reckless* discussion which has all the dangers of inflammatory mob oratory. . . . The only solution I can see is that, if wise liberals are very careful *not* to shock, wise rulers should be brought to see that, in a most difficult time of transition, they are our only hope for the future.[181]

Ward then turned to his fears and misgivings about Tyrrell. He thought that Tyrrell was the one person who had most thoroughly grasped the mediating principle, but now he was in trouble and even "spoke to me quite calmly of going into schism." Ward was worried that Tyrrell would do something reckless, and he appealed to the baron to restrain him. "But don't say I have referred to the schism possibility."[182]

This exchange points up the chilling of a relationship and the increasingly divergent views of Ward on one side and von Hügel and Tyrrell on the other. They would always have much in common, but henceforth Tyrrell, at least, would never see eye to eye with Ward. The principal difference stems from their attitudes toward authority. Ward always presumed in favor of those who exercised authority—as in his letter where he simply assumed the sagacity of rulers—whereas von Hügel and Tyrrell regarded authorities with caution and suspicion. The upshot was that Ward, in turn, regarded von Hügel and Tyrrell ever after with caution and suspicion, and in that atmosphere the Tyrrell-Ward relationship deteriorated from friendship to obliging respect.

At the beginning of April 1900 two totally unforeseen factors entered the picture to hasten events toward a final interdict against Tyrrell. One was Robert Dell's apologia of Mivart in the *Nineteenth Century*, in which he upbraided the Jesuits, neo-scholastics, and narrow party politicians for hurting the church and Rome's potential to be the center of Christian unity. In the same breath he complimented Tyrrell as "an English Jesuit father whose views seem to be as much out of harmony with the spirit of his Society as his abilities are superior to those of his *confrères*."[183]

This compliment could only have infuriated Tyrrell's enemies, and a call seems to have gone out for Tyrrell publicly to repudiate Dell's insinuations. But, as Tyrrell told Ward on 7 April, he declined to recover his reputation "by an onslaught on Dell. I said that I was too much in agreement with his main contentions to do so honestly . . . that the best refutation of Dell would have been the fact of my being allowed a free pen in advocating wider and more sympathetic lines."[184]

On 19 April, however, Gerard sent Tyrrell some cogent reasons for answering Dell. He appealed to the significance of Tyrrell's vows and the manifestation of God's will therein—how it seemed contrary to God's will that an individual who had been allowed to pledge himself so deeply to the Society should assume an individualistic position so completely at variance with it, and how the assumption of such a position of "superior enlightenment" is often the beginning of evil. Gerard agreed that Tyrrell's doctrine was theologically justifiable, but he also saw that the general's attitude was understandable, "& since he backs it with his authority, the one for us to adopt," namely, that although Tyrrell's explanations of Catholic doctrine had done much good for certain people, they had done harm where they were misunderstood. "Therefore it is necessary to let people see that your meaning is not that which some would foist upon you." There was no question, he said, of Tyrrell having to say what he did not believe, "but of letting men see the other side of your mind, which like the other side of the moon has recently been out of sight." Gerard's clinching argument was one of Tyrrell's own dicta: as for enduring the pain of submission to external authority, "Did not you yourself write recently 'It is the desire to climb up by some other way, rather than go through the one door of self-denial, that is the source of all corruption?'"[185]

Tyrrell yielded and executed an answer to Dell entitled "Who Are the Reactionaries?" In it he first credited Dell with a sincere desire to be complimentary but also with "a complete, though scarcely credible, obliviousness" about the embarrassing and awkward position in which Dell placed him relative to his order. For one could hardly feel complimented by a public assurance that he is totally unsuited for his vocation, as a Jesuit would necessarily be who is "absolutely out of harmony with the spirit of his order." Even if it were true, Tyrrell complained, it was not the sort of truth one cares to have told to the public. But as far as he was concerned, it was not true. Dell, he said, wrongly imagines that a nar-

row unaccommodating spirit is the spirit of the Society. Just as one
should not define the spirit of Christianity by the ideas and cus-
toms of a particular group of Christians in an isolated time and
place, so it is not legitimate to define the spirit of the Society of
Jesus by the sayings and practices of individual members. One
must study the spirit of the founder. For Ignatius that is "notoriously a spirit of elasticity and accommodation—the antithesis in
every respect of that which forms the theme of Mr. Dell's stric-
tures."[186] Since that is the spirit of the Society, Tyrrell went on, he
could not be justly accused of disharmony for holding a doctrinal
opinion tolerated by the theology of the church with which the
theology of the Society professes to be identical.

But just as Tyrrell disclaimed allegiance to that narrow spirit attributed by Dell to the whole Society, so he disclaimed allegiance
to "that diametrically opposite extreme of 'liberalism' which to
some hasty minds seems the only conceivable alternative. Indeed, I
have always looked upon the popular representatives of this school
as the worst enemies of solid theological advance." Extremism is
always detrimental to the truth, as it fails to recognize the legitimate place and function of an opposite view, "and, in general, the
extremists on either side are the ultimate authors of their own grie-
vances." As to the terms "liberal" and "conservative," no sane person could disavow them in their root meanings, but as they had become the properties of sectarians each bent on destroying every
opinion but their own, no wise person could even think of himself
under those labels.[187]

Tyrrell allied himself with the position of Newman in his *Apologia* (1864), namely, that in confrontations with "high ecclesiastics"
events have shown, as Newman put it, "that they were mainly in
the right, and that those whom they were hard upon were mainly
in the wrong"—as in the case of Origen (whom Newman admired)
versus Theophilus of Alexandria and Pope Vigilius, who though
unsavory characters, were on the whole right.[188]

As to orthodoxy *versus* heresy, said Newman, that is often a
question of opportuneness. The critic forgets to ask whether the
time is right for his message, and knowing that no one else will
voice it in his lifetime, he pushes it forward against the voice of authority and so spoils in his own century what, cleansed and purified, belongs to the next. To the world he may come off as a mar-
tyr of free speech, whereas he really ought to be silenced; and
authority, for silencing him, may come off as tyrannical and indifferent to the cause of truth and justice, especially if it happens to
be supported by extremists.

The parallel to Tyrrell's situation *vis-à-vis* Rome is uncanny, and, seeing it, Tyrrell quoted Newman: "Such a state of things may be provoking and discouraging at the time, in the case of two classes of persons; of moderate men who wish to make differences in religious opinion as little as they fairly can be made; and of such as keenly perceive, and are honestly eager to remedy, existing evils,—evils, of which divines in this or that foreign country know nothing at all, and which even at home, where they exist, it is not every one who has the means of estimating."[189]

Ironically, within a year Tyrrell would charge "high ecclesiastics" with promoting a heretical conception of the church's constitution. Meanwhile he wanted to see himself on the side of ecclesiastical authority, as it pruned away what was harmful or useless. "The 'inhibited' branch of writing," he told Ward as he began this essay, "is really the most important one and that for which I am best fitted, so that I am extinguished for the most part of me." But Tyrrell could not bear to let any part of himself fall away unnoticed. Thus, "I may . . . find a sort of issue in ethics and kindred subjects where my modernity will be less detected; besides which, anonymous work will always be possible if due secrecy be observed."[190]

But for this essay there was no question of secrecy. Tyrrell had composed it "in obedience to His Paternity," consequently His Paternity had to approve it for publication.[191] In fact, he rejected it, and so, Tyrrell told Ward, it had no chance of ever seeing light.[192] Ward was disappointed—and perhaps von Hügel too, who found it "full of deeply stimulating and suggestive writing"[193]—for Ward believed that Dell, like Mivart, had to be answered. And since Tyrrell was prevented, Ward again stepped in with "Liberalism and Intransigeance" in the June *Nineteenth Century,* an answer that Tyrrell found "curiously parallel to his own."[194] More on this presently.

The second unforeseen factor that hastened the interdict against Tyrrell was the Jesuit general's ill health. On 16 May Fr. Rudolf Meyer, the American assistant to the general charged with the affairs of the English Province, wrote to Fr. John Gerard to suggest that the general's illness was aggravated by the Tyrrell affair, that the articles sent up were unsatisfactory, but that the general sincerely desired "to save Father Tyrrell." Therefore the general advised that Tyrrell publish a brief statement noting that, in the incriminated article, "three things must be distinguished—dogmas of faith, Catholic truth, and theological opinion." Tyrrell should make clear that, as to the first two, there could be no question about his position—"all loyal sons of the Church are bound to accept them"; and that, as to the third, he "subscribes to the common opinion of

Catholic theologians; and that his article must be thus interpreted, i.e. he only meant to say that we must not require more than the Church requires through her recognized spokesmen."[195]

Tyrrell complied—in his own way—and wrote to Ward on 31 May that his revised version was on the way. "After six months of groaning and labour the seven hills have been delivered of a lean little mouse whose ineffectual squeak will be heard in the W. Register of Saturday."[196] It actually appeared on Friday, 1 June 1900, thus:

"A PERVERTED DEVOTION"

DEAR SIR,

Owing to some apparent ambiguities of expression in my article of December 16th, 1899, entitled "A Perverted Devotion," which have been distorted in an unorthodox sense by certain superficial readers, I have been asked to state: that in the said article *three things must be distinguished—dogmas of faith, Catholic truths, and theological opinions: that as to dogmas and Catholic truths, all loyal sons of the Church are bound to accept them, and that consequently there can be no question as to my position on this score;* but that as to theological opinions, whether touching the matter in hand or others, I wish it to be clearly understood that I hold whatever all theologians hold, unanimously and in common; and that where, as occasionally happens, they disagree, I follow no opinion that has not such a weight of theological authority in its favour as to make it safely and solidly probable; and that in this sense readers must interpret the article in question, *wherein I meant simply to say that we should not require more than the Church requires through her recognised spokesmen.*

I am, etc.

May 30th, 1900   G. TYRRELL[197]

Discreet Departure: Richmond-in-Swaledale

Upon publication of his "retraction," Tyrrell escaped from the turmoil of Farm Street to the peace and quiet of the small Jesuit mission of St. Joseph and St. Francis Xavier at Richmond. From there he wrote on 6 June to let the baron know that he was "on supply" for a fortnight or so, was finding the "grave-yard tranquility of the place" a relief after so much strain and worry, and that in the latest *Weekly Register* he could find "the mouse of which the labouring mountains have at last been delivered . . . & so the curtain falls on the feeble little farce. Of course they will never forget or forgive."[198]

Meanwhile the baron was waiting for the absconder's return, as he was hoping for a heart-to-heart talk. Finally on 7 July he submitted to the drudgery of a letter. He first complimented Tyrrell on his "retraction"—"so little yours, however, as to be barely grammar. . . . Yet I was, of course, very glad that it amounted to so little—indeed it would be impossible to specify what it amounted to." He then proceeded to what was really on his mind—a painful letter to Ward on the events just passed, on the differences he felt between them, and the difficulty of trying to reconcile those differences within a disaffected climate of thought and feeling. In such a climate explanations only serve to multiply and intensify differences. But to Tyrrell he explained that the differences were not so much of policy—what to say or how to say it—but of interior attitude, "as to the estimate and practice of the driving forces of religion."[199] He went so far as to imply that Ward's religion was politically based indirection, whereas his own and Tyrrell's expressed itself in direct and heartfelt action.

A case in point was Ward's answer to Dell, in which he intended to mediate between the extremes but wherein he left no doubt as to which side he was on. Ward began with the wholesale exoneration of authority and apologized for the right by trying to make the note of intransigence to be merely a misreading by the extreme left. How tolerant authorities really are, he said, is proven by the fact that such men as Newman, Bremond, Georges Fonsegrive, and others are allowed to write with the approval of church authorities, and one was even given the cardinal's hat. Ward referred with contempt to recent agitations in the press as the "vague extravagances" of "comparative tyros in the theological arena," and declared that no sane person could or ought to take them seriously.

> At a time when the Church shows so much zeal and devotion throughout nearly all Europe; when one saintly Pontiff has reigned for twenty years in succession to another saintly Pontiff who reigned for thirty; when the morality of the Roman Curia is above suspicion; when the much-abused Jesuits are living heroic lives and winning converts in many countries;—a vague denunciation of the existing Catholic system as signally corrupt is so ludicrous to those who know the facts of the case, that it might very well be simply dismissed as of no account.[200]

Even before receiving von Hügel's letter of 7 July, Tyrrell had lost confidence in Ward's position and hesitated to continue associating with it. On 18 June he sent Ward a long and pointed statement of his own mind on the true mediating position and asked Ward to comment.[201] The distinctness of his position relative to the extremes, he explained, was not merely in degree of toleration but in kind. It lay in striving to conciliate all positions, in regarding both extremes as inevitable factors of social and ecclesiastical progress, in taking what is good in each and rejecting what is bad, and interpreting the extremes to each other—not in taking sides and speaking for one side to the other. Such a role cannot be predetermined with an *a priori* program but must adjust to the drift of conflicting forces. The leaven of progress moves inevitably from below upward, and no one can say where it will end. But it was clear to Tyrrell that the rapid currents of the nineteenth century would precipitate crises in the church in the twentieth century, and he was anxious that the church not be caught unaware and so be panicked into factional strife and schism.

Unfortunately Ward's response is lost, but his drift may be gathered from developments to be reviewed in the next chapter. For the present, Maisie Ward's substantive opinion will suffice. According to her, Ward was convinced that Tyrrell had thrown in his lot with the radical liberals. The only question was when. Ward thought that the joint pastoral letter issued by the Catholic bishops of England at the end of 1900 was decisive. The present writer leans rather toward Maisie Ward's opinion that the reception accorded "A Perverted Devotion" had far more to do with the change.[202] She pointed out that Tyrrell enjoyed strong support from his English superiors and censors, but that the flaw in his character showed in his reception of criticism from higher up. "He sent the attack on to my father endorsed, 'My dear Ward, who could bear this.' For some days he stopped saying Mass."[203]

This last detail is undocumented, but assuming it as fact, it shows the depth of Tyrrell's pain. The joint pastoral merely added external justification for Tyrrell's radical disaffection that was already an interior reality. But to place Tyrrell in the liberal camp was also unjustifiable, unless one defined "liberal" very broadly. Tyrrell would not place himself there, as he told Ward, and only a person who himself pledged allegiance to the right would interpret divergence as allegiance to the left.

Tyrrell for his part did not reach clarity on the precise point of divergence between himself and Ward until early 1904. It came at the end of a lengthy discussion over doctrinal development that began with Ward's answer to Mivart—actually with two preliminary drafts that Tyrrell read and criticized.[204] He saw in them that Ward was not and perhaps could not speak for him. So in early March 1900 he began to set down his own views. They were eventually published as a pseudonymous brochure, *The Civilizing of* the *Matafanus*.[205] Three years later, when Ward published *Problems and Persons*, a collection of essays including his reply to Mivart, Tyrrell took the occasion to expand his criticism into a two-part review article entitled "Semper Eadem."[206] The *Month* published part 1 in January 1904 but rejected part 2 over confusions and disagreements generated by part 1. Ward and Tyrrell strongly disagreed over the meaning of Newman's *via media*, and John Gerard, then editor of the *Month*, became confused over the exact target of Tyrrell's criticism. Tyrrell's letter to Ward of 19 January 1904 makes the issue clear:

> I reminded him [Gerard] how in offering the article to him I had said that it was "neither an attack, nor a defense, of *any* school, neither of 'liberal theology' nor of those whom you (J. Gerard) call 'theologians of the wooden old school'; but an attempt to clear the *Status Quaestionis*. If it was *against* anyone it was against those who hoped they had found a *via media*,—"liberal" Catholics who failed to distinguish themselves *in principle* from the extreme left; or against Ward who— *meo judicio*—had failed to distinguish himself *in principle* from the extreme right."[207]

There the Ward-Tyrrell relationship remained.

By 12 July 1900 Tyrrell had returned from Richmond to Farm Street.[208] A retreat he was to have given in Dublin to young Jesuits preparing for ordination fell through. In its place he was allowed to direct a retreat for an institution of women in London, 22 to 31 July. It was his last.[209]

In the midst of that retreat Tyrrell wrote Bremond that he was still under interdict and could not publish outside the *Month*, and to Ward he wrote that even to give retreats he had to receive permission from Rome each time—"a polite way of making the thing impossible."[210] "The latter is good," he quipped to Bremond, "because it gives me more time; and the former because it gives the charm of illegality to what else were an irksome duty; and I doubt not that some day what is written in darkness will be brought to light."[211]

A few days after this retreat, on 3 August, Tyrrell met with Baron von Hügel for the last time before escaping again to Richmond, where he would remain until finally dismissed from the Jesuits on 19 February 1906.[212] Five and a half years would go to writing and studying, much of it in areas previously closed by reason of his ignorance of German. But with prodding from the baron, Tyrrell quickly assimilated that language and choice bits of its scholarship. His writing bore the mark of his study, but he never sold himself wholesale to any one scholar. Rather what was already within was simply drawn out and given expression through the instrumentality of French and German scholars. With this study and writing Tyrrell passed beyond Wardian liberalism to that period subsequently caricatured as modernism, in which emerged his new apologetic for Roman Catholicism.

CHAPTER 4

The Parting of Ways

THE EMERGING APOLOGETIC

For five and one-half years of self-chosen exile at Richmond in Yorkshire, George Tyrrell enjoyed the leisure to read what he liked—or what Baron von Hügel liked—and to write about what he read. It was a period of profuse productivity both in publications and in correspondence. Almost everything he wrote he published, by hook or by crook, with or without his name, with or without ecclesiastical approval. His writings are characteristically unsystematic and occasional. What progression or continuity is in them rests entirely within the subjective experience of their author. Tyrrell's overall aim in public and in private was to elaborate a *modus vivendi* for liberal Catholics in an illiberal church. His public writings reveal his thought, his private writings his feelings. To examine both is to lay bare not only his apologetic and underlying philosophy but also the inner history of a remarkable man.

Setting Tyrrell's Mind

In 1896 Tyrrell had written on the title page of his breviary, "Thou shalt see from afar the land which the Lord God will give to the children of Israel, but thou shalt not enter therein."[1] In a letter of 19 January 1902 to Maude Petre, he added, "from that conviction I have never swerved since long before that date. Still I am very satisfied with my destiny as a wheel in God's will, & find sufficient reward in the interests of life, its ups & even its downs; nor would I willingly purchase so dull a thing as personal safety at the sacrifice of such entertaining dangers.[2]

During the Richmond years there are recurring references to Moses as a figure in whom the Jesuit in exile found sympathy. Like the biblical prophets, Tyrrell saw himself as a thankless mediary for the progress of truth. As he himself had appropriated and was credited for the ideas and wisdom of forgotten heroes, he knew that he in turn would be ground beyond recognition, only to be reincarnated generations later in the common acceptance of truths for whose proclamation he had been sentenced to die on Mount Nebo.[3]

A pathetic melancholy runs through most of Tyrrell's works and letters. It was due no doubt—given the events of his life—to that deeply felt kinship with Moses. Edmund Bishop sensed it all too keenly when he read Tyrrell's *Autobiography and Life* a few weeks after its publication.[4] Bishop himself, a rare and promising lay Catholic theologian, had been ground under in the antiliberal campaign of Pius IX. The pain of that experience welled up again as he read Tyrrell's story and filled the margins with poignant annotations:

> "Rome" *is . . .* an embodied and *organized egotism:* one of the greatest (I am apt to think: *the* greatest—as a *system*) the world has ever seen.
>
> how one knows the style,—the hollowness, the unChristianness of the system (and those who "work it,"—when they are *on the work*).
>
> Our "Church" is full of,—is it "bristling with," or all afire with?—"*scandals.*"
>
> The S.J. *man is* (in *so far as a true blue S.J.*) at the least a potential *fanatic.*
>
> . . . the depths of the desert misery of our modern R.C.-ism.
>
> The tragedy of it all,—the *tragedy!*
>
> It—what follows—is *too sad.* I cannot go on.[5]

The Civilizing of the Matafanus

Von Hügel was the first to notice and name Tyrrell's melancholy as he read the manuscript version of *The Civilizing of the Matafanus* in August 1900. He connected the tone with the constraint to Tyrrell's freedom due to ecclesiastical pressures. "I return herewith the 'Walla-Washee Tribe' paper," he wrote, read with

> rare intellectual delight. . . . There is of course a profound and pathetic melancholy running through the paper, which does not become

less so to one, because one realises how inevitable, indeed well-grounded it is, and because one cannot but ask oneself how long this constraint and trial is to last, and with what results. . . . With your sensitive nature and delicate health, and immense need of indefinite activity and self-communication, a long course of silence and repression would be too painfully trying to yourself, for me to be able to bear to think of it as probable.

In the same letter von Hügel noted that Tyrrell was "evidently not thinking of publishing" the paper. "What a pity that such a decision should be necessary!"[6] Tyrrell was forbidden at this time to publish outside the pages of the *Month* unless he cleared himself through Jesuit censors in Rome—something he was not about to do because, as he told his friend and literary agent Alfred Rayney Waller, "even though their theology be unimpeachable"—which in Tyrrell's opinion it was not—their "English is Ollendorfian."[7]

If Tyrrell had not been thinking of publishing this paper, the thought was planted by von Hügel and soon blossomed into deed.[8] Tyrrell answered the baron on 7 September and confessed that he felt "so encouraged by your appreciation of my theological romance. . . . I wish I could devise some way of publishing it anonymously," or perhaps have it "Frenchified" for *La Quinzaine*.[9] The baron answered that the possibility of misinterpretation would only be compounded by a translation, and he was anxious that Tyrrell's circumstances be improved and not worsened "for the sake of souls at large, even more than for your own."[10]

But on the very day of von Hügel's letter, Tyrrell was already writing to Waller to initiate his first clandestine operation: "I wondered if in the event of its [the cloud of repression] not lifting at all Duckworth wd. care to risk an anonymous volume of the 'Hard Sayings' type. The anonymity would have to be all the stricter as the authorship would be so palpably evident."[11] Tyrrell was probably referring to what eventually was published as *Oil and Wine*, but less than a week later he wrote again to Waller with an unequivocal proposal for the masked appearance of the *Matafanus*:

The situation is really this: I ought not to saddle the SJ with the responsibility of a work which the great majority of its representatives would shudder at—if they could understand it. Were I to wait till I could find censors advanced enough to approve of its publication I should have to wait at least 100 years. But I think it is just now, & not at that remote date, that the ideas might help a few here & there in the right orientation of their minds in approaching the Christian & even the Catholic problem.[12]

But the little volume was delayed by a new round of conflicts and did not appear until January 1902—and then under Waller's name. Meantime it experienced a complicated redaction. As part of its concealment Tyrrell at first proposed to publish under the pseudonym "Stephen Grey." Then, because so many had read his manuscript, he decided to change his characters' names from rough savage to smooth Latin sounds, and the title to *The Civilizing of the Cimmerians: An Essay in Development*.[13] But Tyrrell was dissatisfied with the new arrangement, so on 16 April 1901 he suggested to Waller that he redact the manuscript by supplying

> such connective tissue as below indicated, and then publish the document under your own name. . . . Thus we shall have a double document like those of the Pentateuch—a narrator & digestor working on a previous document. This is quite sufficient accordg. to Biblical critics to constitute you the *author*—the more since you do professedly what the sacred redactors did tacitly. . . . Possibly you might invent savage names instead of Latin. I changed only because so many had read the M.S. that the names wd. strike them at once.[14]

So Waller changed "Cimmerians" to "Matafanus" and "Sagittarius" to "Alpuca." But Tyrrell's heart was in the old sounds, and when he and some half dozen readers had seen the new names in print, he repented and earnestly implored Waller "to reconsider the restoration of the original names in all their barbaric wildness—Shishibamba, Walla-Washies & the rest. Appearing under your name and in the Pentateuchal form of a redaction of the public MSS. of an unknown Moses I am technically safe enough not to mind (though I do not desire) being suspected. Those who have read both forms are unanimous in regretting the old familiar names."[15] Waller, however, asserted his privilege as final redactor, and the published version appeared with his own inventions and with the final title, *The Civilizing of the Matafanus: An Essay in Religious Development*.[16]

The content of this booklet and of two related works written in close conjunction during the first half of 1900 suggests that Tyrrell's principal theological preoccupation was the problem of doctrinal development: the nature and scope of the initial revelation, the receptive organ thereof, and the subsequent tradition and its authority. *The Matafanus* is a similitude in the Swiftian style of some earlier essays.[17] Its aim was to set at rest those who were finding "the present condition and past history of Christianity . . . perplexing and disappointing in the absence of some such explanatory conception."[18]

Presupposing as a hypothesis the possibility of a supernatural revelation such as that ascribed to Jesus Christ, Tyrrell's allegory described the transmission of that revelation to the crude ore of a humankind endowed with a woefully inadequate vehicle of conceptualization and expression. Once the initial revelation had been committed to language, it followed the natural laws of psychological and social development. Tyrrell postulated that if one could understand the very human problems connected with natural development, one might find the fate of any kind of revelation committed to those natural processes not quite so disappointing. Even if Christ were no more than a great teacher, the resistance he met in trying to propagate truths far in advance of social standards would have yielded such results as described in this allegory. But given that Christ is much more than a great teacher, indeed the bearer of God's own revelation, the difficulties of his task are infinitely compounded and the conditions of this allegory are more nearly realized.

As a tribute to his source of inspiration and as a hermeneutical hint, Tyrrell quoted as a preface the cave scene from Plato's *Republic*. Parallel to that, his parable describes the attempt of a cultured group of philanthropists (the Society for the Spread of Civilisation amongst the Savages) to civilize and moralize a tribe of savages (the Matafanus). The revelation by which civilization was to be induced was, of course, the society's ways and means of right living. Initial forays by their own members to try to communicate the truth were unsuccessful because they failed to establish any medium of communication, any common measure between the known and the unknown. The savages, instead of being awed, were *over*awed, to the extent that it hardly occurred to them to try to imitate these superhuman powers. By attempting to reveal truth in its fullness, the pioneers had overshot their mark. An objectively untruthful picture could have done more to win the savage mind than the blinding light of full truth. They needed to temper the light to tender eyes. What they needed was a mediator, someone with experience of both cultures.

A savant of the higher culture hit upon the idea that such a creature might be fashioned by hypnotic suggestion. So they selected out of the tribe a particularly apt specimen (Alpuca), gave him through hypnosis a complete thought-transference from the savant, and reinjected him into the tribe in hopes that he might leaven the mass.

As subject of a split personality, with half his brain in light, the other half in darkness, Alpuca struggled to utter a message he himself only half understood, and at which his hearers shook their heads. At first he tried to explain his fate to intimate friends, but they thought him a "victim of over-strained nerves." Finally, to prove he had access to hidden sources of knowledge, he resorted to miracles, which in themselves would have won him no credit, but his already obvious moral integrity inspired confidence in all his actions. Followers gathered and, through invidious comparison, began to form low opinions of their priests and pow-wow men, a development Alpuca discountenanced because he did not want to excite the "jealousy of that exclusive and arrogant faction, ever nervous of the communising of those secrets on which its power and influence depended."[19] This class was the greatest obstacle to the progress of civilization, although in an earlier stage it had been the cause of what little advance had been made beyond mere barbarism. But progress ended back then because that first revelation became "the property of an exclusive caste wherein the faith of each member was supported by the faith of all the rest," and to guard their own status they opposed the "discoveries and advances of others outside their own clique, and thus essentially shut themselves off into a fruitless and unprogressive insolation."[20]

There follows an account of Alpuca's mission, its ups and downs, with a predominance of the latter, the anguish of thwarted expression: "hopeless as the endeavor to render a Beethoven's sonata on the Jew's harp, or to reproduce Raphael on a stable door with a lump of chalk."[21] This failure, along with the rising and increasingly organized opposition from the "official guides," conspired to impress on Alpuca heavy thoughts as to the "whence" and "whither" of his life and mission. He began to suspect that what he had to say might have to be left to the discovery of some future age, for it seemed quite clear that his own age would surely do him in without a fair hearing. So he determined to leave a record with his trusted friends, who, though they helped in its production, understood it hardly better than his fiercest opponents.

The record fell into two parts: the first concerned the origins, life, and death of Alpuca himself; the second, what he taught and revealed. The verbal accuracy required when one describes objects for their own sake was not thought important, as this description was for the sake of something else that the record merely symbolized. It was this "something else" that concerned Alpuca most, because he foresaw that future wranglings and misunderstandings would throw his meaning into jeopardy. Had his account been strictly historical, knowledge of the primitive language combined with a facility for logical analysis and reading of evidence would suffice. But as his truths dealt with transcendent realities only hinted at through crude and narrow forms, a true interpretation in future ages would depend on more than logic, grammar, and analysis; it would come with the growth of the savage mind toward sympathy with higher standards and ideals. "Hence, not through any addition to the record, but through an increased transparency of the reading mind, the truth would shine more clearly and distinctly in later ages." Thus what was needed for growth toward an authentic understanding was growth in civilization. "It was, then, to a certain 'spirit' that Alpuca left the interpretation of his record."[22] Alpuca is then duly murdered.

Centuries later the Matafanus had grown into "a vast semi-barbarous people walled round . . . like the Chinese empire." In their midst still existed, "albeit in a languid and declining state, a goodly remnant of the once all-powerful sect of the Alpucas." Outsiders regarded the Alpucas with skeptical contempt for their pretensions and pointed to the "contrast between the stagnant and unprogressive character of the Alpuca intelligence and morality, and their own which was so manifestly and marvellously advanced upon former ages."[23]

What accounted for this state was that after Alpuca's murder, an attempt was made to exterminate all his followers. As a result they formed a secret community dedicated to preserving Alpuca's record. So long as disciples of only one or two removes from Alpuca still lived, precise literal adherence to the record was not felt to be urgently important. But as they died off, preservation of Alpuca's mind and thought rested on the accurate preservation and interpretation of the document. Hence the first stage of development was a movement from a vital and flexible to a harder and more literal reading of the doctrine, and from a living of its substance to establishing Alpuca's claim to bear a special revelation.

A struggle ensued and resulted in schism. The orthodox strengthened their opposition to the innovators by pointing to supposed defects in the record and the opportunity these afforded to unbelief. Gradually isolating themselves from the rest of the world, the orthodox lost influence in proportion to their refusal to be influenced. But they justified their conduct by blaming the one-sidedness of their opponents, and though they sometimes lost ground momentarily, they often won in the end. Yet just as often they resorted to the tactics of their adversaries and so put themselves in the wrong. "In sticking to the *whole* of the legacy of Alpuca—shell and kernel, sound and sense—they were infallibly right." But when they did as their opponents did and "claimed an equal authority for each part torn away from the whole which gave it its life and meaning . . . they made themselves ridiculous"—this, through a "continual tendency . . . to forget that life was the end of knowledge."[24]

It is difficult to be precise about the period of composition of *The Matafanus*, but from parallel passages and phrases in Tyrrell's correspondence, one can guess that the work was begun at least by the end of January 1900 and finished in rough draft not long thereafter. There are in fact so many parallels in Tyrrell's correspondence during the first half of 1900 that one can hardly avoid concluding that the story of Alpuca was a similitude on Tyrrell's own life as well as on the life of Jesus and the fate of Christian revelation. A recounting of select parallels will display the feeling behind the work and thus give a better idea of its underlying critique.

The reader will recall that in early January 1900 Tyrrell received his first real check from Jesuit authorities in Rome, who were afraid that they had another Mivart on their hands. Tyrrell was censored and driven to consider a program of diplomacy and accommodation to avoid Mivart's fate and especially the condemnation of all his past work. He even considered keeping silence for several years, but that would have done violence to his nature. "While I have a personal dislike, inability and contempt for diplomacy," Tyrrell wrote to Frank Rooke Ley, "my reason tells me it is the necessary condition of success. Truth and justice *ought* to be conclusive arguments with ecclesiastical authorities—but they are not;—never have been. . . . It is easy to be moderate when one's own skin is not touched. . . . Still, I confess that I have made things worse, and never better, by giving expression to irritation."[25]

To cope with the situation Tyrrell formulated a stoic *modus vivendi* and passed it on to Bremond, who was preparing to make his final religious profession on 2 February 1900. On 31 January Tyrrell wrote to congratulate him "in the sense that a man may be congratulated who from a sense of duty & principle sacrifices himself in fulfillment of what he believes to be a binding engagement entered upon in good faith . . . and not evidently invalidated by a substantial error. This is a frigid statement of what I nevertheless believe to be a far more heroic act in your case than in the case of those who still take the Society at its own valuation, and for whom profession is a crown & not a cross."[26]

Then, in the heat of the Mivart explosion, Tyrrell wrote to von Hügel in vehement terms about "these Ultramontanes"—their "savage ferocity," "shameless untruthfulness," "arrogance," and "tyranny." Still they were part of the system, the ore that had to be taken whole if one wanted its gold. "It is as though a savant were to give a course of scientific lectures to bushmen & then leaving them a synopsis, to go his way. Christianity in the hands of the Roman Church is like the synopsis in the hands of the savages; they may grow to some intelligence of it in the course of ages; and savages though they be, at least they & they alone possess the authentic record."[27]

Von Hügel's answer of 4 March urged Tyrrell on the one hand to rise above bitterness and preserve the "splendid *verve* and strong, mellow tone" of his writings for the sake of those who depended on him, but on the other hand not to cower before the rantings of the ultramontanes. Newman, Duchesne, Blondel, and Laberthonnière, the baron reminded Tyrrell, all remained productive amidst their troubles and were an annoyance to their opponents, who evidently felt themselves hit without really being able to hit back. Loisy was a case in point. According to Duchesne, Loisy's whole attitude of mind and treatment of subjects was so different from that of his antagonists "that they slip about the premises, trying to find a common starting-point and measure, and failing utterly. Good." But the baron had his own hypothesis to explain the "ever vivid wrath and vindictiveness" of Roman authorities and especially their "deep anti-English animus." It was due to "that old affair, the Temporal Power and its abolition and England's having made the latter possible."[28] This theme Tyrrell pressed repeatedly in subsequent correspondence and writings, as it were a thorn in Rome's flesh.

Tyrrell agreed that he must take Mivart as an object lesson and hold his temper, and perhaps even "subside into silence now; for, as you say, it is wonderful how much I have been allowed to do; and I cd. still go on writing quietly & supplying other people with matter." But Tyrrell was overstating his capacity for silence in the face of real or imagined outrage, and in the next breath he announced what would be much more his subsequent comportment.

> The best policy, I half think, would be not to oppose but to fan the flame of this "authority-fever"; to get them to declare the infallibility of every Congregation, of the General of the Jesuits, of every Monsignorino in Rome; to define the earth to be a flat plate supported on pillars, & the sky a dish-cover; in short, to let them run their head full tilt against a stone wall, in hopes it may wake them up to sober realities.
>
> The "reductio ad absurdum" is God's favorite argument—to let evils work themselves out & so manifest their true nature. Nothing else ever carries widespread conviction.

. . . I try to see God in it all. One seems to see the Church of the future struggling for birth in the Church of the present—pained & paining; and looked back upon, these crises are as natural as the sloughing of a snake's skin, though at the time they are as agonising as parturition.[29]

Here again is evident Tyrrell's stoic resignation to his fate, as truth worked itself out in a slowly grinding process in which the *reductio ad absurdum* seemed an inevitable and painful means.

The Civilizing of the Matafanus, therefore, written neither under censorship nor with a view to publication, stands as the first formal prognosis of the struggles Tyrrell saw before him. They were all here in capsule: the intellectual, emotional, and even the physical cost of trying to receive, assimilate, live by, and propagate a message to people who would not and perhaps could not hear, let alone understand—to people who found the new strange and the strange inimical. Like Alpuca, Tyrrell was fated to prophesy and suffer a prophet's reward. He would resign himself to opprobrium and to leaving behind a record, a prophecy to be verified by secret assimilation and eventual common acclaim in the church of the future. But unlike Alpuca, he would not be silent before his shearers. The mordant criticism of radical factions that he here muttered under his breath would be shouted from the housetops and in his own name eight years hence in *Medievalism: A Reply to Cardinal Mercier*.

MORE ON THE DEVELOPMENT OF DOGMA

Much of what Tyrrell had expressed in the high symbolism of the *Matafanus* he set about reducing to straight prose. All during 1900 he was elaborating in various ways the theme he set forth in "The Relation of Theology to Devotion": the distinction between revelation and its expression. But while in "The Relation of Theology to Devotion" he emphasized the priority for the life of devotion of the intuitive *sense* of revelation as it appealed to the imagination of the *profanum vulgus*, he now became preoccupied with the church's apologetic of revelation, that is, with the distinct, conceptual, rational *knowledge* of revelation. In that article he defined the deposit of faith as God's way of putting truths, namely, in the imaginative language of the common man, so that the deposit was practically defined as the form of sound doctrine. But as will be seen, Tyrrell soon changed his mind on this definition.

Among his essays, those of immediate interest are "Non Tali

Auxilio," an unpublished essay that unfortunately now seems to exist only in reported form in a Louvain doctoral dissertation; "The Mind of the Church," a two-part article in the *Month* for August and September 1900; and various parts of *Oil and Wine,* a collection of essays completed by December 1900 but not released to the public until 1906.[30] Among his correspondence, the letters to Wilfrid Ward are of primary importance.

Available evidence does not allow a precise chronology of these works, but "Non Tali Auxilio" seems to have been completed before "The Mind of the Church" and, written freely and not for publication, perhaps formed the working paper for the carefully chiseled "The Mind of the Church." The latter was obviously completed in its two parts by August and September and underwent modification in one crucial point between its appearance in the *Month* and its reappearance the following year in *The Faith of the Millions.* The vignettes of *Oil and Wine,* also not written for publication—at least under the circumstances of their composition Tyrrell had little hope that they would ever see type—[31]ran parallel to all his productions of 1900 and so will be used comparatively as background material.

Apart from Tyrrell's personal interest in the problem of revelation and dogma, what seems to have provoked him to write about it were some "recent" and "not too lenient" criticisms of the Catholic use of the term "the Mind of the Church" as involving "what might be called a fallacy of personification."[32] It is not possible to identify the stern critic beyond doubt, but he might well have been Adolf von Harnack, for on 16 June Tyrrell wrote to von Hügel:

> I have been reading Harnack—in English of course—and have been impressed with the madness of supposing that we can go on ignoring so plain a fact as the growth of Catholicism out of a germ as unlike Catholicism as a wall-nut is unlike a wall-nut tree. It will take all our wits & more learning than at present, alas! the Church can command anywhere, to show that the out-growth is a real & legitimate development; and yet our theologians go on dreaming & romancing about a full-fledged apostolic Catholicism; & are anxious to anathematize the very notion of development by putting Newman's Essay on the Index. Surely we are nearing the stone-wall against which we seemed [*sic*] fated to bang our heads before we wake up.[33]

All that the Catholic press had to offer as antidote was the theory of "literal unfolding" as represented by the likes of Canon James Moyes, then editor of the *Dublin Review.*[34] Tyrrell criticized Moyes's position in a long letter to Wilfrid Ward of 13 March 1900 and outlined his own position, which was basically that found in the *Matafanus* brochure, in "Non Tali Auxilio," and in "The Mind of the Church." According to Tyrrell, Moyes allowed no real development of the deposit of faith, as a seed might develop into a tree, but only a kind of evolution as a moth's wings unfold after the chrysalis breaks, or as a folded cloak is unfolded. By implication, then, every dogma known today was "known by every pope since Peter; at least *in confuso* or, as it were, in small type needing only a closer glance." Thus there is development not in the actual knowledge of revelation but only in the *mode* of apprehension. Tyrrell thought that Moyes could not admit real development in the church's knowledge for fear that such an admission would destroy the theory of the immutability of the deposit of faith. But that does not necessarily follow, said Tyrrell, for it is one thing to say that truths themselves have not developed, and another to say that *knowledge* of those truths has not developed. "We shd. all agree that when we speak of the growth of an idea we really mean that growing subjective accommodation of our mind to reality,—and not that eternal realities change." Hence Moyes's admission of development from confused to distinct knowledge, while it does not add to the *thing* known, means real growth in *knowledge of* the thing—development from "potential to actual knowledge" is a substantial change. "Hence, keeping strictly to the *depositum fidei*,[35] I believe that the sub-apostolic Church (I leave out the apostles, as being founts of revelation) did not & could not know all the potential contents of the deposit; that questions since asked & answered could not then have been asked or answered."[36]

At the time of this letter to Ward, Tyrrell still allowed that the apostles *possibly* knew explicitly the future developments of Christian revelation, but not so the subapostolic church, including the popes. For that would have required not only the power of logical analysis (no problem here), but also that intensified vision which results only from the natural growth of experience and from a supernatural growth in faith and grace under the guidance of the Holy Spirit who presupposes the former (here is the problem).

To explain to Ward how he conceived this growth, Tyrrell returned to his parable of the philanthropist who wants to bring his culture to a savage tribe, has little success, then before dying leaves a record in the coarse tongue. The parallel of this metaphor to Christ's life and revelation, said Tyrrell, fails in that, where the philanthropist's mind is fairly adequate to the reality he preaches (since, even though it is a higher reality, it is a human reality and out of his own experience), the same cannot be said of Christ's human mind. For *as man,* Christ has direct but not comprehensive or adequate intuition of the truth he preached as it exists in the mind of God. Christ clothed his *human apprehension* of eternal realities in the language of the *profanum vulgus* of Galilee.

After the philanthropist dies, the opposition is gradually vanquished, and the great record becomes an oracle to all future generations. But what will happen, Tyrrell explained, is that, when the immediate disciples die off, their followers will be at a loss for an authoritative interpretation, and much of the record will then seem nonsense. But because some of it is obviously so valuable and they are not sure where to draw lines, they will force interpretations of the rest. In time, as civilization progresses, much that was at first inexplicable will be understood, as later generations with their increased experience and perspicacity will be in a better position than the first disciples to interpret their benefactor's mind. But living languages change rapidly, so it is considered advantageous "to preserve the original meaning of the record—the sense it conveyed to the first hearers, for that is their *depositum fidei.*"[37]

The parallel to Christian revelation is this far applicable: As the mind of the church developed, many realities that at first were hidden came to light. But the parable fails in that Christ left to the church not only his revelation but also his Spirit, who guides the church in her understanding of that revelation but does not add to it. By the "mind of the Church," Tyrrell understood not only the church's dogmatic intelligence at any given stage of development but also the principle active in that and future development, namely, the Holy Spirit, whose function as the "*active mind* of the Church" is to safeguard and interpret the revelation of the Man-Christ.[38] So that, unlike in the parable, there occurs not only natural growth in the church's mind, according to laws governing the growth of any mind, but there is also supernatural growth due to the influence of the Holy Spirit.[39] To resume the parallel: since living languages change, the sense that Christ's words conveyed to his first hearers must be preserved, for that is the *depositum fidei.*

If here the reader is quite confused as to what exactly Tyrrell meant by the deposit of faith, the confusion is only a reflection of Tyrrell's own mind on this point. He was wavering on whether to place emphasis on the *sense* of Christ's words, or on the sense of Christ's *words* as being the deposit of faith. It is also not clear from his letters to Ward of 13 and 16 March where the deposit is preserved. That question he asked and answered in "The Mind of the Church."

Before examining that article, however, a quick review of coordinate correspondence reveals Tyrrell's underlying attitudes, hopes, and motives. In a letter to von Hügel, Tyrrell had referred to his six-month long confrontation over "A Perverted Devotion" as a "feeble little farce,"[40] but to Bremond he suggested that it involved repercussions far beyond his private concerns, "that many really good and religious people will be lost to the Church through this 'tug-of-war' crisis, which is now upon us."[41] Sadly, Tyrrell wrote to von Hügel that he saw the church starving to death before a groaning board of food, "yet we hang back through a timidity which vaunts itself as faith & prudence but is in reality unfaith & shortsightedness."[42] To Ward, Tyrrell explained that he wanted not to identify with either party in the tug-of-war, but that decision set him apart in a sobering and lonely position.[43] Von Hügel remarked these feelings in "Who Are the Reactionaries?" as sounding "that enchanting note of spiritual aloofness and pathetic, patient, brave loneliness, which is ever characteristic of one side and aspect of all spontaneous and deep religion."[44] And upon receiving a message of support from the Italian scripture scholar, Padre Giovanni Semeria, Tyrrell confessed:

> It is no small consolation that here and there the level plain of Catholic intransigeance is broken by some lonely peak that catches the light of that coming day which for the many is as yet buried below the horizon. This . . . is not merely a poetical trope but rather the true and sober philosophy of the unpleasant situation in which not a few find themselves just now. God knows it is hard to be patient—hard, not to spoil a good cause through some momentary lack of faith in the irresistible power of fact against fiction,—hard, to be content that hereafter others shall appropriate with approval what we have been censured for gathering; and to acquiesce in the doom: E contra videbis terram et non ingredieris in eam quam ego dabo filiis Israel . . . Vidisti eam oculis tuis et non transibis ad illam.[45]

Overlaid with the issue of abuse of authority was the issue of doctrinal reconstruction in the light of historical and biblical criticism. It was the imagined destructive influences of criticism that Tyrrell addressed in "The Mind of the Church." He was, of course, acquainted with the matter from secondary sources, but now at von Hügel's instance he was meeting the critics firsthand. "I have just finished Loisy's studies on the Gospels," he wrote Bremond on 16 July, "and his still more admirable article on inspiration. Doubtless the inquisitors of some future day will build up his sepulchre, & will say: 'See how the Catholic Church was ever the first to welcome new light!'"[46] Tyrrell was convinced that the really destructive influence in the church was the ultra-Vaticanist view of infallibility, and he was alarmed that it had simply played into the hand of Harnack, who was about to trump even the legitimate understanding of papal infallibility as an outgrowth of ecclesiastical infallibility. "I have been saddening my soul lately," Tyrrell wrote to the baron on 6 June, "by going over the miserable story of the Vatican Council again. . . . I have been looking for a 'way out'; but so far have not succeeded." What struck Tyrrell was "the apparently *radical* opposition of principle between vaticanism & anti-vaticanism; between viewing the pope as the *mind* of the Church, and as merely the *voice* of that mind. But I may ask you some day to read what I am writing on the question."[47]

Tyrrell was ill-equipped to meet Harnack's criticism, and to date he had found no Catholic author who even tried, let alone succeeded. Newman, in his theory of doctrinal development, certainly had anticipated the need to meet critics on their own ground, but he himself had not explicitly done so. One author who did was the Anglican William Hurrell Mallock.[48] Tyrrell found Mallock invaluable as an impartial rationalist showing that the form and growth of the Roman system could be explained by natural laws, abstracting from without necessarily denying the legitimate Catholic assumption of infallible assistance of the Holy Spirit. It was to Mallock, therefore, that Tyrrell allied himself in "Non Tali Auxilio" and "The Mind of the Church."[49] It is time to see how.

Tyrrell's thesis was that it would be a great gain to apologetics if it could be shown that a divinely assisted infallible church—and, by corollary, a divinely assisted infallible pope—is not inconsistent with natural laws. In Blondellian fashion, Tyrrell asserted that of course the *conception* was not present in the earliest church, but the reality was. The early church believed in an "inspired" (in-spirited) church and only later, with the passing of the prophetic period, in a "divinely assisted" church. The distinction is modern, the outcome of much reflection on past controversies, questionings, and obscurities. Practically in Blondel's words Tyrrell explained, "We have a dull subconsciousness of principles, and we act upon them consistently and regularly, long before we come to define them. Action naturally precedes the theory and criticism of action in every department. Thus, though we seek in vain in early times for the terms of the distinction between inspiration and assistance, we are not wrong in trying to find a practical recognition of it."[50]

Modern theologians tell us that revelation, in the strict sense, ceased with the apostles, that the deposit of faith was closed with the death of Saint John, and that thenceforth doctrinal issues were decided by ecumenical council. This understanding may be a correct reading of history, but it does not prove what ought to be and will not satisfy the rationalist. Certainly the apostles, as firsthand witnesses, were distinguished from prophets, as in disputes they pronounced judgment not out of a new revelation but simply by appeal to what they had witnessed. Apostleship was regarded as *sui generis* in many ways, and the disappearance of the last eyewitness marked an epoch, a transition to a different order, analogous to that of Christ's passing to his Father. But Christians were not at first conscious of the transition. Only with the passing of true inspiration marked by the growing prevalence of conflicting "prophecy" would they have become aware of the new order and new system. Without apostles to settle disputes, the church's whole concern was to conserve her sources, as she would henceforth have to depend on her memory and understanding of them for guidance, rather than on the intuition of new truths. So she fixed the canon of inspired writings and limited the deposit of faith to the teaching of Christ and the apostles.

In further disputes, recognized authorities would then be appealed to not as inspired oracles but as witnesses to and preservers of the deposit of faith. In matters of lesser import the decision of local bishops and councils sufficed. In matters threatening unity, the whole church represented by bishops in council became the final court of appeal. Even apart from any claim to "assistance," a general council would be felt more likely to be right than any local synod. Indeed, error on the part of this final court would have been judged wholly incompatible with Christ's promise of protection and of the Holy Spirit's assistance in bringing to her memory all that Christ had said to her. Thus the church gradually came to an explicit recognition of a divinely assisted and infallible church.

With this introduction, Tyrrell turned to examine the notion of "the Mind of the Church" that is involved in the concept of an ecumenical and final authority. If that final authority rests ultimately on the teaching of Christ and the apostles (the deposit of faith), where, Tyrrell asked, is this deposit to be found?

Never was it contended that Christ or the apostles committed the deposit of faith to the chance letters of Paul or to the narratives of the evangelists. Rather, just as Christ had chosen and guaranteed the living voice of the apostolic college as the means to disseminate his doctrine, so they in turn would entrust their teaching not to paper but to the living voice of some corporation that would succeed them. What the doctrinal authority of the Twelve was and whether anyone conceived of an infallible teaching corporation in the early church are open questions. However, in a short time, by the process of dissension and appeals to higher and more representative tribunals, the church came explicitly to recognize an ultimate court of appeal whose decisions had to be regarded as irreversible and infallible under pain of ecclesiastical anarchy.

Thus the ecumenical council and not the mind of each individual bishop nor of synods of bishops was recognized as the full and adequate receptacle of the deposit of faith and indeed as "the organ of the Holy Spirit." As individuals, the members of this body were fallible, but joined together they were infallible. Thus "the Mind of the Church" is more than a logical abstraction. There is something more to the whole than the mere sum of the parts. The sum adds a quality not present in the parts singly. This is the case, for example, in the compilation of testimonies from a crowd of witnesses. It is likely to be more complete and accurate than the testimony of one or two. So, too, with the historic and dogmatic truths of Christianity. No single mind sees them as fully as does the collective mind of the church.[51]

The ecumenical council follows the same laws as are operative, for example, in a group of students who gather after a lecture to reproduce the lecturer's mind by comparing separate understandings and eliminating personal accretions, diminutions, and distortions. The composite contains no more information than was possessed potentially by the whole assembly from the beginning, although much that was potential has now become actual. But there is no denying that individual students received an absolute increment of knowledge not present even potentially before the conference.

Notice, however, that the presupposition for growth and development in the collective mind is the growth and development in the minds of the individual members. The Holy Spirit, whose mission is to guide the church into all truth, operates in each believing soul as well as in the deliberations of councils, the difference being that in the latter case the guidance is infallible, in the former case fallible.[52] The attribute of infallibility cannot be claimed except for the court of final appeal, and then only in matters of extremest moment where the unity of the church is threatened. This understanding is in strict accord with a fundamental principle of God's economy: while we should expect that he made sufficient provision for his church, more than sufficient we should not look for. "God, like Nature, *non deficit in necessaris*. The individual has the collective Church to fall back upon; but the collective Church has only God."[53]

Tyrrell next explained how the original revelation develops in the mind of the church according to the natural laws of psychology that govern the individual mind. He used the example of a great man who on his deathbed wants to leave his son the fruit of his full life as guidance. There are the obvious problems of reducing the whole to the mind of the boy. That done, there will still be much the boy will understand only with time and experience. While there is no change in the deposit, the child's understanding of it develops in three ways: (1) by analysis and distinction of the terms of the expression, (2) by fuller coordination with his other knowledge, and (3) by the increased power of mental insight due to accumulation of further experience and reflection.

The collective mind of the church follows the same pattern. To illustrate this truth Tyrrell appealed to the example of the philanthropist and the savage tribe as he had in the *Matafanus* and his letter to Ward of 13 March 1900. But if one allows the third mode of development to the deposit of faith as Tyrrell understood it prior to these articles, would not one have to discount its immutability? For growth in understanding of revelation must necessarily be accompanied by new expression, and if the deposit of faith be identified with the form of sound doctrine, where is the essential deposit? Tyrrell commented on this difficulty in a letter to Ward of 2 October 1900 and said that his previous notion of the deposit would not allow the third kind of development, and rather than try to explain *that* away, he reconsidered his notion of the deposit of faith.[54]

Thus Tyrrell asked *the* question: How essential to the deposit of faith are the *ipsissima verba* of Christ and the actual symbols and expression by which he conveyed his revelation to the mind of the apostles? From the Catholic standpoint, the New Testament documents are contingent on the church's memory. If these writings had perished, we would still have possessed the whole substance, if not the form of Christ's doctrine. But what is the substance without the form? What remains the same? Tyrrell answered with Vincent of Lerins's example of how the infant-self is preserved identically in one's own person even though one cannot remember that earliest self: "so the mind of the nascent Church lives identically in the maturer mind of the present Church, though the remembrance of those earlier stages may be obscure and faulty." So with the deposit of faith, the substance remains the same, though the words and form might change. "No new expression of the Christian idea can reveal more truth and fact than Christ intended to reveal to the Apostles, but it may give far clearer expression and illustration to

the same facts and truths."[55] What grows and develops and yet retains its identity is the *expression* of the Christian idea. Thus in the
Month version of "The Mind of the Church" Tyrrell concluded that
"by the 'deposit of faith' we do not mean any primitive document,
nor yet that expression which the faith received in the minds of its
first hearers: *but the present-day expression of the faith,* in which
that former expression is at once lost and preserved as the child is
in the man."[56]

But there is a discrepancy here. We should expect Tyrrell to
conclude that what remains identical is the mind of the church and
the truths committed to her memory, *as distinct from any expression,* whether yesterday's, today's, or tomorrow's. Wilfrid Ward
remarked on this discrepancy, and Tyrrell replied on 2 October
that the phrase was indeed misleading. He corrected it for the reprinted version: "By the 'deposit of faith' we do not mean any
primitive document, nor yet that expression which the faith received in the mind of its first hearers: *nor yet* the present-day expression of the faith, in which that former expression is at once lost
and preserved as the child is in the man; *but rather those identical
truths and realities which were expressed and seen less perfectly
(relatively to me) through the earlier form, more perfectly through
the later and more transparent forms.*"[57]

The deposit of faith is only what Christ showed us in the beginning, and the recipient of this deposit is the collective mind of the
church.[58] One will not find the deposit in documents or in the past.
The words of scripture and the commentaries of the fathers are
dead words, "except in so far as the Church takes them on her lips.
It is her living breath that gives them their inspiration."[59]

Finally Tyrrell turned to the question of tradition, or, as he put
it, "the 'mind of the Church' regarded as *memory,*"[60] as a *natural*
guarantee for the truth of dogmas. Analogous to the professor's
lecture faithfully reconstructed by the conference of students, the
church over centuries of conferences sifts and tests individual ec-
centricities and variants on the great truths living in the church's
memory. In such a worldwide and time-honored society, even
apart from any promise of supernatural assistance, there is a strong
presumption in favor of the church's tradition. But given such assistance, *a fortiori* the Catholic appeal to the church's living tradition is wholly reasonable and consistent.

This conception of the deposit of faith and of the mind of the
church as its recipient, Tyrrell concluded, lifts revelation and authentic dogmatic development above the slings and arrows of biblical and historical criticism, for those are scientific disciplines

whose subject is *not* the mind of the church and the unchanging truths committed to her memory but the words and forms in which those truths find expression. The mind of the church is the organ of tradition, the organ of growth, the organ of the Holy Spirit.[61] It is the collective mind of the *whole* church, priests and laity as well as bishops and pope. If there is a growth in the mind of the church, it is because there has been growth in the individual minds. No single mind or factional group of minds may usurp the whole heritage.

This two-part article, Tyrrell explained to Ward, was

> but part of a train of thought whose fuller development should lead to a clear sundering of two absolutely incompatible understandings of the Papal infallibility. . . . The test question is: If the Scriptures & the Fathers & all written documents were destroyed (all allow that these are contingent) where lies the *depositum fidei?* In the pope's single brain, or in the collective brain of Christendom? If in the former, then the Pope may say *L'Église c'est moi;* the spirit works directly on his mind; & only through it on the Church. If in the latter then the Pope is infallible in declaring the general mind in cases of sufficient magnitude to threaten unity; in such matters as formerly justified an ecumenical council; when he publicly & notoriously does investigate the *depositum fidei* contained in the general mind.[62]

PRIMING FOR THE JOINT PASTORAL

The occasion for that "fuller development" leading to a clear sundering of minds on the question of papal infallibility was the English bishops' joint pastoral of 29 December 1900. But several other issues preempted Tyrrell's attention and prevented him from expressing himself publicly on the matter until two months later. These other issues require a preliminary review.

First, there was Tyrrell's ambiguous position in the Society of Jesus. He had no real assignment. Superiors were unsure what to do with him. In August 1900, when he took up residence in Richmond, he was uncertain how permanent that would be.[63] He was sure only that he wanted to escape from Farm Street and London society in order to take stock of his life. On 8 August he wrote to Maude Petre from Richmond to explain that he felt "horribly selfish" in fleeing from his responsibilities in London, but perhaps his present leisure would promise a greater return for others in the end. "I need all my wits about me just now," and added that he would stay until Sydney Smith, editor of the *Month*, "begins to grumble at my absence."[64]

For five and a half years Tyrrell succeeded in holding out

against the grumblings of friends who tried to lure him out of his hermitage. Their usual protest was (1) that they needed him close by, and (2) that the solitude was not good for him. His usual response was (1) that he could not stand the madness of London society, and (2) that converse with his friends and those who came to him—those unusual cases who would not go to partyline priests—would only get him into worse trouble because of the unusual cures he prescribed. Moreover, until his superior general lifted the ban against his preaching and giving retreats and completely exonerated him, he had no intention of displaying himself as a mannequin before the public eye, draped in clerical garb and playing the official role, but forbidden to say anything of meaning.

Second, there was the matter of his reading and writing. Richmond was at least an escape that gave him time to read, ponder, and write. During the last few months of 1900 he read mostly in philosophy and philosophy of religion. In general his reading confirmed him in a more liberal view of Catholicism and so widened the breach opening between himself and accepted tradition, especially as represented by members of his own order.

Maurice Blondel claimed almost exclusive attention. Tyrrell labored through two readings of *L'Action* and through a couple of essays sent by von Hügel.[65] Tyrrell's penchant was to rush his latest findings into print. But in the case of Blondel he resisted the urge simply because Blondel resisted; Tyrrell found Blondel's thought tortuously intractable, or perhaps it was simply his style. Only once did Tyrrell give in, and then only to defend Blondel against a "mischievous travesty" of his position. In a letter to the editor in the *Pilot* for 27 October 1900, Tyrrell objected to several charges levied at Blondel. These shall be considered later. What interests here is a parenthetical remark—"(and it is eventually with this Society M. Blondel must reckon)"—whose significance would be lost on one ignorant of Tyrrell's domestic circumstances.[66] It was a direct jibe against the increasingly painful realization that his own religious order was the major bulwark and bastion of all that he opposed in the church's theology. To the initiate, this remark lies heavy with meaning, as it draws the line between Tyrrell and the Society of Jesus.

It was also at this time that von Hügel introduced Tyrrell to Eucken and Henri Bergson who, next to Blondel, must rank as most formative for Tyrrell's philosophy of religion. Tyrrell also began to explore psychopathology, notably the works of Pierre Janet, probably in connection with von Hügel's project on mystical experience.[67] The only other author mentioned in Tyrrell's correspondence at this time was Coventry Patmore. Tyrrell reviewed Basil Champneys's biography of Patmore for the *Month* and found his ideas illuminating.[68] But they were merely supportive and not formative, and so may be passed over without grave loss.

"Tracts for the Million"

While Tyrrell was doing all this reading and not much publishing, John Gerard, his provincial superior, was trying to coax him back into the orthodox line of apologetic journalism. Tyrrell complied by sending a seemingly innocuous "Tracts for the Million" to the *Month* for November 1900.[69] To those unfamiliar with Tyrrell's concurrent correspondence, the article might seem a mere platitude on the present and future state of Roman Catholic apologetics in England. But to the knowing, it seethes with feelings on a host of issues. Following a summary of the article, its true character will be revealed from correspondence.

The article took its title from the well-meaning but—in Tyrrell's view—misguided belief that the apologetic now required in England should be addressed to the uneducated masses currently threatened by a tide of unbelief. Agnosticism, Tyrrell said, is today such a universal threat only because some fifty years ago Catholic apologists turned exclusive attention to the Anglo-Roman controversy in hopes of an unending string of spectacular catches of the W. G. Ward and Newman species instead of addressing more fundamental and substantive issues. Unfortunately, attention remains riveted on that now largely dried-up stream. Meanwhile world interest has shifted without our noticing, so that world opinion is now no longer even Christian, let alone Roman Catholic.

In the ages of faith it was possible to secure the masses against the relatively isolated contagion of unbelief simply by requiring an act of confidence in the church. The reasoning here was compelling, for the beliefs of the masses are dependent far more on authority and common opinion than on any rational argument. But the ages of faith are gone, and it is no longer possible to secure the masses from what is no longer an isolated contagion. Besides, officialdom's position on how to meet the new godlessness is a babel of spurious opinions.

To correct the situation, some have suggested a series of tracts for the million. Fine. What can be done in this line should be done. But caution is in order about what might be expected from such a project. In the first place, even if capable authors could be found to write the tracts, how could the uneducated comprehend them?

The problems are too subtle and intellectual. We are led to overestimate the competence of the masses by the fact that they have learned by rote some clever bits of reasoning to be applied in certain cases, so that they *seem* to understand what they only repeat. As we ascend even to the summit of clerical training, we find more and more of this reasoning by rote, which renders the subject critically incompetent, a deficiency that is only more easily concealed by the pulpit and professorial chair where logic alone seems paramount.

In the second place, and more important, such a project is aimed at an illusory target. The true cause of unbelief in the uncritical is the decay of popular consensus for belief and ultimately the disagreements and countercharges of critics who form public opinion, and not the reasons alleged by the latter when they attempt a criticism that is beyond them. The faith context today is much the same as in early Christianity when the Gospel had to be made compelling in a context of unbelief and even hostility. Then it was not the "persuasive words of human wisdom" but a certain show of power that won the crowd—experimental, not rational, proof of the Gospel. In the later ages of faith, the church held ascendency over the many by her ascendency over the strong, wealthy, and learned few. Today our approach must be the same: to hold the many, we must hold the few who lead and form public opinion.

Still, intellectual difficulties must be met on their own ground, even if by inadequate and sophistical reasoning. So that, while tracts for the million seem an impossibility, they also seem a necessity. Those astute enough to understand the difficulty might be little inclined to take up the task. Fortunately "God's universal method in the education of mankind" is equal to the challenge. At every level of enlightenment are some sufficiently advanced to be able to help the rest, but not so far advanced as to speak practically another language. Let those at each level who feel called to such efforts put forth their very best with a view to helping minds that are most like their own. Granted that such tracts will not contain the fullness of truth, still they will contain a truth tempered to eyes not yet ready for the full sun. It was thus that God used the Law and the prophets to prepare for Christ and his Gospel. But none should be forced to condescend to a level of writing that seems from the author's viewpoint mere sophistry and vulgarity. At the same time each must recall that "the superiority of his own taste and judgment is more relative than absolute, and that in the eyes of those who come after, he himself may be but a Philistine."[70]

Tyrrell's real point, therefore, was a plea for tolerance. While tracts for the million should be offered, they should not be the only fare on the market. There are also sophisticated minds that need help.

In fact most readers missed Tyrrell's irony and thought his tracts for the million a capital idea. Chagrined, Tyrrell wrote to Maude Petre that he never had any intention to produce such tracts, yet he was getting inquiries from all sides asking when he would begin. "Very few have a sense of irony. The way to 'convert' England is to educate our priests and make them sober and pure, and to look after the spiritual wants of our perishing millions; and to leave Prostestants alone until we are in a position to set them an example. Christ only said one thing about proselytising, and it was not complimentary; but He said, 'Let your light so shine,' etc."[71]

Tyrrell's Correspondence: The Explosive Mix

Behind the cool prose tailored for censors and the Catholic audience of the *Month* lay a good deal of heat that would build to flash point at the instance of the joint pastoral. The tension is clear in Tyrrell's correspondence on several particularly burning issues centered around the Society of Jesus and its failure for himself and the church.

Tyrrell felt deeply about the cause for which he had entered the Society. He wanted to work for the spread of faith, and he had chosen what he considered the most apt instrument to that end. Now, when he was faced with evidence that the present Society had departed from her founder's original conception, that her burning spirit of vitality and accommodation had atrophied, and that what he thought he had to contribute was neither asked for nor desired, he felt betrayed. Fair became foul. He wanted not to care about the old hag—to use his figure—but he did care.[72] And for years the memory of "what might have been" sustained a fading hope for reconciliation.

In those years Tyrrell dreamed of producing a work on Ignatius's *Spiritual Exercises*, for he always regarded them as "the finest fruit of Christian teaching and as of a very high 'apologetic' value for that reason," and he wanted this study to be "the work in which all the others were to culminate."[73] But in the summer of 1900, in an act symbolic of divorce, he sent his project up in flames and wrote Maude Petre claiming no regret, as "it would only have created a false idea of the teaching and principles of the existing S.J. which would be neither fair to the Order nor to the public."[74]

But some nuns, Maude Petre among them, convinced Tyrrell to let them try to reconstruct his thoughts on the *Exercises* from notes taken during a retreat which he preached to them. At one point as he was going through their version "with red ink," he confessed to Petre that "the old fire would kindle now and then with the beauty of so grand a theme, and the thought of what could be made out of it if one were free and had a religious public worth writing for." But, he added, "personally I hope I do not care a straw whether this is done or not."[75]

That was the beginning of November. Shortly thereafter, something occurred—one can only surmise what—to end Tyrrell's vacillation and to harden him toward the Society of Jesus. In a discussion on the question of temporary religious life, prompted by Petre's suggestion, Tyrrell replied that he would propose the same for religious orders. After the founder's death his followers cling to the letter of his rule and slay his spirit. "Where more than with us? The most 'liberalising' Order ever conceived has become the one block in the way of the Church's expansion."[76] For Tyrrell obstructing the church was the Society's most grievous sin, and the sudden realization of that accounts for the hardening of his position.

On 12 November Tyrrell wrote to thank the baron for sending Archbishop Mignot's pastoral on apologetics. He was delighted to be able to lend it to some of the leading Jesuits at Farm Street "to show them that the episcopate is waking up while the Society slumbers on with lamps untrimmed" (an invidious comparison that Tyrrell did not believe for a moment). As for himself, he said, "I find my own *interior* position getting harder every day as the idea takes clearer and firmer shape that all that stands in the Church's way may be summed up in the one word 'Jesuitism.'" Not that Jesuits were the only transgressors, but Tyrrell found their influence abroad in the church "like an atmosphere—'jesuits & jesuited persons' as the Elizabethan penal statute says."[77]

The culprit, said Tyrrell, was Claudio Aquaviva, fifth superior general from 1581 to 1615. His legislative additions represented a deviation from and substitute for Ignatius's spirit and began a trend

> to check the "liberalism" to which S. Ignatius had given impetus. . . . Can you imagine (e.g.) S. Ignatius writing this rule for the Professor of Theology: "He shall not quote heterodox authors save to refute them; nor shall he ever praise them; and if they have said anything well, he shall try to show that they have borrowed it from Catholic sources"? All that we now groan under in the way of government by prying,

keyhole listening, letter-opening, secret delation, unexplained punishments, suppressions, etc. is simply canonised in the Aquavivian legislation of the S.J., and passes thence to all the modern congregations
(esp. female) which mimic our institute; and thence, to all those who
are educated under that influence in schools and seminaries, & thus to
the devout clergy & laity—for indeed it is the high moral repute of the
Society that gives it all its power for evil.[78]

Aquaviva's deviation raised for Tyrrell the personal question:
"Can I seeing all this, live a lie? And my only answer is that I have
more right to eat the bread of Ignatius than the rest of them." This
assertion Tyrrell was able to make because he saw the distinction
between Jesuits and Jesuitism. But the ethical problem taking
shape before him was, Could he go on calling himself a Jesuit
when the content of that term in the public view had been usurped
by Jesuitism? In private he would say no, but there were his public
responsibilities: "Nothing short of absolute cogency would justify
me in a step so fraught with distress to others, & triumph to my ill-
wishers; so calculated to undo whatever little I have done to widen
the narrower-minded."[79]

What solidified Tyrrell's indictment against the Society of Jesus
during the first weeks of November 1900 was not only his own
troubles but the fact that on top of these he was called on to aid a
number of priests whose faith was being eroded by forces they
could neither understand nor cope with. Most shattering to them
was that they found the church herself unable to cope. In fact, the
whole unbending policy of officials seemed bent on disaster. The
situation, Tyrrell wrote to Bremond on 13 November, was aptly
described by Archbishop William Magee[80] to his Anglican con-
freres: "'The Bishops are fighting over the papering of the attics
while the basement storey is in flames.'" What saves the clergy is
either their lack of intelligence and ignorance of the very existence
of intellectual difficulties, or their preoccupation with "money-get-
ting & parochialism; but where any intelligent priest comes in contact with doubt he is so ill-prepared to resist the virus that he takes
the disease in its worst form. The number of these 'Blanco Whites'
is already large & will be daily larger."[81] And of course their bishops and superiors are the last persons they would go to for help.

What remained for Tyrrell was only belief "not as with faith,
but as with science" in the irrepressible energy of truth to work itself out "as infallibly as the roots of a tree make for the water
through or round every obstacle." With Patmore, he could say only
"I believe in the Christianity of ten thousand years hence" or in the
"latent & undeveloped Christianity of the present, as distinct from

its halting expression." This affirmation, he concluded, "is not prophecy or *a priori* prediction but a simple statement of what I see going on—unless it be prophecy to predict that a stone that is in process of falling will come to the earth."[82]

Three days later Tyrrell's anxieties had escalated. He complained to Maude Petre of the church's role during the French Revolution, of "religion lending itself to be a mere political tool, an instrument of scared tyranny, in hopes of being paid back with temporal power. But these are gruesome topics." He could not avoid feeling the "unreality of Euckenism or Hügelism in the face of the perishing multitudes," that his continued identification with the Jesuits "gets more & more of an acted lie," and that the distinction on which he lived would no longer bear the strain. He was not yet ready to bolt, but he held out little hope for the future.[83]

The next day, 17 November 1900, Tyrrell posted to his provincial, John Gerard, perhaps the most poignant letter in the entire corpus of his correspondence. It warrants quoting at length for several reasons: (1) it is a crystal clear description of Tyrrell's subjective state on all the issues troubling him, and as such it gives invaluable background to his current writings; (2) it is a statement "for the record," written as it was to his religious superiors; and (3) it demonstrates how utterly candid he was with English superiors, whom, in contrast to his Roman superiors, he respected for their fair play and personal concern. The occasion for writing was to explain why he could not contribute the kind of tracts that James Britten of the Catholic Truth Society wanted, higher in quality but basically "controversial, slashing, aggressive, after His Paternity's own heart."

> As I said in my article, I believe such tracts do *some* good. . . . Yet this is working at the extremities & outgrowths of the evil, and not at its root; it is banking out the tide with sand-ramparts, checking its inroad here & there only, and only for a time; nor can we forget the unhealthy habit of mind created in the crowd by the controversial method. I quite admit the existence of a class of unbelievers (of every grade of culture) whose unbelief is irreligious or even anti-religious, with whom controversy is justified, not for their own sake, but for the sake of believers whom they disturb. But I also know that there is a large class of reluctant unbelievers (again, of every grade) who are affectively & often effectively, religious-minded. In Rome where every man is either a Catholic or a freemason, Christian or anti-Christian, the existence of such a class is inconceivable. Nay, we have theses to prove its impossibility; *e purchè si muove!*[84] Now the great *scandalum pusillorum* here, to-day, is the unbelief not of the irreligious but of the religious, the sincere; and those who disbelieve, as every modern sem-

inarian does, in the possibility of honest doubt, are incompetent to go to the root of the evil. We need never hope to win the irreligious intelligence of the country; but if we fail to get hold of the intelligently religious minds the rest of our success is but forking out the waves. But to deal with these best minds, needs a sympathy, a breadth, a subtlety, which the coarse-minded dogmatism of foreign theologians would not tolerate for a moment, and it is they eventually who rule us & prescribe for countries of whose condition they are as ignorant as they are of Christian charity & truthfulness; they are the veritable descendents of those who kept the key of knowledge & would neither enter themselves, nor suffer others to enter. You suggest that I should keep clear of theology & confine myself to philosophical points; but unless one keeps to astronomy or pure mathematics, what corner of the whole domain of philosophy is there where these theologians have not put up their notices to trespassors? Agnosticism is essentially a religious problem; even were it merely philosophical, has not every line of Aristotle been imposed upon us by these fanatical theologians as a test of orthodoxy? We are allowed to amuse ourselves with the stars, or with chemistry (provided we don't touch on matter & form v. atomic theories) or with anything that has nothing to do with the one burning question of God or no God. Supposing I could throw cold water on evolution, how would that help any man towards faith? In short, the first condition for doing any real good in the matter, would be a liberty which Rome has too little faith in the tenableness of her own position to tolerate. She is as afraid of the light, as Peter was of the wind & waves. Things must get much worse before they can get better; they must slowly work out God's favourite argument of the *reductio ad absurdum* before the dormant good sense of mankind will be wakened. And to speak my mind candidly I believe it is the mission of the Society of Jesus to help the Church to wake up by running her head against a stone wall—a heroism which will prove rather costly. . . . Furthermore even if I had the fullest liberty I am not at all sure that I should know what to do with it; I should know the right direction but not much more. Therefore I don't want any of my liberties back again. I will write for the Month till the next delation; and then I will throw down the cards, and turn to some other game. But what other? Even preaching, retreat-giving & such publicly exposed work, unless it is to be a mere useless reverberation of "that which was from the beginning," is rendered impossible where the supreme government is controlled by the secret delations of the stupid, the envious, & the place-hunters, with the old & inevitable result of "art made tongue-tied by authority, and Folly, doctor-like, controlling skill." I am sure you have yourself suffered enough from this kind of government to feel that what I say is not red passion but the quiet grey truth.

Tyrrell then quoted at length from letters he had received from troubled priests. The quotations represent rare remnants of letters *to* Tyrrell, and as they indicate most poignantly the kind of burdens he was called on to bear for others, they are of great interest here. "One of the best and most active" priests, who had devoted his life to writing for the church, had written to express his discontent with Tyrrell's "The Mind of the Church":[85]

"May I speak quite openly to you. I was born a Catholic, and hope to die one. But I stagger like a drunkard under the theological difficulties that weigh upon my mind. It has been my lot to be thrown among intellectual men for many years now, and I need not conceal from you—I cannot conceal from myself—that to their clear-stated objections my replies have been taken as 'Chinese.' Why? Was it the fault of the defender, or the weakness of the defence? Modesty makes me fear it was the former; but if the defence was strong, why should not the defender have been strong in its strength? So I began, I was forced to begin, to ask questions of myself and to cease 'in Worten Kramen' [*sic*] as Goethe puts it.[86] When I saw the title of your article my hope rose. I devoured it—you know with what result" (sc. negative. G.T.) Later: "When such objections are pointed at me, I know not how to blunt them. . . . Difficulties are not doubts, thank God; yet they are gadflies and we would delightfully sweep them away. They are stinging endless priests now-a-days, and what these shall do when stung to madness, who shall say? I do not myself like to think. I fear a great outburst of rage and secessions must come on us soon, if no salve be applied. Que voulez-vous? Will men cease to think in a free land? We can no longer be convinced by being burnt. It seems to me the Church is in an evil case. She has lost the intellect of Europe; she is fast losing the intelligence. She may, like a pool, continue to hold water. But it will become stagnant water, of which men will decline to drink. With all her storied past, people now ask, is she merely a stained-glass window, letting in a mellow light & shadowing forth painted forms which look like men and are—painted shades? Or is she fact & truth & life? The latter: then let her speak and act. We ask her for bread & she gives us a stone, a stony silence. God only knows in how many years of arduous press-work on her behalf, I have striven for her. But everywhere I meet law, administration, what Charbonel [*sic*] (poor fellow) called "Chinoiseries administratives" (—may I translate: administrative mandarinities);[87] but teaching, intelligent guidance, intellectual comprehension, nowhere. Just a shibboleth, just a recitative, just a command, just a shrug of the shoulders, and a 'serva fidem'—nothing more. This is little help to a mind distressed. I have grown afraid even to undertake a defence of her. I enter a labyrinth with no clue in my fingers. I cannot find my way even among her own teachers. They are hopelessly entangled, ravelled like a wind-tossed skein of silk. What is wrong? If we have a deposit of revealed truth 'once communicated to the saints,' in God's name, what is it & where is it? I have asked bishops & priests & no one can tell me, and I cannot find out for myself. This is no mere Jeremiad. I feel acutely." etc. etc. In a subsequent letter: "I have found these thoughts current among priests, who, I fancied, had never thought in their lives. For the past . . . months I have been preaching up and down—, and I assure you I think I have heard the passing bell of a dying creed. This is strong language; but the passing bell rings very loud in my ears everywhere."

Tyrrell quoted another priest to the same effect and cited two others in like straits. Then:

What saves many of our priests is their engrossment in parochialism & the complete suspension thereby of their mental growth; others are saved by their natural stupidity which makes them practically deaf & blind & senseless to any line of thought but that which they have learned by rote at the seminary. It is well for them; & well for the mass of the equally uneducated laity; but ill for those who go to them seeking guidance in mental perplexity. But when a fairly intelligent priest happens to come in contact with modern doubt, the fabric of his seminary theology collapses like a card-house. Why so? Because though it means much in "Chinese," it means nothing in English. He has no interpreter's key; no bridge to pass from one world to the other; & is scared, confused & panic-stricken. And this because one uniform seminary course is imposed on the whole Church without respect to varieties of period, language, nationality; because the world has been developing one sort of culture; & we another; so that mutual understanding has become impossible. There is not a single priest at Farm Street or, I fancy, in all London to whom I could recommend an educated agnostic to go with any hope, I do not say of being satisfied but even, of being understood. I should without hesitation send such an one to Gore, or to Scott-Holland, or to James Ward;[88] or to Baron von Hügel; or I myself in difficulties would go to them; but if I turn to the Church, who ought to be my first support, "I ask for bread & she gives me a stone"—a farrago of mediaevalism warmed up. And every year from S. Beuno's there is turned out a fresh relay of coinage from the same unchanging mould, more curious each time, as the world in which it must circulate moves rapidly fowards. I have entertained myself these few months writing myself clear on this & kindred topics and as I approach the conclusion, the *Mene Thecel Phares* of that present system of ecclesiastical management, for which so many well-meaning people are fighting tooth & nail, stands out clearer on the wall.[89] What it will cost in the way of scandal & loss of faith, God knows; whether it could have been avoided if gentler counsels had prevailed in the past, who can tell? I think so, but I am not sure. Ill as I can express or defend my own faith, it remains not weaker but stronger after the failure of every support on which I have hitherto leant; my whole trouble is for others. There is nothing private in this except what I have quoted from the private letters of others. You will differ profoundly from my view of the situation; but I am content to wait only ten years for this whisper in the ear to be shouted from the housetops. You are as helpless to change things as I; even the General, were he awake to the existence of this century & country & not wrapt in dreams of medieval Spain, could do nothing radical or sufficient, since our ultimate government is that of the Latin majority in our general congregations. A pope who should dismember us into self-governing provinces would be our best friend; our next-best, one who should end us honourably before we end ourselves shamefully.

Ever yours faithfully, G. TYRRELL.[90]

Other letters written toward the end of 1900 could be cited, but they only confirm the explosive mix of Tyrrell's feelings. It is now quite clear how the joint pastoral of 29 December 1900 could have ignited the bomb that exploded on the new year and thrust Tyrrell into a whole new round of confrontations.

THE JOINT PASTORAL

Prenote On Terms "Apologetic" and "Philosophy of Religion"

In reference to Tyrrell's works up to 1901, it is fitting to use the terms "apologetic" and "philosophy of religion" somewhat interchangeably. But from this point on discrimination between them is required to match Tyrrell's own awareness. Before the joint pastoral Tyrrell had wished to remain aloof from extreme factions and to mediate between them. Now, however, given the charged atmosphere induced by censure, unexplained punishments, and defections in faith and morals among clergy and educated laity, the pastoral jarred Tyrrell from his mediating position and landed him squarely on the left. Heretofore his apologetic aim had been primarily pastoral. Now it became polemical and bitter as he sought to represent another point of view opposed to that of the "Philistines" who sought to discredit him and "usurp the whole heritage for themselves."[91]

To be true to that shift, the term "apologetic" must now be reserved for works composed from the leftist view *over against* the right, and the term "philosophy of religion" for those works that, even in the heat of battle, Tyrrell was able to compose from a coolly philosophical point of view, where his starting point was not the obverse side of doctrinaire ultramontanism but the experience of transcendent realities common to all religions.

There is, of course, some artificiality in this division, as elements of apologetic and philosophy of religion are inextricably enmeshed in each of Tyrrell's works. Still, it seems possible and helpful to clarity to classify some works as more apologetic, others as more philosophical, depending on their underlying motive.

Origin and Exposition of the Pastorial

To say the least, the new century opened auspiciously. On 29 December 1900 Cardinal Vaughan and the fifteen bishops of the Province of Westminster issued "A Joint Pastoral Letter on the Church and Liberal Catholicism" and published it in the official diocesan organ, the *Tablet*, for 5 and 12 January 1901.[92] Provoked by the outspoken views of Mivart, to whom Tyrrell had been linked by authorities in Rome,[93] Vaughan drew up a plan of response and sent it to Archbishop Merry del Val for Rome's approval. On 30 June 1900 Merry del Val replied that he had brought the matter to the pope, who was anxious "that you should make the stand in a full doctrinal pronouncement upon the whole subject, clearly expounding Catholic doctrine without any regard to persons, whoever they may be," and that the pope was "quite ready to follow on and express his approval in support of your action." But he did not think it advisable for himself to act directly. Merry del Val then added, "And I think every one feels that it is your place and duty to speak first in defence of Catholic principle in your own diocese, together with the other Bishops or at all events with the support of the majority of them." But to ensure that it be done right, Merry del Val made a generous offer:

> Now, as to the best way of insuring the efficacy of the document. It is essential that your letter or declaration should be unassailable in its force and that you should be able to issue it with the certainty that every word of it will be supported here as expressing the teaching and mind of the Church. To attain this end, I hardly think that under the circumstances you can reckon upon much help in England, especially as it will not be easy to obtain absolute discretion before and afterwards from the persons who might be called upon to cooperate with you in the drawing up of the document. And if anything transpires as to the persons who have worked with you, your statements will be set aside by many as simply the expression of the opinions of individual teachers. Would it not be well then, either that you should draft the document and then send it here to be revised by competent

persons with the knowledge and approval of the authorities; or that you should allow such persons to draft the document and send it to you for your sanction, and final publication? I could get this done for you without any one appearing in the matter, and if you accept the suggestion I would set about doing so at once, for there is no time to be lost. . . . Of course it would be your declaration and none of the cooperators would appear at all. Your task would thus be facilitated and you would speak with the assurance that the Holy See was entirely with you.[94]

How could Vaughan refuse? Whether he did or did not remains obscure. What is clear is that the pastoral did receive the promised papal approbation, and it was certainly "unassailable in its force," indeed noticeably similar in style to the encyclical condemning "modernism" in 1907.

The pastoral opened with a broadside against "Liberal Catholics" who "take leave to discuss theology and the government of the Church with the same freedom of speech and opinion" as they use in other matters, but with the evil intent either to belittle and despise or utterly to reject the authority of the church and "to substitute the principle of private judgment for the principle of obedience to religious authority." Such affronters are "ignorant of the true character of the Church," "wanting in filial docility," and "infectious" enough to "stir our pastoral vigilance" to defend "the rights and liberties of the Church" against them.[95]

The import of this volley could not have been lost on Tyrrell. On the previous 6 June he told von Hügel that he had been saddening his soul "by going over the miserable story of the Vatican Council again."[96] Thus he would hardly have failed to see that the pastoral was redrawing the old battle line of Pius IX between the ultramontane infallibilists and the liberal minority.

The pastoral expounded on three main points: (1) what is meant by the "Teaching Church"; (2) to what extent one's mind must conform to the mind of the church; and (3) the meaning of development and the deposit of faith. The burden of its argument rested on the traditional distinction between the *Ecclesia docens*—that small body of men, chosen and assisted by the Holy Spirit, who represent the authority of Jesus Christ—and the *Ecclesia discens*—the large body of faithful who are taught, guided, and guarded by the "Divine Teacher" speaking through the audible voice of the smaller body.

God, the bishops asserted, did not abandon mankind to private judgment in matters of salvation, but guaranteed the presence and authority on earth of a "Divine Teacher." This teacher is none other than God himself, who once spoke through the lips of the Sacred Humanity, but after Jesus' ascent spoke through the mouth of Peter and the apostles and now continues to speak through their legitimate successors "until the consummation of the world." "The *Ecclesia Docens* is fully conscious of her Divine mission and needs no dictation from without as to the course she should pursue."[97] Just as she does not proclaim the doctrines contained in the deposit of faith on the score that specialists in theology, philosophy, or the natural sciences have been consulted, neither could she conceive of fixing the cardinal points of revealed truth according to the changing opinions and fashions of the day. As to the role of the *Ecclesia discens*, this body consists first of all not only of the laity but also of priests and bishops in their individual and private capacity. The church may indeed encourage even the faithful laity to lecture and write on religious topics when she sees that they are fit to serve her in this way. However, they do not do this in their own right, but in strict subordination to authority. What they teach must be the church's doctrine, not their own.

On conformity of mind, the pastoral stated that all have an obligation to think as the church thinks and to assent to whatever she presents for acceptance. It distinguished two kinds of assent: "the assent of faith," to be given not only to revealed doctrines but "also to the decisions of the Church concerning matters appertaining to or affecting revelation" and as such either defined or universally held by the church; and "the assent of religious obedience," to be given to the teaching that does not fall under the head of revealed truth, or even under the endowment of infallibility, but to that covered by the church's "daily magisterium" which "comprises all that is necessary for the feeding, teaching, and governing the flock." Included would be the pastoral letters of bishops, diocesan and provincial decrees, many acts of the supreme pontiff, and all decisions of the Roman congregations.[98]

As to development and the deposit of faith, the church as "Divine Teacher" is identical with herself in every age; that is, as she is continuous and indefectible in her existence and constitution, so is she in her doctrine. But these are attributes of a living organism animated by the Holy Spirit. Thus the church admits only such development and progress as is compatible with no essential change in her dogmas. Truths held only implicitly can by degrees become explicitly realized and defined, as one or other becomes the object of special attention due to controversy or hostile attack.

First Shock

As one writer put it, "the reaction to the Pastoral was immediate and loud, and it lasted for well over six months."[99] The reactions of Tyrrell and von Hügel were certainly immediate, but not immediately public. Just two days after the pastoral was issued, von Hügel analyzed for Wilfrid Ward the great defect of that document. "The double apprehension that we all have to be ever learning" and not to be simply passive or merely receptive "is as impossible in religion, and therefore also for a religious- and intellectual-minded layman, as it is impossible in any other subject-matter, or for any other class of men, if they are at all made of one piece, and if they are to be centres of conviction. . . . The absence of any consciousness of these two, I think essential concomitants of all fruitful present-day faith amongst the educated, whether priest or layman,—would strike one painfully."[100]

Tyrrell saw the pastoral's underlying exegesis to be precisely that of the majority faction of Vatican I and precisely what he had opposed in his articles on "The Mind of the Church." There Tyrrell had emphasized that the church was a collectivity of minds that included priests and laity as well as bishops and the pope. If there is growth in the mind of the church, it is because there has first been growth in these individual minds. On 2 January 1901 he wrote to Maude Petre:

Isn't this horrid about Abbé Loisy? And now there comes the bishops' encyclical on Liberalism. Not that one wants Mivartism; but that there is never a word from authority on the other side; never an admission that there are difficulties to be dealt with; always the old rule-of-thumb method of repression: "Don't read; don't think; trust us; we know everything." They don't see that the ground has shifted and that the question is: Why should we trust you? If they showed that *they* had read and digested; they might command some confidence when they forbid us to read. But they show themselves as ignorant of the world they live in as any seminarian.[101]

A shift had occurred in Catholic thought. Tyrrell felt it; officials did not. He described the shift on 5 January to Frank Rooke Ley, and began with a phrase similar to one he used six months earlier to describe his feelings on Vatican I:

I have just been making myself ill over the Joint-Pastoral; more perhaps on account of the felt spirit of the thing, than of anything said. . . . They have as a body no ghost of an idea what it is all about;

and one cannot deal with difficulties one has never felt. "Authority" is their one note—their whole tune. They do not see that it is a question-begging note; that it is the existence, or at least the right limits of their authority, which has been brought into question.[102]

Actually, Tyrrell was more than ill. He was angry. The pastoral was a too-vivid example of what he had hinted at in "Tracts for the Million": "the absolute incompetence of our clergy as a body to meet the incoming flood of agnosticism" and "the deep somnolence of our Bishops," and, in the face of these problems, his own helplessness. Vatican theologians, he commented to Rooke Ley,

> have so tied us up in matters outside their own department that we have not the liberty needed for apologetic. If you deny or impugn the "Clockmaker" argument or "prime-motor" argument for the existence of God, you come under some condemned proposition or other. So that really one cannot stir. I should like to deal with the Joint-Pastoral in the *Nineteenth Century*, but my speech would betray me. It is a great opportunity for a strong and temperate protest against Reaction on the Rampage.[103]

Distracting Maneuvers

Despite the desire announced here to express himself publicly on the matter, Tyrrell in fact did not publish his views until March, and then only pseudonymously. Von Hügel never did publish his views. Of course the baron, unlike his excitable friend, did not feel compelled to rush into print at the slightest provocation. Moreover he was at that time beset with family problems and laid every other concern aside. But for Tyrrell to have been silent for so long is simply out of character. If he had wanted to publish in the *Nineteenth Century*, he would have had to wait until February in any case, and in the meantime find a way to publish that would compel notice without his identity being suspected. But his *Nineteenth Century* article did not appear until May. Surely a man of such proven resources could have devised a way before then unless other considerations prevented him.

A clue as to what forestalled Tyrrell's reply is given already on 18 December in a letter to Petre. The whole question of his status as a member of the Society of Jesus was coming to a head. John Gerard, who had been pleading Tyrrell's cause in Rome, was about to be replaced as provincial by one of less independent means, "Fr. Colley, Stonyhurst born & bred, & no idea outside Stonyhurst. . . . I shall soon get ordered out to foreign missions; but they can hardly forbid my ink & paper." But the issue was more radical than the replacement of Gerard, for with Gerard's removal, Tyrrell was forced to face more urgently the question of whether or not to remain a Jesuit.

> My position as an SJ is becoming such a lie; & bound as I am, there is no way out, but by an act of schism; so powerful is the SJ influence at Rome that dispensation cd. not be had against their will; & they are afraid to let me out much as they (at Rome) wd. wish to be rid of me. For the sake of others & to avoid scandal I could stay on in external communion if they would give me common & reasonable liberty, but I feel no inclination whatever to allow them to decorate their wigwam with my scalp, and I feel that the next aggression will finish me. One would submit gladly to the occasional mistakes of a government one respected & felt to be in the main on God's side; but the Society everywhere puts itself before the Church & I have no beliefs in its corporate sincerity of purpose; in fact I regard it as the chief obstacle to the progress of the Church for whose sake alone I originally entered it. Things might have dragged on under Fr. Gerard, but now I must look out for squalls. The only thing that wd. save me wd. be if the Pope cd. say a word in favour of my work.[104]

The first squall on the horizon was the mission scheme. No one could fail to take it seriously—certainly not the new provincial, since the suggestion came from Cardinal Vaughan, and certainly not Tyrrell, since to him it meant moral suicide.[105] Reginald Colley was in an impossible situation. What could he do with a priest whom Rome judged unfit to preach, direct retreats, or hear confessions, except on the mission where he could do no harm? But Tyrrell was not about to let curial officials get away with such bigotry, nor would he allow them to dispose of him quietly in that fashion. He demanded that the general exonerate him totally and publicly. The alternative, he told Colley over and over again, was "that I must leave the Society and justify my action in the eyes of the world. . . . I have occupied myself here with a complete and detailed review of my relations with the Society and my experiences and observations of twenty years; and I am simply waiting for further developments to add the final chapter to the tale. Still, it is my deepest, if faintest, hope that I may never have occasion to take a step so painful to myself & to many that I love."[106]

After one month and seven exchanges of correspondence, the issue ended in a stalemate. At least for the moment Tyrrell could remain in Richmond. "I have been too worried to write before," he told Maude Petre on 29 January. "To-day, however, I have had my seventh letter from Fr. Colley, in which, at last, he admits the wisdom of leaving me in peace." Tyrrell concluded with a blistering assessment:

> As I said to him, it seems to me marvellous that never having spoken 5 words to me in his life he shd. consider himself *ex officio* competent to diagnose my spiritual state and prescribe for it without any hesitation. Even "infallible assistance" presupposes the use of ordinary means such as experience, observation & reflection. A few à priori spiritual maxims seem to be his whole stock in trade for governing men. "Spiritual pride" "ambition" "indocility" are the headings under which the most complex cases are to be classed without qualification or even enquiry. After all to "become as a little child" does not mean to become a little goose for the benefit of the nearest fox. It is the duplicity of parents that eventually destroys forever the simplicity of children. In truth I have been a little child too long & have trusted these guides who have proved unworthy of all trust. No effort of my will could ever again make me trust the Society or regard it otherwise than the prison-house in which I have been put for my sins. I am attached to it as a bird to a limed twig; but in no other sense.[107]

A second squall complicated the first. An extract from *External Religion* had appeared in translation and without Tyrrell's knowledge in the liberal Italian Catholic paper *La Rassegna Nazionale*. This extract "excited" the general, Tyrrell told Petre, because supposedly the pope had forbidden ecclesiastics to publish in that journal.[108] Fr. Rudolf Meyer, the general's assistant for the English-speaking provinces, sent an inquiry to Colley, demanding that Tyrrell recant or explain himself. Tyrrell replied petulantly to Colley on 23 January 1901, "I am responsible for a book called 'External Religion' which is perhaps what Fr. Meyer means by 'The Externals of Religion.' I never heard of the 'Rassegna' in my life.[109]

Tyrrell could have let the matter drop there. But, Colley and the mission scheme vanquished, he decided to take the battle into the general's camp. "I see, by the W. Register," he wrote Petre on 4 February, "that the Archbp. of Genoa contributes an article to the *Rassegna*, to wh., accordg. to our General, the Pope has 'forbidden priests to write.' The untruthfulness of our superiors is inexhaustible."[110] Tyrrell then wrote to the editor of the *Rassegna* to get the facts on the supposed prohibition. The editor replied that he had no knowledge of the prohibition and as evidence enclosed copies of the *Rassegna* in which both the archbishop of Genoa and Tyrrell's friend John Spalding, bishop of Peoria, had contributed.[111] These publications patently would not have been possible, Tyrrell told Colley on 18 February, if the prohibition were in any way public, and if it were not, the general's complaint had no foundation. So if the general wanted a recantation, he must first produce a public document or proof of the prohibition, "as I cannot act on a mere rumour in the face of such reasons for doubting." Better still, "from other informations [sic] that I have received . . . His Paternity had better drop the matter as quickly as possible or he will have a hornet's nest about his ears; but this is just the last thing he will do."[112] To the general Tyrrell wrote directly, "I have grave fears his Paternity is misinformed about the prohibition; the Editor of the R. is very angry about what he considers a malicious libel and wants to trace it. Before I act on the supposition of the prohibition can I have some better evidence of its existence than a mere report contradicted in so many ways?"[113]

At the same time Tyrrell wrote to the editor of the *Rassegna* and requested that he print a notice *from himself* in explanation of the mistake about the insertion of the translated chapter. On 20 February Tyrrell summarized the whole episode for von Hügel and concluded: "That is the last stage of this storm in a tea-cup. I suspected at once that it was the story of Americanism over again—of the endeavour of the orthodox to enhance their reputation for orthodoxy by slandering those who differ from them in anything. Don't think my mind is as full of all this ecclesiastical nonsense as my letter is. It is a surface storm which leaves the deeps of one's life untroubled."[114]

There was a further stage in this episode. Rome answered Tyrrell that the article by the archbishop of Genoa in the *Rassegna* was "in no way a contribution but simply a protest against the misrepresentations of his Lordship's Pastoral by the Rassegna," nor was Bishop Spalding's article a contribution but an "unauthorized appropriation." Thus Tyrrell explained the "explanation" to Semeria on 17 May 1901, and asked him to check "the accuracy of these confident statements."[115] Presumably Semeria answered, but the only extant reference comes in a letter from von Hügel of 28 May 1901. He had just visited Semeria in Genoa and reported that Semeria had no idea who had translated the extract and got it inserted into the *Rassegna*, that he sent his regrets for this fresh annoyance, all the more as the translation was badly done (although the review was well meaning and generally competent), "so that the game seems hardly worth the candle." The baron added, "The Archbishop of Genoa *has* written in it; i.e. a letter of his was published in it, by himself or at least with his consent."[116] The only clear resolution of the conflict was that Tyrrell was sufficiently satisfied of Rome's duplicity that anything more she would say could not possibly rekindle his burnt-out hope.

So he turned to more substantive matters—editing his *Month* articles for a two-volume collection, writing his autobiography for Maude Petre, and composing a review article for the *Month*.[117] But the real issue at hand was the joint pastoral, and it is this affair that now claims attention.

The Public Campaign

The joint pastoral was issued on 29 December 1900. A month later Tyrrell had formulated a public reply, but not until May did it go to press. The delay, as seen above, was due in large measure to wranglings with Jesuit superiors. But there was the further problem of finding a suitable outlet for the kind of cold-blooded criticism that would tell. Tyrrell's aim was to expose the extremism of the pastoral in the whitest light possible as a challenge to the extremists to deny it. The only Catholic journal to which Tyrrell would even consider contributing was the *Weekly Register*. But under Dell's editorship the previous year, it had grown "rabid and superficial" and so would not compel the notice of the orthodox.[118] But perhaps an airing in the *Nineteenth Century* would. Already on 5 January Tyrrell informed the *Register*'s new editor, Frank Rooke Ley, of his intentions, "but," he added, "my speech would betray me."[119]

A convincing disguise was needed. Nothing is more revealing of Tyrrell than the correspondence around his disguise and article, for he managed to maneuver his way into the pages of the *Nineteenth Century* almost without attracting the notice even of Lord Halifax, who put his name to the article.

Charles Lindley Wood, second Viscount Halifax would be a perfect disguise. Who would suspect a man of his stature to front for someone else, and that someone a Roman Catholic, a Jesuit, and Tyrrell at that? Moreover Halifax was acquainted with controversy. As president of the English Church Union, he had defended the Anglo-Catholic position against both the ritual prosecutions attending the Act for the Regulation of Public Worship (1874) and threats to the Catholic heritage and doctrine of the Church of England. He was also acquainted with Tyrrell—although only by letter—and it seems that no one knew this. In July 1897, amidst the furor raised by Leo XIII's rejection of the validity of Anglican orders,[120] Halifax opened correspondence with Tyrrell to thank him for "The Prospects of Reunion" and to voice his hopes for reunion. Again in early 1900, on the occasion of Tyrrell's censure for "A Perverted Devotion," Halifax wrote in sympathy. In a brief but pathetic note of 12 February, Tyrrell thanked Halifax for his support, then

added, "One cannot help feeling that there are deeper spiritual interests wherein worshipers on Sion and Gerezim may be more closely
united than worshipers on the same mountain. May I hope to meet
you some time when you are in London?" In fact, when Halifax in
early July 1901 proposed a meeting, Tyrrell declined on the grounds
that the *Tablet* "would certainly publish a rumour about 'A certain
leading Anglican connected with the E.C.U.' and the *Church Times*
would predict the speedy accession of a well-known Romanist to the
English Church." Besides, "it has often been convenient to me when
asked by the curious if I knew you, to be able to say, I never laid eyes
on you."[121]

But the stage was set for a joint operation. Only an opportunity
was wanting. That came at the instance of publication by the Anglican bishops of a joint pastoral at the same time and on the same
subject as that issued by the Roman Catholic bishops. Never one to
miss a cue, Tyrrell wrote to Halifax immediately, asking him first
to "treat this letter as quite confidential," then pointing out that, before continuing efforts at reunion, Halifax had "a right to demand a
much more definitive statement, first of the *limits* of Papal infallibility; then of the limits of non-infallible authority, papal or episcopal, than has hitherto been accessible," for the pastoral's argument "leads logically to unqualified absolutism of every authority
whatsoever, civil or ecclesiastical. I cannot help thinking that a letter or an article from yourself noting a few plain answers to a few
plain questions would just now do much to clear the ground for
better, mutual understanding. If you like I will send you a brief
statement of the problem as it strikes me."[122]

Tyrrell set to work at once on "Halifax's" article and without
waiting for a reply sent it completed on 28 January, explaining that
of course it was "written from an Anglican standpoint" and appealing to Halifax's interest: "Not till the questions in my paper have
been clearly & definitively settled will it be time to negotiate
peace" between England and Rome. Then follows a passage that
betrays Tyrrell's real motive for courting Halifax: "Rome just now
attaches great importance to what comes from you & those round
you." Their mistaken *"idée fixe* that you represent the whole
Church of England & therefore the whole nation . . . will lend
weight to what you or yours may say beyond what would attach to
the smothered protests of men like myself or Wilfrid Ward."[123]

Halifax responded favorably by return mail and Tyrrell immediately replied that he could "use the M.S. anyway you like. . . .
The great point is to put the matter so clearly strongly and publicly
that it shall not be hushed up." Again Tyrrell appealed to Halifax's

interest, saying that converts from Anglicanism must better understand what they are in for. "They enter Newman's Church and find
themselves landed in Dr. W. G. Ward's"—not through fraud but
"through the hazy-mindedness of those who receive them." One in-
structor "files infallibility down to a molehill; and the first confessor they go to afterwards heaps it up into a mountain. Let us then
know clearly its true dimensions: and then we can discuss its
credibility."[124]

Illness prevented Halifax from moving quickly on the joint project, but Tyrrell wrote again on 17 February to say that the delay
was perhaps fortuitous. Not only would Queen Victoria's death
and funeral have diverted attention, but the rumored papal ratification of the joint pastoral "will give more point to whatever you
may decide to say—if anything." To be sure that Halifax grasped
the urgency of the matter, however, Tyrrell pointed out that the
crux of the problem with the joint pastoral was its "'pastoral' metaphor drawn from the behest: 'Feed my sheep.'" If the metaphor is
to be pressed rigorously, the pope "or the Eccl. Docens—for with
us the distinction is trivial . . . stands apart from his flock, as a
being of another species: he is rational & active; they are passively
driven or led." If the metaphor is to be limited and the pope is to
be regarded as "only the principal sheep, a member of the flock
that he leads," then in what sense can he be called shepherd? This
was not a question of doctrinal subtlety "but of the very constitution of the Church,—of the very nature of the rule of faith . . . ;
we must settle what it is the Pope claims, before we discuss the validity of that claim."[125]

On the same day Tyrrell made the same point to Rooke Ley
and drew its implication for theologians. The joint pastoral, he lamented, made "a distinct line of theological cleavage with Jesuitism . . . on one side, and Newmanism on the other." Under these
circumstances there was no point in fighting about "whether we
are to accept more or less the results of criticism until we have established the place of criticism with regard to ecclesiastical
teaching."[126]

Thus Tyrrell outlined what would henceforth be his program.
His philosophy of religion would deal with the nature of faith, his
apologetic with the nature of the *rule* of that faith, that is, the question of authority: Who has the right and power to formulate beliefs
and impose them on the church, and with what limits? Tyrrell's
aim in the whole discussion of the joint pastoral was to set in bold
relief not only these questions but the answers given in recent history. These fell into two mutually exclusive categories: "Jesuitism"
on one side and "Newmanism" on the other.

Wilfrid Ward had written wonderfully of Newman's position on the matter in the 16 February issue of the *Weekly Register,* and Tyrrell wrote at once to congratulate him. But, he asked, "is it what our bishops say: is it what they say at Rome? These are rhetorical questions needing no answer for the answer is obvious. The Pope has blessed and approved the Joint-Pastoral."[127] Further, Tyrrell had serious misgivings about Ward's view expressed in a letter that the joint pastoral was "merely a false analysis" on the part of the bishops.[128] "But I reply," Tyrrell wrote to Halifax, "that a false analysis when acted on & approved presently becomes a false doctrine; just as a false analysis of good art becomes later an authoritative rule productive of bad art."[129] In a word, Tyrrell wrote vehemently to von Hügel on 20 February:

The bishops have mounted on metaphors as witches on broomsticks, and have ridden to the devil. It is the "sheep & shepherd" metaphor that does the trick. The sheep are brainless; passive; their part is to be led, fed, fleeced & slain for the profit of the shepherd for whose benefit solely they exist. Apply this to the constitution of the Church & where are you to stop? And then there is the "Divine Teacher" fallacy: Christ is God; Peter is Christ; the Pope is Peter *ergo* he is, we dare not say, God: but a Divine Teacher. There is not an attempt even at qualifying or limiting the Pope's delegated power. In Heaven's name, one asks, why doesn't he work miracles & raise the dead? Why is he not exposed on the Altar for worship? Is he really present in the Blessed Sacrament? Yet these are the legitimate developments of the exegesis & principles of the Joint Pastoral which Leo XIII has blessed and approved. And there is not a man among us with sufficient freedom or authority to raise a protest against this rabid nonsense, this very drunkenness of absolutism! It seems like a horrible dream.[130]

Tyrrell solemnized his position in a letter to the editor of the *Pilot* and put the final period to an eight-week controversy that was aired in its pages.[131] It appeared in the 2 March number and was signed, ironically, "A Conservative Catholic." In weighing the joint pastoral, Tyrrell insisted, one must remember two points. First, that it is final and decisive only for those who already accept the absolutism it enunciates, but "not for those who, in the light of history, distinguish between the Pope as the voice of a theological clique and the Pope as the voice of the universal Church past and present." Second, one must remember its main purpose and distinguish that from its *obiter dicta.* When it strikes down the school of Mivart, no one should think that it has also struck down that school "which looks to Newman for its principles, if not for all its conclusions—a school which should rather be called conservative, first, because it stands for antiquity against innovation: and then because he is the true conservative who, however reluctant, will not hesitate to part with any superfluous cargo that he foresees will endanger his vessel—whose motive is conservative, though his method be liberal."[132]

Then silence fell on the issue for nearly two months, silence broken only by what Tyrrell described to von Hügel as "an intolerably offensive article from the pen of Fr. Joseph Rickaby" in the *Month* for April. Rickaby laid the cause of dogmatic deviation in liberals to their moral deviation. "At this rate," Tyrrell quipped, "they must be numerically stronger than is generally supposed," and he told von Hügel that he had written Rickaby for an explanation why then liberals were so few and why "we have not 9/10 of the clergy & the Cardinals on our side."[133]

Of import, however, was the "Halifax" article. It was finally in the works. Halifax had composed an introduction and conclusion for Tyrrell's text, and on 15 April Tyrrell returned the composite with his own connecting links. He noted how personally urgent it was that the absolutist sense of the Vatican decrees be excluded. "But now they are trying to impose that sense as a test of orthodoxy, if not of actual communion. Were it so imposed I should be simply roofless."[134]

The article appeared, at last, in the *Nineteenth Century* for May 1901. In posing "a few plain answers to a few plain questions," its underlying aim was to expose the uterine malignancy of "Jesuitism" whose outworking Tyrrell had traced back even behind the legislation of Aquaviva to Alfonso Rodriguez, whose ascetical teaching had for centuries been a staple of religious and priestly formation. In discussing obedience, Tyrrell observed to Halifax, Rodriguez spoke of "obeying the Superior as Christ himself," but then he slips imperceptibly "from the modified to the literal and absolute sense of the simile," making it "impossible for nuns and novices ever to imagine that they can have any rights or liberties against one who is so inextricably identified with God." Our present ecclesiastical absolutism is simply an "extension of these fallacies into the realm of Church polity. It is too easy and pleasant a doctrine not to be patronised by those who want to govern irresponsibly and without criticism. But easy ways are seldom God's ways."[135] It was this misconception that lay behind the "Divine Teacher" fallacy.

The article asked and answered three basic questions: (1) What are the limits claimed for papal infallibility? (2) What assent are Catholics required to give to matters that are not *de fide divina* but *de fide ecclesiastica?* (3) What is the relationship of the laity and lower clergy, the *Ecclesia discens,* to the *Ecclesia docens?* Much of Tyrrell's reply was drawn from "The Mind of the Church" and correspondence already considered, so brevity is in order here.

In limiting the pope's authority, Tyrrell distinguished, as he did in "The Mind of the Church," between "assistance" and "inspiration." The pope and bishops singly are divinely *assisted,* the former infallibly under certain conditions, the latter fallibly; but no one is *inspired* in the sense of being able to add anything to revelation. Their assistance is a special providence that presumes and guides the use of ordinary means and in no sense abrogates the natural order of things or dispenses people from "keeping their powder dry." "Two conditions, therefore, are required for an authoritative decision—the use of natural means and a special Providence directing that use. If the former condition be absent the latter is simply impossible."[136]

As to the Vatican Council's definition of papal infallibility, that was merely a further precision, wrought by casuistry, of what was implied all along by the doctrine of ecclesiastical infallibility and therefore cannot be extended beyond the limits of the latter. What the *letter* of the definition means is that the pope inherits the infallibility formerly ascribed to ecumenical councils. As the council was "a desperate and final remedy," a court of last appeal, when the essential unity of the church was at stake, so now the pope is infallible only in like circumstances—"when every other ordinary means has been tried in vain," not when, anticipating extremities, he intervenes in controversies not clearly and substantially detrimental to unity, nor when he gives his episcopal or patriarchal opinion as *primus inter pares.*[137]

The *spirit* of the definition is another matter. Those who pushed it through and subsequently developed it in the schools of Rome are governed by the same principles of exegesis exemplified in the joint pastoral: Christ left to his church all that was necessary for the pastoral office; but this, that, or the other is easily seen to be necessary; therefore the church has the necessary power. Thus the notion of "unqualified viceregency" and no hint that the pastoral powers of Peter and later popes and bishops were of any lower order than that of Christ. And thus the pale of infallibility comes to include all affairs of the church's "daily magisterium," for it is inconceivable that the pope as a "Divine Teacher" could sanction a belief that is untrue, or direct worship and devotion to what is superstitious or unreal. This crude literalism was impossible as long as the fullness of power was attributed only to an ecumenical council, but as soon as it was equally vested in the person of a single bishop, literalism followed as night follows the day.

This literal notion of "Divine Teacher" leads to the second question about assent. The pastoral states that Catholics are bound to give the assent of faith not only to revealed doctrines (*de fide divina*) but "also to the decisions of the Church concerning matters appertaining to or affecting revelation" (*de fide ecclesiastica*). Given the substantial unity of truth and the interlacing of natural with supernatural knowledge (for example, the Aristotelian philosophy of substance and accidents in the explanation of the doctrine of transubstantiation), it is hard to see any limit to this *fides ecclesiastica*. The whole realm of secular knowledge jostles up against revelation at every point, and in claiming to settle some points regarding revelation, the church virtually claims to settle all. The pastoral speaks of "the vast fields of profane science and speculation open to" the Catholic philosopher, but if infallibility is at work every day in that indefinitely wide range of matters "necessary for the feeding, teaching, and governing the flock," how is he free? "He can neither breathe nor move, lest he knock up against some condemned proposition."[138]

Tyrrell also found problematic the pastoral's insistence that "religious assent" or "obedience of interior judgment" be given to noninfallible authoritative decisions. Certainly the church as guardian of revelation has a right to impose her teaching on those whose education has been entrusted to her, and these are duty bound to assent as long as clearly contradictory evidence does not make them duty bound to a still higher rule of assent. That such a higher rule exists is evident in the pastoral's implying that the Holy Office may make mistakes—for example, by condemning an opinion today and tomorrow admitting it as true. Can one even speak of interior assent to an authority that both proposes and disposes? Assent to such decisions can be at most conditional and probably never final. "But of this and similar limitations there is no indication . . . just because the Sacred Congregation or the local bishop, no less than the Pope, is a 'Divine Teacher,' of whom it has been said: 'He that heareth you heareth me.'"[139]

The third and last obscurity that Tyrrell wanted clarified was the relation between the *Ecclesia discens* (the laity and lower clergy) to the *Ecclesia docens* (now virtually equivalent to the pope). The pastoral, said Tyrrell, treats those two entities practically as two distinct moral personalities or corporations:

> The *Ecclesia discens* is conceived as wholly passive and receptive, and the *Ecclesia docens* as active and communicative; they are related

literally as sheep and shepherd; as beings of a different order, with different, if not divergent, interests. . . . The mind and will of the Church is conceived as residing in the Pope, united, for solemnity's sake (not for validity's), with the Episcopate. There the faith is deposited; there it is to be studied and elaborated; and then the results of this thought and study are to be transmitted to the passive, unthinking *Ecclesia discens*. . . . In no sense, therefore, does the safeguarding and elaboration of the faith take place in the mind of the laity or the lower clergy.

But this view is irreconcilable with what the pastoral elsewhere admitted about religious practices originating for the most part with the laity and only being guided, approved, or checked by the *Ecclesia docens*. "Historically, it is evident that the doctrines and beliefs are but the theoretical implications of devotions; that all through the *lex orandi* has been the *lex credendi*," that change has originated from below, and has been only criticised and formulated from above. "If this be so, then the relation of the *Ecclesia discens* and *docens* is not mechanical, but organic, it is the whole Church that thinks and wills and acts." And the pope is infallibly assisted not as apart from that organism but as one with it, for it is the whole organism that is the immediate recipient of divine assistance. This concept, Tyrrell asserted, is an older theology that does not conflict with the letter of the Vatican decrees. It accords with the denial of papal dependence on episcopal consent and with the validity of extraconciliar definitions *ex cathedra*. All it demands is that "the Pope should *ex professo* put himself in vital touch with the mind of the Church preparatory to declaring infallibly what that mind truly is."[140]

To conclude on the point of distress, Tyrrell took a broad swipe at that root evil that had fed every fiber of the church's being. In reaction to the Reformers' revolt against ecclesiastical authority, Counter Reformers appropriated Ignatius's teaching on obedience and extravagated it via the "Divine Teacher" fallacy into a revealed basis for that obedience due not only to the inspired apostles but to all legitimately constituted authorities, civil as well as ecclesiastical. A simplistic application of the proof text, "He who hears you hears me" (Lk. 10:16), led to such a divinizing of authority that little or no attention was paid to the limits and conditions under which authority may be considered divine.

The ascetical works emanating from the Jesuit order make straight for this unqualified absolutism: the superior is God and there is an end of it. "On his side nothing but rights; on the other, nothing but duties, or, rather, one all-comprehensive duty, namely, passive, mechanical, uncriticising obedience."[141] When one considers the all-pervasive influence of that order in the post-Reformation church—how it has insinuated itself into other religious orders and congregations, especially the modern ones, and controlled the education of the secular clergy—it is hardly going too far to call this conception of authority "Jesuitism." And it was only by the heroic struggles of the defeated minority at the Vatican Council that the Roman Church narrowly avoided setting her seal on that system. All subsequent developments, however, have been in that direction.

After-Words

With this article Tyrrell placed himself decisively in the line of the defeated minority of Vatican I and allied himself with the party of Acton and Döllinger who had fought to keep alive "an older theology" against the onslaught of "wholesale innovation" and indeed "heresy."[142]

To ensure the kind of discussion that would meet headon the issues raised by "Halifax," Tyrrell had ready for press a provocative essay in which he christened the "older theology" as "amended Gallicanism" and pitted it against the new Roman absolutist theology. "Lord Halifax Demurs," Tyrrell's reply to himself, appeared unsigned in the *Weekly Register* for 3 May. The value of Halifax's criticism, Tyrrell said, lay "in putting side by side two almost incompatible views of papal infallibility." In the one view—so congenial to the mind of the Anglican—not the Holy Father but the whole church collectively is the immediate recipient of divine guidance. Granted that the *Ecclesia docens* has a function of its own from which the *Ecclesia discens* is directly excluded, namely, to gather up, formulate the church's thinking, and impose the results authoritatively on the *Ecclesia discens*. Still, "it is the whole organism which teaches and the whole organism which is taught; so that *indirectly* the *Ecclesia Discens* teaches, and the *Ecclesia Docens* is taught." They are coprinciples of one self-teaching, self-governing organism. The church collectively is the proper and immediate vicar of Christ and shepherd of the sheep; the pope and episcopate are vicar only in a derived and secondary sense. This notion might be called "an amended form of Gallicanism," as it implies a rather democratic and complex notion of church polity, compared with the monarchic conception whose simplicity "is just what draws into the Church those who are wearied with the unworkableness of so vague and unwieldy a rule of faith as that of ecumenical consensus."[143]

In the monarchic conception, the pope alone is directly and primarily the vicar of Christ; the episcopate, only insofar as headed by him. In all that concerns the teaching, governing, and feeding of the flock, he receives a strictly supernatural *charisma,* "which makes his guidance as absolute as sure and as infallible as that of Christ Himself." As Cardinal Henry Edward Manning, a sober exponent of the "common interpretation," put it in his pastoral on the Vatican Council, "Divine assistance is [the pope's] special prerogative depending on God alone; independent of the Church which, in dependence on him, is endowed with the same infallibility."[144] "There can be little doubt," Tyrrell concluded, "as to which of these views is the badge of orthodoxy, even if it be granted that 'amended Gallicanism' saves the letter of the Vatican decrees." The whole effort in doctrinal development "has been to extrude the quasi-democratic conception and to vindicate the monarchic," or as Manning put it, "to preclude all ambiguity by which for two hundred years the promise of Our Lord to Peter and his successors has in some minds been obscured."[145] But the more Tyrrell looked at these two views, the farther apart they stood; nor could he imagine any synthesis that could transcend and save them both.

On the day that this article appeared Tyrrell wrote to Rooke Ley of the *Weekly Register* to clarify several points that, posing as the devil's advocate, he had deliberately left obscure. First his remark about Manning was ironic understatement aimed at showing that the "common interpretation" was extremist and that Manning was a sober and solid expositor thereof, neither shrinking from the extremest conclusions of his principles nor exaggerating their essential implications. Second, Tyrrell had to explain that his own position was that of "amended Gallicanism," even though he had posed as *advocatus diaboli* to *both* views so as not to implicate the *Register:*

> I call it "amended Gallicanism" because, personally, I believe that there was a truth as well as an error in Gallicanism, namely its protest against the absolutist view of infallibility; its error was the denial of the sane view. Hence an "amended Gallicanism" is just what I want. . . . If . . . anyone . . . can show us a *via media* or a higher synthesis let us have it by all means. But if controversy issues simply in a clearer recognition of the need of choosing one alternative or the other, and of abandoning the shilly-shally muddle-headed position, it will also be a great gain.
>
> Hence my pose in the W.R. is that of one who impartially and dispassionately recognises the actual situation and sees the seal of or-

thodoxy *all but* set upon the view which he cordially dislikes. If I have
misinterpreted the orthodox position let them say so.[146]

But no one of the "them" was saying anything in public, and
Tyrrell was enormously disappointed. He was convinced that he
had accurately stated their position and that he could annihilate all
objectors. "It is strange no maximist has come forward to repudiate
my statement," he wrote to Rooke Ley three weeks later.[147] Cardinal Vaughan reacted privately but gave Tyrrell only the blandest
satisfaction: "As to Lord H. I have no thought of answering his article & think it best left alone. He alone stands in it erect, as Pope H.,
while bishops of his own communion and of ours are prostrated or
scattered before him."[148] "Which of course is very true," Tyrrell
reacted, "but why?"[149] The attitude evident here toward even discussing such matters with "Halifax" is patent in a remark to Wilfrid
Ward of Dr. Victor J. Schobel, professor of dogma at the diocesan
theologate at Oscott: "You must take it for granted that a Protestant, like Lord Halifax, cannot read a Catholic document aright."[150]

Von Hügel's reaction was ecstatic. He wrote from Milan on 28
May, "I have not yet told you how much struck I have been by
your remarks about the Joint P. . . . The point that that document
really puts the Pope outside of the Church is most strikingly
true. . . . Not since Newman have we English-speaking Catholics
had anything like as sweet and deep an 'organ-voice,' as adequate
an expression of the truest, most constitutive forces within ourselves, as is that which God has now given us in you."[151]

If extremists did not reply, moderates did—H.I.D. Ryder of the
Birmingham Oratorians and Wilfrid Ward.[152] However the discussion, in Tyrrell's view, was not advanced. On 17 June he reported
to the baron that Ryder and Ward had attacked his *advocatus diaboli* standpoint, but that he had replied as "S.T.L." in various letters and insisted

> that there are two incompatible theories of infallibility sheltered by
> the Vatican decrees of which only one, the absolutist view of Manning
> & the Joint Pastoral, can be regarded as the "badge of orthodoxy." I
> made this view as absurd as was compatible with the show of defend-
> ing it against the other which I stigmatised as "Amended Gallicanism."
> On the whole I managed to give away the Joint Pastoral pretty well;
> though I am satisfied that neither Ryder nor Ward are clear about
> their own position & are trying to blow hot & cold at once.[153]

Ward's rejoinder, "Doctores Ecclesiae" in the *Pilot* for 22 June,
was another case of special pleading. He accused "Halifax" of mis-

understanding the functions of a pastoral "in the economy of the Church" and of being "beside the mark, because his most extreme interpretations . . . have long since been universally rejected."[154] To which Tyrrell, writing as "E.F.G." in the 6 July *Pilot*, retorted that a pastoral letter is not, as Ward claimed, directed to "educated theologians" but to the faithful at large. "If, then, it puts before these a doctrine which is saved from absolutism only by limitations which have to be sought for in books of theology, it must be allowed that such half-truth is as dangerous and mischievous as any heresy."[155] Even some people of Ward's own persuasion found his argument weak. James Britten, editor of the Catholic Truth Society publications and friendly with a number of bishops including Cardinal Vaughan, wrote to Ward and backed "E.F.G.'s" reply: "I confess I think the writer in this week's *Pilot* makes a practical point. It is an ungrateful task to be continually protecting those in authority from the consequences of their own utterances—and, after all, *they* do mean what they say, and the average man knows they do, even if he does not accept it as binding upon him to accept it."[156]

Von Hügel told Ward more directly that "Halifax's" paper was in its substance unanswerable and that Ward's attempt, though well meaning and useful in other respects, "was not *really* an answer." What is one to say about such a document, supposedly well thought out and representing the thought of the entire English episcopate, if it must be defended by fetching arguments from outside? At the least, it leaves itself "strangely open to misconception" and "legitimate attack."[157] And to Tyrrell he made it clear that he understood "Halifax" not to have attacked the authorities and interpretations marshaled against him by Ward but simply to have stated that for the pastoral and the theory it supported, these authorities and interpretations did not exist. "And, since the good W. can nowhere show even the roots of such limiting powers in the Pastoral, it is clear that his defence is a failure, and only helps confirm his antagonist's specific contention."[158]

Ward's final comment—not really a reply since it came in a lengthy article in the *Edinburgh Review* on A. J. Balfour's Cambridge University Address of March 1900—sought to limit the sphere of infallibility by ascribing fallibility to many details of church teaching but infallibility to the whole.[159] But Tyrrell remarked to Maude Petre that this was a "whole-sale climbing down" necessitated by the official church's ignoring of development and projecting the present backward to apostolic times. How can we go on admitting error in nearly every detail of the church's guidance taken singly and still maintain infallibility as to the whole? "I feel sure that the Infallibility doctrine will have to be restated in the terms of Halifax's article."[160] To Ward himself Tyrrell wrote that, although Ward's latest remarks implied principles pointing toward "a radical change of view as to the sphere of ecclesiastical infallibility," this change would not happen through such analyses and refinements as proposed in the recent *Weekly Register* controversy but "simply through the opening up of the past by historical research." The church or the pope cannot pretend to be infallible "in departments where they have erred over and over again." As to infallibility in matters touching the rule of faith and the nature of the church, we rightly point out that no error in doctrinal detail can be so deadly as an error here:

> & yet we forget that the mechanical "creationist" view of the Church still held by men like Gallwey & Humphrey & Lescher, who believe that Christ said the First "Mass" & that S. Paul paid triennial visits *ad limina*, is only a survival of what was once universally held. When history has done its work it will be hard to imagine men ever trusting the Church as she now demands to be trusted—with that naïve faith in the Pope which is just what attracts so many converts to us desirous of certainty in matters of quite secondary import, or less. I think we shall be drawn back to the view I put forward in the "Walla-washee" romance.[161]

By early September Tyrrell was ready to admit that the whole discussion had fallen flat. "As to the Joint Pastoral," he wrote to Ward, "I think the issue of all the correspondence is that it will be quietly shelved & forgotten in some cupboard together with the bones of King Edmund."[162] But to von Hügel on 22 September he announced that he would "like to sum up the whole in some more coherent & complete form."[163] Two years later he realized his wish in *The Church and the Future*. That book was the final fruit of the controversy surrounding the joint pastoral.

So the curtain falls on this act. As Loome puts it so clearly, the effect of the joint pastoral and the ensuing eight-month controversy was twofold: (1) By its vituperative characterization of liberal Catholics as men "wanting in filial docility and reverence," beset by "rationalism and human pride," "allured by fashion, curiosity, or a desire to taste of forbidden fruit," and full of little but "sneering and profane conversation and carping criticism," the pastoral reintroduced a tone not heard since the liberal Catholic controversies in England over thirty years before.[164] Tyrrell reacted in kind and became bitter and hardened in his attitude particularly toward the Jesuits, on whom he laid the blame for this "reaction on the rampage." (2) It raised again, in a more acute form, a question that had lain dormant since the first Vatican council; the nature of the teaching church and indeed the nature of Catholicism itself. The joint pastoral was the new paean summoning the forces of the ultramontane majority against the liberal minority and their conception of Catholicism. Thus it shifted the ground of the discussion. Whereas before Tyrrell and persons like him saw their liberalism primarily in terms of a pastoral and apologetic role *vis-à-vis* the modern world, they now discovered that their "liberal Catholicism" rested— at least in the minds of church authorities—in their failure to have learned the lessons of the Vatican council and to have assimilated that conception of Catholicism elaborated by the exegesis of the ultramontane majority. Tyrrell had grasped the lay of the land in an instant. He saw that confronting the joint pastoral would entail more than mere border skirmishing, for the question it raised was not a "question of detail" but "of the very constitution of the Church,—of the very nature of the rule of faith."[165] And so, although the curtain falls, it is only for a change of set. The drama would run through Tyrrell's life and beyond, but for Tyrrell's part it would climax in *The Church and the Future*.

CHAPTER 5

Drawing the Lines
of Conflict

A SENSE OF FOREBODING

Truth is better served when a certain detachment and serenity prevail in the discussion of momentous ideas. Truth was not well served in the exchanges between George Tyrrell and his superiors. In fact there was so little serenity on either side that from the beginning of 1901 Tyrrell increasingly described the exchanges in battle imagery. Violence of any kind repelled him, but where principles were concerned he would meet violence with violence. With the poor and unlearned he was the first to bend, but with religious leaders his demands were uncompromising. It was this characteristic that drew him into conflict. He entered into it with a sense of foreboding, but once in it he fought tooth and nail, accepting its results as something that had to be.

During the first half of 1901, as Tyrrell saw it, he had scored an impressive string of victories: squelching Colley's mission scheme, silencing the general's demand for a repudiation of *External Religion*, getting him to drop the Roman censorship requirement, and airing a trenchant criticism of the joint pastoral without being detected. Heady with victory, he launched a two-pronged attack just about the time that the uproar over the joint pastoral was subsiding. This new offensive would bring him into conflict not only with Jesuit authorities but with ecclesiastical authorities as well. Previously he had engaged the latter only indirectly through Jesuit

166

superiors. Now he would engage them hand to hand, and, judging by his identification with the prophets, he knew the price he would pay.

THE *OIL AND WINE* AFFAIR

The occasion of this new round was the disposition of a collection of new essays that Tyrrell had completed by December 1900 but had not yet published because of the Roman censorship requirement. But at the beginning of February 1901, the Jesuit general dropped that requirement and in its place appointed thirty-two censors from among the English Jesuits—"after his own heart," Tyrrell retorted,[1] and "of whom 27 are no better than pious raw Stonyhurst schoolboys. . . . I am now 'free' to write," Tyrrell commented facetiously to von Hügel, "i.e., the chances are 27 to 5 that each of the four censors who have to sit upon me will be incompetent to understand & therefore sure to condemn."[2] Nevertheless, toward the end of June Tyrrell was willing to experiment and see if he could get his new book past the censors and even the cardinal. His tactics would be the same as those that won him success in recent skirmishes with Colley and the general.

When one studies Tyrrell's correspondence with his provincial on this affair, the distinct impression emerges that after the removal of Gerard from office and the accession of Colley, Tyrrell saw the latter as nothing more than the long arm of Rome and to be treated accordingly. Thus he seems to have approached Colley with a carefully thought out scheme based on a prediction of what the provincial's reaction would be. Tyrrell's method was really an attack from the rear after a show to the face. Colley, who had only the benefit of each letter in turn and was still naive enough to presume candor and goodwill from his subjects, found himself flipped on his back before he had the slightest inkling that the danger was not what he saw before him. In a word, Tyrrell seems deliberately to have manipulated Colley into passing the book as the lesser of two evils.

On 20 June 1901 Tyrrell informed Colley that he had made a present of his manuscript to his Anglican friend Fr. Robert Dolling, that the latter now wanted to "turn it into money for the benefit of the poor" and so would like to have the selling power of Tyrrell's name. But this request Tyrrell said he refused due to the annoyance of submitting the book to censorship. Instead, he proposed—he could only propose, since he had given the manuscript unconditionally—that Dolling publish it anonymously with a preface signed by himself to the effect that the author had for his own reasons rejected the manuscript and left it to Dolling's disposal. Of course the book would be for Anglicans only, as Catholics would not buy a book without the *imprimatur*, and the title would have to be changed to avoid a chance association with the author of *Nova et Vetera.* "If any other precaution occurs to you please let me know, as I am sure my friend will respect any reasonable desire of mine . . . though I cannot expect him to attend to the mere *fiat* of authorities which he does not yet recognize."[3]

In plain language, Tyrrell was informing Colley that he was about to publish a book covertly, but that the cover would not last long, for anyone who could read carefully would see Tyrrell behind the words. Colley thought Tyrrell was asking permission for this venture and balked. Tyrrell responded on 27 June with his first threat to take his case to the public. "The Institute forbids us to publish anonymously; or to get others to publish for us in our own name." This prohibition, Tyrrell agreed, was reasonable in ordinary cases. But "it does not forbid us to give away M.SS. which others may publish in in [*sic*] their own name. This would be tyrranical & unreasonable and therefore, not to be regarded."[4]

Having weakened Colley with that bit of bullying, Tyrrell introduced his real intention. It was "only as a favour and not as a right" that he was asking Dolling to consult the wishes of the Society. It would be to his financial advantage if the book could pass censorship and be published under Tyrrell's name, but that would probably "lead to much more trouble than the present arrangement. It might however be worth seeing how far the censors would be disposed to go; and if you wish I could get one of the copies sent to Fr. Knight."[5]

Colley apparently answered with an accusation about disregarding solemn obligations, for on 1 July Tyrrell replied by defending his action as a regard for still more solemn obligations, "or as a recognition of the invalidity of obligations taken in substantial ignorance of circumstances, or invalidated by the non-fulfillment of conditions." He began now to refer to the Jesuits no longer as *his* but as *your* Society and to the general as *your* general. He said that no man had tried harder to cling to his faith "in your Society," but now he had been "forced to let go" and admit his error. Again Tyrrell threatened "to put all this in evidence some day."[6]

Apparently Colley agreed to submit Tyrrell's manuscript anonymously to the censors, but Tyrrell had serious misgivings. "It is impossible that they shd. not know who the author is," he told Colley, "or that knowing it, they will not be extra-nervous and timid in the light of recent events."[7] Still Tyrrell sent a copy, along with the preface he had suggested to Dolling—"as it were a little mouse to four cats."[8] There the matter stalled until the middle of October, when Tyrrell lost patience over the censors' delay and again resorted to threats to extract his manuscript and a judgment. Of this later.

Meantime a matter from which Tyrrell had been smarting since the beginning of 1900 required redressing, namely, the unexplained punishment doled out by Rome and the damage done thereby to his good name. In Tyrrell's mind the issue of the *Oil and Wine* affair and of the joint pastoral controversy were one and the same: the nature of the modern Society of Jesus and his relation to it, or "Jesuitism" over against the liberal spirit of Ignatius and Newman.

Tyrrell had been turning these matters over and over for some time now, and had prepared an apologia for publication. Also, since January 1901, he had occupied himself with his autobiography and sent it to Maude Petre chapter by chapter. His hope, he told her, was that the story might "piece together this battered personality of mine into some flattering semblance of unity and coherence."[9] Then Henri Bremond, whose own relationship to the Society of Jesus was extremely tenuous, came to Richmond in July, and for a full week he and Tyrrell "talked incessantly without any prospect of nearing the end."[10] All of Tyrrell's recent writing and conversing worked together to clarify and harden his line of resistance.

At the same time Tyrrell was distressed at finding himself so alone in his valuation of the Society, a conclusion he arrived at by following a dispute in the press between Jesuit loyalists and radical critics. He was convinced of the utter hopelessness of the argument and interjected a vitriolic assessment with an unsigned article, "Jesuits and Their Critics," in the 2 August issue of the *Weekly Register*.[11] He pointed out that only the plain truth could give the Society's well-wishers what they really wanted: ideal Jesuitism in place of the perversion wrought by its absolutist methods. But the kind of sane and searching criticism the Society needed, it had never yet received. Critics from without, from Pascal down, lacked inside knowledge and were moreover driven by passion and party spirit, while critics from within had no teeth whatever, and those who had been in and left were usually bitter and biased. "Only a Jesuit— could such be found—of sufficient intellectual detachment, historical sense, and critical ability, working under conditions of complete liberty, could do for the Society of Jesus what Mommsen has done for Rome, or Pastor for the renaissance Papacy."[12]

Of course, Tyrrell felt that he himself did not possess the requisite freedom for objective criticism, but at least as long as he was in the Society he would never tire of saying so and would resist the pressure toward that conformity that he felt had crippled so many of his fellow Jesuits. Resistance, however, would not be easy. On 4 August he wrote to Bremond that he felt keenly the pressure to conform, to take the easier and pleasanter way, to swim with the tide and take the Society at its own valuation. "Indeed, I feel within myself a capacity of narrowness that few would credit me with."[13] So he had constantly to remind himself "that in resisting the pressure I am in harmony with a far wider & more authoritative consensus. . . . Hence your visit confirmed my faith in better things & in the need of energetic resistance of evil." Then, referring to the affects of that evil in his companions at Richmond, he continued:

> I feel very kindly towards these spoilt lives—as towards maimed creatures of every sort. In the world they might have led unselfish & happy lives; whereas the flowers of their soul have been neglected or uprooted; & the weeds brought out in all their rank profusion. Against the charge that our training tends to destroy individuality some point to the collection of oddities we turn out. But surely oddity is not individuality; or eccentricity the same as originality. Those are the result of destructive agencies—the irregularities of ruins—; these; of constructive. Nothing more surely produces grotesque deformities than the endeavour to produce an impossible uniformity. And then it is pathetic to see the faith of the poor victims themselves in the system which has blighted them; & how sincerely they would burn all its opponents! As long as one looks to the Jesuit one is irritated; but when one thinks of the underlying strangled humanity one weeps with Dante:
>
>> "Now think thee, Gentle reader, for thyself
>> "If I could keep the tears from starting forth,
>> "Beholding, close at hand, our human form
>> "So twisted & distorted back-before, etc., etc.[14]

On 16 August Colley visited Richmond on his yearly rounds of the province. Tyrrell happened to be out, so Colley left word that Tyrrell should visit him in York three days later. But Tyrrell sent word that what he could say to the provincial was not worth the price of a return ticket and that it would only pain Colley to hear opinions and sentiments so opposite his own. "As far as I can see with my present light there is not the slightest prospect of a reconciliation between myself and the Society," but he hoped "to maintain peaceable external relations" for the sake of those who could never understand a rupture. But this, he pointed out, would depend on being allowed "reasonable liberty to use my pen." Then came another slightly veiled threat: "Though my faith in the Society is gone & my hope & affection on their last gasp; yet while a spark of hope is left I should be sorry to be hurried to practical decisions of an irrevocable kind."[15]

Colley yielded and Tyrrell reported the victory to the baron: "It is only by playing on the motive: "ne majus scandalum oriatur"— only at the point of the bayonet that I can get on at all." The provincial was "most kind & sympathetic; accepting the situation & promising to do his best to make things run smooth."[16]

Having secured Colley's "cooperation" on his Jesuit status, Tyrrell was ready for the next skirmish: clearing his name and getting *Oil and Wine* past the censors. On 15 October he wrote to Colley and complained about the "protracted dilatoriness" of the censors (they had had the book now three and a half months) and the "wild & malicious gossip" circulating in London to the effect that Tyrrell had left the Society or was about to leave. To counter those rumors, he told Colley, he had requested to preach at Farm Street Church but had as yet received no reply. He could only conclude that there was some inhibition of which he had not yet been told and that would therefore prevent his preaching in Richmond and everywhere else as well. Then another threat:

> Having no other means of self-defense, I propose now to write an open letter to one or two influential Catholic friends stating my side of the case as simply & briefly as I can. . . .
>
> I think this is *most* undesirable from many points of view; but I will not let my name be dragged in the gutter through consideration for those who have shown no consideration for me. Your general failed ludicrously to justify his charge of heterodoxy against my article; while he gave no reason whatever for stopping my ministerial work—a species of justice unknown among civilised men who refuse to punish a criminal without first connecting the punishment with some fault and allowing the condemned a chance of explaining & defending himself.
>
> If this step produces no fruit, then, in God's name, I will go home to my friends and publish my "Apologia pro vita sua."[17]

The very next day Colley sent Tyrrell the censors' opinions on *Oil and Wine* and reported that his request to preach was being considered and that he himself would follow up on the matter.[18]

Tyrrell replied at once to the censors' criticism and said he would certainly attend to their "*definite* objections where they refer to page & line," but that he could not correct "'a vein of thought running all through the book' or 'impressions that might be given by the book as a whole.'"[19] But perhaps a preface could be so worded as to forestall such objections. One censor said yes, the other no, and Colley cast the deciding vote.[20] *Oil and Wine* was passed, and Tyrrell could relish another albeit momentary victory. Further trouble on this publication lay ahead, but for the time being he could turn to affairs on another front.

Tyrrell was confident that an invitation to preach at Farm Street would be forthcoming, but there was still the unexplained prohibition against giving retreats, which he thought had come from Rome. It was two years since he had given a retreat, and gossips began to speculate about the reasons. As rumors grew "virulent & universal"—just how virulent will soon be seen—Tyrrell felt that the pretext of avoiding scandal was no longer a valid reason for holding back and he must do something "to bring things to a crisis." On 3 November he disclosed his move to Bremond. He had written to the general's assistant, Rudolf Meyer, and reminded him that for two years the general had given no reason for the prohibition to give retreats, that this had resulted in "grave defamation of my character," and that if the general felt any obligation in conscience to correct this evil he should do so or else state the charges. Tyrrell told Bremond that he expected no answer and felt he would be left no choice but to ask for release from the Society. Perhaps, he mused, an open letter to the general in a public newspaper to this effect would be "a new & startling event in history" and open the way for a sensational series.[21]

Meanwhile the invitation to preach at Farm Street arrived, and Tyrrell went down to London on or about 4 November. He returned a fortnight later and reported to von Hügel that he had made the rounds of "the chief centres of gossip and told the plain unvarnished truth; and where I could not go I wrote it plainly, as an open letter."[22] But illness struck and had forced him to cancel his sermon at the last moment. "After all the sermon didn't matter," he wrote Maude Petre; "the announcement served my purpose & the disappointment drew attention to the fact."[23]

Shortly upon Tyrrell's return to Richmond, a letter arrived from the general's assistant explaining (1) that the general had nothing to do with Tyrrell's removal from London and from his ministries there—the reasons for that were best known to the then provincial—and (2) that the provincial's action concerning retreats had been prescribed by the general, but even here he allowed the provincial some latitude later on. As to motives, there were the following considerations: (1) The general never once impugned Tyrrell's personal orthodoxy or his good intentions, but he did find some of Tyrrell's writings imprudent, as did Englishmen of high standing both inside and outside the Society. (2) And if not in England, at least in Italy these writings were turned against the Society and the church by men of questionable standing. (3) But even more problematic than these writings were things said by Tyrrell during retreats and at other times, which disturbed the consciences of not a few and gave rise to grave complaints from persons whose authority could not be ignored. (4) Finally, the general did not understand Tyrrell's statement: "I cannot delay . . . those steps which I have resolved to take for the vindication of my character," but he sincerely hoped that Tyrrell would not commit himself to such action against the Institute as would compel his superiors to take steps that they would rather not take.[24]

Colley, who was at the novitiate in Roehampton making his retreat at the time, also received word that the general wanted him to clarify some of the points Tyrrell had raised. So Colley wrote to Gerard, who had been provincial at the time of the prohibition. Gerard's response of 23 November gives a heretofore unknown side of the story.

DEAR FR. PROVINCIAL—P.C.—

I did not tell Fr. Tyrrell that he was taboo for retreats, and therefore did not, of course, assign reasons. In the first place, I desired, so far as possible, to avoid driving him to extremity, and secondly, although as you know, I have little sympathy with his petulant attitude, I have in my own mind quite as little for the course adopted by his Paternity; which seemed to me very ill-advised & arbitrary, & for which I felt I could offer no reasons which would hold water for a moment with so acute a man as Fr. T.

In particular, the verdicts of the censors, the documents which professed to substantiate the worse charges upon which presumably the very severe sentence was founded, were, especially No. 2., in my judgment simply outrageous and considerably more deserving of blame than the article censured.[25]

My intention therefore was to leave Fr. T. alone till he had sufficiently devoured his soul—& meanwhile I tackled him, as if from myself alone, in a correspondence which became a bit sharp, upon what I gathered from the whole affair to be really wrong—I found him sadly impracticable and could not flatter myself that I had done much good, but was confirmed in my judgment that it was well I had not told him more.

As to the move to Richmond, it began somewhat casually, he going on a temporary visit, & then suggesting that he should rusticate for a season. I jumped at the idea as [sic] just about the same time the Cardinal expressed a hope he would not be placed in London on account of his imprudence in speech, especially with persons who require steadying. If T. knew this it would make him wild—

Yours ever in Xt,
JOHN GERARD, S.J.

I thought it better, as explained above, to speak to him as from myself alone, seeing that the mention of Father General is as a red rag to a bull.[26]

The next day Colley wrote to Tyrrell that the general had "never forbade your giving retreats" and that as far as Colley's position was concerned, "I did not think of asking you to give any Retreat as the reasons assigned by you against undertaking any spiritual work seemed to apply a fortiori to retreats." Colley knew this latest disclosure would infuriate Tyrrell, so he added a postscript: "If any injustice has been done at least take such measures for a remedy as are constitutional and do not ruin all by an act of rebellion which as you know must involve very serious consequences."[27]

Tyrrell did not disappoint. The next day he sent what is perhaps the most important of all his communications with his English superiors. In it he indicated why the retreat issue was of such grave importance and then rebutted slanderous charges against him. The letter must be quoted in full, not only because of its intrinsic importance but because it offers a contrary explanation for evidence that at least one recent writer has distorted into the suggestion that Tyrrell was homosexual.[28]

MY DEAR FATHER PROVINCIAL

So many unpleasant slanders were in circulation about me that, for the sake of some of my non-Jesuit friends, I felt bound to do what I could to refute them. By coming to London I proved that I was not forbidden to come to London; by preaching I proved that I was not forbidden to preach; and in addition I went in person to some of the principal centres of Catholic gossip and corrected false reports by a simple statement of the not very sensational truth—namely that I was under no sort of inhibition save a qualified restriction as to retreats the reason of which had never been given to me; that as to writing, whatever difficulties had arisen from my article "A Perverted Devotion" had been long since adjusted & that I enjoyed now the same freedom as any other Jesuit. Preparatory to such a statement I wrote, for the first time in all these troubles, to Fr. Meyer to ask whether His Paternity felt bound to give me a reason for a restriction which in the case of one, like myself, often asked for retreats, could not fail to give rise to grave defamation of my priestly reputation. In reply I was told that "certain" persons had complained of "certain" things, but I was not told *what* things, so that I could judge of the truth of the delations, or defend myself, or amend my ways if necessary. This is gross & indefensible injustice and deserves no mercy. His Paternity also implied, what you say more explicitly, namely, that there was no general prohibition in the matter. Why then was not this made plain from the first? Surely I made it clear enough to you & Fr. Gerard that it was the existence of such a general prohibition, on no assigned reason & with no opportunity of self-defense, that made my relation to the Society one of irreconcilable hostility! It was as inconsistent with such a prohibition, which I am now told, was non-existent, that I refused all spiritual work of a like nature. I had rather fancied that home authorities were more friendly to me than foreign, & had tempered the severity of His Paternity's judgment. It seems now to have been just the contrary—so little can one understand or follow these crooked methods of government by secret delation! Frankly, I never liked giving retreats or preaching; and now, least of all since I have learnt how slanderous delation is encouraged & protected by His Paternity. Still, I think you owe it to my reputation to appoint me to give some one, more or less public retreat which may be well advertised, and I on my part will engage to back out at the last moment, as I did with regard to the sermon the other Sunday. His Paternity is naturally alarmed, not having a presentable case, because I said, what is undeniable, that no authority, civil or ecclesiastical has any right to stand between me & my good name. He even uttered some vague threat of pains and penalties as though the Society could give or take aught that I cared about. I have no thought of overt "rebellion"—as you call it; and every wish for peace within the limits of principle; though I can never belong to the Society internally in the light of my disillusionment as to every qualification which attracted me to her. If however, I am *forced* out I will justify myself openly & before all. I have no sympathy, nothing but contempt, for the vulgar attacks on the Society made by those who know not what they say; but if I have to choose between hurting the Society & hurting those who have trusted me & stood by me, there can [be] no question as to the issue of my choice. For God's sake do what you can to prevent such an issue; for if I have to write about the Society I think my words will live & burn.

And now let me say how much I resent what is said now by some big men in the Province; that the recent exodus of scholastics[29] is traceable to my baleful influence. Of the last nine or ten who left only two were even in communication with me by word or letter. Of the rest I knew nothing save by hearsay. Poor Thorp had been allowed to pass through his noviceship & take his vows in defiance of our Constitutions with bad habits still upon him, in which he was persevering when, somewhere in '94-5, he fell into my hands; and after great difficulty I broke him from the habit altogether. He left the Society not while under my influence, but after I had broken off all intercourse with scholastics feeling myself no longer a trusted member of the Society. From Jan. 1900 I had nothing to do with him. With H. Gardner I had very little to do. I believe he admired me & misquoted me, as young men will, in defence of his many erratic opinions. He left for faults that should have been evident to his novice-master. I always wanted him to leave; tho' at the last, as he had stayed so long & also foolishly wanted to stay, I told him not to *ask* for dismissal but to wait till he was sent away. Stapleton wrote to me once or twice about his moral difficulties, but I never knew him further. Smith, Lickert, Brand I had absolutely nothing to do with; perhaps they might have stayed if I had—for I know why they went. For I have unfortunately had a sinister experience of the moral state of our Scholastics.

When I entered the Society & till I was a priest I believed at least in the Society's repute for purity; but that last illusion is shattered beyond hope. The cynical indifference of superiors to the souls of the unfortunate boys they have entrapped into vows—made in substantial ignorance; the old-womanish folly & blundering of novice-masters, the incompetence of the spiritual fathers who are selected merely as unfit for anything else (e.g. Fr. Parkinson, Fr. Sheagh, Fr. Martyn Parker etc.) are no doubt answerable for the lamentable sepulchre full of dead men's bones. And then I am told it is I who have taught these young men sodomy & self-abuse! And as for the unfortunate lay-brothers who cares about them otherwise than about servants? I wonder how much the empty formality of manifestation[30] has taught you as to their state; or whether you suspect that those who say least have most to say? It is because I know these things through the confidence of the wretched boys themselves and have tried wherever I could, to help them out of the mire into which their spiritual guides had suffered them to sink, that I cannot but burn against the injustice of such things as are said about me by Fr. J. Brown & Fr. J. Rickaby in their desire to destroy an influence of which they were jealous. God will judge them; but meantime let them take care that their words do not reach my ears in any indictable form. It is hard for you to whom the Society is as divine as the Church, to imagine that I can enjoy perfect spiritual peace under her disfavour. Yet so it is; nor does it ever cross my mind for a moment to identify His Paternity with God—else I should soon be an atheist. Still no internal frailities [*sic*] or corruptions to which all human institutions are liable, can alter my faith in the great ideals & principles of S. Ignatius or make me cease to regret that things are as they are; & that I have to live alone—as it were a lodger in my own house. I would ask you to leave me in the Catalogue at Farm Street, as it will enable me to deny the report that I have been banished from London. Also, I should like to come South for a weekend four or five times in the year (my friends will stand the expense)

to allay gossip & to attend the meetings of the Synthetic Society if
they should be resumed this year.

Ever yours faithfully
G. TYRRELL, SJ[31]

"So there is the whole drama in a nut shell," Tyrrell wrote to Bremond after digesting it for him. "And the moral is: when dealing
with cowards you must growl & show your teeth. This also I have
learnt *à l'ecole de Jack*."[32]

In reply to that onslaught, on 4 December 1901 Colley invited
Tyrrell to preach the ordination retreat for the diocesan clergy at
Oscott the following Lent.[33] Tyrrell accepted, but he told Colley
that any further retreat work or nonprinted utterances he would
undertake only as an occasional exception, "as may be necessary to
repress gossip and sinister interpretations of my inactivity."[34] He
added that he expected Mgr. Henry Parkinson, rector of St. Mary's
College, Oscott, and some of the bishops to object. But Colley assured him that Monsignor Parkinson "thinks there is no one who
would be more cordially welcomed as your [books?] are in great
demand among the students."[35] Tyrrell seems indeed to have been
highly regarded, not only among seminary students but among faculty members as well, at least to judge by what one professor reported to Wilfrid Ward concerning the opinion of colleagues at
another seminary. In their view Tyrrell was the only writer who
could interest the students in theology, since apart from him "the
general attitude is fear of thinking *at all* on dogma, and consequently a total want of interest in it. . . . If Tyrrell were generally
suspect it would be a most serious thing for the young theologians
and priests."[36] Eventually, however, Tyrrell declined to give the retreat because, he told Bremond, "I am too feeble physically; more,
because I find I am a *signum contradictionis* there & that every
word would be subjected to a theological microscope."[37]

THE TYRRELL-VAUGHAN-COLLEY EXCHANGE:
THE FATE OF *OIL AND WINE*

There the matter rested. From this time on Tyrrell never altered
his position on the Society of Jesus and its Jesuitism. He suspended
correspondence with his Roman superiors until February 1904,
when he opened the negotiations that would end in his dismissal
two years later. But those events go beyond the scope of this study,

and our concern must return to the postscript of the *Oil and Wine* affair.[38]

The fate of *Oil and Wine* was actually determined long before it became tainted by being linked to "The Relation of Theology to Devotion." That article had just been reprinted in *The Faith of the Millions* with Cardinal Vaughan's *imprimatur* given on the trust of Jesuit censors. When those volumes appeared, Tyrrell wrote forebodingly to von Hügel, "My new vols . . . have been very well received & reviewed; though I hardly doubt they will be denounced eventually on account of 'Theology & Devotion' which my censors were too obtuse to understand in all its profound malignity."[39]

In fairness to the censors' capacity to understand, it should be remembered that they were always under pressure either directly from Tyrrell or indirectly from him through his superiors—Gerard in the case of *The Faith of the Millions* and Colley in the case of *Oil and Wine*—who were trying hard on the one hand to appease Tyrrell and accommodate him to a system from which he was totally disaffected, and on the other hand to prevent a scandal. And now, although most reviewers were indeed favorable toward *The Faith of the Millions,* one at least detected the underlying "profound malignity" and called it "Liberalism Again."

That review appeared unsigned as the lead article in the 7 November number of the *Church Review,*[40] a copy of which was found among Cardinal Vaughan's papers after his death.[41] So it is most probable that the cardinal had understood the import of his *imprimatur* being connected with liberalism and rued his decision, especially in view of the recent Mivart affair and the joint pastoral. Next time he was not going to trust Jesuit censors. Accordingly, when *Oil and Wine* appeared for the cardinal's *imprimatur,* he sent notice that one Jesuit censor would have to be replaced by one of his own men. "There is a new hitch about my wretched book," Tyrrell wrote Maude Petre on 12 December. "I have not yet decided what to do, but I don't see how anyone can blame me if I refuse to submit afresh to all the tedious annoyance of censorship."[42] A week later he wrote directly to Vaughan to that effect and asked for the new censor's name so that he might know what to expect. "If he names *Moyes* or *Gildea,*" Tyrrell wrote Petre, "I don't think I should go on."[43]

A few days later Tyrrell received a note from Colley saying that the cardinal had given as reason for his action the fact that "a passage in *The Faith of the Millions* had been found fault with, referring to Our Lord's nearness to us in the Blessed Sacrament."[44] Predictably, that passage occured in "The Relation of Theology to Devotion."[45]

This news angered Tyrrell and touched off a brief but heated exchange with Vaughan that, Tyrrell told Bremond on 31 December, ended "in a propitiatory note from him yesterday" and that would be eulogized in a new essay entitled "Rome's Opportunity." It would be composed "from a Gallio's standpoint" to show how the church was "playing straight into the hands of agnosticism. I shall treat the S.J. as the 'brain' of the Church & conclude: 'If the light that is in thee be darkness, how great must the darkness be!' My aim is, if possible, to alarm Rome."[46] More on this shortly, but first the end of the *Oil and Wine* affair.

If Tyrrell extracted a note of propitiation from the cardinal, he was a long way from extracting an *imprimatur*. The proofs of *Oil and Wine* finally rolled off the press and were in Vaughan's hands by the second week of March 1902. On 20 March Vaughan wrote to Tyrrell, "I read through the greater part of them; but found myself in such conscientious difficulties that I sent them to be revised by censorship in Rome."[47] And to Colley Vaughan wrote that he found the book "full of mischief—& inaccuracy—and calculated to do more harm than good."[48] But Vaughan would not act until he heard from Rome. Further, he informed Colley that Tyrrell had intimated alternative plans to publish if he were refused an *imprimatur*. Colley wrote at once to Tyrrell to forestall a possibly precipitous move. He expressed sympathy and regret about the cardinal's hesitation, but "we must wait patiently till he gets an answer from Rome and be ready to obey whatever is ordered. God will bless your work all the more for your patience & obedience in this matter."[49]

Rome replied with astonishing haste. Five days after Vaughan informed Tyrrell that he had sent the proofs, he returned Rome's judgment. Two of the censors were positively adverse and he was only waiting for the opinion of the third. He added that he trusted Tyrrell would "bear this trial with all the patience and humility that mark a great Christian character."[50]

Tyrrell answered on 25 March with a letter that Vaughan amazingly interpreted as an expression of loyalty and virtue. To one who knew Tyrrell it could only be interpreted as a duplicitous attempt to slight the cardinal and gain the upper hand:

MY LORD CARDINAL

Whatever the verdict of your Italian censor, it is plain to me on reflection that a book which puzzles Y[our]. E[minence]. will puzzle the average Catholic intelligence of this country. For this reason I will not publish it, but have given it as a present to my Anglican friend Mr Dolling on the understanding that if he should ever care to publish it for the benefit of Anglican readers it must be under his own name & with a preface to say that it has been repudiated by its anonymous author

I think I need say no more on the subject here & now

Your Eminence's Servt. In Xt
G. TYRRELL S.J.[51]

The next day, not suspecting what Tyrrell's provincial would immediately grasp, Vaughan enclosed this letter with a note to Colley: "You will be glad to see the enclosed—which please *return to me*."[52] And to Tyrrell he wrote, "I hasten to thank you for your note just received and to say that it fully justifies the high opinion which I have formed of your loyalty and virtue."[53] Colley consulted Gerard, to whom Tyrrell had already sent a copy of Vaughan's accolade.

"This is a beast of a case," Gerard replied to Colley. There could be no question of allowing vicarious publication of a work condemned by episcopal authority. But the principal awkwardness came from the cardinal's apparent sanction of Tyrrell's plot, so that now if it were to be stopped, Jesuit superiors would have to intervene and thus once again bear the whole odium of suppression. Gerard advised Colley to make sure the cardinal understood what was going on.[54] Colley spoke to the cardinal and at the same time advised Tyrrell not to let Dolling publish the book, as the true authorship would be detected at once, "and it wd never do for you even to connive at the publication of a book written by you wh. authority has decided to be likely to do harm rather than good."[55] What was making Gerard and Colley extremely nervous was not so much the publication of a book that the cardinal found questionable (yet apparently publishable under Dolling's cover), but that Roman ecclesiastical officials had condemned.

On the question of harm, Tyrrell answered Colley that Catholics would have no business with a book published under Protestant editorship, and Protestants could not suppose it to represent authorized Catholic teaching. "Indeed it will instruct the latter to see what Catholics may *not* say." And as to *objective* harm, he suggested recalling that the book had been passed by Jesuit censors, "who are at least as good judges as any three anonymous foreigners." Besides, he had given the book to Dolling unconditionally, and if trouble were made, he would ask Dolling to publish an ac-

count of the whole transaction—"for the truth is always less scandalous than its palliations. For this end I have kept copies of the
whole correspondence from first to last."[56] Tyrrell sent this letter
on 2 April.

On the same day Dolling wrote to Tyrrell to say that Colley had
just been to see him and convinced him that "for the sake of the
Society the book must not be published at once . . . , but I take
the book and I put it away for three years."[57] Under Gerard's direction, Colley asked Tyrrell to explain to Dolling that their agreement was from the first out of order, that superiors who were not
consulted could not now be expected to sanction it, and that the
cardinal did not want the book published, even anonymously, despite his letter to Tyrrell.[58] Tyrrell simply forwarded Colley's letter
to Dolling and left the final decision up to him. Dolling honored
Colley's request, and *Oil and Wine* was not printed for public circulation until April 1906—after Tyrrell had been dismissed from
the Society of Jesus. However, during 1902 Tyrrell had up to two
hundred copies printed and distributed privately at his own
expense.[59]

The result of this whole affair was that Tyrrell's self-image as a
Roman Catholic theologian was dealt a critical blow. He concluded that, at least as far as church officials were concerned, he
could no longer be regarded as an authorized exponent of Catholicism. But if that were the case in England and Rome, it was not the
case elsewhere, and he would continue working underground. It
was a momentary setback, and Tyrrell paused only long enough to
take stock.

On 3 April Tyrrell was ready for another confrontation. On that
date he wrote Maude Petre that his posing as an authorized exponent of Catholicism had all along made him dimly aware of dishonesty, "of 'special pleading' for a cause that neither asked nor liked
my services." But now that he saw the situation as it was, he felt
much at rest. "If I see my way to staying on as a priest & Jesuit I
can still work anonymously; & at present I don't see why I need
move."[60] All that was now needed was to clean the slate, honestly
state the premises of those involved, and consistently follow them
out.

Accordingly Tyrrell wrote to Colley to inform him that he
would prepare a work that would undo the harm his past writings
may have done in putting Catholicism in a false light. But perhaps
a more efficacious means would be to get Rome to condemn all his
past writings. That action could be easily arranged, and he would
not find it hard to recognize "the external rights of the present

Church-government to have its own way & to run the ship on the rocks if it chooses."[61] At the same time he wrote to Vaughan and offered to repudiate all his past writings, since all the points censured in *Oil and Wine*, "with one trifling exception," could be found over and over again in his other works, not merely under Vaughan's *imprimatur* but under strong eulogies in his own hand.[62] To the many Anglicans who had "been deceived through regarding me as a worthy exponent of Catholicism," he told Vaughan, and to the many Catholics who had been kept in the church by his books, it would only be consistent and fair to withdraw them and publish his reasons.[63]

Vaughan did not think much of Tyrrell's proposal and replied through Colley that it was not to be thought of, as it would give great scandal. Tyrrell was not disappointed. He had only made the proposal as a point of debate to embarrass his opponents with their inconsistency. "I think they will leave me alone another time," he wrote to von Hügel on 12 April, "but of course this double censorship, which H [is]. E [minence]. will now always insist upon makes it impossible to publish under my own name."[64]

"ROME'S OPPORTUNITY":
PRELUDE TO *THE CHURCH AND THE FUTURE*

The work that Tyrrell told Colley he would now set about to prepare is undoubtedly what appeared one year later as *The Church and the Future*. That book is an outgrowth of the essay "Rome's Opportunity," which Tyrrell composed toward the end of 1901 and revised during the early part of 1902 but never published. The importance of this work therefore hinges on the importance of *The Church and the Future*, and it is as illuminative of the latter that it now deserves attention.

"Rome's Opportunity" was left in rough typescript in the hands of Katherine (Kitty) Clutton, niece of Maude Petre and a zealous admirer of Tyrrell. On the folder in which Clutton kept the typescript, she had written:

> *very very private—*
>   G.T. gave me this before the row started. T. sat down and faced the whole difficulty. I first woke up to the position by hearing the talk of two seminarians my brother & WJ Williams. They were extra intelligent.
>   Do keep it to yourself or I shall feel I am doing what Bishop Amigo told my sailor brother G.T. had done. "Delivered over the fleet

to the enemy" by his criticism of "Pascendi." G.T.'s comment on this was "Perhaps I only pointed out to them that this was what *they* had done."[65]

First mention of this essay was made in a letter to Bremond of 31 December 1901. In it Tyrrell said he was writing an essay *in memoriam* of his mortal struggle with Cardinal Vaughan and the Jesuits over censorship of *Oil and Wine*. A month later he gave Bremond the gist of that essay but said "it would be suicide to publish it in its present form" as G.T. was

> writ large over every page. . . . I will however expand it, for its own sake & for the sake of a few readers who will not be scandalised. You shall see it sooner or later. Oddly enough, as the present system tumbles daily into greater ruin, I seem to see clearer vistas of a possible reconstruction, through the rents of its walls. Perhaps, like her Master, the Church must die and rise again. To human view, the gates of Hell prevailed against Him on Calvary & the disciple said: *Actum est,* as they will say when some critical Longinus shall thrust his spear into the heart of the Gospel.[66]

Tyrrell's essay began in the same prophetic-apocalyptic key. He saw the Gospel's description of the last days realized to a degree in "those recurrent periods of transition when an old world with its old order of things breaks up and gives place to a new heaven and a new earth."[67] The modern world with its crumbling faith, Tyrrell asserted, was in such a stage. But where, he asked, could one look for hope in rebuilding the faith? The Eastern churches have stagnated in their original doctrinal formulations, and as state religions their sole aim is conservative rather than progressive. What holds them together is external support. Remove that support and they would fall in a heap before the onrush of modern ideas. As to mainline Protestantism, its essential spirit of denial of any final authority outside of scripture has resulted in the gradual destruction of the old Catholic tradition without provision for a substitute that could Christianize nations as in the past or keep them Christianized in the future. Protestantism has sped off in the direction of liberal individualism, Romanism in the direction of authoritarianism. Anglicanism alone sees the difficulty and struggles for a workable synthesis. But having cut itself off from its roots, it is losing strength and bleeding to death.

Looking at all representatives of Christianity and seeing their essential strengths and failures, Tyrrell argued that it was still impossible not to feel that the fate of Christianity was largely bound up with the fate of the Church of Rome, the mother and mistress of European Christianity from whom Protestantism itself sprang. This conviction made it critically important to examine the current failure of the Roman Church to see what grounds there might be for believing that Rome was playing straight into the hands of agnosticism and reverting to tactics that led to the breakup of Western Christianity in the sixteenth century and were today preparing for a similar disaster in relation to the modern world.

The root evil operating in the Roman Church today, Tyrrell averred, was the same as that which led the church from the Renaissance on to regard every opposition as rebellion and to drive the critical spirit from her midst as an implacable enemy, instead of keeping it as a friendly ally to play a legitimate and necessary role. Had the Roman Church believed what she always says "from the teeth outward—that religion has nothing to fear from facts . . . Christianity might not be so imperilled as it seems, and that though Rome might be slightly protestantized, Protestantism had never existed."[68]

Tyrrell called that root evil "protectionism," by which he meant simply that legitimate element of protection needed to some degree in every stage of life perverted into an end rather than a means. The Roman Church is supposed to be a school for religious development after the pattern of Jesus Christ, but, dominated by the spirit of protectionism, she warns her charges away from every symptom of spontaneity or originality and thus hampers growth toward self-movement and mature independence. The result is a decay and paralysis of those very faculties that Christianity purports to develop. She has become a school of crippled souls rather than a school of saints. There are, of course, many saints in the Roman Church, but they do not justify the system. Saints are what they are in spite of the system. One must look to the average product for validation.

Where does this spirit of protectionism come from? Tyrrell asked. Not from any sort of deliberate and reflex consciousness on the part of authorities, for they have been reared in it and are now psychologically incapable of conceiving any other mode of operation. Today "it has all the blind strength of world-wide and ancient tradition—a sort of *Kirche[n]geist*" propagated and prolonged by clerical class-interest whose self-interest makes the hierarchy instinctively hostile to every movement of self-helpfulness on the part of the laity.[69]

But the church's power over the laity is increasingly weakened by the conditions of modern life, so that today one can see protectionism best in the spiritual education of the clergy where Rome has it all her own way. Candidates are recruited from fully protected convent schools and thrust immediately into seminaries where the sum total of character building consists in maintaining ignorance of evil, negative innocence, and practices of piety. Their sole mental preparation consists in an external grasp of the formulated orthodoxy of the catechism, wherein alien beliefs are treated with blinkered scorn and bigotry. Then, armed with wet "squibbs and crackers," they march out against the invading hordes. Occasionally an intelligent priest is impressed by the ineffectualness of these weapons and finds himself hard pressed to justify a system that so arms her clergy, but he has a faith in the faith of others, which makes him diffident of his own criticism. Hence "we find Romanists individually open to conviction and reason, but corporately intractable and obstinate."[70]

While the laity becomes more and more independent from the convent schools and in consequence more and more exposed to modern ideas, the clergy continue in their isolation to develop a theology in the jargon of another era that has no vital connection with the thought system of today, no passages or bridges connecting it with other departments of human interest. "Roman Catholic theology stands in the world of present-day thought like a well-preserved ruin in the midst of London—the dead in the midst of the living."[71] So an ever-widening breach forms between the laity and their clergy.

Nothing, Tyrrell continued, would contribute more to an even wider breach than the education of women. Previously they were "the natural guardians of religious tradition among the laity, and in virtue of their mental incapacity, the strongest conservative influence. . . . As long as the *tabula rasa* of the female mind offered its blank surface to the priestly scribe," religion was safe. "But if mothers begin to perceive that the priest is not educated, their children will not be taught to look up to him as an oracle of superterrestrial wisdom or to interpret his obscurities as proof of his sublimity or profundity."[72]

A further cause of schism between clergy and laity is the exclusion of the latter from their rightful participation in the work of the church and the limiting of their role to subscriptions of obedience. Indifference to the fate of ecclesiasticism is a foregone conclusion of noninvolvement.

The chief patron of this "disease of which the Roman Communion is perishing," Tyrrell charged, is the Jesuit order whose Gregorian University in Rome, governed by a *ratio studiorum* that has remained substantially unaltered since the sixteenth century, is taken as the model for all seminaries.[73] The philosophical manuals produced at Stonyhurst College, for example, are simply "the results of a frantically Quixotic effort to make the Sun not merely stand still, but go backwards to the days that gave birth to the *Ratio Studiorum*." For the whole aim is "to show that all that is good in modern philosophy was anticipated in the Middle Ages," and thus "that there has been no true progress since the protective hand of Rome was shaken off."[74]

Such prophylaxis is a vain attempt to maintain an artificial environment. It may prevent the decay of a live one. Moreover it can be effective only so far as it can be kept up always and everywhere; otherwise it does nothing but prepare for disaster. Should a ray of light break through and chance to fall upon a mind that, though intelligent, has been embalmed with nothing but medieval thought and categories, it crumbles to dust. If this be the case among Jesuits, if they who are the eye of the whole Roman body are in darkness, how great must the darkness be!

Efforts must be directed to cultivating a vitality that can adapt itself to every environment. But in this effort one cannot expect help from Romanism. Many have been fooled into thinking so by Rome's apparent stability over against the rapid disintegration of other denominations. But one must know whether that stability is "the immobility of vital resistance or the rigidity of a corpse." To most all that is apparent is that "whereas other creeds crumble under the touch of criticism Rome goes on her way as it were blind, deaf and insensible to the very existence of criticism, and that in this she is but logical, once her claim to infallibility be allowed." But in fact "it is by default and through the exhaustion of her rivals, that she seems to stand out as the sole surviving heir of historical Christianity."[75]

If, however, historical criticism sobers up and does its work and undeniable facts become commonly accepted by non-Romans, Rome herself will have no future except as transformed into something that is no longer Romanism. At present there is no answer to the problem that Anglicanism sees and attempts vainly to solve, namely a flexible embodiment for the spirit of Christ. The best hope lies "in the honest and fearlessly scientific criticisms of the Church's history from first to last."[76]

Up to now Rome has been more responsible than anything else for the disruption of Christendom, and so the responsibility falls on her more than on others to hasten the day of reunion by recognizing and correcting the errors of her method. But if she tries to defer that day by piling up her vain barriers, the tidal forces of religious life and progress will in the end burst through and destroy her because "in this her day she did not know the things that belong to her peace, and did not use her unique opportunity."[77]

Born of bickering over excessive censorship, "Rome's Opportunity" was the child of the very system it condemned, namely, protectionism. As such it did not rise above that system but only pointed out what was wrong with it. It was the black surface over which Tyrrell laid *The Church and the Future*, his positive restatement of Catholicism based on his own liberal instincts, reflection, and study of historico-critical sources. But it will not do to proceed with that side of Tyrrell's apologetic before looking at the parallel development of his philosophy of religion, for it was on this that his restatement of Catholicism rested.

CHAPTER 6

Tyrrell's Philosophy of Religion

PROPAEDEUTIC TO "ENGELS"

Tyrrell's first elaborate yet tentative statement of his philosophy of religion was printed in early July 1902 for private circulation under the title *Religion as a Factor of Life* and the pseudonym "Dr. Ernest Engels."[1] It appeared in red paper covers, a color Tyrrell thought "rather appropriate to the dangerous character of the booklet." Concerning the pseudonym, Tyrrell explained to his agent, A. R. Waller, that a foreign name would really throw the hounds off the trail, and if later he could get an American to publish it "with corrected spellings . . . a German-Americanist would be a fairly workable scapegoat."[2]

"Engels" was an attempt to locate the essence of religion in the will rather than in the intellect and thereby to lift religion above the passing storms of critical argument. It was a hybrid of all that Tyrrell had been reading—largely under von Hügel's direction—following the censure for "A Perverted Devotion" and "The Relation of Theology to Devotion." On 3 January 1902 Tyrrell wrote to von Hügel that he should not expect to find in this "imperfect essay at a synthesis . . . anything that I have not derived from you directly or indirectly—saving blunders and paralogisms."[3] And three months later: "My theory is an amalgam of Loisy, Blondel, Munsterberg [*sic*], Eucken, etc.—nothing being my own but the amalgamation; someday you shall read it—for your sins."[4]

As von Hügel's lifework was in the direction of mysticism, most of the authors he recommended to Tyrrell were in service of that same interest. They all in one way or another advanced the view that knowledge of ultimate reality is attainable not through the intellect but through intuition, a power that involves all faculties simultaneously. Thought and conceptual expression are only a more or less faithful representation of reality, a practical emolument of human nature enabling one to engage the physical environment. True human nature is expressed in the vocation to grow morally toward an increasingly intimate will-sympathy (love) with fellow humans and ultimately with God, while thought and its expression are subordinate and instrumental to that end.

The following account of the development of Tyrrell's philosophy of religion returns to the beginning of 1900. As it unfolds, sight must not be lost of all that was said in the preceding chapters concerning that development and the concurrent storms that embroiled Tyrrell in endless controversy and resulted in his polemical apologetic. Otherwise a significant aspect of Tyrrell's personality would be missed, namely, his astonishing capacity to distance himself from emotionally involving conflicts and to plunge himself quite regularly into the wholly other realm of philosophical and theological reflection.

Taken for granted as bedrock for Tyrrell's philosophy of religion is the perduring influence of Thomas Aquinas and John Henry Newman. What interests here is the galaxy of modern scholars and spiritual writers who figured in Tyrrell's reeducation and moved him to attempt a restatement of traditional philosophy and theology that would do justice to post-Enlightenment thought. For convenience and manageability, Tyrrell's galaxy may be divided into greater and lesser lights, the latter being those who interested Tyrrell briefly and helped fill out what he gathered from the former.

Lesser Lights: Arnold, Juliana of Norwich, Récéjac

It is not practical or particularly helpful to analyze all the minor influences on Tyrrell, but from his correspondence it is possible at least to discover which authors Tyrrell was reading and the drift of their influence.

One such figure, whom some would classify as a major influence, was Matthew Arnold. Tyrrell had read Arnold as early as 20 July 1899, for, in a letter of that date to Bremond, Tyrrell described the roots of his faith in terms straight out of Arnold's *Literature and Dogma:* "As for my faith, so far as it must necessarily be rooted in some kind of experience and not merely in propositions and principles accepted on hearsay, it rests upon the evidence of a Power in myself and in all men 'making for righteousness' in spite of all our downward tendencies."[5] Bremond thought Arnold's influence on Tyrrell so great that he told Loisy that fully one-third of Tyrrell's ideas could be found in *Literature and Dogma.*[6]

Bremond exaggerates here, but that Tyrrell found Arnold's thought congenial is readily attested to by the numerous references and allusions in Tyrrell's publications subsequent to 1900. Alec Vidler plays down the significance of these references. He notes that they are "critical, and do not express any consciousness of indebtedness on Tyrrell's part."[7] But perhaps he has overlooked Tyrrell's indicative little preface to Amédée de Margerie's *Saint Francis de Sales,* published by Duckworth in 1900.[8] Tyrrell certainly did criticize Arnold's vague liberalism, just as he criticized Adolf von Harnack and Auguste Sabatier,[9] but he endorsed Arnold's premise that religion is concerned primarily with life and conduct and is based on experience. Along with this premise he admired Arnold's antipathy to rationalism in religion, his insistence on the inadequate, analogous, and nonscientific character of religious affirmations and on the falseness of the common antithesis between natural and revealed religion, and his abandonment of the attempt to prove the truth of Christianity from prophecies and miracles.

In the preface to *Saint Francis de Sales,* Tyrrell singled out Francis as the embodiment of several of these themes. They also fitted neatly what von Hügel was passing on from Eucken. Francis, Tyrrell observed, was a person who had found religion in life and whose life was religious, a person who had roundly integrated all his faculties, not exaggerating one over the other—"or, to revert to Matthew Arnold's idea, in him the interests of Hebraism and Hellenism were reconciled in a way that had seemed impossible in ruder times." Francis self-consciously pursued this integration on the basis of the principle of action and thereon founded his order. Not that he wanted a purely active order. Rather, his uniqueness lay in subordinating action to contemplation, not merely as a rest or diversion "but as a direct means or instrument both for forming the soul by securing the healthful balance of its faculties, as well as for feeding its thought and love with the fuel of experience and information."[10]

Von Hügel recognized in this preface the effect of his encouragement on Tyrrell and heavily scored his proof copy. On 4 March

1900 he wrote from Rome, "Then the St. Francis of S. pleased me too so much—with its doctrine of perfection having to be sought in the proportional development of all the faculties of the soul."[11] In the same letter von Hügel expressed appreciation also for a copy of the first of what he hoped would be a lengthy series of articles by Tyrrell on Juliana of Norwich and her *Sixteen Revelations*, which was then rapidly gaining popularity.[12] The series, however, stopped short at two. The first appeared in the *Month* for January 1900, the second followed in March.[13] It is not without significance that, as Tyrrell had selected "A Change of Tactics" with the new title, "A More Excellent Way," for the lead article of volume 1 of *The Faith of the Millions*,[14] his choice to introduce volume 2 was the combined article entitled "Juliana of Norwich." One would underestimate Tyrrell if one did not at least consider the possibility that by so pairing these articles he meant to imply that the mystical way of Juliana was in fact a more excellent way of integrating what rationalism had torn asunder.

Tyrrell's appropriation and interpretation of Juliana's *Revelations* as the authentic way to truth was embryonic of what later developed into his theory of knowledge in *Religion as a Factor of Life*. According to Tyrrell, what was important for Juliana was "the light of wisdom" born not of rational argument or conceptual knowledge but of contemplation. She had a prescription for the modern mind against "the evil of our own day, when to be passably well-informed so taxes our time and energy as to leave us no leisure for assimilating the knowledge with which we have stuffed ourselves."[15] In her own fourteenth-century way she faced and solved the apparent discord between the truths of faith and the facts of daily living by appealing to "revelations," or insight received in contemplation. But, Tyrrell suggested, what she called "revelations" are what we mean today by "inspiration," for "revelation" implies some form of conscious communication or control of one mind by another and "inspiration" implies the conscious control of one will by another will. And for Tyrrell Juliana's "revelations" had much more to do with the will than with the mind.[16]

There is, of course, an intimate relationship between the will and the mind, Tyrrell explained, between Juliana's will-stimulated "inspirations" and the concepts in which she formulated them. In the ordinary mind-will interaction, the will naturally inclines toward what reason presents to it as good, that is, as in accord with the divine will. But in the extraordinary process—and this notion is a commonplace of mystical theology—God who created the will can bypass the medium of knowledge and work directly on the human will, inclining it toward will-sympathy with the divine will "without violating that liberty of choice (which no inclination can prejudice)."[17]

Tyrrell suggested, however, that the latter process might not be as extraordinary as is commonly thought, and indeed it might be the ordinary process. Possibly this process underlies what is referred to as "instinct" and indicates the true path of life-knowledge. For in the case of instincts, whether animal or spiritual, it seems that the craving for satisfaction precedes any clear idea of the satisfying object. The mind, for example, craves a unified experience, and this craving initiates the mental groping for such ideas as will satisfy the craving. Parallel to this, man's natural religious instinct seeks interpretations in the various manmade religions of the race and finds itself satisfied and transcended by the Christian revelation. Thus in the case of instincts, "we find will-movements not caused by the subject's own cognitions and perceptions, but contrariwise, giving birth to cognition, setting the mind to work to interpret the said movements, and to seek out their satisfying objects."[18]

Tyrrell found support for his interpretation in Ignatius of Loyola's method of discerning God's will. "St. Ignatius almost invariably speaks, not, as we should, of thoughts that give rise to will-states of 'consolation' or 'desolation,' but conversely, of these will-states giving rise to congruous thoughts." The mind is "magnetized by even our physical states of elation or depression, to select the more cheerful or the gloomier" thoughts "according as we are under one influence or the other," and by a sort of inductive process, the subject eventually settles upon a rationally conceived course of action because on the whole he feels at peace with that decision.[19] Ignatius was convinced that such a feeling would be incompatible with a decision not in accord with God's will, which, Tyrrell held, is communicated directly through conscience. But whatever the revelation, of which the will-states of consolation and desolation are indicators, Tyrrell concluded that the attempt to express it in the conceptual framework of language and imagery can yield only inadequate results.

In that same letter of 4 March, von Hügel suggested more food for Tyrrell's thought: Jérôme-Édouard Récéjac's *Fondements de la connaissance mystique.*[20] The baron had not yet read the book himself—it was not unusual for him to recommend books he had only glanced at—but he noticed that Récéjac tried to present mystical "visions (of a spiritually enlightening and moving kind) to be both true and divine *and* simply interior, mental,—which seems to me to get this important matter exactly right."[21] He was referring to Récéjac's opinion that a person at the peak of mystical activity consciously senses a being at once *excessive* (in the twofold sense of overwhelming and exterior) and *identical* with the self; that is, a being "exterior" enough to be God, yet interior enough to be self.[22] Récéjac also defined mysticism as the tendency to draw near to the Absolute morally and by the use of symbols, an idea proposed by Kant, adopted by Blondel, and echoed in Tyrrell's writings on ethics and in *Religion as a Factor of Life.*[23]

Tyrrell responded to von Hügel on 10 March 1900 that he had not yet seen Récéjac's book but was reading Paul Lejeune's *Vie mystique.*[24] He complained that the irritation caused by his quarrels with authorities "untunes me & throws me out of sympathy with what is after all the only satisfying side of religion."[25] It was more than a year before Tyrrell got around to Récéjac, but he was delighted with what he found. On 3 April 1901 he wrote to Maude Petre:

> He is with me in finding the divine and specifying element of our nature in disinterestedness; i.e., in our love of what does not concern us as separate units, but only as identified with the All which lives in us; in our desire for the *existence* of the good and the true and the fair— of the Kingdom of God, not as of something we want to have for ourselves but of something we want to exist, whether we exist or no to enjoy it. This is just what you find so inhuman in me or rather in my theory. Had I been Moses I don't think I should have felt not entering the Land of Promise one bit, so long as I knew that Israel would do so one day. I do not justify this, but I understand it; just as I could understand a man committing a mortal sin rather than that one dear to him should do so.[26]

This note of "disinterestedness" describes a puzzling, enigmatic side of Tyrrell's character. On the one hand, it explains how Tyrrell could identify with Moses, not out of a sense of self-sacrifice but out of utter disregard for his own fate. For Petre, it was this characteristic that made Tyrrell at once so attractive and so annoying; it also made him heedless of danger to himself.[27] Because he lacked self-regard, he was often unaware of the regard others had for him and the store they set by his words. "All my life," he told Petre, "I have been hurting people simply from not realising that they cared so much about me, or what I might say."[28]

On the other hand, Tyrrell himself suggested that disinterestedness lies at the heart of Christian faith, for in facilitating identification with the struggles of others through lack of self-regard it could allow one to become a slave to duty. And Tyrrell identified faith above all with *doing* what one conceived to be the will of God out of an unswerving sense of duty.[29] Hints of this idea have already been seen in various of his writings up to this point—for example, in *Oil and Wine*—but it will be explicitated in *Religion as a Factor of Life*.

Three years earlier Tyrrell would have attacked Récéjac from a narrowly orthodox position, just as he had attacked Auguste Sabatier.[30] But now he linked the two and drew both into his mediating cause. On 6 May 1901 he wrote to Petre, "Récéjac's book on mysticism . . . puts religion well out of reach of philosopho- & scientific attacks. Of course he is *nearly* A. Sabatier; but says much that *must* be noticed."[31]

Tyrrell's receptivity toward Récéjac and Sabatier comes as no surprise. Even in his orthodox period he felt the cogency of Sabatier's argument, and contact with it marked his first sympathetic leanings toward liberal Protestant views. Indeed, once Tyrrell declared himself in favor of the Kantian immanentism of Blondel and Laberthonnière, convergence toward the line of Sabatier as represented by Récéjac was a foregone conclusion. But as much as Tyrrell liked Sabatier's psychology of the origin and development of dogma and found it adaptable to a Catholic position, he never espoused Sabatier's radical subjectivity. Albert Houtin in *Histoire du modernisme catholique* maintained that Tyrrell's works "might be considered a reply to the work of Sabatier, but adapted to the mentality of those in the Catholic Church who acquired a taste and a desire for an external social bond, a liturgy of symbols, and above all for historical continuity."[32]

It could be enlightening to view Tyrrell's thought against the backdrop of Sabatier's, but one would have to do Tyrrell the justice of distinguishing his thought as carefully as he himself did from that radical subjectivity that would make dogma a wholly arbitrary symbol of divine mystery and truth. Tyrrell always felt that there was a very fine line between the objective, representative value of dogma and its purely symbolic character, and he always argued for divine guidance in the framing of dogma. But he was never satisfied with his own explanation of the complex interaction by which God and man cooperated in the process. He commented to that effect in a letter of 17 June 1901 to von Hügel. After admitting that Récéjac's theories of symbolism had rearoused the desire to write a treatise on materialism in religion, Tyrrell continued: "At present there is no *firm* line between those [various theories], with their somewhat sceptical consequences, & the admissions of S. Thomas as to the analogical character of our super-sensual conceptions. Yet one feels that there must be a difference. But the problem is so purely philosophical that I am afraid we must wait till the end of the world for its solution."[33] More on this presently.

Greater Lights: Loisy, Blondel, Eucken, Bergson

Tyrrell was not lying idly by from the time that Récéjac was first recommended to him until a year later when he finally got to the book. The time rescued from squabbles with church officials and from writing he spent in a thorough study of Blondel's *L'Action*, Bergson's *Essai sur les données immédiates de la conscience* and *Matière et mémoire*, as well as essays by Loisy and Eucken. All of these works, with the possible exception of *Matière et mémoire*, were, as usual, recommended by von Hügel.[34] But in mentioning again the baron's role in Tyrrell's reeducation, it ought not be over-emphasized. There is no question but that Tyrrell was flattered by the baron's attention and paid great heed, but at the same time he demonstrated a mind of his own. If most of what he read had been channeled to him by the baron, the catch was entirely Tyrrell's own.

High on Tyrrell's agenda for his Richmond leisure was to learn something about biblical criticism. Naturally he turned to the baron for advice. On 2 April 1900 Tyrrell asked, "What should I read of Loisy—short of everything?"[35] Von Hügel replied from Rome: "(1) 'Les Evangiles Synoptiques.' (2) The series of articles on Renan's 'Histoire du peuple d'Israel.' (3) The series on select passages of the 4th Gospel. (4) A series on points in the philosophy of Religion, appearing at this moment, under a pseudonym."[36] He promised to try to procure all of these for his friend, but at that time the baron was making his way back to England, so the actual transaction did not occur until 12 July, when Tyrrell visited him at Hampstead.[37]

On 26 July Tyrrell wrote Bremond that he had "just finished Loisy's studies on the Gospels and his still more admirable article on inspiration."[38] Fourteen months later he had completed, "with great refreshment," Loisy's expanded second edition of *Études bibliques*. He especially liked Loisy's "luminous treatment of the Fourth Gospel which," he quipped, "deserves the honour of the Index more than anything I have seen for a long time."[39] Finally, on 3 January 1902 Tyrrell reported to von Hügel that he had "carefully read & studied" Loisy's *Études bibliques*, his *Religion d'Israël*, and his article on Genesis and the Babylonian myths—"whence I draw the principle: Inspiration means the progressive spiritualising & refining of those gross embodiments in which man expresses his own ideas & sentiments about God."[40] It was this notion of inspiration that Tyrrell elaborated in his "Engels" book. He continued to read Loisy's works as they appeared, but only the ones read up to the early part of 1902 had any significant bearing on his philosophy of religion.

At the head of the list of those who influenced Tyrrell's philosophy of religion, both in content and formulation, would have to be placed Blondel, Bergson, and Eucken. Von Hügel had introduced Tyrrell to all three. As seen in chapter 3, Blondel's impact on Tyrrell was immediate and strong, but up to the middle of 1900 Tyrrell's knowledge of him came largely through Laberthonnière. In November 1899 the baron had promised Tyrrell a copy of *L'Action* to keep, but he went off to winter in Rome without having made good that promise. When he returned to Hampstead in the spring, he discovered the oversight and delivered the book on 12 July 1900.[41]

Tyrrell plunged into it almost at once. "I am attacking M. Blondel's 'L'Action'—the toughest task I ever encountered," he wrote to Petre on 15 August.[42] Three days later he sent Raffalovich his first impressions, the sum and substance of what "Engels" would soon say:

> What delights me is his analysis of the dilettante sceptical attitude of the modern who at once despises & tastes every dish on life's table. He shows that such a man in spite of his denial of any end in life, lives for an end; & cannot accept incoherence as the last word—cannot refuse to answer the "moral problem" in some way or other, tho' with his lips denying that there is such a problem, still more, that there is a findable answer to it. In fact the book is a splendid but miserably obscure apology for faith & mysticial religion. I must try to dress it up in English some way or other.[43]

Amidst the obscurity, he told Bremond, there were "pregnant & pithy sentences in nearly every page worth writing down & developing."[44]

By 7 September he had completed the first reading and announced his triumph to the baron:

> It has taken me three weeks, but surely it will repay thus to have opened the ground. I now see why the Baron de Retours [*sic*] accused me of being a reader of Blondel, for we seem, if I may say it without

arrogance, to reach most identical conclusions independently, and from most opposite approaches—a fact which vouches for the "naturalness" of those conclusions far more than had we followed the same methods. To put it more truly he reaches by a methodical research what I stumble on by luck, or, at best, by instinct. Hence it is a great strength to me to discover that I have been unconsciously talking philosophy.[45]

Tyrrell used "accused" ironically here, as the "accusation" was really a compliment paid by Baron J. Angot des Rotours in a recent review article of Tyrrell's essays.[46] Angot's "accusation" was to the point. Tyrrell's reading prior to the composition of *External Religion* consisted of several essays by Blondel and Laberthonnière— although in the above letter Tyrrell seems to be pleading total innocence of Blondel.

In the same letter Tyrrell expressed how regretful it was that "so epoch-making a book should be practically buried in the obscurity of its style" and thus kept from those who need it most, namely, the scholastics. It would do little good to translate *L'Action,* he said, but its substance could be turned into English "with transparent simplicity." "What will happen will be that middlemen like myself—literary jackals—will learn from him, and translating his thought to the multitude, will get credit for it, & so enter into his labours when he is forgotten." Tyrrell was itching to do a series of articles on *L'Action,* "but I must go over it & over it before even thinking of such a thing."[47]

But the *daimon* to write was upon Tyrrell. All he needed was an excuse. It soon presented itself in the form of a particularly "mischievous travesty of Blondel's position" in the *Pilot* for 20 October 1900.[48] Tyrrell was irked that the author had accused Blondel of being Kantian and abstract simply because he was not a raving Thomist. In a pseudonymous letter in the next issue of the *Pilot,* Tyrrell tried to explain that Blondel was original and therefore easily misinterpreted.[49] He was neither Kantian nor Thomist but aimed to reconcile Kantian idealism with Thomistic realism along with the endless conflict between natural science, ethics, and metaphysics by, in Blondel's words, shifting "the very center of philosophy . . . to action, because that is where the center of life is found." From the vantage point of "action" one can see that the seeming irreconcilables are simply the imperfect and heterogeneous aspects of the same reality that is the nexus of ethics and metaphysics. One need not—indeed must not—choose one or the other: ethics or metaphysics, speculative reason or practical reason, idealism or realism. As Blondel put it, the "Science of Action" shows that "idealism and realism are . . . equally worthless, one without the other, and equally foundations the one of the other."[50] But Blondel perturbs scholastics because in speaking to the modern mind he speaks in modern language.

Tyrrell took particular umbrage at the charge that Blondel was abstract, because he could not imagine anything being more abstract than scholastic categories and was in recent years increasingly irritated at their encroachment upon even liturgical worship over against the simplicity, immediacy, and concreteness of scriptural language.[51] Blondel's whole mission, Tyrrell pointed out, was to revolt against "a religion that worships God indirectly through the mediation of abstract ideas" and to seek God "directly with the true mystics, as a will, an action, a life, mingling with our own will, action, and life."[52] And if, as the reviewer admitted, "Blondel is to be classed at all with Newman, it is just because they are both essentially 'concrete' thinkers, conscious of the infinite inability of our mental conceptions to cope with the inexhaustible reality of the concrete."[53]

Blondel's theological dilemma, Tyrrell explained, arises no doubt from his overdependence on Augustine, whose writings spawned the *de auxiliis* controversy that, in turn, led to "refinements" of the meaning of "supernatural." For Blondel, as for Aquinas, the vision of God is a requirement of man's rational nature and is "supernatural" only in the sense that man's created faculties of themselves cannot attain it.[54] They have a natural aptitude for it, but God must give himself. Recent Roman theology, however, has limited the "supernatural" to what exceeds not only the faculties and powers of created nature but the very exigencies of nature.[55] But even here Blondel only *seems* to be in conflict, for to save Augustine and Aquinas certain Jesuits—"(and it is eventually with this Society M. Blondel must reckon)"—have devised a system that views man as having an exigency if not specifically for the present historical and "supernatural order" of adopted sonship in Christ, at least of some inferior substitute for it; so that if man were stripped of the supernatural altogether, he would be in an unnatural state. Or, as Tyrrell summed it up, man "has no right to the royal robes of adopted sonship, but he cannot go naked." Blondel's logic of action leads to the same conclusions: that is, not specifically to the Christian answer to man's natural craving but to a generically divine answer. It so happens that God's answer in Christ "meets the cravings of our nature not only abundantly but superabundantly, giving 'more than we desire or deserve.'"[56]

Here, in a word, is practically the whole of Tyrrell's understanding of Blondel, as well as the entire thrust of his own philosophy of religion. But as yet Tyrrell was insecure in his grasp of Blondel and wrote to von Hügel to explain that only the need for prompt action prevented his seeking the baron's advice before publishing the letter. "I only hope in trying to save him [Blondel] from his friends I have not myself misrepresented him in any way."[57]

The baron reassured Tyrrell by return that he had done Blondel "excellent service" in pointing out that Thomas, too, had taught that the exigencies of man's rational nature postulated supernatural grace, and by showing "how the abandonment of his most wholesome view of Ss. Augustine and Thomas has forced some of your people to construct a theory,—surely 'fearfully and wonderfully made.'" He went on to summarize a recent paper by a German whom he did not identify but who argued compellingly along Blondel's lines that scholastic natural theology "is the true and direct offspring of Greek intellectualism," that so far as it is demonstrable by reason it is a mere analogue of religion, but "that part which is real, actual religion, is conditioned at least as much by action and by grace as by the pure reason." The baron concluded with the strong plea "that a certain friend in the wilds of Yorkshire could make up his mind to master German! He wd. find this not so very hard, and wd. very soon find himself repaid a hundredfold!"[58]

On second reading, Tyrrell found Blondel much more luminous. But there were "one or two clues" that he had not yet uncovered, "and so," he wrote to von Hügel, "I lay it aside for some months that 'unconscious cerebration' may do its accustomed work." And again forgetting how much of Blondel had already seeped into his thought, he continued, "The enclosed extract from one of my last set of Oxford Conferences is curious as showing how I was groping after Blondel before I knew him.[59]

This comment was Tyrrell's last word on Blondel until April 1902, when he read "À propos de la certitude religieuse," a reply to Abbé E. Péchegut, a curé of Boissel, Tarn, published in *La Revue du clergé français* for 15 February 1902.[60] On 12 April Tyrrell wrote to tell the baron how delighted he was to find that Blondel's reply "fell in exactly with what I was at the time engaged upon—a study of religion as *a* factor of life."[61] "Engels" was largely completed by that time, but Tyrrell was able to place copious extracts from Blondel's "reply" into the lengthy notes at the end.

If von Hügel could not get Tyrrell to do battle at once with Rudolf Eucken and his German, he did manage to recruit Maude Petre and thereby draw Tyrrell to his side. In September 1900

Petre had gone to the Continent for a retreat and to attend the chapter meetings of her religious congregation. For reading material she brought along, "by Baron von Hügel's great desire," his favorite work of Rudolf Eucken, *Der Kampf um einen geistigen Lebensinhalt.*[62] "It is very hard," she noted in her diary for 10 September, "but I am gaining by it." For several months she struggled through the difficult German, aided by several letters and lengthy discussions with the baron. In her diary for 8 November she summarized one of their discussions in words that are fairly echoed by the title of "Engels." She noted that they had "discussed Eucken chiefly—and, above all, the point 'religion all? or one among other things?'" and that they were in fair agreement, "though he dips rather to one side, I to another; he giving more prominence to the independence of nature & science and the outside world—I seeking instinctively more unification."[63]

On 26 September von Hügel had sent Petre an extraordinarily long analysis of *Der Kampf* and specifically of Eucken's key concept of *Wesensbildung.*[64] Four days later he wrote to Tyrrell with invidious intent:

> Maude Petre has been giving me very great pleasure. She is evidently getting deeply into, and getting ever so much out of Eucken. How I wish you too could study him! I think you would find him perhaps as rich and certainly more uniformly lucid than, Blondel. And there is in E. the same deep seriousness, the same touching sense of God within us and around, of our mysterious being and responsibility, and of the sustaining solidarity of all humble, self-denying seeking after truth and goodness throughout the ages.[65]

Tyrrell replied that Petre had been giving him very great pleasure too: she "feeds me like a little bird with choice worms & flies from Eucken which I gulp down greedily & wish I could feed myself."[66] Petre had forwarded to Tyrrell the baron's long exposition along with an excerpt from *Der Kampf* that she had translated. On 16 November Tyrrell wrote to thank her for that and for "the Baron's wonderful letter."

> It is the best evidence I have seen [yet?] of the deep power of his mind. I shall keep it some time in order to appropriate its contents. I think I see Eucken's drift pretty clearly. I expect Wesensbildung is equivalently "soul-feeding," or the building up of our spiritual substance by voluntary acceptances of materials in the way of light & good impulse offered us by God—much as a caddis-worm builds its house. These materials are offered to us both by religion & by culture, whose relation is like that of man & wife in the Catholic *ideal*—equal-

ity, independent personality, complementariness, a certain priority of the husband; yet neither for the sake of the other *directly* but for the sake of the Whole, i.e., of the dual society which they constitute; & whose good is indirectly the good of each separately. The Whole of wh. E. speaks is, I think, the whole man the whole of human life which is a process of soul-feeding. This is only a rough first impression, an assimilation of his thought to my own.[67]

Tyrrell was tempted to try more Eucken, if he could find him in any digestible form. "Has Eucken, I wonder, been done into French in any form?" he asked the baron on 17 June 1901. "Your terrible German language stands as an iron barrier between me and all I should best like to read. But I might as well cry for the moon as hope for the leisure to master it."[68] But the baron would not be put off. "I really cannot resign myself, without protest, to your not mastering German," he replied on 6 August. Again he stooped to invidious comparison and described how he himself at the age of forty had mastered Hebrew and how Duchesne and Loisy had taught themselves English and German amidst pressing professional duties. He softened momentarily and promised to send the few items he could find that had been translated into English and French, but added, "Of course, all this . . . gives but a very partial and superficial idea of a mind, so delicate and deep, so sensitively religious so continuously growing both in insight and in power of expression. But it will be better than nothing."[69]

"The *Euckeniana* you promised me have not yet arrived," Tyrrell replied on 22 September. "I don't say this to hurry you; but in case they may have strayed in the post." Then, as if to appease: "I have actually *begun* German; but Oh! what a language! Hebrew seems a simple task in comparison."[70]

When the Euckeniana began to arrive shortly thereafter, Tyrrell found them not as clear in places as he had hoped but overall most enlightening. The essay on Hegel, he told Petre, was "most illuminative" and supportive of his own understanding in sections where he was most unsure of the meaning.[71] By 3 January 1902 Tyrrell had finished the article on Augustine and a little book by Smith on Eucken, called *Truth and Reality,* and reported to the baron that he was delighted especially with Eucken's estimate of Augustine. "From all I can at least gather E's general trend—perhaps better than I shall for years, be able to do by first-hand reading of him."[72]

Tyrrell was too modest. On 10 July 1902, eight months after he had taken up German in earnest, he reported to von Hügel that he had almost finished reading *Der Kampf,* a difficult book of exactly four hundred pages.[73] The baron could only have been pleased. By this time, however, *Religion as a Factor of Life* was already in print, so Eucken's influence on Tyrrell's philosophy of religion was only secondary and little more than a reinforcement of what he had already got from Blondel, namely, an emphasis on the whole of human life rather than on any one dominant faculty.

Parallel with his study of Blondel and Eucken, complementing and illuminating them, was Tyrrell's study of Henri Bergson. No one's philosophy could have been more suited to Tyrrell's current views. At first an apostle of Spencer's evolutionary theory, Bergson very early abandoned that philosophy as too narrow in its conception of man and the world and converted to the metaphysico-spiritualistist tradition of Maine de Biran and Félix Ravaisson. Tyrrell had read the first three of Bergson's principal works: *Essai sur les données immédiates de la conscience, Matière et mémoire,* and *L'Évolution créatrice,* the first two prior to the publication of *Religion as a Factor of Life.*[74]

Bergson's philosophy constitutes an assault on most of the "isms" of his day, and a defense of all that would appeal to Tyrrell: spirit *versus* materialism, intuition *versus* rationalism, freedom *versus* determinism, creativity *versus* mechanism, and philosophy *versus* scientism. Taking "intuition of duration" as a starting point, Bergson elaborated an original, exhaustive, and convincing critique of science in which he showed why science does not and cannot give a true picture of life or of reality as a whole. For Bergson, "science" is a comprehensive term that included all of conceptual knowledge, which is enlisted to cope with reality in a practical but not living way. Science is a product of an intelligence that evolved solely to assure man's physical survival and his dominion over nature. Caught in the materiality of space and time, intelligence views all reality as quantitatively measurable; and, as its function is to dominate and manipulate matter for practical purposes (ultimately of survival), it seeks to express reality in manipulable formulas and communicable concepts that serve as substitutes for the real. The inevitable result is a mechanistic explanation of the universe. All reality is conceived—*because* conceived—as static, homogeneous, discontinuous, and predictable. The vital, dynamic, novel, and unforeseeable are not allowed. The very nature of intelligence renders it incapable of adequately comprehending life, becoming, spirit, and freedom.

Although man's *natural* mode of knowing is through intelligence, Bergson maintained that the human mind is capable of another mode, namely, intuition—a direct contact or coincidence with inner realities. The former mode provides knowledge only of relations; the latter, of the things related, namely, absolutes. Intuitive thinking is not bound by space and time but occurs in duration and thereby is capable of grasping the inner dynamism of being.

Most philosophies, Bergson asserted, neglect intuition, which is the knowledge proper to philosophy, and base their metaphysics solely on what is rationally conceivable. The true philosophy must be both empirical and intuitive. It must on the one hand arise out of experience and be subjected to the experimental method. But, on the other hand, it must admit intuitional knowledge as not only an integral part of man's experience but at once the highest and most fundamental part. Philosophy must begin with life, with the whole and the concrete that are accessible only to the perception of intuition. The intellect's view of reality is too physical. It subdues reality by dividing it into discrete concepts, and reality, like Humpty-Dumpty, once divided can never be reconstructed in its wholeness. Out of no amount of *dis*creteness can one recreate *con*creteness.

To philosophy Bergson's ideas were a revolution of Copernican proportions, and Tyrrell welcomed them like the springtime thaw.[75] Tyrrell had already revolted against scholastic rationalism and was only looking for a flexible framework in which to construct the new. *Religion as a Factor of Life* demonstrates how thoroughly he entered into the Bergsonian horizon. All of the above stated themes constitute the basic harmonic structure of Tyrrell's philosophy of religion.

Bergson's *Essai* was first recommended to Tyrrell at a meeting with Baron von Hügel on 3 August 1900.[76] By the end of November Tyrrell had procured a copy and on 18 December wrote to Petre that Bergson's *Essai* was illuminating Eucken's *Wesensbildung* and Blondel's "obscurer psychology." "His 'point' is the complete dissociation of the worlds of *quantity* & *quality*; & the detection of [numberless?] unperceived intrusions of the former category into the latter. The issue is all in favour of liberty & spirit & Wesensbildung."[77]

The following 6 May 1901 Tyrrell wrote again to Petre that he was plunging into Bergson's *Matière et mémoire,* and three weeks later was finding "new vistas in all directions."[78] On 17 June he told von Hügel how "wonderfully attractive" Bergson's theory was, how it "clears many dark corners of psychology & philosophy" and "offers a good basis of Eucken's 'character-building' doctrines." But he still felt insecure about Eucken's thought and was about to turn to Hugo Münsterberg as to an interpreter—"tho' if I spend my life in these preliminaries I don't know when I shall get to work on my unpublished Oxford conferences which I hope to expand into a Prolegomena of Catholic ethics—after which I shall die content—unless," he added, "it were for an oft-dreamt-of never-to-be-realized treatise on materialism in religion. Récéjac rearoused the idea with his theories of symbolism."[79]

More Lesser Lights: Münsterberg, Zamoyska, Hatch

A few weeks earlier the baron had written to Tyrrell to urge him to study and write about Hugo Münsterberg's *Psychology and Life* (1899). It was a voice compatible with Bergson and the baron's interests. "Even tho' written in often horribly German—, indeed pigin-English [*sic*]," the baron observed, "it is surely a book of the most stimulating kind. He is a convert from the pedantry of solemn belief in the ultimate character of technically scientific truth. And the place he assigns to science in the spiritual-moral purification and constitution of man's personality, is, to my mind, exactly right."[80] Münsterberg was in Tyrrell's hands by 22 September, but by that time he had nearly completed a first draft of *Religion as a Factor of Life*. Nonetheless, he told the baron, Münsterberg too would "eventually . . . be worked into my *olla podrida*."[81] A month later he reported to Petre that Münsterberg was delightful and supportive of "much that I have contended for in my 'Ethical Preludes' which is now finished as far as the Oxford lectures went but needs 2 more chapters, & infinite notes & interludes."[82] Tyrrell did indeed assign Münsterberg a place in "Engels," a place made conspicuous by the absence of the names of others to whom Tyrrell owed far more. In fact, Münsterberg is the *only* modern author cited in the text. There he is seated alongside of Augustine, à Kempis, Aquinas, and Saints John and Paul. Even in the notes and appendix, of all to whom Tyrrell owed most only Blondel is cited, and that belatedly.[83]

Possibly Tyrrell expunged the more significant names from the final copy, as when he eliminated Loisy's name from *The Church and the Future* to save his already beleaguered friend from the slings and arrows that were bound to strike anyone too closely associated with that book.[84] Tyrrell did confess to having expunged one name—"so as to make it self-subsistent"—that of Countess Madame Hedwig Zamoyska of Poland,[85] but on the more significant names he was silent.

If Madame Zamoyska's thought did not significantly revolutionize Tyrrell's, her little *Sur le travail*[86] provided a certain moral impetus in the composition of *Religion as a Factor of Life*. In fact,

Tyrrell sometimes referred to his own work as a "study of Mdm. Zamoyska" or as "suggested" by her. Madame Zamoyska's book, he told von Hügel, "fell in exactly" with what he was working on at the time—"a study of religion as *a* factor of life—as it was "founded on a recognition of life as consisting in a threefold labour sc. of the spirit, of the mind, & of the hand." He also noted that it fell in exactly with Blondel's reply to Péchegut as well as with the conception of Eucken and the baron himself "that the religious interest though principal is not *all;* it is the head of our organised interests; but not the body & members; that it needs a body in order to have a *raison d'être.* Instinctively this good woman has seized the true philosophy of religion; though she is not reflexly aware of the 'infiltrations du protestantisme' which permeate her system. I will send you some of her documents as soon as I have written a little notice about them."[87]

The "notice," entitled "Un Noviciat De Vie Chretienne Dans Le Monde," appeared in the *Monthly Register* for May 1902 and served as a point of synthesis for all that Tyrrell had been reading and writing about in the past months.[88] But for those unaware of this context, Tyrrell explained to Petre, his "Zakopani article was *à propos* of nothing & led to nothing . . . ; but I did not want to waste the labour & it was good enough for the M.R."[89] One might surmise that Madame Zamoyska herself would have found surprising if not wholly unintelligible Tyrrell's philosophical dusting of her pragmatic principles by which a young woman could live a Christian lay vocation in a socially stratified world. But perhaps not. In a letter to Tyrrell of 4 June 1902 von Hügel pointed out an interesting connection between the countess and Tyrrell's "context." Abbé Albert Lamy, a student and friend of Blondel and of Ollé-Laprune, told the baron that the countess "spends part of every year in Paris, and is an old friend of M. Ollé-Laprune's. And Lamy thinks (and I take it, correctly) that she got a good part of her ideas from that source,—hence the same source as that to which B. too is indebted."[90]

Before passing on, mention must be made of the most singular contribution of Madame Zamoyska to the "Engels" work, namely an emphasis on the primary role of scripture *vis-à-vis* the sacraments. She solidified for Tyrrell some rather romantic and almost pietistic notions of the pristine simplicity of liturgical practices in the early church that he had acquired from Edwin Hatch's *Influence of Greek Ideas and Usages upon the Christian Church* (1888). In his review of *Sur le travail* Tyrrell applauded Zamoyska's proposal to teach her girls to turn to the scriptures "as to the fountain of all healthy religious inspiration . . . rather than to any of those streams deriving from them." This proposal, he said, was perhaps "the most attractive and original feature" of her program and the one "best calculated to wake an independent, as opposed to a merely useful, interest in religion." Her instinct for the sources was equally active in the matter of the sacraments. In teaching her students not to distract themselves during mass with rosaries or other spurious devotions but intelligently and sympathetically to follow the rite, "she shows at least an instinctive perception of one of the root-causes of religious decay—the gradual formalising of the most vital and soul-stirring act of worship ever known to mankind."[91]

Hatch would have been sympathetic. Tyrrell had read his work sometime before 15 August 1900, because in a letter of that date he suggested to Maude Petre that she would find Hatch "far better than Harnack" and could get a copy of the book from the baron.[92] Tyrrell thought that Hatch's thesis that "the Church passed from the Sermon on the Mount to the Nicene Creed" through contact with the Greek "artificial habit of mind" ran away with him.[93] But in substance Tyrrell was with him, and from this point on one can see Tyrrell in his correspondence regularly casting rueful aspersions on the Roman Catholic tendency to stress the *ex opere operato* power of the sacraments in reaction to the Protestant emphasis on the Word, while at the same time casting wistful glances to Hatch's charismatic times.

Nowhere did Tyrrell express himself more intensely on this understanding than in his letter to Maude Petre of 20 November 1901. He had just returned to Richmond from Farm Street, London, where he had gone to set straight the rumors about his relationship to the Society of Jesus:

> Maud[e], I *could* not live in London; it seemed a lower, poisoned air, & God went from me for all those days. A famine-stricken city, & I a poor wretch with a false repute of bread in my pocket & everyone tearing after me for a bite. Perhaps in this wilderness one may learn at last to turn stones into bread; but till then I am better out of the way— unheard & unseen. What use is a "sympathetic hearing" which leads to nothing? And whom have I ever found straying & brought back? And then the inadequacy of our Jesuit garrison piling sand banks against the flood! . . . No one seems to care about "souls" i.e., about making men *better* ethically, morally, religiously; at best it is to get them to perform certain rites, which, frankly, I think of little consequence for all I have seen come of them. If it could but stand in the air & hold together how good were that Old Bible-Christianity centered round that

dear Personality which is dying out of our midst—how accessible to the simplest, how satisfying for the subtlest!—a fragment indeed of the old Catholic spirit before politics had poisoned the wells of life. God gave us Bread & men have turned it into a stone, & the Fish into a scorpion.[94]

This idea, purged of raw emotion, is reexpressed in "Engels," which by this time was in rough draft.

Maude Petre was not, as some have suggested, a sponge for every drop of Tyrrell's wisdom. As devoted as she was to Tyrrell, she was no sycophant. She exercised critical and independent judgment. On this very matter, for example, she took issue with Tyrrell. In her diary for 15 November 1900 she wrote:

What however strikes me somewhat is that he [Hatch] seems to put down to *Greek* influence what was, in fact, simply the working out of the inevitable law of all human things, which pass from the spirit to the letter. A certain artificial element entered the Church not only because of Greek influence, but because of the natural process of formalization, just as the same element creeps into a religious order. And, further, however often a man may react against it, it creeps on again like a destiny—it is the fate of mankind and of individual men. Also, I think in the dislike he feels for that formal period of the Church he probably idealizes the earlier times of spontaneous speaking & preaching. Are we so sure that some of those early Christians, contemporaries of the apostles, were not as noisy and shallow as we find in certain modern sects?[95]

One might lay these conflicts between Tyrrell and Petre to the unavoidable differences between born-and-bred Catholics and converts. But converts are often zealous to excess in swallowing their new religion whole and unmasticated and apologizing for it. Tyrrell had tried that, but his critical mind could not be denied for long. It soon forced upon him a distinction between theory and practice that Rome did not appreciate—and understandably so, as Tyrrell pointed out that it was Roman and particularly Jesuit practice that prevented the church from becoming what it was in theory. Tyrrell's neophyte zeal then turned to apologizing for what seemed to him "a more excellent way," but lacking support from official Catholicism, he faced the impossible task, as he put it, of trying to make his "way" hang together in mid-air.

COMPOSITION AND EXCURSUS OF "ENGELS"

Scribal Development

What eventually appeared as *Religion as a Factor of Life* Tyrrell conceived initially as merely a "chapter on philosophical presuppositions" to introduce a much larger work on Christian ethics. The latter work began as a second set of Oxford Conferences delivered during Lent of 1900, but Tyrrell got bogged down on his introduction and never published his "Ethical Preludes" in book form. Their publication is not to be regretted, as he himself, without false humility, condemned them as "incoherrent [sic], dry & dreary."[96] He was much more interested in the philosophical prolegomenon.

On 16 July 1901, one month after he told von Hügel that Bergson was clearing many dark corners, Tyrrell wrote to Petre that he had completed four chapters of his "Ethical Preludes" but was "floundering hopelessly in a psychological *excursus* of a Bergsonian tendency showing the function of habit & determinism in relation to action & personality." He regretted his dependence on such a "disputable philosophy," yet he needed it to state his presuppositions.[97] Two weeks later he told Raffalovich that he was producing a "synthesis of everything . . . after which humanity will have nothing more to discover."[98] On the same day to Petre he confessed that his "Preludes" had "wandered away into a complete philosophical synthesis" with "no prospect of ever getting back to my point which was the bearing of habit—by which we merge ourselves in the determinism of nature—upon character & freedom."[99]

On 22 September Tyrrell informed von Hügel that he hoped to finish a rough draft in about a month and then go on emending it as "a sort of mental journal" of his reading and reflection. As the manuscript emerged, he had it typed and sent to Petre "so that in the event of my demise it may not fall into the hands of the destroyer." But to keep his mind unfettered, he felt it necessary to suspend any thought of publishing it, "as the prospective censor exercises a bad influence on one's intellectual sincerity." He saw deficiencies and lacunae in his presentation, but on the whole he was satisfied and surprised to find more intellectual coherence arising out of his instinctive views than he had dared to hope. As to his expression, no one contributed more than Bergson. Had it not been for him, Tyrrell told the baron, he would not have had the courage to formulate what he really felt on the problem of knowledge and to reject "the representative & picture theories altogether, so that the problem of the correspondence of thought to reality becomes non-existent."[100]

Petre was reading Tyrrell's manuscript in installments and acknowledged a certain enthusiasm over it.[101] On 2 November 1901 Tyrrell sent the concluding pages with a cautionary note, "I am afraid your delight with my M.S. will be tempered when you pass from easy preliminaries into the 'dark night' of my 'Presuppositions'; yet I could not build in the air."[102] By that date, therefore, Tyrrell had roughed out the body of "Engels," but he would continue working it over for several months longer.

If Petre was enthusiastic over Tyrrell's manuscript—*"pioneer work*," she called it, "leaving necessarily much that is uncertain behind it . . . a vista that is being opened, not a complete scheme of philosophy"—[103] she was also perplexed. She disputed, for example, Tyrrell's views on the interrelation of souls, how the individual's freedom and personality grow in proportion to relatedness to other persons and to being dissolved into one superpersonal reality, not losing but gaining thereby one's own personality. The idea of the immortality of every soul as a center of consciousness, she confessed, terrified her as much as it attracted Tyrrell. It seemed to hedge on pantheism and threaten the loss of personal distinctness. Yet she had to agree that "if there be truly a *super*-personal unity it will *not* lessen personal distinctness—we must lose our soul to find it again more fully."[104]

Apparently Petre and Tyrrell carried on an exchange over these difficulties not only by letter but also in person, as Tyrrell spent a couple of weeks in London during November to further his campaign of exoneration. But nothing more appears in writing until the following 2 March 1902, when Tyrrell sent another query and explanation:

> As to your All-in-One and One-in-All problem, I should like to know in what sense you understand it. Is it an antithesis? For myself everything converges to the conviction that the difference between you and me is only that of severed tracts of experience in the same personality, such as exists between my sleeping and waking self; save that here there are a few connecting links that make the personal identity evident, but there, there are none such owing to the perfect physical discontinuity of our brains. Read Pierre Janet in the light of that hypothesis and you will see how many mysteries disappear. But how this squares with theology God only knows; though I am not sure but I learnt the idea first from St. Paul.[105]

It was Janet, Tyrrell admitted later, who reinforced his conviction "that the doctrine of separate souls stuck into separate bodies like swords into scabbards won't do; & that I am you as much as the somnabulic [sic] & normal personalities are the same, tho' ignorant of one another."[106]

Petre was also perplexed about Tyrrell's views on habit in relation to freedom and personality. His language led her to believe that he understood habit as an automatism, whereas she held to the old doctrine that habit is a strength.[107] But Tyrrell, too, regarded habit as a strength. If his explanation was not clear, the confusion may be laid to his Bergsonianism.

For Bergson, habits formed a kind of protective crust in which nearly all of one's conscious and intelligent but largely insignificant daily actions are carried out. Beneath this crust, undisturbed by trifles, is seated one's fundamental self, seething and forming itself through intercourse with unrational, unbound, and free feelings. Routine actions are called forth not so much by constantly changing feelings as by unchanging images that are bound up with these feelings. For example, Bergson explained,

> in the morning when the hour strikes at which I am accustomed to rise . . . this impression, instead of disturbing my whole consciousness like a stone which falls into the water of a pond, merely stirs up an idea which is, so to speak, solidified on the surface, the idea of rising and attending to my usual occupations. This impression and this idea have in the end become tied up with one another, so that the act follows the impression without the self interfering with it. In this instance I am a conscious automaton, and I am so because I have everything to gain by being so.

So far Tyrrell was with Bergson. Petre was not. Bergson went on. Our routine actions, he explained, however habitual and even predictable, are nonetheless conscious and even intelligent. They seem to be preprogrammed responses to external impressions, but in fact they arise out of a solidification in memory of certain sensations, feelings, or ideas that past experience has proven to be the most salutary responses to similar stimuli. Associationists may base their hypotheses on this seeming determinism, but Bergson demurred that such actions taken together are "the substratum of our free activity, and with respect to this activity they play the same part as our organic functions in relation to the whole of our conscious life."[108]

This notion parallels what Tyrrell wrote to Petre in an important letter of 24 June 1901, in which he seemed to make habit play the role of determinism. The latter he defined as the laws of nature, fixed and respected by God for the sake of man's free development:

Were there no determinism, no fixed laws of divine action in the world, were all immediately dependent on divine caprice, we should go mad as surely as in a world of mere chance and fortuity. I assume, therefore, that for the development of our personality by self-government and self-direction, stable laws and uniformity are absolutely necessary. A father who listened to every cry; who gave his children everything for asking; who laid down no laws or rules or conditions by which, as far as possible, they should help themselves to what they needed, would destroy their characters. In crises unforeseen he might come to their aid, but he would make such crises as rare as possible, and would be inexorable in exacting the normal and universal conditions. In fact he would put them *en rapport* with a certain "determinism," or set of laws, to which he would bind his own will no less than theirs. . . . Is it not in virtue of nature's uniformity (i.e., the stable determinism which God has set between us and Himself as a bridge) that, in material matters the race has risen to a control over nature and to a high degree of self-government and independence? And is it not the same in higher matters? and in regard to individuals? As a fish needs the water, so a free agent must swim in an ocean of determinism. It is to our freedom what air is to the bird's wings. . . . I think the mischief of superstitious prayer lies in its contempt of natural means and co-operation; in its ignorance of the dignity of law; in its expectation of a *miraculous* answer involving a breach of uniformity; in not remembering that God has, of our good, freely bound Himself to respect His own laws and therefore to work within limitations. To deal with us at all personally He must take on Himself limits like our own. I think as we understand things better we pray less and less for temporal benefits or even for miraculous providences of any sort, and trust ourselves rather to the "determinism" which, harsh and ruthless though it seem, is but the will of Him whose wisdom reaches from end to end and disposes of all things sweetly. We begin with: "If it be possible, let the chalice pass," and end with "Since it may not pass, Thy will be done." Though God condescends to the simpler faith, I cannot doubt but that the stronger pleases him better, the faith of Job or of Christ's *Calicem quem dedit mihi Pater nonne bibam ex illo.*[109]

In a letter of 6 December 1901 Tyrrell suggested to Petre a tentative reconciliation of their views by paying less attention to Janet, who fails to distinguish between physiological and spiritual subconsciousness. With him it is all physiological, "an affair of brain-layers." With Tyrrell the physiological exists solely for the practical expression of the true self and is not part of the true self. The latter, with all its acts of knowing and willing including the physiology, constitutes what Tyrrell referred to as "that full personality which is the resultant of all our past acts, and which is the *implicitum* of the present act could we rightly analyse it." He wanted to call it the "subconscious self," but that term had already been appropriated by the physiologists. All this, Tyrrell observed, accorded with the Thomistic-Aristotelian principle, "habit is for the sake of (free) action,"—a principle that Petre seemed to invert. "You say the act passes the habit remains. I don't think the act passes."[110]

Tyrrell was here supplementing and correcting Janet with Bergson. The latter held that each act, though posited in the external world of clock time and therefore belonging to the past, is nevertheless an act of a personality that belongs not to clock time but that *endures.* The act is absorbed as part of the personality and *in situ* interpenetrates with all other acts and endures along with the personality of which it is a "part," but no longer separable or divisible. But he distinguished two selves: the real, fundamental self and its spatial-social representation or external projection. This latter self is the seat of habit and occupies itself with the vast majority of our acts of social intercourse. The real self is reached only by deep introspection. But the moments when we thus grasp our true selves are rare, and that is why we are rarely free.[111] The problem is that we usually succumb to the comfort of inertia and indolence or to the safety of social motive. We thus hide behind habit or determinism and let some serious case run its course when our full personality ought to erupt and intervene. So that, Bergson asserted, we look in vain for evidence of the true and free self in the ordinary actions of life. Rather, "it is at the great and solemn crisis, decisive of our reputation with others . . . that we choose in defiance of what is conventionally called a motive, and this absence of any tangible reason is the more striking the deeper our freedom goes."[112]

Bergson thus assigned the rationally accountable action to the realm of determinism and the spontaneous, unreasoned action, performed in a moment of crisis, to the realm of freedom, where only deep and searching reflection can show that action to have agreed with and expressed one's true self. For Tyrrell this deepest self— what he wanted to call the "subconscious self"—was a kind of reservoir in which past experiences, captured in felt responses to these experiences, are stored and allowed to ruminate, interact, and build up energy for some future spontaneous expression.

Here, especially, Tyrrell had some explaining to do for Petre. She tended to regard the subconscious self as the fuller and realer self insofar as it came to clarity of expression in the future. But

Tyrrell regarded the subconscious self rather as "the accumulation of past life, the formed or dead matter which gets pushed behind and congested as life goes on," as he told her in a letter of 30 May 1902 in which he again attempted a reconciliation of views. Perhaps, he suggested, the subconscious self was both—"the 'not-present,' and therefore the past and the future, both of which characterise our present choice; the one by way of obscure memories, the other by way of obscure anticipations." The two of them agreed that full consciousness is the higher state, and the subconscious self is fuller, realer, and better to the extent that it moves toward conscious actuation. But, Tyrrell cautioned, within the "not-present" subsconscious self, one ought to distinguish between the buried past and future selves. The former is automatic and mechanical, the seat of habits, and represents what a person was. The latter is the not-yet fully appropriated self, the seat of ideals, and represents what a person tends to become. The latter is higher than the former, as ideals are higher than attainments, but as not yet actuated, ideals are lower. Good habits have no such superiority at all, since they represent only what a person was.[113]

Tyrrell had an insight here into the relationship between habitual and free acts, between habits and ideals, between the buried past and the future self, between the subconscious and the fully conscious self. It was a polar relationship whose polarities, however inexplicably, found paradoxical unity in some superpersonal "I." One could wish for a less confusing formulation, but however clearly stated, paradoxes can never be done justice. Tyrrell himself was dissatisfied. He realized that he was dealing with a problem that had no final solution, but a problem that would open itself to progressively greater insight. He continued to struggle with it, as his journal for 1904-6 shows,[114] but he did not advance his formulation significantly.

To continue with the development of "Engels," on 5 December 1901 Tyrrell wrote to Bremond to tell him of his recent foray into the London lairs of fable. Then:

I hardly dare tell you what I am writing now it is so dangerous & yet so necessary. Perhaps if I ever succeed in bringing it to full birth it may enlist your sympathy. I met so many moribund Catholics in London in search of a *modus vivendi* that I determined on a book or series of reflections for the spiritual help of people in that condition. On the analogy of "How to live on sixpence a day"; this might be entitled: "How to live on the minimum of faith." A non-controversial, non-apologetic retreat for *bona fide* agnostics was an old idea of mine. This is an effort in a like direction. Needless to say the work will never get beyond the MS stage & will be circulated under most horrific oathes of secrecy. It will *not* have Cardinal V[aughan]'s *Imprimatur*.[115]

Again to Bremond on 17 February 1902 he wrote that he was "in labour with a suddenly conceived synthesis of many thoughts" that had been gathering in his mind "without apparent connection" but were in fact the offspring of one seed.

It is utterly unfit for publication this century. We must put religion high above all scientific, historic, & even ethical uncertainties; & free it from that "body of death" to which theologians & apologetes have tied it. As long as it rests on a foundation of sand it cannot be believed, or "lived"—that is my thesis. I do not say religion can be altogether indifferent to positive knowledge; any more than a snail can be indifferent about its shell; but the shell is not the snail, who can make itself another as often as one is broken. This, as written, sounds a latitudinarian commonplace; but I think I can give it a Catholic sense.[116]

This description fits perfectly what Tyrrell included as the appendix to "Engels," in which, by applying the principles elaborated in the body of the text, he tried to show that the chief formulations of Catholic faith and morals belong to the scientific sphere and can therefore develop without substantially affecting the deeper truths that they only symbolize.

For all of Tyrrell's protests against publishing such an advanced excursus, he could hardly bear to keep any thoughts to himself, particularly if he had labored over their formulation. His eventual decision to publish the book—but privately—seems to have been triggered by three considerations: (1) he was currently under stress from the recensoring of *Oil and Wine* and vowed that he would be less scrupulous about clandestine publications in the future; (2) his recent publication of *The Civilizing of the Matafanus* showed that he could print privately for a very reasonable sum; and (3) intimations of mortality. In a letter of 25 February 1902 he told Petre: "I have no intention of publishing my study of Mdm. Zamoyska. Nothing that really represents me could (or indeed *ought*) to pass theological censors. If I felt that after my demise it would get a chance of being read I shd be satisfied. But my friends will be so careful about my reputation for orthodoxy that all will be lost. However it only cost £7 to print 500 Matafanus; & so I think I will print some things for private circulation in the course of time."[117]

On 2 March Tyrrell wrote to A. R. Waller for the name of the "cheapest printer" he knew and complained that the cardinal was going to sit on *Oil and Wine* "& press all the juice out of it."[118] A month later he reported that the cardinal had indeed "sat down with all his weight on my poor book," so Tyrrell felt justified in extruding himself in another direction: "As to the other document I thought of printing for private circulation I will send it you [sic] as soon as Wilfrid Ward disgorges it."[119]

On 14 April Tyrrell recounted for Bremond the whole recensorship business, then added that *Oil and Wine* "belongs in substance to three years ago; & I am so much more interested in its younger brethren that, except for the objective injustice of the whole transaction, I mind its assassination less than you wd. think."[120] By 23 April he had retrieved the manuscript from Ward and sent it to Waller with a note saying:

> Herewith is the M.S. I spoke about. There are perhaps 50 people in the world who wd. be interested in it & no sane publisher wd. take a present of it. Hence I want it multiplied in the cheapest way possible for private circulation—bare legibility is all I demand. The notes are either to be massed at the end, or else, if not more expensive, to be embodied in small type in the text. . . . Now that my muzzle has been so unfairly tightened I feel no scruple in biting in any way that a chance offers.[121]

In that same letter Tyrrell promised a preface for a new edition of *Mother Juliana of Norwich*, which he figured would cover the printing fees for "Engels." But he needed cash immediately, so he appealed to his standby, Maude Petre. On 3 May 1902 he informed her of his plan to print for private circulation what he now was calling his "Study of Religion"—"having expunged the Zakopani references. You have found me good pay before, & so I will ask you to lend me £7 which I have already earned this week by a Preface to a new edition to Mother Julian but may not realise for some little time."[122] By the last week of May "Engels" was in proofs. After going over them Tyrrell wrote to Petre that, though "deadly dull," they were more satisfactory than he had thought.[123] To celebrate his performance, he told Waller:

> I am inclined to make Ernest Engels a D.D. . . . & to omit 'For private circulation' which is true without being said & will only attract curiosity. So the title-page might run thus:
>
>
>
> Religion as a Factor of Life
>
> A Study
>
> by
>
> Dr Ernest Engels
>
> 1902[124]
>
>

Three hundred copies were printed by William Pollard & Co. and were in Tyrrell's hands by 8 July.[125] "The get-up is distinctly satisfactory," he wrote to Waller. "I don't know that it matters about copyright. I shd. be rather glad if anyone thought it worth pirate-ing."[126]

Tyrrell was not at all confident about this work. It was really his first effort at a philosophy of religion, and, as he well knew, it was quite a brew from a multitude of sources, some conscious, most lost to his memory but at one with him. He felt he had something to say, but "Engels" did not say it quite right. "I send you another of my 'cries,'" he wrote to Bremond on 23 July. "There is less in it than I had hoped. The Appendix gathers up the somewhat obvious fruit of the laborious & tortuous fore-work & notes. And yet, and yet, there is something I want to say if I could only bring it clear in my own mind & which keeps my faith vigorous amid the ruins of my orthodoxy."[127]

Actually, three months earlier Tyrrell did manage to distill and clarify the essence of "Engels" into a thirteen-page preface to a new edition of *Juliana of Norwich.* Just a week after "Engels" had been sent to press, Tyrrell notified Waller that the preface for *Juliana* would come out looking like "Engels," "but I hope much simpler & clearer."[128] That being the case, it requires no separate treatment but its clarity can elucidate "Engels." Thus parallel passages from the preface to *Juliana* are interspersed throughout the following presentation of Tyrrell's philosophy of religion.

Exposition of Religion as a Factor of Life

Beneath the life of those senses which reveal to us that world of appearances, which the unreflecting so easily confound with the reality which it only symbolises; beneath the life of the understanding, whose forms and frames (contrasting in their permanence and universality with the unsteadiness and uncertainty of that chaos of fleeting phenomena which they but classify and set in order) have seemed to some to merit the name of Reality; beneath even the life of the higher, though self-centred and self-regarding emotions and sentiments, aesthetic or spiritual; deep down at the very basis of the soul, is to be sought the only life that in an absolute and independent sense deserves the name of "real," because by it alone are we brought into conscious relation with other personalities, and made aware of our own. Whatever else we call real is so, but in some secondary and derived sense. Only in so far as it resembles a person can we think of it at all, and only in so far as it affects a person, ourself or another, can we desire it or care about it in any way. It is precisely by love and its dependent affections that we are brought into conscious and active relation with the whole world of personalities outside our own, so as to make therewith in some sort one many-membered spiritual organism. It is love which at once saves and yet overcomes that separateness and individual distinction which is of the very essence of personality, and thereby welds the several grains of corn into one living bread.[129]

A full and integrated life, Tyrrell premised, involves the harmonious interaction of three labors: of the heart, the head, and the hands. For this interaction to occur, one labor may not be developed at the expense of the others, yet there is a proper ordering that must be observed. In amplifying this premise, Tyrell's aim was threefold: to describe the interrelationship of the principal factors of life, to locate therein the place proper to religion, and thereby to show that true religion is not victimized by the changing circumstances of the other factors of life.

Tyrrell's listing of the three labors indicates from the outset his opinion of their proper ordering. "We are nothing else but wills," he said, quoting Augustine, and it is in relation to other wills that we find our deepest spiritual reality.[130] In will-relations we live, and move, and have our being, whether the relations are of agreement or disagreement, of love or of hatred. Each will exists in a triangular relationship: to other wills taken singly, to the whole world of wills taken collectively, and to that transcendent yet immanent Will that is the center and bond of the will-world.

This last relationship is the foundation of the religious sentiment, which in turn includes and regulates the sentiments that proceed from all other relations. "Religion is the principal element in the life of the affections," Tyrrell asserted, "and, therefore, in the whole organism of human life," but it is not the only element.[131] For itself to be healthy it needs the well-balanced cultivation of all other interests, and in this it has everything to gain and nothing to lose. Some would accord a certain priority to the head in relation to the members, Tyrrell observed, because the human organism can do quite well without one or other member but not without the head. But at the same time, if one's intelligence is not governed by religion, one's whole life lacks foundation and finality.

Hence in the interests of even nonreligious activity, as well as for its own sake, a certain explicit and separate exercise of religion is essential. The religious effort "religionizes" all other aspects of life—intellectual, practical, and moral. It governs and controls them, not for its own sake but for the sake of life, which is bigger than religion and of which religion is but one element, albeit the highest.

WHAT IS THE "RELIGIOUS EFFORT"? It is not theology. It might be defined as prayer in the widest sense, but that definition is too vague. To answer that question, one must first answer the question, What is religion? In its public, exterior sense, Tyrrell answered, religion is a school for training the spiritual faculties. Its aim is to instruct the mind and form the will and affections so as to determine action, feeling, and attitude, first in relation to God directly, then to all the other things viewed in relation to him. Whatever instruction religion offers to the mind "is not in the interest of intellectualism, but of life and action; . . . its chief aim is the shaping of the affections and sentiments."[132]

Sentiment or affection is the mainspring of conscious life. It is created and modified by perception and, by reason of that perception, gives birth to some sort of self-adaptation. Feeling in its most elementary form is the inclination to advance or to withdraw in response to a touch. Where there is no feeling, as in the case of habitual mechanical actions, the inclination is running parallel to the touch. Where there is feeling, action has somehow been checked, so we may say that "feeling is equivalently the consciousness of the impeded conversion of perception into action." In that case, the "feeling" itself is spontaneous. It depends not on our choice but on our natural or acquired state at the time. What is of our choice is the direction in which we seek outlet for the feeling. That freely chosen outlet makes what Tyrrell called "a furrow in the sensorimotor field," thereby modifying the nature of all future feelings.[133] Future reactions to the same stimulus will not be so abrupt but will tend to run along that same furrow and become less conscious, less sentient, more automatic and habitual, unless we consciously choose to seek outlet in another way. But we must first be awakened by feeling.

"Feeling, therefore, is repressed and indetermined action."[134] Give it a channel and it becomes a force. We are self-directive and free insofar as we feel, but we need to perceive and understand the context in which force has to be adapted. So that, although feeling is central and the mainspring of life, it is but one part of the indivisible movement of life blended of perception, feeling, and action.

To say that religion is a matter of feeling is to say only that religion controls the mainspring of life. It is not the whole of life. It is a kind of life and a kind of feeling or group of feelings that have their perceptual antecedents and resultant actions. The same is true of the virtues commonly associated with religion: faith, hope, love, reverence, penitence. Each is a kind of feeling arising from a certain perception and finding release in a certain action. Thus it is just as or even more correct to speak of religion as a sentiment or affection than to speak of it as consisting in beliefs or good works. For it seems that the locus of religion is the internal will-attitude rather than the perception that precedes or the action that follows it.

EXPERIENTIAL REFERENT OF RELIGIOUS AFFECTIONS. As feeling, religion is an experience of attraction and repulsion in accordance with certain stimuli. Tyrrell's next point of inquiry concerned the nature of these stimuli. To what element of our experience do religious affections refer? Not to one that is set alongside or above the other elements of our experience, but to one that pervades and unites all the rest—the whence and whither of all being and movement, of which our own is but an infinitesimal fraction.

To digress briefly, it should be noted that in Bergson the really real belongs not to the realm of extensible and divisible space and time but to the realm of duration, all of whose denizens are interpenetrable. This same understanding would hold true *a fortiori* of the Absolute. Consequently, if Tyrrell were following Bergson here, he would be led to conclude that the element to which religious affection refers—namely, Absolute Reality—cannot be an element of the extensible world of objects, but one that interpenetrates all reality and is therefore perceived in all and through all. That, in fact, is Tyrrell's conclusion.

Before our understanding gathers up and abstracts from our experiences a distinct thought about God or gods, Tyrrell argued, there is an underlying datum that pervades our total experience and is coperceived along with but not apart from our other perceptions. Consequently this datum can religiously modify our actions without giving rise to distinctly religious acts. It might be described as the sense of the Absolute, or a sense of the intrinsic and ultimate value of truth, goodness, and beauty. But to perceive this datum as absolute implies simultaneously one's own subordination to a universal order and interest. This sense, like others, may be sharpened and intensified by exercise, by positively seeking the Absolute, or it may be dulled by misuse or abuse. But to the extent that it is intensified, it will draw on the understanding, whose function is "to map out in small, and by aid of symbols, the wilderness of our experiences for the better guidance of our conduct, and to supplement our natural foresight by a power of more or less scientific and infallible prediction of the absent and distant."[135] Our sense of the Absolute, then, seeks to know itself through the symbols provided by the understanding, and the Absolute becomes an object, the chief of all objects in our artificial scheme of "things."

Tyrrell's language here is not as careful as his meaning requires, and lest he be misunderstood, a qualification must be added.[136] In saying that the Absolute becomes an object, Tyrrell did not mean that God-in-himself is reduced to the level of object, but that our *concepts* of God are on the level of object. These, through symbolic representation, mediate understanding of the diffused and undifferentiated *sense* of God to the intellect.

TYRRELL'S SCHEME. In rough outline this is how Tyrrell's religious psychology works: A feeling or sense gives rise to an idea or explanation of that sense, its whence and whither. This idea in turn produces a feeling about the fitness of the explanation. If the feeling is good, we are inclined in the direction of the explanatory idea; that is, we judge that it is true, at least relatively and tentatively, until we can come up with a better explanation. Conversely, if the feeling is bad, we judge that there is little correspondence between the explanation and the feeling that gave rise to it. Thus, feeling passes judgment on explanatory hypotheses and acts as a criterion of truth.[137]

In the case of religious affections, a vague sense of the absolute claims of truth and justice generates a feeling of reverence and worship. This sense in turn drives the understanding to formulate an explanatory hypothesis (e.g., theism). In the measure that this hypothesis corresponds to reality, we experience an enrichment and strengthening of and control over the original feeling. In other words, we can in a way gather up that feeling and channel it in a profitable direction. This new feeling of enrichment then demands a further and fuller explanation, which in turn gives rise to new ideas and new feelings about those ideas, and the process continues in a never-ending spiral of stimulus-response.

As to the role of understanding in this process, we can conclude that it is *through*, but not *by* or *in*, the understanding that we come into contact with reality—*through* it insofar as our schemata symbolize reality faithfully. But the map is not the wilderness, and the *objective* world of images and their relations is only a shadow-world by which one can guide and determine one's relation to the substance-world, the real world. The range of real interaction between one's own and other realities of the substance-world is indefinitely and unknowably broader than what comes under one's knowledge and control. In Blondellian terms, the *réel en soi* (the real in itself) is infinitely more than the *réel connu* (the real as known). Only *in* the living self, as actively willed and thereby continually multiplying and modifying the virtually infinite relations of will-sympathy with all other beings, only in *life* is true reality given to us—that *réalité réelle* (real reality) of which the *réalité connu* (reality as known) is but the symbol.[138] It is because God and other realities are *in* us that we to some extent know them, not conversely as intellectualism alleges. The "outsideness" (and even the "insideness" so far as it is a spatial figure) is verified not of the realities but of their symbols in the *objective* world, where alone such relations of inside and outside obtain.[139] "In other words," Tyrrell asserted, "in religion as in other matters, it is under the guidance of sentiment that the mind fashions its symbolism of the realities whose action gives birth to the sentiment, and thus is enabled to bring itself into closer relation with those realities; whence an access of sentiment, demanding a fuller symbolism; and so forth without end."[140]

ANALOGICAL NATURE OF CONCEPTUALIZATIONS. No one pretends that the conceptual and material symbolism of our relations to God are adequate or more than analogous or not constantly in need of revision as our relations change. Nonetheless, our symbols possess an equivalent or *practical* truth in the measure that they guide our conduct in the right direction. Life is the test of truth, and religion is true insofar as it aids the life of correspondence with the Absolute and thereby gives a fuller, deeper, wider life to the soul.

But, while practically true, our schemata and hypotheses about God are in theory and speculatively false simply because they are not exhaustive. They suit us and guide us safely to a knowledge of that portion of divine action which is universal and constant relative to our own limited experience and duration, but they would mislead a being capable of universal experience.

Understanding cannot reach God in himself, in his reality, just as it cannot reach underlying substances or subjects, which are represented to the understanding by changeable symbols. Understanding can reach only God's manifestations and effects. Through will and action we experience (directly contact) substance and subject as realities that cannot be pictured in terms of sense. So, too, with God. While his attributes and effects belong to the order of science (conceptual knowledge), he himself belongs to that order with which the will is in direct contact, the world of "will-values" and history, not to the world of science.[141] True reality is given only *in the self*, not as *knowing* that reality directly but as actively *willing*, as continually modifying and multiplying the *relations* between realities. It is only because God and other realities are *in* us that we to a limited degree know them. Substantial realities are interpenetrable, so that "outsideness" and "insideness" apply only to the symbols of reality, to the objective, spatial world.

The following passage from Tyrrell's preface to *Juliana of Norwich* illustrates his meaning:

> As the blind man who feels his way to the fire tests his conjectures according as they bring him an increase or decrease of warmth and comfort, so in his gropings after God man brings religious doctrines and systems to the test of life and love; nor does he heed the rudeness of the earthen vessel so long as it is sound enough to hold the treasure of religious truth. For purposes of navigation the astronomy of Ptolemy is as true as that of Copernicus; and many a belief less accurately representative of the realm of the outer senses and the understanding is far truer to the facts of the spiritual order—far truer to the ultimate realities—than one more consonant with current fashions of thought.
>
> Nor need this surprise us when we remember that the outward and apparent world can never be representative, but at most symbolic, of the inward and real; that it yields us at best a rude algebra, giving results of practical sufficiency and possessing the correspondence of a chart to the locality through which it guides the traveller's wandering steps. Only through the visible effects of their action in the world of appearances are personalities revealed to one another, and made aware of their mutual agreements and disagreements in thought, aim, and affection.[142]

REALITY AND THE SPIRITUAL LIFE. Our own reality is revealed to us in willing and acting, and we notice and account other things as real insofar as they seem to oppose their wills to ours. Our existence from moment to moment is a single "willing" by which we respond to every momentary transformation of surroundings. However we may analyze that single act into a sum total of past and present willings, it is one simple act by which we adapt ourselves to our total situation—the past behind us, the present around us, and the future before us.

Through the world of corporality, of which senses, memory, and understanding take account, we are made aware of other wills by the sensibly evident results of their action. "It is in our *felt* relation to these other wills that our spiritual life and reality consists."[143] All wills together make up a world of wills in ceaseless commotion, like motes in a sunbeam, each changing its relation to all as moment by moment likes and dislikes interact. Whenever we find a will or wills in accord with our own, we experience a sense of reinforcement and expansion of our own spiritual life and being in proportion to the nature and extent of agreement and to the nature and number of wills in agreement. On the other hand, we sense spiritual impoverishment and contraction whenever we confront an opposing will-force.[144]

To this world of wills, certain personalities are what first principles are to science: principles of unification and classification. Persons can be grouped according to their will-attitudes, as expressed in the deeds and aims of certain personalities. Terms such as "Christian," "republican," and "vivisectionist" imply a common end toward which wills are set in agreement. The function of history is to show the order and connection of these governing deeds, aims, and personalities.[145]

But groupings of concordant wills implies disagreement with contrary will-attitudes. Simple will-union cannot be taken as an end in itself or as a motive for action. We must always ask: *Agree with what?* Throughout the universe of will-attitudes, the difference between good and evil, true and false, gives a rule of choice higher than the blind rule of love; even if we would want to follow the impulse to be in will-union with all persons, we could not. We might err in perception and judgment of what is true and good, but we can never err as to the absolute and imperative character of these will-attitudes; we can never doubt that we *ought* to be in sympathy with persons of good will and out of sympathy with persons of bad will.

> Now this imperative character of the Absolute is simply the force of that supreme, eternal, eventually irresistible Will, which we call God—that will to which the whole will-world must be subordinate, and in union or agreement with which each created will is saved and realised, even were it at variance with all the rest. This love of God, this dynamic union with the Infinite Will, is the very substance and reality of our spiritual living and being; other lovings and agreeings belong to the perfection, but not to the essence of our blessedness.[146]

But of that supreme will we know nothing except as manifested in those who live by it. We only feel it "mingling and conflicting with our own in each concrete action that is submitted to our freedom."[147] This sense of continual action of the divine will on our own, drawing us towards good and away from evil, Tyrrell defined as conscience.

RELIGION AS THE LOCUS OF KNOWLEDGE OF THE DIVINE WILL. One can live religiously without performing any distinctly religious acts simply by obeying conscience and following one's sense of the absolute will. But religion begins as soon as one separates out this sense and conceives this all-pervading, governing will apart from and above all others. In other words, religious sentiment precedes religion—a notion Tyrrell had expressed in *External Religion* and in "The Relation of Theology to Devotion." This notion is also consistent with the psychological dynamic of sentiment and idea explained above. The sentiment gives rise to an expression (external religion) or conception to which the religious sentiment again reacts and is either intensified or diminished according as the conception does or does not prove an apt guide toward more perfect harmony with reality. But this process is also different from that involving the origin and test of ideas, for the latter is a process of the individual, while the former is a process of a society. Religion is a matter of public sentiment and public ideas, and the individual born into a society is educated under the influence of those public sentiments and ideas. In the individual, sentiments are learned from ideas, for the latter are directly communicable, while the former can only be the individual's interior response to the idea. Thus the individual in the first stages of education takes in religious ideas by force of imitation, but they remain dormant in the mind until sentiment, of which ideas are the mental expression, is in some measure realized. But the public idea becomes a private possession and part of the individual's personality only when that individual has responded with a sentiment appropriate to the idea.

The force of individuality, on the other hand, precludes perfect correspondence between private sentiment and public formulation. There will always occur a disparity that stands as either an implicit or explicit criticism of the public formulation, depending upon whether the individual consciously and publicly expresses the disparity or not. Criticism is a necessary consequence of the eccentric polarity between the individual and society. But few people ever rise to the level of maturity required for *judicious* criticism, which alone is productive rather than destructive. Therefore, Tyrrell concluded, it is generally better for our own sentiment to be in bonds to some extent than to seek full liberty of expansion without a plan of expansion, for on the whole we gain from public religion far more than we lose.

In a long footnote inserted at this point, Tyrrell explained the curious parallel he found between Blondel's dynamic psychology of idea and sentiment and the Ignatian process for discerning the will of God. To Tyrrell, Ignatius's *Spiritual Exercises* were based on the view that thoughts are created by feelings, not *vice versa*. Tyrrell observed that Ignatius did not speak as an intellectualist would of the "consolation" or "desolation" that springs from true or false thoughts. He inverts the causal relation and speaks of thoughts that spring from consolation as coming from the good spirit and thoughts that spring from desolation or depression as coming from the evil spirit. The former presumably are true, the latter false. Tyrrell's terms are different, but his idea is the same: as the individual's will draws near to the divine will (or reality), which is the center of the soul's life, a deepening of sentiment or a sense of spiritual fullness and reinforcement results. Ignatius called this "consolation."[148]

Our cooperation with inspiration consists in seeking some mental expression in which to capture the sentiment. "Without such a containing vessel this welling-up of living waters from the secret depths of the soul . . . is quickly dissipated and forgotten, or else is contracted into some existing form of expression, with loss to its fulness and originality—so much only being fixed as is banal and ordinary."[149] The same is true of artistic and ethical inspiration.

The sentiment captured in inspiration is at root love in some form or another—or hate, for the antagonistic passions equally inspire and stimulate the imagination to devise some concrete expression for the world of appearances. But "love is, at root, the effect of person on person, spirit on spirit, so that all inspiration, artistic as well as religious, is in some sense from beyond, above, and behind Nature—it is an event in the world of freedom and spirit." This understanding is admitted of the gift of genius, which is often described in terms of grace, that is, as a gift that the genius cannot command, "an inspiration, or expansion of the sentiment, giving birth to an illustration, or mental expression, rational or imaginative."[150]

Religion may be considered as both an activity of the individual soul and a social activity. As the former, it is simply the movement of one's will-attitude in relation to God's will and to all other wills so far as accordant with God's. The measure of religion is the extent to which God's will is understood and loved. The individual taken alone will be practically and naturally religious to a greater or lesser degree. But in society the individual can develop a theoretical religion that can help gauge his or her level of accord with the divine will through those notions about God and rules of religious conduct that are the same for all peoples and that express the accumulated wisdom and experience of the ages. Through social intercourse one can attain a practical guide possessed of an inerrancy not otherwise attainable.

But the map is not the wilderness. As an attempt of the understanding to represent and chart paths through the wilderness of the world of wills in relation to the divine will, religion has a double truth: (1) speculative, insofar as it strives to represent its object as it exists independently of its relation to the practical needs of life; and (2) practical, insofar as it furnishes a guide to goodness and truth. Conceivably, a religion can be practically true and speculatively false, or speculatively true and practically false for souls unprepared for its reception.[151]

REVELATION AND INSPIRATION. Precisely as a work of the understanding—that is, as a theology—religion is an effort as purely human as ethics or logic. The difference is that its object is *given* to it, not all at once, but progressively by "revelation," from which springs the natural desire of and effort at new expression or "inspiration." Tyrrell explained how this connection works by appealing to the Gospel account of Peter's confession of Christ's divinity. Up to that moment in Peter's life, he had been in will-union with Christ, but his sense of Christ's position in the will-world in relation to the supreme will, as perhaps that of more than a prophet, was inadequate. Now, by revelation, Peter apprehends Christ's position more truly, "as it were, a second sun in the firmament"—not by conception of the understanding, but by will-experience, by an interplay of God's Spirit in both Christ and Peter, by the action of the divine will in Christ eliciting a response of the divine will in Peter.[152] The revelation was God's; the response *in confession*—the wording and communication of the revelation—was Peter's.

The formulation and communication of revelation Tyrrell called "inspiration." But, he noted, we have become so accustomed to apply the term "revelation" to the communication of the truth revealed that we forget we have never received that truth by revelation ourselves. Once revelation has been conceptualized by inspiration, it has been thrust into the public forum of ideas, and it is there that we as members of society first encounter it. Many of us "believe" in Christ's divinity because it has been revealed to Peter. But to how many has it been revealed personally? And yet the purpose of such communicated revelations is not merely to instruct our intellect and guide our conduct but to awaken in us an inspiration corresponding to that of which Peter's words are the mental expression. Thus we should come to a "sense" and not merely an idea of the reality disclosed. Only in this way does religion become real and a personal experience.[153]

At the same time, if one is to maintain membership in society, one's personal inspiration must remain subject to critique by the public standard. The latter may be far beyond our personal capacity to respond, or it may lag behind. In either case it is the norm and guide. And while we may challenge the norm and go beyond and develop it, we may never contradict it. Authorized formulas must always remain verified in our internal experience.

More strictly, the terms "revelation" and "inspiration" belong to the prophetic office as exercised in the interests of public and external religion. It is a decidedly minority function, not the function of the multitude. The prophet or revealer is one who has attained a high degree of sensitivity to and will-union with the supreme will and all accordant wills. He gathers into his own soul the converging rays of light and warmth, and, urged by interior burning, is compelled to mirror them outwardly again with the new focus of his own utterance. "Such modifications are rightly called 'inspired,'" Tyrrell observed, since they proceed from the workings of God's will and Spirit in the prophetic soul; "the words and mental forms are human, but the force that weaves them into a more spiritual expression is of God."[154] All prophets have contributed to the progressive revelations of God, because God's Spirit has worked for ages through the spirit of man. But only in the human soul of Christ did God's Spirit find his fullest and definitive organ of utterance.

The aim of prophetic utterance is the amplification of life, the more perfect harmonizing of the created will with the uncreated. Increased religious vitality, then, is the test of every religious utterance. But, Tyrrell warned, we must not be too literal in applying the test. The expression (the letter) should not be taken for the reality (the spirit), for it is the latter that enlivens and quickens through the former. The former belongs to the level of science and is therefore subject to the same methods of criticism, and on that level there can be conflict. But between science and the reality of religion there can be no conflict, because they are on entirely different levels of being. The matter of religion (revelation) is never touched in the collapse of its form (inspiration).

THE DOMAIN OF RELIGION. In a convoluted disquisition on the function and domain of religion, Tyrrell first put the question of how the boundaries of religion are to be marked off from those of ethics or morality. He was preoccupied with this question and looked at it in various ways throughout the second half of his book. Only at the end did he state himself very clearly on the question.

Tyrrell's initial response was that to some extent the domains of religion and ethics are coextensive because God is given to us not apart from, but as permeating, the will-world. Yet our actions, as related to the universal and nonreligious claims of right and truth, become religiously qualified as soon as we discern in human experience "the equivalent 'personality' of God" to which all other wills are subordinated.[155] Human actions then take on the new quality of being either accordant or discordant with God's will, and so they become religious as well as ethical. The field of religion, then is defined by our relation to the Universal Will distinctly perceived, and it includes yet transcends the field of ethics, just as our duty to God includes yet transcends our duty to neighbor and self.

Religion, like the regulative sciences, supposes a certain spontaneous activity, a chaos of energies, which it seeks to reclaim to service—not to impede but to develop and channel more profitably. Until these energies are harnessed, we are enslaved to the passive determinism of our nature. It is the role of ethics to school these impulses into harmony and to mold us into free personalities. But if that is the role of ethics, Tyrrell asked, what is the role of religion, or how does religion relate to this schooling process?

Religion, Tyrrell suggested, *results from* that ethical action by which our will tames our initial chaos, but religion cannot be equated with that action. The process is this: We are born into a society and learn by imitation the patterns of behavior considered ethical by that society. Gradually our wills awaken and we respond appropriately to those patterns. Thus we are brought into will-union with all persons of like will. Then, insofar as we *know* that we will what others will, a certain sympathy and mutual love results. There is of course also the contrary sense of hatred for what is judged evil. The very reality and substance of our spiritual lives consists in the sense of our ever-changing relation to other wills, of loving and being loved, hating and being hated. But this sense of relatedness to other wills is not yet religion. For above all other wills and loves is the will and love of God. Acknowledging and participating in that will and love is the life of religion. It is exercised in the same acts by which we act ethically—we cannot do *what* God wills without in that very act bringing our will closer to his—but not until we *know* that what we will is also what God wills are we thrust into the will-relationship with God in which love and the religious life uniquely consist. "The ethical act entails the religious result, and if done in view of that result, puts on a religious character." It is chiefly by conduct, then, that our union with God is determined and fostered; and as our actions do not pass away, but are built into our spiritual substance as an eternal possession, "our union with God, our growth in grace and love, admits of an endless accumulative progress."[156]

Ethical conduct, therefore, may be considered prayer in the

widest sense, in that it is action done in conformity with but ignorance of God's will. But even prayer in the strict sense is directed to ethical conduct, since its explicit aim—and this is the "religious effort"—is the adjustment of our will to God's, and out of this adjustment comes action in acknowledged conformity with that will. Yet however closely conduct and prayer are related, they are distinct and separable, and in fact are sometimes separated. One's whole life must be *for* God by ethical conduct or prayer in the widest sense, but only part of one's life can be *with* God by prayer in the strict sense. To put it another way, one can do what God wills and love what God loves without knowing or loving God; or, one can love the law without loving the Lawgiver.

THE MYSTICAL LIFE. The love that binds wills cannot be conceived statically. As described above, it is a process of continual adjustment and readjustment. It is essentially a "becoming," even when two wills *seem* at rest because they are moving along parallel tracks. The love that binds the human and the divine will cannot be conceived statically either. "Relatively to us, and conceived, as we must conceive it, manwise, the Divine Will is ever transforming and developing itself; and our union with it involves a like self-transforming on our part. The mystical life consists in this process."[157] It is a *conscious effort* involving practices of religious asceticism aimed not merely or directly at "religionizing" our conduct but at increasing personal love or converse with God. It is not a passive process of waiting till we are moved, but an active process in which we seek by memory, reflection, and inquiry to multiply the chances of our hearts being touched anew by some aspect of the divine personality. "No otherwise are human affections deepened. A certain leisureliness is the condition of any very firm and lasting bond between soul and soul."[158]

ORGANIZED RELIGION. It is through self and other selves, through the world of freedom and will, that we get to know and love God as a personality. The hidden God is not to be sought in hypostatized idealization such as Truth and Righteousness, but in concrete actions and will-attitudes. We are not moved to love by colorless abstractions but by concrete deeds that reveal to us the living will and reality that underlie and give birth to them. Just as in the arts and sciences we seek to perfect ourselves by studying the masters, so in religion we turn to masters, to saints and prophets, to study and appropriate their Godward attitudes. We study their lives and find in their concrete deeds and words food for our souls, for it is there that their will-attitudes are revealed.

In its organized form, the society of those who love God is called the church. Its head or unitive principle is the perfect humanity of Christ, which those who have put on Christ communicate to us in an infinite variety of ways throughout ages and cultures. This society, this many-membered Christ, is the school to which we go to perfect ourselves in divine love and bring our wills into ever greater sympathy with God's.

To this end the whole apparatus of Christianity viewed as an external religion is directed. Its two principal components, as Thomas á Kempis pointed out, are "the table of the Divine Word and the table of Sacramental Grace."[159] These are the sources of the soul's nourishment and the standards for will-conformity. All private devotions are effectual only insofar as they fall in with these divinely given standards.

Both tables, Word and Sacrament, are called "means of grace." But before discussing the interrelationship of the means, Tyrrell wanted to be clear about their effect, namely "grace." Swayed by Bergson, Tyrrell rejected the traditional notion of grace as a *qualitas physica* with the attendant notion that the soul resembles a static, bodily substance susceptible of different shapes, modes, and accidents. Even the more congenial notion of grace as the indwelling of the Divinity in the soul he found too materialistic and spatial. He preferred the description of grace as the love of God or charity, a relation of will-agreement between ourselves and God that creates not merely a community of aims such as might pertain between persons who love the same thing but never heard of each other, or who are possibly even at variance with each other, but a community of those who love the same thing and one another in consequence.

This definition, Tyrrell maintained, not only saves the older notion of indwelling but also casts aside the old semimaterialism that viewed the will as a separate or superadded "faculty" and recognized it as merely another name for the free, personal ego. Thus, union of wills and loves equals union of persons equals indwelling. This way of putting it, he thought, also clarified how grace is a sort of strength imparted to the soul and is therefore spoken of as a quality or property. For when persons are bound in love, their strength seems more than doubled, as in the case of the martyrs, or Paul who could say, "I can do all things through Christ who strengthens me."[160]

THE DIVINE NATURE. Lastly, Tyrrell asked what is meant by Saint John's dictum, "God is Love." In answer, he first appealed to the New Testament notion of love as found in 1 Corinthians 12, where Paul rebukes the schismatic spirit and exhorts the Christian community to seek that one gift which is better than all, to which all others are subservient, and which is the most precious manifestation of the Spirit, namely, unity or charity—the *unum necessarium*, the very soul of the community, that which abides even when faith and hope have passed away. But charity is more than mere unity, which may obtain by coercion. As the Latin word implies, "Charity means a mutual 'dearness,' the affection that binds persons to persons, and overcomes that separateness which attaches to the very idea of personality—overcomes without destroying."[161] It is an internal, not an external connectedness; a sameness of being and substance, not merely a relation to some mutual yet distinct aim. Sameness of aim may be the cause or the result of love-union, but it is not the thing itself.

What it positively is, Tyrrell answered, we cannot say, for its fullness is as great a mystery as life itself. But we can say this much, that it is a sense of a fundamental "sameness," which is just as real as that "otherness" which is the essence of personality. Nor is it so much a bond that is made and unmade by circumstances, as one that is revealed or obscured.

Christian revelation pictures God as a trinity of distinct persons in one substance, and indeed it is only as person (implying will) that we can enter into relations of friendship with God. But in saying that God is love or dearness, we should think not so much of the divine personality, which is the center of the hierarchy of wills, as of the divine nature that is the superpersonal bond of dearness that overcomes the "otherness" of the three personalities without destroying them, and by extension is the superpersonal bond also of all who by grace are members of that family by adoption.

That Divine Nature is the common and hidden ground from which we all spring in our several individualities; and which is revealed to us by every new tie of "dearness," that binds us to another personality. It is the bond of the will-world, as distinct from the elements bound together in it. If, on one side our spiritual life consists in a continual development of our individuality and distinctness, on the other, it consists in a parallel development of our sense of sameness—of a convergence towards, as well as of a divergence from, a common centre, eternally approachable and eternally unattainable.[162]

THE CHURCH IN RELATION TO WORD AND SACRAMENT. Having clarified the meaning of Christian grace, Tyrrell turned to the question of the means of grace and the interrelation between the two tables of Word and Sacrament. There are two ways a Christian is united with God: individually or person-to-person, and corporately through solidarity with fellow believers, that is, through the Christian church. The Word is related to the first mode of union, Sacrament to the second. The Word appeals to the individual intelligence and is effective of personal union with God; Sacrament appeals to the corporate mind and is effective of corporate union. In the former, the individual's cooperation is essential. One cannot be inspired to will-union with Christ by the scriptures, the liturgy, the preaching and teaching of the church without that mystical "effort" by which one strives to throw oneself into that spiritual attitude revealed in the scriptures.

But we are also related to the divine will corporately, as parts of the many-membered Christ composed of all who are in will-sympathy with Him. Christ's words, "No man comes to the Father but by me," may be referred not only to the invisible Church (members conceived individually) but also to "the visible Church, of which Christ as man is the Head and unitive principle, and which is the effective sacrament and symbol of the spiritual Church."[163] Nor can anyone not visibly united with the visible Christ through his visible Body share the corporate graces and privileges.

The sacraments are the means of this visible union. Through them the church distributes the riches of divine love bestowed on her corporately. On our part, they are acts of union with her, which, like all acts, abide in our soul and endure as a permanent element of our personality. "By each of them we are rooted more deeply in that sacred soil, and draw a richer nutrient from it."[164]

But chief of all the sacraments is the Eucharist. It is *par excellence* the Sacrament of incorporation. Its combination of ministry of Word with ministry of Sacrament ordered to individual and community makes it the ideal "spiritual exercise." First the soul individually is brought into harmony with the soul of Christ by confession, prayer, praise, being instructed and exhorted, but especially by hearing the Gospel. Then in the sacred mysteries the individual is drawn into the great interchange of love between God and redeemed humanity and thus is made one in the church: "I in them and thou in Me, that we may be perfect in one."[165] But as commonly formalized, the Eucharist has fallen from its original conception—"not by enactment or deliberate alteration, but under the spoiling hand of time, whose fossilising influence is ever hostile to that spirit of life of which flexibility is the essential condition."[166]

THE CHURCH AND DOGMA. What Tyrrell held on the matter of dogma he summarized clearly in his preface to *Juliana of Norwich*.

> Hence it is that religion, whether viewed as a doctrine or as a life—whether as a perception of the nature and relations of that spiritual world which flows from and centres round God and is seized by faith, or as a vital reaction of love evoked by that perception—embodies and expresses itself, more or less sacramentally, in terms of that outward world which is seized by the senses and the understanding. It identifies itself with a certain body of statements—philosophical, ethical, historical—not directly in the interests of the mind, but in those of the heart; not because they are coherent with current conceptions of the order of phenomena, but because they are practically true to the facts of the real order, and guide us into closer will-union with God and man.
>
> But though the religious and the mental values of such statements are distinct, even as the spiritual and the natural effects of sacramental bread or water are distinct, yet, like these, they are tied together within certain definable limits; nor can religion suffer the denial of any natural truth that enshrines a supernatural value, unless when the earthen vessel is destroyed only to be replaced by one more worthy of her heavenly treasure. Still, she cares nothing for the affairs of the mind, nor even for ethical propriety of conduct, save as an expression and instrument of the life of the spirit, as furthering union with the Divine Will. Love, Charity, Eternal Life: this is her meaning in all that she says, this, the inspiration under whose influence she chooses her words and weaves her own garment from the materials she finds to hand; and it is for the sake of such inward meaning that Faith clings to the otherwise indifferent beliefs of the natural order in which that meaning is embodied—clings with a certainty that is truly not of this world, but supernatural.[167]

As a school of dogmatic teaching on faith and morals, the church under the impulse of inspiration presents the finest conceptual expression of the will-world in Christ that humankind's collective understanding has devised. As the joint work of Old Testament prophets completed by Christ and enunciated by the church, it is given us as an external and authoritative standard by which to measure our personal religious understanding.

The aim of the church's utterance is purely practical: to provide a map to guide our attitudes in the will-world. To the extent that the map so functions, it is true. If it hinders, it may be that we have forgotten its purely practical aim and take it too literally and thus abuse it. Doctrine is meant to stimulate, not suppress, personal initiative. Of primary importance is the truth of the relations of the spirit-world, not the truth of the symbols that express those relations. If the church pronounces on a point of history, science, or philosophy, it is only because she sees that some relation of souls to God is at stake. When she sees that the threat has passed, she turns to other matters. "Her interest in history and science is somewhat analogous to that of a poet, who is not pleased when he finds that he has been using some ignorant blunder as a vehicle for his most solemn self-expression; as a point of science it does not interest him, but he is unwilling to reconstruct his masterpieces, and may not find the truth so flexible to his purpose as the blunder was."[168]

REVELATION AND ETHICS. Tyrrell anticipated the charge of rationalism to which he laid himself open by his position on the "purely practical aim of religion." He could be read as denying all mystery in revelation and admitting nothing as true whose direct bearing on ethical conduct is not apparent.[169] But he asserted that such a reading would ignore the distinction between religion and ethics and would treat religion as simply the servant of morality, whereas conduct is the servant of religion, for it is through conduct that we engage in the work of God and bring our wills into communion with his. "We do not love in order to labour, but labour in order to love. This love and sense of will-union is the very substance and basis of our spiritual being; our conduct is at best its manifestation, and belongs to our surface life. . . . Love is not a part of conduct, but a spring or motive. It is that which acts."[170]

Making conduct the servant and at best the manifestation of religion might seem to contradict what Tyrrell said about religion resulting from ethical conduct.[171] But the contradiction is only apparent if one sees that the relationship Tyrrell drew between ethics and religion is reciprocal, analogous to the reciprocal relationship between ideas and feelings. Presuming an ethical society, one born into that society first *learns* ethical behavior. Feelings appropriate to the learned behavior should follow in due course, and at that time one becomes bound by love to all of like aim. Love in turn should inspire and motivate increasingly generous response to ethical imperatives as revealed in the words and actions of Christ and his saints. Generous response to revelation in turn leads to increased will-sympathy or love. Hence, Tyrrell concluded, in saying that all revelation is directed to love and the life of religion, he places himself "in strict opposition to those who say that it is directed solely to conduct and the 'religionising' of life," and so he acquits himself of the charge of rationalism to which he is open if this reciprocal relationship is not kept in mind.[172]

So far, then, as revelation is inspired by God, it is a word to the heart, not to the head. It proceeds from and is directed to love of God. Of course one who *loves* will want to *know* the will of the beloved, hence the conceptualization and formulation of the spiritual life—for example, in the Nicene Creed. But even the articles of the creed, taken as an organic expression of God's relation to man, have an immediate if not always apparent bearing on man's conduct: they determine more fully and completely our will-attitude to God and so are plainly directed to love.[173]

Of course, revelation does have its say in the matter of ethics, as ethics certainly bears on divine love. Will-union with God implies a desire to know and do *what* he wills, so far as it lies within our power of response. Our judgment may err in ethical conduct, but the persistent desire to please God by ethical perfection cannot but lead to a progressive refinement and spiritualization of originally crude conceptions. But just as in the case of science, Tyrrell asserted, religion is not concerned with ethics for its own sake but only because it bears on divine love and because love is exercised by conduct. Religion concerns itself with the rights and wrongs of moral problems only under the formality of "the will of God." It transcends the sphere of ethics or of any branch of mere knowledge, "just as the self or will-life of the spirit transcends its life of thought and self-utterance."[174]

Religion's interest is therefore the will of God, an interest that lies on the plane of faith and that at once embraces and transcends ethics, which lies on the plane of understanding. The better one comprehends this transcendence of religion, the more absurd will appear the fears of those who fret about reconciling faith and understanding—as if the two were ideally harmonious and complementary parts of the same thought-world but whose coherence is obscured by our ignorance. The fact is that they belong to two different worlds. They do indeed enjoy a certain complementarity, but they can no more clash than can history and poetry. Only the expression of religion, its embodiment in the categories of the understanding, is exposed to such conflict. Exploding the poet's science and facts may disembody his sentiment, but it will not destroy it.

Religion, which relates our will to God's by love, is the crown of our will-life but not the whole of it. It is the regulative head, but not the body. As the head is nothing without the body, religion is disembodied without the whole of our will-life—our social, friendly, familial relationships of all kinds—which it brings into order, deepens, strengthens, and purifies. The cultivation of these "secular" interests is as essential to religion as the body is to the head. "Hence, the love of God and of our neighbour are but complementary parts of one and the same precept which governs the fundamental life of the soul—the life of Charity or will-union."[175]

But religion, Tyrrell concluded, is not the mere "religionizing" of behavior. That is, at best, the fruit of religion. Rather, religion is a distinct life apart, albeit in harmony with conduct, thought, and all outward activity. Its direct concern is the deepening of the bond between our will and God's, an effect producible by certain external acts of religion, whose norm is the chief act of the church's worship, namely, the Eucharist. This act is normative because the Eucharist, with its ministry of Word ordained to the soul's individual capacity and its ministry of sacraments ordained to the soul's corporate capacity, expresses and fosters the fullness of human life. It is plain, then, that anyone who wishes to live a full life must pursue religion as a distinct and separate endeavor. "A prayerful life is not enough if it be a life without prayer and explicit commerce with the Divine Will."[176]

Aftermath: Benedictions and Maledictions

Despite "horrific oaths of secrecy" under which "Dr. Engels" distributed his book, at least one fell into the hands of the "Philistines." M. Eugène Franon, director of the seminary of the Institut Catholique of Toulouse and ecclesiastical watchdog over philosophical publications, managed to secure a copy through an antiquarian bookdealer. Referred to as "le philosophe distingué du Bulletin," Franon was a vicious opponent of the new anti-intellectualist philosophy and one of Tyrrell's chief refuters.[177] His review of "Engels" appeared in *Bulletin de littérature ecclésiastique* for June 1903 and called the book an "inestimable compendium of agnostic and symbolist theology."[178] Franon said that he could not conceive anything "less reasonable nor more disconcerting" than M. Engels's theory of religion. Deduced *a priori* from a psychology and a systematic metaphysics, said Franon, that theory was worth exactly what that psychology and metaphysics are worth: nothing! Is it not in effect a mutilation of human nature to reduce it to a matter of the will? According to M. Engels, the Absolute is an object of our experience—one of the more preposterous propositions that defy demonstration. And does M. Engels prove it? By no means. "All he proves is the possibility of founding on experience a religion from which nothing follows."[179] As for M. Engels's theory of Christianity, how radically it departs from traditional teaching is apparent to anyone from the first glance, since from the outset it implies the denial of the supernatural character of Christianity. It is true that M. Engels admits revelation and inspiration—he even speaks of them as the two chief factors of theological development. But what notion does he have of them? A purely naturalist one. That is evident from his view of miracles and of dogma. By not accepting miracles he eliminates the transcendent character of Catholicism, and by interpreting dogma merely symbolically he destroys Catholicism altogether.

If such defenders of orthodoxy as Franon noticed the radicalness of "Engels's" departure, they did not guess the identity of the real author, at least not until the publication of *Lex Orandi*, which incorporated much of "Engels" verbatim. Even then no one seems to have uttered the name right out loud.[180] Even the Roman authorities seem never to have discovered the book's true author. Romolo Murri's Italian translation, *Psicologia della religioni*, published in Rome in 1905 under the pseudonym "Dr. Sostene Gelli," was placed on the Index on 5 July 1909, but it was listed under "Gelli, Sostene [*pseudonymus*]" with no cross-reference to Tyrrell.[181]

Tyrrell and von Hügel took great pains to limit "Engels's" ambit to select friends, so very few copies went into circulation. Tyrrell was still swamped with copies shortly before he withdrew them altogether in favor of *Lex Orandi*.[182] As the recipients were friends and sympathizers, their responses are predictably sympathetic, but to Tyrrell's surprise also enthusiastic. Heinrich J. Holtzmann, the German Protestant biblical scholar, wrote to thank von Hügel for sending a copy and praised it as "one apologetic of Catholicism from new points of view which is also partially acceptable to us. I will see to it that the *Theologische Jahresbericht* for 1901 gives it the notice it deserves."[183] Julius Goldstein, a disciple of Eucken, also wrote von Hügel:

Doctor Engels has sent me through you a very interesting and valuable little book. Unfortunately I do not know the man's address. May I ask you therefore to be so very kind as to communicate to the author my most sincere thanks for the joy he has given me with his work on a subject which always requires re-thinking and re-presentation according to the newest resources and conceptions of philosophy and science. As a philosopher I found especially interesting and gratifying the connection with Blondel and Münsterberg. Then too his whole

manner of handling this difficult subject with marvelous clarity together with a fervor of feeling is simply outstanding. When I have my
Habilitation [as Professor in Darmstadt] behind me, I hope to be in a
position to review this work in the supplement to the *Allgemeine
Zeitung*.[184]

Joseph Sauer, who had received his doctorate in 1900 under Franz
Xavier Kraus in Freiburg and was currently delivering his first public lectures, wrote, "I am astounded, delightfully astounded over
the profundity, over the philosophical depth and the clarity and
persuasive power with which the fundamental problems of philosophy of religion are handled here in so tight a space. My eyes flew
over the little work, so attractive did I find its presentation; many
parts I went over again and again. Who is the author anyway? May
I ask you please to forward him my most sincere thanks?"[185] And
Eucken wrote, "Philosophically Tyrrell and I stand side by
side. . . . In substance I can go with him all the way."[186]

But Eucken also sensed a divergence. Tyrrell sensed it too, and
explained it partly by his own scholastic prepossessions but mostly
by his adoption of the leading ideas of Bergson.[187] Indeed it was
Bergson, more than Blondel or anyone else, who led Tyrrell to
sever his ties to the traditional apologetic and to reject the mediating liberalism of Newman and Ward that tried to synthesize faith
and reason by making them merely different poles on the same
spectrum of reality rather than placing them on two different levels
of being altogether. But more of this presently.

Other reactions from Italy, France, and England were forwarded by von Hügel, but the letters seem to have perished. In
substance they were all enthusiastic, and Tyrrell was understandably elated. On 1 October 1902 he wrote to Waller that he was now
"encouraged to work out something less tentative on the same
lines."[188] But, he complained to von Hügel, "It would have been so
much more encouraging had it been possible to put my name to
'R'; & not necessary to speak the truth under one's breath, as it
were something obscene."[189]

How was Tyrrell to get his name put to it? His first plan was to
serialize "Engels" for the *Month*. After the recent row with
Vaughan and censors over *Oil and Wine*, Tyrrell had cowed them
into passing and publishing a two-part article entitled "Mysteries a
Necessity of Life."[190] He thought that by now the censors were so
intimidated that he could sneak an expurgated "Engels" past them
as well.[191] So he set to work, breaking "Engels" into chapters, rear-
ranging materials and purging it of as many inflammatory referen-

ces as integrity would allow. "I have resolved to send an unbroken stream of articles into the *Month* until I am stopped," he told von Hügel on 4 December, "and *I mean to doctor up* 'Engels'—even the Appendix—for that purpose. They are so very dense, so long as one avoids the 'male *sonans*' that one can say anything 'male *significans*.'"[192]

But the baron did not share Tyrrell's enthusiasm. Discerning readers of the *Month* might unmask "Engels" and bring ruin on Tyrrell's head. As early as the previous August, when the baron had spent three weeks at Richmond with Tyrrell and Maude Petre, reading and discussing *Oil and Wine* and *Religion as a Factor of Life*, he had expressed nervousness about Tyrrell's publishing pseudonymously, "lest it should lead to a catastrophe."[193] Then the following winter in Rome he had spent much time and energy in sensitive negotiations with friends and ecclesiastical authorities over the cases of Loisy and Marcel Hébert. He knew what could happen. So in a postscript to his letter of 4 December 1902 von Hügel suggested that Tyrrell write instead on the baron's first hero of Catholic and orthodox reform, Nicholas of Cusa, but not try to publish "Engels" in the *Month* in any form. He closed with Hügelian flattery: "with my heart prayerfully and affectionately full of you my intensely alive, immensely impulsive and hence astonishingly, most meritoriously and fruitfully balanced Friend!"[194]

But Tyrrell would not be put off. He replied the next day that he felt some urgency about getting at least the substance of the appendix into the *Month*, "just because so many *ordinary* Catholics need such a *modus vivendi* now. However I will think it over & over before I venture."[195]

Further thought led Tyrrell to reject his original plan in favor of a more elaborate one involving one pseudonymous work, which would allow him to say all that he dared not say in the *Month*, and one work that would carry the archbishop's *imprimatur*. The former work was eventually published in the spring of 1903 under the title *The Church and the Future* and the pseudonym "Hilaire Bourdon." Tyrrell referred to it as "a cousin of Dr. Engels,"[196] although it was of another cut altogether. It is analyzed in the following chapter.

The other book arose out of Tyrrell's earlier breakdown of "Engels" into chapters for the *Month*. The baron may have cut short that plan, but the labor would not be lost. As soon as Tyrrell saw "Bourdon" off to the printer, he announced the resurrection of "Engels." To von Hügel on April 1903 he wrote, "I am writing a sort of expurgated & amplified Engels for the orthodox multitude which I am going to offer to the censors. . . . It is called *Lex Orandi;* & will be a *tour de force* when finished."[197] By 14 June "Engels" had been transformed. On that date Tyrrell sent A. L. Lilley copies of "Engels" and "Bourdon" with the note, "The Red [the color of "Engels"] has been just recast with a view to publication under my name—should censors prove manageable; of which however there is very small hope."[198]

Lex Orandi: *"Engels" Redressed Wins* Imprimatur

Tyrrell's plan now was to secure the benediction not only of Jesuit censors, which would have been the case had he serialized "Engels" in the *Month,* but of the cardinal himself. This was clearly a superior plan if it succeeded. With the cardinal's *imprimatur* on *Lex Orandi,* Tyrrell would be virtually assured immunity against ecclesiastical proceedings in the event that his cover on "Engels" were blown. Publication in the *Month* would have provided little protection, as the recent *Oil and Wine* debacle proved, and Tyrrell would almost certainly have shared the fate of Loisy, whose *L'Évangile et l'Église* had been condemned by Cardinal François Marie Richard de la Vergne the previous 3 February.

Feeding *Lex Orandi* to the censorial process was a bold move. Possibly Tyrrell was counting on sneaking by while the watch was still exhausted from the last confrontation and anyhow reluctant to cross swords again so soon with so fierce an opponent. Tyrrell was optimistic. On 9 August he notified both Waller and von Hügel that he was withdrawing "Engels" for the present. He had incorporated much of it "rather brazenly" in *Lex Orandi,* and it would jeopardize his chances for an *imprimatur* if authorities noticed the parallels. "I more than half suspect that the powers know all about it as it is; but the fiction of secrecy must be kept up *pro forma.*"[199]

Eleven days later Tyrrell sent Bremond the news that *Lex Orandi* had passed the Jesuit censors "with 3 *superavits* and 1 *vix attigit.*[200] But now the difficulty is to get a Diocesan blessing."[201] For that step the manuscript had first to be set in print. At this point Tyrrell made subtle but insidious revisions in the spirit of "Bourdon." The proofs of *Lex Orandi* have been very troublesome," he confessed to the baron. "I feel it will be my last say & I want to say all I can and as well as I can; to get in as much as will fit of Bourdon under the *Imprimatur.*"[202]

Church politics was another factor favoring Tyrrell's scheme. Cardinal Vaughan had died on 19 June, so Tyrrell had now to deal with Vaughan's successor, Archbishop Francis Bourne. The relationship between Westminster diocesan authorities and the English Province Jesuits had been most cordial, and it would have been most unseemly for the new archbishop to inaugurate his reign by such a contrary act as rejecting a book that highly respected Jesuit censors had passed. He did not disappoint. On 19 November Tyrrell wrote to Lord Halifax, "I have told Longmans to send you a copy of *Lex Orandi*, which has got the new Archbishop's imprimatur; some things in it may please you, but on the whole it is heavy, owing to the need of obscurities and circumlocutions in order to evade the snares of the Philistine. Still, I hope it will tell slowly, and with a few."[203]

Lex Orandi fell beneath Tyrrell's expectations. It was not the *tour de force* he anticipated. So much of the underlying psychological and philosophical prepossessions were either omitted or so disguised that the real value and singular contribution of "Engels" was drastically diminished. Disappointed, Tyrrell wrote to Lilley on 30 November, "This is just to accompany *Lex Orandi* which, you may notice, is Dr. Engels' 'Religion as a Factor of Life' in water. It will not interest you save as having won ecclesiastical approval & being therein a sign of the times—yet not so very significant; because it only means they (the approvers) are too far behind the times to twig its smothered liberal implications. Still it has got to be born, poor puling weakling: whether it will be overlaid remains to be seen."[204] Von Hügel's only extant reaction was, "What a refined, pretty-looking book: and short too!"[205] He promised to read it carefully and report his impressions, but he did not get around to that until the following August and September, when he did so *viva voce* during his month-long visit to Tyrrell in Richmond.[206]

The public reaction to *Lex Orandi* was comparatively mild, not at all what one might have expected had Tyrrell given the public "Engels" full strength—if indeed the public could have assimilated it. Reactions were also predictable. Tyrrell's friends applauded, his enemies disapproved. Franon called it by the same phrase he used to describe "Engels": a compendium of agnosticism.[207] Père Jules Lebreton, S.J., whom Tyrrell regarded as among the fairest of his adversaries, respectfully maintained silence until Tyrrell's departure from the Society of Jesus was made public. Lebreton's review in the 5 March 1906 number of *Études* expressed astonishment that Tyrrell's writings, which he said presented a system that "imperils the foundations of the faith," could have received an *imprimatur*. That they did, Lebreton could only assign to "a regrettable error."[208]

Archbishop Bourne seems by hindsight to have concurred. Apparently he had not carefully scrutinized *Lex Orandi* but had simply approved the Jesuit sanction and then afterwards repented. According to Tyrrell, Bourne blamed Fr. Alexander Charnley, the superior at Farm Street and prefect of censors, for affixing his *nihil obstat* to the book.[209] In a letter to von Hügel of 6 February 1904, Tyrrell expressed his "profound distrust of that gentleman [Bourne] who is a dangerous gossip & a trimmer." Of an exchange with Bourne over *Lex Orandi*, Tyrrell continued, "He tells me had he seen Ch. XXIII. of *Lex Orandi* he had refused his *Imprimatur*. I have told him that if he will suggest any amendment I will put it in the 2d. edition if I can do so with sincerity."[210]

Chapter 23 was based largely on Loisy's form criticism of the Gospels. It began by distinguishing in creedal statements between their historical and religious value. "It is only for the sake of the latter that the Church interests herself in the former," Tyrrell asserted,[211] and went on to illustrate his point with the dogma of the virgin birth. Without denying the historicity of the Gospel account, Tyrrell clearly played down the traditional Marian emphasis and gave the dogma a Christological interpretation.

The religious value of this dogma, he insisted, is to be sought in the influence it has exercised on the hearts of Christians and saints. Theologically there is no essential connection between it and the Incarnation. That is, its religious significance is not that Christ was born of a virgin, but that Christ was born of woman. It tells us not what virginity did to enhance Christ, but what Christ did to enhance Mary and through her all humankind. She is "the highest expression and embodiment of Christian sanctity which the Holy Spirit has brought forth in the hearts of the faithful; and . . . the revelation of a new aspect of the Divine Goodness with which we are thus put into fuller and more fruitful communication." Thus this dogma has fed and fostered the Christian spirit as much as any other dogma, "yet, plainly . . . it is not the physical facts that matter, but the religious values which they symbolise."[212]

This notion, Tyrrell observed, is operative in the way that the saints assimilate Christ's spirit and communicate it to us in other ages and conditions than those of Christ's mortal life. Through them we learn not what Christ did historically, but what he would have done in our age. The same notion was at work in the evangelists. Full of Christ's spirit and mind, they "might conceivably have been inspired to reveal Him to us, not in strictly historical narrative, but in such fact-founded fictions as would best characterise and portray His personality to those who knew it not. Such literary devices were in no wise disreputable at a time when they were recognised and expected." If the Gospel narratives embody "actual events of the phenomenal world," Tyrrell concluded, "and not merely . . . sacred or inspired legends," still it is important not to confound their religious and historical values and thereby subject our faith to needless assault.[213]

Tyrrell's devaluation of the assumed facticity of certain biblical narratives was far in advance of the times. Even many post-Vatican II bishops and theologians would be hard pressed to match their theological currency against this devaluation. It is easy, then, to understand Archbishop Bourne's agitation and Franon's indictment of *Lex Orandi* as an "inestimable compendium of agnostic and symbolist theology."[214]

The peculiar significance of *Lex Orandi* in Tyrrell's theological development lies in its clear and careful orchestration of a theme hinted at in his October 1902 article, "The Limitations of Newman," and resolved in his two "Semper Eadem" articles.[215] That theme was a declaration that the theory of development devised by the mediating liberal school of Newman and his loyalists had failed to effect a plausible synthesis between faith and reason. Intellectually the synthesis made sense because Newman and Ward put faith and reason on the same plane of reality. But in Tyrrell's view faith and reason required no synthesis since they lie on two different planes of reality and therefore cannot come into direct conflict. The conflict is merely apparent. Ward's representation of the theory, Tyrrell charged, failed to distinguish adequately between the roles of intellect and will in religion, between external religion and real religion, between what is conceptually known and consciously willed on the one hand and what is instinctively felt on the other, between symbol and what is symbolized. Ward's theory gives the lead to the head and makes the *lex credendi* the *lex orandi*. But in real life, action is primary and gives the lead to the heart. It makes the *lex orandi* the *lex credendi*. Moreover, any theory that gives the lead to the head cannot provide a criterion to distinguish true from false developments of belief, for a criterion that lies on the same plane of reality as that which it is supposed to judge is no criterion at all. It can decide only what beliefs are reasonable, not what beliefs are true.

The whole question, Tyrrell told Ward, is, Who are the real teachers in the church? Answer: the saints, who in their deepest selves (that is, in conscience) are in direct contact with the voice of God. The saints originate what the whole church eventually comes to profess. The theologians and ecclesiastical authorities only gather up and distribute the fruit of prayers, the labors of the saints. The few saints always precede the multitude. Only in the course of time, under guidance of the Holy Spirit, what made the saints holy becomes pared down and embodied in a form assimilable by the multitude; what is angular or spurious is cast off; "what is believed always, everywhere, and by all" is saved and made the rule of faith.

> *Non in dialectica,* says Ambrose, "It is not through disputation that God has chosen to save His people;" it is not through theologians nor by theological methods, though these have their due place, but by the Holy Spirit, by the Spirit of Holiness working in His saints and servants, that He has promised to lead His Church into all truths. . . . If we hear the Shepherd's voice it is because we are already His sheep in some degree, and because the Christ that is within us recognises the Christ that is without us. Herein lies the religious or supernatural element of faith; the reasons we give to our mind are but afterjustifications of an impulse that derives, not from reason, but from the sympathetic intuitions of the Spirit of Holiness. . . .
>
> When once we realise clearly that the Church is guided into all truth not by the precarious methods of theological dialectic, but by the Holy Ghost; that life and not logic is the ultimate criterion as to what beliefs and forms of belief are fit to survive; that eventually, and in the last resort, it is the Saints and their followers who discriminate between false and true, food and poison; that the doctrinal authority of the Pope and Bishops rests not on a special theological skill, but on an instinctive discrimination between holy doctrine and unholy, i.e., on the guidance of the Holy Ghost; then only shall we be delivered from the spiritually disastrous snare of confounding intellectual perplexities and entanglements with doubts against faith.
>
> No theory of doctrinal development however true, however subtly flexible, can alleviate this ailment or supply us with a firm and simple principle of discrimination so long as it looks on that development as more or less principally an intellectual or theological movement, led and controlled by the mind in the interests of speculative truth; so long as it gives the lead to the *lex credendi,* to the head rather than the heart; so long as it makes sentiment wait upon the idea; life and action upon knowledge; forgetting that we must live and act in order to discover the laws of life and action, and that we must keep Christ's commandments, if we would know His doctrine.[216]

There is real and authentic development in the lived relation between God and man. But this development depends on and correlates to the development of the Spirit of Holiness in the church at large, whose movements the theory follows as a shadow follows the movements of the body. But in this case the shadow, too, is animated. As in a dance, "it co-operates with and reacts upon the movement which it follows."[217]

Here Tyrrell took Harnack to task. For Harnack the external expressions of the Spirit through time are so much refuse behind which are to be found the authentic unchangeable essence of religion, pure and undefiled, the simple homogeneous sentiment of the fatherhood of God and the brotherhood of man. But this notion, Tyrrell charged, implies that always the same changeless substance is revealed beneath various changes of costume. At the same time it denies that charity or the spirit of divine love, in both the individual and the church at large, is susceptive of a true development— "not merely of an increase of intensity, but of an endless unfolding and closer co-ordination of multiform possibilities latent in its first germ." It also ignores the chief function of doctrine in the work of development, which is both to characterize and to fix each stage of the process and so prepare for the next stage. It is not merely a case "of setting new melodies to words ever the same. The music grows with, and answers to, the growth of the theme; as the Church prays, so she believes."[218] *Lex orandi, lex credendi.*

CHAPTER 7

The Church and the Future

SETTING THE SCENE

The most decisive work of George Tyrrell's foreshortened career was *The Church and the Future*. It was also the most daring and personally costly. It ended one period and ushered in the last. It was the climactic and inevitable conclusion to all his reading and writing prior to 1903, and at the same time it determined his future direction. Up to this point Tyrrell had struggled mightily to find a *via media* between orthodox and liberal extremes. Now he declared that effort dead. He rejected the mediating school of Newman and Ward and proclaimed a new era of apologetics born of the radical and practical principles of his philosophy of religion. Not until 1907 would Tyrrell find new accomplices—Döllinger and Acton—to replace Newman and Ward; nevertheless, the publication of *The Church and the Future* proleptically ratified the pact.[1]

It was also ratified *sub rosa*. Not only did Tyrrell conceal his authorship by publishing under a pseudonym (Hilaire Bourdon) and making the book seem to be a translation from a French original, but prior to his open divorce from the Jesuits and the Roman Church he distributed only a handful of copies to a carefully defined circle of his most trusted friends.[2] This secrecy, however, he maintained not out of cowardice, nor because he could not or did not want to face the agony of separation from the old alliance. Indeed he found keeping up false appearances even more torturous than making a clean break. In fact at one point, only eight months after the appearance of "Bourdon," his hatred of pretense led him

246

to take the first steps toward legal separation from the Jesuits.[3] But he quickly repented of that move and let matters drag on for two more long and excruciating years.

Why then did he maintain secrecy? Why submit to the pain of a false position? When one has lost faith in a position, is it not time to leave it? He had "two honest alternatives," Maude Petre wrote in her introduction to the 1910 edition of "Bourdon," "to leave the Jesuits or to keep silence, whereas he did neither."[4] More than once he confessed that he would find either of these alternatives easier than the compromise he settled on. Compromise was not in his nature, but compromise he did. For as long as conscience would permit, he strove to achieve the impossible with all the success that the impossible promises. He tried to live on both sides of an impassable fence, simply because people he loved and who loved him lived on both sides. He had to think about them more than about himself; that was his nature. A rupture from the Society of Jesus, and even more so from the church, would mean a serious loss of influence and credibility—not credibility about his own person but about the cause for which he labored, namely the church. It would also represent a victory for the ultramontanes who were insisting that the liberal gospel according to the likes of George Tyrrell had no place in the Church of Rome.

Tyrrell's position was precarious. Not only did he have to speak out, but he had to maintain ecclesiastical standing. He was convinced that his liberal conception was nearer the truth than was the reactionary, conservative conception and therefore required a place in the church. To demonstrate his position he himself had to try to remain both in the church and in the Society of Jesus, despite his disaffection from the latter, for, in the mentality of the time, to leave the Society was tantamount to leaving the church. Driven by duty and affection he straddled the fence until his strength and temper gave out. To those on the right he strove to represent the light of his own truth against the darkness of the reactionaries. To those on the left he tried to prove by his own presence that they, too, could live within the Church of Rome along with the likes of James Moyes, William Gildea, Merry del Val, and the Vatican theologians. He needed to prove that the Church of Rome was ecumenical enough for both conceptions, and that, in the event of divorce, the onus of responsibility would rest squarely on those of the extreme right. These divided feelings tore him apart.

The Church and the Future was a hybrid of two basic movements in Tyrrell's thought: the one, apologetic, fueled and ignited by the joint pastoral controversy and by the struggle with Jesuit and ecclesiastical officials over censorship; the other, religious-philosophical, Tyrrell's natural habitat, prepared from afar by his study of Butler, Aquinas, and Newman, and more recently recast by contact with the new philosophy of Blondel, Laberthonnière, Bergson, Eucken, and a host of related scholars. The questions addressed in this book were the same as those addressed in previous published and unpublished writings, only now the questions were more intense, and answers were sought with greater urgency. The contents of the two streams were channeled into one, but now into the mix were introduced new data, the fruit of Tyrrell's most recent studies and personal experiences. The latter accounts for the urgency of the book.

Once "Engels" was under way, Tyrrell turned his attention almost exclusively to the most recent developments in biblical and historical criticism. It was a foreign environment. By background and intellectual tooling, Tyrrell was unfit to deal with the issues raised—historical facts that seemed to collide head-on with the ultramontane conception of the constitution of the church and even sideswipe his own liberal conception. Yet the issues had to be faced and somehow incorporated into Roman Catholic ecclesiology if the church was either to remain credible to those still inside or to regain credibility with those on or beyond the fringe.

"Bourdon" is Tyrrell's attempt to face and incorporate the new to save the old. It was conceived and born in less than two years. Consequently one ought not expect to find a completely developed and mature ecclesiology. Rather one should expect a developing outline, a tentative groping, a first effort. Beginning tentatively was always Tyrrell's way. He was an essayist in all senses of that word. He was constitutionally unable to think in terms of tracts and tomes, and all his writings were nothing more than first essays. To him there was no such thing as an ultimate solution in any case, so why not offer whatever one has to hand in the realization that it only leads to the next offhand offering.

Furthermore Tyrrell did not intend *The Church and the Future* for the general public. He conceived and executed it as a private study, an attempt to answer some questions that were personally involving for himself and those like himself who were trying to find room in the church for the new. It was strong medicine for the few, not food for the many—not that the many did not need it, only that they were as yet unprepared to assimilate it.

One may wonder why Tyrrell bothered to write the book at all. Simply answered, he felt compelled to write it. But the reasons behind his compulsion are many, various, and complex. Some of them, as already indicated, were tied in with apologizing for his resistance to the ultramontane apologetic and with fashioning a new Catholic apologetic. Primarily he wanted to register another view of the nature of the church and church teaching, a view that, because of its opposition to the majority view, could not be approved but he hoped would at least be tolerated for the sake of the minority. Tyrrell knew well that authorities have to guard the welfare of the majority, but not at the expense of the minority. To save the minority was also vitally important—important ultimately for the welfare of the majority—for it was among the minority that many of the most creative minds were to be found, and it was there that the future of the church was being worked out and lived before that future became the generally accepted and officially approved present. The other, more particular, immediate, and existential reasons for writing *The Church and the Future* will emerge in the tracing of its development.

A TROUBLED GESTATION

Engaging Historical Biblical Criticism

ALFRED FIRMIN LOISY. In a way, "Bourdon" began and ended with Loisy, the leading French scripture scholar. That his name appears nowhere in the book is no indication that he was not behind the book or that Tyrrell did not want to give the devil his due. The fact is, Rome was already stoking the devil's fire, and Tyrrell did not want to make it any hotter by associating Loisy's name with such obviously anti-Roman sentiment. So he expunged Loisy's name from the page proofs. On 19 April 1903 Tyrrell wrote to explain the late deletions to Waller, who was again serving as underground agent. It would not be fair to Loisy, Tyrrell said, to connect his name with "Bourdon," "for I am sure he does not go near so far in the liberal line as, I think, his principles may be pushed and as I push them in the sequel; yet a reader might infer that I was simply a defender and exponent of Loisyism."[5]

Privately, however, Tyrrell did acknowledge his debt. On the occasion of receiving two gifts from Loisy—*Le Quatrième Évangile* (1903) and *Autour d'un petit livre* (1903), the latter written in defense of the recently condemned *L'Évangile et l'Église*—Tyrrell wrote to express his thanks. His curiosity about the first book, he told Loisy, had been roused to a high pitch by von Hügel on their long and frequent walks, but of course he had also read everything

Loisy had previously published on the matter. "To me this manner of reading the fourth gospel is just the pivot, the cardinal point about which the whole battle between the causes of static & dynamic Catholicism must move."[6] Tyrrell was referring here to Loisy's insistence on symbolic and mystical *versus* a rationalist interpretation of scripture.

Loisy expressed that idea most pointedly in the conclusion to his article "L'Évangile selon Saint Jean":

> The Fourth Gospel, unique within the Bible for the originality of its conception, the depth of its development, and the intensity of mystical feeling that penetrates it, had everything to fear from its modern critics. Applying, as they did, the narrow logic of critical philosophers and meticulous historians, they could not help but misinterpret the Gospel's true character. Saint John was the farthest thing from a philosopher working out a system or a historian curious about factual material. He was above all a witness to Christ, and his testimony is a portion of the witness by which the Spirit of Truth attests to the Word made flesh. In many respects Christian tradition had a far better understanding of this Gospel than contemporary criticism does. That is why Catholic commentators, without losing sight of the various approaches of rationalist exegesis, wisely chose to enter more deeply into the spirit of the ancient Fathers, which is the spirit of the Fourth Gospel. Had they not done so, they too would have risked, by their exegesis, compromising the most profound religious thought expressed in human language.[7]

Tyrrell had read that article in September 1901 and saw its import. It "deserves the honour of the Index more than anything I have seen for a long time," he told von Hügel with relish.[8] Canon A. L. Lilley, Tyrrell's Anglican sympathizer who had carefully followed Loisy's career, summed up its significance in the March 1903 number of the *Commonwealth*.[9] "As a critic," he said, "Loisy is led to the most radical results." He could not abide Harnack's arbitrary separation of Christ's teaching into the relative and absolute, into what was eternally true and what was historically conditioned. Only what is true for actual men is actually true, but this truth is apprehended only through an experientially determined intellectual medium. The absolute and relative are separable in thought but not in life, and "religion is a life." Nor could Loisy admit the notion that Christ intentionally accommodated his teaching to the intellectual capabilities of his hearers. "Jesus spoke," asserted Loisy, "in order to say what He thought true, without the least regard to our categories of relative and absolute." It is not necessary to search out the truths uttered by Jesus that in their very form have eternal value. For

> the full life of the Gospel does not reside in a single element of the teaching of Jesus, but in the totality of His manifestation which has its point of departure in the personal ministry of the Christ and its development in the history of Christianity. What is truly evangelical in the Christianity of to-day, is not what has never changed, for in one sense everything has changed and has never ceased changing, but that which notwithstanding all external changes, proceeds from the impulse given by the Christ, is inspired by His spirit, serves the same ideal and the same hope.[10]

This summary is a fair suggestion of Loisy's position and of what Tyrrell absorbed and reexpressed in his own way.

Loisy had stood as a signpost at the crossroads. He pointed out, Tyrrell told him in a letter of 12 October 1903, that of the ways available

> one alone was really open & permeable, and that a labour of radical reconstruction was the only condition of keeping one's Catholicism. Each day of reflection & study deepens that conviction and also shows that seeming losses and impoverishments have been real gains in spiritual & religious richness. . . . Needless to say our older men *will* not read you and our younger men *may* not. But whenever I lend your works to these latter they are absorbed as water by a thirsty soil. These poor starved intelligences are in many cases hungering for bread & receiving stones. This is the most hopeful sign of coming redemption: the old teaching falls on dead ears; unconsciously, if not consciously, the young men are, & therefore the future is, with us. About 2 days ago one of our ablest men, to whom your name was anathema, took your *Études* from my room in a spirit of hostile curiosity. Being fundamentally honest-minded the result has been a complete bouleversement of his whole attitude. However grievous, the opposition of Bishops in these days can only advertise and underline your teachings. Strange they should not see this.[11]

On the same day Tyrrell wrote more graphically to von Hügel, "As I said to Loisy to-day, the young men are with us & therefore the future is with us. The complaint at our English Jesuit theologate of late years is not that the students are heterodox (they are too blinkered for that) but that they simply *will not* listen to their professors or take interest in the old codex-grinding work. Those that come here by any chance (I have 3 cases in mind) & pick up Loisy in my room (I see to that) drink it up with the eagerness of dipsomaniacs."[12]

Tyrrell began his own heavy sampling of Loisy during the summer of 1900, coincident with his separation from the scriptorium at Farm Street. More and more he found in Loisy inspiration and materials with which to construct his own ark against the flood. On 3 January 1902 he reported his progress to von Hügel. "What I am fullest about is . . . the manner in which, Loisy excepted, we Churchman [*sic*] evade" the implications of biblical historical criticism. "The conclusion will soon be drawn for us by outsiders and we shall find ourselves with no *modus vivendi* if we now burn the boats that L. has prepared for our escape."[13]

Tyrrell went on to explain how Loisy viewed inspiration as "the progressive spiritualising & refining of those gross embodiments in which man expresses his own ideas & sentiments about God," and how this view applied to various points of New Testament revelation. "Christ's whole 'revelation' was little else but a further correction of the better sort of religion which he found in Israel." The words of the "Our Father," for example, were not new but were given new meaning. The Father was no longer "ours" in the nationalistic sense but in the catholic sense, the sacred name was no longer a ceremonial taboo but required a spiritual and practical reverence for the nature behind it, and no longer was there a zeal for a kingdom of this world but for the kingdom of God in men's hearts. Paul was clear on this understanding when he distinguished the true from the carnal seed of Abraham, but we shrink from the consistent application of this principle "because we secretly think the *material* sense is *true*, & the spiritual, *unreal*." But the real reason for Rome's hostility to scriptural criticism was this:

> that nothing which Fathers, Councils or Tradition have said of the Church's infallibility is half so strong as what they said of the infallibility of Scripture; and that if the latter conception has to be gravely modified the former cannot hope to escape a corresponding modification. Yet both modifications are "insuppressible" and the more obstinately the truth is resisted, the more disastrously will it avenge itself at last, and the Church will have to "begin with shame to take the lowest seat."[14]

Harnack's answer to the *quid inde?* of historico-critical studies was that they enabled one to peel back the husk of tradition and find the kernel of Christianity deposited by the historical Christ. Loisy countered that historical studies could never uncover the essence of Christianity, as if it were a body of truths committed to verbal transmission. For Loisy, Jesus was indeed the Messiah prophesied by Isaiah and the prophets, but as such his only concern was to herald the final judgment and the coming of the Kingdom and to call men to repentance and salvation through himself. Jesus came not to impart any final *truths*, but to impart a *spirit*, to initiate a religious *movement*. Jesus, his teaching, and the language of the Gospel were part of history with all the conditions and limitations of the time. The scriptures may be a vehicle of transmission for the spirit of Christ, but they contain no deposit of faith to be explained and developed but never changed. For Loisy development of doctrine implied real change and not simply an accumulation of reformulations to keep pace with changes in culture and language so as by *accidental* change to remain *essentially* the same. This view of development is obviously at odds with Newman's, but it was the one that Tyrrell felt the evidence pointed to, and for all his procrastination it was the one he eventually adopted—not, however, without his own modification, as will be seen.

PAUL WERNLE. In 1901 Tyrrell took up seriously the arduous task of learning German—"for the 9th time in my life," he told Petre.[15] The first theological work in German on which Tyrrell tested himself was Paul Wernle's *Die Anfänge unserer Religion* (1901). He wrote to von Hügel on 3 January 1902 to say that he was at it, and again on 12 April to say, "I finished Wernle's 'Anfänge' & liked it better as I went on and saw what might yet be built out of the seeming ruins."[16] Indeed the book was an exercise in destructive criticism and concluded much more about what is not known than what is known of the origins of Christianity as a religion. But Wernle was not apologizing. He argued that many features of the old picture of Jesus deserved to be destroyed. But from the historico-critical residue he was not able to construct a new image. On the question of Jesus' divinity Wernle's silence roared so loudly as nearly to drown out his one positive assertion: that Jesus is at any rate the *way* to God.

GIOVANNI SEMERIA. Tyrrell was finding the critical atmosphere too rarified, and his head was swimming as a result. The previous October his ebullient Barnabite friend, the Italian scripture scholar Giovanni Semeria, had paid him a visit at Richmond and given him a firsthand whirl around in criticism. Initially Tyrrell took the tour almost as a lark—in the spirit of Semeria who, born and bred in the faith, could gambol about the most sacred tenets without ever touching the roots. "How wonderfully buoyant in the midst of the ruins he is creating!" Tyrrell said of him to Bremond.[17] But Semeria left Tyrrell with a mare's nest of apprehensions. In his letter to von Hügel of 3 January 1902, following mention of Wernle's *Anfänge*, Tyrrell described Semeria's effect on him:

> Semeria's short visit was like a sudden burst of sunshine to me. But his hopefulness is too obviously physical in its basis to be solidly reassuring. For one who begins life with the fulness of popular Catholicism the disillusionments of criticism are not so costing as for one who has climbed up somewhat laboriously to that position at the cost of a good deal of needless intellectual torture & is now forced step by step down to the level of sane Christianity. I feel that S. does not, perhaps cannot, know experimentally the horrors of pure negation; that his sense of the extremest possible issue of honest criticism is more "notional" than "real." In all else, I felt abundantly in sympathy with the humour of the man, and his all-saving sense of the ridiculous—that salt for lack of which so much corruption has invaded theology.[18]

ALBERT HOUTIN. Shortly thereafter Tyrrell received another "burst," but this time without the cushion of humor, and this time not from biblical criticism as such but from a history of the effects of criticism in France. It was Albert Houtin's new book, *La Question biblique chez les Catholiques de France* (1902), a present from the baron.[19] Houtin, whose career was strangely similar to Loisy's, was an ardent admirer and disciple of Loisy and consulted the latter as he composed *La Question biblique*. In large measure that book was about Loisy and his influence in the church. Houtin's biography of Loisy, not published until 1960, contains a telling passage that bears on Loisy's effect on Tyrrell and on the general effect of historical criticism as assimilated and practiced by Loisy. Recounting an alleged confession by Loisy on the occasion of a serious illness in March 1907, Houtin wrote, "I knew that he was no longer a Christian, though he always claimed to be something of a Catholic, but I believed that he was like me a spiritualist and deist. He told me that twenty years ago he had ceased to believe in the soul, in free will, in the future life, in the existence of a personal God."[20]

Houtin described the effect that Rome feared: loss of belief in the divinity of Christ, if not altogether in God. If it could happen to Loisy, why not to simpler folk who were much less prepared? Historical criticism was a new venture for everyone, but particularly for Catholics, and Rome had every right to treat it cautiously. At the same time, she had an obligation to educate herself in the new method so as to provide intelligent criticism and guidance in its use and gradual assimilation. But her reaction was largely negative, fueled by ignorance, fear, and panic.

La Question biblique, provoked by the politics behind the new

Roman Biblical Commission, was a history of that reaction.[21] Houtin purported to give only the facts, but the arrangement of those facts, together with his wit and irony, led Tyrrell to question Houtin's success in avoiding suspicion of a certain "animus."[22] Houtin's book, Tyrrell wrote to Bremond on 9 April,

> makes me feel that we live on the verge of a revolution & are but suffering the ordinary & normal phenomena of such conditions. I am also learning . . . not to hate the authors of our sufferings anymore than one hates the wild beasts of the forest, since they are alike determined by necessary causes. Still one may wish them slain or trapped, or otherwise restrained from hurtfulness. What I fear in my own case, is, lest I should give them the triumph of seeing their head-shakings and predictions verified. To this, they goad one continually, & the only safe rule is to do nothing for mere anger's sake; though at times one's wisdom is sore tempted.[23]

Tyrrell really needed no incentive to anger, because at that same time *Oil and Wine* was in the process of being quashed by Cardinal Vaughan. Nevertheless he found more than enough incitement in Houtin's book. The reactionary repression of Houtin's principal malefactor and his school, Bishop Charles-François Turinaz of Nancy, Tyrrell complained to Petre, was "really responsible for the extravagances of the opposing school." The episcopacy's blind intolerance of even moderate liberalism has destroyed confidence in their competence and sincerity, so that one can no longer see any limit to disintegration. The moderates have ceased "to exercise restraint on their immoderate disciples, and what might have been an orderly and dignified retreat from untenable positions has become a pell-mell flight." At the same time Tyrrell doubted more and more that anyone could find "an honest *via media* with clearly defined limits, such as W. Ward is trying to tinker up out of J. H. N[ewman]."[24]

Tyrrell then outlined for Petre the negative elements of the problem. It was the skeleton of what would soon become "Bourdon," part 1:

> I find now three millstones with which Catholicism is weighted to destruction, and yet, cut them away, and what remains? They are first the political conception of the Church as embodied in the "court of Rome" and the claim to temporal power; secondly, the "protection" system, which adapts the environment to the organism and not conversely, and is embodied in Jesuitism; thirdly, the tyranny of theological schools as embodied in scholasticism. But Catholicism, minus Politics, Jesuitism, and Scholasticism, equals Protestanism; and with that equation I am not quite satisfied.[25]

In "Bourdon," part 2, Tyrrell tried to rebalance that equation and show how those three millstones could be cut away without the church floating off into airy Protestant latitudes.

The next day, 12 April, Tyrrell wrote to von Hügel of Houtin's book: "That authority should blunder now and then were natural; but to see it always & systematically on the wrong side suggests a sort of inverted infallibility that is hard to account for on natural principles until one digs down to the 'the roots of all evil,'" namely the "three millstones" of ecclesiastical politicism, scholasticism, and Jesuitism. Turinaz is right in seeing that the old system is gravely threatened, but, Tyrrell charged, it is he and his kind who by avoiding reform in the past have forced the progressive movement "into an attitude of antagonism: *Ipsi viderint!*"[26]

Two days later Tyrrell advised Bremond on a plan for securing release from the Jesuits and urged patience against the ineluctable vindication of time.

> I believe in patience because things are moving very fast towards liberty, a fact of which these violent repressive tactics are the best evidence. The old men feel that the reins are slipping from their senile grasp, & they are clutching at them with the anger & energy of despair. Pope Canute cannot keep out the tide with a pitchfork or a crozier. Houtin's "La Question Biblique" (which the Baron sent me) shows his Holiness skipping back step by step, with very bad grace & much cursing & swearing, before the encroaching waves. So far, he has only wet his feet & caught cold; if he doesn't move faster he will be presently drowned. Personally, I have not much difficulty in waiting because I have so much to do in order to unlearn all that the S.J. has taught & to fill up the appalling lacunae in my education caused by ten years (noviceship 2, tertians[hip]. studies 7) waste in the best part of my life.[27]

First Signs of Inner Turbulence

So Tyrrell plunged deeper into the unknown sea of historical criticism and allowed himself to be tossed and turned by conflicting waves and crosscurrents. The upshot was fear and bewilderment. As long as matters were kept on the speculative level— philosophy was Tyrrell's natural habitat—he remained high and dry, but what he had to deal with now were historical facts, or at least with what were so construed. Theories can be alternately taken up and set aside by whim, but facts have to be faced and living adjusted to suit the relentless forces of nature.

On 27 April Tyrrell wrote to Petre of perhaps his most fearsome specter—the effect of criticism on the doctrine of the Incarnation: "You are right in feeling that I am working down to that root gradually, instead of beginning there. But, odd as it may sound to you, I have been afraid to touch the basis of all lest I should find myself houseless & homeless in the wilderness. But the ostrich policy never answers for more than a time with me. Only can one go on in outward communion with the Church, knowing that one could not sign the tests that authority might propose at any moment?"[28] Yet Tyrrell was fully, almost fanatically, committed to offering himself as a sacrificial victim for the cause. For him the whole meaning of the present was found in struggle, but a struggle that, contrary to the hopes of Ritschlian liberals, would be redeemed in an otherworldly future and not in this life. It was the notion of the prophets. On 20 May he wrote again to Petre:

> Were it not for its pessimism, its despair of the world, its contempt of l'avenir, I should say Bouddhism was better than our fussy strenuous struggling reforming Christianity which crucifies gods & men in the belief that the world can be made better & conquered to God. It is only that wild yet irresistible fanaticism that saves me from A'Kempis & the Bouddha. At all events I think the world like the flesh is intended to be struggled with & not fled from & that in the grip of conflict the muscles of the soul are developed & our personality brought out in a way which men arriving at tranquilty could never effect. There is great energy in the crucifix as contrasted with the slumberous Bouddha—magis. And yet—[29]

For Tyrrell incarnationalism was a problem overburdened with consequences. What was to be expected from this life by reason of the Catholic doctrine of the Incarnation? Did God become man to convey a message of ultimate triumph of love over hate in this life? Or was his message simply that the ultimate value of the present life consists in that struggle, and that that value would be redeemed in the kingdom to come? Still, was not one to expect some tangible signs already in this life and see that struggle was progressing gradually toward that ultimate redemption? Tyrrell emphatically believed both in progress and in final consummation of the struggle, and he was convinced that the authentic Christian message preserved in the mind of the church was the most effective medium for progress.

BENJAMIN KIDD. Tyrrell had long ago pondered the value of engaging in the struggle for progress, but recently Benjamin Kidd's *Principles of Western Civilization* (1902) stirred the question again.

In a review for the April 1902 number of the *Month*, Tyrrell praised the book's apologetic value but questioned Kidd's contention that the unselfish sacrificial principle of true progress was not to be sought in modern Roman Catholicism.[30] Privately and consistent with his own thinking, Tyrrell had to concede that one could find plenty of evidence in present-day Catholicism to support Kidd's contention. At the same time—but in the pages of the *Month* Tyrrell could only imply this—Kidd's error lay in identifying current "officialism" with Roman Catholicism.

Roman Catholicism, as opposed to Protestantism, Tyrrell argued, did in fact preserve the most universalizing and ecumenizing principle of progress.[31] This principle lay in what could be gathered from Christ's teaching on the Kingdom of God—that progress for the individual is precisely relative to the individual's service of the whole. But this belief by no means implies a subjection of the individual to the convenience of any other individual or of the state. Christ's revelation of the infinite and absolute value of the individual makes such a notion intolerable. To serve others the individual himself must be strong and capable. Christ's teaching forbids not only murder but any curtailment of one person's spiritual development for the sake of another's. "It demands the greatest possible equality of external opportunity for all; and therefore will not tolerate the exploitation of the future in the interests of the present. Yet it is a principle given us rather by sentiment than by reason—one of Pascal's 'reasons of the heart.'" This principle, Tyrrell asserted in the spirit of "Engels," was a fact of that underlying will-world and had been operative in all true social evolution, although it had been felt rather than known and had often been more obscured than explained by the creeds and institutions in which reason sought rightly but vainly to embody it. "The old pagan categories still dominate our thought, and we strive to encase the spirit of Christian liberty in the political conceptions of Aristotle—conceptions shaped by a belief in the paramount ascendency of the Present."[32]

To offset Kidd's assessment of the effectiveness of Roman Catholicism, Tyrrell would offer another ecclesiology in *The Church and the Future*. There he would argue that Christian revelation is prophetic and spiritual, in no sense legal or dogmatic, and that therefore political categories are wholly inadequate for its transmission.

VINCENT ROSE. Toward the end of May 1902 Tyrrell made the literary acquaintance through André Raffalovich of one of the less notorious French scripture scholars, the Dominican Père Vincent Rose of the University of Fribourg in Switzerland. A target of both praise and blame, Rose generally managed to retain his place on episcopal white lists and to avoid outright censure. He was pronounced passing clean, for example, by Célestin Douais, bishop of Beauvais and professor at the Institut Catholique of Toulouse, but he was pronounced unclean by the Jesuit Père Julien Fontaine for making the Christ of the Gospels too human, a charge soon to be levied against Loisy.[33]

Raffalovich had sent Tyrrell a copy of Rose's *Études sur les Évangiles*,[34] and on 4 June Tyrrell sent his thanks with the observation that Rose was a welcome complement to Loisy. The latter, Tyrrell said, was engaged in assimilating the good results of criticism rather than in rejecting the spurious. Rose conversely. Yet Rose was absolutely candid, liberal, and capable of dealing with the critics on their own ground. "Still I can fancy the shock it will be to many to realize how much of a *prima facie* case there is against the stories of the birth & the resurrection; for indeed R. does the Devil's advocate with alarming skill."[35]

Ironically, *Études sur les Évangiles* appeared with Cardinal Richard's *imprimatur*. Tyrrell pointed this fact out to von Hügel, and he observed that as a moderate book its significance lay in its method and tone rather than in its conclusions: "& here it is Card. Richard who makes the *faux pas* of an *imprimatur*. I really believe these men are too absolutely ignorant of the *status questionis* to discern good from evil, unless some officious Jesuit points it out to them."[36]

It is quite clear, however, that Tyrrell himself was not sure how much was good and how much evil in the new studies. He was confident that their aim was true, but their weapon was too strange in his hand for comfort.

Consultations at Richmond

On 5 June 1902 Maude Petre took up residence at 24 Newbiggin in Richmond.[37] During June she and Tyrrell spent many hours together reading and discussing Eucken's *Der Kampf* and William James's *Varieties of Religious Experience* (1902). The state of Tyrrell's faith in the face of historical critical assaults also came up for discussion. On 29 June, while Petre was away briefly, Tyrrell wrote ostensibly to reassure her about the state of his faith: "I am not really unhappy at all. If I never were more confused as to 'what is truth' I was never more deeply confident that it is something infinitely better than we dream. . . . I am content to be much in the dark; perhaps I prefer it, as God seems nearer."[38] But was he not rather trying to reassure himself with some whistling in the dark, or did he really feel that he had severed the spheres of faith and knowledge in himself as cleanly as his articulations of the process in "Engels" would lead one to believe? The fact is, what was now assailing Tyrrell's knowledge was at the same time recoiling on his faith-experience—a result in perfect accord with that reciprocal relationship between faith and knowledge that "Engels" also described.[39]

Nor was contact with the baron any antidote. On the contrary, von Hügel's easy play with ideas and disturbing historical facts on the broad base of a pious faith acted as a deceptive invitation for Tyrrell to try the same. But von Hügel was already many years at this sort of study, and Tyrrell was taking his first faltering steps.

The baron spent three weeks in Richmond, from 18 August to 6 September, reading, walking, and talking with Tyrrell and Petre. Tyrrell's reflections on that visit are telling. After the baron's return to Hampstead, Tyrrell wrote to him to say "what a great help & pleasure your visit has been to me & how greatly it has stimulated my flagging interests & filled me with hope & desire to work on through thick & thin."[40] But to Bremond Tyrrell showed another side to that story: "The Baron has come & gone, & left me, as usual, with more to think of than I can digest. I wish he wd. draw up a list, not of what he doesn't believe but of what he does. A few months ago Dr. Engels seemed to me an ultra-liberal; now he seems an ultra-montane. Were it not for men like Caird & Eucken I don't know where I should be, but these men have touched what Jesus Christ touched." If Tyrrell was convinced that Jesus Christ had touched something, he was feeling less and less sure of what that was, and in fact almost despaired of finding it anywhere but in mystical experience. His letter to Bremond continues:

> Doubtless God speaks in history, but it is a polysyllabic word of which we miss the ends & therewith the meaning; & unless he is to be found within each soul he is practically unfindable. I think honestly that when I live for that inward God of my ideals I find some sort of peace & life & that elsewhere I find none. And that experimental proof is perhaps all I have a right to expect. It is as near as I can get to reality. I read more & more, & write less & less everyday.[41]

This closing remark comes close to understatement. The baron had deluged Tyrrell with more suggestions for his reading, which will be looked at shortly.

Apparently Bremond had pressed Tyrrell for more details on

the baron's beliefs and unbeliefs, because on 25 September Tyrrell replied that he would not even attempt to speak briefly on the baron's Christology, except to say that "he considers my religion too 'Christo-centric'" and in the spirit of chapter 19 of *Oil and Wine* "insists much on Christ as the *Way, not* the End." As to his own views, Tyrrell said only that he was presently "incubating a Christological egg" and did not want to disturb it by premature investigations.[42]

Actually Tyrrell carried his "Christological egg" throughout his lifetime and only by the by gave readers hints of what the formed fledgling might look like.[43] Chapter 19 of *Oil and Wine* is as good a hint as any and deserves brief notice. It shows that even prior to Tyrrell's contact with the disturbing elements of biblical criticism, which told him more what he did not know about Christ than what he did know, he tended to deemphasize Christ's divinity in favor of his humanity.

The essay, called "The Sacred Humanity," takes off on a revealing quotation from Augustine: "No creature should hold us back from God, since not even our Lord Himself, in so far as He vouchsafed to become the Way wished to hold us back, but went from us lest we should cleave weakly to those things done and suffered by Him, in time, for our salvation instead of hastening onwards more quickly by means of them."[44]

For Tyrrell it was precisely as man that Christ's instrumentality was helpful and necessary, "for no man hath seen God at any time, that he should have any adequate or proper conception of the Divine nature." It was necessary that the Word, "the reflex of the Father," be made flesh, so that those who see him also see the Father. "The human mind . . . conceives God humanwise or not at all," for there is no way to knowledge of the Father except by the "flesh." Likewise, "the object of our love must be, not merely a personality but a human personality," and therefore "the highest humanity is the highest image we can possess of the unimaginable divinity."[45]

But for all of Tyrrell's talk of Christ's humanity, he was far more comfortable with the humanity of the risen Christ, the Christ in the realm of the Spirit, than with the humanity of Christ in the flesh of Jesus of Nazareth. It was particularly in that humanity that Tyrrell found biblical criticism troubling, and he needed some respite.

A Retreat into Philosophy of Religion

For two months following von Hügel's visit Tyrrell retreated into the familiar and more comforting haven of philosophical theology. Among the works von Hügel left for Tyrrell to read were Eucken's *Der Wahrheitsgehalt der Religion* (1901), Ernst Troeltsch's *Die Absolutheit des Christentums* (1902), "Die Grundprobleme der Ethik" (1902), and "Die wissenschaftliche Lage" (1900), Fichte's *Die Bestimmung des Menschen* (1800), and Bernhard Duhm's *Das Geheimnis in der Religion* (1896); later he forwarded Troeltsch's "Geschichte und Metaphysik" (1898).[46] On 8 September the baron dispatched a list of six more books, all of which Tyrrell would eventually read, but two of which he attacked almost at once: Richard Falckenberg's *Grundzüge der Philosophie des Nicolaus Cusanus* (1880) and Georg Wobbermin's *Theologie und Metaphysik* (1901).[47]

All of these works were to tell in some way on "Bourdon." Fichte's *Die Bestimmung*, Tyrrell told Petre on 10 October, "is quite wonderfully what I have been trying to say for years. . . . It leaves one convinced of the sole reality of the will & spirit & the dreariness of all else."[48] Four days later he told the baron that no book had ever satisfied him quite as much. "It has all the contemplative earnestness of Augustine's Confessions; and gives the grateful relief of clear shape to many of my own vague imaginings. . . . It would help many a soul in search of a firm basis of faith."[49]

Duhm reinforced all that Tyrrell had been saying about the inadequacy of human understanding and categories for the expression of religious truth. And now that scientific criticism was confirming his half-felt suspicions with unavoidable concreteness, he was even more firmly convinced. All these recent rumblings erupted into an article for the *Month*, "Mysteries a Necessity of Life."[50] It does not go beyond Tyrrell's previous writings in any essential way, but in his letter to von Hügel, Tyrrell drew the connection between Duhm and that article: "Duhm's Geheimnis I only read *after* I had written a very cautious brace of articles for the *Month!* on "Mysteries, a necessity of Life"—a point which we spoke of, climbing down the green bank by the old bridge, one day. Even if it is rejected, I will have 100 copies printed. In principle I am with Duhm, tho' I try to save theology within its due limits."[51]

If nothing substantially new was advanced in this article, its emphasis—particularly against the background of Tyrrell's recent studies and the visit from von Hügel—betrayed Tyrrell's state of mind and stands as a manifesto of the one thing in life of which he was still sure: mystery. Who could deny this? Faith is what it is precisely because of mystery. But it is hard to avoid the impression of special pleading, as if Tyrrell were saying, "I find myself hopelessly confused. Now how can I turn this into virtue?"

Back to the Critics: Another Hügelian Prescription

HERMANN GUNKEL. Though Tyrrell had found a moment's rest
in philosophy of religion, troubling historico-critical studies were
never far way. On 16 September he informed von Hügel that he
had finished the introduction to Hermann Gunkel's *Genesis* (1901)
and was at the text. By 14 October he was close to the end.[52] Tyrrell
had shared the centuries-long unquestioned assumption that the
scriptures were transmitted in written form. Now Gunkel challenged that assumption and argued for oral transmission. Tyrrell
found the argument "fascinating" and convincing, and there is no
evidence that the ensuing readjustment in his thinking on this point
particularly disturbed him.[53] But it was another straw added to the
rapidly increasing burden of readjustment.

JOHANNES WEISS. Johannes Weiss's *Die Predigt Jesu vom
Reiche Gottes* (1892) was another matter. Until he read that book
Tyrrell had been resting more or less comfortably with the liberal
notion that Jesus was really a modern man in ancient dress who paraded around a philosophy of religion that resembled "Engels"
stripped of local color. Truth to tell, Tyrrell had himself criticized
liberal Protestantism, but he had also assimilated enough of its
spirit to have felt the full force of this new critique. Contrary to
liberal claims, Weiss argued compellingly that Jesus was not a
modern man, but a man of his times who thought in the eschatological categories of his times. For Jesus the Kingdom of God was not
a religious experience, it was "never something subjective, inward,
or spiritual, but . . . always the objective messianic Kingdom,
which usually is pictured as a territory into which one enters, or as
a land in which one has a share, or as a treasure which comes down
from heaven."[54] Coincidentally or not, Weiss's book represented a
double father-murder. On the one hand it ended the liberal domi-
nance of the school of his father-in-law Albrecht Ritschl. On the
other hand it repudiated the conservative orthodox position of his
own father, Bernhard Weiss.[55] Tyrrell, who was trying to walk between the two, was suddenly left without a hold, caught the blow
squarely in the middle, and was thrown for a headlong *bouleversement*.

LOISY *versus* HARNACK. Weiss's ideas penetrated the thought of
many subsequent critics, including Loisy's. On 10 November 1902
Loisy's *L'Évangile et l'Église* went on sale in Paris bookshops. On
the same day the baron received four copies from Loisy and immediately distributed them.[56] One of these copies went to Tyrrell

along with Loisy's *Études évangéliques,* which was issued simultaneously. On 17 November Tyrrell replied with thanks to the baron, but said that he had already received a copy of *L'Évangile et l'Église* from Loisy and had finished it "with great pleasure"— although its polemical nature made it less pleasing than his more disinterested works. "I see he makes great use of Weiss in the first two essays. It will surely be translated; & as the only solid answer to H[arnack] *ought* to win him golden spurs if our authorities were not stone blind."[57]

In the area of philosophy of religion Tyrrell was discriminating, so he did not swallow Loisy whole. He was quick to notice weaknesses in Loisy's arguments against Harnack, on which Loisy received plenty of adverse comment in the press.[58] But it was the only solid Catholic rejoinder to Harnack. As Tyrrell observed to Bremond, *"L'Église et l'Évangile* [*sic*] leaves one more door of escape open if our brethren do not succeed in shutting it."[59] But on matters of historical criticism, particularly with regard to scripture, Tyrrell's background did not allow an equally critical and independent judgment. Here he was at the mercy of Loisy and Weiss.

Even von Hügel, who, compared to Tyrrell, was an expert in biblical criticism, was set back on his heels by Weiss's little book. He described the impact in an important letter to Tyrrell of 26 November 1902: "I do not know what book taught me a more fundamental historic-religious lesson—or indeed, one which goes deeper and ranges further than the point he brings home to one with conclusive power." The baron confessed that until he read Weiss he had been clinging to the notion of the Kingdom of Heaven as "centrally interior and already present." But now "we all—Casciola, Fawkes, you, I—must manfully learn to realise and admit that that view is simply *not true.* . . . It is *not* the originally directly taught and intended doctrine," although as proven true by experience we must acknowledge it as coming from "our Lord's immense stimulation, enrichment and revelation of the soul's inner life." But the doctrine of the interior and already-present Kingdom is such an enormous modification of his original message that we are driven to two conclusions:

> The conception of human life as, even fundamentally and permanently, not simply present and not solely spiritual and moral, cannot be simply a popular mistake and caricature of the real truth, unless the very substance of Xtianity has ceased to be *normative* to us. And the Church's at first sight *omnium gatherum* sort of a Kingdom of Heaven presentation, and its putting this ever into the future, will be, in some important respects, more primitive, *because of these very features,*

than a Tolstoian sublimation and contraction of it all to one unchanged, indeed immutable point.[60]

Tyrrell might have found company in von Hügel's misery, but
misery was not the sort of company he needed. He would have to
look elsewhere for assistance in solving the conflicting exegeses.
Oddly, he turned to Loisy. On 20 November Tyrrell wrote to thank
Loisy for the books and to express his pleasure at seeing *Études
évangéliques* published "under the present straightened circumstances." But he assured Loisy of "many sincere though fettered
& timid admirers in the Society"—and even its corporate attitude
was not altogether hostile, "though of course it is determined by
expediency and opportunism rather than by any interest in truth or
religion." Still "oculi omnium in te sperant: your work is rooted too
deeply in public intelligence & sympathy to be possibly uprooted
now, by any tempest of ecclesiastical opposition." What was especially pleasing, however, was "the manner in which you have assimilated and rendered helpful instead of harmful the somewhat
disconcerting position of Weiss' *Predigt Jesu vom Reiche Gottes*, a
book which had given me considerable pause."[61]

For Tyrrell, Loisy cut the straight draft of Weiss, for although
he was with Weiss in opposing Harnack's liberal notion of the
Kingdom, he went on to interpret how the meaning and spirit of
Jesus' preaching came to be embodied and expressed, however
imperfectly, in the Catholic Church. The Kingdom preached by
the historical Christ, Loisy contended, was not purely personal and
already interiorly present, a matter of subjective experience, but
was rather collective, objective, and future.

In his chapter on "L'Église," Loisy charged Harnack with being
grossly unhistorical in his contention that the essence of Christianity
is restricted to faith in God the Father and that the whole development of the church—its structure, dogma, and ritual—is superfluous. While conceding that Jesus did not establish an ecclesiastical constitution that was to endure through the centuries, Loisy
objected that Harnack's conception of "an invisible society formed
for ever of those who have in their hearts faith in the goodness of
God" was even more foreign to Jesus' teaching. Historical criticism
shows that Jesus' gospel "contained a rudiment of social organization, and that the kingdom also was announced as a society. Jesus
foretold the kingdom, and it was the Church that came." As soon
as the Passion closed Jesus' ministry, the church was there, "enlarg-
ing the form of the gospel" because "it was impossible to preserve
as it was."[62]

If Jesus did not foresee and establish the church in its present form, Loisy argued, it was nevertheless a necessary consequence of the work of Jesus, an organic development out of his religion and identical with the spirit bequeathed to that first group of disciples. "To reproach the Catholic Church for the development of her constitution is to reproach her for having chosen to live, and that, moreover, when her life was indispensable for the preservation of the gospel itself." Just as one's identity "is not determined by permanent immobility of external form, but by continuity of existence and consciousness of life through the perpetual transformations which are life's condition and manifestation," so the church, to be identical with the religion of Jesus, "has no more need to reproduce exactly the forms of the Galilean gospel, than a man has need to preserve at fifty the proportions, features, and manner of life of the day of his birth, in order to be the same individual." And if the church and its development were necessary for the preservation and preaching of the Gospel, development was *a fortiori* necessary for the church's dogma and ritual. Up to now, Loisy observed, emphasis had been laid only on the unchanging object of faith. But the time had come to emphasize the undeniable fact that the church's *expression* of faith is continually changing and to formulate accordingly a doctrine of development.[63]

Assessing Tyrrell's Condition

For a long time now, Tyrrell had found congenial the liberal thesis of the Kingdom of God, that the Father through Christ was to be found within—the largely interior, personal, and spiritual notion of Ritschl and Harnack. This notion was reinforced and supported by Blondel's and Laberthonnière's new apologetic of immanentism and the new value and life philosophies of Fichte, Dilthey, Bergson, and Eucken. Then suddenly an antithesis struck Tyrrell in the form of historically supported contentions that the Kingdom preached by Jesus was external, objective, and future, standing over against man as a judgment and a call to repentance. These contentions were affirmed by Weiss and to some extent by Wernle, Gunkel, and Loisy. Finally Loisy arrived with a comforting synthesis: the Kingdom is both objective and personal, external and spiritual, future and present. The objective, external, and future Kingdom is yet to be realized completely, but it is personally, spiritually, and presently available in a form most faithfully approximating the Spirit of Christ in the Roman Catholic Church. It seemed a neat compromise. It fit in beautifully with the separation between religion and ethics, will and intellect, and faith and reason that Tyrrell had so sedulously achieved in "Engels." All that belonged to the external, objective, and future Kingdom could with impunity be subjected to the scrutiny of historical criticism—that Kingdom, after all, belonged to the preaching of the historical Christ as recorded in the Gospels. However, all that belonged to the spiritual, personal, and present Kingdom still lay beyond the reaches of any authoritative challenge other than one's own faith experience. This interior Kingdom is the realm of freedom. But if it is the realm of freedom, it is at the same time the realm of the most searing kind of personal honesty and responsibility. It is the realm, Tyrrell would argue, to which the Gospel calls every person.

A FIRST SYNTHESIS. But any synthesis in this life is as labile as life itself. It stands only long enough to be confronted by a new antithesis. Thus, while Tyrrell struggled mightily to achieve a passable resolution, what he came up with satisfied him only long enough to say so. In early December 1902 he conjured up a first synthesis of the Weiss-Harnack antithesis (the outward-future *versus* the inward-timeless views of the Kingdom of God) in a long footnote to "Religion and Ethics," one of the articles stemming from his second set of Oxford Conferences.[64] Harnack's notions about the present interior Kingdom of God, Tyrrell explained, were fine, except that he confused the essence with the means. Weiss, on the other hand, was very good on the description of the future and outside Kingdom. By pitting the two critics against each other Tyrrell figured to find the truth in the mean. What the historical Christ meant by the new heaven and new earth is difficult to say, except that he implied some abrupt and general renewal. He foretold "a new environment or world for which we must begin to prepare ourselves," but he was not clear on its nature. He was clear, however, on the preparation required for it, and here Harnack's description fits in. Not external rites or sacrifices but only the practical living out of that inward spirit of grace and love that resulted in the apprehension of the fatherhood of God and the brotherhood of man can prepare mankind for the true Kingdom. Then "from the spiritualizing of the preparatory conditions we can infer a corresponding, though as yet mysterious, spiritualizing of the conception of the coming Kingdom." But what Harnack considered the essence of the Kingdom is only the condition, and however well that condition or preparation is lived, it remains an "imperfect mode of life" and will only "receive its full development [change] in an altogether new environment hereafter."[65]

"Environment" is the key word in Tyrrell's synthesis. The future, outward Kingdom of God consists neither in the present, inchoate eternal life of faith and charity in the individual, nor in any conceivable future development that depends in any way on the right living of that inchoate life. It consists in the environment where that future development takes place, "that will-world of which God is the central sun," that "society and communion of the saints."[66] The life lived in the Kingdom of Heaven will be a wholly other and mysterious change and development out of the virtuous life lived in the present. But Tyrrell identified the Kingdom neither with the old virtuous nor with the new mysterious life, but with the mode or environment in which that life is lived.

Yet he wanted to preserve some continuity between the two lives and the environments in which those lives are lived, since after all there does seem to be some sort of identity retained between the person who lives the one life here and the other life hereafter. Both lives arise from God's creative activity, not our's. But that new environment "in which present mysteries shall give place to vision, and vague aspirations to attainment is causally continuous with that interior life we now lead as Christians"—although it is not, as Harnack implies, a mere extension and deepening of the present life, "but a development and transformation such as that which changes the grub into the moth."[67]

The key to this conception, Tyrrell told von Hügel in a letter of 4 December, he found in Fichte, who

> makes a certain future *Zustand* the term for which the inner life of conscience is making—a change of nature, connoting a change of environment; for the two are correlative. The future Kingdom, given us in apocalyptic clothing in the Gospel, is, I suspect, the natural *development*, not merely extension, continuation, deepening, of that inner kingdom of love which Christ describes in its own terms. His emphasis is on the life of love (as opposed to legalism) as being the true preparation for the future development of the spirit into something over-human in an over-natural environment. The *nature* of that development & of the pure will-world or society of spirits—all that he leaves *mysterious;* & paints in terms of current eschatological fancies; but as to the *via* he is clear and decisive.[68]

A NOTE ON DEVELOPMENT. Tyrrell was evidently preoccupied with the problem of development. As a direct result of reading Loisy, his position on development shifted from the liberal Catholic notion of Newman—that the expression of dogma changes so that the content might remain identical—to the notion that the content itself changes as the mind of man changes. For Loisy development meant essential change: There is no such thing as an absolute *teaching* handed on unchanged by tradition. Tradition and anything belonging to tradition are elements of history. But a primary property of history is change, so it is pointless to search for an absolute essence of the Gospel or of Christianity as Harnack had done. There is no absolute form of the Gospel that is valid for all times and places. The only element of the Gospel that is absolute is its life, its soul, the Spirit of Christ that was communicated to humankind through the risen Lord.

At this time, therefore, Tyrrell adopted the notion that the deposit of faith was a Spirit, an Idea, which was subject to growth and development according to a living organic model as opposed to an architectural model. In the latter, ideas are added to the original deposit quantitatively, as additions are made to an original structure without essentially changing that structure. But in the organic model, additions of ideas mean a qualitative change: the moth is not the same as the grub, nor the grown man the same as the baby. They are both quantitatively and qualitatively other. To speak of the Idea of the *depositum* as both developing and remaining the same, as Newman did in his *Essay on the Development of Christian Dogma* (1845), seemed to Tyrrell unreal.[69] With Tyrrell's revised organic model, in which development means change, an earlier form cannot be the criterion by which to judge a later form's conformity to the Spirit of Christ. The only criterion is the conformity of the present expressions to the Spirit of Christ perceived in conscience and religious experience. It is simply a question of whether or not a particular expression leads to holiness. It is the principle: *lex orandi, lex credendi.*[70]

THE BARON REPENTS. Apparently von Hügel considered his letter to Tyrrell of 26 November momentous enough to require a response by return post. When that did not happen, he began to wonder if he had said something amiss. On 4 December he dispatched a feeler—which crossed Tyrrell's reply—to test whether there was reason to suspect "that you are in interior trouble and trial,—of a specially strong kind or degree." He hoped that he was wrong and that Tyrrell would take it as a sign of affection if he disclosed his intimations. He felt all the more pressed to do so because "at Holy Com[munion]. yesterday" he felt "two clear pricks of conscience,—one a big one, and one a little one." The big one was that perhaps he had urged too much or too rapidly on Tyrrell "the Wernle-Troeltsch-Weiss-Loisy contention as to the large element of Hereafter and Non-Morality in the First Form of Christianity." Perhaps painful memories were stirred of how adversely his urging had affected his daughter Gertrud a few years before.[71] At any rate he was now deeply aware of how he himself had been dealt with so mercifully by God who fed him leisurely and in fragments that he could manage. He also feared lest his urging had given the impression that he now regarded "the Wernle-Troeltsch-Weiss-Loisy contention" as somehow overshadowing the "Blondel-Münsterberg-Fichte line." He wanted to be sure that Tyrrell understood that he still regarded the latter line as "the very centre of religion" and "the deeper truth," which the former line could but help to deepen, clarify, and enrich.[72]

The "small point" of conscience concerned von Hügel's recent criticism of Alfred Fawkes for making light of Loisy's apologetic against Harnack. Tyrrell had appreciated Fawkes's criticism and described it to the baron as "very firm & sane and quiet."[73] But the baron regarded Fawkes as too reactionary against the ultramontanes, and he had little patience with him.[74] Fawkes and his kind are "busy with the abuses and blind-alleys of our system" and therefore do not welcome anything that appears to give it fresh sanction. "Yet it is surely evident that this [Loisy's] sanction would turn out to be of a kind which, in the very act of sanctioning would also renovate the Catholic conception." Moreover, "I have so far a right to speak, since not only have I worked long and hard at these things, but because I do not think *any* discovery cost me, emotionally, as much to finally accept as this one." At the same time, with some diplomatic equivocation, the baron wanted to convey the impression that he did appreciate Fawkes (as far as his gifts went) and agreed with Tyrrell's estimate of him. He could excuse some excesses because he knew how much it cost himself personally to keep from becoming reactionary, and how much more pressure a priest like Fawkes was under. "And he writes with an admirable clearness and elegant forcefulness."[75]

This "small point" was not as small as the baron would have it seem. He was worried that Tyrrell's association with a reactionary like Fawkes would jeopardize his position in the church. To the extent that Tyrrell's position were jeopardized, the baron's own position would be jeopardized, and he would have to take protective measures. Should Tyrrell be excommunicated, the baron would have seriously to reconsider his association with him.

As it turned out, their friendship endured all the strains to the end. But it did not remain unchanged. There was a decided cooling. For Tyrrell *The Church and the Future* was a declaration of independence. Although he continued to seek and consider the baron's advice, he was far less deferential. For his part, the baron in giving advice grew far more circumspect, and guarded his words carefully. But however one reads the evidence, neither von Hügel nor Tyrrell could be convicted of acting out of base motives.

Tyrrell responded immediately to the baron's solicitude of 4 December. His answer, dated 5 December, is worth quoting at length.

I cannot thank you too much for this last mark of your affection. My letter of yesterday will show that your telepathy was not altogether at fault, & that my mind had of late been much filled with the problem in question. Weiss' book impressed me profoundly—not with a new idea but by a complete confirmation of an old half-faced suspicion. Still the temporary bouleversement of my ideas did not in any appreciable way affect my general faith or hope or even, good spirits. Indeed I am too accustomed to such crises of alternating night & day to doubt but that the sun will appear again, & that seeming loss of truth is the condition of fuller gain. We get our food in blocks & periodically like the lions in the Zoo & not like babes in a continual stream from our mother's breast; and I am not sure that I don't sometimes long for a good tough block and rejoice when it comes. Now and then,—now, for example—it is so tough & big that one's courage is for the moment baulked; but my letter [of 4 December] will have shown you that I have flung myself upon it and am trying to assimilate it though it should cost me every tooth in my jaw. And then, my dear kind friend, as to your "economizing" with me for my own peace sake [sic], I don't think you understand how absolutely & indeed culpably, little I have ever cared about my own soul, my present or future peace, except as a condition of helpfulness to others. It is a natural affection that has been left out of my composition for some strange purpose. Like Moses I had rather be damned with the mass of humanity than saved alone or even with a minority; and so I could not bear to think that there were faith—or moral—difficulties pressing on others of which I knew nothing; and that I owed my stability to any sort of ignorance or half-view. All the best help you have given me—and surely I have grown from a boy to a man since I knew you—has been in opening my eyes to an ever fuller & deeper knowledge of the data of the great problem of life. I have never troubled you or anyone with my inward autobiography; but I feel sure if you knew all you would have no anxiety for so non-personal a being as myself. Perhaps when S. Catherine is safely in circulation I may explain myself more fully.

As far as may be known, Tyrrell never did explain himself more fully. He ended this letter by asserting again his temptation to put "Engels" into the *Month* against the baron's earlier advice. But he promised to "think it over & over before I venture."[76]

TYRRELL'S GREAT DEPRESSION: CHRISTMAS 1902. The whole effort was taking its toll. If Tyrrell did not care about his own welfare except as an aid to others, he nonetheless felt the pains of growth and decay. One book that comforted him at this time was Eucken's *Der Wahrheitsgehalt der Religion* (1901). In his letter of 4 December Tyrrell suggested to the baron that he start prospective converts to Eucken on this book rather than on *Der Kampf*. It was so much clearer and explained much that was presupposed in *Der Kampf*. It also showed "where I am at variance with E. in following, partly, my scholastic prepossessions; partly my continuity bias; mostly, the leading ideas of Bergson."[77] By 18 December, however, Tyrrell was feeling a bit lower and more ambivalent. *Der Wahrheitsgehalt*, he wrote to Petre, "is truly a grand book & gives me something to hold on to when all else slips from under our feet. But I get on very slowly & wearily for all that. Weltbildung at 42 is not very hopeful work."[78]

As the feast of Christmas 1902 approached, Tyrrell's interior state was building toward a crisis. Confusion over what and how to believe and the pain caused by that confusion were only heightened by the concrete juxtaposition of the material signs of the coming celebration. Nineteen centuries of art and lore had simply and richly captured the mystery of the Incarnation and etched it on the hearts and imaginations of generations of simple folk. Now, with one quick blow, criticism had turned all that to dust. The cost to faith, the implications, the responsibility were staggering considerations. The bells of Christmas tolled in Tyrrell's frame with a shattering hollowness. On 29 December he ventured the following to Bremond:

> It has been a bad Xmas for me and "lampades nostrae extinguuntur" has been on the tip of my tongue all the while. Saying the midnight Mass for the nuns for whom it was all so real, life-giving, factual & tangible I could fain have cried out "date nobis de oleo vestro," hankering after the flesh-pots of Egypt & loathing the thin & windy manna of criticism & truth. And then appealing to my emotional feebleness, round came the Waits at 2.a.m. with their "Glad tidings of great joy" till I could have damned all the critics into hell, if they had left me such a receptacle. However they wound up with a somewhat dolorous rendering of "So long Thy power hath blessed me" etc. and so I went asleep with a vague hope that in some, as yet unguessable, way we should find the synthesis and that the angel-faces of the beliefs loved long since & lost awhile, would shine out on us again glorified & eternalised. After all, it is the fault of the official guardians, & not ours, that the said lamps have burnt so low, tho' it [is] we who suffer the

darkness. Had they been steadily replenished & trimmed, needful changes had been effected noiselessly & without cataclysms.[79]

"*Bourdon*" Aborning

In this frame of mind Tyrrell made his final disposition of "Engels" and his synthesis on behalf of the ordinary Catholic. One could question the wisdom of such a decision at that time. But Tyrrell felt something had to be done. Criticism was raising questions that could be neither avoided nor postponed. The authorities' program to meet those questions by repression and suppression could only in the long run cause more harm than would an immediate confrontation. A confrontation may scandalize thousands today, but Tyrrell thought that price worth paying to save millions tomorrow. If he could not act with ecclesiastical approval, he would act without it. Two days after Christmas he wrote to his literary agent, A. R. Waller, "I am going to enlarge Engels and try to find a publisher for him. Longmans is shy; he wants my name but he'll not get it."[80] Two and a half months later *The Church and the Future* went to press.

During those two and a half months Tyrrell's correspondence diminished to a trickle as he threw himself wholeheartedly into his urgent cause.[81] But the letters he did write are crammed with the themes of his synthesis. They show, moreover, how intimately the genesis of "Bourdon" was involved in the thought and fate of Loisy.

LOISY'S FATE AFFECTING. On 8 January 1903 the baron enclosed three letters for Tyrrell and Petre to read "and carefully return."[82] We are not told the content of the letters, but they very likely concerned Loisy and how *L'Évangile et l'Église* was being received in Rome. Rumors were rife about an imminent condemnation. Loisy responded by asking Archbishop Mignot to intercede. Mignot replied on 22 December 1902 that although "the situation is tense," the danger of condemnation was still too uncertain to make an appeal to Cardinal Rampolla advisable. There was no doubt, however, that Loisy was accused of writing an all too human history "after the fashion of a Sabatier." On 27 December Loisy wrote to von Hügel of Mignot's sentiments, and this letter was no doubt one of those forwarded to Tyrrell.[83]

The 1 January 1903 issue of *L'Univers* opened a campaign in the French press against Loisy. It was spearheaded by the Dominican professor of scholastic philosophy at the Institut Catholique of Toulouse, Abbé Hippolyte Gayraud. Four more thrusts from Gayraud followed in *L'Univers* for 2, 4, 9, and 10 January. Loisy, von Hügel, and Mignot were in communication on all these developments, and Tyrrell was kept abreast by von Hügel.[84] Tyrrell returned the three "most interesting" letters to the baron on 11 January and commented:

> I am still young & inexperienced enough to marvel at the fatal blindness that makes Rome devour her most serviceable children, not in exceptional deliria of puerperal fever but steadily & systematically, so that honestly & unequivocally the Church seems to be invariably on the wrong side. Of course Ward says this is all proof of her far-reaching wisdom; an excuse that might come from a disciple of Hartmann, for certainly it [is] an unconscious & unintentional wisdom. We might at that rate say that Nero & Decius were guided by the Holy Ghost.[85]

Tyrrell went on to report that his pen had not been entirely idle. The storm that broke upon him at Christmas, about which the baron had been "prophetic though not telepathic . . . registered itself in a fat essay on the Nativity—which you, poor devil, will have to read some day or other for your sins." That essay was never published as such, but its content was no doubt worked into the Christological sections of "Bourdon" and subsequent works. It was a response to the frustration Tyrrell felt over officials' failure to "keep their lamps trimmed." "Had they done their duty by Truth steadily from the first, adjustments would have been made insensibly which wd. have saved these revolutionary changes of posture which will destroy the faith of millions."[86]

MORE HÜGELIAN PRESCRIPTIONS. What was keeping Tyrrell from moving on to his grand synthesis was the backlog of readings assigned by the baron. In early January 1903 Tyrrell sent the baron an accounting. He had again been over Eucken's *Wahrheitsgehalt* ("which I think has impressed me more deeply than any book of late years"), had read Percy Gardner's *The Historic View of the New Testament* (1901) ("eminently satisfactory & clear"), had laid aside Samuel Eck's *D. F. Strauss* (1899) half read ("baulked my German"), was now at Johannes Volkelt's *Immanuel Kants Erkenntnistheorie* (1879) ("coercively clear" and "quite to my keenest taste"), and had talked Herbert Lucas into getting Father Provincial Colley to read Joseph Turmel's *L'Eschatologie* because it was "so staggeringly historical & so hopelessly irreconcilable with ultra-infallibilism." Of the other recommended readings, Tyrrell said, he managed to secure all except Dilthey's *Einleitung in die Geisteswis-*

senschaften (1883), which was out of print. Referring probably to Troeltsch's *Die Absolutheit des Christentums,* Tyrrell went on, "Troeltsch's problems give me most pause; they are those *towards* which, rather than *from* which, my mind seems to be working; the question of the relation of Christianity to other religions is just the *whole* question." "Bourdon" would incorporate Troeltsch's position on this question. Then, so as not to miss anything, Tyrrell asked the names of some articles or brochures "on the immortality-belief" by Jules Touzard that the baron had mentioned.[87] Von Hügel immediately forwarded copies of the articles as well as his own annotated copy of Dilthey's book.

A THUNDERBOLT: CONDEMNATION OF *L'ÉVANGILE ET L'ÉGLISE.* Tyrrell seemed bent on reading forever and well might have, had not a sudden bolt from the storm gathering over Loisy jolted him into action. The press campaign against Loisy produced the desired effect. On 17 January Cardinal Richard, under advice from an examining commission, signed an ordinance of condemnation of *L'Évangile et l'Église* and forbade the book to be read by anyone under his jurisdiction. The reasons given were that the book had been published without *imprimatur* and that it was of such a nature as seriously to trouble the faithful on the fundamental dogmas of Catholic doctrine.[88] Four days later von Hügel received the news from Loisy. When and from whom Tyrrell heard it is not known, but on 26 January he wrote to von Hügel:

> Many thanks. I will read Touzard at once & the marked parts of Dilthey afterwards; not all, because the Δαιμονιον [Demon] is crying write! Write! anent a certain difficulty that must be faced; & I have tried to stifle him with books on the pretext that one cannot write anything till one has read everything. . . .
>
> This deplorable old Richard! Is he in secret a disciple of Harnack that he wants to stifle the only competent Catholic opponent. And such a time to choose! When union & mutual toleration in face of a common foe is a matter of life & death. There must be more than mere *intellectual* limitations in a man like Gayraud. As for Batiffol he has realized your worst predictions. And all this comes to encourage one at the end of a week which brought me three fresh cases of "faith-failure"—all *good* & intelligent Catholics!
>
> Eppur si muove! In truth there is a fundamental "principiell" [*sic*] enmity between Loisy-Catholicism which *may* live & Gayraud-Catholicism which *must* die. So far Gayraud is only a little sharper & more consequent than his fellow-schoolmen. He sees that L. is trying to slip a healthy baby into the cradle of the puling heir—to accomplish a

quiet revolution. G. is too ignorant to see that the heir is doomed & so he gives the alarm with all his lungs. The result will be an empty cradle & an heirless estate. Meantime what will become of "Ginx's Baby" i.e., of the man in the street, when "the Churches have killed their Christ"?[89]

The next day Tyrrell wrote to Loisy to express his sympathy.

That the blow was not altogether unexpected does not make it lighter. . . . The déraison of these violent tactics is, that no one's position is changed either pro or con; and that an antagonism of thought which is harmless, is transformed into an antagonism of sentiment which is full of harm, especially now, in France where union and mutual toleration is all-important in the face of foes who accuse the Church of being the enemy of light and liberty. *Epur* [sic] *si muove.* Facts are stronger than Cardinals; nor will the whole Curia be able to prevent the tide of history coming in and sweeping down all barriers that are of sand instead of rock.[90]

The *affaire Loisy* drove Tyrrell into action and catalyzed "Bourdon." Tyrrell felt himself questioned by all the questions that this action against Loisy raised. "Am I solvent?" "Am I Catholic?" "We are no longer Christian," Loisy wrote of himself and Tyrrell in his journal for 3 June 1904; "we believe neither in the infallibility of the pope nor in the kingdom of heaven."[91] Of course Tyrrell did believe in both infallibility and the Kingdom of Heaven, but certainly not as interpreted by "officialism." That, therefore, was the question "Bourdon" sought to answer: Could one disagree with officials and still remain a Catholic? Tyrrell explained himself on 1 February 1903 to Maude Petre: "Am writing all day like mad. Heard from Loisy. The Pilot is right about him. It is 'mors et vita duello conflixere mirando.' My God! What will the issue be? I am now summing up the *whole* situation as seen from my chink in the door of eternity. 'Am I solvent' is the question I have been choking down for years. Now others put it to me & I must answer it."[92]

The *Pilot* for 31 January had carried an article "From our French correspondent" erroneously claiming that Loisy had surrendered to Rome. It also linked Newman with Loisy and made Bremond an accomplice.[93] Tyrrell warned Bremond on 1 February and added, "I am simply swamped with correspondence. If I had invented this religion, people could not hold me more responsible for it."[94] The next day he wrote the baron, "I don't think the *Pilot* article will do any good. The Church is being driven fast to what you Germans call an Entweder-Oder."[95]

The baron replied on 11 February with an interpretation of that

Entweder-Oder.[96] He had been urging Loisy not to give permission for a translation of *L'Évangile et l'Église* or to publish a second edition at this time. The important thing, he insisted, was to do nothing that might provoke Rome into ratifying Richard's condemnation. If a Roman condemnation could be prevented, he reasoned, Richard's condemnation would fall flat.[97]

The baron's advice irritated Loisy. For years he felt himself— not without justification—an object of ecclesiastical persecution, and he was in no mood to play the fox's goose. Furthermore, whatever premonitions the baron might have as to Rome holding fire, his own premonitions were that Rome was only holding fire until the best advantage could be gained. Loisy had little confidence in von Hügel's diplomacy. In these matters he usually sought the advice of Mignot, who now warned him that Rome would only use his silence against him. But the baron would counsel no counteroffensive until he had solid evidence of Rome's intentions.

That evidence would gradually accumulate to the point of no ignoring. On 8 February, while visiting the duke of Norfolk at Arundel Castle, von Hügel happened to glance at a copy of the latest *Tablet.* It contained a list of the forty consultors of the revised Biblical Commission.[98] The strength of the original twelve, who were qualified men and would have treated Loisy fairly, was now diluted with twenty-eight men who were either scholastic trained and knew nothing of historical criticism or were of no professional repute whatever. It was depressing news. But, the baron wrote Tyrrell three days later, "other, sadder things" were happening that convinced him that in the foreseeable future diplomacy and expediency would be the only criteria for official decisions. This situation would leave two hopeful alternatives: either officials would become alarmed and issue "merely hortatory documents or decisions with big loopholes for later escape," or they would "really take the plunge into a decision so hopelessly narrow" as to precipitate reaction. "Alas, alas: that any men or body of men should think, they simply *hold* the final truth and final statement of it *hic et nunc.*"[99]

The second alternative, Tyrrell replied, was what he had been counting on for many months now.

> I do not believe that Gayraudian Catholicism can ever be explained away or stretched to hold the new wine; it must burst. I have not now time to give a reason for this Faith that is in me. Only in one thing do I fancy I have the advantage of you; & that is in my sense of the absolute inelasticity of the present "official" theology. It has run itself into

a corner in a manner that forbids us to draw parallels from past con-
cessions. It *can't* retreat except by suicide. . . .

Their *whole* system stands or falls with even the smallest & rotten-
est part—thanks to scholastic rationalism.[100]

Such an attitude could only lead to choosing up sides, separating them by an impassable moat, and lofting killer missiles back
and forth. The baron believed in holding position within the ranks,
even if that meant conceding a temporary victory, in the hope and
belief that the truth would eventually infiltrate the opposition silently like a leaven. But for that to happen, a mixing, not a separation, must occur. On 24 February the baron wrote to Tyrrell to that
effect. He did not say directly that he was "surprised" and "disappointed" in Tyrrell's attitude; rather, he used the case of Fr. Herbert Lucas, whose attitude was similar. The question he posed to
Lucas was whether the scholastic pioneers were not right in remaining in the church in the face of condemnations for adapting
theology to Aristotelianism. They neither ignored the condemnations nor lost faith in the ultimate triumph of the substance of their
efforts but continued to work quietly in ways and degrees left
open to them. Would we not do well to imitate them even though
the parallel between their circumstances and the present was not
perfect? The baron enclosed in this letter the additions that Loisy
was preparing for the second edition of *L'Évangile et l'Église* but
cautioned Tyrrell to keep their existence absolutely secret. Loisy
did not want Cardinal Richard to think that he had blithely forged
ahead with a second edition without the slightest regard to ecclesiastical thunderings. Besides, Loisy had informed Richard that he
was withdrawing his book and abandoning the projected second
edition, also that "he condemns with the Cardinal, the errors deduced from his book, by writers who had placed themselves at a
different point of view from that which he had himself taken up in
writing it."[101]

"I sometimes think L[oisy] is almost naif in his surprise that the
'official' theologians are so furious with him," Tyrrell replied on 28
February.

Does he realise that their syllogistic card-house is so delicately poised
that to touch a single card brings it *all* to the ground? . . . Apart from
the blow to Loisy personally, I should hardly regret the Roman condemnation—I have no hope of the officials' candour, but every hope
in their self-interest; not till they make themselves thoroughly ridiculous will they learn their lesson. With quite an opposite animus I often
reechoe Mgr. Dun[n]'s aspiration *à propos* of the Mivart controversies:

"I wish they wd. define the moon to be made of green cheese & *force* these fellows to swallow it" (i.e. the definition, not the moon).[102]

BRIEF SURCEASE: SOHM'S *KIRCHENRECHT*. A nervous calm fell over the battlefield after Loisy's answer to Richard. Nothing could be heard but the whispering and shuffling of slippered diplomats on the one hand and the scratching of pens on the other. Loisy was preparing his defense, and Tyrrell his *magna carta*. The latter was using the brief respite to gather grist for his mill from Rudolph Sohm's *Kirchenrecht*, an impressive if tendentious historical treatise on the beginnings and development of church structures.[103] "Sohm's Kirchenrecht has swallowed me up at present," Tyrrell wrote to the baron on 28 February. "To my ignorance it is the most convincing book & more illuminative, in the *positive* line, than aught I have yet read. If he is right, what radical reconstructions of Catholicism will be forced on us! How Cardinal Vaughan would revel in his anti-Anglican conclusions (Die römische Bischof. §. 31.) all heedless of their cost. I think that section wd. make a beautiful C. T. S. tract. Britten would swallow the bait eagerly."[104] What Tyrrell meant is that people who believed in the miraculous origins of church structures would see in Sohm's data confirmation that those structures were directly from God. Tyrrell looked at the same data and saw them as overwhelming evidence of the presence of a merely human element in the establishment of those structures. He would say as much in "Bourdon."

"BOURDON" IS BORN

First Drafts

Maude Petre's diary for 19 February 1903 contains without comment the following entry: "He gave me this evening the MS. of the first chapter of 'Gayraud v. Loisy or The Theory of ecclesiastical Inerrancy.' Should he die I am to 'publish it *coute que coute*.'"[105] This manuscript was undoubtedly what "Bourdon" would call part 1, "Catholicism as Officially Stated; or, The Theory of Ecclesiastical Inerrancy." On 6 March, less than two weeks later, Tyrrell expressed to Petre relief that he had cleared his position, except for a very practical question. He concluded that, as a rule, people who think as he did ought to remain in the Society of Jesus. The question was whether his case was an exception and whether or not he was really bound to speak out and suffer the consequences.

> It is a question of choosing between evils. The "scandal" reason is a fallacy—a bit of Jesuit sophistry. To live in peace & then to leave a mine to explode when I am safe from hurt is cowardly. The Bible I lent you the other day falls open always at the same place and tempts me to superstition. "An adamant harder than flint have I made thy forehead; fear them not neither be dismayed at their looks—speak to them whether they will hear thee or whether they will forbear etc etc etc."
>
> It is not however my forehead but my stomach that is unequal to the task; & so I reply *Spiritum rectum innova in visceribus meis.*[106]

This note is too similar to "Bourdon's" conclusions to be coincidence, and it is safe to infer that by 6 March 1903 *The Church and the Future* was in script. All that remained undone were a few pages of appendixes and epilogue and some tidying up.

On 15 March Tyrrell notified his agent Waller that "a cousin of Dr. Engels has written a brochure of a very tentative character for private circulation" and was wondering whether he could negotiate for its printing. He was bigger than "Engels" but would prefer a more casual and "floppy" dress. Also the printers could save themselves trouble if they eliminated their label. "Pollard must have sworn a bit over enquiries after the *Factor.*"[107] The next day Tyrrell wrote to Bremond, who had been spending the better part of the year away from Paris to consider his status in the Society of Jesus. After advising Bremond against precipitous action, Tyrrell continued about his own latest brewings:

> I have been writing "Catholicism Re-stated" by an Evangelical. Perhaps it will be in print by the time you arrive. I think you will like it; it is plain & naked, as I really think. Have you read a gruesome book, "La Maison du Peche" by Marcel [*sic*] Tinayre? It gave me the blues for a week. Yet its interest is based on a false disjunction: Calvinism or Paganism. Of course Paganism is the more Christian of the two. But surely there is a midway—the Christianity of the future that is yet *in fieri.*[108]

Meanwhile Tyrrell was having his say about the church of the future typed and prepared for the printers. On 18 March he promised Waller the typescript in a few days, but the very next day he sent the body and promised the appendix presently: "I think it better meantime to get forward with what is already done as the book will be needed during this Loisy crisis."[109] It would be more economical and thorough to send troubled inquirers a complete and enduring explanation of a *modus vivendi* than to try to handle their problems by letter or consultation. But two hundred copies would be more than enough, for, Tyrrell told Waller a week later, "there are hardly 200 for whom the book will be useful & not harmful—at least, in this generation. The problem in its entirety is rarely felt at present, nor its solution needed. Were I free as a bird & had I the Pope's express permission I would not *publish* the book at present. It is a medicine for the few that are ailing not a food for the many who are well. If a man's house will last him his lifetime it is no use showing him what he must do when it tumbles."[110]

Parenthesis: A Christological Controversy

Tyrrell could not, however, dismiss every inquirer with a cold text, however much of his life's blood was therein enshrined. His fellow laborer and sympathizer Giovanni Semeria, for example, deserved a personal response. Semeria had sent a list of questions on various scholastic arguments concerning the existence of God, God's personality, miracles, the scholastic conception of the soul, and the God-man problem in Christ. One wonders whether Semeria realized what he was asking of the man. While "Bourdon" was going through the press, Tyrrell took time to address these questions. On 29 March he returned a long answer, with the leader that his delay was due not to lack of time but to "perplexity as to what to say."[111] Not surprisingly, part of Tyrrell's reply bears directly on ideas in *The Church and the Future* and possibly also on that missing essay on the Nativity.

First, as to miracles: they do not compel assent in the order of knowledge because God can intervene only by becoming part of the finite order—a self-limitation that is admittedly mysterious, but no more so than the Incarnation. "Hence the *possibility* of miracles could only be proved by their actual occurrence; their occurrence, only by showing that the effect is beyond the possibilities of Nature; and this supposes a perfect comprehension of Nature." So all we can say is that we do not *know*.[112]

As to Christology, the problem is to reconcile Christ's humanity with his divinity. Growing consciousness of Messiahship or divine sonship, even ignorance or error about the end of the world, are not incompatible with his divinity—as he himself confessed: "Of that day and hour the Son knoweth not." These admissions do not undermine the doctrine of the Incarnation, but they do contravene certain theological accretions, for example, that Christ as human possessed infused knowledge and enjoyed the beatific vision. The difficulty goes back to the fathers who held that Adam before the fall enjoyed all this wonderful psychology *by reason of his essential nature.* Hence Christ as sinless and perfect man had to enjoy what Adam lost by sin. But the Jesuit-Jansenist controversy changed theologians' view of human nature. They agreed that Adam's endowments were *preter*natural, and that sin stripped him of these honors while leaving his *essential* nature intact. But they failed to apply this amendment to Christology, so we still have Christ's "perfect manhood" requiring all these wonders and making of him "a plexus of psychological miracles which practically take him out of the category of our humanity & destroy the whole helpfulness of our doctrine of his pure manhood." It is a deep-seated docetism that makes Loisy's theses difficult even for theologians, despite the fact that his theses do not conflict with the Christology of the New Testament or of the creeds. "I wish indeed I could write a book on these matters but I have no liberty. I will soon send you a new secret brochure which will show you better where I stand."[113]

Meanwhile von Hügel was engaged in a discussion with Blondel over Loisy's Christology. Periodically he would apprise Tyrrell of developments with a batch of letters from the two contenders as well as copies of his replies. One such installment was sent on 3 April with the apology, "I am quite ashamed again to trouble you with a Blondel-Hügel batch of letters; but I want you to know his objections, & like to think of your knowing too whereabouts exactly I am, on these points." The baron also included "3 *admirable* articles fr. Troeltsch, on his usual problem, but clearer than he has ever been: he is growing fast, & will do wonders before he has done."[114]

What began as a discussion, however, soon escalated into an argument, with Loisy and von Hügel siding against Blondel. It was an important and personally painful encounter for the baron, as it involved matters on which he felt most deeply: Christ, his humanity and divinity, his knowability as an historical figure and his mysteriousness as outside history, and all these considerations to be seen in relation to the church. There was also Blondel himself, whose personal friendship von Hügel cherished and which now seemed jeopardized.

The crux of the dispute was Blondel's charge of an historicism that allowed Loisy to treat Christ's knowledge as purely human and imply that to the historian there was little evidence for divine omniscience in the earthly Jesus. Von Hügel, on the defense, appealed to Blondel to take the Incarnation seriously. If God became man in Jesus, he became fully man and enjoyed the same passions and limitations of knowledge belonging to that state.

Von Hügel and Blondel registered their dispute in articles, and eventually on 19 March 1904 the baron wrote what he considered a crucial letter to Blondel.[115] He told Blondel that he sensed in him little understanding for what Loisy was doing because he lacked a certain instinctive sympathy for that kind of work. That deficiency was not a fault, the baron assured him, only a lack of feel for the purpose and function of a study that concerns the relative and contingent, that is, the historical.[116]

Much confusion abounds over Loisy's Christology. What is clear is the distinction he made between what is and what is not accessible to the historian. Granted that Christianity is based on historical facts, Loisy insisted, those facts neither cause nor explain Christian faith by which the believer appropriates the spiritual significance of those facts. Historical criticism cannot establish the existence of the spiritual realities, which are the objects of Christian faith. Von Hügel largely agreed with this position and criticized Blondel for not sufficiently distinguishing between historical phenomena and their spiritual significance. Blondel, whose mind-set was metaphysical and not historical, could not allow this distinction, because it led him to conclude that therefore the Christ of faith and the Christ of history are two really distinct persons. Von Hügel drew no such conclusion, because for him the distinction was merely between *methods* by which one knows, which does not lead to a distinction in the ultimately integral *object* of knowledge itself.

In a letter of 8 April Tyrrell gave the baron a synopsis of "Bourdon's" view of the controversy. As Tyrrell's mind was no less metaphysical than Blondel's, it is no surprise that he inclined to that position—"it appealed to my somewhat incurable Christ-centrism which survives & thrives upon all that should overthrow it." But Tyrrell's better sense of historical method also gave him an appreciation of von Hügel's position.

> Of course neither Blondel (nor even Loisy, nor perhaps even you) will follow me in my radicalism though I think I make out my case sc. that the most liberal Catholicism is essentially distinct from Protestantism & has its right place in the Church. But when I turned to your reply wondering what you would find to say I saw how much deeper & keener your criticism was than mine, & how you saved all that I liked in B. & without any sacrifice of the rights of scientific criticism. I have only one unclearness about Loisy's view remaining & that is that it [is] too indiscriminately conservative,—that it does not give us what Newman tried (vainly, I think) to give us, a *criterion* to distinguish

true from false developments. B. calls it a theory of evolution rather than of development. In a sort my objection . . . is *Nimis probat.* The "Fawkes" school sees the same weakness. I am anti-Fawkes in regarding the "catholicising" of Christianity as a *per se* result of the spirit of Christ, & not as a perversion or accident; but I perceive in that "catholicising" process (as in the Scriptures) a divine & a human; an inspired & an uninspired, element; and I apply the "quod semper etc" test in a *practical* way sc. Beliefs & institutions which are universally proved, experimentally, to foster the Christian spirit ipso facto are proved to be true to that spirit. And by Christian Spirit I mean that spirit which spoke from the beginning in the prophets & men of faith & found its most docile organ in Christ & which still speaks in the corporate life of the Church so far as holiness is found there. i.e. I make the Saints and not the theologians, the teachers of Christianity. The Spirit of Christ rather than Christ himself is the creator of the Church—or rather of the whole organism of the pre- and post-Christian Church of which Christ is the bond, & of which no part, not even Christ, exhausts the potentialities of that spirit. I think when you read my brochure you will see that this offers a very workable criterion to distinguish mere results from true developments. It also, I believe, coincides with your admirable defence of the need of the twofold Christ— subject & object—glorified & terrestrial—; it leaves his human sanctity in the same category as ours, while allowing room for a mysterious relation between his humanity & that spirit of which it was the most perfect, *but infinitely inadequate,* utterance, & whose utterance (as the spirit of *human* sanctity) needs *all* humanity for its organ.

When you deny "concupiscence" to Christ I need a distinction. There is natural & blameless passion whose absence were a defect; & there is a passion which is the fruit of past carelessness or sin, personal or ancestral. To deny the former to Christ is open to the same objection as docetan views as to his knowledge. Are not ignorance & passion the two roots of our temptation? & how is Christ tempted as we, how is his sinlessness admirable, if he lacked either root? Our chastity is usually at best a reconquered chastity; his must have been at least a self-preserved chastity. If ever there was a blunder of thought surely it is the idea of *necessary* (intrinsically) virtue![117]

A week later the baron responded with a further clarification of his twofold subject-object Christ. The model is based on man's psychological "I-me" structure. The object *me* is what is phenomenally accessible to history. It is the revelation of the subject *I*, which is not directly observable. The "Christ-subject" is the *I* that is not accessible to direct observation, but it reveals itself in the "Christ-object," which is historically accessible. The baron enclosed a further letter in which Blondel thoroughly rejected this "clarification" as involving a "confusion of thought" underlying the

Christ-subject conception. Von Hügel demurred that confusion would result only if one failed to distinguish the knowledge one has of the Christ-subject from the empirically observable data that is available in the case of the Christ-object. The "I-me" parallel is apt, but is not to be pressed too hard. "But I am sorry to find B., so absolutely closed to a reconsideration along these lines—at least, for the moment."[118]

Two and a half months later Tyrrell outlined for Petre a further synthesis of the Christological question. It was probably the final one that underlies "Bourdon." Evident in it is all the intellectual pain and perplexity of attempting to conceptualize a paradox. It is as if Tyrrell tried to situate Loisyism on both sides of a chemical reaction at equilibrium: on one side, Loisy's theological and immanent Christ, the Christ who was comforting precisely because of his immanence; on the other side, Loisy's historical and human Christ, but external because not yet living in that eschatological realm that allows him entry into hearts and to that extent not comforting. Still, Tyrrell urged, there was a comforting aspect about the human Christ: his complete identity with the human condition. The kenosis doctrine means that he "shared all our groping & darkness & uncertainty & blameless ignorances—to me, that were more than his sharing physical pain & weariness. The theological Xt lived in a blaze of absolute certainty about everything—like a Roman Cardinal." Still, "the dilemma presses: the more human, the less present & immanent." Then, criticizing some notes Petre had prepared for a joint publication, he continued: Is not your solution Caird's conception? "God revealed not merely in the historic Christ of the critics but in the Christ of the developing Christian conscience—in the Catholic idea of Christ. This is also Bourdonism."[119]

In Print

By 19 April "Bourdon" was in proofs. On that day Tyrrell returned the proofs to Waller, having expunged Loisy's name so as not to add to his troubles.[120] Nowhere in the book can be found acknowledgment of the one who in so many ways inspired it. Seven weeks later "Bourdon" appeared in gray paper wrappers. Printed by Turnbull & Spears of Edinburgh, it carried "a French title along with the English one, to veil, as far as possible, the true authorship."[121] And on the first page, to further dissemble, was printed: "Three of the longer chapters have been synopsised and relegated to the Appendix; and a few inconsiderable adaptations have been introduced with the Author's approval."

Beneath those wrappers can be found much that has already been seen, albeit scattered piecemeal and in other contexts. The new historical context detailed above and the synthesis forged by force of that context make *The Church and the Future* a new book. It is both old and new, just as Tyrrell wanted the church to be.

To recapitulate briefly, the point of departure of *The Church and the Future* was the age-old dispute between ultramontane and liberal forces as to the nature of ecclesiastical authority, where it is definitively invested, and what the answer to the dispute says about the nature of the church as a whole. The dispute erupted into full view during the pontificate of Pius IX and called forth the definitions of Vatican I on papal infallibility. These were then parlayed into extreme interpretations by the ultramontane majority, while the views of minority liberals were for the moment suppressed. In England liberal views surfaced again just before the turn of the century. St. George Mivart stood as their most strident spokesman. The Mivart affair in turn called forth the joint pastoral of the English hierarchy, a distillate of infallibilist views that the moderately progressive Leo XIII surprisingly sanctioned. This act lit the fuse.

Tremendous strides had been made throughout the nineteenth century in all areas of scientific research, and not least in church-historical and biblical criticism. While most of this work was done by Protestant scholars, mainly in Germany, their methods and conclusions could not help but seep under the Catholic ramparts, however impenetrable church authorities tried to keep them. In fact the level of seepage rose dramatically during the pontificate of Leo XIII, who did so much to lift the church out of a siege mentality and to extend an authentic missionary spirit to all sectors of life. In academic and seminary circles much that had been written off as fallacious and heretical simply because it was developed within the enemies' camp came to be regarded with new eyes and eventually accepted as undeniable truth. The door having once been opened to promising vistas, it seemed an outrage to slam it shut again. Granted that the overwhelming majority of Catholics, cleric as well as lay, still had not a clue as to what the new learning promised by way of consequences for the old, those who had been allowed a taste of the new would not forget its savor.

The joint pastoral, even with papal weight, could not reverse a process that already had a generation of momentum behind it. Although ultimately ineffectual, it alerted church authorities to the forbidding presence within their camp of a rival, more powerful authority. Clearly nothing but wholesale extermination would do.

Leo XIII, now old and ailing, ceded control to a more rabid faction, and the campaign was launched.

In early 1900 Tyrrell felt the pressure, as he was silenced for "A Perverted Devotion." Von Hügel, with his communications network, was daily relaying alarming information on what was being prepared for those most threatening to Rome's authority. Loisy was a primary target. The condemnation in January 1903 of *L'Évangile et l'Église* was the alert that sent Tyrrell to his arsenal. His tactic was to criticize the orthodox view and file a liberal one and to show how the latter could protest against the former without becoming Protestant. This tactic was the program of *The Church and the Future*.

A VIEWING: *THE CHURCH AND THE FUTURE*

Tyrrell divided his book into three parts, followed by three short appendixes and an epilogue. The first two parts contain the substance. Part 1 is a negative critique of official Catholicism; part 2 is a positive restatement of Catholicism on liberal lines; part 3 argues the need for honest criticism in the church and infers possible consequences of that criticism. The appendixes elaborate several points made in the body of the text: (1) on the nature of ecclesiastical authority, (2) on discerning true from false developments in doctrine, and (3) on the changing view of scriptural infallibility and the consequences for ecclesiastical infallibility.

Part 1: "Catholicism as Officially Stated; or, The Theory of Ecclesiastical Inerrancy"

To commemorate the Loisy-Gayraud controversy, Tyrrell originally titled this part "Gayraud v. Loisy or the Theory of Ecclesiastical Inerrancy."[122] The dispute, as Tyrrell described it, was between "official" and "liberal" Catholicism, or between two theologies and those who hold them—those who presently sit in the chair of Moses and want to impose as binding in conscience the "official" doctrine of ecclesiastical inerrancy with all its consequences and those who call for a radical reinterpretation of that doctrine. It was a dispute over the rule of faith, over who defines it, how it is defined, and whether and with what authority it can be imposed. The liberal Catholic cannot deny *every* sort of ecclesiastical inerrancy and remain a Catholic. Hence it is not a dispute as to the *fact* of ecclesiastical inerrancy, but as to its limits. The limits and nature of ecclesiastical inerrancy are "just the one dogmatic point which a Catholic may dispute without *logical* suicide." Even officials dispute the rule of faith, as is obvious from their various opinions on the infallibility or noninfallibility of, for example, the bull on Anglican orders or the canonization of a saint. "Hence, a Catholic may always dispute the *limits*, so long as he believes in the fact, of the Church's inerrancy, and can point to some rule which he stands by in all its consequences."[123]

Belief that there is such a rule of faith and the assent to it cannot be based on the authority of the rule itself but is always a matter of private judgment. It is based on "those *reasons* of heart and head which compel my assent."[124] The rule of faith for Protestants is the Bible—one particular *phase* of the church—and the Protestant is this or that kind according to the mode and limits he allows to the Bible's inspiration. For the Catholic the rule of faith is the mind of the living church itself, not a particular phase of that mind. The difference between Protestant and Catholic therefore lies in the *nature* of the rule, not in the exercise of private judgment as to its limits.

With the scope of the dispute defined, Tyrrell moved on to consider the difficulties that had been accumulating against the "official" doctrine of inerrancy, difficulties that were not purely philosophic or scientific—as, for example, those derived from Voltaire, the Encyclopedists, Kant, Hegel, and Schopenhauer: the *absurdi* of scholastic manuals. But they were difficulties of almost entirely a positive and historical character, derived from church historians, scripture critics, and comparative religionists: "Gunkel and Holtzmann, and Weiss and Harnack, and Sohm and Weizsäcker; and . . . many Catholic workers on the same lines."[125] The difficulties, said Tyrrell, are not speculative but factual. They may be ignored or denied for a time, then perverted and distorted, but finally they must be admitted.

DIFFICULTIES FROM BIBLICAL CRITICISM. On one side stands the "official" theory of inspiration. It is prescribed in the encylical *Providentissimus Deus*, a condensation of the teaching of Franzelin who faithfully relays the teaching of the Vatican, Tridentine, and other councils, which in turn are only slightly developed expressions of patristic teachings. On the other side stands the liberal theory of Gunkel, Jülicher, Weiss, and Holtzmann. The two are absolutely irreconcilable. Eventually the results of criticism will be accepted, and the doctrine of inspiration of scripture will be maintained, if at all, only in a greatly modified sense. "The theological schools, the popes, the councils, the fathers," Tyrrell charged, "have been mistaken; and this not merely in a detail of doctrine, but as to what might be called a secondary 'rule of faith,'" because until quite recently they have taught "*semper ubique ab omnibus* . . . that the Bible is a miraculous book, dictated by the Holy Ghost; free from error in all its original parts." But not even a theologian's power to juggle words can square this view with criticism.[126]

The indirect consequences of this erroneous interpretation of scriptural inerrancy are even more serious for the theory of ecclesiastical inerrancy. Not only is the latter based on the former, but the teaching of the fathers and councils on the inerrancy of the church "is as nothing to what they have said concerning the inspired authority of the Sacred Scriptures." If they were wrong there, *a fortiori* the theory of ecclesiastical and papal inerrancy must fall. "To prove the Church's inerrancy from Scripture we cannot begin by assuming the Church's doctrine as to the inspiration of the New Testament. We must treat the New Testament as a mere document subject to the ordinary laws of criticism." But if we do that, we see that the texts adduced from scripture to prove ecclesiastical and papal infallibility can no longer support the burden imposed on them by the doctrine of literal inspiration.[127]

Acceptance of the results of criticism also has serious consequences for other doctrines that rest largely on the scriptures, for example, "that Christ was, if not God . . . , at least an inspired and infallible prophet of God, whose doctrine is infallibly preserved in the Catholic Church." Apart from the philosophical difficulties brought against the proof value of prophecy fullfilment and miracle texts, biblical criticism has robbed those texts of nearly all apologetic value. "For apologetic purposes we must take the Bible as it is estimated by those whom we would convince, if we are to have a common basis of argument." Criticism has shown that the New Testament writers have both consciously and unconsciously doctored their accounts into agreement with Old Testament "prophecies" in order to convince the Jews of Christ's Messiahship. As to miracles, critics ask, Did they really happen? Was there a real interruption of the established laws of nature by special intervention of the First Cause? Or was it merely an unusual occurrence that was lifted from the category of the strange to that of the miraculous?[128]

The personal valuation that the "official" apologist gives these texts is beside the point, however true it might be. If he is to enter into dialogue with the outside world, he must take the scriptures "at their present scientific and public valuation or else set about changing that public valuation."[129]

DIFFICULTIES FROM HISTORICAL CRITICISM. Many people experience the Catholicism of today as manifestly different from that of the apostles, yet they desire to reconcile this admission with their fidelity to the church. Newman effected a reconciliation with his doctrine of development, but many within and without the church regard his attempt as a *deus ex machina*. "Officials" themselves have never cordially accepted it. The only development they can allow is a development of distinctness of analysis, a kind of literal "evolution" like the unfolding of a garment. The supposition is that Christ and the apostles delivered to the church the complete deposit of faith. All the major and minor premises of modern Catholicism "were revealed to St. Peter and passed on to St. Linus, who, had he been Socratically interrogated about any of the dogmas or Sacraments, would have answered in substantially the same way as a D.D. of the Gregorian University." This assumption is the "explication" theory as distinct from the "development" theory. But the contentions of such non-Catholic investigators as Harnack, Sohm, Wernle, Hatch, and Gardner, as well as of "the few Catholics of the more liberal school, who have followed them timidly at a distance," have shown the "explication" theory to be preposterously inadequate. They have shown [how] the dogmas and sacraments, the theologies of Christ, the Trinity, and Mary, and the whole hierarchical institution have developed through quite natural influences from their early amorphous and undogmatic forms into what today is understood as Catholicism.[130]

Pace Newman, "officials" are right in their criticism of the development theory to the extent that the theory as understood today would have been regarded as novel and therefore heretical in the Middle Ages. "Vincent of Lerins meant 'explication' and nothing more, since the old-world physiology conceived manhood as a mere 'explication' of boyhood, and considered that a microscope would have detected the full-formed oak in the acorn." In short, "the theory of development is itself a development which may be further developed, and must begin by proving itself Apostolic, at least in germ."[131]

Having stated the problem confronting the "official" theory, Tyrrell described what that theory is: the theory of charismatic authority. That authority, he charged, came gradually to be centered in the single brain of the Roman pontiff, who became by consequence not only the one through whom development is expressed but the one who effects whatever development occurs in the mind of the whole church. But the real tyrant is not the pope. It is the theological schools, the *sensus theologorum* that controls the minds of the various congregations and commissions on whom the pope depends for advice.

Now the consensus of experts would be a valuable, although purely natural, criterion of religious truth. But in point of fact it is an artificial consensus based on one school of thought and enforced from without by "the deposition of dissident professors; the suppression of dissident publications; the creation of strong corporate bias, etc., etc." The basis of this school is scholastic theology; scholastic theology is chiefly metaphysics; and metaphysics, "by reason of its necessary obscurity, is the department where mediocrity and slovenliness of thought can most easily mask itself under the semblance of profundity, and where the intellectual charlatan can lie longest undetected."[132] What can be expected from a monolithic system fed on obscurity, mediocrity, and slovenliness except more of the same?

But the real power for evil of this school arises from its alliance with the newly defined authority of the Roman pontiff.

> It is manifestly impossible that the pope should think for the whole Church and be wise with its collective wisdom; hence he must necessarily rely upon his consultors and be content to reinforce their opinions with the seal of his own ecumenical authority. It is as thinking for the pope that the theologians have become omnipotent. *En revanche* it is their corporate interest to defend the extremest views of papal infallibility and ecclesiastical inerrancy; to maintain the apostolicity of their views; to deny all true dogmatic development; to impose the past as a mould on the present and future; to push the present back into the past in the very teeth of history—in short to introduce an intellectual theocracy of the most fanatical type.[133]

Plainly, Tyrrell concluded, we are forced to consider this "official" view of the limits of the church's inerrancy irreconcilable with established facts and must therefore seek out another view that will justify adherence to the church along with honest acceptance of facts.

Part 2: A Liberal Restatement of Catholicism

RELIGION AS A SPIRIT. Protestants take the Bible, Catholics the church as the ultimate rule of faith. Whatever rule of faith is chosen, its authority cannot rest on its own witness but must come from beyond the rule itself. What ultimately authenticates the rule of faith is what Tyrrell sought to answer in this section.

Naturally, what authenticates the rule of faith is not what "officials" think it is. Their view of the nature and purpose of the church's doctrinal vicegerency is open to two very serious criticisms. First, they assume that Christ's mission was as directly dogmatic as it was prophetic, "that by Faith he meant orthodoxy, correctness of theological position," that we are to believe things intellectually perplexing because their revelation has been authenticated by miracles, and if Christ fell foul of Jewish authorities, it was because he set up a countertheology, not because he disdained the arrogant pretensions of theology as such. So we are taught that Christ committed to the church the whole creed, leaving her merely its "explication" and application for later times.[134]

But the Christ of the Gospels shows himself to be quite other. Indeed he taught *with authority,* but not *from authorities* as the scribes did. He taught "as one inspired with the prophetic spirit, like those prophets whose sepulchres were built up in scholastic commentaries that guarded the bones of their teaching but could not enshrine its spirit." His teaching was directed to the poor and common folk, not to intellectuals and theologians. He taught not a theological system but a way of life. The Gospel "was in fact a recall from intellectualism and outwardness to inwardness and vitality of religion in view of the coming Kingdom of God: 'Repent, for the Kingdom of Heaven is at hand,' is the whole substance of Christ's teaching in epitome."[135]

Christ taught about that coming Kingdom in the apocalyptic language of his milieu and thus left its exact nature and spiritual value veiled in the half-light of mystery. But he was quite clear about our spiritual preparation for that coming. The Kingdom of Heaven now present within each of us prepares for that future external Kingdom that will constitute the environment for that new life to come in its maturity.

There is no doubt that Christ's teaching about the preparation is "altogether practical and not intellectual; prophetic and not theological." Still, any practical teaching implies a theory of life, a doctrine of God, the world, and man and their interrelations. These implications must not be slighted but must be given their due. Intellectualism, however, inflates the theoretical implication out of all proportion, "as though conduct were shaped by theory, rather than theory by conduct." The fact is, people live without a theory of life and love without a theory of love, although in living and loving they do imply "a whole creed of mysteries beyond any compass of their explicit understanding." But "the fact that mysteries were necessarily implied in the practical teaching of Christ does not make him primarily and directly a teacher of mysteries, and still less a theologian."[136]

If intellectualism is to be avoided, so, too, is its counterfallacy sentimentalism, which claims that religion is such a matter of the heart and affections that dogmatic beliefs are utterly arbitrary. Religion is an affair of the *whole* soul. Conceptual formulation of the mysteries of faith are essential to a social and communicable religion. "Christianity without dogma is almost as impossible as Christianity without mysteries." The Johannine and Pauline writings were the beginnings of philosophic reflection on Christ's teaching, "but that teaching itself was of another order."[137]

Intellectualism and orthodoxy confuse faith with intellectual submission to a revealed theology. But of that Christ

> seems to take no account; but much of Faith as a dawning, though yet imperfect, vision of other-world realities and of the coming Kingdom and Judgment; not as an extrusion of our own theological system by the intrusion of another theology divinely guaranteed by miracles, but as the strengthening of a prophetic faculty higher than cold reason, which sees now through a glass darkly what it will come to see at last, as he saw it, face to face. For though dim, Faith is a vision, an intuition of the *whole* soul, dependent largely on moral and affective dispositions; nor should it be, as it so often is, confounded with that "belief on testimony" which is after all only an inference of the understanding, and of which it might be said: "Thou believest that there is one God; thou dost well; the devils also believe and tremble."[138]

Tyrrell's second criticism was that "officials" conceive the church's doctrinal vicegerency in an unqualified or very exaggerated form. He did not question the proposition that the church does authoritatively continue Christ's teaching. His question was in what sense and with what authority. In the apostolic church, authority was charismatic; the teacher was the Holy Spirit At some later point the corporate authority of a community or of its officials was substituted for the authority of the Spirit speaking through inspired but unofficial individuals. The first letter of Clement implies that this transfer was instituted by Christ with a view to times when the spirit would grow cold. But criticism sees the Catholic system to be a device of later times, instituted to meet conditions never foreseen by those who expected an imminent parousia. Granted that the transfer of Christianity from a charismatic to an institutional phase was wholly necessary for its survival, and granted that authority had to be transferred to the institution, two questions concerning this transfer have to be answered: (1) In what sense, if any, is this corporate authority divine? (2) What are its limits?

The first question brought Tyrrell to confront the Protestant contention that the "'institutionising' of Christianity," however justifiable, was a purely human undertaking and that the Catholicizing of Christianity was a corruption and not a legitimate development. The underlying and fallacious psychology of Protestant counterexpectations, Tyrrell charged, is that the church today is to be governed by the same outpouring of gifts of the Spirit as in apostolic times. But Protestantism in its essential principle "is in conflict with the psychology of the individual and the multitude, in its vain effort to perpetuate what of its very nature is as evanescent as a thunderstorm or a spell of fine weather." Weather changes, and the conditions that prevailed while the Bridegroom was present will not suffice to keep his spirit alive in his absence. Protestants seem to want the constant presence of the Bridegroom. But that would only keep Christians in a state of infancy. Hence Jesus' words: "It is good for you that I go away."[139]

But without contending that the Catholicizing of Christianity was a corruption—and by "Catholicizing" Tyrrell meant the transformation into an institution with graces attached to offices rather than the converse—we may see it as "a purely human work, the result of man's co-operation with the Spirit."[140] It cannot be considered purely and simply a divine institution, and it is doubtful if Christ himself ever contemplated such a transformation.

The only sense in which the institutional church is divine is as a product of the same Spirit that gave us the Jewish religion and Christ. In Christ that Spirit found its highest, although not its exhaustive, utterance. Naturally that Spirit "will express itself differently in an individual and in a society; in a human heart and life, and in a system of doctrine, discipline and ritual; yet it may be unmistakably the same Spirit and governing principle."[141] Insofar as the institutionizing process was carried out under the suggestive, selective, and corrective influence of that Spirit on the natural workings of human transactions, the church is divine. It is divine in the same sense that the Bible is a divine book possessing divine authority. But in no sense was it delivered whole and entire by divine fiat on the day of Pentecost. The modifications that criticism has forced on conceptions of the Bible must also be applied to conceptions of the church. If this means that theology in both matters must break down, it does not mean a breakdown of Catholicism. "Catholicism is a divine institution possessing divine authority," a "joint-effect . . . of the same spiritual out-pouring, or up-welling, that gave us Christ and the Charismatic Christianity of his immediate followers."[142]

In answer to the second question, on the nature, scope, and limits of ecclesiastical authority, Tyrrell employed the religious psychology developed in *Religion as a Factor of Life*.[143] In general, he began, "it is the failure of inspiration that renders an institution necessary."[144] But that does not make the institution the essence of the church's life, nor even does it consist in the charismatic gifts evident in the apostolic church. Both were mere expressions of the church's life and were given to serve that life. What underlies both institution and charisms is the *caritas Dei*, the law of love, the supreme gift of the Spirit that remains, as Paul says (1 Cor. 13:13), when everything else will have passed away.

That *caritas Dei*, which found its highest utterance in Christ, has become the soul of the church.

> I do not suppose that any "official," from the Cardinal Secretary downwards, nor any theologian would care to dispute the proposition that the Church is before all else a school of Sanctity and Charity; that her sole *raison d'etre* is to reproduce the pattern of Christ as exactly as possible, in as many as possible; that this simple end is professedly the ultimate justification of all her institutions, her hierarchy, her sacramental system, her dogmatic system, of all her battlings and diplomacy in defence of the temporal power; of all the pomp and parade of the Court of Rome in its palmiest days; of all the ceremonial, the purple and scarlet and fine-twined linen of bishops and prelates and cardinals; of all that is mere worldliness, if not sanctified by that end, and mere fraud and hypocrisy if it only pretends to be so sanctified. Pass through the courts and halls of the Vatican Palace amidst the outward semblances of earthly vanity and secular power, and ask yourself the ultimate *Why* and *Wherefore* of all that you see and hear going on around you; or ask the first Monsignore or Cardinal who will deign to notice you, and he will have to answer you, as gravely as he can, "Our sole thought and aim is, that men may love God and love one another as much as possible in the Spirit of Christ. We do not care about temporal power for its own sake, or for money, nor even for spiritual power over men's minds and wills; nor for our own dignity and position; nor for the system and institution which we defend; but we desire purely and simply to make men holy and Christ-like, and we are convinced that these are lawful and expeditious means to that end."[145]

It is therefore primarily a way of life that has been committed to the church's care, not a body of doctrine; Christ rather than Christology; a living spirit rather than a system of ideas.

But what precisely is that "spirit"? It is not the Divine Spirit itself, Tyrrell answered, but the human spirit *as influenced by* that Divine Spirit and as inspired with certain aims and ideals. By transference, "spirit" comes to mean also "the personified aims and ideals of the spirit so worked upon."[146] But here Tyrrell meant the religious attitude of the soul of Christ as the perfect expression of that Spirit.

In the "heroic" stage of Christianity, enthusiasm was the rule, as nearly all were in direct contact with that Spirit. But as the initial shock diffused its force and general enthusiasm fell below the heroic, social helps assumed greater importance. Then the direct promptings of the Spirit no longer sufficed. The Spirit that once spoke to hearts had now to be kept alive by expressing and conceptualizing his earlier utterance for the benefit of posterity. In the absence of the more vivid personal inspiration and enthusiasm, wills had to be stirred rather by an appeal to minds. "Thus, no doubt, it was that the 'depositum fidei,' . . . came gradually to be considered as a system of doctrine rather than as a spirit."[147]

RELIGION AS A DOCTRINE. Defining the relationship between the spirit of man governed by the Divine Spirit in Christ and the doctrinal expression of that spirit so governed occupied Tyrrell throughout most of his life. The question arose again here. Much of his discussion is consistent with what has been seen in the preceding chapters—how the adequate organ of the Spirit's voice is the mind of the whole church and how the intellect provides a conceptual map that is to guide yet not hinder the human spirit. But a few emendations and refinements require comment.

In the appendix to *Religion as a Factor of Life* Tyrrell provided a liberal interpretation of the articles of the creed. Now he was asking what sort of truth these articles represent. Liberal Protestants, he noted, maintain that these articles, as well as all other religious expressions, are merely symbolic and purely regulative of the Christian's actions. But to the Catholic they are much more. Indeed they are symbolic and analogous, practical and regulative; but universally accepted religious expressions have a real ontological foundation—although not in the world of time and space but in the spiritual and "metempirical" realm of the Absolute. "There alone it is that the ontological values of these doctrines are to be sought, which err, not as overstatements, but as immeasurably defective understatements of the truth."[148] Doctrine does have a profoundly divine foundation and truth, but this ontological reality is in no way to be equated with its intellectual "figuring-forth," however necessary the connection between the ontological reality and its universally accepted and authoritatively approved symbol.

Christianity as a doctrinal system, that is, as a construction of the understanding, has a twofold truth: in relation to the world of outer experience and in relation to the spirit of Christ (not to be confused with the Spirit of Christ) and "the order of eternal realities of which that spirit is the product." Under the former aspect doctrine is "a necessary fallible approximation to natural truth; under the latter, it is an infallible approximation to supernatural and eternal truth." The reason is this:

> The Spirit of Christ seizes from the chaos of current beliefs—theological, ethical, historical—those that are most appropriate for its own embodiment and progressive expression, and weaves them into a garment adapted to the present state of its own growth. If the choice and the weaving is its own, the matter chosen is the work of fallible man in his quest for truth. It is in the former, in the choice and the weaving, that the product of inspiration is to be sought; and not in the "beggarly elements" of man's devising; in the heavenly treasure, and not in the earthen vessel—*Spiritus est qui vivificat, caro non prodest quidquam.*[149]

For Protestants, what is *spiritually* true is somehow less than real—as when they say that Christ is spiritually present in the Eucharist, meaning that he is not *really* present. "Officials" of the Roman Church have adopted that same convention. But in fact what is spiritually true is really true, truer than liberal or materialistic representations can ever possibly be. Thus Tyrrell concluded that his views were really less liberal and materialistic and more spiritual and real than those of the "official" theology, which found itself unwittingly on the side of liberal Protestantism. For although he gave doctrine a primarily pragmatic truth, he founded it ontologically in the order of absolute reality rather than in the order of appearances, where one finds the matter or "reality" of popular thought.

DOCTRINE AND ECCLESIAL AUTHORITY. At this point Tyrrell took up the question of the value of doctrine and the nature of the authority behind it. He first recalled the underlying ecclesial process by which vaguely felt realities of the eternal order are gradually communicated from soul to soul in a community of like wills, how these communications are refined and developed into ever truer symbolic representations of those will-realities, and how the whole process is guided and dominated by the principle developed in the course of history, namely, the spirit of Christ. Doctrine, as a harmonious expression of that spirit, he argued, can claim our submission only to the extent that its expression is in "harmony with the spirit of Christ in its present stage of development." Nor can that expression be regarded as final. It develops and "can come to an end only when the development of charity, and the collective religious life of the Church comes to an end,—only when the infinite treasury of Christ's spirit is exhausted."[150]

External norms are essential for a religious society. They embody the *consensus fidelium*, the wisdom of the ages, and thus they possess a certain infallibility, even in the natural order. The educational advantages of such external and social standards are obvious, but they can be vitiated by abuses. The danger is that norms expressed in some particular stage of social development become apotheosized and regarded as final and adequate for all possible stages, past, present, and future, to the detriment both of individual personalities, which are racked and distorted into an artificial mold, and of the community at large, which falls into a dull mechanical uniformity. But if abuses can be checked, the benefits of social norms for personal and communal development are great. Each society has its characteristic store of wisdom to be appropriated by its members. This appropriation is the primary condition of self-education. This task done, the individual may go beyond the norms "to effect those original and personal modifications and enrichments of the same, by the accumulation, criticism, and selection of which the corporate mind of the community is gradually developed." But to strike out in some or other private direction without having first appropriated the common mind is to be merely eccentric, not original; it is to be content with something less rather than something greater that comprehends and includes the common mind; it is not to have gone beyond it but to have failed to come so far.

> The general mind is a rule and standard by which we have to correct a certain inborn *unlikeness of defect*, by which we are separated from the common type. Personality means a certain self-wrought *unlikeness of excess*, by which we surpass that type, remoulding what we have received to our own individual image and likeness. Disobedience may be described therefore as that sort of wilful and irrational eccentricity by which a man refuses due respect to the gathered experience and reflection of the community to which he belongs; and from this the notions of obedience, and of authority, its correlative, are straightway deducible.[151]

Simply because the spirit of Christ and the appropriations of truth revealed to the mind of the church are constantly growing and developing throughout the ages and spreading as the community spreads, the Catholic system with its central ecumenical authority is necessary to gather up, formulate, and propose (not impose) for the guidance of each that truth which has come thus far in its development under the influence of the Spirit.

But how does such an ecumenical authority tally with the interpretation of the Vatican Council or with the actual history of the development of the Catholic organization? Taking his cue from Rudolf Sohm's *Kirchenrecht*, Tyrrell argued that the successors to the apostles failed to trust in the providence of Christ's Spirit working in the community and instead claimed the same miraculous charism for teaching and governing possessed by the apostles. This claim along with another badly understood claim, that *unity must* characterize any doctrine that purports to be divine, led inevitably through confrontation with counterclaims to a narrowing down of the miraculous charism to the single person of the Roman pontiff.

> As long as the office of "Divine Teacher" was claimed by more than one, the claim was again and again disproved by their differences; hence the only hope was that it should be disclaimed by all except one. . . . Paradoxical though it may sound, this clinging to the more or less *miraculous* charismata of Apostolic days is in principle Protestant, . . . and is inconsistent with the Catholic: *Securus judicat orbis terrarum.* The latter is an appeal to the more or less *natural* criterion of a multitude of counsellors—the highest criterion being the consensus of all. To call it a "natural" criterion is however not to exclude the action of the Holy Spirit which, in the form of Divine Charity, or the spirit of Christ, is shed abroad in the hearts of the faithful. If in each of these singly this spirit is a supernatural grace, yet it cannot be called a *charisma* in the sense of a miraculous gift of gnosis or prophecy or interpretation. To determine the implications of this spirit by conference and intercourse is to have recourse to natural means; and yet the utterance of such a council or conference may be regarded as the voice of that spirit which is diffused through the multitude. The interpretation can never be adequate or final for all times; but it is never false, and it is the highest public rule of truth at present procurable.[152]

In almost all aspects of church government, natural means are adequate. Only when these fail—which is rare—may we expect God to work miracles. Thus nearly all *ex cathedra* pronouncements are true by virtue of natural rather than miraculous means, so that "the claim to miracle is squeezed to its smallest dimensions, and all but extinguished."[153]

History has for centuries prepared the way for a final abandonment of the charismatic claim. "Each breakdown of that claim in its wider form has been remedied by some unconscious concession to the 'institutional' and democratic principle, i.e., to the logically necessary consequences of the Catholic idea."[154] The real experts in Christianity (which does not equal theology) are the saints (not theologians), and sanctity is found throughout the Christian body. Thus the natural method that Tyrrell saw for arriving at truth led him to conclude that the principle of government and teaching in the church is essentially democratic.

The episcopal system, for example, possesses an indirectly divine character not by reason of divine intervention but by reason of its spontaneous creation of the united Christian people, in other words, in consequence of the democratic principle. Its validity is sealed not by its own claim to apostolic succession—which history questions—but by approbation of the united church, whose apostolic continuity remains unassailable.

As to the papal office, "the Pope as Czar and absolute theocratic Monarch by divine right must, under the logic of the Christian idea, give place to the Pope as really, and not only in name, the 'servus Servorum Dei,' as the greatest, the first-born among many brethren only because he is the most widely and universally serviceable and ministrant." With the emergence of an organic as opposed to a mechanical conception of society, papal primacy will be reconciled with the church's fundamentally democratic character, and an impossible centralization will give way to a freer and more spiritual unity.

> But all this transformation will depend ultimately and radically on the abandonment of the claim to an oracular power, by which the Pope becomes the mouthpiece of God not *through* the Church, but *to* the Church, and claims her absolute subjection as to God himself. It will depend on the recognition of the entire Christian people as the true and immediate *Vicarius Christi*, the only adequate organ of religious development, as that *orbis terrarum* whose sure verdict is the supreme norm of Faith for the time being, and in whose life and growth the truth of Christ lives and grows from generation to generation, "ever ancient ever new."[155]

The foregoing exposition represents the substance of *The Church and the Future*. There are two more sections to part 2 that require only brief notice. Section 3, titled "The Future of Officialism," simply recapitulates previous arguments and draws conclusions just seen. The last section, on "Catholicism and Heterodoxy," considers the relationship between Roman Catholicism and other Christian and non-Christian religions.

However much negative criticism Tyrrell brought against current Roman Catholic "officialism," his position on the Roman Church as a whole remained unaltered. He held the church up as the highest and truest institutional development of the Christian spirit.

On the relationship of other religions to Catholicism, he adopted Ernst Troeltsch's position in *Die Absolutheit des Christentums*, namely, that Christianity is an ideal and absolute religion toward which the whole world is evolving but will fail within history to realize. That is, as an ideal for the whole world, it will never be the attainment of more than a fraction. In this view, the official position that regards other religions as anathema becomes intolerable. It is tantamount to the Calvinist tenet of election by divine favoritism of a faithful remnant from the reprobate multitudes. Rather we must recognize the essential unity of all religions insofar as they are valid expressions of the *caritas Dei,* even if we are convinced that some religions are truer expressions than others. If Christianity is the ultimate religious expression, it is not the only valid religious expression. It is simply "the highest expression yet attained of the religious instinct" and "the fullest embodiment of that spirit of Christ which is striving for utterance through all religions however uncouth and barbarous."[156] Just as civilization, liberty, and knowledge are the universal destiny of mankind, so is Christianity. But it is an adult state, and children and babes will always constitute half the race.

Part 3: The Ethics of Conformity

Given views of the church so discordant from those of officialism, Tyrrell had to face the question, What place, if any, can a liberal dissenter have within the Catholic body today? He was not concerned with the radical liberal who goes as far to the left as "officials" go to the right. Both positions are reprehensible: officials doctor facts to agree with their own utterances, while liberals doctor their utterances to agree with facts.

Tyrrell was concerned with the "really honest liberal" who "admits that the doctrine of ecclesiastical inerrancy must be restated so as to render such equivocation unnecessary."[157] Real honesty puts a liberal in a difficult position. For if he rejects the Protestant and individualist view of Christianity as opposed to the social view and regards the mystical body of Christ as the authentic organ of the Christian spirit, no position other than the Catholic position is possible. But his interpretation of Catholicism puts him in opposition to the "official" interpretation and to those who hold

the power of anathema. How is the honest liberal to meet the dilemma and at the same time maintain his integrity? First, conscience forbids him either to secede or needlessly to get himself
thrust out. If he does not agree that wholehearted adherence to officialism is the very essence of Catholicism, he is bound to stay and
do all he can to further a saner position. "Officials" will exploit all
the resources of authority—censorship, the Index, the Inquisition,
secret delation—to try to drive him out. But he must evade their efforts and thus seek to break their power.

Nor need he worry that such "evasion" is dishonest. "Persecution and evasion are correlatives; the former justifies the latter. Per-
secuted in one city, the liberal Catholic will flee to another; repressed in one way, he will break forth in another." If his argument
is to be met only with a hail of stones, "he may prudently decline
martyrdom." But persecution is what he may expect, "and indeed
when those who sit in the seat of the Apostles pronounce him no
true Catholic he may be pardoned if he recalls the parallel im-
peachment of those Apostles and their Master by those who sat in
the chair of Moses."[158]

The liberal ought not court this possibility needlessly, but the
occasion may arise where a victim seems required and where
someone must speak out and suffer the consequences. In that case,
he may rest secure that, though severed from the body of the
church, he is drawn closer to her soul; and though thrust out of visible communion with the orthodox, he cannot be separated from
the love of Christ or from the communion of humanity.

There Tyrrell rested his case. Unfortunately the gallery was
empty of those who needed to hear his argument most. In itself it
was a masterpiece of apologetic. But for extrinsic reasons it was
lost to the generation for which it was meant.

"BOURDON'S" RECEPTION

Tyrrell and his friends exercised the greatest caution in dissemi-
nating *The Church and the Future*. The author's identity was kept
from even some of his most ardent sympathizers, as the risk in
printing the book at all was extremely grave. As well as may be
known, not a single copy of "Bourdon" escaped the circle until
several years later. Consequently there is no record in the press of
"Bourdon's" reception. But one can easily extrapolate an answer to
how "officials" would have received him from the reception they
accorded a less-guarded offspring.

Late in 1903 Tyrrell published the anonymous and now infamous *Letter to a University Professor*, later republished as *A Much-*

Abused Letter.[159] This work was largely a development of part 3 of "Bourdon" on "The Ethics of Conformity." Late in 1905 sections of the *Letter* were leaked to the Italian press, and Jesuit officials soon learned the author's name. Shortly thereafter Tyrrell was dismissed from the Society of Jesus and was well on his way to excommunication.[160] From this extreme reaction to "Bourdon's" offspring, it is safe to say that official reaction to "Bourdon" would have been no less violent.

If ultramontane reaction to *The Church and the Future* cannot be documented, the book's reception by Tyrrell's sympathizers can be, but only from correspondence, since "Bourdon's" ambit was severely restricted. The keynote to distribution was, extreme caution and safety in small numbers. Thereby its movements could be accounted for by one man, Tyrrell himself.

The first reference to "Bourdon" after publication appeared in a covering letter of 14 June 1903 from Tyrrell to Canon A. L. Lilley, whom Tyrrell had met two weeks earlier at a meeting of the Synthetic Society in London.[161] Tyrrell had spoken to him about "Engels" and "Bourdon" and now sent him copies with the warning to be extremely discreet, as the Red Book ("Engels") had just been recast with a view to publication under his own name—"should censors prove manageable; of which however there is very small hope"; and the Grey Book ("Bourdon") "must ever remain shrouded in mystery." But if Lilley could "suggest any quarters where it might *tell* I could cause copies to be sent. I don't want to wake those who are sleeping comfortably unless some very definite good is to be hoped."[162]

Four days later Tyrrell also warned Bremond, who by this time had carried his self-imposed exile from Paris to London and the Jesuit community at Farm Street. He had received a copy of "Bourdon" from Maude Petre. "For God's sake," Tyrrell urged, "don't communicate it to Thurston or any of our Farm St. people, or leave it about under their eyes; or acknowledge it should you ever meet it in the hands of another. If however you know any place where it would do good & not harm tell me & I will provide."[163] It is interesting that even Thurston, with whom Tyrrell remained on friendly terms, was not to be trusted. Evidently by this time Tyrrell's views had advanced so far beyond the scope of Thurston's sympathy that he was now classified among the somnolent.[164]

Tyrrell's agent A. R. Waller was keeping the stock of the "Grey Books." On 20 June Tyrrell wrote him for fifty copies, which "will probably do me for many a long day. . . . There are so many it would simply upset to no purpose & but a few who being already upset it might set up."[165] In fact, Tyrrell told Petre the next day, "I only see openings for 8 copies in the whole world."[166] Five library copies were to be distributed as customary, but none was to be released for reviewing. "I am the more careful just now," he continued to Waller, "as I anticipate some rough ecclesiastical weather"— probably a reference to troubles he expected with censors over *Lex Orandi*—"though the death of H[is] E[minence] ought to bring eventual calm."[167]

Predictably, the fullest and most important response to "Bourdon" came from Baron von Hügel. His reaction was mixed. On the one hand, he found the forcefulness and brilliance of Tyrrell's presentation beyond praise. On the other hand, he saw it as hazarding an open conflict, especially now when the Loisy affair indicated that Rome was laying in arms.

Cumulative evidence indicates that the baron was becoming increasingly alarmed. Events seemed to be moving toward excommunications—was it not stated in "Bourdon's" conclusion? For the baron that was a fate to be avoided at all costs short of abandonment of principle. And from this point on, the picture that emerges of von Hügel's role in the modernist conflict is that of an inept horseman who belatedly discovered that he had given rein to wild horses and now was vainly struggling to contain them without either breaking their spirit or denying them the right to run.

On 22 June von Hügel sent Tyrrell an extraordinarily long critique. He saw in the book "five closely interconnected theses" that were "of most living, poignant importance and interest." Two of them had been driven home "with an extraordinary force and consistency," but the other three fell somewhat short.[168]

The first thesis consisted of a presentation of the Catholic view of the Christian church and a criticism of Protestant and Anglican views. Here the baron found Tyrrell at "the very heighth of your merit and success" in bringing out "more persuasively than ever, a truly Catholic because cooperatively corporate, conception of the Church." The description of the building up of the Christian body by interaction of spirit with spirit into an ever fuller expression of the Spirit of Christ that even Christ himself could not exhaust "could not . . . be truer and more nobly put." And the implications of Tyrrell's "profoundly catholic" conception of the church leading to an eventual collapse and final abandonment of the claim to charismatic teaching power was the most "startlingly impressive part of this whole noble argument" and "quite impregnable."[169]

The second convincing thesis was "that the inerrancy claimed for the Church by the first Thesis, will have to be conceived in a mode corresponding to the change necessitated in our conception of Biblical inerrancy." Tyrrell's argument, in its main contention, was "quite unanswerable."[170]

Then there were the less satisfactory theses. The third, in which Tyrrell proposed that the deposit of faith about which the church is inerrant is the spirit of Christ and not a body of statements, was also what the baron wanted. But von Hügel found that the statement of the thesis slipped from a superior emphasis on *all* the faculties of the soul working in harmony to a lower untenable deemphasis of the role of reason and understanding in favor of immediate intuition. He pointed out that the wholly admirable position begun on page 34 and worked up so finely to the position on page 81 slipped "off the rails" on page 111, where Tyrrell asserted "the complete subordination of the pure isolated understanding to the whole commonwealth of our spiritual faculties; of the brain, to the heart and affections." The baron acknowledged the difficulty of maintaining proper balance, but it had to be done if one were to avoid simply reacting against intellectualism and establish a position both higher and deeper than either intellectualism or sentimentalism.[171] "You are abundantly right," Tyrrell replied on 27 June; "it is not only untrue to what I have said elsewhere but to what I meant to say there. Instead of 'completely subordinated to' I meant 'co-ordinated with'; but in negating the false supremacy of intellect my rhetoric thrust it down too low."[172]

The fourth thesis concerned the relation of Roman Catholicism to non-Catholic and non-Christian religions. Tyrrell had stressed the need for Roman Catholicism to recognize that the spirit of Christ works in all peoples and all religions and that therefore, if Christianity be confessed as the highest religion, it can no longer be confessed in the exclusive sense hitherto assumed. This argument, along with what Tyrrell contended about missionary efforts, the baron found quite admirable. But why was it necessary, he chided, to declare "one universal religion" to be a "crude dream"? Was it any cruder than the dream of a universal language or a universal empire? "Whilst too weary to argue it out, I must, in honesty, put upon record, that it hurt my poor instincts a bit, to find that formal repudiation of so touchingly grand a conception there."[173]

By the "crude dream of one universal religion," Tyrrell explained, he meant "*one* in its dogmatic symbolism; in the *stage* of moral & mystical development: not merely one as it is now & always has been." Its crudeness, he said,

lies in the ultra-montane supposition that Catholic truth is as definite (or should be) as geometrical truth which is the same for all men. If, as long as man's mind grows, religious truth will be still ever at the horizon relative to his, then, clear midday understanding, uniformity of expression & cultus would be possible only if all men stood on the same intellectual & moral level—i.e., spoke the same language (using "language" as the index of inner life). Such uniformity of development seems to me to exclude that graduated range of variations which is a condition of all evolution. Hence I feel that the *one universal religion* is, like the Pole Star to an arctic explorer, a thing to make-for, but never to be reached; an inspiring ideal (like that e.g. of infinite moral or mental perfection in man). Here I doubt if we really differ except in some turn of expression.[174]

The fifth and final thesis concerned the knowableness and conceptualization of God. Again the baron largely agreed, but some modifications or additions were wanted "to prevent the impression that God may, after all, be something less than (human) spirit, reason and will." One questionable passage occurred on page 187:

It is only in the secondary cause, in man, that the unnamable, unimaginable influence of the First Cause takes the form of *mind* and *will;* being in itself something that is prior to all mind and will, infinitely greater, infinitely different; not to be thought of as a spirit ruling over spirit, as a man rules over men. Hence, that God is the Author of our thoughts does not mean that He has thought them; nor has He willed what we will; or said what we have said; or done what we have done.

Of course, the baron continued, it is impossible to define God as such. But at the same time "any Hébertian evaporation of all attribution, however analogical it may have to remain . . . must be most vigilantly avoided by us."[175] Tyrrell assured the baron that he saw the danger of Hébertianism, but what he was addressing on that page was the counterextreme of anthropomorphism. What he wanted was the mid-air position between the two, such as that offered by Aquinas's view of analogy as outlined "in my Synthetic paper." Some may see this suggestion as mere word juggling, "yet I don't think that the *super*-will, *super*-personality etc which we predicate of the Absolute are mere x or y so long as we allow that they are inclusively though super-excellently *will* & *personality*. Hébert seems to think that 'non-personal' means 'impersonal'; 'non-conscious,' 'unconscious.'"[176]

Having said all this, the baron apparently felt that he might have given the impression of discounting "Bourdon" more than accepting it, and the prospect pained him as a devoted teacher is pained at seeing his most promising student slipping from the ways of his master.

I feel as though I were committing a mean action by apparently discounting my acceptance of your noble, touching, deep and singularly courageous book in this, to me painful way. But indeed, I doubt whether it is, if only because I know so well how solid and fundamental is my adherence to, and profit from, all the substantial parts, all the fully deliberate and entirely self-consistent utterances of your noble confession of Faith. And certainly, your first two Theses are throughout of a clearness, and your third is of a rich, deep, tender spirituality such as I would not know where to match.[177]

Then follows a fretful note of caution: "You have elected to run a . . . risk of grave consequences. . . . But I think that risk was clearly worth running,—on condition, of course, that what has been so bravely written, get most discreetly placed."[178] Von Hügel wanted to have it both ways: freedom to criticize and freedom from grave consequences. But given the current ascendancy in Rome, no one could have it both ways. If extreme discretion were exercised, who but the already converted would hear the criticism? If the criticism reached the circles that needed it, grave consequences would follow. Martyrdom was a foregone conclusion of public criticism. Tyrrell saw this inevitability and admitted it. Von Hügel felt it but vainly hoped to avoid it.

For discreet placement of the book, the baron included a list of names, some of them designated as definite recipients, others as questionable or definite negatives. Among the elect were Loisy, Houtin, Mignot (with some slight reservations), Eucken, Troeltsch, Holtzmann (again, with some reservations) and longtime friends of the baron, Fr. Christian van den Biesen, a Dutch professor of scripture at St. Joseph's College, Mill Hill, and Dom Cuthbert Butler, then resident in Cambridge, later abbot of Downside. Among the doubtful cases were Fawkes, Turmel, Semeria, Don Brizio Casciola, Giovanni Genocchi, and Dom Odilo Rottmanner, the Augustine expert from Munich. Blondel was also questionable, because since their Christological controversy, it seemed that the book might simply distress him. "I am old enough to have to repent of several cases where I have urged souls beyond their grace: as regards my own views, I feel I have, until a fresh outlook is gained by B., done all I ought to do: he is so near God, anyhow: may I become as good as he is!" To be excluded were Harnack, Duchesne, Goodrich, Williams, and Barry.[179] The exclusion of Fr. William Barry is curious, since, as will be seen shortly, he was the principal clerical inquirer who provoked Tyrrell into writing *The Church and the Future* in the first place. Whatever Tyrrell finally decided, the baron requested a list of recipients so he might know to whom he could mention the book.

Tyrrell did not immediately answer the letter, but kept the baron in torment over its reception. So von Hügel wrote again on 26 June, as though to appease: "Bourdon strikes me as greater at a little distance now, than it looked when I read it: and yet, then already it impressed me deeply. The division as to 'The Future of "Officialism"' is also excellent; and I ought to have specially noticed it when writing my letter.—That increase of impressiveness at some distance like that, is, I think, one of the surest tests and signs of the livingness and true greatness of a work: this one certainly has that quality in a rare degree." In the same note the baron removed Blondel from the list of the doubtful to that of the excluded—on the strength of Bremond's counsel that Blondel has "a distinctly intolerant side" and for the time being at least is not to be pressured lest he retrench or even turn against us. The baron felt that Bremond was right because Blondel did not acknowledge the receipt of a copy of the baron's Synthetic Society paper. "He is a rare, great soul: but I doubt whether either you or I can, at present, make him grow." In a postscript, the baron added Lilley to his list of recipients and revised his opinion on Casciola: "Bremond and I both agreed that Don Br. Casciola is *exactly* the man actually to require a copy."[180]

Tyrrell had already on 14 June sent a copy to Lilley, who received it enthusiastically. On 23 June Tyrrell wrote in appreciation of his approval and encouragement, "for when one steps out alone into what is at least relatively a new position one feels cold naked & feeble & in need of buttressing up." As an example of what he was up against, Tyrrell enclosed a letter with the explanation:

> The enclosed—which please destroy—will show how little it ["Bourdon"] satisfies the man whose queries & difficulties called it into existence, one who cannot divest himself of his ingrained scholasticism yet finds facts indigestible. What he really wants is some reading of facts that will give him back his antiprotestant slings & stones. Can a man when he is old enter again into his mother's womb? Can he face the bitterness of criticising his life-long categories?
>
> By all means lend the book to anyone whom it will help. I wish to Heaven I could spread it more widely; but were I to become the hero of another Mivart-drama it would mean the end of my influence in that world where it is most needed & the cancelling of whatever little I may have done in the past towards letting daylight into the darker corners of Catholicism.[181]

Evidently the caution Tyrrell displayed just a few weeks earlier was breaking down. Well, Tyrrell was always too bold for caution and anyhow had an irrepressible urge to disseminate his ideas, especially once they were in print and once he was satisfied that he had said well what he wanted to say. Von Hügel had just given him that assurance. But he had also cautioned him, and Tyrrell passed the warning on to Lilley. On 25 June he sent Lilley two more copies of "Bourdon" with the note, "Von Hügel has been cautioning me to be careful about my neck; & does not think the elaborate mendacity of the title-page etc enough to baffle the inquisitive or the inquisitorial."[182]

Evidently, too, the author of the letter enclosed for Lilley was Fr. William Barry, professor of theology at the major seminary at Oscott and friend of von Hügel. Such is gathered from Tyrrell's irenic reply to the baron's letters of 22 and 26 June. Tyrrell finally answered these on 27 June and explained why Barry, contrary to the baron's advice, would have to receive a copy of "Bourdon":

> You warned me especially against Dr. Barry; & I know the man to be indiscreet and unbalanced & not a really liberal mind in any sense. Well, he wrote to me about Loisy's book first with great sympathy; then later in a sort of fluster attacking him on the grounds that such conclusions spelt protestantism & yet how could we deny facts etc. Then I took the line that a far extremer acceptance of critical results than L's would not spell protestantism necessarily; that the *Entweder-Oder* of Renan & the Ultramontanes was a fallacy, & I promised him I would make my contention good, which I did in the form of this H. B. book. Hence he being the occasion of it, is necessarily in the secret. However I am quite certain that under all the circumstances he will keep the affair as a *secretum commissum;* it would need a peculiar degree of treachery to do otherwise; & I have reason to believe him a very sincere well-wisher. The book has not satisfied him very much, just because it robs him of some of his anti-Protestant slings & stones; but his theological castles are all in ruins & he has no love for the officials.[183]

In this same letter Tyrrell enclosed a list of those to whom he would send copies of "Bourdon." "My own feeling said *No* to Blondel," he explained. "I feel that he is not *detached* from his system sufficiently to bear patiently any facts or suggestions that might entail reconstructions. Does he read the N.T. critics at all? To know of them, & even of their results, at *second* hand is but dream-knowledge compared with even an imperfect first-hand aquaintance—at least, so I have found it. The speculative mind needs continual cold douches into the realm of fact if it is not to become fevered & delirious; yet such douches are not pleasant."[184] Tyrrell was no doubt recalling here the ghost of Christmas past.[185]

Tyrrell also suggested that von Hügel save any criticisms of the book that he might receive from recipients until the two met—this to save time for von Hügel's own much interrupted work on Saint Catherine. Tyrrell said that he did not care a bit about compliments on the work. All he was interested in was "to stick a seed or two where it will germinate some day or other, & to communicate the idea to those who have more liberty to utilise them than I have." To that end, he said, French or German translations would be welcome, if they could be arranged. But he knew that would be difficult to manage because most publishers would not touch the book without an *imprimatur*.[186]

On 11 July Tyrrell sent Don Brizio Casciola a copy of "Bourdon" with a covering letter that demonstrates Tyrrell's deftness at dissembling. "At Baron von Hügel's instance I am sending you M. Hilaire Bourdon's 'The Church and the Future.'" Tyrrell had asked the baron if he might thus use his name. Not only would it draw attention away from the real author, but it would "secure an interest" by reason of the baron's recommendation. Presumably the baron agreed. "Needless to say," Tyrrell continued to Casciola,

> the book has not been published in France nor secured any episcopal Imprimatur there. Hence the author is desirous that it should fall into no hands but those that can be trusted not to betray one who endeavors however feebly and unsuccessfully to bring relief to those very few Catholics who are sufficiently versed in the data of the religious problem to be anxious about its solution. If you think it could be translated, as it were, from the original French into Italian, with any profit to souls the author will give all liberty in the matter.[187]

On the following day he sent Loisy a copy with a similar caution, then added:

> I do not expect that you will consider it successful as a construction or synthesis; but you may possibly find it suggestive were it only as a theme of criticism. At all events it attempts to take into account all the chief data of the problem of ecclesiastical Christianity and draw its conclusions with respect to what is agreeable or disagreeable, convenient or inconvenient to the writer's private prepossessions & hopes; and as such it will, I trust, win your respect if it fail to gain your assent.[188]

Casciola apparently could not assent to at least two important aspects of Tyrrell's synthesis without some clarification. First, he found that making the imminence of the parousia *the* leitmotiv of Christ's preaching, as Weiss did, vitiates Christ's doctrine of self-renunciation. Secondly, the discussion on development was too obscure. Tyrrell responded immediately on 15 August with important clarifications. On the first criticism, he explained that taking the immediacy of the parousia as the leitmotiv of Christ's teaching does not void his general doctrine concerning unworldliness, poverty, self-abnegation, and self-sacrifice, because only *certain* features of that doctrine "derive from that 'optical illusion'—those namely which would make *continued* social life impossible." Christ did not invent the belief in the imminence of the parousia. He found it already present and widespread among the people with whom he dealt. They were a worldly people convinced of an imminent parousia, and Jesus simply used their belief—"and most probably shared this useful illusion"—as an *ad hominem* argument for unworldliness. But that he so used this illusion does not mean that he thought the transitoriness and futility of worldly aim the only or the true argument for unworldliness. As to Christ's true argument, Tyrrell suggested:

> The positive or direct motives of his doctrine of renunciation were not those of Bouddhist asceticism which are of the "vanitas vanitatum" order; very much akin to those that would be created by the conviction of a near *Parousia,* but those that spring from a great belief in the value of life, in the dignity of the soul as such, and irrespective of external circumstances of wealth birth and education; and which lead by consequence to an asceticism whose motive is the love of others and a hatred of egoism and self-indulgence. H.B. has followed J. Weiss in his "Predigt Jesu vom Reiche Gottes" partly because that view seems *at present* critically stronger; but still more because it is the one most difficult to reconcile with received beliefs, and he wanted to face the problem in the most difficult form.[189]

As to Casciola's second criticism on the obscure explanation of development, Tyrrell acknowledged his lack but added that "Bourdon's" aim was to offer a corrective to Loisy.

> He felt that whereas J. H. Newman had at least attempted to furnish a very complex criterion of doctrinal development, Loisy had given us none at all, and had exposed himself to the objection: *"qui nimis probat, is nihil probat."* He felt that L. and J. H. N. were wrong in making *doctrine* the direct subject-matter of development, which *he* finds rather in the inward spiritual life of Christians whereof *doctrine* is only the mental expression and register, a matter of altogether sub-

ordinate and dependent impostation; that . . . the true criterion of
doctrines is whether they are found to be *semper, ubique,* in *omnibus*
fruitful of a Christian life.

The capacity to engender Christian living is admittedly a "searching and very radical criterion," Tyrrell told him, "which would
sweep away a great deal that now cumbers us." The real teachers
of Christian life are no longer the theologians, but the saints—"not
only the 'official' Saints—but all the Christlike men and women
who together with Jesus of Nazareth constitute the mystical
Christ." And although the synoptic gospels offer a poor criterion
of Christ's teaching, they "do give us an easily applicable criterion
of his spirit and ethos that enables us to say e.g. that political Catholicism is a corruption; that the Pope-king is a monstrosity; that
the 'theologians' are the scribes and pharisees risen from the dead
etc."[190]

Unfortunately, most reactions to *The Church and the Future*
are not extant, as Tyrrell had requested that the baron deliver them
viva voce. That opportunity came late in the summer of 1903,
when the baron again took his vacation with Tyrrell in Richmond
from 18 August to 3 September. In his diary of 20 August he wrote,
"Fr. Tyrrell came: read him letters for an hour; and then an hour's
walk w. him."[191] No doubt some of those letters had to do with
"Bourdon."

Fortunately, however, one review escaped their conferences.
Von Hügel transcribed it in a letter to Tyrrell of 10 to 12 November 1903. It came from Joseph Sauer, the baron's friend from
Freiburg im Breisgau. Sauer's reaction to "Bourdon" was even
more enthusiastic than was his reaction to "Engels." Not for a long
time, he testified, had any book gripped him as this one had, and
he found himself returning to it again and again, "not to run
through the book hastily, but to stroll through his logical train of
thought marked by the strictest progression." The work displayed
"the power of attraction of a great thinker," and it would not be
going too far to say that many parts are simply breathtaking, even
with repeated readings. And, although the author goes very far in
his criticism and demands, "I have not found a single point, despite
the severest scrutiny, where, from the standpoint of the historian or
philosopher, I would take exception." Its trenchancy and logic
were astounding, yet the presentation was at the same time filled
with warmth and sympathy. "Can we hope to see wide circles, or
perhaps even the official Church, drawn to this ideal conception of
Christianity," he asked in conclusion, "or will it remain forever the

promised land, which man, because of his sinfulness, may only view and admire from afar?"[192]

LAST WORDS

This question about the church of the future (the ideal church) and its relation to the church of the present (the real church) occupied Tyrrell throughout the remaining few years of his life. And although he would go to his grave in an Anglican churchyard, cast out from the church that he loved, he would not cease to proclaim and propagate his vision of the church of the future. Still, he never proclaimed that church as some kind of Camelot, but always as real gold accompanied by but never freed from dross. As historical, the church of the future is at the same time the church of the past. Even if the revolution should come, even if the church should be led ineluctably by its current policies to a *reductio ad absurdum*, as Tyrrell constantly predicted, any future rebuilding would incorporate the old, as the future always embraces and comprehends the past. But will the church of the present ever embrace and comprehend the church of the future? Will the real church ever realize its ideal? Or will the ideal ever remain a *terra promissa* that, with Moses, we can only gaze at from afar but never enter?

Tyrrell's final answer to that question puts the final period to this study of the genesis of his apologetic. Entitled "The Church and Its Future," it formed the last chapter of his last work, *Christianity at the Cross-Roads.*[193] In many ways it was the same as his first answer, yet it was also different, as it, too, both comprehended and went beyond Tyrrell's past.

"If Christ be more than a teacher," Tyrrell began, "the Church is more than a school; if He be more than a founder, the Church is more than an institution." The question implied is, How is the church both a school and an institution and also more than that? Put simply, Tyrrell's answer was that which has become popular in today's church through Otto Semmelroth, Karl Rahner, and Edward Schillebeeckx, namely, the church is a sacrament. It is Christ's *mystical* body—"an extension of that human frame through which His spirit and personality communicated itself to His disciples, as it were sacramentally, i.e., in the way that a personality makes itself felt, as opposed to the way in which a teacher imparts a doctrine." Through the church, animated by Christ's spirit, we are brought into immediate contact with Christ, not metaphorically but actually. In the church, he finds "a growing medium of self-utterance, ever complementing and correcting that of His moral individuality. . . . Thus it is through the instrumentality of the Church and its sacraments that His personality is renewed and strengthened in us; that the force of His spirit is transmitted and felt. The Church is not merely a society or school, but a mystery and sacrament; like the humanity of Christ of which it is an extension."[194]

This view of the church, Tyrrell asserted, "stands or falls with the Catholic conception of Jesus, as the name of the Divine Spirit acting the role of a man; and not merely as the name of a man, conforming himself to the inspirations of that spirit as to those of another personality." Where this conception of the spirit and personality of Jesus fails, the church is "but a society of the disciples of a bygone prophet . . . whose personality and example grow less and less intelligible and illuminating as he recedes into a remoter past." The Catholic conception of the abiding presence of Jesus makes the church a sacrament rather than a society, "a sacrament not invalidated by the meanness of the 'beggarly elements' through which the Spirit is communicated."[195]

A religion, to be truly Catholic, must contain something for everyone. It must support all kinds and conditions of persons at every stage of their relgious progress.

> The process of the race repeats itself in the individual. Man does not begin, but ends by being spiritual and personal; first that which is earthly, afterwards that which is heavenly; milk for babes, meat for the strong. The law is but a pedagogue to lead us to Christ, though the fruit is implicit in the seed and Christ in the first whisperings of conscience. A Catholic religion will lead the soul through externalism to internalism. Ideally, the value of the lower is absorbed into and saved by the higher. Practically, in existing Catholicism, it is not so. We find these different sorts of religion ranged side by side, each subsisting with its own alloy—the religion of fear, the religion of hope; the religion of external and of internal obedience; the religion of abstract and exclusive mysticism, and that of inclusive and world-embracing mysticism. In his *Mystical Element of Religion* Baron F. von Hügel has shown that, if the ideal synthesis of the institutional, rational and mystical elements be unattainable, owing to a sort of natural antipathy between them, yet the perpetual struggle after that ideal is essential; that the health of a religion consists in the balancing and holding together of principles that tend to fly asunder and become independent and exclusive.[196]

The church is an alloy of base and noble metals, "violently held together by a continual synthetic effort." In practice, the effort has been a work of instinct and experience rather than of premeditated purpose, and it has "all the imperfection and clumsiness of tentative gropings." But with all its imperfections, Catholic Christianity is more capable of conforming itself to the exigencies of historical processes than any of those forms that have narrowed themselves to the development of some particular facet of Catholicism however excellent.[197]

Catholicism is the most integral and widely influential of all religions, but precisely because it is that, it is also the most exploited. The power of this religion to lead the soul to the perfect stature of the Christ-possessed personality is equally well turned by the exploiter into a means of subjecting the consciences and personalities of its members to the divine right arrogated to himself. At the present time in the Roman Church, exploiters hold the reins of power.

Will that church reform itself? "Will the Roman bureaucracy, that exploits even the Papacy, ever resign their revenues and their ascendancy? Modernists do not believe it for a moment." Their whole hope rests "in the irresistible tide of truth and knowledge" and "in such inward and living Christianity as may still be left in a rapidly dying Church." And as long as the modernist can cherish such hopes, why should he leave his church? Where else could he find the true Catholicism of which he dreams? He may find this or that element better developed elsewhere, but it is always isolated from the whole and purchased at the expense of integral Christianity. Such a religion is less Catholic in fact and far less in potential.[198]

As in the past, the spirit of Christ working in the general mind will again save the church from her oppressors within and without.

> Deliverance comes from below, from those who are bound, not from those who bind. It is easy to quench a glimmering light caught by the eyes of a few; but not the light of the noonday sun—of knowledge that has become objective and valid for all. It is through knowledge of this kind that God has inaugurated a new epoch in man's intellectual life and extended his lordship over Nature. Shall He do less for a man's spiritual life when the times are ripe? and are they not ripening? Are we not hastening to an impasse—to one of those extremities which are God's opportunities?[199]

A Lament

We have reached finally the end of the story we set out to tell: of how George Tyrrell, born and raised an Evangelical Protestant, converted to Roman Catholicism as a young man and joined the Society of Jesus to serve in the best way he could the cause of the

Gospel, and of how in that cause he was led to confront the growing rift between official Catholicism and the secular world by developing both a philosophy of religion and a new and coordinate apologetic for Roman Catholicism. We have seen the fierce opposition he faced and how he faced it. Coming both from within the church he loved and from within the Society he joined to serve the church, that opposition drove him into a love/hate relationship that gnawed at his interior and contributed substantially to his physical as well as his spiritual suffering.[200] Now and then he would release the pain and frustration that he felt—not only for himself but for the many troubled Catholics who sought his help—by writing an article or a book or a letter. Occasionally he would also scribble some lines in his private notebooks, a verse or two. One verse, written probably in 1903, has come down to us, as he recopied it in a letter to Henry Clutton of 10 October of that year. It is a paraphrase of Catullus's *Carmina LXXVI*, "Si qua recordanti." Tyrrell dedicated it "Ad meipsum foedo Societatis amore paene perditum."

> Whatever joy may yet be won
> From consciousness of duty done,
> Of loyal faith, of truth unstained,
> Of oaths by no deceit profaned.
> All this in after years of thee
> Fruit of the fruitless love shall be.
> For when was costly word or deed
> Too costly if it served her need?
> All squandered on a thankless w——!
> Why worry about her any more?
> Screw up your mind, & bid her pack,
> And get your pluck & spirit back.
> "Old love dies hard" you will complain
> But by hook or crook it must be slain.
> No safety else! Your love must go;
> So away with it! Whether you can or no.
> O God if thou doest pity know
> For mortal man's extremest throe;
> If thee I ever served aright,
> Rid me of this pestilential blight
> Whose poison-sleeps my limbs oppress
> And wrap my heart in heaviness.
> To win her back no prayer I waste;
> Not God himself could make her chaste.
> For my own health alone I pray;
> God purge this loathesome love away.[201]

There is another story to be told—of the purge itself, of how Tyrrell remained true to the principles laid down in his philosophy of religion and apologetic and how these gradually seared him free of the dross of "officialism" but only to intensify his love of religion in general and of Roman Catholicism in particular, that ideal Catholicism, the Pole Star to be made for but perhaps never to be reached. *The Church and the Future* was Tyrrell's decisive statement. It set him at the *Scheideweg* where he and officialism parted company. It only remained for officials publicly to ratify that act. Of that book he wrote to Baron von Hügel, his closest associate in the process leading to expulsion from the Society of Jesus and excommunication from the church, "In my own inward history the book ends a painful process of necessary readjustment, and I feel as one who, after much uncertainty, has at last chosen a path that is clear, however difficult & uninviting in many ways."[202] To have come to an end of ambiguity at last was an enormous relief. All other suffering was henceforth at least tolerable, because he was clear as to its origin and issue.

The open map before him showed two divergent paths. Officialism took one, Tyrrell the other. The full story of their antithetical journeys awaits the opening of Roman archives.

Funeral procession for George Tyrrell in the village of Storrington, Sussex, 16 July 1909. Among the mourners (left to right): Sir William Tyrrell (hand on hat), the abbé Henri Bremond (reading), and Baron Friedrich von Hügel.

Epilogue

The story of the judgment of ecclesiastical officials on the life of George Tyrrell and of his reaction covers the period from January 1904 to July 1909 when Tyrrell died. It was a period of consuming emotional involvement that left Tyrrell little time to pursue positive theological interests. As in wartime, when advancement is limited to technical armaments, so it was with Tyrrell during these years: his technique of negative criticism was honed to a fine edge in *Medievalism: A Reply to Cardinal Mercier*, published in 1908. But in the positive line, his works consisted almost entirely in clarifications and elaborations of what he had produced prior to 1904. The one possible exception, as will be seen, was the work he left in manuscript at his death, *Christianity at the Cross-Roads*. The barest outline of this final period follows.

CONFUSED EXIT FROM THE SOCIETY OF JESUS

On 17 December 1903 Cardinal Merry del Val and the Congregation of the Holy Office issued a decree signed by Pope Pius X that placed five of Loisy's works on the Index of Forbidden Books.[1] Loisy would be expected to make an unqualified submission and absolutely repudiate the condemned works or suffer excommunication. By coincidence, on that same day Tyrrell completed and sent to the *Pilot* an article called "L'Affaire Loisy" in which he tried to bring out that, just as the Galileo condemnation saved us from theological tyranny in physics, so a condemnation of Loisy would save us from theological tyranny in the domain of historical criticism of religion.[2]

The news of Loisy's condemnation broke in Paris about Christmas Day and unleashed a storm of articles and letters to editors throughout Europe. Loisy managed to escape excommunica-

319

tion for the time being by offering to give up his post at the École Pratique des Hautes Études.

In the midst of this furor, Tyrrell quietly and quite privately prepared a letter to Fr. Luis Martin, his superior general in Rome, clearly stating his views about the Society of Jesus and offering to apply formally for release if the general so wished. He sent the letter on 8 February 1904.[3] The general replied on 15 February and with genuine concern urged Tyrrell to consult Rome on his charge that the Society was "leagued with those who are doing everything to make faith impossible."[4] As the general had missed Tyrrell's point that Rome was the Society's partner in league, Tyrrell tried again on 23 February to clarify his position, but promised at the same time "to reconsider the whole question once more with all possible diligence."[5]

Shortly thereafter a report in the *Giornale d'Italia* that a certain Jesuit was about to leave the Society was immediately picked up by the English press and applied to Tyrrell, although the report might have referred to Henri Bremond, who had been released from the Society in early February. Tyrrell was infuriated and suspected that the general himself might have planted the report to precipitate Tyrrell's departure. To satisfy his suspicion Tyrrell wrote the general on 9 April, and the general replied on 24 April that he had nothing to do with the report.[6] There the matter rested until August of the following year.

At once Tyrrell set to work on an essay that grew out of von Hügel's request that he prepare a statement in the event of Loisy's excommunication. But the essay spoke more of Tyrrell's own case than of Loisy's. It bore the title "Beati Excommunicati," to which Tyrrell appended, "And they shall cast you forth from their Synagogues. And they cast him out. . . . Jo IX." He dated it "18.V.1904" and below this date wrote, "cf 18.V.1879," the date on which, twenty-five years before, he had been received into the Roman Church.[7]

The intent of the essay was to foretell the fate and describe the condition of those in the church who could neither abide the absolutist methods of officials nor keep silence if silence could be interpreted as resignation to those methods. They will be cast out and deprived of the sacraments. Still they may consider themselves "beati," because God does not tie the grace of salvation to the sacraments. The church has always admitted in *theory* the possibility of salvation outside the sacraments. And today in practice

the thoughtful Catholic no longer regards her [the Church] as a sharp-edged sphere of light walled round with abrupt and impenetrable darkness, but rather as a centre and focus from which the light of religion, spread over all ages and nations, shades away indefinitely and is mingled in varying degrees with that darkness which can never wholly conquer it. He cannot stand so far from the focus as not to share some measure of its influence, however qualified; in a word, he cannot suffer complete, inward, spiritual excommunication.[8]

Tyrrell never published this essay in English. It was only by accident that it appeared in translation in *La Grande Revue* for 10 October 1907, just two weeks prior to Tyrrell's own excommunication.[9]

Upon completing this essay, Tyrrell wrote on 25 May 1904 to von Hügel concerning his next project: he had threatened the general to vindicate himself in an open letter to the press.[10] In early June—after Bremond, who had been vacationing in Richmond, departed—he set to work. He dated the letter's inception 11 June and its completion 26 June.[11] He had anticipated that it would establish a compelling case against his remaining in the Society, but it did not. "I have tried to make out a case for myself," he wrote the baron on 3 July, "and all I can see is that my position is not yet so demonstrably dishonest as to force me to go."[12]

For more than a year Tyrrell rusticated in Richmond and turned over and over the question of leaving the Society. Maude Petre, whose own future was now inextricably bound up with Tyrrell's, spent a good portion of that year in Richmond, discussing options and plans. At some point the question became no longer whether he should leave, but when and how. Exactly when this development occurred is not known, but Maude Petre noted in her diary for 12 August 1905, "He tells me that a letter of mine finally decided him."[13]

On 6 August 1905 Tyrrell wrote both to his provincial, Fr. Richard Sykes, and to the general and announced his intention to seek canonical release from the Society. To Sykes he proposed as a canonically sufficient reason: "'Ne scandalum gravius eveniat.' For no fear of even the extremest ecclesiastical censure would justify my remaining in a false position & facing the consequent censure of my conscience. If I have to leave without canonical release (as I will, if necessary), I shall owe it to myself & to my friends to publish all the reasons for so drastic a step; and this could not be without great pain & scandal to many." He also requested the copyrights and plates of published books "or some equivalent," as he proposed to "live mainly by my pen."[14] He told the general to expect from Sykes the official forms requesting release. "The Society has become an avowedly reactionary institution," he added, and "I am, and always will be, impenitently progressive. As such, my position in her ranks is dishonest; unfair to her and to myself."[15]

The general replied on 22 August that such arguments were not canonically sufficient, that he himself had no authority to release a solemnly professed father, but that he would seek the necessary dispensations from the Sacred Congregation of Bishops and Regulars.[16] To bolster his case Tyrrell then sent the general the very long letter he had composed in June 1904. It stated the case more forcefully, but canonically the argument was the same: disenchantment and radically differing assessments of the Society's goals and means.

On 12 October the general informed Tyrrell that the Sacred Congregation was willing to grant secularization, but that they wanted him to apply to them directly.[17] Friends advised Tyrrell that it was customary, though not absolutely required, for the one seeking secularization first to find a bishop who would receive him into his diocese. This Tyrrell set out to do, but he was not optimistic about finding *any* bishop, let alone a benevolent one. He wrote the general on 14 November to explain the delay and express regret if an orderly and peaceful exit should prove practically impossible.[18] The general replied on 25 November that if Tyrrell was annoyed at the scarcity of benevolent bishops, still worse annoyances would likely await him in his new state and new relationship to ecclesiastical authority.[19]

Tyrrell took this warning as a threat and was outraged, so much so that he did not trust himself to reply until more than a month later. Finally on 31 December he wrote and protested vigorously the intertwining of Jesuit and ecclesiastical interests. He could see its unpleasant consequences for himself, he said, nevertheless he hoped that his separation from the Society would not also mean a conflict with Vatican officials.[20] The general, pained at Tyrrell's accusation, replied on 7 January 1906 that he was not threatening but merely warning Tyrrell in a paternal way of the difficulties he could expect. Nor had he any intention of fomenting those difficulties.[21]

Be that as it may, the general went on, a more immediate concern prompted his letter. It was to ascertain for the archbishop of Milan whether or not Tyrrell was the author of some quotations from a certain "Lettera confidenziale ad un amico professore di antropologia" in the *Corriere della Sera* (Milan) of 1 January 1906.[22] Tyrrell answered by return post that his absolute rule regarding anonymous writings was never either to affirm or deny authorship. Nevertheless, he could agree with the substance of the quotations. He then escalated the confrontation: "What I do want to know *at once* & with a view to external arrangements is whether you will now, on your own initiative, send me out of the Society. I will neither ask for dismissal nor apply for secularization, but will throw the whole onus on y[ou]r P[aternity]. If you do not dismiss me I return to Richmond as before—liberavi animam meam. If you dismiss me I go to London & begin my life's work."[23] Three days later Tyrrell wrote again to say that on second thought—because it might affect the general's disposition on the question of dismissal— he would acknowledge responsibility for the substance of the "Letter to a Professor," though not for its free adaptation.[24]

On 20 January 1906 the general sent Tyrrell a demand for a written repudiation of the "Letter to a Professor" that could be published in the papers. Failure to comply, the general warned, would constitute sufficient reason to consider dismissal.[25]

Tyrrell replied on 24 January that he could not repudiate the "Letter to a Professor," but he enclosed a statement for the press containing as much explanation and apology as conscience would allow. In it he made the following points: (1) the adaptations and changes of the translation were not his, he had not read them, nor did he know the author; (2) the original letter was perfectly private, an *argumentum ad hominem* adapted to the presuppositions of the recipient, not to those of the writer; (3) he did not consent to its publication in the *Corriere* since it was "medicine intended only for some"; (4) the extracts torn from their context and presuppositions may seem startling and sensational, "yet read carefully they contain nothing that has not been said over & over again by Saints & Doctors of the Church"; (5) finally, the Society of Jesus was absolved from any responsibility "for a private letter never destined for publicity & never submitted to its official censorship."[26]

On 1 February 1906 the general closed the correspondence. He said that Tyrrell's proposed statement was inadequate and that since Tyrrell had declared himself unable to do more, the general was unable to do anything but grant Tyrrell's request for dismissal made several times explicitly and now implicitly. He enclosed the form of dismissal. Further requisite forms, he said, would be sent through Tyrrell's provincial.[27]

On 7 February Sykes informed Tyrrell that the dimissorial letters had arrived. They stipulated (1) that Tyrrell could receive communion but not celebrate mass; (2) that only the pope through the Congregation of Bishops and Regulars could lift the suspension; (3) that he was dismissed because of the "Letter to a Professor"; and (4) that to be reinstated by the church he would have to apply to the Congregation of Bishops and Regulars, and to be reinstated by the Society he would have to apply to the general.[28]

On 19 February 1906 in London, Tyrrell signed the letters of dismissal and wrote to the general as follows:

> Y[OUR]. P[ATERNITY].,
>
> I shd. like to assure you, now that I stand outside the Society, how completely I realise that we have both of us been driven to this unpleasant issue by the necessities of our several minds & consciences; & Y. P. still more by the exigencies of a most difficult position.
>
> You may depend that whatever explanations I may ever be forced to give of what has happened will make this quite apparent. Nothing cd. be further from my sentiments than any sort of personal rancour or resentment. I feel that it is a collision of systems & tendencies rather than of persons; & that many such collisions must occur before the truth of both sides meets in some higher truth. And tho' you may say *Absit!* I do not doubt that in the deepest principle of all we are nearer to agreement with one another than with many of our respective fellow thinkers.
>
> I thank you for your promised prayers & holy sacrifices. My own sacrifices must now be of another—& more expensive if less valuable—sort, but such as they are I will offer them for you.
>
> Yr. servt. in Xt.,
> G. T.[29]

On the same day Tyrrell addressed the following notice, probably to Sykes:

> In my letter of Dec. 31, 1905 to H[is]. P[aternity]. I withdrew explicitly & *tot verbis* my request for separation from the Society & threw the entire responsibility on H.P.; nor have I ever since either explicitly or implicity renewed that request.
>
> Finally, I remark that a censure, to be valid, requires gravis sui on the part of the delinquent, & that of this H.P. as well as my own conscience acquits me. My submission to the censure is therefore merely forced & external & lest the ignorant be scandalised.[30]

It is not known whether Tyrrell ever sent this notice. The point is one that Tyrrell wanted to make in his own favor with his friends, but the general's letter of 20 January 1906 indicated that the sufficiently grave matter for dismissal would be Tyrrell's refusal to repudiate the published excerpts from "A Letter to a Professor." Neither morally nor legally was Tyrrell's case compelling. One suspects that Tyrrell knew it, as there is no indication from correspondence that he did in fact try to make this point with his friends.

The news of Tyrrell's departure drew considerable comment in the press. Tyrrell himself was staying with various friends and relatives away from London and so was not following the comment closely. But he did not like what he was hearing, so he tried to end the discussion with a brief explanation in the *Daily Chronicle* for 23 February 1906 along the lines of his last letter to the general. He concluded with an appeal for broad-mindedness: "While I am most grateful to those who take up the cudgels for me I had far rather be left defenceless than that anything should be said to offend my Jesuit and pro-Jesuit friends, who are very many and very dear; or that would seem to refuse to the opinions and tendencies of others that broad tolerance which, in the name of Catholic liberty, I claim for my own."[31]

LEX CREDENDI

That appeal, however, did not prevent even the *Daily Chronicle* from trying to make news where there was none. Just prior to the appearance of Tyrrell's *Lex Credendi* in April, the *Chronicle* carried the following notice: "Considerable interest attaches to Father Tyrrell's new book. . . . It is a sequel to his *Lex Orandi*, which was criticized from the Roman Catholic standpoint as not being orthodox. Now comes his reply, that of a Roman Catholic priest who is no longer a Jesuit. Father Tyrrell is regarded as one of the ablest writers in the English Roman Catholic Church."[32] However, as a sympathetic reviewer for the *Month* pointed out, despite the close connection between *Lex Orandi* and *Lex Credendi*, it is misleading to see the latter as a reply to criticism of the former.[33] Tyrrell did reply to some criticisms in a few pages added *après coup*, but the body of the work was composed and published as two series of articles without deference to criticisms of *Lex Orandi*.

Tyrrell's interest shifted in this work from philosophy of religion and ecclesiastical apologetic based on that philosophy to the devotional content of Christianity. "It is the purpose of these paragraphs," he explained, "to consider, not the teachings of Christianity, but Christ; not the implications of His life, but the life itself; in other words, to give more definite meaning and content to the term, 'the spirit of Christ.'"[34] Thus, despite the continuity with *Lex Orandi*, the affinity with Tyrrell's earlier devotional works, *Nova et Vetera* and *Hard Sayings*, is strong.

The first part, "The Spirit of Christ," lays the foundation for the second part, "The Prayer of Christ." In *Lex Orandi* and *Religion as a Factor of Life* Tyrrell granted that rightful ecclesiastical authority is steward to both theology and devotion. Now he addressed the underlying question: "By what norm is that stewardship to be judged?" His answer: the spirit of Christ—by which he did not mean the Holy Spirit but the "complexus of ideas and sentiments" expressed in the words and deeds of Christ whose life is "the classical or regulative manifestation of the Spirit by which all other manifestations are to be tried and measured." In a sense, therefore, the *Holy Spirit* or the *Spirit of Christ* "was itself the Revelation, the *depositum fidei.*" But the *spirit* of Christ is the *normative manifestation* of revelation. It is the concrete manifestation that serves as the source of study and discernment, not the spirit of Christ in itself.[35]

Of course Christ's deeds and words as depicted in the New Testament are the primary source for discerning his spirit, but we find it also manifested in the life of the church, especially in the lives of the saints who have discerned and adapted the spirit of Christ for their own time and place. The saints are therefore secondary manifestations of Christ's spirit and as such guide the church in its "really fruitful and lasting decisions. . . . The Pope is in theory no irresponsible absolutist who can define what he likes, who can make truth and unmake it. He is but the interpreter of a law written by the Holy Ghost in the hearts of the saints. He is bound by this living book." By following the lead of the saints, the church came to formulate its creedal expressions. Thus "the *Credo* is but the 'explicitation' of what is latent in the *Pater noster.*"[36]

In the appendix to *Religion as a Factor of Life* and in *Lex Orandi* Tyrrell had elucidated the articles of the creed. Now he turned to Christ's prayer, the perfect prayer as the manifestation of that perfect Spirit by which all true theology and devotion must be guided and inspired. The phrases of the prayer are not to be taken singly and literally, Tyrrell explained, for in that form they are no more than statements of tradition already set down in the books and liturgy of the Hebrews. They are to be taken "as part of a complex, organic whole, each in the light of all the rest, and all in the light of His whole life of action and utterance; we must look to the sayer as well as to what is said. . . . For a prayer is a vital utterance, or it is nothing."[37] Moreover, it is to be taken not as a prayer that Christ himself prayed, but as one that he taught his disciples to pray. Therefore we are justified in attaching more importance to the actual form of the words than we would otherwise be allowed to do.

In this spirit Tyrrell meditated through the Lord's Prayer, clause by clause, showing how it is the supreme comment on the overwhelming mystery of redemption. In the end, he concluded that the prayer of Christ is purely and simply the expression of love, of that emptying out of self by which the life of God himself takes flesh. As a prayer taught to Christians, it invites the Christian to go and do likewise—to rise above "the self-interested individualistic standpoint" and devote oneself "freely and disinterestedly to the service of goodness, truth, and love," to become a secondary manifestation of that Spirit who revealed himself definitively in Christ.[38]

Tyrrell's self-conscious appropriation of this mystery is evident in his letter to Maude Petre of 15 February:

> Recent experiences give one an inward understanding of His [Christ's] life-tragedy which will abide or fall away according as one has or has not courage to follow in the same track. I feel what it costs to scandalise those who have *trusted* us; to be condemned, not by the wicked but by the good and well-meaning; and that through an ignorance that is inculpable and fated. It is only because one believes that somewhen or other angels will come and prevent the worst that one goes on at all; and each step is forced on one and never really accepted. Nemo tam cordialiter senserit passionem Christi quam is qui contigerit pati similia—at least we can get up our little ant-hill Calvaries and make our sums of proportion better than before. It is a better route to the knowing of Christ than theology.[39]

THE *CELEBRET* QUESTION

After signing the dimissorial letters, Tyrrell remained in London for one week. During that period and for several weeks after he was deluged by sympathetic letters, visits, and offers of lodging from Jesuits as well as non-Jesuits, even from Jesuits who were not of his mind. But he decided to quit the entire scene for an indefinite period to give himself the time and distance he needed to let matters settle and plan for the future.

At 9:00 A.M. on 27 February 1906, Tyrrell left Victoria Station for Paris and an open-ended stay with Henri Bremond. After a few days in Paris the two of them went on to Freiburg im Breisgau. For Tyrrell, getting away from London was in itself a great relief. But no sooner was he away than he was overwhelmed with a sense of loss, a loss that centered in the deprivation of his priestly privileges and a loss that would pain him till his death.

From time to time, to recover his loss, Tyrrell would consider again seeking a bishop who would have him on tolerable terms. And quite possibly he would have followed through and found a bishop, or perhaps he would even have returned to the Society, had ecclesiastical opponents allowed him to rest quietly. But shortly after he arrived in Freiburg hostilities opened against him in the press, instigated, it seems, by direct order of Pius X. "Know once & for all," Tyrrell wrote to Maude Petre on 9 March,

> that it is now perfectly plain that all my correspondence with the General from Aug. 6 to Jan. 1. has had *nothing* to do with my expulsion. A mot d'ordre (this is strictly confidential) was given by the Pope to the General of the Dominicans (which I have read) & therefore also to the other Generals as well as to the bishops, to help him to crush out this liberal neo-Catho. movement. A book of Pere Rose (on the Gospels) on the point of appearing was withdrawn in consequence. I & Hummelauer were shot out. Bonomelli was crushed. The Archbps. of Milan, Turin, Piedmont & others simultaneously wrote violent pastoral charges. Articles against me have appeared in the *Civiltà*, the *Études;* in Batiffol's *Bulletin*, & I believe some others. Also articles against our set in a score of "safe" periodicals. Even apart from the Corriere's indiscretion my life in the S. J. was not worth a pfennig. I am glad to have got out of it so decently, & really when I look back & think of its noisome moral atmosphere, I shudder & wonder how I could *ever* have so twisted my mind as to justify my adhesion.[40]

On 12 April Tyrrell and Bremond returned to Paris to consult friends on strategy. Meanwhile Tyrrell had written on 7 April to Cardinal Domenico Ferrata, prefect of the Sacred Congregation of Bishops and Regulars, regarding the completion of Tyrrell's secularization. A longtime friend, Mother Mary Stanislaus of the English convent of Bruges, had recently informed Tyrrell that Archbishop Désiré Joseph Mercier of Malines was interested in receiving him. This step now seemed desirable for two reasons: not only did Tyrrell want his priestly privileges back, but as long as he remained simply "expelled" from the Society and not yet under a bishop, he was bound to reform and seek readmission. He seems also to have been under the impression that the general could simply recall him. So he requested Ferrata either to allow Mercier to receive him or to grant him a *celebret* by special dispensation. Otherwise, Tyrrell warned, he would go to the press with the whole story.[41]

On 24 April Tyrrell returned to England to await Ferrata's reply. He took lodgings at 14 Lydon Road, Clapham, near the Shelleys, old friends from his pre-1900 days at Farm Street. By 4 May Ferrata had not replied, so Tyrrell wrote again, protesting the silence and again threatening to expose the whole affair.[42] This letter, too, went unanswered. But on 18 June 1906 Cardinal Ferrata gave Archbishop Mercier permission to receive Tyrrell and grant him a *celebret* "on the condition . . . that the same Fr. Tyrrell make a formal promise not to publish anything on religious questions nor even to hold epistolary correspondence without the explicit approval of a competent person appointed by your Lordship."[43]

This news reached Tyrrell in France, where he had returned to spend the summer and autumn. He interpreted the condition to mean that his private correspondence would be subject to censorship. Infuriated, he composed and had printed 150 copies of an open letter to Cardinal Ferrata.[44] He actually distributed only a few copies, but the one he sent to Ferrata he purposely numbered 67. He dated it 4 July 1906 from London.

In it he reminded Ferrata of the two unanswered letters to which "courtesy, charity, justice demanded a reply." Then on the censorship issue he said: "If this is to be the condition of my reinstatement I decline finally and categorically to be reinstated on a condition so dishonouring both to me and to the tribunal which imposes it." Moreover, he argued, it was contrary to the spirit of the Gospel to use the right to say mass "like an ecclesiastical decoration or title as a mere instrument of government and moral coercion; and I will live and die without it, rather than condone such a profanation." Finally, he pointed out that to impose a penal condition on his reinstatement implied that his suspension was penal. Yet he had never been convicted of heterodoxy or of any other crime against the church. He would "accept this present *impasse* as permanent rather than plead any further with authorities who have already treated my pleadings with a seemingly contemptuous silence and at whose hands I have suffered such an indignity and outrage as is implied in" the condition laid down for reinstatement.[45]

It was a decisive move, but to make it even more decisive Tyrrell sent two copies of the letter to Cardinal Merry del Val on 20 July and asked him to have it "translated to His Holiness"—not to seek redress or any sort of answer, but only to explain "why I should consider it idle to seek such redress or to engage in further negotiations or correspondences." Further, he announced plans to publish an open letter "to all those who, through any writings of mine, have been drawn towards or preserved within the pale of the Roman Church," informing them "that so far as they have supposed my life's work to be approved by that Church's official guides they have been utterly deceived" and that only diplomacy or lack of opportunity "has prevented or still prevents the utter condemnation of me and my books." Then, he said, he would draw up a syllabus of all the modern difficulties to which he had been striving to find remedies and drop them in the lap of His Holiness and say:

> Tell us plainly what we are to say. We have a right to look to Your Holiness for positive as well as negative guidance; for construction of truth as well as destruction of error. . . . Since you possess the knowledge, you cannot and dare not withhold it. . . . Of what use is a bea-

con, if it is not kindled at the moment when it is most needed? All
eyes are on Rome, but her light is out. Of what use is personal and independent infallibility and divine assistance, if life and death questions, clamouring for insistent answer, and involving the loss or gain to
the Church of thousands of the most deeply religious intelligences of
the day—if such questions are to be referred to laborious commissions, whose lengthy deliberations issue in a pair of critical platitudes
once in four years. . . .

In the face of such questions as I shall put, silence or an indefinite
answer will be equally impossible; equally fatal to all belief in the honesty, candour and good faith of the Holy See. We shall therefore hear
the truth and learn exactly where we stand; and we all agree that that
is supremely desirable.

I owe this last service to the Church, as a strict duty of reparation
to all those whom I have unintentionally deceived through so many
years as to the real mind of the Church's official guides. I am determined they shall know the truth as clearly as those guides themselves
know it.[46]

The "syllabus" turned out to be the publication in early No-
vember 1906 of *A Letter to a University Professor*, under the title *A
Much-Abused Letter*. It included, along with copious notes and an
epilogue, a lengthy introduction detailing the correspondence with
Fr. General Martin, but it did not list the objections to which the
Letter was an answer, and therefore Tyrrell did not challenge
Rome to provide the answers that he allegedly failed to provide.
Nor did he bring up the burning issue of the irregularity of his dismissal from the Society. The dismissal itself was canonically sound
enough, but to dismiss a religious priest without a bishop to autho-
rize his functioning as a priest seems to have been canonically irregular—unless, of course, he had been convicted of a crime against
the church. That was not the case. And despite Tyrrell's anger at
this irregular deprivation, he did not in turn wish to provoke authorities while there remained any chance at all of finding a
bishop.[47]

The climate of feeling towards Tyrrell in England was beginning to sour, however. The appearance of *A Much-Abused Letter*
turned many previously sympathetic Jesuits against him, as they
became aware for the first time of "a certain class of his writings"
and felt therein betrayed.[48]

Tyrrell returned from France in late October and took up residence with the Shelleys at 16 Old Town, Clapham. During much
of his stay in France and now for the next six weeks he worked
with von Hügel on the latter's two volumes of *The Mystical Element of Religion*. But the climate of London, with its noise and dirt

and odious associations, aggravated Tyrrell's gradually deteriorating physical condition, so on 4 December he fled to Storrington and a home rented by Hattie Urquhart, sister-in-law of his cousin William Tyrrell. There, he told Dora Williams, he hoped "above all to pull up the appalling arrears of literary work which have accumulated all these idle months. . . . I shall not emerge until something is accomplished."[49]

What emerged by early May 1907 was a manuscript to be published in July as *Through Scylla and Charybdis*. Of the thirteen chapters, nine were reprints of earlier articles. The four new chapters did not significantly advance the substance of Tyrrell's apologetic. But that was not his intention. He was merely trying to clarify his position against recent criticism and misinterpretation and show how he had tried to avoid the errors of both the old theology ("Scylla = the rock of tradition; authority, etc.") and the new ("Charybdis = the whirlpool of progress; liberty, etc.")[50]

For some time now Tyrrell and Petre had been considering Storrington as a permanent base of operations.[51] In those considerations the question of the *celebret* surfaced again. To deal with it Tyrrell sought the help of Fr. Xavier de la Fourvière, superior of the Premonstratensian Priory in Storrington, in May 1906. Father Xavier took an immediate liking to Tyrrell and offered him residence and assistance in trying to regularize his status. Tyrrell declined the offer of residence for the time being, but he allowed Father Xavier to petition Bishop Peter E. Amigo of the Southwark diocese for at least a temporary *celebret*.

The case perplexed local canonists, so Amigo referred the matter to Rome. On 4 January 1907 Tyrrell sent Petre the following assessment:

> If I am "expelled" he cannot give me a *celebret* without Rome's leave; if I am "released" he can. But no one knows which it is, the story & the very formula is [*sic*] so mixed. *I* think the formula is not expulsory, but permissive; but this is impossible to prove. Martin [the general] says in his letter: "Since you cannot repudiate nothing remains *but to accede to your oft repeated request for* release." Now the fact was, I had (Dec. 31) formally withdrawn such requests. But he wanted to thrust the *onus* on me, & not to be responsible for an act of expulsion which nevertheless it really was. So I believe it was a wilful muddling of the issue.[52]

On 15 January Tyrrell reported again to Petre:

> The Southwark canonists say that, from an inspection of my documents, it is clear that the General, while intending to expel me, did

not dare do so, but simply released me on the fiction of an implicit renewal of my petition for release, and that any bishop could have received me without asking Rome; but that Malines having asked Rome confuses everything and makes an *impasse* without precedent. Again, so much the better. It is far better not to have what they could and would so easily take from me.[53]

How true that last statement was, Tyrrell would learn a few months hence. It was not a case of Tyrrell having lost something by accident that he never would have lost by intention. It was only that the intention to deprive Tyrrell of his clerical status was rendered canonically messy by the accidental handling of Tyrrell's request for release, thus rendering him for the nonce clerically neutered.

Another reason, however, lay behind Tyrrell's temporary acquiescence. In the first few months of 1907 he was preparing *Through Scylla and Charybdis*, in which, as he put it, "I throw down my cards on the table."[54] He wanted to have his last say, and that would not have been possible if he had to work under the conditions that a *celebret* would impose. The book was scheduled to appear from Longmans on 22 July.[55] On 20 July Tyrrell wrote to Father Xavier whose own superior, the abbot of Leefe in Belgium, was prepared to intercede with Rome. Tyrrell told Xavier that the conditions under which he would accept reinstatement were these:

Since there has been no charge alleged or proved against me, there must be no question of any condition that would be interpreted as penal; but only of such conditions as are obligatory on every priest in virtue of the common laws of the Church. When the Holy See restores me my rights as a Priest, I will engage faithfully to render the duties dependent on those rights; that is to say, I will not publish any sort of theological teaching, nor will I disseminate such teaching by epistolary correspondence, or in any other way equivalent to publication, without due authorisation. (But till my rights are restored I will regard myself as free from all corresponding duties.)

My principles will not allow of any further concession.[56]

However, unknown to Tyrrell, Rome had determined a course of action that would seal his fate. On 3 July 1907 the rumored syllabus *Lamentabili sane exitu* was issued by the Holy Office of the Inquisition. On 4 July Pius X approved it. On 17 July the text appeared in *L'Osservatore Romano*. Von Hügel received a copy on 22 July, along with a copy from Longmans of Tyrrell's *Through Scylla and Charybdis*. After lengthy study to determine the precise authority and intent of the syllabus, Tyrrell and von Hügel concluded that, though it did not augur well, neither did it call for countermeasures. But when Canon James Moyes asserted in the 27 July issue of the *Tablet* that the syllabus required absolute internal consent under pain of mortal sin, Tyrrell could not stay his hand. His letter to the editor, signed "A Roman Catholic," appeared in the *Church Times* for 2 August and simply pointed out the absurdity of a position that would make assent to a noninfallible document, issued by a fallible tribunal and without the claim of papal infallibility, the condition of one's eternal salvation.[57] Tyrrell did not give his name, as he did not want to exacerbate the situation and end once and for all his chances of receiving a *celebret*.[58]

There was still a chance. On 13 August the prior at Storrington forwarded to Cardinal Ferrata Tyrrell's statement of 20 July along with a personal attestation of Tyrrell's good intentions. On 29 August the prior informed Tyrrell that Ferrata had accepted the statement, had simply reproduced it for Tyrrell's signature, and demanded no extraordinary conditions beyond those imposed on all priests. Aware of the unpredictability of his cast of characters, the prior urged Tyrrell to sign at once. Tyrrell did so and returned the following signed statement to the prior on 30 August: "In accordance with the conditions prescribed by the Holy See I hereby undertake, from the date on which I receive permission to celebrate Mass and for as long as I may retain permission, not to publish any sort of theological teaching, nor to diffuse such teaching by correspondence, or in any other manner equivalent to publication, without due authorisation."[59]

In a letter of that same day Tyrrell pointed out to Petre that he was careful in his statement "not to promise silence absolutely (as the formula seemed to imply) but conditionally on the *celebret*. If they notice that, I dare say they will refuse." He was rather disturbed, moreover, by a report in the *Times*'s "Court News" of 30 August that the *Giornale d'Italia* had published a notice to the effect that Tyrrell's capitulation was practically a *fait accompli*. "That means they [Ferrata and the Holy Office] are excited and have blabbed and boasted of my *submission* already."[60] On 31 August the *Daily Chronicle* announced the alleged submission but expressed doubt about the reports from the Vatican press in view of the fact that Tyrrell's essay, "Plea for Greater Sincerity," was about to be published and a complete edition of his works in Italian was being prepared.[61]

Tyrrell immediately wired Petre in Storrington to prevent the prior from dispatching the signed "submission," but she was too late. He then sent denials of "submission" to the *Giornale d'Italia* and the *Daily Chronicle*. His statement in the *Daily Chronicle* of 2 September was as follows:

> The Vatican Press, in its eagerness to score a triumph, mistakes proposals for agreements. There never was any question of my "submission" to the common canonical law of censorship obligatory on all priests. It is to the censorship of my private correspondence that I have refused, and will refuse, submission, as contrary to canon law and to natural right. If the Holy Father thinks I have yielded on this point he has been misinformed—not by me. If, however, he has withdrawn that requirement, then, in restoring me to my ordinary canonical rights, he subjects me to my ordinary canonical duties—however unwelcome. The latter do not exist for me so long as I am unjustly deprived of the former.[62]

At the same time he wrote to Cardinal Ferrata to protest the false impression created by the premature disclosures to the press and to clarify once again the fact that it was not the imposition of the *common* laws of censorship but of the censorship of his private correspondence that was in question. To the latter, he said, he never had submitted as the Vatican press implied. "This inordinate thirst for 'submissions,'" he concluded, "this desire to humiliate and degrade, is suicidal and disastrous. I should be obligated if you would explain this letter to the Holy Father. So far as an *impasse* has, I fear, been created by this unexpected development, I think we had better regard it as final. Indefinite relations are equally unsatisfactory to both sides, and paralyse action."[63]

Ferrata did not reply. Instead the 23 September issue of the *Corrispondenza Romana*, the short-lived but celebrated unofficial bulletin of Vatican politics, devoted itself to "Il caso Tyrrell." It first denied that there had ever been a question of censoring Tyrrell's private correspondence *in the ordinary sense*. It then detailed the order of negotiations with Rome.[64] Tyrrell rebutted with a letter to the *Daily Chronicle* of 25 September. He pointed out that as soon as he heard of the censorship condition for his *celebret* he wrote to Cardinal Ferrata on 4 July 1906 "to say I would accept the common obligations of a priest as to censorship, but no censorship of my private correspondence." If Cardinal Ferrata did not mean this in the ordinary sense, then was the time to say so. Instead he kept silence for nine months "and left me without mass, where a word would have set things right had I really been mistaken, as is now pretended."[65]

A few days later Tyrrell wrote again to Ferrata to demand that he publish *all* of the correspondence from 4 July 1906 to the present. When no reply came, Tyrrell wrote for the last time, on 11 October, and threatened to publish the entire correspondence himself.[66] He never carried out this threat. Only he would have been the loser by it. Besides, his attention was now turned to a far more serious issue, one that would change the face of Catholicism for generations.

PASCENDI DOMINICI GREGIS: THE VATICAN OFFENSIVE

On 8 September 1907 Pius X issued the antimodernist encyclical *Pascendi dominici gregis*. It was published on 16 September in Rome.[67] On 18 September Tyrrell was summoned to von Hügel's residence where a copy of *Pascendi* arrived the next day from Count Francesco Salimei, the baron's future son-in-law.[68] For three days Tyrrell and von Hügel studied and discussed the document. On 21 September Tyrrell showed the baron a draft of his reply composed at the invitation of the *Giornale d'Italia;* he had a similar invitation from the *Times.* Tyrrell then fled to Storrington to escape reporters and interviewers. His *Giornale* letter appeared on 26 September, and his *Times* article appeared in two installments on 30 September and 1 October.[69] The former, as von Hügel put it, was "very strong, indeed vehement," and he wrote on 30 September to caution Tyrrell against a note of bitterness which had not been present in the draft he saw on the 21st. Bitterness was entirely understandable, said the baron, but it could only hurt in the long run.[70] Indeed the letter received mixed reactions even among Tyrrell's Italian admirers. Some of them were not sure they could any longer stand by him.

The *Times* letters were considerably more extensive but perhaps not noticeably kinder than the *Giornale* letter. After summarizing the encyclical in his first installment, Tyrrell began the second with the following salvo:

> If the foregoing synopsis of the controversial part of the Encyclical seems startling and incredible, it is only because brevity required that the argument should be stripped of its flowing rhetorical robes and revealed in its simple nakedness. . . .
> As an argument it falls dead for every one who regards its science theory as obsolete; for all who believe that truth has not been stagnating for centuries in theological seminaries, but has been steadily streaming on, with ever-increasing force and volume, in the channels which liberty has opened to its progress.

No modernist should be surprised at the encyclical, he asserted; it is merely the logical consequences of the principle of unbridled authority reacting to the Reformation principle of unbridled liberty. Nor should he quake before the forces it commands.

> Neither the engineered enthusiasm of *la bonne presse,* nor the extorted acquiescence and unanimity of a helplessly subjugated episcopate, nor the passive submission of uncomprehending sheeplike lay multitudes will deceive him into thinking that this Encyclical comes from, or speaks to, the living heart of the Church—the intelligent, religious-minded, truth-loving minority.

As to its authority, the modernist will not be deceived. For him it is

> not a question of form or formula, but of fact. Not even the extreme theologians will pretend that an encyclical of this kind has the slightest claim to be considered an ecumenical and so far "infallible" utterance. It is a disciplinary measure preceded by a catena of the personal opinions of Pius X. and his immediate *entourage.* Why this "compendium of all heresies" was not considered worthy of an *ex cathedra* pronouncement is not easy to explain, except by a certain fear of cutting off all means of retreat in the event of victorious assault. The new theory of *quasi*-infallible utterances, claiming all the force, and accepting none of the responsibilities of ecumenical decisions, demanding absolute inward assent to avowedly reversible propositions, is of no account with the "modernist," on whom, therefore, the "Roma locuta est" of the journalists falls flat. As for censure, suspension, and excommunication, they belong to the logic of the position, and he will expect them as a matter of course. They were the portion of his spiritual ancestors, who in past ages so often saved the Church, sick unto death with the pedantries of scholastic rationalism and the *rabies theologorum.*

Nor will the modernist be moved from his Catholicism by any act of juridical violence. If he understands the logic of his position, he "realizes that union with the Church depends on inward reality more than on outward form." His faith is secure against the word of an angry bishop.

> Much as he may prize the sacramental bread of life, he prizes still more the unleavened bread of sincerity and truth. To secede would be to allow that his calumniators were in the right; that Catholicism was bound hand and foot to its scholastic interpretation and to its medieval Church polity: that the Pope had no duties and the people no rights. It would be to abandon what he believes to be the truth at the moment of its greatest betrayal.[71]

But what the modernist regrets most, Tyrrell concluded, is the church's lost opportunity of showing herself to be the savior of nations. Rarely had the time been more ripe and people more expectant "in the hope that she might have bread for the starving millions, for those who are troubled by that vague hunger for God on which the Encyclical pours such scorn." Just when the rigid wall between Protestants and Catholics was beginning to soften and Protestantism in its best thinkers was growing "dissatisfied with its rude antithesis to Catholicism and was beginning to wonder whether Rome too had not grown dissatisfied with her rigid medievalism"; and just when "the 'modernist' movement had quickened a thousand dim dreams of reunion into enthusiastic hopes . . . lo! Pius X. comes forward with a stone in one hand and a scorpion in the other" to the great scandal and wholesale alienation of her most religious and educated members. This step cannot "tell otherwise than disastrously on the less educated," for "the scandal of the strong is ever the greatest scandal of the weak."[72]

All three letters were signed. Tyrrell knew and was ready for the consequences that would befall a priest who publicly attacks the Holy Father in the secular press. On 10 October 1907 *La Grande Revue* published in French translation Tyrrell's "Beati excommunicati," which he had prepared in the spring of 1905 in the event of Loisy's excommunication. Now it was against the day of his own excommunication.[73]

In a letter dated 22 October 1907, Bishop Peter Amigo of Southwark, informed Tyrrell that he had been deprived of the sacraments with his case reserved to Rome. He was told that it was because of his two articles in the *Times*. No further explanation.[74]

The question was in everyone's mind, and many put it to Tyrrell: Why had he gone so far as to provoke excommunication? He answered the question over and over in various ways, in his mind and in writing, but his letter to Augustin Leger of 24 December 1907 is the fullest and most carefully considered answer. "You have asked me about the motives of my ecclesiastical suicide," Tyrrell wrote.

> They were various—diplomatic, religious, personal, human; I felt that Rome was trading on the assumption that the idea of absolute obedience had so triumphed that she might say or do anything, however reckless. I felt that one should show that resistance was still a contingency to be reckoned with; and I think my bad example has been sufficiently followed to make Rome (not the Pope) pause in her wild career of destruction. As already suspended, I had less to lose in the venture than other priests. Again, all whom I had ever brought to or

kept in the Church would have been scandalised had I silently accepted a document denying every reason I had given them. I felt I should show them that I could reject that document and yet remain a Roman Catholic. Again, I felt it would be better to come out in public, and act as my own accuser and defender, than wait to be tracked down by inquisitors and be condemned for some outrageous travesty of my position. Again, the secrecy and diplomacy of my conformity has always been odious to me, and I have maintained it solely to avoid the *scandalum pusillorum*, but seeing that the Encyclical augments that scandal by a travesty of my views, that restraining motive is gone and I can "deliver my soul" and resume my self-respect. Again, I have felt the moral badness of Rome and the Curia so deeply and acutely these late years that I cannot take active service, as a priest, under such a *canaille*. I feel as a French monarchist officer who throws up his commission rather than serve under a government of *apaches*. The Montagnini and the Benigni revelations have extinguished every spark of respect for the present *personnel* of the Roman See. Again, if *everyone* submits to Rome's repressive measures there will be no remedy, but only a reinforcement of present evils. . . . I take it for granted that only a very few of my friends will approve of my action. But, on the whole, I believe it was objectively as well as subjectively right, and I do not regret it.[75]

Tyrrell was not the only one to fall. Pius X was, if his own words are to be believed, after blood. It is hard to know whether he was reacting to the teachings of "modernists" or also to his recent political disgrace in France over the law of separation of church and state. In any case, on 17 April 1907 he delivered a violent speech at a consistory for the creation of new cardinals. Phrases from the forthcoming *Pascendi* were scattered throughout:

> You can see clearly, O Venerable Brethren, that We, who must defend with all our strength what has been handed down to Us, are right to be troubled by this new attack, which is not a heresy, but the compendium and poison of all heresies. . . .
> We count a great deal on your work, Venerable Brethren, in letting our bishops, your suffragans in your own districts, know who these sowers of tares are, in joining Us in the struggle against them, in informing Us of the danger to which souls are exposed, in denouncing their books to the Holy Office and meantime using the facilities allowed you by canon law, by solemnly condemning them; urged on in this by the high obligation you have assumed to help the Pope in the government of the Church, to combat error and defend the truth, even to the point of bloodshed.[76]

On 28 October 1907 in Rome the book *Il programma dei modernisti: Risposta all'enciclica di Pio X "Pascendi dominici gregis"* appeared anonymously.[77] The next day the pope excommunicated everyone who had anything to do with its publication. Almost at once Tyrrell was at work on a translation of it for T. Fisher Unwin. The volume set side by side two documents, "The Programme of Modernism" and *Pascendi*, and asked readers to decide for themselves: "What manner of spirit is this? A spirit of light or of darkness; of peace or of strife; of sweetness or of bitterness; of gentleness or of violence; of comprehension or of exclusiveness?"[78] Tyrrell's translation appeared in January 1908 with an introduction signed by A. L. Lilley but based on a text supplied by Tyrrell.[79]

On 6 November Cardinal Andrea Carlo Ferrari, archbishop of Milan, forbade his priests to buy or read *Il Rinnovamento*, a review under the editorship of a group of laymen. On 23 December Ferrari excommunicated the editors, directors, authors, and collaborators. The excommunicated would have included Tyrrell, as he had several articles already published in the journal and was currently preparing for it a review of Lord Acton's *History of Freedom and Other Essays*.[80] In December 1909 *Il Rinnovamento* went under. The condemnation of December 1907 and subsequent condemnations of individuals connected with the review sent its members scurrying for personal justifications and counterjustifications.

The demise of *Il Rinnovamento* was a critical blow to Tyrrell, for although he did not identify with its political orientation, still the group associated with it was fervent in supporting the struggle for freedom of religious investigation and expression. With yet another arm of support gone Tyrrell would limp along less confidently and more painfully, with neither home nor employment, until his own death in 1909. *Pascendi* was having the desired effect.

A FINAL RIPOSTE: *MEDIEVALISM*

After his excommunication in October 1907, Tyrrell moved his personal effects out of the priory, where he had lived since the previous May, into the garden cottage of Maude Petre's Mulberry House in Storrington. Henceforth, much to the prior's discomfort, Mulberry House was to be Tyrrell's home base. Here and elsewhere, particularly in his extended stays with the Shelleys and Bremond, Tyrrell continued to study and write. But now his writing turned almost exclusively to a clarification and defense of the modernist cause against its assailants.

Ironically Tyrrell's loudest and most incisive shot was aimed at one who only months before was seeking to assist him: Cardinal Désiré Joseph Mercier, archbishop of Malines, whose Lenten pastoral of 1908 endorsed *Pascendi* and singled out Tyrrell as "the most penetrating observer of the present Modernist movement—the one most alive to its tendencies, who has best divined its spirit, and is perhaps more deeply imbued with it than any other."[81] Several other ironies stand out. First, it is ironic that Mercier, a scientist-philosopher who studied under Jean Martin Charcot in Paris and founded the Institut Supérieur de Philosophie at Louvain to promote the study of neo-Thomism after the mind of Leo XIII, should now turn against one who was so close to him in spirit. It was further ironic that whereas the encyclical, virulent as it was, contented itself with naming errors without naming names, a diocesan pastoral that opened by thanking God that its diocese was untainted by modernism should deem it necessary to single out an individual about whom virtually no one in that diocese ever heard or cared. Further, in a diocese where, as Mercier admitted, interest in religious matters was at a low ebb, and where people were content to live out their lives with no further knowledge of their religion beyond what they learned for first communion, it is ironic that their bishop should try to initiate interest by pointing out the errors of an inquiring spirit. Beyond these ironies was a contention that particularly angered Tyrrell. Mercier made modernism a form of Protestantism and found it unsurprising that the "parent-idea of Protestantism" should be found in Tyrrell, "a convert whose early education was Protestant"[83]—as if to say, once tainted, always tainted, and not even the cloak of Catholicism could cover the sin of Protestantism.

All these ironies make no sense except in some such hypothesis as this: No other prelate had identified himself as closely as Mercier did with one who was now ecclesiastically unclean. To prove himself clean, he had to perform the ritual sacrifice and bind himself by *Blutkitt* to the antimodernist regime. He was after all a recipient of the red hat at that secret consistory on the previous 17 April, when Pius X, with more rhetoric than sense, called for the shedding of blood. Pius X blessed Mercier's act with a letter of commendation.

Tyrrell's riposte was swift and biting. He called it *Medievalism: A Reply to Cardinal Mercier*. It took the form of an open letter, which he began in late April while in France with Bremond and dated 17 May 1908 from London. For those firmly committed to Tyrrell's cause, *Medievalism* gave cause for loud cheering. It was Tyrrell in his best polemical form. Indeed it is a masterpiece of polemics. He pointed out to Mercier all the ironies of his position and concluded with an address that left no doubt that Tyrrell, at least, knew how untrue to himself Mercier had allowed himself to be:

> Your Eminence, I call this a reply, yet strictly it is not so. Your Lenten Pastoral was not addressed to me, nor did I know of its existence till Lent was over and chance put it into my hands. I have thought it, however, more respectful and straightforward to write *to* you, rather than about you or at you, and to ensure that my words shall reach you before they reach any one else, so that you may have ample time to keep them from the readers of your Pastoral should you think fit.
>
> I am not so sanguine as to imagine that they will make the slightest impression on you, though from certain lines in your Pastoral I would fain believe that you were not all Cardinal, but had still some vulnerable heel of humanity in which a more skilful marksman than myself might lodge a shaft. Indeed, it is no impeachment of your sincerity to suspect that, in the depths of your subconsciousness, you agree with me more than you dare admit to yourself. For I know from personal experience how deep and sincere may be the conviction which, regarding the official view as identical with God's view, makes it a matter of conscience to shut one's eyes and ears to every suggestion of the possibility of any other view. I conceive it a false conscience, but as conscience in any form I respect it.
>
> Your Eminence's Fellow-servant in Christ,
G. TYRRELL.[83]

Medievalism went through four editions (1,450 copies) within a year and was immediately translated into French and Italian. Tyrrell received many letters of appreciation,[84] but probably the most satisfying was the response of Edmund Bishop. Von Hügel heard of Bishop's reaction from Robert Dell and reported it to Tyrrell in a note of 22 September: "Dell delighted me by telling me how *enthusiastic* that all-but-unsatisfiable, intensely fastidious Edm. Bishop is over your 'Mediaevalism,'—one among many."[85]

While von Hügel regularly reported to Tyrrell the positive response his book was provoking in many readers, the baron's own reaction was considerably more detached. He had a penchant for taking the long view of things, and in that perspective the scene of an excommunicated priest taking on the central authorities of the church was simply tragic, particularly in view of personal harm suffered and the dissipation of a gift for more spiritual pursuits. The baron wrote Tyrrell on 27 June, shortly before *Medievalism* appeared, concerning his misgivings. First he denied that he was upset about Tyrrell's answering "a man in his position"—although it is hard to imagine that the baron was not at all concerned about this. Rather, he had the feeling that "the other side" was "beginning to discover the immense difficulties of *their* position." Therefore "we should not keep prodding them too directly and continually, nor move on to further points before they have digested earlier ones." But then, to the personally tragic point:

> As to yourself in particular, I ever feel that (brilliant as are your controversial, polemical hits) God has made you for something deeper and greater, and that not *there*, but in mystical intuition, love, *position*, do you give and get your full, most real self. —So I am most glad that if somehow you *must* have one more directly polemical work, you are keeping it back for leisurely and repeated revision. Of course, even so I feel a bit sad over it; for it can hardly fail to strengthen that quite secondary habit of polemics, and to create a fresh situation and additional occasion for a repetition of this class of literature.[86]

Tyrrell replied by return post:

> MY VERY DEAR FRIEND,
>
> I think you had equally sombre presentiments about poor *Lex Credendi* which you have never recovered, though I had hoped you wd. like it best of all my books. I do not say the same of this. For this time I have tried to put everybody out [of] my head and be *myself* for better or for worse. It is necessary for my sincerity to say why & in what degree I still think it right to belong to so mendacious & immoral an institution as the Roman Church; why I still hesitate to follow Fawkes; why I dislike certain schools of Modernism. Because I am exactly *myself* I am sure to please nobody entirely, everybody partly. It is however my farewell to all specifically Catholic writing—a parting shot. . . . I do not believe a bit that Rome is growing moderate. She only couches [*sic*] to spring.[87]

Considerable tension had arisen between Tyrrell and von Hügel in recent months over courses of action. Just before this disagreement over *Medievalism* they had quarreled over their comportments toward Alfred Fawkes, who had recently given up his Catholic priesthood and reverted to the church of his birth. Von Hügel, who thought Fawkes a reactionary in any case, was for shunning him. Tyrrell, who liked Fawkes but did not especially like some of his ideas, refused to alter his behavior toward him by reason of his irregular status.

But prior to both of these issues was the more serious one of what stance to take toward Loisy. On 31 January 1908 Loisy's two latest books appeared: *Les Évangiles synoptiques* and *Simples réflexions sur le décret du saint-office Lamentabili sane exitu et sur l'encyclique Pascendi dominici gregis*. Two weeks later, on 14 February, Archbishop Léon Adolphe Amette, successor to Cardinal

Richard, who had died on 28 January, forbade his clergy and laity under pain of serious penalties to read, buy, sell or possess *Le Programme des Modernistes* (recently published by Nourry) and under pain of excommunication reserved to the pope to read, possess, print, or defend *Les Évangiles synoptiques* and *Simples réflexions*. One week later the bishop of Langres, Loisy's canonical superior, sent Loisy a summons from Rome demanding his unconditional submission to *Lamentabili* and *Pascendi*. If he failed to comply within ten days, he would be excommunicated. On 7 March 1908 Loisy was excommunicated.

In the *Tablet* for that day a letter from the baron appeared in defense of Loisy. Had the baron known of the excommunication, it is doubtful that he would have allowed the letter's publication. Not that he wanted to abandon Loisy, but he had to be cautious because he was on the brink of publishing his own life's work, *The Mystical Element of Religion*. The previous autumn he had promised to write openly for *Il Rinnovamento* if its group would stand by Loisy and Tyrrell. Now he was hedging on that promise, and he wrote to Tyrrell on 25 March to explain himself:

> As to my own work,—I have got the first of my 3 papers on L's book sent off and accepted. I have decided neither to sign nor even to put my initial; but to put some non-telltale letter. After all, it is of importance to me, with my book now coming, that I should not rile and irritate them more than I can help, compatibly with decent loyàlty to my friends & convictions,—and this latter I can live up to without such signatures. —It is true that I stand pledged for a review of L's book in the 'Hibb. J.' for July; and *that*, Jack & Hicks both say, *must* be signed. But July is more that 3 months hence; I will try and be as judicial and sober as possible; and possibly they will, after all, be content with, say, the initial H.[88]

The baron's timidity on supporting Loisy to protect his own book sent Tyrrell reeling. How long could he himself count on the baron's support? Angered and disillusioned, he wrote on 1 April to Maude Petre:

> I observe that to the many who have asked me: Why doesn't von H. speak out? When is he going to speak? I have answered *on his assurance* that he wd. do so in 2 or 3 months. I observe that it was he who at Levico & elsewhere urged the Rinn. people to face not only the condemnation of their work but the privation of the sacraments, & who was scandalised at Scotti's timidity—not to say at Wilfrid Ward's & Battifol's [*sic*]. . . . I conclude that if he does not stand fire now he is a lost man as far as I am concerned; nor do I think he will keep many of his friends. I cannot imagine how he can have the face to

back down before the Rinnovamento people. It is the rudest shock yet to my dwindling faith in human nature—von Hügel with all his preaching of stress & strain & friction, a coward! It only remains to discover that Christ kept a mistress, or that you have been delating me to Rome. The man who has been a sort of Conscience to me never existed! I had a mind to write to him; but after all it would not make him different, tho' it might make him act differently.[89]

Tyrrell did write to von Hügel a few days later, but he turned nearly about-face. Perhaps he reflected on the significant differences between his and Loisy's cases and saw that the baron had to treat them differently. For one thing, Loisy's excommunication was "nominative." So he was not only out of the church but was to be shunned as much as possible, especially regarding theological projects. Tyrrell's excommunication was "minor." Therefore he was still in the church but could not receive the sacraments. Secondly, their personal relationships differed. The baron vigorously disagreed with some of Loisy's philosophical-theological opinions (for example, his excessive immanentism) while at the same time respecting his historico-critical talents and personal integrity. With Tyrrell, however, there was almost complete unanimity in philosophical-theological matters, and, more important, a much deeper spiritual and affective bond.

Undoubtedly, too, Tyrrell realized that at this precarious point he dare not bite *any* friendly hand. Moreover, he had just finished reading Loisy's latest book, *Quelques lettres sur des questions actuelles et sur des événements récents* (1908), and realized how much the baron had compromised himself by allowing Loisy to publish therein twelve letters he had written to the baron. Tyrrell referred to Loisy's letters in his letter of 6 April: "You are not badly committed, but still decidedly committed by Loisy's letters to you; & this reconciles me more to your determination to sign nothing— not even the sober & judicious Hibbert article." Still, Tyrrell had misgivings: "I am so much afraid your action may be misunderstood by the Rinnovamento & other people whom you have encouraged in an opposite course. Still I would not wish you to emulate my foolhardiness or to sacrifice your work or your sacraments for anything less than some *very great* gain to the cause of truth. Had I believed as much as you do in the Modernist cause I shd. have probably acted differently."[90]

Von Hügel saw directly the point of Tyrrell's indirect criticism and wrote on 16 April to say that he had decided after all to do the "reasonably courageous thing" and sign his *Hibbert* article and initial with "H" the last of his three *Rinnovamento* articles. This decision momentarily lifted Tyrrell's spirits. But in the next paragraph the baron explained that he might be forced, "before I have finished my little life-work, to discriminate myself from him [Loisy]."[91] Dismayed, Tyrrell wrote to Maude Petre on 24 April, "Von H. wants now to 'dissociate' himself from Loisy in his signed article for the sake of his 'own poor little work.' It is enough to make one a Jesuit again."[92]

Compared to recent days, Tyrrell's days as a Jesuit were halcyon indeed. One more arm of support was about to fold in the group surrounding Ernesto Buonaiuti and his review *Nova et Vetera* to which Tyrrell had lately contributed. Pressure from the Vatican had scattered its undisciplined forces, and Tyrrell registered his distress to Petre: "N. & Vetera have taken a bad schismatic turn & the 'Lettera d'un Prete Modernista' are very terre-a-terre & cruely [*sic*] Positivist. What shd. have been a quiet incubation has become a conflagration; the mob has got hold of us. It is exactly the story of 1789."[93]

Moreover, the vigilance committees ordered by *Pascendi* to be established in every diocese were by now operating with a vengeance and undermining by secret delations whatever solidarity still remained to the battered modernist cause. "Modernism has been defeated, utterly crushed," Houtin wrote to Loisy in April 1908. "The reign of terror holds sway in every diocese and the young men have gone underground."[94] Nowhere was the defeat more complete than in the diocese of Southwark, wherein Tyrrell resided when in England.

LAST WORDS

Tyrrell returned to England from France at the beginning of May 1908 and took up residence with the Shelleys in Clapham. On 1 August he moved down to Mulberry House. During these months reports of ecclesiastical violence arrived in Tyrrell's mail with alarming regularity. In letters of 24 August and 18 October to von Hügel he enumerated recent blows to the modernist cause in general and to his own spirit in particular: Amigo had begun to extort signatures to *Pascendi* under pain of suspension from those priests delated to him by informers;[95] the Pope had "now cut off French ecclesiastics *absolutely* from the Universities";[96] and tongues in Storrington were clucking over Tyrrell's presence there with Maude Petre and her frequent reception of the sacraments at the priory. In fact, Tyrrell said, he had received "a very unpleasant letter from the Prior" asking him to leave Storrington. In reply he sent a note to the *Tablet* exonerating the priory from any sympathy with his views, but the *Tablet* refused to publish it, so he sent it directly to the prior.[97] He also sent a copy to von Hügel, which the latter pronounced "so firm, dignified and even kind: how right!"[98]

One result of the campaign of violence in the Roman Church was to make Tyrrell pine for the leeks and onions of his former church. Actually, from the onset of his ecclesiastical troubles, the thought of returning to Anglicanism was never far from his consciousness. But as often as the temptation arose, he set it aside by the more urgent conviction that, as he wrote to one vicar, "I feel my work is to hammer away at the great unwieldy carcass of the Roman Communion and wake it up from its medieval dreams. Not that I shall succeed, but that my failure and many another may pave the way for eventual success."[99]

It was to that eventual success—to the church of the future— that Tyrrell was committed. He could gain nothing by joining Anglicanism, except perhaps a moment's peace. For him Anglicanism was indeed "an integral part of the Church Catholic." Still, it was "merely a recession from Romanism" and "a lower form of organism."[100] There were other strong reasons against joining. One was that for Tyrrell to remain a Roman Catholic was to remain a thorn in Rome's side. But, more important, there was the scandal he would cause by deserting all those with whom he struggled in the modernist cause. Finally, a secession would justify Rome's position and facilitate her designs. The papalists would have their way, and that Tyrrell could not allow, as long as a breath of life remained.

He could commit himself neither to Anglicanism nor to Romanism but only to Catholicism—that is, to the Catholic Church without papalism. The latter he saw as a medieval excrescence that sooner or later would have to suffer the knife of historical criticism. Döllinger and Acton had the same view and exerted themselves in trying to reverse the ultramontane momentum at Vatican I. When they failed, their cause passed to the schismatic Old Catholic sect, but they themselves rejected sectarianism, as did Tyrrell after them.

Thus in late 1906, when disaffected clerics approached Tyrrell to help them found an Old Catholic colony in England, he promised support but refused to join.[101] He was not interested in a new religion, only in purifying the authentic tradition from those elements that made it into a new religion. Indirectly an Old Catholic colony recognized by the Church of England could possibly support Tyrrell's own interest. He figured that both churches could strengthen each other in their nonpapal forms of Catholicism and thereby strengthen his voice against papalism in the Roman communion.[102] In the summer of 1908, however, the Lambeth Conference rejected recognition for the Old Catholics, and for Tyrrell one more arm of support fell away.[103]

Mixed in with Tyrrell's motives in this venture was one that arose out of a negative and destructive side—the desire to get back at Rome by strengthening Rome's opposition, a cause of distress to Baron von Hügel. He had heard of his friend's association with the Old Catholics not from Tyrrell himself (which leads one to suspect that Tyrrell was not especially proud of it), but from the Rev. Gerald Christopher Rawlinson, an Anglican sympathizer of the modernist cause. When the baron brought the rumor to Tyrrell's attention and suggested that he write to Rawlinson to check it, Tyrrell answered sharply:

> You plainly take R.'s rumour seriously, since you write so elaborately on the subject. There is no smoke without fire; & the fire is this—that I have expressed & feel great interest in the understanding between Anglicans & O. Catholics. Of two evils I had rather see England O.C. than Papist. Is it possible that in the light of the last five years you can deny that *as against Rome* the Old Catholics were in the right or that Rome was on the Devil's side as usual? However your attitude towards the lost sheep of the House of Israel is not one that I pretend to understand. I could not join the O. Catholics only because they bear the seeds of the papacy in their bosom. . . . You are wrong in supposing that *Rome* would rejoice if I joined the O.C. No, she would & does *dread* that & so I don't mind these rumours. The idiots of Westminster are terrified lest the O.C.s should impregnate the Anglicans with "real orders." That is the sort of rubbish their silly heads are stuffed with. They think the movement might become "serious" if I took it up. What Rome loves is a proof of the "Rome or Agnosticism" alternative. That one should give up as little as possible & keep to the nearest thing instead of rushing to the furthest extreme, annoys her. Do you know I sometimes think it annoys you? & that you would rather see me an atheist than an Anglican? However neither you nor Rawlinson need fear—I am afraid I have not faith enough left to join any body or anything.[104]

Tyrrell's reaction pained the baron and sent him searching for its provocation in his own behavior. He concluded that Tyrrell was perhaps thinking about his aloofness from Fawkes, who had recently returned to Anglicanism, as against his intimacy with Loisy, who was rumored to be agnostic. On 7 December he replied to Tyrrell that, of course, if Loisy were to join some atheist body, he would mind that step "out of all proportion more than I mind F.'s action." Sometimes, he agreed, conscience requires secession. But "I feel still that the reform of the Roman Church is *the* point for us whom Providence has made . . . members of that Church" and that secessions, for whatever good they may have done to the seceders and to the body formed or joined by them, only "helped further to narrow the Church which they left." He closed with a touching and perceptive counsel:

> As to Faith, Friend . . . of this I am sure . . . you are a mystic; you have never found, you will never find, either Church, or Christ, or just simply God, or even the vaguest spiritual presence and conviction, except in deep recollection, purification, quietness, intuition, love. Lose these and you lose God; regain these, and you could as soon doubt Him as you could deny that you have hands and feet. And your helping others, *any soul alive*, depends upon your keeping or regaining those convictions, hence these dispositions; not all the wit, vehemence, subtlety, criticism, learning that you can muster (and *how* great they are!) will ever, without those, be other than ruinous to others as well as to yourself. And this is why,—this, that you may be able to help and build up, and, in doing so, find happiness; and be saved from endless pulling down, and thus, finding the restless bitterness of an essential self-contradiction,—that I so long for you to turn again to teaching, and hence to practising, that deep great spiritual life which is your one strength, joy and significance.[105]

How Tyrrell took the baron's advice is not known, as his reply is missing.[106] But from early March 1909 the baron noticed "a marked change of tone . . . as to Rome, Anglicanism, Old Catholics" in the direction of his advice. He did not speculate on the cause of that change, but the present writer suggests that a violent illness suffered by Tyrrell in the first week of March threw a scare into him and contributed to a certain softening.[107]

Tyrrell had been staying with the Shelleys in Clapham when the illness struck. The first doctor called in diagnosed the case as serious and related to kidney disfunction. But Tyrrell made a remarkably sudden recovery and two weeks later obtained a second medical opinion, which confirmed his wish to believe that the illness was nothing more than a severe attack of influenza of "no worse than a chill combined with one of those so-called 'migraines.'"[108] But events were to confirm the first diagnosis. Tyrrell was approaching the last stages of Bright's disease, and his last arm of support was about to fall. Before that happened, however, he would produce what von Hügel called "the deepest and most characteristic of his books, *Christianity at the Cross-Roads*."[109]

Perhaps the illness provided incentive for Tyrrell to take

seriously the baron's exhortation of 7 December that he leave off destructive criticism and begin again to think and write construc- tively. In any case, subsequent to that illness Tyrrell began to con- sider positively the gold he found embedded in the ore of Roman Catholicism and to use it as a touchstone against which to measure any other religious expressions. Thus he wrote to advise the baron on 7 April 1909 concerning the "apparent allies" in the modernist cause. Few of them, he said, "have really grasped or believed in the Modernist position. . . . They do not believe that modernity has anything to learn from the Church, but only that the Church has everything to learn from modernity." As for the modernist princi- ple of reformation from within:

> I have perhaps less hope & faith than you in the success of the scheme. But against that I hold first of all that a right course should be followed sometimes in the face of *certain* failure; that though we know an evil to be inevitable we should take care that we at least did our best to prevent it. . . . Not that I yet accept this pessimism; but that I should not abandon the Church even if I did. If there is a new religion coming, it is well below the horizon; and our guesses at its shape & form are idle. The premature attempts to hook it from the womb of Time will only procure grotesque & short-lived abortions. Modernism i.e. the reformation of existing forms of Christianity, is the best way to prepare for it.[110]

In the second week of March 1909, up from his sickbed, Tyrrell set out on several projects: two lectures for which he was prepar- ing new material and a new book on Christological questions over which he had ruminated for several months.[111] The first lecture, "Divine Fecundity," was a carefully worked apologetic on the im- manence of God and the evil of natural disasters. He delivered it on 25 March in Kensington Town Hall to a group called "The Quest Society" and three days later reported to the baron, "I wasted a very careful essay on what proved to be only a society of senti- mental theosophists under a new name—people who long to be rid of reason in order to be free to believe in their gnostic ravings; pseudo-mystics of the worst types; mostly *mulierculae*."[112]

The next evening Tyrrell delivered another original lecture, this time to a sophisticated and appreciative audience, students and professors of King's College, London. He called the lecture, "Reve- lation as Experience: A Reply to Hakluyt Egerton." "Hakluyt Eger- ton" was a pseudonym for Arthur Boutwood, an Anglican layman who had recently published a book-length criticism of *Through Scylla and Charybdis*.[113] It was an honest and fair criticism, the kind Tyrrell always welcomed. He merely used the lecture to deal with Boutwood's objections and thereby to clarify his own thought.

Boutwood's principal concern was Tyrrell's description of revelation and the distinction he drew between theology and revelation: "Does it consist in certain divine statements; or in certain spiritual experiences about which *man* makes statements that may be inspired by those divine experiences, yet are not divine but human statements?"[114]

Tyrrell took up this question by first analyzing the revelation that is attributed to Jesus. Since we hold Jesus to be God, he argued, we hold his statements to be divine statements. But this way of speaking about Jesus' revelation requires more theological precision, since strictly speaking God who is spirit does not "make statements" any more than he walks or talks as men do. Therefore, strictly speaking, Jesus' words are not revelation but only the occasion for revelation. The revelation occurs in a wordless, immediate communication or experience between the divine nature of Jesus and his human nature. This experience he then expressed in his own human categories and language. Without that inward divine communication, Jesus' words could have no more authority than the words of an angel or a prophet.

Revelation in the ordinary human person, Tyrrell went on, occurs in much the same way as it occurred between Jesus' divine and human natures. That is, it is not experienced as *statement*. It is tempting to think this way, because then one could simply line up all the statements that are divine revelation and deduce from them their logical consequences and construct thereon a whole system of thought. And so far as it is logically deduced, that system "will possess the divine certainty of those revealed statements, and will therefore serve as a criterion for other departments of human knowledge which must be squared with all this divinity. That, I need not say, is exactly the claim of scholastic theology." Rather a truer idea of revelation is found in the notion of the "indwelling spirit of Christ, present to all men at all times—a revelation that consists in felt promptings and guidings of the finite by the infinite will, and not in man's spontaneous or reflex interpretations of those promptings."[115]

We may loosely refer to inspired expressions of those experiences as "revelation," but theology requires greater precision. With the mystics, we really must distinguish between God's action and man's reaction and realize that "the *inspired* statement is not strictly a *divine* statement" and therefore that it is not an infallibly adequate expression of the revelatory experience. It follows then that another expression of the same experience could be better, even without being in logical or intellectual agreement with the first. "In short," Tyrrell concluded, "we are delivered from what I have elsewhere called 'the dogmatic fallacy' that gives to divine authority the intellectual value of such utterances."[116]

Tyrrell then turned to Boutwood's assertion that such a subjective conception of revelation as Tyrrell's cannot show that God is revealed immediately in the revelational experience or indeed that experience is even revelational. The real question, he said, and the one that lies at the heart of orthodox presuppositions about God is

> what do we mean by God? Is God primarily a term of action and secondarily an object of contemplation and statement; or conversely: Is God primarily an idea or truth deduced from experience and subsequently a term of action [the orthodox position]?
> . . . If God is what religion teaches; if He is to man's soul what light is to his eyes, or air to his lungs; if he [sic] is the correlate and coprinciple of his spiritual life, the medium in which the soul lives and moves and has her being, is it conceivable that we should hold Him merely by a slender thread of obscure inference; or that it should be necessary to *prove* his existence before we begin to live our spiritual life? No; all we need do is to prove to men that they necessarily believe in him; that they affirm him in every movement of their spiritual and moral life.[117]

Tyrrell proposed to demonstrate such a proof by showing that in moral action, the moral person experiences a Power (which is not himself) that "makes for Righteousness," and that we can call that Power God. It is only to the Power that makes for Righteousness that man renders absolute worship and obedience. He is not moved to worship and obedience by omniscience and omnipotence. If the Power that makes for Righteousness is also omnipotent and omniscient, well and good, but as Newman rightly maintained, "the world apart from man's inner moral experience might give us the idea of a vast though scarcely infinite power and intelligence, but not of God." The Power that makes for Righteousness is available to every person's experience and is the core of all religion. Other objective attributes are logical deductions and the product of man's mind and really do not get man beyond his mind.

> Hence I conclude that if experience gives us a Power that makes for Righteousness it gives us God—it gives us, not a statement or an

idea but a thing, a term of action, of obedience, worship, self-sacrifice, about which we more or less spontaneously frame ideas and statements. Experience is revelational. It reveals God as every cause is revealed in and with its effects; it reveals Him not in a statement but in the moral and religious impulse that proceeds from Him.[118]

Nor is this moral impulse anonymous, as Boutwood claims. It reveals a cause that one is impelled to worship and obey. That is precisely what we mean, or ought to mean, by God.

As to Christ, the believer experiences him as Conscience incarnate. His words bear eternal life. They have a "sacramental spiritual efficacy beyond their merely intellectual value," and therefore Christ is accorded the same worship and obedience as that Power which makes for Righteousness.[119]

With regard to creedal statements, we know their truth only by appeal to faith. Appeal to intellect and reason is irrelevant. If it were not, unbelievers and evil persons, for whom reason works equally well as for good persons, could be brought to faith simply on the strength of logical argument. Rather the critical element in knowing the truth of creedal statements is faith, and so we are thrown back again on revelation as an inward experience. Creedal statements are "not divine statements but human statements inspired by divine experience."[120] For these inspired human statements to come alive with religious meaning, faith experience is a prerequisite.

Rev. Albert A. Cock, a young Anglican divine and lecturer in education and philosophy at King's College, was in the audience that night. He later met and became fast friends with Tyrrell and with Baron von Hügel. Some forty years later he recalled that evening with Tyrrell and described the lecture as "a brilliant statement of his general doctrinal position as he had reached it in his new book on *Christianity at the Cross-Roads.*"[121]

Certainly Tyrrell's latest conception of the problem of revelation and inspiration underlies the whole of *Christianity at the Cross-Roads,* but there is considerably more to the book than that. It is an apologetic for his modernist position against the charge that his position lined up squarely with Protestant liberalism. So throughout the book, on each successive issue, Tyrrell demonstrated how his position is radically Catholic and differs essentially from Protestant liberalism.

Originally Tyrrell meant his new work to be a synthesis of Christology based on the results of historico-critical investigation of the New Testament. However, when William Ralph Inge, in the *Quarterly Review* for April, sketched the history of modernism in the Roman Church and linked it with Protestant liberalism,[122] Tyrrell added to his original idea the apologetic task of clarifying once again the nature of modernism and its radical difference from Ritschlian liberalism and at the same time stressing its preservation of all that is most truly Catholic.

This clarification he attempted by appealing to that aspect of the historical Christ which had been largely ignored by early nineteenth-century critics and only lately discovered by Johannes Weiss and Albert Schweitzer, namely, the eschatological message of Jesus. Because liberal Protestants ignored it, Tyrrell argued, they lost the real Christ of history who proclaimed the wholly otherness and giftedness of the Kingdom of God. The Christ of Harnack is merely an ethical teacher whose teachings in no way differ from those of Jesus' milieu. "The Christ that Harnack sees, looking back through nineteen centuries of Catholic darkness, is only the reflection of a Liberal Protestant face, seen at the bottom of a deep well."[123]

The eschatological "idea" of Jesus, the totally new creation proclaimed and verified in the resurrection, Tyrrell asserted, is preserved in the Roman Church and particularly in her sacramental system and constitution. The Catholic Church,

> is identical and continuous with the Apostolic band that Jesus gathered round Him. Its later independent organization and externalism were contained in the idea of Jesus. There is no chasm; no need for a bridge. The temporary disorganisation of Apostolic Christianity, consequent on its separation from Judaism, was an abnormal state of affairs. The "idea" was bound to reassert itself as it did. Of that reassertion Liberal Protestants speak as of a deplorable relapse into the legalism from which Christ had made us free. What Christ freed us from was not externalism, but its abuse; not the letter, but its oppression of the spirit; not the priesthood, but sacerdotalism; not ritual, but ritualism; not the Altar, but the exploitation of the Altar.[124]

Admittedly there are many "beggarly elements" in the externalism of Catholicism, but it is only in externalism that the church can realize her true nature. For by nature she is a sacrament of the spirit and personality of Jesus abiding in her. Nor is that sacrament invalidated by the meanness of the "beggarly elements" through which the Spirit is communicated. The essential element of the Catholic Church is that she is the re-presentation of Christ above all in her sacraments. She is not the re-presentation of an ethical system, which Jesus at most adopted and transmitted but in no sense originated.

There is much in Tyrrell's acceptance and presentation of the results of then-current biblical criticism with which one could take issue. But even Dean Inge, who disagreed with Tyrrell more often than he agreed, did not allow particular discrepancies to obscure the argument of the book as a whole. He found Tyrrell's *Tendenz* persuasive: "If some external force were to compel all Christian bodies to federate to-morrow, it is perhaps more likely that they would make Rome their capital than that they would create a new city in the wilds. . . . No other existing ecclesiastical centre could be seriously considered."[125] But he did not have Tyrrell's faith that the present abuses were no more than accidental consequences and not symptoms of senile decay. Inge knew better than most that in keeping the gold the church also kept the ore. But Tyrrell's point was that she kept the gold and did not cast any of it out to suit the demands of a passing age as some more limited institutions had done. Above all she maintained in herself and in her Christ that transcendence of outlook which is of the essence of religion and enables the believer to survive the most searing trials of his faith.

DENOUEMENT

Christianity at the Cross-Roads was Tyrrell's last and most characteristic work. He signed the preface 29 June 1909 at Clapham.

The next day he returned for the last time to Mulberry House in Storrington. At 8:00 in the evening of 6 July he fell critically ill. It was the onset of the last stages of Bright's disease. Sometime that evening he suffered a stroke that paralyzed his left side and impaired his speech. Over the next ten days he suffered violent headaches, nausea, and internal bleeding, and he became increasingly comatose until the evening of 14 July, when he lost consciousness altogether. The next morning, 15 July 1909, at about 9:00, he died.

Maude Petre was beside Tyrrell almost constantly during those days. On 9 July, when she recognized the seriousness of the illness, she telegraphed Baron von Hügel. He came at once. They faced a dilemma. The issue had become no longer what they could do to preserve Tyrrell's life but what he would want them to do to preserve his integrity. They knew that he would want the comforts of the last sacraments, but he had made it very clear that he would not want them at the cost of unqualified submission to Vatican demands. If Tyrrell received the sacraments and nothing were said about the circumstances, authorities could claim that he had died piously renouncing all his writings and endorsing *Lamentabili* and

Pascendi. If Tyrrell received the sacraments without making an unqualified submission, he could certainly be denied Catholic burial, and other penalties could be imposed on the administering priest. Canon law, however, did allow any priest to absolve a dying man at least conditionally if the man showed signs of repentance or could be presumed to have a penitent disposition. There, of course, lay the hitch. Authorities might claim that any sign of repentance meant submission to their demands. What von Hügel and Petre would do about this dilemma would be determined later. What they actually did in the moment is best told in the baron's words as he described the situation to Lilley. He wrote from Storrington on 13 July:

> On this Friday [the 9th] two trained Nurses had been installed. And the question of the Sacrs. was on. He had had a paralytic stroke on the left side . . . which rendered his articulation most thick, and the mind was very wandering. No possibility then of ascertaining *now* what he would wish. We decided according to the tenour of many a conversation,—recent ones, too— . . . to call in, next morning at once [the 10th], a Southwark Diocese Secular Priest, a friend of his, with full faculties, and to put to him what we were confident Fr. T. would wish done. —This Priest came at 1, midday; and, since the whole decision wd. have to be based upon interpretation and construction,—he made me take the responsibility for the following interpretation. Fr. T. would certainly wish to receive the Sacrs. and would certainly be willing and eager to confess, and to express penitence for, any and all excesses of speech or of writing, any unnecessary pain or scandal given to anyone,—and this also in specific instances that might occur to his memory. But he would as decidedly, refuse any unlimited, absolute retraction, any unbounded submission; and would, sadly but firmly elect to die without the Sacrs. if such a condition were insisted on. The Priest fully accepted these three positions; and saw T. twice, offered to hear his conf., and T. seemed very pleased to see him, apparently recognizing him, and spoke much,— possibly his confession,—but it was impossible to make out what T. was saying, or whether even he realised the situation in general. The Priest gave him conditional Absolution, and asked to be sent for again, if he got still worse, for Extreme Unction; and, if he got better, for H. Com. Throughout Sunday T. lay restless, with the pain in his head, dozing a little now and then,—semi-aware, apparently of persons and things, but with still a curiously high degree of strength about him. The night to Monday [the 12th] was so alarmingly bad, that Miss Petre, on the Dr.'s advice, sent at 8 a.m., not for the distant Secular Priest but for the Premonstratensian Prior here, who, as you know, used to be so friendly, and then became so hostile to him. The Prior, in the presence of 3 witnesses, Mr. W. Tyrrell, Miss Petre, and

her sister, Mrs. Sweetman Powell, administered Extreme Unction to him, without attempting to extract even a merely interpretative recantation from him,—a proceeding which would, it is true, have been physically blocked and impossible.

The baron was sorry that they had to call in the prior at that point—not that they doubted his good-heartedness, but that, if Tyrrell pulled through, "it will be from this quarter that trouble will arise."[126] Just what trouble he had in mind is not clear.

The baron wrote this letter not merely to inform Lilley, who by friendship had "a right to the above confidences," but to have a record of those days "for future reference, if necessary"—perhaps to cover the possibility of a charge that after Tyrrell's death his friends released only a cosmetic version of the story. To disseminate the facts against rumor concerning the circumstances of Tyrrell's reception of the sacraments—that he made no unconditional retraction—von Hügel, Petre, and Bremond (who had arrived the evening of the 12th and attended Tyrrell to the end), immediately upon Tyrrell's death composed a statement that appeared in the *Times* and the *Daily Mail* on the morning of the 16th.[127] It was essentially along the lines of von Hügel's letter to Lilley. That same day von Hügel sent the following justification to Edmund Bishop: "Miss P. and I were, of course, well aware of the unpopularity of what we were doing,—especially by this letter to the Papers. But we felt that the most elementary loyalty to our friend and to the great cause for which we have all laboured in common strictly *demanded* such a prompt declaration, so as to anticipate the upspringing to legend, which would have arisen in 24 hours, incapable of eradication any more."[128]

That letter to the press proved to be double-edged. On the one hand it did forestall rumors and prevented officials from claiming the victory they wanted. On the other hand, victory having been removed in death, officials could claim it in burial. Evidently acting on orders from Rome, the bishops of Southwark and Westminster refused permission for Catholic burial.[129] After several days of fruitless appeal, Maude Petre and the baron arranged for burial on 21 July in the Anglican churchyard at Storrington.

Early on that morning Bremond offered a requiem mass at the high altar of the priory church for the repose of George Tyrrell's soul. At 12:30 P.M. a group of some forty friends and relatives assembled outside the garden house where Tyrrell's body lay. Bremond, wearing no sign of liturgical office, addressed the group briefly: "Catholic burial has been refused him by our ecclesiastical Authorities, and we will make no comment on this decision, accepting it as he would have told us to do. We wish for nothing that would suggest a schismatic or sectarian attitude, such as he abhorred. But we cannot let him be borne to the grave without prayers over his body, and will bless the grave, in the Parish Cemetery, wherein he is to lie. And when we have laid him to rest, I will venture to speak a few words."[130] He asked that he be the only one to speak so as to avoid the least suspicion of a demonstration against authorities.

The mourners then processed in silence through the small village to the churchyard, Bremond leading, William Tyrrell and Baron von Hügel accompanying him, followed by the coffin and finally the other mourners. At graveside Bremond prayed over the grave the traditional Roman Catholic burial prayers, omitting the conditional absolution so as to give no cause to interpret the ceremony as an official act of the church. He then blessed the grave and coffin and read a final eulogy:

> You see the place we have lovingly chosen for him, since another place was refused to us. You see the place. He used to like it, and many a time, when he was living in the Priory, here he came, reciting his breviary in the very same path beside which they have dug his grave. As you see, it stands half-way between two Churches, the one in which he died and the other in which he was born. On this side, separated from us by a tiny wall, the Catholic Church; on the other, the Church of Keble, of his friend of friends, Dolling, and so many of you who have been so discreetly kind and so courageously true to him. . . .
>
> . . . No greater mistake could have been committed about him than the mistake of those well-meaning opponents who looked upon him as the modern apologist of private judgment and of individualism in religion. He wanted a Church, both from the sense of the necessity of a social organisation of the Christian idea, and still more, perhaps, from his profound belief in, and his intense love for, the sacramental side of religion. No dogma was dearer to his heart than the dogma of the communion of Saints, of which I confidently repeated to his dying ears the . . . simple formula: *Credo in communionem sanctorum.*
>
> . . . We to whom he openly said the worst that was in him and sometimes did not entirely succeed in hiding the best, we knew the pathetic struggle which seemed, at times, to absorb his activities, and we knew, too, without the slightest hesitation, what would be the end of the struggle. We knew that, for him, the Roman Catholic Church, as a fact, stood for the oldest, and the widest body of corporate Christian experience, for the closest approximation, so far attained, to the still far distant ideal of a Catholic Church.
>
> . . . He clung to the Church of his conversion with the same deep-rooted conviction and the same love with which he clung to the Gos-

pel and to the Divine person of our Lord. The most admirable book, soon to be published, which occupied his last months—which shortened his precious life—will stand as a lasting monument of his faith. The book is called "Christianity at the Cross-Roads." Let me read just a few sentences of it: ". . . It is impossible to deny that the revelation of the Catholic religion and that of Jesus are the same, not only in substance, but largely in form. . . . It was in the form of such a tradition that He necessarily embodied His Gospel, and the Catholic Church has preserved the earthen vessel with its heavenly treasure, while those who have broken and cast away the vessel seem to have lost much of the treasure. Ought we not still to keep it, while carefully distinguishing it from its contents?"

Bremond then bade farewell on behalf of Tyrrell's many French, Italian, and German friends and the poor and simple everywhere who were always so close to Tyrrell's heart. He ended with an exhortation to hope: "To realise that we shall never hear him again on earth would entirely darken our lives, if he had not taught us his own bitter, but triumphant, optimism, and the present duty of hoping against hope. Hope! This must be our parting word and feelings."[131]

Over the grave was placed a simple marker with the words:

Of your charity
Pray for the soul of
GEORGE TYRRELL
Catholic Priest who died
July 15 1909, Aged 48 years
Fortified by the Rites
of the Church
R.I.P.

This inscription was in accord with the wish Tyrrell inserted into his will the previous 1 January: "If I decline the ministrations of a Roman Catholic Priest at my death-bed, it is solely because I wish to give no basis for the rumour that I made any sort of retractation of those Catholic principles which I have defended against the Vatican heresies. If no priest will bury me, let me be buried in perfect silence. If a stone is put over me, let it state that I was a Catholic Priest, and bear the usual emblematic chalice and host. No notes or comments."[132]

Three days after the funeral Bishop Amigo suspended Bremond from exercising his priestly privileges within the Southwark diocese. Within a week Cardinal Merry del Val made Bremond's local suspension universal.[133] On 30 July Merry del Val wrote to

Amigo to ascertain whether and what steps should be taken against von Hügel and Petre. Amigo and Bourne consulted Bishop John Cuthbert Hedley of Newport, a senior bishop in England and longtime friend of the baron. Hedley replied to Amigo, "As far as I can see, no public sentence or canonical censure can be passed either on Baron von Hügel or on Miss M. D. Petre, in regard to what they are alleged to have said or done in connection with this matter." The possible charges were that they had prevented or suppressed a retraction and/or that they prevented access of a priest who could have made Tyrrell's duty clear to him. "Whatever may be suspected," Hedley concluded, "I do not think that either of these charges can possibly be proved." Moreover, "I know F. von Hügel, and as he denies them, I believe him."[134]

Amigo forwarded Hedley's letter to Bourne and suggested that "perhaps the best time to act will be when poor Tyrrell's book is published. So far though Miss Petre's conduct is strange, we have nothing positive to go by. I am glad that you will have the responsibility as the book will be published in Westminster."[135] Bourne was not a narrow man and generally observed a nonaggressive policy toward "modernists" in his diocese.[136] When he reported to Merry del Val the results of his investigation, he included Hedley's opinion and supported it as "wise and prudent." He added that refusal of Catholic burial had "shown people the horror of dying under the censure of the Church." Moreover, he said, the presence and effectiveness of modernism in England were neglible and advised that further pursuit of the matter would very likely arouse sympathy for the accused. But he concluded by asking Merry del Val to let him know if there were "any further information that you would wish to have or any action that you desire me to take."[137]

Meanwhile Petre and von Hügel collaborated on preparing the manuscript of *Christianity at the Cross-Roads* for publication. Petre composed a brief introduction. Von Hügel, in a letter to her of 14 September, requested that she omit his name from the introduction. Edmund Bishop, he told her, had argued forcefully against it, because instead of helping the cause, it would "simply add to their irritation, as showing a continuance of plotting, etc." It would be so important, not just for their own spiritual safety, "but *because of the truths and the future we stand for*" to avoid condemnation and the pressure to subscribe to *Lamentabili* and *Pascendi.*[138] Yet he admitted to feeling mean about not adding his name. It would leave Maude Petre to bear the responsibility alone.

The book appeared from Longmans sometime in late October

or early November. Petre went to France in late November to consult Bremond about his assistance in preparing Tyrrell's autobiography for publication. When she returned and, on the morning of 1 December, went to the priory church for mass, the prior rushed into the church and forbade her to receive communion. Upon being questioned about his authorization, the prior admitted that he had no orders from the bishop. She immediately appealed to Amigo, but he answered that she could help him decide between her and the prior by declaring her sincere acceptance of *Lamentabili* and *Pascendi*. When she refused, Amigo responded that he would not compel the prior to admit her to the sacraments, since she was suspected of holding modernist opinions and had not given any assurance to the contrary.

She began to communicate at Greyshott in Surrey in the diocese of Portsmouth, where she went periodically to visit her sister. But Amigo manipulated a prohibition in that diocese as well. However, as she had not been explicitly forbidden to receive the sacraments elsewhere than the priory church, she continued to receive at various neighboring parishes. On 1 September 1910 Pius X signed the *motu proprio, Sacrorum antistitum,* which settled on a formula for an oath against modernism to be taken by all clerics in major orders and professors of Catholic faculties of philosophy and theology. It was not aimed at the laity. Yet Amigo pressed it on Petre. At her refusal to take the oath, Amigo deprived her of the sacraments.

Meanwhile Petre labored with great devotion over the two volumes of Tyrrell's *Autobiography and Life* and saw them through the press in late summer or early autumn of 1912. On 17 June 1913 the Congregation of the Index placed them on the Index of Forbidden Books.[139]

This was the judgment of the highest ecclesiastical authorities on the life and writings of George Tyrrell. His end and the end of modernism seemed complete and utter. Yet the modernism for which Tyrrell stood and gave his life merely went underground for a time. Anyone who has studied both him and the documents of Vatican II will recognize his principles reborn on nearly every page. Thus was fulfilled the prophecy that Tyrrell applied to himself and inscribed in his breviary in 1896: "Thou shalt see from afar the land which the Lord God will give to the children of Israel, but thou shalt not enter therein."

List of
Abbreviations

Abbreviations Used in the Notes and Bibliography

AAW	Archives of the Archdiocese of Westminster
AL	Maude Dominica Petre, *Autobiography and Life of George Tyrrell*
BL	British Library
BN	Bibliothèque nationale, Paris
CCR	George Tyrrell, *Christianity at the Cross-Roads*
CF	George Tyrrell, *The Church and the Future*
EFI	George Tyrrell, *Essays on Faith and Immortality*
ER	George Tyrrell, *External Religion*
EPSJ	English Province of the Society of Jesus
FB	Fonds Bremond
FL	Fonds Loisy
FM	George Tyrrell, *The Faith of the Millions*
FvH	Baron Friedrich von Hügel
GT	George Tyrrell
GTL	George Tyrrell, *George Tyrrell's Letters*, ed. MDP
HP	Friedrich von Hügel Papers
vH&T	Maude D. Petre, *Von Hügel and Tyrrell*
HS	George Tyrrell, *Hard Sayings*
LC	George Tyrrell, *Lex Credendi*
LO	George Tyrrell, *Lex Orandi*
LP	Alfred Leslie Lilley Papers
MDP	Maude Dominica Petre
NAF	Nouvelles acquisitions françaises
O&W	George Tyrrell, *Oil and Wine*
PP	Maude Dominica Petre Papers
RFL	George Tyrrell, *Religion as a Factor of Life*
SAUL	St. Andrews University Library
TSC	George Tyrrell, *Through Scylla and Charybdis*
WFP	Wilfrid Ward Family Papers
WP	Alfred Rayney Waller Papers

Notes

PREFACE

1. The widespread success of the antimodernist campaign led to a general and uncritical acceptance of the meaning given by *Pascendi* and other antimodernist documents to the terms "modernism," "modernist," and their various linguistic forms. Scholars of the modernist period continue to debate over the content of these terms, but on one point they all agree: the meaning given by the antimodernist documents is a caricature of what the modernists understood of their own aims and activities. It is beyond the scope of this study to enter into the debate, but I acknowledge its importance by placing "modernism" and related terms in quotation marks wherever it seems necessary to call attention to the historiographical problem of a term's meaning or to alert the reader to regard a term over against the meaning given it by the antimodernist documents. Wherever a term carries a neutral meaning—where it designates the period, controversy, or participants without further connotation—it is not set off by quotation marks. For a history of the terms "modernism" and "modernist"

prior to their adoption by *Pascendi*, see Jean Rivière, *Le Modernisme dans l'Église* (Paris: Librairie Letouzey & Co., 1929), pp. 13–34. For more recent discussion, see Alec R. Vidler, *The Modernist Movement in the Roman Church* (Cambridge: At the University Press, 1934), pp. 270–71; Thomas Michael Loome, "The Meanings of Modernism," *Tablet* 225 (5 June 1971): 544–47; J. Derek Holmes, "Some Notes on Liberal Catholicism and Catholic Modernism," *Irish Theological Quarterly* 38 (1971): 348–57; Mary Jo Weaver, "Wilfrid Ward, George Tyrrell and the Meanings of Modernism," *Downside Review* 96 (January 1978): 21–34; Loome, *Liberal Catholicism, Reform Catholicism, Modernism*, Tübinger theologische Studien, vol. 14 (Mainz: Matthias-Grünewald-Verlag, 1979), pp. 23–196; and Darrell Jodock, "A Response to Thomas Loome's *Liberal Catholicism, Reform Catholicism, Modernism*," in *Current Research in Roman Catholic Modernism*, ed. Ronald Burke and George Gilmore (Mobile: Spring Hill College Press, 1980), pp. 9–16.

2. Pope John XXIII, however, as Padre Angelo Roncalli, professor of patrology in 1924 at the Pontificio Ateneo

362

Lateranense (now the Lateran University), was no stranger to the modernist controversy. In fact, he was relieved of his post at the Lateran, after only one term, on suspicion—he believed—of modernism. Meriol Trevor tells the story from an eyewitness, that shortly after Roncalli became pope in 1958, he went to the offices of a certain congregation to find out why in his early years a routine promotion had been so long delayed. There in his personal file he found against his name the damning words: "suspected of Modernism." At once he seized a pen and with a flourish wrote on the file: "I, John XXIII, pope, say that I was *never* a Modernist!" Meriol Trevor, *Pope John* (New York: Macmillan, 1967), p. 132 n.

3. Friedrich von Hügel (hereafter FvH) to Maude Dominica Petre (hereafter MDP), 13 March 1918, in FvH, *Selected Letters, 1896-1924,* ed. Bernard Holland (London: J. M. Dent & Sons, 1927), p. 248.

CHAPTER 1

1. See, for example, MDP, *My Way of Faith* (London: J. M. Dent & Sons, 1937), p. 292; Ronald Chapman, "The Thought of George Tyrrell," in *Essays and Poems Presented to Lord David Cecil,* ed. W. W. Robson (London: Constable, 1970), pp. 142-43; FvH, *Selected Letters,* p. 334.

2. Here I am in complete agreement with Ronald Chapman's observation that the key to GT's thought is the man. GT's writings were exceptionally personal, so much so that if one does not grasp GT's personality as it interacted with his peculiar circumstances, one will almost certainly misread him. See Chapman, "Thought of George Tyrrell," p. 140.

3. Quoted in MDP, *Autobiography and Life of George Tyrrell* (hereafter *AL*), 2 vols. (London: Edward Arnold, 1912), 1: 94; see also Anne Louis-David's note in GT, *Lettres de George Tyrrell à Henri Bremond,* trans. and ed. Anne Louis-David (Paris: Aubier Montaigne, 1971), p. 26, n. 1; and *AL,* 1: 2.

4. Gabriel Daly, "Some Reflections on the Character of George Tyrrell," *Heythrop Journal* 10 (July 1969): 258.

5. GT cautioned the reader of his autobiography with this observation about the relationship between his mother and father: "Perhaps my mother did not understand him, or . . . she unconsciously irritated him, and . . . my impressions deriving mostly through her, are less than quite just." *AL,* 1: 9.

6. Ibid.

7. Chapman's observation in "Thought of George Tyrrell," p. 166, is to the point: "Examined as a whole Tyrrell's thought is seen, for all its critical negations, to be a search for security, to be ultimately in the interests of conservatism."

8. *AL,* 1: 10.

9. *AL,* 1: 12, 16.

10. Specifying the religion of GT's birth is something of a problem in that his father was High Church Anglican while his mother was Evangelical. But since his mother was the dominant influence in his early years, it seems sensible to name Evangelicalism as GT's earliest religion.

11. *AL,* 1: 17-18.

12. *AL,* 1: 20.

13. *AL,* 1: 25.

14. *AL,* 1: 43.

15. Ibid.

16. *AL,* 1: 53-55.

17. *AL,* 1: 59.

18. *AL,* 1: 58-59.

19. *AL,* 1: 60.

20. *AL,* 1: 92-93.

21. *AL,* 1: 92.

22. *AL,* 1: 68.

23. *AL*, 1: 55, 79.
24. *AL*, 1: 79–80.
25. Joseph Butler, *The Analogy of Religion, Natural and Revealed, to the Constitution and Course of Nature* (London: John and Paul Knapton, 1736). On GT's assessment of his early reading of Butler's *Analogy*, see GT, *Medievalism: A Reply to Cardinal Mercier* (London: Longmans, Green & Co., 1908), p. 99; and Raoul Goût, *L'Affaire Tyrrell: Un Épisode de la crise catholique* (Paris: Émile Nourry, 1909), pp. 10–11, where Goût quotes a letter to himself from GT.
26. *AL*, 1: 94.
27. *AL*, 1: 97, 98.
28. *AL*, 1: 111–12. *Foris Te quaerebam et intus eras*: "I was seeking you without, but you were within," my translation. All translations given in the notes and text are mine unless otherwise identified. GT loved to quote Augustine. This particular sentence seems to be a variation on Augustine's famous saying, *Sero te amavi, pulchritudo tam antiqua et tam nova, sero te amavi! et ecce intus eras et ego foris, et ibi te quaerebam*: "Too late have I loved you, O Beauty ever ancient, ever new, too late have I loved you! And behold you were within and I without, and there I was seeking you." *Confessions*, bk. 10, chap. 27.
29. *AL*, 1: 104.
30. *AL*, 1: 116.
31. *AL*, 1: 119.
32. *AL*, 1: 122. *Quoniam in me . . .* : "Because he has hoped in me, I will deliver him; I will protect him because he knows my name; he will call to me, and I will hear him; when he is in distress, I will be with him, I will rescue him, and I will glorify him." Ps. 91: 14–15.
33. *AL*, 1: 129–30.
34. *AL*, 1: 128–29. *Nova et Vetera* (London: Longmans, Green & Co., 1897) was GT's most popular devotional work. *Benignitas et humani-*

tas Dei Salvatoris nostri (from the Vulgate version of Titus 3:4): "the graciousness and human-heartedness of God our Savior."
35. *AL*, 1: 132.
36. *AL*, 1: 139. *Per fas et nefas*: "by fair means and foul."
37. See *AL*, 1: 140.
38. *AL*, 1: 141–42, 229, 149. GT was not quite so derelict in his duty as he leads one to believe. Shortly after he entered the Society of Jesus in September 1880, his mother and sister moved in with Uncle Arthur Chamney in London to be near GT. His mother was at this time suffering from cancer of the breast. In 1881 she quietly converted to Roman Catholicism and soon thereafter moved with Louy to Bonn to allow the latter to perfect her German. But as the cancer progressed and the end approached, she determined to return to Dublin and Miss Lynch. She got only as far as London. Fr. Edward Purbrick, GT's provincial superior, told GT to spare no expense in obtaining help and comfort for his mother. Before he could act, however, she lapsed into a coma and died on 14 May 1884. That same year Louy converted to Roman Catholicism, then returned to Bonn where she married a certain Herr Thoenes, a widower with a young son. In 1893 her husband died and left her in dire circumstances. She herself was not well, and the question arose whether GT ought to leave the Jesuits to support his sister. But they wished to keep him, so they agreed to support Louy with a lifelong annuity. That arrangement did not last long, however, as Louy died on 13 July 1897 at the Convent of St. Augustine. See *AL*, 1: 278–80.
39. *AL*, 1: 152–54.
40. *AL*, 1: 155, 139.
41. *AL*, 1: 133.
42. *AL*, 1: 158.
43. *AL*, 1: 189.

44. *AL*, 1: 176, 191.
45. See GT's explanation, *AL*, 1: 202.
46. *AL*, 1: 204, 212.
47. *AL*, 1: 218.
48. *AL*, 1: 226–27.
49. *AL*, 1: 224–26.
50. *AL*, 1: 233.
51. "Father M" was doubtless Fr. Thomas Rigby (1842–1912). Identification was facilitated by an excerpt from *The Printed Catalogues of the English Province of the Society of Jesus*, kindly supplied by Fr. Francis Edwards, S.J., archivist of the English Province.
52. See pp. 30–31, 37–38 below.
53. *AL*, 1: 249, 273.
54. "I think, however, at the end of the year I had the repute of being one of the better men in the logic and ontology class." MDP added, "His reputation, I am told, stood much higher than he was aware—too high, indeed, for him even to excite any jealousy." *AL*, 1: 251.
55. *AL*, 1: 250.
56. The identity of "Father T" is less certain than that of "Father M" above, but he was probably Fr. Joseph Rickaby, a known friend of GT. See *AL*, 2: 59.
57. *AL*, 1: 278.

CHAPTER 2

1. *AL*, 1: 243. For a helpful history of neo-scholasticism, see Gerald A. McCool, *Catholic Theology in the Nineteenth Century* (New York: Seabury Press, 1977).
2. Leo XIII, "Litterae Apostolicae 'Gravissime Nos,' quibus Constitutiones Societatis Jesu de doctrina S. Thomae Aquinatis profitenda confirmantur," *Allocutiones, epistolae, constitutiones, alique acta praecipua*, 7 vols. (Bruges: Desclée, de Brouwer & Co., 1887–1906), 5: 133–43. For GT's reaction to this episode, see *AL*, 1: 244. His placement of Leo XIII's letter in "1895 (1894?)" is of course mistaken.

3. See chap. 1, n. 51.
4. GT to A. L. Lilley, 23 June 1903, Lilley Papers (hereafter LP), St. Andrews University Library (hereafter SAUL), Scotland, MS 30765. GT's letters in this collection number 118 and cover the period 14 June 1903 to 21 June 1909. Lilley, vicar of St. Mary's, Paddington and a foremost figure of Anglican modernism, corresponded with numerous Roman Catholic and Anglican modernists. See pp. 320–21 below and chap. 7, n. 174; and Alec R. Vidler, *A Variety of Catholic Modernists* (Cambridge: At the University Press, 1970), pp. 126–33.
5. *AL*, 1: 251.
6. In a letter of 26 May 1906 to Raoul Goût, GT recalled the "profound revolution" in his thinking effected by his reading of Newman, a point to be considered in chap. 3, esp. pp. 73–74. The fate of the original letter is unknown, but it is published in *AL*, 2: 209–10. Goût translated into French GT's "great letter" of 11 June 1904 to Luis Martin, superior general of the Society of Jesus, and included it as an appendix to his *L'Affaire Tyrrell*. See also *AL*, 2: 485–99.
7. See *AL*, 1: 248.
8. On 13 August 1901 GT wrote to MDP, "I have just recovered all my errrant MSS. in defence of scholasticism that have been circulating at S. Beuno's since my student days. Now for a bon-fire!" Petre Papers (hereafter PP), British Library (hereafter BL), London, Add. MSS 52367, published in part in *AL*, 2: 46.
9. [GT], "Aquinas Resuscitatus," *American Catholic Quarterly Review* 16 (October 1891): 673–90. On 3 December 1891 GT wrote to Herbert Thurston: "I was ineffably surprised to hear of the appearance of my miserable essay in the *Catholic American Quarterly* [*sic*]. Fr. Clarke told me many months ago that he was going to offer it to them; but as

I had heard nothing more about it, I concluded that he had forgotten as usual, and I was too disgusted to make any further enquiries about it. I think I might at least have had the privilege of correcting the proofs myself, and of receiving a copy of the periodical in question; for there ought to be a limit to freedom, even in America." Published in Joseph H. Crehan, S.J., "More Tyrrell Letters—I," *Month*, n.s. 40 (October 1968): 181.

10. See GT to Thurston, 3 December 1891, published in Crehan, "More Tyrrell Letters—I," p. 181. For a useful, if unobjective, appraisal of the Tyrrell-Thurston relationship, see Joseph H. Crehan, S.J., *Father Thurston* (London: Sheed & Ward, 1952); Crehan, "More Tyrrell Letters—I"; and Crehan, "Tyrrell in His Workshop," *Month*, 2d n.s. 3 (April 1971): 111-15, 119.

11. [GT], "Cramming and Other Causes of Mental Dyspepsia," *Month* 67 (November 1889): 410-19.

12. Ibid., pp. 412, 417.

13. Ibid., p. 416.

14. GT, "A Symposium on Immortality," *Month* 56 (February 1886): 195-205, a review of *Immortality: A Clerical Symposium*.

15. Ibid., p. 200. For a fine exposition of GT's thought on the knowledge of God, see Joseph W. Goetz, "Analogy and Symbol: A Study in the Theology of George Tyrrell" (Ph.D. diss., King's College, Cambridge University, 1969).

16. GT, "The Contents of a Pre-Adamite Skull," *Month* 67 (September 1889): 56-73; "Among the Korahites," *Month* 72 (May 1891): 81-93; "A Long-Expected Visitor," *Month* 74 (January 1892): 61-70; "A Lesson from the Skies, on Universal Benevolence," *Month* 76 (November 1892): 387-97.

17. GT took up the study of German seriously in 1901 at the urging of Baron Friedrich von Hügel. Within a year he was able to read difficult scholarly works.

18. GT to Thurston, undated, but from internal evidence, Crehan places it at 16 April 1892. Published in Crehan, "More Tyrrell Letters—I," pp. 183-84.

19. "Prussic acid," a common name of hydrocyanic acid, is intensely poisonous but a painless way to die. The letter from GT to Thurston is undated, but Crehan places it at September or October 1891. Ibid., p. 179.

20. GT to Thurston, 15 November 1891, published in ibid., pp. 180-81.

21. *AL*, 2: 40.

22. *AL*, 2: 41-42. MDP does not reveal the source of this statement.

23. Crehan, "Tyrrell in His Workshop," p. 114. Crehan conjectures that the source of MDP's story was Joseph Thorp, one of GT's students, who left the Jesuits in 1901, as Crehan said, "largely owing to his sympathy with Tyrrell." See Joseph Peter Thorp, *Friends and Adventures* (London: Jonathan Cape, 1931), p. 37. Fr. Charles Coupe and Fr. Bernard Boedder were the other two professors at Stonyhurst. GT was at odds particularly with Boedder. Crehan reports that "in some of the encounters Fr. Boedder told Tyrrell plainly that his views if taken to their logical conclusion would end in agnosticism." Crehan, "Tyrrell in His Workshop," p. 114.

24. *AL*, 2: 42.

25. *AL*, 1: 275. GT's reminiscences must be read critically, because he tended to telescope the development of his positions and reflect later ones into earlier ones. "Cramming and Other Causes of Mental Dyspepsia," for example, does not hint of hostility toward Thomistic psychology and cosmology.

26. GT always held the place of authority in religion very high. He criticized only its abuse, as will be seen in subsequent chapters.

27. Reported in *AL*, 2: 42, but MDP did not give Mazzella's addressee. One presumes that he replied to GT, but he might also have written to Jesuit and/or ecclesiastical officials in Rome and/or England.

28. Ibid.

29. [GT], "The 'Tabula Aurea' of Peter de Bergamo," *Blandyke Papers* 68 (February 1896), published for the first time in *Heythrop Journal* 10 (July 1969): 275–79.

30. [GT], "The Hypostatic Union," *Month* 85 (December 1895): 588–90, a review of *S. Thomae Aquinatis . . . doctrina sincera de unione hypostatica Verbi Dei cum humilitate amplissime declarata* by J. B. Terrien, S.J. Loome, *Liberal Catholicism, Reform Catholicism, Modernism*, p. 220, attributes this unsigned review to GT on the basis of a letter to Thurston in which GT asks to review Terrien's book for the *Month*. The letter is published in Crehan, "Tyrrell in His Workshop," p. 111. It is undated, but Crehan places it in the summer of 1895.

31. GT to Thurston, summer 1895, published in Crehan, "Tyrrell in His Workshop," p. 111.

32. GT, "Mr. Balfour and the Foundations of Belief," *Month* 83 (April 1895): 457–72; 84 (May 1895): 16–32, a review of *The Foundations of Belief* by Arthur James Balfour.

33. T. H. Huxley was incensed at Balfour's book because he thought it completely misrepresented his views. See Maisie Ward, *The Wilfrid Wards and the Transition*, 2 vols. (London: Sheed & Ward, 1934), 1: 352.

34. See chap. 6.

35. GT, "Mr. Balfour," pt. 2, p. 27. GT was here doubtless following Newman (see Newman's *Grammar of Assent*, chap. 9, par. 3) and anticipating Michael Polanyi, "Faith and Reason," *Journal of Religion* 41 (1961): 237–47; and Polanyi, *Personal Knowledge: Toward a Post-*

36. Thomas Aquinas, *Summa contra gentiles*, 1. cc. 4, 5.

37. GT, "Mr. Balfour," pt. 2, p. 20.

38. Denzinger-Schönmetzer, *Enchiridion Symbolorum*, 3004, 3026.

39. GT, "The New Sociology," *Month* 84 (August 1895): 502–22, a review of *Social Evolution* by Benjamin Kidd.

40. See, e.g., GT, *Christianity at the Cross-Roads* (hereafter *CCR*) (London: Longmans, Green & Co., 1909), pp. 39–45. *CCR* was published posthumously.

41. GT, "New Sociology," p. 518.

42. Ibid., p. 522.

43. GT, "An Apostle of Naturalism," *Month* 85 (October, November 1895): 215–28, 358–73, a review of *Modern Science and Modern Thought, Problems of the Future and Other Essays*, and *Human Origins* by Samuel Laing, reprinted in GT, *The Faith of the Millions* (hereafter *FM*), 2 vols. (London: Longmans, Green & Co., 1901).

44. *FM*, 2: 158, 160, 212.

45. *FM*, 2: 212–13.

46. *FM*, 2: 214.

47. GT to André Raffalovich, 24 August 1904, Raffalovich Papers, Blackfriars Library, Oxford. On Raffalovich and his relation to GT, see Louis-David's note in GT, *Lettres de Tyrrell à Bremond*, p. 159, n. 2.

48. GT to Abbé Ernest Dimnet, published without date in *AL*, 2: 164–65. The fate of the original letter is unknown.

49. GT, *Nova et Vetera* (London: Longmans, Green & Co., 1897); *Hard Sayings* (hereafter *HS*) (London: Longmans, Green & Co., 1898).

50. GT, "A Change of Tactics," *Month* 86 (February 1896): 215–27, reprinted as "A More Excellent Way" in *FM*, 1: 1–21. MDP regarded this essay as "one of the noblest presentments of his abiding ideal of the Catholic Church." *AL*, 2: 50.

Critical Philosophy (New York: Harper Torchbook, 1964).

51. Wilfrid Ward, "The Rigidity of Rome," *Nineteenth Century* 38 (November 1895): 786–804. On 14 April 1895 Leo XIII addressed a letter to the English people, *Ad Anglos regnum Christi in fidei unitate quaerentes*, in which he professed benevolence toward the Anglicans and exhorted all sides to end hostilities and work toward union with Rome. The Anglican press attacked the chauvinism of the letter. See Augustus Jessop, "The Celestial Empire of the West," *Nineteenth Century* 37 (June 1895): 961–67. Ward's article was a response to Jessop.

52. *FM*, 1: 4, 6. GT's chauvinistic tone is typical of Catholic writers of this age from the pope on down. See, e.g., Sydney Smith, S.J., "Leo XIII's Letter to the English People," *Month* 84 (May 1895): 5–6.

53. *FM*, 1: 9.

54. GT's emphasis here is prophetic of several of the decrees of Vatican II. See John Oliver Nelson, "A Response," in *The Documents of Vatican II*, ed. Walter M. Abbott, S.J. (New York: America Press, 1966), p. 577.

55. *FM*, 1: 11, 12. GT's essay, "The Clergy and the Social Problem," *American Catholic Quarterly Review* 22 (January 1897): 151–59, was composed while he was still at Stonyhurst and addressed the question of church-state relations. On the involvement of clergy in social issues, GT argued that the priest has a universal ministry extending beyond individuals to all people collectively, to society, and to the state. Like Christ, the priest must concern himself with the welfare of all peoples and use his influence against any unethical solutions proposed by the state. As the priest has always had his part in politics, *a fortiori* he is bound to interest himself in social questions. GT accused Protestantism of causing the separation of church and state.

56. *FM*, 1: 15.

57. *FM*, 1: 16–17. GT undoubtedly had in mind English Catholics as the "rationalistic and unimaginative people" who disparage mysticism. It would not be too farfetched to assume that the fathers at St. Beuno's felt themselves fingered by GT's criticism, as his complaints about the mechanical forms of meditation taught in the noviceship were well known. In a later article, "The True and the False Mysticism," *American Ecclesiastical Review* 21 (October 1899): 389–403, reprinted in *FM*, 1: 273–98, he wrote: "Perhaps one of the strangest misapprehensions is that which identifies 'mysticism' with that 'subjectivism' in religion which is distinctive of the Protestant spirit. It is commonly assumed by Protestants that the mediatorial principle of Catholicism is asserted not only in the definition of dogmatic truths by public authority to which private judgment must submit; . . . not only in the communication of certain special and super-abundant graces through sacramental channels; not only in making communion with the Church to be a condition of union with God, as one member of a Body, through the intercession of Christ and the saints; but also in that mediation is pressed to such an extent as to forbid the soul either to speak to God directly in prayer or to receive from God, and through conscience, any light or direction which it may obey without sanction of the Church. Hence, in every mystic of the Middle Age they at once hail a harbinger of Luther. So superficial a travesty were scarce worth mention, were it not that some Protestants have so persistently claimed mysticism as their own, that they have bred a distrust of it in less well-informed Catholics." *FM*, 1: 280–81.

58. *FM*, 1: 20.
59. GT to Thurston, 7 August 1896, published in Crehan, "Tyrrell in His Workshop," pp. 114-15.
60. GT, "A Perverted Devotion," *Weekly Register* 100 (16 December 1899): 797-800, reprinted in GT, *Essays on Faith and Immortality* (hereafter *EFI*) (London: Edward Arnold, 1914), pp. 158-71.
61. GT to Bremond, 18 January 1900, Fonds Bremond, Bibliothèque nationale, Paris, Nouvelles acquisitions françaises (hereafter FB, BN, NAF). GT was, of course, referring facetiously to Ward's article, "Rigidity of Rome." GT's letters to Bremond, originally in the care of Père André Blanchet, S.J., were left at his death in the care of Aubier Montaigne Press, Paris, which deposited them in the Bibliothèque nationale. As the letters have not yet been foliated or assigned an acquisition number, they will be cited by date only. They have been published in French in GT, *Lettres de Tyrrell à Bremond*.
62. Ward, "Rigidity of Rome," p. 793.
63. Five years after Leo XIII's letter to the English people, Roman officials apparently thought that the waging of peace had gone too far and issued a new order. GT discussed it in a letter to FvH of 10 March 1900, PP, BL, Add. MSS 44927.106: "The facts, so far, are these. First a letter from our General retailing complaints against *all* our English S.J. writers as 'too anxious to conciliate the enemies of religion' and as not 'speaking strongly & boldly enough in condemnation of heretics & unbelievers'; exhorting them to remember the best traditions of the SJ and walk worthy of the vocation wherewith they are called. That is, of course, an order to emulate the violent & mendacious tone of the Civiltà. Second: a letter telling me not to write any more except for the *Month*, until my article on Hell had been examined & censured."

GT's article on Hell was "A Perverted Devotion." "Civiltà" refers to *La Civiltà Cattolica*, the Jesuit-edited periodical that proposed always and in all matters to reflect the thinking of the Holy See.

CHAPTER 3

1. See pp. 43-47 above.
2. See GT to Abbé Ernest Dimnet, published without date in *AL*, 2: 164-65. Dimnet had summarized and reviewed GT's *FM* in "Une Meilleure voie," *Revue du clergé français* 31 (1, 15 June, 1 July 1902): 5-23, 129-49, 35-72, so the letter would have followed shortly thereafter. Dimnet's article was reprinted in *La Pensée catholique dans l'Angleterre contemporaine* (Paris: V. Lecoffre, 1906), which was placed on the Index almost as soon as it appeared. See Louis-David's note in GT, *Lettres de Tyrrell à Bremond*, p. 128, n. 3.
3. GT to MDP, 11 July 1901, PP, BL, Add. MSS 52367, published in part in *AL*, 2: 163.
4. GT, "A Life of de Lamennais," *Month* 89 (January 1897): 19-27, a review of the *Abbé de Lamennais and the Liberal Catholic Movement in France* by William Gibson, reprinted in *FM*, 2: 80-95.
5. *FM*, 2: 82.
6. *FM*, 2: 86.
7. *FM*, 2: 94-95.
8. "Digamma" [GT], "Keeping up Appearances," *Month* 89 (February 1897): 132-41 (see *AL*, 2: 60); GT, "Socialism and Catholicism," *Month* 89 (March 1897): 280-88, a review of *Socialism and Catholicism* by Edward Soderini; GT, "Round *versus* Russell," *Month* 89 (April 1897): 358-70.
9. GT, "The Prospects of Reunion," *Month* 90 (July 1897): 1-15, reprinted in *FM*, 1: 40-67.
10. On 7 September 1909, two months

after GT's death, FvH wrote to Canon George Newsom in reply to a request for help on a memorial article on GT: "Among all his published Papers, there is nothing to which he himself (in numerous confidential conversations) attached greater importance than 'Theology and Devotion' . . . and 'From God or from Men?' . . . To these two papers I would, myself, add: 'The Prospect[s] of Reunion' . . . as containing the very soul of what, later on, he developed sometimes with vehemence and indeed some bitterness. I love these three Papers through and through." Published in FvH, *Selected Letters*, p. 166. Newsom's memorial appeared as "George Tyrrell," *Church Quarterly Review* 69 (October 1909): 114–45. George Ernest Newsom (1871–1934), a friend of GT in his later years, was then professor of pastoral theology, King's College, London. For more on Newsom, GT, and FvH, see Thomas Michael Loome, "'Revelation as Experience': An Unpublished Lecture of George Tyrrell," *Heythrop Journal* 12 (April 1971): 120–23.

11. FvH to GT, 19 October 1897, PP, BL, Add. MSS 44927.5–6, published in MDP, *Von Hügel and Tyrrell* (hereafter *vH&T*) (London, J. M. Dent & Sons, 1937), p. 13.

12. FvH to GT, 20 September 1897, PP, BL, Add. MSS 44927.1–2, published in *vH&T*, pp. 10–11.

13. Diary of FvH, 9 October 1897, Hügel Papers (hereafter HP), SAUL.

14. Loome, *Liberal Catholicism, Reform Catholicism, Modernism*, pp. 144–62.

15. Ibid., p. 151.

16. FvH to H. I. D. Ryder, 18 August 1890, Oratory Archives, Birmingham, England, VC 20, quoted in Lawrence F. Barmann, *Baron Friedrich von Hügel and the Modernist Crisis in England* (Cambridge: At the University Press, 1972), p. 5.

17. FvH to J. H. Newman, 13 De-

cember 1874, quoted in Barmann, *Von Hügel*, pp. 5–6.

18. See FvH's *mémoire* of Charles de Smedt sent as a letter to Père Hippolyte Delehaye, S.J., 15 September 1920, published in Loome, *Liberal Catholicism, Reform Catholicism, Modernism*, pp. 436–40.

19. Diary of FvH, 27 and 30 October 1897, HP, SAUL.

20. GT, "Wiseman: His Aims and Methods," *Month* 91 (February 1898): 142–50, a review of *The Life and Times of Cardinal Wiseman* by Wilfrid P. Ward, reprinted in *FM*, 1: 22–39.

21. Ward's epilogue is chapter 31, "The Exclusive Church and the Zeitgeist," in Wilfrid P. Ward, *The Life and Times of Cardinal Wiseman*, 2 vols. (London: Longmans, Green & Co., 1897), 2: 533–83.

22. *FM*, 1: 27.

23. *FM*, 1: 30.

24. The phrase "wish to believe" appears occasionally in GT's writings. It is taken from Wilfrid Ward's essay by that title in his *Witnesses to the Unseen and Other Essays* (London: Macmillan & Co., 1893), pp. 156–309, which GT reviewed in *Month* 81 (June 1894): 222–33. By "wish to believe" Ward (and GT) meant not a flabby disposition to believe whatever is thrown up but a critical disposition, free from bias and prejudice, that will allow an objective discernment between what is to be held *per se* and what *per accidens* in Catholic belief and practice; between what is to be ascribed to Catholics as such and what to local, national, or individual circumstances; between what is due to the use and what to the abuse of principles and laws.

25. *FM*, 1: 37.

26. See GT, "The Oxford School and Modern Religious Thought," *Month* 79 (December 1893): 560–68; 80 (January 1894): 59–68, a review of *William George Ward and the Oxford*

Movement and *William George Ward and the Catholic Revival* by Wilfrid P. Ward; see also GT, "Witnesses to the Unseen: The Wish to Believe," *Month* 81 (June 1894): 222–33, a review of *Witnesses to the Unseen and Other Essays* by Wilfrid P. Ward. A cache of sixty-two letters and six cards from GT to Ward dating from 12 December 1893 to 20 May 1909, along with GT's unpublished MS, "Who Are the Reactionaries?" was recently discovered by Mary Jo Weaver. Weaver kindly allowed me access to them before publication as *Letters from a "Modernist,"* ed. Mary Jo Weaver (Shepherdstown, W. Va.: Patmos Press, 1981). They are preserved among the Ward Family Papers (hereafter WFP), SAUL, MS deposit 21, VII.294. Hereafter citations to these letters will include reference to *Letters from a "Modernist"* only if there is a question about the date. In January 1910 Ward made copies of a small portion of the letters and sent them to Lord Halifax. These are preserved among the Hickleton Papers, part of the Halifax Papers, 1861–1933 of Charles Lindley Wood, second Viscount Halifax, in the Borthwick Institute of Historical Research attached to the University of York.

27. GT to Ward, 22 September 1898, WFP, SAUL, published in *AL,* 2: 99. MDP supplies a footnote indicating that the epilogue referred to in this letter is to be found in *W. G. Ward and the Oxford Movement.* The date and context of the letter, however, indicate that the epilogue is that of *Cardinal Wiseman.*

28. Ward, "New Wine in Old Bottles," in *Witnesses to the Unseen,* p. 81. See also Maisie Ward, *The Wilfrid Wards and the Transition,* 1: 183.

29. GT, "'Liberal' Catholicism," *Month* 91 (May 1898): 449–57, reprinted in *FM,* 1: 68–84.

30. *FM,* 1: 80. Cf. Ward, *Witnesses to the Unseen,* pp. 81–84.

31. *FM,* 1: 82. What GT meant by this he drew out in a later ironical article, "Tracts for the Million." See pp. 133–36 below.

32. GT, "Sabatier on the Vitality of Dogmas," *Month* 91 (June 1898): 592–602, a review of *The Vitality of Christian Dogmas and Their Power of Evolution* by Auguste Sabatier, reprinted in *FM,* 1: 115–35.

33. *FM,* 1: 130.

34. *FM,* 1: 131.

35. *FM,* 1: 132.

36. GT, "The Church and Scholasticism," *American Catholic Quarterly Review* 23 (July 1898): 550–61, reprinted as "The Use of Scholasticism" in *FM,* 1: 205–27.

37. *FM,* 1: 227.

38. GT to FvH, 3 July 1898, PP, BL, Add. MSS 44927.35.

39. GT, "Rationalism in Religion," *Month* 93 (January 1899): 1–16, reprinted in *FM,* 1: 85–114.

40. *FM,* 1: 91.

41. *FM,* 1: 95–96; J. H. Newman, "On the Introduction of Rationalistic Principles into Religion," in *Essays, Critical and Historical,* 2 vols. (London: Longmans, Green & Co., 1919), 1: 47, italics GT's. Later GT would depart substantially from this restriction of revelation.

42. *FM,* 1: 111–12.

43. See chap. 6 below, esp. pp. 216–45.

44. GT, "Authority and Evolution: The Life of Catholic Dogma," *Month* 93 (May 1899): 493–504, a review of *La Vie du dogme catholique: autorité, évolution* by André de la Barre, S.J., reprinted in *FM,* 1: 136–57. De la Barre elaborated a view of doctrinal evolution similar to one GT had forwarded in "Ecclesiastical Development," *Month* 90 (October 1897): 380–90, which was not republished in *FM,* probably because of its virulently anti-Protestant and orthodox tone.

45. *FM,* 1: 143.

46. GT, *External Religion: Its Use and Abuse* (hereafter *ER*) (London: Sands & Co., 1899).
47. The influence of Maurice Blondel, a point to be pursued later (see pp. 74–85 above, and 195–99, 216–36 below), is evident already here and in "Authority and Evolution." See *FM*, 1: 157.
48. *ER*, pp. 31–32; all citations are to the 1906 ed. Passages like this prompted Henri Bremond to say that fully one-third of GT could be found in Matthew Arnold's *Literature and Dogma* (1873) (see pp. 189–90 below). It is quite certain that GT had been reading Arnold about the time he wrote *ER*, but exactly what he read is not certain. Despite his liking for Arnold, GT never identified God and man the way Arnold did, as the quoted passage shows.
49. *ER*, pp. 33, 34. Sebastian Moore, *The Crucified Jesus Is No Stranger* (New York: Seabury Press, 1977), based on Ernest Becker's anthropology and Carl Jung's model of the human person, draws out these themes in remarkably similar language.
50. *ER*, pp. 35–36.
51. *ER*, p. 49.
52. *ER*, pp. 86–87.
53. *ER*, p. 156.
54. *ER*, pp. 158–59. GT was here attacking the current theories of liberal Protestant theology, particularly those arising from the Hegelian branch of liberal Protestantism, according to which Christianity is justified by an *Aufhebung* into philosophy, rather than *vice versa*. GT's acquaintance with the neo-Hegelians came most likely through Edward Caird, *The Evolution of Religion*, and Benjamin Kidd (see pp. 40–41 above). Some of the ideas expressed throughout *ER*, but particularly in this final lecture, GT had discussed previously in *HS*; see the following chaps.: "The Hid-

den Life," "God in Conscience," "'Quid erit nobis?,'" "The Divine Precept," "Idealism: Its Use and Abuse," and "The Mystical Body." *ER* is in fact *HS* over again, but in more systematic dress and going beyond *HS* in its language and emphases, no doubt the result of GT's current reading of Blondel and Lucien Laberthonnière.
55. See Mary Alice Forbes, *Rafael Cardinal Merry del Val* (London: Longmans, Green & Co., 1932), p. 55.
56. Ibid., p. 95. Forbes does not identify the addressee. Gary Lease, "Merry del Val and Tyrrell's Condemnation," in *Proceedings of the Roman Catholic Modernism Working Group of the American Academy of Religion*, ed. Ronald Burke and George Gilmore (Mobile: Spring Hill College Duplicating Service, 1979), p. 17, identifies the recipient of this letter as Denis Sheil, who was Merry del Val's cousin, closest friend, and a priest of the Birmingham Oratory. Lease provides an enlightening discussion of the state of current research on Merry del Val.
57. *ER*, p. 96.
58. *ER*, p. 98.
59. *ER*, p. 99.
60. GT to MDP, 2 January 1901, PP, BL, Add. MSS 52367.
61. *FM*, 1: 80.
62. "Feeling" is a misleading translation for *Gefühl*, an idea that received currency in liberal Protestantism from Friedrich Schleiermacher. For him *Gefühl* is the response of some *tertium quid* "faculty" of the soul that is properly the religious "faculty" responsive to the direct action of God, just as knowledge is the response of the faculty of knowing and action is the response of the faculty of willing. But *Gefühl* underlies knowing and willing and is their base of integration. See Gerhard Spiegler, *The Eternal Covenant: Schleiermacher's Experiment*

in *Cultural Theology* (New York: Harper & Row, 1967).

63. See John J. McNeill, *The Blondellian Synthesis: A Study of the Influence of German Philosophical Sources on the Formation of Blondel's Method and Thought*, Studies in the History of Christian Thought, vol. 1 (Leiden: E. J. Brill, 1966).

64. See pp. 31–32 above and chap. 2, n. 6.

65. See p. 52 above; and Barmann, *Von Hügel*, pp. 5–8.

66. Léon Ollé-Laprune, *De la certitude morale* (Paris: E. Belin, 1880); Ollé-Laprune applied his understanding of true philosophy to apologetics in his *Ce qu'on va chercher à Rome* (Paris: A. Colin, 1895).

67. See Ferdinand Brunetière, *La Science et la religion*, rev. ed. (Paris: Perrin, 1916).

68. Lucien Laberthonnière, "Le Dogmatisme moral," *Annales de philosophie chrétienne* 38 (August–September 1898): 531–62; 39 (October–November 1898): 27–45, 146–71, reprinted in *Essais de philosophie religieuse* (Paris: P. Lethielleux, 1903), pp. 17–110.

69. Laberthonnière, *Essais*, p. 103; quoted in Édouard Lecanuet, *L'Église de France sous le troisième République*, 4 vols. (Paris: J. de Gigord, 1930), 4: 530–31.

70. Bremond's first three articles were combined into a volume titled *L'Inquiétude religieuse* (Paris: Perrin & Co., 1901). The other articles were "Les Sermons de Newman," *Études* 72 (5 August 1897): 343–68; "Newman," *Études* 93 (20 December 1902): 851–53; "Autour de Newman," *Annales de philosophie chrétienne*, 4th ser. 5 (January 1908): 337–69. Bremond's first three books on Newman were *Newman: La Vie chrétienne* (Paris: Bloud & Gay, 1902); *Newman: Le Développement du dogme chrétien* (Paris: Bloud & Gay, 1904); and *Newman: Psychologie de la foi* (Paris: Bloud &

Gay, 1905). These were translations or summaries of selections from Newman with introduction and commentary. His last book, *Newman: Essai de biographie psychologique* (Paris: Bloud & Gay, 1906), aroused much interest and comment and went through four editions within a year. It was translated into English by H. C. Corrance under the title *The Mystery of Newman* (London: Williams & Norgate, 1907); GT wrote the introduction. Wilfrid Ward gave it a scathing review: "Two Views of Cardinal Newman," *Dublin Review* 141 (July 1907): 1–15. See Henry Hogarth, *Henri Bremond* (London: SPCK, 1950), pp. 6–8.

71. The 287 extant pieces of mail that passed between them from 8 March 1897 to 25 September 1904 are collected in Bremond and Blondel, *Henri Bremond et Maurice Blondel: Correspondance*, ed. André Blanchet (Paris: Aubier Montaigne, 1970–71).

72. A glance at the periodical literature of the time is instructive on the centrality of Newman to the figures of the "modernist movement." See, e.g., "A. Firmin" [Alfred Loisy], "Le Développement chrétien d'après le cardinal Newman," *Revue du clergé français* 16 (1 December 1898): 5–20; Loisy's remark in his review of *Jean Adam Möhler . . . sur les origines germanique du modernisme* by M. Vermiel, *Revue d'histoire et de littérature religieuse* 18 (November–December 1913): 569–71, that Newman had replaced Ernest Renan on his list of favorite authors; Wilfrid Ward, "Newman and Sabatier," *Fortnightly Review*, n.s. 69 (1 January 1901): 808–22; quotation from Florimund Dubois, uncritical commentator on the emerging apologetic who mixed fact with hearsay, in B. D. Dupuy, "Newman's Influence in France," in *The Rediscovery of Newman: An Oxford Symposium*,

ed. John Coulson and A. M. Allchin (London: Sheed & Ward, 1967), p. 155. Newman was in fact so often invoked by "modernists" that there was danger of his being condemned along with the "modernists." Discussion on this possibility was aired largely in the *Times* (London) during November 1907. GT contributed "The Condemnation of Newman," *Guardian*, 20 November, 11 December 1907, pp. 1896–97, 2060 (see also GT's correction in *Guardian*, 27 November 1907, p. 1957); "Cardinal Newman and the Late Encyclical," *Times* (London), 2 December 1907, p. 8. GT's contention that Newman, too, had been condemned is supported by Anton Michelitsch, *Der biblisch-dogmatische "Syllabus" Pius' X . . . und dem Motu proprio vom November 1907*, 2d ed. (Graz: Styria, 1908), pp. 386–87. This commentary was approved by Cardinal Merry del Val, Pius X's secretary of state.

73. Maurice Blondel, *L'Action* (Paris: F. Alcan, 1893; reprint, Paris: Presses Universitaires de France, 1950). See Wilfrid Ward, "Liberalism and Intransigeance," *Nineteenth Century* 47 (June 1900): 972, where he remarked on the similarity of ideas and their relationship to GT.

74. Blondel thus combined into his category of "action" the three categories used by Schleiermacher to describe human psychology. Traditional psychology up to Schleiermacher operated with the two categories of knowing and willing. But trying to explain man's certitude about divine truths that cannot be demonstrated by reason on the basis of only two categories, which were more or less separate and distinct, albeit interacting, led to too many cul-de-sacs. Schleiermacher therefore posited a third "faculty," "feeling," as the specific "faculty" responsive to divine revelation. Cf. Friedrich Schleiermacher, *The Christian Faith*,

2 vols. (New York: Harper Torchbooks, 1963), 1: 8–9, as bearing a striking resemblance to Blondel's more refined explanation. Resemblances are not surprising when one realizes that both Blondel and Schleiermacher were responding to the same Spinoza-Kant-Fichte-Schelling-Hegel-Schelling line of discussion. References in Blondel's correspondence indicate that he had read Schleiermacher.

75. Blondel, *L'Action* (1950 ed.), pp. 470–80. Henri Bouillard, *Blondel and Christianity*, trans. James M. Somerville (Washington, D.C.: Corpus Books, 1969), pp. 174–93, claims that the term "Logic of action," invented by Blondel, was changed to "method of immanence" in his "Lettre sur les exigences . . . du problème religieux," *Annales de philosophie chrétienne* 131 (January 1896): 337–53, 467–82, 599–616; 132 (July 1896): 131–47, 255–67, 337–59, reprinted in *Premiers écrits* (Paris: Presses Universitaires de France, 1956), in English as *The Letter on Apologetics and History and Dogma*, trans. Alexander Dru and Illtyd Trethowan (New York: Holt, Rinehart, & Winston, 1964). The change was in response to a critical review by Leon Brunschvicg in *Revue de metaphysique de morale*, reprinted in *Études blondeliennes*, ed. Jacques Paliard, 3 vols. (Paris: PUF, 1951–54), 1: 5–95. Blondel subsequently dropped the term "method of immanence" as well because Catholic criticism too readily connected it and its author with the heresy of immanentism.

76. The similar function of GT's external and internal elements of religion should be noted.

77. Blondel was criticized for an anti-intellectualist tendency in his early writings. Consequently he sought in *La Pensée* (Paris: Alcan, 1934) and subsequent writings to modify his position and bring it more into line

with traditional Catholic philosophy. But he never departed in any essential way from the principles of *L'Action;* he merely made his words sound more scholastic—as GT had advised on more than one occasion that he should do if he wanted to gain a hearing among Catholics. See GT to FvH, 6 December 1897, 29 June, 31 December 1898 (this last letter misdated 1897 by MDP is out of proper sequence in the folios), PP, BL, Add. MSS 44927.10,32,12. Actually, for Blondel as for Schleiermacher, thought and action were never rival principles but were always to be taken together: action is not a blind drive, but always includes thought; and thought cannot attain its philosophical goals unless it is fed on action. Thus even toward the end of his life, when he reconsidered the rational proofs for God, Blondel asserted that these proofs are valid only on the basis of a prior affirmation of God out of one's experience as an active being.

78. See Maurice Blondel, *Le Problème de la philosophie catholique* (Paris: Bloud & Gay, 1932), p. 13.

79. Blondel, *Letter on Apologetics,* p. 127.

80. See Henri Dumery, *Blondel et la religion: Essai critique sur la Lettre de 1896* (Paris: Presses Universitaires de France, 1954), p. 4 n. In *Le Problème,* p. 19, Blondel explained that the "Letter on Apologetics" was "improvised month by month during the course of my first year's teaching at the Faculty, when I was in the grip of an emotion and a danger which threatened all my reasons for thinking and living." He added that the "Letter on Apologetics" "contains some ill-chosen expression. . . . To a prejudiced mind, it could easily give the impression, in spite of an intention which is plainly the very opposite, that in criticizing 'methods' I am tampering with 'dogmas,' and that in speaking of 'contemporary

requirements in apologetics,' I am actually ranging myself among the apologists (where it is entirely a question of methodology, and where I am seeking not to weaken but to fortify and vivify the methods which I criticize only in so far as they are found in isolation, so as to lead men's minds to the vital point on which the convergence, the organization and the efficacy of the proofs all depend." Translation from Dru and Trethowan, introduction to Blondel, *Letter on Apologetics,* p. 123. The "Letter on Apologetics" did give that impression to prejudiced minds, and that is why it was delated to Rome. But, Blondel explained, he appeared to "call in question not so much the true features [of scholasticism] as the caricature of it which alone my criticism envisaged." *Le Problème,* pp. 28–29, trans. Dru and Trethowan, ibid., p. 122.

81. See n. 75 above.

82. Gregory Baum, *Man Becoming: God in Secular Experience* (New York: Herder & Herder, 1970), pp. 1–36.

83. Following Blondel, the Belgian philosopher Joseph Maréchal developed "transcendental Thomism," which strongly influenced such theologians as Karl Rahner and Bernard Lonergan, who in turn profoundly affected contemporary apologetics, not least of all by their work at Vatican II. See Baum, *Man Becoming,* p. 27; and "The Pastoral Constitution on the Church in the Modern World," art. 2 in *The Documents of Vatican II,* ed. Walter M. Abbot (New York: America Press, 1966), pp. 213–14.

84. Laberthonnière, "Le Dogmatisme moral"; Laberthonnière, "Le Problème religieux," *Annales de philosophie chrétienne* 33 (February–March 1897): 497–511.

85. FvH to GT, 19 October 1897, PP, BL, Add. MSS 44927.5–6, published in *vH&T,* pp. 13–14.

86. Diary of FvH, 27 October 1897, HP,
SAUL. FvH's daughter Gertrud, now
twenty years of age, was undergoing
a religious crisis occasioned in great
part by the free way in which her
father shared with her his vast learning, questioning, and perplexities
about the immediate future of the
church. Gertrud's doctor prescribed
a six-month-long change of environment, by which he apparently meant
away from her father. She stayed
behind in England that winter, and
GT guided her back to health and
advised FvH to be more careful
with her in the future. See the exchange of letters dated 6 December
1897 (published in part in *AL*, 2: 45),
11, 16 January, 16 February, 22, 25
March 1898, PP, BL, Add. MSS
44927, published in part in *vH&T*,
pp. 15-28.

87. GT to FvH, 6 December 1897, PP,
BL, Add. MSS 44927.7-11, published
in part in *AL*, 2: 45, 90-91. The "little brochure" was almost certainly
the lengthy "Letter on Apologetics."
GT cited it (*FM*, 1: 259) as "helpful
to Catholic truth" in "What Is Mysticism?" *Month* 90 (December 1897):
601-11, a review of *Psychologie des
saints* by Henri Joly, reprinted in
FM 1: 253-72.

88. GT to FvH, 6 December 1897, PP,
BL, Add. MSS 44927.10, published
in part in *AL*, 2: 90-91. *Piis auribus
offensiva*: "offensive to pious ears."

89. Ibid.

90. FvH to GT, 26 January 1898, PP,
BL, Add. MSS 44927.16, published
in *vH&T*, p. 23.

91. The point made earlier about Newman's centrality is highlighted by
Blondel's comment in a letter of 16
June 1897 to Bremond: "If you
would like to see a kind of equivalent (if one can speak of such an
equivalence), a Germanic and Lu-
theran equivalent to Newman, I
would recommend the works of
Rudolf Eucken, professor at Jena."
Bremond and Blondel, *Correspondance*, 1: 48; see also pp. 123-24.

92. See GT to FvH, 11 January 1903,
PP, BL, Add. MSS 44928.65. Also
see Dru and Trethowan, introduction to Blondel, *Letter on Apologetics*, p. 56; and René Marlé, S.J., *Au
coeur de la crise moderniste* (Paris:
Aubier Montaigne, 1960), p. 18. On
Blondel and Eucken, see Maurice
Blondel and Auguste Valensin, *Correspondance, 1899-1947*, ed. Henri
de Lubac, 3 vols. (Paris: Aubier,
1957-65), 1: 40-41; 2: 100.

93. See pp. 199-202 below.

94. FvH to GT, 22 March 1898, PP, BL,
Add. MSS 44927.23.

95. Diary of FvH, 26 April to 20 May
1898, HP, SAUL, mentions the following works: J. G. Fichte, *Die Bestimmung des Menschen* (Berlin,
1800); Ernst Troeltsch, "Geschichte
und Metaphysik: Erwiderung auf
Kaftans Angriff gegen die Selbständigkeit der Religion," *Zeitschrift für
Theologie und Kirche* 8.1 (1898): 1-
69; Rudolf Eucken, *Die Lebensanschauungen der grossen Denker*
(Leipzig: Veit & Co., 1890): Hermann
Lotze, *Grundzüge der Religionsphilosophie*, 2d ed. (Leipzig: G. Hirzel,
1888-91).

96. Diary of FvH, 1 to 17 May 1898,
HP, SAUL. Subsequently FvH and
Eucken carried on an extensive correspondence. Eucken's letters to
FvH are among the HP, SAUL,
which also has a microfilm copy of
the small fraction of FvH's letters
to Eucken preserved at the University of Jena.

97. FvH to GT, 23 May 1898, PP, BL,
Add. MSS 44927.26; diary of FvH,
20 May 1898, HP, SAUL.

98. FvH to GT, 21 and 28 June 1898,
BL, PP, Add. MSS 44927.30,31; diary
of FvH, 20, 28 June 1898, HP, SAUL.

99. GT to FvH, 29 June 1898, PP, BL,
Add. MSS 44927.32. The date of this
letter was fixed by MDP, executrix
of these letters and of all of GT's
papers. GT dated the letter simply
"Weds." from Wimbledon.

100. An English version of FvH's "Historical Method and the Documents

of the Hexateuch" appeared in *Catholic University Bulletin* 4 (1898): 198-226. FvH did not attend the conference but had his Barnabite friend Giovanni Semeria read the paper for him. Semeria was a scripture scholar who early in his career attracted the notice of church authorities. GT first met him in Richmond in autumn 1901. To Bremond on 3 November 1901 GT wrote, "I have seen Semeria in the flesh. How wonderfully buoyant in the midst of the ruins he is creating!" FB, BN, NAF. For more on Semeria and FvH, see Barmann, *Von Hügel*, references listed in the index, esp. pp. 55-71.

101. Alfred Firmin Loisy, *Mémoires pour servir à l'histoire religieuse de notre temps*, 3 vols. (Paris: Émile Nourry, 1930-31), 2: 481, quoted in Michael de la Bedoyère, *The Life of Baron von Hügel* (London: J. M. Dent & Sons, 1951), p. 104. There is perhaps a note of contempt in Loisy's remark. If so, it would not have been there at the time of the congress. But when he composed his *Mémoires*, he was excommunicate, bitter, and not wholly objective in his recollections. On the congress, see also Loisy, *Choses passées* (Paris: Émile Nourry, 1913), pp. 210-11.

102. Bishop Eudoxe-Irénée Mignot to FvH, 3 September 1898, quoted in Bedoyère, *Baron von Hügel*, p. 104. On Mignot's role during the whole modernist crisis, see Barmann, *Von Hügel*, references listed in the index.

103. GT to FvH, 29 June 1898, PP, BL, Add. MSS 44927.32-34.

104. FvH to GT, 26 September 1898, PP, BL, Add. MSS 44927.39-42, published in FvH, *Selected Letters*, pp. 71-74. The similarity evident in this letter between the psychologies of FvH and Schleiermacher is not surprising in view of the fact that FvH was influenced by Hermann Lotze, a mentor of Eucken at Göttingen. Lotze followed Schleiermacher in emphasizing feeling over the intel-

lect as the faculty that apprehends the Good—for Lotze, a higher category, than the True, which the Good comprehends and exhausts. Rudolf Eucken, in *Rudolf Eucken: His Life, Work and Travels*, trans. Joseph McCabe (London: T. Fisher Unwin, 1921), p. 59, referred to Lotze as 'undoubtedly the most important thinker of those decades [1844-81]." For Eucken's admiring assessment of Schleiermacher, see his *The Problem of Human Life*, trans. Williston S. Hough and W. R. Boyce Gibson (London: T. Fisher Unwin, 1911), p. 509.

105. FvH to GT, 26 September 1898, PP, BL, Add. MSS 44927.41-42.

106. Ibid., fol. 42.

107. Ibid.

108. GT to FvH, 28 September 1898, PP, BL, Add. MSS 44927.45, published in *vH&T*, pp. 36-40, and in GT, *George Tyrrell's Letters* (hereafter *GTL*), ed. MDP (London: T. Fisher Unwin, 1920), pp. 44-47. The similarity of this passage to GT's psychology in *Religion as a Factor of Life* (hereafter *RFL*) (Exeter: William Pollard & Co. [1902]) is striking. See pp. 216-21 below.

109. GT to Bremond, 29 October 1898, from Wimbledon College, published in *GTL*, pp. 50-51. C. Kegan Paul was on friendly terms with people as different as GT and Cardinal Henry Edward Manning. In a letter to MDP of 18 August 1901, PP, BL, Add. MSS 52367, published in *AL*, 2: 52, GT reproached Kegan Paul for "a sort of intemperate reaction against his former gods who after all had their good points. C.K.P. suppressed this side before me; & I think is one of my deepest sympathisers. Indeed it was he drew me forth from darkness to light in some sense; being the first whose good opinion really encouraged me to believe that I had a chance of a hearing outside the narrow Catholic circle. But to others he simply rants

against modernism & glories in what ought to be our shame. I once, for 2 or 3 years had the fever in a mild form, so I can understand."

110. FvH to GT, 21 November 1898, PP, BL, Add. MSS 44927.60–63, published in FvH, *Selected Letters*, pp. 74–76. FvH mentioned also that he had been thinking of thanking a number of people in his preface but specially GT "for looking over the proofs, and putting this latter service in such a way, as, if necessary, to reassure any timid Catholics as to the substantial orthodoxy of what I say." Obviously GT's orthodoxy was not then notoriously in doubt, whereas FvH's was, at least in his own mind, as his letter to GT of 26 January 1898, PP, BL, Add. MSS 44927.18, published in *vH&T*, p. 24, shows. Ten years later the "little book" had grown to Hügelian proportions: *The Mystical Element of Religion as Studied in Saint Catherine of Genoa and Her Friends*, 2 vols. (London: J. M. Dent & Sons, 1908). GT never did write the introduction, doubtless because at the time of publication he was excommunicate, although he worked closely with FvH throughout the book's gestation. GT was not even mentioned in FvH's preface, but in the preface to the 2d ed. (1923) GT received acknowledgment: "Father Tyrrell has gone, who had been so generously helpful, especially as to the mystical states, as to Aquinas and as to the form of the whole book, for so many years, long before the storms beat upon him and his vehemence overclouded, in part, the force and completeness of that born mystic."

111. FvH to GT, 31 December 1898, PP, BL, Add. MSS 44927.64–69. See, e.g., *HS*, p. 2.

112. See diary of FvH, 23 December 1898, HP, SAUL. The title of Blondel's article was not given in the correspondence but was almost certainly "L'Illusion idéaliste," *Revue de metaphysique et de morale* 6 (November 1898): 726–46, reprinted in *Premiers écrits*, 2: 97–122. The following evidence supports this conclusion: (1) this was Blondel's only publcation that year; (2) FvH mentioned it in his diary for 17 January 1899; and (3) there is an obvious reference to this article in GT to Bremond, 11 January 1899, FB, BN, NAF.

113. GT to FvH, 31 December 1898, PP, BL, Add. MSS 44927.12–13, published in part in *vH&T*, pp. 55–56. On the dating of this letter, see n. 77 above.

114. GT to Bremond, 11 January 1899, FB, BN, NAF. GT's last remark could indicate a proclivity toward immanentism greater than FvH's. *Hominem non habeo:* "I do not grasp him." Typhoid fever at age eighteen left FvH nearly deaf.

115. FvH to GT, 4 December 1899, PP, BL, Add. MSS 44927.92–97. *Orate ut vigiletis:* "Pray, so that you can watch." Besides Blondel and Laberthonnière, the only authors of notable influence mentioned by GT in the two years prior to publishing *ER* were Matthew Arnold (see pp. 189–90 below) and William James. In a letter to MDP, undated, but probably from the summer of 1899, PP, BL, Add. MSS 52367, GT mentioned James's *The Will To Believe* (1897). That work among others puts James within the ambit of Blondellian sympathizers. James and Blondel knew and admired each other's thought; they corresponded, and Blondel, at least, lectured on James. See Frederick J. D. Scott, "William James and Maurice Blondel," *New Scholasticism* 32 (1958): 32–44; and Jacques Flamand, *L'Idée de mediation chez Maurice Blondel* (Louvain: Édition Nauwalaerts, 1969), p. 77. Avery Dulles, *A History of Apologetics* (New York: Corpus Books, 1971), pp. 203, 270, also notes a connection between James and Blondel and the "modernists."

116. According to present information Bremond's side of the correspondence is not extant.

117. MDP to Canon Alfred Leslie Lilley, quoted without date in MDP, *My Way of Faith*, p. 269.

118. See Hogarth, *Henri Bremond*, p. xiii. For a critical assessment of Bremond's part in the modernist crisis, see Roger Aubert, "Henri Bremond et la crise moderniste," *Revue d'histoire ecclésiastique* 72 (1977): 332-48.

119. MDP, *My Way of Faith*, p. 260.

120. GT to Bremond, 6 July 1898, FB, BN, NAF. Crehan, *Father Thurston*, p. 57, reports that "Bremond had been a friend of Tyrrell since his days at St. Beuno's, for Bremond was at the time studying theology with the French Jesuits in exile at Mold, and contacts were frequent between Mold and St. Beuno's." Unfortunately Crehan supplies no supporting documentation. At any rate, the content and tone of GT's "first letter" would seem to argue to a prior acquaintance, but not necessarily friendship.

121. See FvH to GT, 26 September 1898, PP, BL, Add. MSS 44927.39-42, published in FvH, *Selected Letters*, pp. 71-74; and diary of FvH, 8 February 1899, HP, SAUL.

122. GT to Bremond, 2 October 1898, FB, BN, NAF. Beatrice Portinari (1266-90) of Florence, believed to be "Beatrice" of the *Divine Comedy* and *Vita nuova*, was Dante's lifelong inspiration.

123. GT to FvH, 20 November 1899, PP, BL, Add. MSS 44927.90.

124. GT to Bremond, 29 October 1898, FB, BN, NAF. See Joannes Philippus Roothaan (1785-1853), *How to Meditate*, trans. Louis J. Puhl (Westminster, Md.: Newman Bookshop, 1945); and Antoine le Gaudier (1572-1622), *De perfectione vitae spiritualis*, 3 vols. (Paris: Julien, Lanier & Co., 1856-58).

125. GT to Bremond, 11 January 1899, FB, BN, NAF.

126. See pp. 136-37 below.

127. *AL*, 2: 78.

128. Diary of FvH, 2 May 1899, HP, SAUL.

129. GT to Bremond, 13 June 1899, FB, BN, NAF, brief excerpt published in *AL*, 2: 84.

130. GT to Bremond, 20 July 1899, FB, BN, NAF.

131. Ibid.

132. Ibid. *Frangar, non flectar:* "I will break rather than bend."

133. Ibid.

134. GT to Bremond, 22 December 1899, FB, BN, NAF.

135. GT, "The Relation of Theology to Devotion," *Month* 94 (November 1899): 461-73, reprinted in *FM*, 1: 228-52, and as "Lex Orandi, Lex Credendi" in GT, *Through Scylla and Charybdis* (hereafter *TSC*) (London: Longmans, Green & Co., 1907). pp. 85-105; GT, "A Perverted Devotion."

136. GT to Bremond, 22 December 1899, FB, BN, NAF.

137. Ibid.

138. "Dr. Ernest Engles" [GT], *RFL;* GT, *Lex Orandi* (hereafter *LO*) (London: Longmans, Green & Co., 1903); "Hilaire Bourdon" [GT], *The Church and the Future* (hereafter *CF*) (N.p.: The Author, 1903).

139. *TSC*, pp. 85-86.

140. *TSC*, p. 86.

141. *TSC*, p. 88.

142. *TSC*, pp. 91, 93, 94. See Andrew Seth Pringle-Pattison, *Man's Place in the Cosmos and Other Essays* (Edinburgh: W. Blackwood & Sons, 1897), p. 218. Seth, along with Ward and GT, was a member of the Synthetic Society and a thoroughgoing Hegelian. On the Synthetic Society, see Maisie Ward, *The Wilfrid Wards and the Transition*, 1: 344-79, 417-20; 2: 412-20. On the Synthetic Society, see John D. Root, "George Tyrrell and the Synthetic Society," *Downside Review* 98 (January 1980):

42–59; and Maisie Ward, *The Wilfrid Wards and the Transition*, 1: 344–79, 417–20; 2: 412–20.

143. *TSC*, p. 98. This phrase describes accurately GT's condition around Christmas 1902 when he was composing *CF*. See chap. 7, below, esp. pp. 249–73.

144. *TSC*, p. 95.

145. Jan Hendrick Walgrave in *Newman: Le Développement du dogme* (Tournai: Casterman, 1957), pp. 305–39, argues that GT did not understand the complex psychology underlying Newman's theory of development. Daniel Kilfoyle, "The Conception of Doctrinal Authority in the Writings of George Tyrrell" (Ph.D. diss., Union Theological Seminary, New York, 1970), p. 135, agrees, but suggests, "It should be noted that Tyrrell was not so much concerned with the mind of Newman as with the use to which his theory was being put in the polemical apologetics of the Roman scholastic theologians. Although he probably did not make the distinction in his own mind, Tyrrell was not rejecting Newman, but Newman in the hands of the scholastic theologians of the time." Whether or not GT correctly understood Newman's theory in all its supposed complexity is a question that will never be answered. But nowhere, either in GT's published works or in his correspondence, is there evidence to substantiate Kilfoyle's suggestion. It is therefore at least arguable that GT thought he both understood and was rejecting Newman.

146. *TSC*, p. 95.

147. *TSC*, p. 104.

148. Ibid.

149. GT to Ward, 16 March 1900, WFP, SAUL. This remark occurred in the context of GT's criticism of an early draft of Ward's "Unchanging Dogma and Changeful Man," *Fortnightly Review* 73 (1 April 1900): 628–49.

150. FvH to GT, 8 October 1899, PP, BL, Add. MSS 44927.83–84, published in part in FvH, *Selected Letters*, p. 77. On Basil Champneys and GT, see pp. 133–34 below, and chap. 4, n. 68. It is quite likely that GT's proposal that the saints are the teachers in the church came from FvH. Loome, *Liberal Catholicism, Reform Catholicism, Modernism*, pp. 156–58, notes FvH's poignant affirmation of this view in the margin of his copy of Döllinger's address at the conference for Catholic scholars in Munich at the end of September 1863. Opposite Döllinger's assertion that theologians have a prophetic role in the church, FvH wrote, "Hat dieser § recht? Ich glaube *nicht*. Das Prophetenthum in der Kirche sind die *Heiligen*, ja vorzüglich die *gelehrten* H[eiligen], aber doch immer quâ Heilige noch mehr als quâ Gelehrte: "Is this assertion true? I think *not*. Prophecy in the church belongs to the *saints*, and especially to the *learned* saints, but always more *qua* holy than *qua* learned." FvH's annotation is on p. 47 of his copy of *Verhandlungen der Versammlung katholischer Gelehrten in München vom 28. September bis 1. Oktober 1863* (Regensburg: Manz, 1863), preserved in FvH's library at SAUL.

151. GT, "A Perverted Devotion," *Weekly Register* 100 (16 December 1899): 797–800, reprinted in *EFI*, pp. 158–71.

152. *EFI*, pp. 158–59.

153. *EFI*, pp. 159–60.

154. *EFI*, p. 161.

155. *EFI*, pp. 162–63.

156. *EFI*, p. 163. See *TSC*, pp. 90–96.

157. *EFI*, p. 171.

158. GT to Bremond, 16 July 1900, FB, BN, NAF. *Pendente lite:* "pending judgment." In general GT was well respected and fairly treated by English Jesuits, as he himself admitted and as is attested by the fact that for the past few years he had been chosen to give retreats to Jesuits about to be ordained. There were,

of course, "delators" among the members of the English Province, but had not this initiative against him come from Rome, it is quite likely that GT would have lived out his days within the Society of Jesus.

159. St. George Mivart, "Happiness in Hell," "The Happiness in Hell: A Rejoinder," and "Last Words on the Happiness in Hell," *Nineteenth Century* 32 (December 1892): 899–919; 33 (February, April 1893): 320–38, 637–51. See also Mivart, "The Index and My Articles on Hell," *Nineteenth Century* 34 (1893): 979–90.

160. St. George Mivart, letter to the editor, "The Roman Catholic Church and the Dreyfus Case," *Times* (London), 17 October 1899, pp. 13–14. See also the leader of this issue, p. 9; and Barmann, *Von Hügel*, pp. 74–77.

161. St. George Mivart, "Some Recent Catholic Apologists," *Fortnightly Review*, n.s. 67 (1 January 1900): 24–44; Mivart, "The Continuity of Catholicism," *Nineteenth Century* 47 (January 1900): 51–72.

162. Merry del Val to Cardinal Herbert Alfred Vaughan, 10 January 1900, Vaughan Papers, Archives of the Archdiocese of Westminster, London (hereafter AAW), V. 1/14/24. See Lease, "Merry del Val and Tyrrell's Condemnation."

163. Vaughan to Mivart, 21 January 1900, copy, Vaughan Papers, AAW, V. 1/2/12. Obviously Vaughan had not read Mivart's opinion of Clarke in "Some Recent Catholic Apologists." Rev. Dr. Robert Francis Clarke, S.J. (1844–1906), was a friend of Wilfrid Ward, taught metaphysics and psychology at Kensington College, and was a member of the Pontifical Biblical Commission. Johannes Baptist Franzelin was the papal theologian at Vatican I and drew up the first draft *Dei Filius*, the constitution on the nature of the church.

164. GT to FvH, 10 March 1900, PP, BL, Add. MSS 44927.106, published in part and with some inaccuracies in *AL* 2: 119–20. The words quoted here are those GT quoted for FvH ostensibly from one of the general's letters to GT's provincial. He quoted similar but not exactly the same words to Ward in a letter dated only "Friday," WFP, SAUL, no. 20 in *Letters from a "Modernist."* A likely placement of this letter would be late April or early May 1900 when GT was preparing an answer to Robert Dell's apologia for Mivart (treated below, pp. 104–8). Ward seems to have read GT's answer and offered suggestions.

165. GT to Ward, dated only "Thurs." WFP, SAUL, no. 14 in *Letters from a "Modernist."*

166. Quoted in GT to FvH, 14 February 1900, PP, BL, Add. MSS 44927.99. *Quidquid sentiat Reverentia Vestra . . . :* "Whatever Your Reverence and consultors might think, here in Rome the view is very different."

167. *AL*, 2: 455. *Post . . . :* "After: *Happiness in Hell,* condemned by the church, now we have: *Devotion to Hell,* which is no less damnable." The critiques by the two Italian censors are included in the appendix to *AL*, 2: 451–58.

168. GT to Bremond, 18 January 1900, FB, BN, NAF.

169. It is not unlikely that GT got the substance of Merry del Val's letter to Vaughan from Vaughan himself, as he and GT were in communication. See GT to FvH, 10 March 1900, PP, BL, Add. MSS 44927.106; and Merry del Val to Vaughan, 11 January 1900, Vaughan Papers, AAW, V. 1/14/24.

170. GT to FvH, 14 February 1900, PP, BL, Add. MSS 44927.100. See also GT to Ward, 4 February 1900, WFP, SAUL.

171. GT to Bremond, 18 January 1900, FB, BN, NAF. In fact GT was about to publish *The Testament of Igna-*

tius Loyola, trans. E. M. Rix (London: Sands & Co., 1900), for which he had written the introduction, annotations, and epilogue. See GT to Ward, 24 February 1900, WFP, SAUL. MDP, who played a significant role in the development of GT's philosophy of religion (see chap. 6), had introduced GT to Juliana of Norwich. MDP claimed that GT's "A Perverted Devotion" "received an undercurrent of inspiration" from Mother Juliana. *AL,* 2: 112. Indeed, one can see a similarity in GT's appeal to faith and mystery. He also quoted Juliana in "The Relation of Theology to Devotion," so MDP's advertence is well taken.

172. GT to Ward, 27 February 1900, WFP, SAUL, published in Maisie Ward, *The Wilfrid Wards and the Transition,* 1: 326.

173. GT to FvH, 14 February 1900, PP, BL, Add. MSS 44927.100.

174. GT to Ward, n.d., WFP, SAUL, no. 14 in *Letters from a "Modernist."*

175. GT to FvH, 10 March 1900, PP, BL, Add. MSS 44927.106-9, published in part in *AL,* 2: 119-20. MDP gives the bulk of GT's reply to the censors in *AL,* 2: 121-25. She also reports that one English superior (probably Gerard) lost his office for supporting GT. *AL,* 2: 129.

176. GT to FvH, 10 March 1900, PP, BL, Add. MSS 44927.107, published in *AL,* 2: 119-20. GT reports Gerard's reactions.

177. GT to Ward, 24 February 1900, WFP, SAUL.

178. GT to Ward, n.d., WFP, SAUL, no. 19 in *Letters from a "Modernist."* See also GT to Ward, n.d. (no. 20 in *Letters from a "Modernist"*), 31 May 1900.

179. FvH to Ward, 18 February 1900, published in Maisie Ward, *The Wilfrid Wards and the Transition,* 1: 323-25. The 202 letters of FvH to Ward, dated 1882-1916, are among the WFP, SAUL, VII. 143.

180. Ibid.

181. Ward to FvH, 27 February 1900, in ibid., 1: 325-26. The letters of Ward to FvH are among the HP, SAUL.

182. Ibid.

183. Robert Edward Dell, "A Liberal Catholic View of the Case of Dr. Mivart," *Nineteenth Century* 47 (April 1900): 676. Dell, a recent convert, was editor of the *Weekly Register* from 1899 to 1900 and therefore was the publisher of record for GT's "A Perverted Devotion."

184. GT to Ward, 7 April 1900, WFP, SAUL.

185. Gerard to GT, 19 April 1900, Archives of the English Province of the Society of Jesus (hereafter EPSJ) London. See *TSC,* p. 104.

186. GT, "Who Are the Reactionaries?" WFP, SAUL, MS Deposit 21, VIII. 294, pp. 1, 2, 6, published in *Letters from a "Modernist."*

187. Ibid., MS pp. 11, 14.

188. J. H. Newman, *Apologia pro vita sua,* ed. David J. DeLaura (New York: W. W. Norton & Co., 1968), p. 198.

189. Ibid., p. 260; GT, "Who Are the Reactionaries?" MS p. 18.

190. GT to Ward, 7 April 1900, WFP, SAUL.

191. GT to Ward, 31 May 1900, WFP, SAUL.

192. Ibid.; GT to FvH, 6 June 1900, PP, BL, Add. MSS 44927.116.

193. FvH to GT, 7 July 1900, PP, BL, Add. MSS 44927.121.

194. GT to Ward, 31 May 1900, WFP, SAUL. See Ward, "Liberalism and Intransigeance."

195. Related in *AL,* 2: 128. A week later FvH wrote GT from Rome with news (now three weeks old) from his Bollandist friend François van Ortroy "that you were now *safe;* that the Roman S.J. authorities were going to leave the matter alone; and that I might tell you so as from him, and as a thing which he *knew for certain.* But he was and is a bit nervous . . . that they should not be poked up by anything of a kind to

draw special renewed attention to you, for some little time to come." PP, BL, Add. MSS 44927.113.

196. GT to Ward, 31 May 1900, WFP, SAUL.

197. GT, letter to the editor, *Weekly Register* 101 (1 June 1900): 686, reprinted with MDP's italics in *AL*, 2: 128-29; the words in italics are those transcribed verbatim from Rudolf Meyer's instructions.

198. GT to FvH, 6 June 1900, PP, BL, Add. MSS 44927.115-17, published in part and with inaccuracies in *AL*, 2: 129-30.

199. FvH to GT, 7 July 1900, PP, BL, Add. MSS 44927.121-22, published in part in FvH, *Selected Letters*, pp. 85-87.

200. Ward, "Liberalism and Intransigeance," p. 960.

201. GT to Ward, 18 June 1900, WFP, SAUL.

202. If the joint pastoral were so critical, why did it take GT two months to respond to it? See pp. 132-51 below.

203. Maisie Ward, *The Wilfrid Wards and the Transition*, 2: 188.

204. See GT to Ward, 13, 16 March 1900, WFP, SAUL.

205. See pp. 115-22 below.

206. GT, "Semper Eadem," *Month* 103 (January 1904): 1-17, reprinted as "Semper Eadem I" in *TSC*, pp. 106-32. Part 2 of "Semper Eadem" was published as "The Limits of the Theory of Development," *Catholic World* 81 (September 1905): 730-44, reprinted as "Semper Eadem II" in *TSC*, pp. 133-54.

207. GT to Ward, 19 January 1904, WFP, SAUL. *Meo judicio:* "in my judgment." See also the letters of 4, 12, 14 January, ibid. For a fuller discussion of the Ward-Tyrrell relationship, see Weaver, "Ward, Tyrrell, and the Meanings of Modernism," pp. 21-34.

208. At a meeting on this day, FvH gave GT a copy of Blondel's *L'Action* to keep, which he had promised him on 17 November 1899 but forgot to send. He also included other reading materials, among which were undoubtedly works by Loisy, which GT had asked about on 2 April 1900 and FvH promised to procure in a letter of 27 May 1900. See letters of those dates. PP, BL, Add. MSS 44927.88-89, 110-14; and the diary of FvH, 12 July 1900, HP, SAUL.

209. See *AL*, 2: 130. This was the retreat at which MDP was present and during which she and GT became friends. On this retreat and its results, see p. 137 below and chap. 4, n. 75; *AL*, 2: 77-84; diary of MDP, September 1900, PP, BL, Add. MSS 52372; MDP, *My Way of Faith*, pp. 272-88.

210. GT to Ward, 7 August 1900, WFP, SAUL.

211. GT to Bremond, 26 July 1900, FB, BN, NAF.

212. Crehan, *Father Thurston*, p. 56, writes that GT's departure to Richmond was at the suggestion of his friend John Gerard, then provincial. But it must be noted, contrary to rumor, that GT's exile was self-imposed, and not enforced. On 1 January 1901, GT wrote to Gerard: "I am not at all unhappy or discontented with the difficulties that God sends me. My correspondence, my writing & reading, give me far more to do than I can possibly accomplish. I came here *solely* in order to cope with the amount of my work. I hear now that my absence from London is being interpreted as an enforced banishment, but I have done my best to correct this false impression; nor can I reasonably be expected to direct my movements by the gossip of Farm St. ladies. Still I am entirely at your Reverence's command, whether it be to return to London or to go on the missions, home or foreign. Yours very faithfully, G. Tyrrell." EPSJ Archives. Gerard's own letter of 23 November 1901 to Reginald Colley, his successor in the provincialate, regarding GT's departure

to Richmond, also contradicts Crehan's suggestion: "As to the move to Richmond, it began somewhat casually, he going on a temporary visit and then suggesting that he rusticate for a season. I jumped at the idea at just about the time the Cardinal expressed the hope that he would not be placed in London on account of his imprudence in speech, especially with persons who required steadying. If T. knew this it would make him wild." EPSJ Archives.

CHAPTER 4

1. Deut. 32:51. GT's breviary is preserved in the library of King's College, Cambridge.
2. GT to MDP, 19 January 1902, PP, BL, Add. MSS 52367, published in part in *AL*, 2: 4.
3. See Deut. 34: 1-6.
4. See Edmund Bishop to FvH, 27 January 1913, HP, SAUL.
5. Quoted in Nigel Abercrombie, *The Life and Work of Edmund Bishop* (London: Longmans, Green & Co., 1959), pp. 443-44. Bishop's annotated copy of GT's *AL* is preserved among the Bishop Papers at Downside Abbey by Bath, Somersetshire.
6. FvH to GT, 19 August 1900, PP, BL, Add. MSS 44927.125.
7. GT to Alfred Rayney Waller, 5 September 1900, Waller Papers (hereafter WP), BL, Add. MSS 43680.22. This letter was in explanation of GT's decision to cease contributing prefaces for The Saints series, published by Duckworth, for which Waller was responsible. GT's association with Waller dates from the late 1890s when GT first began contributing prefaces. This open and innocent association soon evolved into covert operations, as Waller became GT's agent for pseudonymous publications. Ollendorf was the inventor of a method for learning a language by means of short and homely questions and answers.

8. GT had already proposed underground work in a letter to FvH of 10 March 1900, PP, BL, Add. MSS 44927.107-8: "I should not find it hard to subside into silence now; for, as you say, it is wonderful how much I have been allowed to do; and I cd. still go on writing quietly & supplying other people with matter."
9. GT to FvH, 7 September 1900, PP, BL, Add. MSS 44927.128-29. *Quinzaine* was a bimonthly edited by Georges Fonsegrive, a recent acquaintance and sympathizer of GT.
10. FvH to GT, 30 September 1900, PP, BL, Add. MSS 44927.133. This last remark only highlights the mutual reinforcement these two offered each other in their identification with self-sacrificing prophets.
11. GT to Waller, 30 September 1900, WP, BL, Add. MSS 43680.23-24.
12. GT to Waller, 6 October 1900, WP, BL, Add. MSS 43680.25-26, published in Thomas Michael Loome, "A Bibliography of the Published Writings of George Tyrrell (1861-1909)," *Heythrop Journal* 10 (July 1969): 286, where Loome misdates the letter 5 October. Loome supplies interesting details surrounding the publication of this and other pseudonymous and anonymous works. The genesis of *Oil and Wine* (hereafter *O&W*) (N.p. [1902]; reprint, London: Longmans, Green & Co., 1907), is covered in chap. 5.
13. See Johannes Jacobus Stam, *George Tyrrell: 1861-1909* (Utrecht: H. Honig, 1938), p. 98. MDP had shown Stam the original MS in 1937, but no one seems to know whether it still exists.
14. GT to Waller, 16 April 1901, WP, BL, Add. MSS 43680.37.
15. GT to Waller, 10 November 1901, WP, BL, Add. MSS 43680.44. Note the reappearance of Moses.
16. "A. R. Waller" [GT], *The Civilizing of the Matafanus* (London: R. Brimley Johnson, 1902), excerpts in *AL*, 2: 391-93, are from the original MS.

17. See pp. 33-34 above, and the essays cited there.

18. "Waller" [GT], *Matafanus*, p. 9.

19. "Waller" [GT], *Matafanus*, p. 41. "An aggressive and insolent faction" is the title conferred by Newman on the ultramontane majority at Vatican I. See Wilfrid Ward, *The Life of John Henry Cardinal Newman*, 2 vols. (London: Longmans, Green & Co., 1912), 2: 287-93.

20. "Waller" [GT], *Matafanus*, pp. 38-43.

21. Ibid., p. 46.

22. These excerpts from pp. 54-58 of the published text parallel those reprinted from the original text in *AL*, 2: 392. The reader may compare the two and estimate the extent of Waller's redaction. In a letter of 3 January 1902, PP, BL, Add. MSS 44928.4, GT told FvH that Waller "translated the merely 'connective tissue' . . . into his own words & for the rest, acted as a redactor of my codex; so that he is at least as much the author as Moses is of the Pentateuch—and what more could authorities desire?" But even some of the "connective tissue" was GT's, as his letter to Waller of 16 April 1901, WP, BL, Add. MSS 43680.37-40, attests.

23. "Waller" [GT], *Matafanus*, pp. 59-60.

24. Ibid., pp. 66, 68.

25. GT to Frank Rooke Ley, n.d., published in *AL*, 2: 149. Rooke Ley, editor of the *Weekly Register* for only two years, published the last number of that journal on 14 March 1902 and nine numbers of its successor, the *Monthly Register*, April to December 1902. As the only liberal Catholic periodical in England, it was the archrival of the only other Catholic and "official" periodical, the *Tablet*, whose legal owner, as archbishop of Westminster, was Cardinal Vaughan. The story of the struggle between the two journals and of the eventual demise of the *Register* can be traced in the Rooke Ley Papers, SAUL. GT was intimately involved with the fate of the *Register*, as it was the only Catholic outlet for airing another point of view. He seems to have written Rooke Ley quite a few letters between 1899 and 1904, which James A. Laubacher consulted for his dissertation in the late 1930s and returned to MDP. Their fate is now unknown.

26. GT to Bremond, 31 January 1900, FB, BN, NAF.

27. GT to FvH, 14 February 1900, PP, BL, Add. MSS 44927.100.

28. FvH to GT, 4 March 1900, PP, BL, Add. MSS 44927.101, 102, 104. FvH's surprisingly aggressive attitude exhibited here toward ecclesiastical authorities would change within three years to one bordering on fear, as those officials found their footing and assumed the offensive.

29. GT to FvH, 10 March 1900, PP, BL, Add. MSS 44927.106-9.

30. See James A. Laubacher, *Dogma and the Development of Dogma in the Writings of George Tyrrell (1861-1909)* (Louvain: Catholic University, 1939), pp. 64-87; GT, "The Mind of the Church," *Month* 96 (August, September 1900): 125-42, 233-40, reprinted in *FM*, 1: 158-204; GT, *O&W*.

31. First mention of these essays is in GT to FvH, 2 April 1900, PP, BL, Add. MSS 44927.111: "Maude Petre has produced an excellent M.S. on 'The temperament of doubt' for which she might easily have been burnt in the ages of faith. I also have produced a good deal of M.S., which will never see type, on kindred topics." See Loome, "Bibliography of Tyrrell," p. 288.

32. *FM*, 1: 158.

33. GT to FvH, 16 June 1900, PP, BL, Add. MSS 44927.119-20. For all the suspicion it aroused in Rome, Newman's *Essay on the Development of Christian Doctrine* (1845) never received the honor of the Index. It is not certain what of Harnack's GT was reading at this time, but a letter to MDP of 15 August 1900, PP, BL,

Add. MSS 52367, indicated that he was at least acquainted with *Outlines of the History of Dogma* (1889) and *History of Dogma* (1886–90). In the same letter GT mentioned Edwin Hatch's Hibbert Lectures of 1888, *The Influence of Greek Ideas and Usages upon the Christian Church*, 7th ed. (London: Williams & Norgate, 1898). Harnack's *What Is Christianity?* did not appear in English until 1901, at which time GT read it. See GT to MDP, 18 August 1901, PP, BL, Add. MSS 52367.

34. On Moyes, see Maisie Ward, *The Wilfrid Wards and the Transition*, 2: 154, 213.

35. I.e., what the church has defined as *de fide divina*, what is known only from revelation and cannot be reasoned to, e.g., the Trinitarian doctrine of three persons in one divine nature.

36. GT to Ward, 13 March 1900, WFP, SAUL.

37. Ibid.

38. Ibid. Cf. *O&W*, p. 173.

39. See GT to Ward, 16 March 1900, WFL, SAUL.

40. GT to FvH, 6 July 1900, PP, BL, Add. MSS 44927.115–16; see pp. 99–112 above.

41. GT to Bremond, early June 1900, FB, BN, NAF.

42. GT to FvH, 16 June 1900, PP, BL, Add. MSS 44927.120.

43. GT to Ward, 18 June 1900, WFL, SAUL. See pp. 109–12 above.

44. FvH to GT, 7 July 1900, PP, BL, Add. MSS 44927.121.

45. GT to Giovanni Semeria, 19 July 1900, Semeria Papers, Provincial Archives of the Italian Barnabites, Rome. The five surviving letters to Semeria were kindly made available to me by Padre Antonio Gentili. The Latin verse is what GT inscribed on the title page of his breviary in 1896. See pp. 113–14 above, and n. 3 above. See also GT's letter to his provincial superior, Fr. John Gerard, 17 November 1900, EPSJ Archives.

46. GT to Bremond, 16 July 1900, FB, BN, NAF. The works of Loisy that GT was reading were suggested by FvH at GT's request. See GT to FvH, 2 April 1900, and FvH to GT, 27 May 1900, PP, BL, Add. MSS 44927.111, 113; see pp. 195–96 below, and chap. 6, n. 36. Louis-David, in *Lettres de Tyrrell à Bremond*, p. 72, identifies the works mentioned to Bremond as "Les Évangiles synoptiques" and "La Question biblique et l'inspiration des Écritures." GT also recommended to Bremond in this letter the essays of Richard Holt Hutton, *Aspects of Religious and Scientific Thought*, ed. Elizabeth M. Roscoe (London: Macmillan & Co., 1899): "a truly catholic mind in every way, kept back by the ethical repulsiveness of our modern ecclesiastical system."

47. GT to FvH, 6 June 1900, PP, BL, Add. MSS 44927.116–17. The "radical opposition of principle" becomes a recurring theme in GT's writing from this point on.

48. See W. H. Mallock, *Doctrine and Doctrinal Disruption* (London: A. & C. Black, 1900). Mallock was among the "outsiders" invited to the discussions of the Westminster Catholic Dining Society founded by Mr. and Mrs. Wilfrid Ward. See Maisie Ward, *The Wilfrid Wards and the Transition*, 2: 148.

49. See Laubacher, *Dogma and Development*, p. 72.

50. *FM*, 1: 165. Cf. "The Mustard Seed," in *O&W*, pp. 168–69.

51. *FM*, 1: 171–73. Cf. "The Catholic Church," "The Voice of the Multitude," "Need of Authority," and "Unity and Variety," in *O&W*, pp. 139–57. GT's use of the word "crowd" must be taken in the sense intended, e.g., in Rev. 19:1, 6. GT later refined his expression by distinguishing between "community" and "crowd," "people" and "populace." See GT, "Consensus Fidelium," *New York Review* 1 (August–

September 1905): 133-38, a review of *Les Legendes hagiographiques* by Hippolyte Delehaye, reprinted as "The Corporate Mind" in *TSC*, pp. 254-63.

52. GT was slightly in error here. The guidance of the Holy Spirit is always infallible. Error lies in the perception and following of the guidance.

53. *FM*, 1: 178. . . . *Non deficit in necessaris:* "God does not fail his creatures in essential matters."

54. GT to Ward, 13 March, 2 October 1900, WFP, SAUL.

55. *FM*, 1: 199.

56. GT, "The Mind of the Church," pt. 2, p. 236.

57. GT to Ward, 2 October 1900, WFP, SAUL; *FM*, 1: 199; italics mine.

58. The reader probably will have noticed long before an inconsistency in the capitalization of "mind" as well as of other words. The inconsistency is GT's. On capitalization he called himself "a hopeless wobbler." GT to Waller, 4 May 1903, WP, BL, Add. MSS 43680.149.

59. *FM*, 1: 200.

60. *FM*, 1: 202.

61. Cf. *O&W*, pp. 143-46, 173.

62. GT to Ward, 10 September 1900, WFP, SAUL.

63. GT had gone to Richmond at the beginning of June "for a fortnight or so" but stayed into July, then spent most of July at Farm Street.

64. GT to MDP, 8 August 1900, PP, BL, Add. MSS 52367.

65. One of the essays was "La Psychologie dramatique du mystère de la Passion à Oberammergau," *Quinzaine* 35 (1 July 1900): 1-18. See GT to FvH, 12 November 1900, PP, BL, Add. MSS 44927.141.

66. "E.F.G." [GT], letter to the editor, "M. Blondel's Dilemma," *Pilot* 2 (27 October 1900): 534.

67. Pierre Janet first appears in GT's correspondence in a letter to MDP of 29 January 1901, PP, BL, Add. MSS 52367, but GT had probably read Janet as early as autumn 1898

when he was engaged in a discussion with FvH on abnormal behavior in connection with the latter's study on Catherine of Genoa and mysticism. GT's letter to FvH of 3 October 1898, PP, BL, Add. MSS 44927.52-53, displays a familiarity with the jargon and method of Janet. But Tyrrell could also have picked up the jargon from Henri Joly's *Psychologie des Saints* (Paris: Librairie Victor Lecoffre, 1897), which relied heavily on Janet and which GT reviewed for the *Month:* "Psychologie des Saints" and "What Is Mysticism?" *Month* 90 (September, December 1897): 329-30, 601-11, the latter essay reprinted in *FM*, 1: 253-72. GT also provided a preface (dated 7 May 1898) to the English translation of Joly, *The Psychology of the Saints* (London: Duckworth & Co., 1898).

68. GT, "Coventry Patmore," *Month* 96 (December 1900): 561-73, a review of *Coventry Patmore* by Basil Champneys, reprinted as "Poet and Mystic" in *FM*, 2: 40-60. GT borrowed some of Patmore's formulations for essays in *O&W;* cf. esp. "God in Us," "God's Life in Ours," "Christ in Us," "God's Jealousy," and "The Path of Counsel," in *O&W*, pp. 203-46. GT synthesized Patmore and Blondel in GT to FvH, 12 November 1900, PP, BL, Add. MSS 44927.141-43.

69. GT, "Tracts for the Million," *Month* 96 (November 1900): 449-60, reprinted in *FM*, 2: 136-57.

70. *FM*, 2: 156. Readers of *The Matafanus* and "Coventry Patmore" will notice how much of both works reappeared in "Tracts for the Million." Particularly evident is the parallel between Alpuca and his task in *The Matafanus* and the apologist in "Tracts," with both of whom GT obviously identified himself. Cf. the conclusion of "Conventry Patmore," *FM*, 2: 58-60.

71. GT to MDP, 12 January 1901, published in *AL*, 2: 166. "N.N.," the name deleted by MDP, in *AL*, 2:

166, was probably Fr. Sydney Smith, editor of the *Month*. GT was so discouraged by the reaction to his article that his promised sequel materialized only as the introduction to *FM*, where he said plainly what he meant. He made the same point in "Two Estimates of Catholic Life," *Month* 93 (May 1899): 449-58, a review of *Helbeck of Bannisdale* by Mrs. Humphry Ward, and *One Poor Scruple* by Mrs. Wilfrid Ward, reprinted in *FM*, 61-79.

72. See GT to Bremond, 22 December 1899, FB, BN, NAF.

73. GT to MDP, 1 November 1900, published in *AL*, 2: 81-82.

74. GT to MDP, 24 September 1900, PP, BL, Add. MSS 52367, published in *AL*, 2: 80.

75. GT to MDP, 1 November 1900, published in *AL*, 2: 81-82. The result of the project was a book of essays, *The Soul's Orbit*, compiled, with additions, by M. D. Petre (London: Longmans, Green & Co., 1904). GT's name did not appear, and the book received little attention. On 11 December 1904, GT wrote to Lilley, "'The Soul's Orbit' is still born according to Longmans. The press ignored it. We are writing frantically all round to get reviews. It is all so much of a toss-up. Had the author been the Rev. M. Petre S.J. the first edn. would have been exhausted by now." LP, SAUL, MS 30793. For MDP's account of the project, see *AL*, 2: 77-84.

76. GT to MDP, November 1900, PP, BL, Add. MSS 52367.

77. GT to FvH, 12 November 1900, PP, BL, Add. MSS 44927.141.

78. Ibid. Extensive searching has failed to produce the exact source of GT's quotation of the "rule for the Professor of Theology," but reference to the "Regulae professorum scholasticae theologiae" of the *Ratio atque institutio studiorum Societatis Jesu* promulgated by Aquaviva in 1599, *Institutum Societatis Jesu*, 3 vols. (Florence, 1892-93), 3: 172-82, shows

that GT's quotation is true to much of the legislation of the day. However, GT shows little historical perspective and sympathy for the complex circumstances that led Aquaviva to draft such legislation. Just as GT recognized that Aquinas was not to blame for the entrenchment of later scholasticism, so GT should not blame Aquaviva for the failure of his successors to modify legislation according to changing circumstances.

79. GT to FvH, 12 November 1900, PP, BL, Add. MSS 44927.142.

80. William Magee (1821-91), Anglican bishop of Peterborough, later archbishop of York, played a major role in the ritualist controversy. He opposed both extremes.

81. GT to Bremond, 13 November 1900, FB, BN, NAF. José-Marie Blanco White (1774-1841), a Spanish writer of Irish ancestry, abandoned the Catholic priesthood and his native Seville for the Anglican priesthood and London. GT wrote of him in "Reflections on Catholicism," *TSC*, pp. 50-51, but he could just as well have had his own case in mind.

82. GT to Bremond, 13 November 1900, FB, BN, NAF.

83. GT to MDP, 16 November 1900, PP, BL, Add. MSS 52367. Before GT learned German he often misspelled Eucken's name. Here and throughout the spelling has been silently corrected.

84. *E purchè si muove!*: "Nevertheless it does move!"—Galileo's rumored reply under his breath to the inquisitors as he rose from his knees after abjuring his scientific findings.

85. GT stressed on p. 7 of his letter that the author was not William Francis Barry (1849-1930), who had written extensively on the Americanist controversy, but a priest "similarly circumstanced." See Barry's autobiography, *Memories and Opinions* (London: G. P. Putnam's Sons, 1926).

86. *Faust*, act 1, line 385: It is night, and

Faust is at his desk, becoming increasingly distraught at the failure of rational explanations for life's meaning. He resolves to have no more of them with "Und tu nicht mehr in Worten kramen": "And henceforth abandon your huckstering in words." The parallel to GT's correspondent is poignant, as he realizes the ineffectualness of neoscholasticism.

87. Abbé Victor Charbonnel left the priesthood and the church over the Americanist controversy. On him, see Felix Klein, *Americanism: A Phantom Heresy* (Atchison, Kans.: Aquin Book Shop, 1951), references listed in the index.

88. All three are Anglicans: Charles Gore (1853-1932), bishop in turn of Worcester, Birmingham, and Oxford, later professor at King's College in London; Henry Scott Holland (1847-1918), publisher of *Goodwill*, later editor of the *Commonwealth*, a member of the Synthetic Society; James Hull Ward (1843-1925), professor of philosophy and psychology from 1887 at Cambridge.

89. GT's reference to Belshazzar's feast in Dan. 5:22-28, is strikingly apt and cogent.

90. GT to John Gerard, 17 November 1900, EPSJ Archives.

91. GT to FvH, 14 February 1900, PP, BL, Add. MSS 44927.100; GT to Bremond, early June 1900, FB, BN, NAF.

92. "The Church and Liberal Catholicism: Joint Pastoral Letter by the Cardinal Archbishop and the Bishops of the Province of Westminster," *Tablet* n.s. 65 (5, 12 January 1901): 8-12, 50-52, published as a booklet, Herbert Cardinal Vaughan and the Bishops of the Province of Westminster, *A Joint Pastoral Letter on the Church and Liberal Catholicism* (London: Burns & Oates, 1900). Indicative of the attention given the pastoral, a German translation appeared only one month after the English publication, *Die*

Kirche und der liberal Katholizismus: Gemeinsames Hirtenschreiben des Cardinal-Erzbischofs unter der Bischöfe der Kirchenprovinz Westminster, Frankfurter Zeitgemässe Broschüren, no. 20.5 (Hamm i. W.: Breer & Thiemann, February 1901). The feeling among the English bishops was not entirely unanimous. On 31 January 1901 GT wrote to Lord Halifax, "One, at least, of our bishops has written to me in confidence to say how much he regretted the tone of the Pastoral tho' to avoid the scandal of seeming disunion he signed it in his own sense." Halifax Papers, Borthwick Institute of Historical Research, Eleven letters (1897-1902) from GT to Charles Lindley Wood, second Viscount Halifax, most of them concerned with the joint pastoral affair, are preserved among these papers.

93. See pp. 99-103 above. Besides the articles by Mivart, a number of other articles published during 1900 gave authorities reason to fear a new ground swell of liberalism: Robert Edward Dell, "A Liberal Catholic View of the Case of Dr. Mivart"; Dell, "Mr. Wilfrid Ward's Apologetics," *Nineteenth Century* 48 (July 1900): 127-36, in reply to Ward, "Liberalism and Instransigeance"; "Fideles," "A Convert's Experiences of the Catholic Church," *Contemporary Review* 77 (June 1900): 817-34; "Fideles," "The Movement for Reform within the Catholic Church," *Contemporary Review* 78 (November 1900): 693-709. GT also reported to FvH on 10 March 1900, PP, BL, Add. MSS 44927.107: "Vaughan is beginning to be dimly conscious of something wrong and is puzzled by the almost complete drying up of the stream of conversions. At Farm Street our returns are but one to five of this time last year." The conversion of England to Rome was a major concern of Vaughan and Merry del Val, and such a falling off of conversions could conceiva-

bly have thrown them into a panic. Whether or not it did and they sought to lay the blame on liberalism are matters for further investigation, but see the important letters Merry del Val to Vaughan, 30 June, 7 November 1900, Vaughan Papers, AAW, V. 1/14/29; V. 1/14/29, 30.

94. Merry del Val to Vaughan, 30 June 1900, Vaughan Papers, AAW, V. 1/14/29.

95. Joint pastoral, *Tablet*, p. 8.

96. GT to FvH, 6 June 1900, PP, BL, Add. MSS 44927.116.

97. Joint pastoral, *Tablet*, p. 9.

98. Ibid., p. 11.

99. Barmann, *Von Hügel*, p. 150.

100. FvH to Ward, 31 December 1900, published in part in ibid.

101. GT to MDP, 2 January 1901, PP, BL, Add. MSS 52367. The reference to Loisy is undoubtedly a late notice of Cardinal François Marie Richard de la Vergne's condemnation of Loisy on 23 October 1900. On that date, by a letter to the editor of the *Revue du clergé français*, Richard forbade the publication of the remaining two articles of a series of five that Loisy was preparing on the origins of Israel's religion. GT heard of the affair almost certainly from FvH. Two letters from FvH to GT of 8 and 12 December 1900 (see diary of FvH for those dates, HP, SAUL) are missing from the collection at the BL; they must have mentioned Loisy's troubles.

102. GT to Rooke Ley, 5 January 1901, published in *AL*, 2: 152–53. For a fine appreciation of the shift, see Ronald Burke, "Loisy's Faith: Landshift in Catholic Thought," *Journal of Religion* 60 (April 1980): 138–64.

103. GT to Rooke Ley, 5 January 1901, published in *AL*, 2: 153.

104. GT to MDP, 18 December 1900, PP, BL, Add. MSS 52367, published in part in *AL*, 2: 143–44, and in MDP, *My Way of Faith*, p. 277.

105. See GT to MDP, 26 December 1900, published in *AL*, 2: 38.

106. GT to Reginald Colley, 7 January 1901, EPSJ Archives.

107. GT to MDP, 29 January 1901, PP, BL, Add. MSS 52367, published in part in *AL*, 2: 139.

108. See GT to MDP, dated by MDP 3 January, published in *AL*, 2: 225. The date should perhaps be 23 January or some date subsequent to GT's letter to Colley of 23 January. GT's dating was not always legible. The original letter is not among the Petre Papers at the BL.

109. GT to Colley, 23 January 1901, EPSJ Archives.

110. GT to MDP, 4 February 1901, PP, BL, Add. MSS 52367, published in part in *AL*, 2: 162, 225.

111. The editor replied, "Del resto non sappiamo come Le abbiano scritto che il Papa ha proibito a qualunque sacerdote di scrivere nella Rassegna; ciò è falso, per quanto da noi si conosca": "Besides, we know nothing about what you have written, namely that the pope has prohibited all priests from publishing in the Rassegna; that is false, so far as we know." Quoted in GT to Colley, 18 February 1901, EPSJ Archives.

112. Ibid.

113. Quoted in GT to FvH, 20 February 1901, PP, BL, Add. MSS 44927.156, published in *AL*, 2: 225–26.

114. GT to FvH, 20 February 1901, BL, Add. MSS 44927.156.

115. GT to Semeria, 17 May 1901, Semeria Papers, Provincial Archives of the Italian Barnabites.

116. FvH to GT, 28 May 1901, PP, BL, Add. MSS 44927.160.

117. As noted earlier, GT's heart was not in republishing his old articles, but FvH urged him to complete the project as his essays were far above the ordinary fare available. GT to FvH, 25 November 1900, and FvH to GT, 26 December 1900, PP, BL, Add. MSS 44927.145, 153. But GT had his own reasons. On 4 February 1901 he wrote to MDP: "It has been

decided that I am to publish two volumes of Month articles, because the undiscerning public will thereby be hoodwinked into thinking that I am free to write as usual, not seeing that it is old matter dished up. I submit to the fraud for the sake of the evidence it will give of my moderateness, in case of an eventual rupture with the S.J." PP, BL, Add. MSS 52367, published in part in *AL*, 2: 162.

118. GT to Halifax, 7 July 1901, Halifax Papers, Borthwick Institute of Historical Research.

119. GT to Rooke Ley, 5 January 1901, published in *AL*, 2: 153.

120. Halifax's efforts must be seen as the groundwork for Rome's 1973 reversal of Leo XIII's condemnation. FvH was also involved with Halifax on this and other issues. See Barmann, *Von Hügel*, pp. 56–62, 108–9, 149–53, 200–27. Thirteen letters from FvH to Halifax (1895–1911) are among the Halifax Papers, Borthwick Institute of Historical Research.

121. GT to Halifax, 12 February, 7 July 1901, Halifax Papers. The letters of Halifax to GT are not extant, but are mentioned in GT's letters to Halifax.

122. GT to Halifax, 17 January 1901, Halifax Papers.

123. GT to Halifax, 28 January 1901, Halifax Papers.

124. GT to Halifax, 31 January 1901, Halifax Papers. Newman's classical statement on the question was delivered in *Letter to the Duke of Norfolk* (1875). GT did not mention that he had read this work, but it is likely. See GT to Raoul Goût, 26 May 1906, published in *AL*, 2: 209–10. In any case, Newman covered the question in his *Apologia*, which GT had read at least seven times. See GT to MDP, 15 February 1901, published in *AL*, 2: 208. The "Halifax" article therefore received a heavy dose of Newman.

125. GT to Halifax, 17 February 1901,

Halifax Papers, Borthwick Institute of Historical Research.

126. GT to Rooke Ley, 17 February 1901, published in *AL*, 2: 153–54.

127. GT to Ward, 16 February 1901, WFP, SAUL. See M. S. Dalton to Colley, 27 January 1901, EPSJ Archives, in which Dalton, a lay friend of GT's, indicated the wish that Colley reveal to GT the secret about the pope's forthcoming blessing of the joint pastoral. See Wilfrid Ward, "Cardinal Newman," *Weekly Register* 103 (16 February 1901): 196–98.

128. Reported in GT to Halifax, 17 February 1901, Halifax Papers, Borthwick Institute of Historical Research.

129. Ibid.

130. GT to FvH, 20 February 1901, PP, BL, Add. MSS 44927.155.

131. The controversy lasted from 5 January to 2 March 1901 and was carried on by a least four different Roman Catholic correspondents, all writing under pseudonyms. "K" of 2 February was almost certainly FvH's Oratorian friend Alfred Fawkes, with whom GT would later become friends. On Fawkes, see Vidler, *A Variety of Catholic Modernists*, pp. 155–60. Fawkes was also very likely the "R. C. Observer" who initiated the controversy on 5 January. "Liberal Catholic" (2, 16 February), who sided with "K" and identified himself as a lay convert, was probably Robert Dell. There are many possible candidates for "Zeta" (19 January, 9, 23 February), the only contributor to defend the joint pastoral, but the Jesuit Sydney Smith seems likely on the basis of a reference in GT to FvH, 2 February 1901, PP, BL, Add. MSS 44927.155. GT's known contributions are these: letter to the editor, "The Anglo-Roman Pastoral," *Pilot* 3 (2 March 1901): 282, signed "A Conservative Catholic"; "The Recent Anglo-Roman Pastoral," *Nineteenth Century* 49 (May 1901): 736–54, signed, "Halifax"; "Lord Halifax Demurs," *Weekly*

Register 103 (3 May 1901): 549–50, unsigned; three letters to the editor, *Weekly Register* 103 (17, 24 May, 7 June 1901): 630, 662–63, 726–27, all signed "S.T.L."; letter to the editor: "The Anglo-Roman Pastoral," *Pilot* 4 (6 July 1901): 23–24, signed "E.F.G.," reprinted in *Weekly Register* 104 (16 August 1901): 198 (on the identification of "E.F.G.," see Barmann, *Von Hügel*, p. 152, n. 2); "Docens Discendo," *Weekly Register* 104 (19 July 1901): 68–69, unsigned. Further information on these letters and articles is given in Laubacher, *Dogma and Development*, pp. xxi–xxii; and three publications by Loome, "Bibliography of Tyrrell," pp. 305–6; "A Bibliography of the Printed Works of George Tyrrell: Supplement," *Heythrop Journal* 11 (April 1970): 166; and *Liberal Catholicism, Reform Catholicism, Modernism*, pp. 222–23.

132. "A Conservative Catholic" [GT], "The Anglo-Roman Pastoral," p. 282.

133. GT to FvH, 17 June 1901, PP, BL, Add. MSS 44927.164. The whereabouts of GT's letter(s) to Joseph Rickaby is unknown. See Joseph Rickaby, S.J., "The Church and Liberal Catholicism," *Month* 97 (April 1901): 337–46.

134. GT to Halifax, 15 April 1901, Halifax Papers.

135. GT to Halifax, 31 January 1901, Halifax Papers. Alfonso Rodriguez (1538–1616) entered the Society of Jesus in July 1557. Pius XI ranked him alongside Bernard and Bonaventure on the strength of his three-volume work, *Ejercicio de perfeccion y virtudes christianas* (Seville, 1609), which up to Vatican II was a staple of formation for religious novices the world over. The work saw at least fifty complete and fifteen partial Spanish editions and was fully or partially translated into twenty-three languages.

136. "Halifax" [GT], "The Recent Anglo-Roman Pastoral," p. 742.

137. Ibid., pp. 742–43.

138. Ibid., pp. 746–47.

139. Ibid., p. 749.

140. Ibid., pp. 749–50, 745.

141. Ibid., p. 752.

142. GT would more consciously identify with Acton and Döllinger during the last two years of his life, i.e., after his excommunication in 1907. On the parallels recognized by GT in this regard and also on his association with and rejection of *Altkatholizismus*, see Loome, *Liberal Catholicism, Reform Catholicism, Modernism*, pp. 40–48; and *AL*, 2: 379–87; see also GT's letters to Arnold Harris Mathew (1842–1919), regionary Old Catholic bishop for England. An error-strewn typescript of forty-five letters from GT to Mathew (1906–9) is preserved in the EPSJ Archives. The last known holder of the original letters was the late Fr. Ralph Baines, S.J. See also GT, "The Home and Foreign Review," *Rinnovamento* 3 (January 1908): 81–94, a review of *The History of Freedom and Other Essays* by John Emerich Edward Dalberg-Acton.

143. [GT], "Lord Halifax Demurs," p. 350. On GT's intention in using the term "amended Gallicanism," see Mary Jo Weaver, "George Tyrrell and the Joint Pastoral Letter," in *Proceedings of the Roman Catholic Modernism Working Group, 1979*, pp. 64–82.

144. Cardinal Henry Edward Manning, *The Vatican Council and Its Definitions: A Pastoral Letter to the Clergy* (New York: P. J. Kenedy & Sons, 1871), p. 97; see also pp. 47–119.

145. [GT], "Lord Halifax Demurs," p. 350.

146. GT to Rooke Ley, 3 May 1901, published in *AL*, 2: 155–57. As will be seen shortly, GT's remark about the *via media* was a swipe at Ward.

147. GT to Rooke Ley, 25 May 1901, published in *AL*, 2: 159.

148. Quoted in GT to MDP, 8 May 1901, PP, BL, Add. MSS 52367.

149. Ibid.

150. Quoted in Maisie Ward, *The Wilfrid Wards and the Transition*, 2: 141.
151. FvH to GT, 28 May 1901, PP, BL, Add. MSS 44927.162.
152. For bibliographical references on these responses, see Loome, "Bibliography of Tyrrell," p. 305.
153. GT to FvH, 17 June 1901, PP, BL, Add. MSS 44927.166.
154. Wilfrid Ward, "Doctores Ecclesiae," *Pilot* 3 (22 June 1901): 774.
155. "E.F.G." [GT], "The Anglo-Roman Pastoral," p. 23. Barmann, *Von Hügel*, p. 152, n. 2, convincingly argues for GT as the author but presents no conclusive external evidence. The following evidence is conclusive: On 16 July 1901, GT wrote to MDP: "A[lfred]. F[awkes].'s answer to me (E.F.G.) in this *Pilot* is good & true." PP, BL, Add. MSS 52367. He wrote again to MDP on 30 July 1901: "This week Ward is to reproduce his 'Pilot' article *Doctores Ecclesiae* & a reply to E.F.G. which of course is G.T." PP, BL, Add. MSS 52367, misdated by MDP 2 August. For Ward's answer, see reference given in n. 159 below.
156. James Britten to Wilfrid Ward, n.d., published in Maisie Ward, *The Wilfrid Wards and the Transition*, 2: 143.
157. FvH to Ward, 22 November 1901, published in part in Barmann, *Von Hügel*, p. 153.
158. FvH to GT, 6 August 1901, PP, BL, Add. MSS 44927.167-68.
159. Wilfrid Ward, "The Time-Spirit of the Nineteenth Century," *Edinburgh Review* 194 (July–September 1901): 92-131, unsigned, revised and reprinted in Ward, *Problems and Persons* (London: Longmans, Green & Co., 1903), pp. 1-65.
160. GT to MDP, 30 July 1901, PP, BL, Add. MSS 52367, fragment.
161. GT to Ward, 1 August 1901, WFP, SAUL. Jesuits Peter Gallwey (1820-1906) and William Humphrey (1839-1910) and Dominican pamphleteer and lecturer Wilfrid Lescher (1847-1917) were all ardent devotées of

papal power. *Ad limina:* "to the threshold," a reference to the requirement that bishops regularly report to Rome in person—since Trent, every five years.
162. GT to Ward, 7 September 1901, WFP, SAUL.
163. GT to FvH, 22 September 1901, PP, BL, Add. MSS 44927.172.
164. Loome, *Liberal Catholicism, Reform Catholicism, Modernism*, p. 37.
165. GT to Halifax, 17 February 1901, Halifax Papers, Borthwick Institute of Historical Research.

CHAPTER 5

1. GT to MDP, 11 February 1901, PP, BL, Add. MSS 52367, published in part in *AL*, 2: 162.
2. GT to FvH, 20 February 1901, PP, BL, Add. MSS 44927.156.
3. GT to Colley, 21 June 1901, EPSJ Archives; GT was still referring to the "M.SS" as "a second series of *Nova et Vetera*." The eventual title was *Oil and Wine*.
4. GT to Colley, 27 June 1901, EPSJ Archives.
5. Ibid. Fr. A. G. Knight was Colley's assistant. GT had little respect for him. See Knight to GT, 13 January 1901, and GT to Colley, 14 January 1901, EPSJ Archives.
6. GT to Colley, 1 July 1901, EPSJ Archives.
7. GT to Colley, 4 July 1901, EPSJ Archives.
8. GT to Raffalovich, 30 July 1901, Raffalovich Papers, Blackfriars Library.
9. GT to MDP, 23 January 1901, published in *AL*, 1: vi.
10. GT to MDP, 16 July 1901, PP, BL, Add. MSS 52367, published in part in *AL*, 2: 163. Although a year later GT would advise Bremond to leave the Society of Jesus (GT to Bremond, 22-25 September 1902, FB, BN, NAF), the upshot of the discussions during July 1901 was the

advice that Bremond should remain and try to adjust his expectations. "His distress comes from a subconscious belief in, hope for, & love of the ridiculous old machine; & I think when that is *all* gone, he will be more at peace." GT to MDP, 16 July 1901, PP, BL, Add. MSS 52367. Bremond's status as a Jesuit comes up throughout the GT-Bremond correspondence until 24 February 1904, by which time Bremond had become a diocesan priest.

11. [GT], "Jesuits and Their Critics," *Weekly Register* 104 (2 August 1901): 133-34. See Laubacher, *Dogma and Development*, p. xxii, for a convincing assignment of this unsigned article to GT. From parallel expressions, one could argue that GT had finished his autobiography by the date of this article.

12. [GT], "Jesuits and Their Critics," p. 134.

13. GT to Bremond, 4 August 1901, FB, BN, NAF. See chap. 2. Doubtless what reminded GT of this side of himself was the reediting of his *Month* articles for *FM*, the appearance of which he announced in this letter.

14. GT to Bremond, 4 August 1901, FB, BN, NAF. The letter was headed "Dom. Imposs. N.N.," a Latin abbreviation for *Domus Impossibilium Nostrorum*. Thus GT referred to Richmond as a "home for impossible cases." See GT to Bremond, 23 June 1901, FB, BN, NAF.

15. GT to Colley, 16 August 1901, EPSJ Archives.

16. GT to FvH, 22 September 1901, BL, Add. MSS 44927.174. *Ne majus scandalum oriatur*: "lest greater scandal should arise."

17. GT to Colley, 15 October 1901, EPSJ Archives.

18. Reported in GT to MDP, 18 October 1901, PP, BL, Add. MSS 52367.

19. GT to Colley, 17 October 1901, EPSJ Archives.

20. Apparently Colley had dispensed with the usual four censors and had assigned only two besides himself. Alexander Charnley and Gerard, GT told FvH, were "supposedly friendly." GT to FvH, 3 January 1902, PP, BL, Add. MSS 44928.4. See Colley to GT, 18 October 1901, published in part in *AL*, 2: 170; see also *AL*, 2: 170-75.

21. GT to Bremond, 3 November 1901, F3, BN, NAF.

22. GT to FvH, 3 January 1902, PP, BL, Add. MSS 44928.3.

23. GT to MDP, 20 November 1901, PP, BL, Add. MSS 52367. The illness may have been arranged. See GT to Colley, 25 November 1901, EPSJ Archives, quoted on p. 175 below.

24. Rudolf Meyer to GT, 19 November 1901, PP, BL, Add. MSS 52368, one of the few surviving letters to GT.

25. See pp. 97-99 above. The opinion of censor no. 2 is included in *AL*, 2: 455-58.

26. Gerard to Colley, 23 November 1901, EPSJ Archives.

27. Colley to GT, 24 November 1901, EPSJ Archives.

28. Unlike those who shrunk from the subject in horror, GT dealt with the moral issue of homosexuality in a sympathetic and balanced way. His attitude is evident in his correspondence with André Raffalovich, a devout member of the Third Order of St. Dominic, author of several books on "unisexuality" (as homosexuality was then called), member of the *Yellow Book* circle, and a friend of Oscar Wilde. See also GT, *Notes on the Catholic Doctrine of Purity* (Roehampton: Manresa Press, 1897), p. 80. Meriol Trevor, *Prophets and Guardians* (London: Hollis & Carter, 1969), first drew attention to the question of GT's sexual orientation. She raised the question on p. 35 and

nine pages later decided that "emotional immaturity rather than sexual inversion" would be a more accurate diagnosis. Unfortunately by this time the sinister question was fixed in her readers' minds, and even Thomas Loome's solid refutation failed to erase it. See Loome, "Tyrrell's Letters to André Raffalovich," pt. 2, *Month*, 2d n.s. 1 (March 1970): 138–40. Trevor's reply, "George Tyrrell: A Rejoinder," *Month*, 2d n.s. 1 (April 1970): 199, only succeeded in showing how subjective was her argument—"from the *tone* of his autobiography . . . and from a published letter to (the young) Laurence Housman." She did not document her source, but perhaps she was referring to one of four letters addressed to Housman or "L. H.," published in *GTL*. Now it may be granted that GT was "emotionally immature," but this category is broad enough to include nearly everyone at some stage of life. And lest the question raised about GT's sexual orientation discredit the witness, it must be said in his defense that even if one could establish that he had some homosexual leanings in his early years (which he admits and which are quite normal), there is no evidence to suggest that he was a true homosexual (type no. 4, 5, or 6 as described in A. C. Kinsey, W. B. Pomeroy, and C. E. Martin, *Sexual Behavior in the Human Male* [Philadelphia: W. B. Saunders, 1948], pp. 636–55). In fact the evidence is to the contrary. See GT to Raffalovich, 15 August 1907? Raffalovich Papers, Blackfriars Library.

29. "Scholastics" here refers to young Jesuits still in training and not yet ordained.

30. "Manifestation" refers to the practice of "manifestation of conscience," whereby every Jesuit is required by rule once a year in private conference to bare his soul to his provincial superior. Manifestation is theoretically of gravest moment because, among other reasons, it is the core principle of government in the Society of Jesus.

31. GT to Colley, 25 November 1901, EPSJ Archives.

32. GT to Bremond, 5 December 1901, FB, BN, NAF. "Jack" was GT's pet Airedale terrier, whose acquaintance Bremond had made during a visit to Richmond the previous 10 to about 17 July. Colley died in office on 12 February 1904. Two days later GT wrote to MDP: "Father Colley, you will have heard, was found dead on Friday. Good for him, poor tired man! He was *in desire* very large and fair and honourable, however hampered by the trammels of his office and vocation." *AL*, 2: 170. Who could say, as GT implied here, that Colley did not die of the burdens of office, to which GT himself contributed not a little?

33. Colley to GT, 4 December 1901, PP, BL, Add. MSS 52368.

34. GT to Colley, 6 December 1901, EPSJ Archives.

35. Colley to GT, 31 December 1901, PP, BL, Add. MSS 52368. The word in brackets is a guess for a hole in the manuscript.

36. Ward to his wife, undated, but from 1901, in Maisie Ward, *The Wilfrid Wards and the Transition*, 2: 221. Ward added, "Hügel *is* rather suspected he says. I, apparently, am not."

37. GT to Bremond, 17 February 1902, FB, BN, NAF. *Signum contradictionis:* "sign of contradiction." As mentioned before, the onset of Bright's disease, from which GT eventually died, can be dated roughly from the time he went to live at Richmond in May 1900. He suffered increasingly frequent attacks that incapacitated him usually for about a week at a time. He

often described the attacks as "migraines," and in between times he always felt more or less "bilious." See Joseph Crehan, S.J., "What Influenced and Finally Killed George Tyrrell," *Catholic Medical Quarterly* 26 (April 1974): 75-85, an article of questionable value; see also chap. 6, n. 95.

38. On GT's negotiations with Rome from February 1904 on, see *AL*, 2: 228-81, 458-506.

39. GT to FvH, 22 September 1901, PP, BL, Add. MSS 44927.174.

40. "Liberalism Again," *Church Review* 41 (7 November 1901): 711, unsigned.

41. Vaughan Papers, AAW.

42. GT to MDP, 12 December 1901, published in *AL*, 2: 171-72.

43. GT to MDP, 21 December 1901, PP, BL, Add. MSS 52367. William Gildea (d. 1915) was a canon of Westminster Cathedral and one of Vaughan's theologians.

44. Colley to GT, 23 December 1901, published in *AL*, 2: 172.

45. See *FM*, 1: 244-46.

46. GT to Bremond, 31 December 1901, FB, BN, NAF. GT was probably referring to Junius Annaeus Gallio (d. A.D. 95?), proconsul in Achaia, before whom the Jews arraigned Paul in the spring of 52 A.D. Note Gallio's reply in Acts 18: 12-17.

47. Vaughan to GT, 20 March 1902, published in *AL*, 2: 172.

48. Vaughan to Colley, 24 March 1902, EPSJ Archives.

49. Colley to GT, 24 March 1902, EPSJ Archives.

50. Vaughan to GT, 25 March 1902, published in part in *AL*, 2: 172.

51. GT to Vaughan, published in part in *AL*, 2: 173. A copy of this letter in Colley's hand, EPSJ Archives, is dated 27 March, but the original letter to Vaughan had to have been written on 25 March, as is obvious from what follows in the text.

52. Vaughan to Colley, 26 March 1902, EPSJ Archives.

53. GT had copied Vaughan's letter and sent it to Gerard, who in turn copied it for Colley. It is preserved in Gerard's letter to Colley of 28 March 1902, EPSJ Archives.

54. Gerard to Colley, 28 March 1902, EPSJ Archives.

55. Colley to GT, 1 April 1902, EPSJ Archives.

56. GT to Colley, 2 April 1902, EPSJ Archives.

57. Dolling to GT, 2 April 1902, published in *AL*, 2: 174.

58. Gerard to Colley, 4 April 1902, and Colley to GT, 4 April 1902, EPSJ Archives.

59. For details of printing and circulation, see Loome, "Bibliography of Tyrrell," 288; Loome, "Bibliography of Tyrrell: Supplement," p. 163; and the letters cited in both.

60. GT to MDP, 3 April 1902, PP, BL, Add. MSS 52367.

61. GT to Colley, 3 April 1902, EPSJ Archives.

62. GT to Colley, 6 April 1902, EPSJ Archives. See GT to Vaughan, 2 April 1902, EPSJ Archives, published in part in *AL*, 2: 174.

63. GT to Vaughan, 2 April 1902, EPSJ Archives, published in part in *AL*, 2: 174; see also GT to FvH, 12 April 1902, PP, BL, Add. MSS 44928.11.

64. GT to FvH, ibid.

65. "Rome's Opportunity" is preserved among the Katherine Clutton Papers in the care of Dr. Arthur W. Adams, Dean of Divinity, Magdalen College, Oxford, to whose kindness I am much indebted. "The row" probably refers to GT's dismissal from the Society of Jesus and/or his excommunication—therefore to events around 1906-7. William John (Willie) Williams along with his sister Dora were two of GT's most faithful friends. "Willie" was author of *Newman, Pascal, Loisy and the Catholic Church* (London: Francis Griffiths, 1906) and numerous articles of a liberal tendency in the Catholic press.

Bishop Peter Emmanuel Amigo was the bishop of Southwark who delivered the notice of GT's excommunication. See *AL*, 2: 313, 341, 365, 436, 446.

66. GT to Bremond, 26 January 1902, FB, BN, NAF. GT referred to *CF* as "Catholicism Re-stated." See GT to FvH, 8 April 1903, PP, BL, Add. MSS 44928.85, published in *AL*, 2: 187–88.

67. GT, "Rome's Opportunity," p. 1.

68. Ibid., p. 5.

69. Ibid., p. 10.

70. Ibid., p. 15.

71. Ibid., p. 17.

72. Ibid., pp. 17–18. GT's comments here on women are, of course, ironic.

73. *Ratio atque institutio studiorum Societatis Jesu* was the official guide for curriculum and teaching methods that appeared in its final form in 1599 under General Claudio Aquaviva.

74. GT, "Rome's Opportunity," pp. 16, 20.

75. Ibid., p. 29.

76. Ibid., p. 31.

77. Ibid.

CHAPTER 6

1. "Dr. Ernest Engels" [GT], *RFL*. See GT to Waller, 30 April, 8 July 1902, WP, BL, Add. MSS 43680.61, 83.

2. GT to Waller, 28 May 1902, WP, BL, Add. MSS 43680.67. For further details of publication, see Loome, "Bibliography of Tyrrell," p. 287.

3. GT to FvH, 3 January 1902, PP, BL, Add. MSS 44928.4.

4. GT to FvH, 12 April 1902, PP, BL, Add. MSS 44928.12, published in *AL*, 2: 176.

5. GT to Bremond, 20 July 1899, FB, BN, NAF.

6. Loisy, *Mémoires*, 3: 268.

7. Vidler, *Modernist Movement*, p. 160.

8. GT, preface to *Saint Francis de Sales* by Amédée de Margerie, trans. Margaret Maitland (London: Duckworth & Co., 1900), pp. x, xiv; see also p. v. The preface, undated, was completed no later than February 1900. See n. 11 below.

9. See, e.g., *FM*, 1: 193 ff.; 2: 60; GT, *Lex Credendi* (hereafter *LC*) (London: Longmans, Green & Co., 1906), pp. 39–42; GT, *A Much-Abused Letter* (London: Longmans, Green & Co., 1906), p. 71; GT, introduction to *The Mystery of Newman* by Henri Bremond (London: Williams & Norgate, 1907), p. xiv; cf. *LO*, p. xxxi; GT, *CCR*, p. 177; *AL*, 2: 398; and *GTL*, pp. 103, 221, 239.

10. GT, preface to *Saint Francis de Sales*, pp. x, xiv; see also p. v.

11. FvH to GT, 4 March 1900, PP, BL, Add. MSS 44927.102. FvH's copy of the preface is preserved, with GT's corrections and FvH's annotations, in the Hügel Library, SAUL, pamphlet box no. 11.

12. GT wrote the preface to a new edition, *XVI Revelations of Divine Love Shewed to Mother Juliana of Norwich 1373* (London: Kegan Paul, Trench, Trübner & Co., 1902).

13. GT, "A Light from the Past," *Month* 95 (January, March 1900): 12–23, 250–58, reprinted as "Juliana of Norwich" in *FM*, 2: 1–39.

14. See p. 44 above.

15. *FM*, 2: 5.

16. *FM*, 2: 23. The position taken on this question in *RFL* is quite different. See pp. 225–26 below.

17. *FM*, 2: 25–26. GT's explanation here shows the influence of William James, whom he had read the previous summer. Cf. William James, *The Will to Believe and Other Essays in Popular Philosophy* (New York: Longmans & Co., 1897), pp. 111–14 and passim. FvH, *Mystical Element of Religion*, 1: 51–53, cites these same pages of James's book as helping him to formulate his theory of the growth of religious experience in man

from infancy to maturity. In a letter of 11 August 1904 to an Anglican friend, Rev. J. H. R. Abbott, GT wrote: "Blessed is the man who is so occupied about living and helping others to live that he cannot and need not occupy himself about the laws and the theory of life. . . . In Ritschl's form the 'value-theory' is very wobbly as a criterion of belief; but I think there is a core of truth in it. Dr. Engels and the author of *Lex Orandi* use it in a modified form, having got at it, not from Ritschl, but from Professor James's *Will to Believe*." Published in *GTL*, pp. 21-22. However, GT's emphasis on will-union, as Charles J. Healey, S.J., pointed out in "Aspects of Tyrrell's Spirituality," *Downside Review* 95 (April 1977): 140, is present already in *HS*, whose introduction is dated 29 June 1898. See, e.g., *HS*, pp. 45-68, 420.

18. *FM*, 2: 28-29. Cf. *RFL*, pp. 4-16, 39-51, where GT elaborated the same theory based on Blondel, Münsterberg, and Bergson.

19. *FM*, 2: 29-30.

20. Jérôme-Eduoard Récéjac, *Essais sur les fondements de la connaissance mystique* (Paris: F. Alcan, 1896).

21. FvH to GT, 4 March 1900, PP, BL, Add. MSS 44927.105.

22. Cf. Récéjac, *Essais*, p. 46. Curiously, FvH never once cited Récéjac in any of his own works even though their ideas on mysticism are largely concordant. This omission is all the more striking in view of the fact that he cited nearly everyone he read. It is likely, but not certain, that he read Récéjac. If he did, it would not have been uncharacteristic for him to have omitted citing the name on the grounds that Récéjac was a priest who had left the church, a point about which FvH was particularly sensitive. In the 4 March 1900 letter to GT, FvH wrote, "I . . . dislike, in

one way, the notion of the book,— as he, poor fellow, is an Abbé who has left the Church."

23. GT had intended his writings on ethics to form the body of what he hoped would be his *magnum opus*, of which *RFL* was to be simply the philosophical prolegomenon. The substance of those writings was prepared as the second set of Oxford Conferences, which were probably delivered during Lent of 1900. The first set, published as *ER*, had been delivered during Lent of 1899. First mention of the second set, which GT referred to as "Ethical Preludes," came in a letter to FvH of 25 November 1900, PP, BL, Add. MSS 44927.144. Eventually GT condemned the "Preludes" as "incoherent dry & dreary" (GT to MDP, 13 May 1902, PP, BL, Add. MSS 52367, published in *AL*, 2: 192), but he continued to work at them piecemeal over the next two years. On 25 September 1904 GT wrote to FvH: "I have finished my 'Ethical Preludes' for the present. They are very heavy & would break any publisher. They run to 87,000 words. At present Miss P[etre]. is to be their guardian. I hope by the collected proceeds of my furtive writings to print them Engelwise some day or other." PP, BL, Add. MSS 44928.208. GT never did publish the "Ethical Preludes" in book form, but MDP claimed (*AL*, 2: 192) that the following articles were taken from them: "Christianity and the Natural Virtues," *International Journal of Ethics* 13 (January 1903): 286-97; "Religion and Ethics," *Month* 101 (February 1903): 130-45, reprinted in *FM* (3d ed., 1904), 2: 313-50; "A Chapter in Christian Ethics," unpublished, refused by the *Month* "as too hard and 'unusual'" (GT to FvH, 21 April 1903, PP, BL, Add. MSS 44928.95), but some printed copies were circulated, of which one is preserved

at University Library, Cambridge; and "Vita Nuova," *Month* 102 (July 1903): 23-38, reprinted in *FM* (3d ed., 1904), 2: 351-80. Apart from some brilliant spots in "A Chapter in Christian Ethics," GT's judgment of the "Preludes" is accurate, and one need not regret their never having appeared as a book. According to MDP, GT did not destroy the original MS, but its present whereabouts is unknown. These articles do not go beyond *RFL*, so they require no special analysis or exposition.

24. Paul Lejeune, *Introduction à la vie mystique* (Paris: P. Lethielleux, 1899), published in English as *An Introduction to the Mystical Life*, trans. Basil Levett (London: R. & T. Washbourne, 1915).

25. GT to FvH, 10 March 1900, PP, BL, Add. MSS 44927.109.

26. GT to MDP, 3 April 1901, published in *AL*, 2: 3-4.

27. See *AL*, 2: 3-14.

28. GT to MDP, n.d., published in *AL*, 2: 4.

29. See GT to MDP, 7 March 1901, PP, BL, Add. MSS 52367.

30. See pp. 59-60 above.

31. GT to MDP, 6 May 1901, PP, BL, Add. MSS 52367.

32. Albert Houtin, *Histoire du modernisme catholique* (Paris: Chez l'auteur, 1913), p. 54.

33. GT to FvH, 17 June 1901, PP, BL, Add. MSS 55927.165.

34. *Matière et mémoire* is nowhere mentioned in FvH's diary or in his correspondence with GT, although the diary for 1901 is missing. But GT to FvH, 11 June 1905, PP, BL, Add. MSS 44929.30, indicates that up to that date FvH had not read *Matière et mémoire*, and for once GT was pressing a work on him. FvH's diary is preserved among the HP, SAUL.

35. GT to FvH, 2 April 1900, PP, BL, Add. MSS 44927.111.

36. FvH to GT, 27 May 1900, PP, BL,

Add. MSS 44927.113. No. 1 is a two-volume work, the second volume much shorter than the first. Alfred Firmin Loisy, *Les Évangiles synoptiques*, vol. 1 (Amien: Rousseau-Leroy, 1894), vol. 2 (Amien: Jourdain-Rousseau, 1896). It is uncertain whether FvH was referring to both volumes or only one. No. 2 is the nine articles serialized under the title, "Ernest Renan, historien d'Israël" in *Revue angloromaine* from May to October 1896. These articles formed the point of departure for Loisy's "La Religion d'Israël," *Revue du clergé français* 24 (15 October 1900): 337-63, which was condemned by Cardinal Richard, who also forbade the *Revue* to publish two projected sequels. Loisy remarked in his *Mémoires*, 2: 5, that this condemnation marked a major turning point in his career. This article and the two unpublished ones were made into a small volume, *La Religion d'Israël* (Paris: Letouzey & Co., 1901). No. 3 was a series of twelve articles that appeared in *Revue d'histoire et de littérature religieuses* from 1897 to 1900. No. 4: the pseudonym "Firmin," under which Loisy published in early 1900, was his middle name, so his identity was an open secret. The list of articles under "Firmin" in the *Revue du clergé français* begins with 1 December 1898, but FvH probably had in mind only those of the current year—at least his list of "Work Done" in his diary for 1900 mentions only the article of 15 March 1900 as having been read. That article was "Les Preuves et l'économie de la révélation." Houtin, *Modernisme catholique*, p. 91, mentions that this article was an "alleged refutation of Auguste Sabatier, with a quotation from Saint Augustine who represents tradition, and with quotations from Ollé-Laprune, Blondel, Abbé de Broglie, and Brunetière, the then-fashionable apologists whose orthodoxy no one questioned." The next "Firmin" article was also the last. It was that one which Cardinal Richard condemned. A full bibliography of Loisy's works is provided by Émile Poulat, "Bibliographie Alfred Loisy," in Albert Houtin and Félix Sartiaux, *Alfred Loisy: Sa vie, son oeuvre,* ed. Émile Poulat (Paris: Éditions du Centre National de la Recherche Scientifique, 1960), pp. 303-24.

37. Diary of FvH, 12 July 1901, HP, SAUL.

38. GT to Bremond, FB, BN, NAF. Loisy's studies on the gospels were very likely the set of four articles titled, "Les Évangiles synoptiques," *Revue des religions* 3 (May-June 1896): 221-38; 4 (July-August 1896): 289-325; 5 (September-October 1896): 385-414; 6 (November-December 1896): 481-501, collected and published as Vol. 2 of *Les Évangiles synoptiques.* The article on inspiration was probably "La Question biblique et l'inspiration des Écritures," *L'Enseignement biblique* 12 (1893): 1-16, reprinted in Alfred Loisy, *Études bibliques* (Amiens: Rousseau-Leroy, 1894). It was this article that cost Loisy his chair at the Institut Catholique in Paris.

39. GT to FvH, 22 September 1901, PP, BL, Add. MSS 44927.173. The article on the Fourth Gospel was no doubt that which had first appeared under the pseudonym "Isidore Després," L'Évangile selon Saint Jean," *Revue du clergé français* 20 (1 November 1899): 484-506. Against the traditional literal interpretation of the Fourth Gospel, this article insinuated an allegorical interpretation comparable to that accepted for the book of Revelation. Presumably that article would have come under the admonition of Leo XIII's recent encyclical letter

"To the French Clergy" of 8 September 1899 against recent innovations in philosophy, exegesis, and ecclesiology. At least Loisy felt himself attacked and responded— again under the name "Isidore Després"—with "La Lettre de Leon XIII au clergé de France et les études d'Écriture Sainte," *Revue du clergé français* 23 (1 June 1900): 5-17. Blondel, too, was very upset by the encyclical, particularly with its allusion to "Catholics [who] thought that they could walk safely in the wake of a philosophy which, under the specious pretext of liberating human reason from any preconceived idea or illusion, denies it the right to affirm anything over and above its own operations, thus sacrificing all of the certitudes of traditional metaphysics to a radical subjectivism. . . . It is a matter of deep regret that this doctrinal scepticism, an alien import and Protestant in inspiration, could have been accepted so favorably in a country once justly known for its love of the clarity of both ideas and language." Quoted in Jean Rivière, *Le Modernisme dans l'Église* (Paris: Librairie Letouzey & Co., 1929), pp. 126-27. See also Bremond and Blondel, *Correspondance,* 1: 231-33. Of course, what GT himself was currently occupied with would have made him equally a target of the encyclical.

40. GT to FvH, 3 January 1902, PP, BL, Add. MSS 44928.2-4. The articles on Genesis and the Babylonian myths would have been "Les Mythes babyloniens et les premiers chapitres de la Genèse," serialized in *Revue d'histoire et de littérature religieuses* from March to October 1901 and republished as *Les Mythes babyloniens et les premiers chapitres de la Genèse* (Paris: Picard, 1901).

41. See FvH to GT, 17 November

1899, 7 July 1900, PP, BL, Add. MSS 44927.88, 121; and the diary of FvH, 12 July 1900, HP, SAUL.

42. GT to MDP, 15 August 1900, PP, BL, Add. MSS 52367.

43. GT to Raffalovich, 18 August 1900, Raffalovich Papers, Blackfriars Library.

44. GT to Bremond, 22 August 1900, FB, BN, NAF.

45. GT to FvH, 7 September 1900, PP, BL, Add. MSS 44927.128.

46. Baron J. Angot des Rotours, "La Religion intérieure d'après un Jesuite anglais," *Quinzaine* 6 (16 July 1900): 141–57. Angot concentrated on *ER* but did not neglect *Nova et Vetera* and *HS*. He described GT as "a priest who preached last year's Lenten Series at Oxford and who is well known today as the most outstanding essayist in the English language. . . . He addresses himself to the more cultivated intellects and to minds that are already critically awakened. And for this kind of reader, what a pleasure to find a mind so open and so sincere!" Ibid., p. 141. Angot also noticed parallels to Newman, Abbé Huvelin, Ollé-Laprune, and Georges Fonsegrive.

47. GT to FvH, 7 September 1900, PP, BL, Add. MSS 44927.128. By reason of its copious citations of Blondel (not, however, *L'Action*), *RFL* could well stand as the fulfillment of that wish.

48. "Philosophy in France," *Pilot* 2 (20 October 1900).

49. "E. F. G." [GT], letter to the editor, "M. Blondel's Dilemma," *Pilot* 2 (27 October 1900): 534. See GT to FvH, 26 October 1900, PP, BL, Add. MSS 44927.137–38.

50. Blondel, *L'Action*, pp. xxii, 28.

51. See, e.g., GT to Raffalovich, 28 October 1900, Raffalovich Papers Blackfriars Library.

52. A nearly identical statement and idea can be seen in *O&W*, p. 238.

53. "E. F. G." [GT], "M. Blondel's Dilemma," p. 534.

54. In footnotes, GT quoted from Thomas Aquinas, *Summa theologica*, P.I.q. xii, art. 1, 4: "For the ultimate beatitude of man consists in the use of his highest function, which is the operation of the intellect. Hence if we suppose that a created intellect could never see God, it would either never attain to beatitude, or its beatitude would consist in something else besides God; which is opposed to faith. . . . Further, the same opinion is also against reason. . . . It is impossible for any created intellect to see the essence of God by its own natural power." English Dominican translation.

55. GT's footnote here reads: "A typical Jesuit, Father Tepe, writes: 'Dona supernaturalia sunt ea quae excedunt vires *et exigentias* totius naturae creatae et creabilis.' Institutiones Theol. Vol. 3, p. 3.": "Supernatural gifts are those that exceed the strengths *and exigencies* of the whole of created and creatable nature."

56. "E. F. G." [GT], "M. Blondel's Dilemma," p. 534.

57. GT to FvH, 26 October 1900, PP, BL, Add. MSS 44927.137–38.

58. FvH to GT, 28 October 1900, PP, BL, Add. MSS 44927.139–40. FvH's concluding remark is merely the continuation of a campaign to get GT to learn German. See FvH to GT, 6 August 1901, PP, BL, Add. MSS 44927.169. A year later GT told Bremond that he was taking up German "as a distraction" and "a narcotic" to forget the church and "purely to please the Baron." GT to Bremond, 30 September, 3 November 1901, FB, BN, NAF. The German whose paper FvH summarized was possibly Wilhelm Dilthey. A year earlier, when FvH was criticizing "The Relation of

Theology to Devotion," he wrote to GT, "I could show you some grand things, analoguous [sic] to these, quoted by Prof. Dilthey of Berlin." FvH to GT, 8 October 1899, PP, BL, Add. MSS 44927.84. The general subject of the letter of 28 October 1900 was again "The Relation of Theology to Devotion," and FvH's diary and list of "Work Done," HP, SAUL, show that he had again been reading Dilthey shortly before writing to GT. Other strong possibilities for the unknown German are Ernst Troeltsch and Bernhard Duhm, whom FvH was also reading at this time and whose works he recommended as compatible with GT's thought. GT himself did not get around to Dilthey until 1903, and it is doubtful that Dilthey had any direct influence on *LO*, which GT was then composing. See GT to FvH, 9 April 1903, PP, BL, Add. MSS 44928.90. But GT did incorporate Dilthey's "historico-philosophic comprehension" in the later chapters of *LC*, See, e.g., *LC*, p. 140; also GT to FvH, 13 November 1905, PP, BL, Add. MSS 44929.62. As for Troeltsch and Duhm, GT did not read them for himself until autumn 1902, when *RFL* was already in print. Still the similarity of ideas is striking. Concerning Troeltsch, GT wrote to FvH on 10 July 1902, PP, BL, Add. MSS 44928.20: "I had also done a chapter on 'the relation of Ethics to Religion' [probably what GT later published as "Religion and Ethics"] exactly on the lines of your friend Tröltsch of Heidelberg. Also on pp. 35 & 74 of 'Dr. Engels' brochure I have touched on the same ideas." Of Duhm, GT wrote to FvH on 14 October 1902, PP, BL, Add. MSS 44928.38: "Duhm's Geheimnis I only read *after* I had written a very cautious brace of articles for the *Month!* on 'Mysteries, a necessity of Life'—a

point which we spoke of, climbing down the green bank by the old bridge, one day. Even if it is rejected, I will have 100 copies printed. In principle I am with Duhm, tho' I try to save theology within its due limits." The parallel between GT's thought and Duhm's is notable. Duhm wrote: "We Protestants have until now greatly concerned ourselves with the investigation of religion. We will also have to have the greatest concern for the investigation and proper appreciation of mystery. For it seems that mystery has practically disappeared from the Protestant religion. We are inclined to identify religion with church doctrine or with the religious *Weltanschauung;* or we regard ethics as the principle element of religion, whereas ethics is only a product of religion and a symptom of its character and can be no more presented as the heart of religion than as the heart of poetry, which also elicits ethics but does not exist for the sake of ethics." *Das Geheimnis in der Religion* (Freiburg: J.C.B. Mohr, 1896), p. 31.

59. GT to FvH, 25 November 1900, PP, BL, Add. MSS 44927.144–45. The "enclosed extract" is missing, but it might well have included the statement: "It is by *doing*, and not by *thinking* or reasoning that we apprehend God and His truth in this life." *ER*, p. 158.

60. Blondel, "À propos de la certitude religieuse: Réponse à Ed. Péchegut," *Revue de clergé français* 29 (15 February 1902): 643–59.

61. GT to FvH, 12 April 1902, PP, BL, Add. MSS 44928.11.

62. Rudolf Eucken, *Der Kampf um einen geistigen Lebensinhalt,* (Leipzig: Veit & Co., 1896). See MDP's diary for 10 September 1900 and passim, PP, BL, Add. MSS 52372, for important discussions on Eucken.

63. Diary of MDP, 8 November 1900, PP, BL, Add. MSS 52372. For the subject under discussion, see Eucken, *Der Kampf*, pp. 334-400.

64. FvH to MDP, 26 September 1900, PP, BL, Add. MSS 45361, published in FvH, *Selected Letters*, pp. 89-96. FvH's letters to MDP are among the Petre Papers in the BL, Add. MSS 45361-62. Eucken's notion of *Wesensbildung* could be roughly translated by "character formation."

65. FvH to GT, 30 September 1900, PP, BL, Add. MSS 44927.134.

66. GT to FvH, 12 November 1900, PP, BL, Add. MSS 44927.143.

67. GT to MDP, 16 November 1900, PP, BL, Add. MSS 52367.

68. GT to FvH, 17 June 1901, PP, BL, Add. MSS 44927.164.

69. FvH to GT, 6 August 1901, PP, BL, Add. MSS 44927.169.

70. GT to FvH, 22 September 1901, PP, BL, Add. MSS 44927.174.

71. GT to MDP, 18 October 1901, PP, BL, Add. MSS 52367, emended and published in *GTL*, pp. 23-24.

72. GT to FvH, 3 January 1902, PP, BL, Add. MSS 44928.4, published in part in *GTL*, pp. 80-83; in *vH&T*, pp. 100-103; and in *AL*, 2: 93, 189. Attempts to identify the work by Smith on Eucken have been unsuccessful. The article by Eucken on Hegel was "Hegel Today," *Monist* 7 (April 1897): 321-39. The article on Augustine was a section from *Lebensanschauungen der grossen Denker*.

73. GT to FvH, 10 July 1902, PP, BL, Add. MSS 44928.20.

74. GT reviewed *L'Évolution créatrice* for the *Hibbert Journal* 6 (January 1908): 435-42. Henri Louis Bergson, *Essai sur les données immediates de la conscience* (Paris: Félix Alcan, 1889); Bergson, *Matière et mémoire* (Paris: Félix Alcan, 1896); Bergson, *L'Évolution créatrice* (Paris: Félix Alcan, 1907).

75. On the appreciation of Bergson by his contemporaries, see Gaston Rageot, "L'Évolution créatrice," *Revue philosophique de la France* 64 (July 1907): 85; quoted in William James, "The Philosophy of Bergson," *Hibbert Journal*, 7 (1908-9): 577.

76. See the note added to FvH to GT, 1 August 1900, PP, BL, Add. MSS 44927.124.

77. GT to MDP, 18 December 1900, PP, BL, Add. MSS 52367.

78. GT to MDP, 6, 25 May 1901, PP, BL, Add. MSS 52367.

79. GT to FvH, 17 June 1901, PP, BL, Add. MSS 44927.165.

80. FvH to GT, 28 May 1901, PP, BL, Add. MSS 44927.162-63. Hugo Münsterberg (1863-1916), a naturalized American citizen, occupied a professorial chair at Harvard in his later years. He received his doctorate at Leipzig under Wilhelm Wundt, who in turn was a disciple of Gustav Fechner, a psycho-physical philosopher and friend of C. H. Weisse. Weisse had also been Hermann Lotze's teacher. Weisse's philosophy of religion had a formative influence on all three: Wundt, Fechner, and Lotze, all of whom are quoted with approval by Bergson, all of whom FvH had read and passed on to GT, who himself read at least Fechner and Lotze. See GT to FvH, 8 April 1903, PP, BL, Add. MSS 44928.89, on Fechner's *Die drei Motive und Gründe des Glaubens* (Leipzig: Breitkopf & Härtel, 1863); FvH's copy with copious annotations is in the Hügel Library, SAUL; GT to FvH, 20 November 1904, PP, BL, Add. MSS 44928.220; and FvH to GT, 4 March 1900, 6 April 1905, PP, BL, Add. MSS 44927.105, 44929.28. All these writers claimed spiritual affinity to Spinoza, Kant, Fichte, and Schopenhauer in their efforts toward an integral view of life and definition of the relationship between matter and spirit, in-

tellect and will, the brain and operations of the mind. Bergson borrowed copiously from Schopenhauer. The following statement from Schopenhauer's *World as Will and Representation*, trans. E.F.J. Payne, 2 vols. (New York: Dover Publications, 1966), 2: 142, demonstrates a typical coincidence of thought among Schopenhauer, Bergson, and Tyrrell: "The defective nature of the intellect here described will not surprise us, however, if we look back at its origin and its density. . . . Nature has produced it for the service of an individual will; therefore it is destined to know things only in so far as they serve as the motives of such a will, not to fathom them or to comprehend their true inner essence." GT read both Schopenhauer and his spiritual progenitor Fichte in German and found their works among the most impressive of any he had read. See GT to FvH, 14 October 1902, 11 January 1904, 19 February 1905, PP, BL, Add. MSS 44928.38, 44928.146, 44929.14.

81. GT to FvH, 22 September 1901, PP, BL, Add. MSS 44927.173. *Olla podrida:* Spanish for "rotten pot," but conventionally it refers to a highly seasoned stew.

82. GT to MDP, 18 October 1901, PP, BL, Add. MSS 52367, published in *GTL,* pp. 23–24.

83. Blondel, "Réponse à Ed. Péchegut," is cited in *RFL,* pp. 39–43. Less than one week after this article appeared, the original MS of *RFL* was already being passed around. See GT to Ward, 21 February 1902, WFP, SAUL. Münsterberg is cited in *RFL,* pp. 9–10, where the reader is referred to his chapter "Psychology and History" in *Psychology and Life* (Westminster: A. Constable, 1899), pp. 179–228.

84. See GT to Waller, 19 April 1903, WP, BL, Add. MSS 43680.147–48.

85. See GT to MDP, 27 April 1902, PP, BL, Add. MSS 52367.

86. Hedwig Zamoyska, *Sur le travail* (Paris: Lethielleux, 1902).

87. GT to FvH, 12 April 1902, PP, BL, Add. MSS 44928.12. See also Blondel, "Réponse à Ed. Péchegut." *Infiltrations du protestantisme* is undoubtedly a satirical reference to Julien Fontaine, S.J., *Les Infiltrations protestantes et le clergé français* (Paris: V. Retaux, 1901).

88. [GT], "Un Noviciat De Vie Chrétienne Dans Le Monde," *Monthly Register* 1 (May 1902): 55–57, a review of the English translation of *Sur le travail* by Hedwig Zamoyska, *Ideals in Practice: With Some Account of Women's Work in Poland.* See also GT, "Religion and Work," *Month* 102 (December 1903): 561–71, a combined review of *Ideals in Practice* by Hedwig Zamoyska and *Gesammelte Aufsätze zur Philosophie und Lebensanschauung* by Rudolf Eucken.

89. GT to MDP, 13 May 1902, PP, BL, Add. MSS 52367. Zamoyska's training school was located at Zakopani in Poland.

90. FvH to GT, 4 June 1902, PP, BL, Add. MSS 44928.14. Abbé Albert Lamy had been a student of Blondel at Collège Stanislas where Blondel, on leave from the Sorbonne to revise his thesis (*L'Action*), had acted as substitute lecturer from January to April 1891. See Blondel and Bremond, *Correspondance,* 1: 42, 235.

91. [GT], "Un Noviciat," p. 57.

92. GT to MDP, 15 August 1900, PP, BL, Add. MSS 52367.

93. Hatch, *Influence of Greek Ideas and Usages upon the Christian Church,* pp. xi, xii; see also pp. 48 ff. and passim.

94. GT to MDP, 20 November 1901, PP, BL, Add. MSS 52367. See also among others, GT to Bremond, 13 November 1900, 26 January 1902, 17 February 1902, FB, BN, NAF; and to MDP, 18 October 1901, PP,

BL, Add. MSS 52367, published in part in *GTL*, pp. 23–24.

95. Diary of MDP, PP, BL, Add. MSS 52372. There was a similar disagreement over Bergson's *Essai* (see diary for 24, 27 January 1901) as well as over Patmore (diary for 7 December 1900) and a host of philosophical and theological questions. I mention MDP's taking issue with GT to counterbalance the picture one gets of her from Crehan, "What Killed George Tyrrell," pp. 75–85. Part of that picture is accurate enough: that MDP was a "liberated woman of the period," "extraordinary," and at times regarded by GT as "a nuisance." But to say that she "had come to live at Richmond to be tutored in theology by Tyrrell whom she adored" is to go beyond the evidence. Theirs was not a tutor-pupil relationship. MDP was as well read in philosophy and theology as was GT—better in some areas. In these matters there was a sharing as between peers. It is true that she was deeply in love with GT—quite one-sidedly so—but her diary shows that for all her temptations she and GT approached nothing faintly resembling an embrace until his deathbed when for the first time they allowed themselves a farewell kiss. To say that she "adored" GT is to imply that in her eyes the master could do no wrong. That implication does not square with the evidence. Crehan's article, however, is by no means preoccupied with the MDP-GT relationship. The burden of his article is to establish Bright's disease as "perhaps *the* major part-cause" for GT's "growing wildness of thought" and "the steps he took in gradually separating himself from the Church," many of which steps "were not quite voluntary acts." Crehan's hypothesis is interesting, but his method suffers from several deficiencies: (1) It is not legitimate

without clinical evidence to subsume every mention of sickness in GT's letters under evidence for the workings of that "dread disease," as if GT never suffered a cold or flu. (2) Nor is it legitimate, in determining intervals between attacks, to fail to take into account the possibility that (a) GT did not mention all his attacks and that (b) not all the letters in which attacks were mentioned were available. (3) Although some changes in personality have been observed in patients with progressive renal failure, there is no hard evidence that GT behaved ideologically any differently after the onset of the disease than he did before. Crehan's hypothesis in this regard is provocative, but he has not established the connection. (4) In clinical observation, "wildness of thought" is associated only with the last stages of the disease, perhaps one to two weeks prior to death. On this I have been assured by a well-known certified specialist in renal diseases and by numerous medical textbooks. See, e.g., the standard text, Maurice B. Strauss and Louis G. Welt, eds., *Diseases of the Kidney*, 2d ed., 2 vols. (Boston: Little, Brown & Co., 1971), 1: 211–60. Apart from these methodological problems, a far graver problem is raised by Crehan's implication that GT *separated himself* from the church—as if excommunication is but an official and legal ratification that Rome resignedly suffers to go out from her in the event of the spiritual suicide of one of her unfortunate children. Rome was anything but passive in her treatment of the so-called modernists. Crehan confesses he is bewildered that modern scholars continue to find so much fodder in one who was "not thought by his contemporaries to be of very great importance." If Crehan's assertion is correct, then it is equally puzzling why Rome thought it necessary to make such an insignificant figure the subject of a decree and an encyclical letter to the universal church and finally to excommunicate him. In a letter of 18 August 1901 to MDP, PP, BL, Add. MSS 52367, GT wrote concerning his unquestioning brethren and previsioned such efforts as Crehan's to rehabilitate him by whatever means: "These good men are so sincere in their 'loyalty' that I am sure they think me a little mad; & believe that with rest & quiet I will return to my right mind. Fr. Gallwey has said as much. 'Bad' & 'mad' are the only two hypotheses that can explain a difference from their views. Of course we are all a little both; & it is easy to find evidence."

96. GT to MDP, 13 May 1902, PP, BL, Add. MSS 52367, published in *AL*, 2: 192. On the fate of the "Preludes" see n. 23 above.

97. GT to MDP, 16 July 1901, PP, BL, Add. MSS 52367.

98. GT to Raffalovich, 30 July 1901, Raffalovich Papers, Blackfriars Library.

99. GT to MDP, 30 July 1901, PP, BL, Add. MSS 52367. MDP misdated this letter 2 August 1901. As much as Bergson's discussion of these matters appealed to GT, he never fully digested it, nor was he ever satisfied with his own expression of it. *RFL* treats the topic of determinism only obliquely if suffusedly.

100. GT to FvH, 22 September 1901, PP, BL, Add. MSS 44927. 173-74.

101. Diary of MDP, 30 October 1901, PP, BL, Add. MSS 52372.

102. GT to MDP, 2 November 1901, PP, BL, Add. MSS 52367.

103. Diary of MDP, 21 November 1901, PP, BL, Add. MSS 52372.

104. Ibid., 19 November 1901.

105. GT to MDP, 2 March 1902, published in *GTL*, pp. 204-5.

106. GT to MDP, 3 May 1902, PP, BL, Add. MSS 52367. On Janet, see chap. 4, n. 67.

107. Diary of MDP, 21 November 1901, PP, BL, Add. MSS 52372.

108. Bergson, *Time and Free Will*, pp. 168-69.

109. GT to MDP, 24 June 1901, published in *GTL*, pp. 203-4. *Calicem quem dedit. . . . :* "Am I not to drink the cup the Father has given me?" John 18:11, New American Bible translation. See GT's pastoral application of this view in two letters from the same period to a friend who was dying of cancer, published in *GTL*, pp. 251-53.

110. GT to MDP, 6 December 1901, PP, BL, Add. MSS 52367.

111. Cf. Bergson, *Time and Free Will*, pp. 99-139, 154-72, 222-40.

112. Ibid., p. 170.

113. GT to MDP, 30 May 1902, PP, BL, Add. MSS 52367, published in *GTL*, pp. 205-6. It is not certain when or by whom GT was introduced to the psychological notion of the subconscious. Crehan, *Father Thurston*, pp. 57-58, n. 2, claims that GT discovered the notion from Frank Podmore, a researcher in psychic phenomena, whom GT mentioned in a letter to Thurston in 1900. However, GT might also have picked up the notion from Janet whom he read as early as autumn 1889. See chap. 4, n. 67.

114. GT's journal seems to have disappeared. All that survives is what MDP published in *EFI*. These unfinished vignettes, sparks tossed from a spinning firework and meant only for the privacy of GT's garden, are where Crehan, "What Killed George Tyrrell," p. 85, finds evidence of GT's "growing wildness of thought" due to the mentally deteriorating effects of Bright's disease. But see n. 95 above.

115. GT to Bremond, 5 December 1901, FB, BN, NAF.

116. GT to Bremond, 17 February 1902, FB, BN, NAF. Cf. GT to Ward, 21 February 1902, WFP, SAUL.

117. GT to MDP, 25 February 1902, PP,

BL, Add. MSS 52367. GT learned in May 1900 that he was suffering from a kidney or liver disease or both. Only in his last months was his condition diagnosed as Bright's disease. See n. 95 above. Since no postmortem examination was made, the precise nature of his illness remains uncertain. As indicated in this letter, GT sensed the seriousness of his condition and lived with a constant awareness of impending death. One could agree with Crehan that GT's illness was a partial factor in some of his decisions. But the disease had nothing to do with the formation of GT's character, and it was the confluence of his character with historical forces within and without the Roman Church that eventually led to his rupture from the Society of Jesus and from the church. His illness certainly influenced such decisions as his employment after leaving the Jesuits and where he might live. It might even have contributed to certain excesses of speech. But GT was given to those excesses at his healthiest, and even if perfectly healthy he would have met the same fate.

118. GT to Waller, 2 March 1902, WP, BL, Add. MSS 43680.54.

119. GT to Waller, 2 April 1902, WP, BL, Add. MSS 43680.55. On the *Oil and Wine* affair, see chap. 5.

120. GT to Bremond, 14 April 1902, FB, BN, NAF.

121. GT to Waller, 23 April 1902, BL, Add. MSS 43680.57.

122. GT to MDP, 3 May 1902, PP, BL, Add. MSS 52367. GT alternately dropped the final "a" in "Juliana," as "Julian" is also an acceptable form.

123. GT to MDP, 25 May 1902, published in *AL*, 2: 176.

124. GT to Waller, 25 May 1902, WP, BL, Add. MSS 43680.65.

125. GT to Waller, 30 April, 29 October 1902, WP, BL, Add. MSS 43680.61, 112.

126. GT to Waller, 8 July 1902, WP, BL, Add. MSS 43680.83.

127. GT to Bremond, 23 July 1902, FB, BN, NAF, published in *AL*, 2: 186.

128. GT to Waller, 30 April 1902, WP, BL, Add. MSS 43680.61. The turbulence of GT's life strongly affected even such a minor project as this. One week after *O&W* was censored, GT accepted Waller's proposal to write the preface, but he insisted that it not go through censorship, GT to Waller, 23 April 1902, WP, BL, Add. MSS 43680.57. The publisher, Kegan Paul, Trench, Trübner & Co., however, wanted an *imprimatur*, which would mean that the entire typescript would have to pass censorship. GT advised against attaching his name to the publication in any way that would make him seem responsible for it. That would draw the attention of Cardinal Vaughan, who would then insist on his right of *imprimatur*, and that, GT argued, "would lose you a lot of Anglican readers to whom it is as the mark of the beast." For the same reason GT proposed that he not annotate the first edition, but wait for the second edition. He justified ignoring censorship on the grounds that "the contract or promise to write it is an old one, and that the present method of double censorship (S.J. and H[is]. E[minence].) is unworkable & negligeable. I could get *nothing* through 2 iron walls—not even the *Pater Noster* if it were in my own hand-writing." GT to Waller, 2 May 1902, WP, BL, Add. MSS 43680.63. The publisher countered that an *imprimatur* would win rather than lose readers, but GT would have none of it and threatened to withdraw his preface. GT to Waller, 20 June 1902, WP, BL, Add. MSS 43680.75. But perhaps not wanting to lose the revenue he

needed for printing "Engels," GT tried another tack. Theological classics, he pointed out, require no *imprimatur*. Moreover, "Mother J. could not be approved *theologically* any more than many of the earlier Fathers of the Church i.e. she is not up to theol. date. It is only present-day utterances, as such, that need censorship. So altogether it is very absurd; unless as regards the Preface. Now *that* is unheard of,—that the Preface of a work should have an independent Imprimatur." GT to Waller, 22 June 1902, WP, BL, Add. MSS 43680.78. Kegan Paul, GT thought, was probably behind the *imprimatur* scheme (see GT to Waller, 20 June 1902, WP, BL, Add. MSS 43680.75; and chap. 3, n. 109), but he died on 19 July 1902, and a few days later GT wrote Bremond, "Poor C. K. Paul is at the 'end of wandering' at last. Anglican, Agnostic, Positivist, Romanist—and now? Well, with God there is neither Jew nor Greek. Let us hope there is rest." GT to Bremond, 23 July 1902, FB, BN, NAF. It is hard to know which argument had the last say. In any case, GT's preface and *Juliana* appeared without Vaughan's *imprimatur*.

129. GT, preface to *Juliana of Norwich*, pp. v–vii.
130. *RFL*, p. 2.
131. Ibid.
132. *RFL*, p. 4.
133. Ibid.
134. *RFL*, p. 5.
135. *RFL*, p. 6.
136. On this very point GT was misinterpreted by at least one reviewer of *RFL*. Whether the misinterpretation was due to GT's carelessness or to the reviewer's antipathetic bias or to both is a moot point. See the treatment of M. Eugène Franon's review pp. 235–36 below, and n. 178 below.
137. See GT's discussion of feeling as a

criterion of truth in GT to FvH, 4 December 1902, PP, BL, Add. MSS 44928.50–51.
138. Cf. Blondel, "Réponse à Ed. Péchegut," pp. 643–59.
139. Cf. Bergson, "The Multiplicity of Conscious States: The Idea of Duration," in *Time and Free Will*, pp. 75–139; see also pp. 232–40.
140. *RFL*, p. 43.
141. For the relation between will and history, GT referred to Münsterberg, "Psychology and History," in *Psychology and Life*, pp. 179–228. Cf. also Blondel, "Réponse à Ed. Péchegut," where Blondel distinguished between *la réalité connu* (*l'objectif*) (the reality known) and *la réalité réelle* (*réel en soi*) (the really real, the real in itself). The former is symbolic of the latter. The *objectif* or shadow-world of images (which is *my* world, "the mind," in the sense that I can grasp the images) is so related to the substance-world that I can guide and determine my relation to it as by a chart or map. Blondel retorted the charge of idealism on those who mistake the *réel connu* (appearances) for the *réel en soi*.
142. GT, preface to *Juliana of Norwich*, pp. x–xi.
143. *RFL*, p. 9.
144. Cf. GT, preface to *Juliana of Norwich*, pp. vii–viii.
145. Cf. Münsterberg, "Psychology and History."
146. *RFL*, p. 11. In his distinction between God and the Absolute, GT followed Hastings Rashdall in *Papers Read before the Synthetic Society, 1896–1908*, for private circulation, presented to the members of the Synthetic Society by the Rt. Hon. Arthur James Balfour, August 1909 (London: Spottiswoode & Co., 1909). God exists in *and above* souls, but the Absolute is a *society* of God and the souls in will-sympathy with him, including all they know and experience, each soul

taken with all its relations to the rest. GT did not broach the question of the nature of the soul, perhaps because that lies in the realm of the *réel en soi*. Likewise he left open the question how the world is different from God. He said only that "God, at a certain point of time, caused the souls to exist; or (if we please) by an eternal act causes that at a certain time they shall appear in the time series." *RFL*, p. 43. GT also left open the question of the eternal "existence" of souls, perhaps because, in the Bergsonian scheme, time belongs only to the realm of extension and materiality, so it makes no sense when speaking of "existence" of souls to ask whether they existed *before* their appearance in time. "Before" and "after" apply only to the world of appearances. See Root, "George Tyrrell and the Synthetic Society," pp. 54–56, for a terse exposition of GT's views relative to those of Rashdall and James McTaggart, a Cambridge Hegelian, on the absoluteness of God.

147. *RFL*, p. 12.
148. *RFL*, p. 47. GT had already included this observation in his *Month* articles on Mother Juliana, "A Light from the Past," but here he gives it psychological foundation. See pp. 190–92 above.
149. *RFL*, p. 48.
150. Ibid.
151. On the separate realms of faith and understanding, see pp. 225–28 below.
152. *RFL*, p. 14.
153. See *RFL*, pp. 48–49.
154. *RFL*, p. 15.
155. *RFL*, p. 16. GT used the term "personality" in Bergson's sense. "It means our freedom, in greater or less degree—our self-possession and deliverance from the determinism of nature. So far as our movement is unconscious, automatic, habitual, we are but part of the mechanism

of the universe. So far as we are perceptive, we are also self-determining. But, at best, our perception takes in an infinitesimal fraction of the whole, present, past, and to come; and our self-determination is correspondingly limited. For the rest, we are but passive; moved, but not self-moving. God alone is all-perceiving and all-free. He alone is, therefore, all-personal, all-active; in no sense passive; determining everything, determined by nothing. Yet even thus carried to infinity the perfection of personality can be affirmed of Him only analogously and defectively." *RFL*, p. 51, n. 11.
156. *RFL*, p. 18.
157. *RFL*, p. 20. Statements like this one led to the article by David F. Wells, "George Tyrrell: Precursor of Process Theology," *Scottish Journal of Theology* 26 (1973): 71–84.
158. *RFL*, p. 21.
159. *RFL*, p. 23. Cf. GT to MDP, 18 October 1901, PP, BL, Add. MSS 52367, published in *GTL*, pp. 23–24; and Thomas à Kempis, *The Imitation of Christ*, bk. 4, chap. 11, no. 4.
160. Phil. 4: 13. Cf. Récéjac, *Connaissance mystique*, pp, 231–38, esp. p. 236; and à Kempis, *Imitation*, bk. 3, chap. 5.
161. *RFL*, p. 28.
162. *RFL*, p. 29.
163. *RFL*, p. 30.
164. Ibid.
165. *RFL*, p. 31. GT misquoted John 17: 23 here. It should read "that *they* may be perfect in one," my italics.
166. Ibid.
167. GT, preface to *Juliana of Norwich*, pp. xi-xii.
168. *RFL*, p. 32. GT was of course arguing what *ought* to obtain, not what in fact *did* obtain.
169. In a letter of 21 February 1902 to Wilfrid Ward, WFP, SAUL, GT mentioned that he was aware—

apparently referring to *RFL*—of coming close to two heresies against which he had written: (1) A. Sabatier's view of dogma (see pp. 59-60 above, and GT, "Sabatier on the Vitality of Dogmas,"), and (2) rationalism in religion (see pp. 58-59, 61-62 above, and GT, "Rationalism in Religion"). He continued, "Against the latter I feel I have raised a firm wall of partition; but as to the former I am not so sure; though I think if Sabatier explained himself better, he might be held in a Catholic sense."

170. *RFL*, p. 33.

171. See pp. 226-28 above, and *RFL*, pp. 16-20, 51-52.

172. *RFL*, p. 33.

173. In the appendix to *RFL*, GT demonstrated the practical aim for religion of each article of the creed.

174. *RFL*, p. 35.

175. Ibid.

176. *RFL*, pp. 36-37.

177. See Jules Lebreton, S.J., "'Lex Orandi' par le P. Tyrrell," *Études* 106 (5 March 1906): 694.

178. Eugène Franon, "Un Nouveau manifeste catholique d'agnosticisme," *Bulletin de littérature ecclésiastique* (Toulouse), 3d ser. 5 (June 1903): 157.

179. Ibid., p. 161.

180. Lebreton, "'Lex Orandi,'" p. 694, hints that he knew.

181. Reported in Loome, "Bibliography of Tyrrell," pp. 287-88.

182. See GT to Waller, 19 March 1903, WP, BL, Add. MSS 43680.139.

183. Transcribed in FvH to GT, 8 September 1902, PP, BL, Add. MSS 44928.27. "This is very satisfactory," FvH added.

184. Transcribed in FvH to GT, 30 September 1902, PP, BL, Add. MSS 44928.33-34. Obviously GT and FvH did not let even their friends know "Engels's" identity.

185. Transcribed in FvH to GT, 13 October 1902, PP, BL, Add. MSS 44928.35.

186. Ibid.

187. GT to FvH, 4 December 1902, PP, BL, Add. MSS 44928.50.

188. GT to Waller, 1 October 1902, WP, BL, Add. MSS 43680.100.

189. GT to FvH, 14 October 1902, PP, BL, Add. MSS 44928.37.

190. GT, "Mysteries a Necessity of Life," *Month* 100 (November, December 1902): 449-59, 568-80, reprinted in *TSC*, 155-90.

191. See GT to FvH, 26 October 1902, PP, BL, Add. MSS 44928.39.

192. GT to FvH, 4 December 1902, PP, BL, Add. MSS 44928.51.

193. Diary of MDP, 24 August 1902, PP, BL, Add. MSS 52372. See also the diary of FvH, 18 August to 6 September 1902, HP, SAUL.

194. FvH to GT, 4 December 1902, PP, BL, Add. MSS 44928.55. See FvH, *Essays and Addresses on the Philosophy of Religion*, 2 vols. (London: J. M. Dent & Sons, 1924, 1928), 2: 97-98. In a subsequent essay, ibid., pp. 118-19, FvH referred to Nicholas's "grandly rich and elastic system in his *Catholic Concordance* . . . as the last word of insight and wisdom," along with Paul's "Stoic image of the body and its members." FvH's interest in Nicholas of Cusa was long standing and profound (see his diaries and lists of "Work Done," HP, SAUL), and had practically nothing to do with the fact that his uncle's home was just down the Moselle River from Nicholas's, as Loome, *Liberal Catholicism, Reform Catholicism, Modernism*, p. 441, n. 14, suggests.

195. GT to FvH, 5 December 1902, PP, BL, Add. MSS 44928.59.

196. GT to Waller, 15 March 1903, WP, BL, Add. MSS 43680.135.

197. GT to FvH, 8 April 1903, PP, BL, Add. MSS 44928.89-90, published in *AL*, 2: 181.

198. GT to Lilley, 14 June 1903, LP, SAUL, MS 30764.

199. GT to FvH, 9 August 1903, PP, BL, Add. MSS 44928.112-13; GT to

Waller, 9 August 1903, WP, BL, Add. MSS 43680.165.

200. A facetious reference to the method of scoring oral examinations in Jesuit scholasticates: *mediocritas* designated the acceptable mean of performance; *superavit mediocritatem* designated a performance beyond the mean; and *vix attigit* meant that the examinee passed by the skin of his teeth.

201. GT to Bremond, 20 August 1903, FB, BN, NAF.

202. GT to FvH, 12 October 1903, PP, BL, Add. MSS 44928.122.

203. GT to Halifax, 19 November 1903, published in *GTL*, p. 130.

204. GT to Lilley, 30 November 1903, LP, SAUL, MS 30768.

205. FvH to GT, 2 December 1903, PP, BL, Add. MSS 44928.129.

206. See diary of FvH for August and September 1904, HP, SAUL. There is no record of FvH's assessment.

207. Eugène Franon, "Un Scolastique anti-intellectualiste," *Bulletin de littérature ecclésiastique* (Toulouse), 3d ser. 7 (June 1905): 165–73.

208. Lebreton, "'Lex Orandi,'" p. 694.

209. See GT to FvH, 3 July 1904, PP, BL, Add. MSS 44928.203.

210. GT to FvH, 6 February 1904, PP, BL, Add. MSS 44928.157–58.

211. *LO*, p. 172.

212. *LO*, pp. 174–75.

213. *LO*, pp. 178–79.

214. Franon, "Scolastique anti-intellectualiste," p. 165.

215. GT, "The Limitations of Newman," *Monthly Register* 1 (October 1902): 264–65; GT, "Semper Eadem;" GT, "The Limits of the Theory of Development."

216. *LO*, pp. 208–9, 211–12.

217. *LO*, p. 213.

218. *LO*, pp. 213–14.

CHAPTER 7

1. On GT's identification with the liberalism of Döllinger and Acton, see Loome, *Liberal Catholicism,* *Reform Catholicism, Modernism,* pp. 28–58.

2. See GT to Waller, 22 December 1903, WP, BL, Add. MSS 43680.184.

3. See pp. 318–24 below; GT to FvH, 12 February 1904, PP, BL, Add. MSS 44928.171; and GT to Luis Martin, Superior General of the Society of Jesus, 8 February 1904, published in *AL*, 2: 228–30.

4. *CF*, p. 8.

5. GT to Waller, 19 April 1903, WP, BL, Add. MSS 43680.147. On Loisy's status at the time, see pp. 273–78 below. See also Loisy, *Mémoires,* 2: 193 ff; and Barmann, *Von Hügel,* pp. 79–118.

6. GT to Loisy, 12 October 1903, Fonds Loisy (hereafter FL), BN, NAF 15662, emended and published in *AL*, 2: 394–96.

7. Loisy, *Études bibliques,* 3d ed., pp. 334–35.

8. GT to FvH, 22 September 1901, PP, BL, Add. MSS 44927.173.

9. Alfred Leslie Lilley, "L'Affaire Loisy," *Commonwealth* 8 (March 1903): 73–76, reprinted in Lilley, *Modernism: A Record and a Review* (London: Sir Isaac Pitman & Sons, 1909), pp. 185–94.

10. Lilley, *Modernism,* pp. 191–92.

11. GT to Loisy, 12 October 1903, FL, BN, NAF 15662, edited and published in *AL*, 2: 395.

12. GT to FvH, 12 October 1903, PP, BL, Add. MSS 44928.122–23. Neither Loisy nor GT dealt adequately with what Paul saw to be the heart of New Testament revelation: Christ crucified and risen. GT was certainly ahead of his time in developing a theology of the Spirit of Christ, but he was also confusing by his failure to differentiate adequately between the spirit of Christ and the Spirit of Christ, i.e., the Holy Spirit, and the work he attributed to each; and he was certainly not equally ahead of his time in developing a theology of the cross. His devotional works ev-

idence the seed of such a theology, but GT did not explicitate it in his foundational-systematic works. There one finds the effects of Christ's Spirit working in humankind curiously detached from the primary work of the Spirit: the creation of divine sonship by obedience unto death. Herein lies the most serious lacuna of GT's theology. See pp. 324-25 below.

13. GT to FvH, 3 January 1902, PP, BL, Add. MSS 44928.2, published in part in *GTL*, pp. 80-83, and *vH&T*, pp. 100-3.

14. Ibid.

15. GT to MDP, 27 August 1901, PP, BL, Add. MSS 52367.

16. GT to FvH, 3 January, 12 April 1902, PP, BL, Add. MSS 44928.4, 12.

17. GT to Bremond, 3 November 1901, FB, BN, NAF.

18. GT to FvH, 3 January 1902, PP, BL, Add. MSS 44928.2.

19. FvH noted in his diary of 27 March 1902, HP, SAUL, that he had sent the book to GT on that day. FvH knew Houtin before GT did, but GT was promptly in correspondence with him.

20. Houtin and Sartiaux, *Loisy*, p. 138, translation in Vidler, *A Variety of Catholic Modernists*, p. 34. Vidler believes that this "confession," while probably not without foundation, must be read with caution. Failure to take Loisy whole and entire led Loome, *Liberal Catholicism, Reform Catholicism, Modernism*, p. 102, to assert: "Loisy . . . fully deserved excommunication since in the end he did in fact hold views incompatible with any traditional conception of 'Catholicism.' Indeed, it would be difficult to call him even a Christian." Strong answers to Loome have been given by Burke, "Loisy's Faith," pp. 138-60, and "Revising the Study of Modernism," *Journal of Ecumenical Studies* 17 (Fall 1980): 670-76;

Nicholas Lash, "The Modernist Minefield," *Month*, 2d n.s. 13 (January 1980): 16-19; and David Schultenover, review of *Liberal Catholicism, Reform Catholicism, Modernism* by Thomas Michael Loome, in *Current Research in Roman Catholic Modernism*, pp. 26-33.

21. On the politics behind and development of the Biblical Commission, see Barmann, *Von Hügel*, pp. 79-93.

22. See [GT], "The Bible-Question in France," *Monthly Register* 1 (October 1902): 277-78, a review of *La Question biblique* by Albert Houtin.

23. GT to Bremond, 9 April 1902, FB, BN, NAF.

24. GT to MDP, 11 April 1902, published in *GTL*, pp. 107-8. Charles-François Turinaz (1838-1918), bishop of Nancy and an avid polemicist, intervened vigorously in all the crises of the times. His *Les Périls de la foi et de la discipline dans l'Église de France à l'heure présente* (Nancy: É. Drioton, 1902) caused a big stir in the French press. See Blondel and Valensin, *Correspondance*, 1: 55-56, 183-84.

25. GT to MDP, 11 April 1902, published in *GTL*, p. 108.

26. GT to FvH, 12 April 1902, PP, BL, Add. MSS 44928.11. *Ipsi viderint!*: "that they might see!"—a reference to the pericope surrounding Mark 10:52.

27. GT to Bremond, 14 April 1902, FB, BN, NAF. The ten years' waste were two years of noviceship, three years of scholastic philosophy, four years of scholastic theology, and one year of tertianship (a kind of third year of noviceship at the end of training). Canute (955?-1035) was a legendary, saintly king of the Danish era who could not brook the homage of his subjects. To prove that he was only a man, he had his throne placed on the sea-

shore inside the tideline. When the tide began to come in, he commanded the waves to stop. When they continued to advance he then and there ordered his people to cease paying him the homage of which he was obviously not worthy. Of course that command was equally effective.

28. GT to MDP, 27 April 1902, PP, BL, Add. MSS 52367.

29. GT to MDP, 30 May 1902, PP, BL, Add. MSS 52367, published in *GTL*, pp. 206-7.

30. GT, "Principles of Western Civilization," *Month* 99 (April 1902): 412-18, a review of *Principles of Western Civilization* by Benjamin Kidd. See also GT to Waller, 2 March 1902, WP, BL, Add. MSS 43680.54; GT to Bremond, 7 March 1902, FB, BN, NAF; and GT to MDP, 9 March 1902, PP, BL, Add. MSS 52367.

31. GT expressed himself to this effect in a letter of 14 August 1902 to Fr. Henry Clutton, a troubled Roman Catholic priest and a brother of Ralph Clutton, MDP's brother-in-law: "I should object to the identification of the Catholic religion with an abuse, however long-standing, whose root is in conditions that may & must fall away sc. in the political form in which the Church has been conceived since the days of Constantine. When she shall be forced to confine herself to purely spiritual ends & methods, curialism & its abuses will cease to have any *raison d'etre*. To say that wilful blindness & dishonesty is of the essence of Romanism is to condemn Romanism altogether. It would be 'absurd' to expect the Curia as now minded & constituted to be other than it is, but to me it is clear that its present energy is the convulsion of a death-agony, a wild grasping, at the reins that are slipping from its hands. That I do not clearly see the course & fruit of the impend-

ing revolution does not hinder my faith in Catholicism & history & the nature of things." The letters of GT to Henry Clutton are among the Katherine Clutton Papers, Magdalen College.

32. GT, "Principles of Western Civilization," p. 416.

33. See Émile Poulat, *Histoire, dogme et critique dans la crise moderniste* (Paris: Casterman, 1962), pp. 266, 430; Julien Fontaine, S.J., *Les infiltrations protestantes et le clergé français* (Paris: V. Retaux, 1901); and the account in Rivière, *Modernisme dans l'Église*, pp. 128-29.

34. Vincent Rose, O.P., *Études sur les Évangiles* (Paris: H. Welter, 1902), a collection of articles that had appeared for the most part in *Revue biblique*. See GT to Raffalovich, "Easter" [30 March 1902], Raffalovich Papers, Blackfriars Library.

35. GT to Raffalovich, 4 June 1902, Raffalovich Papers, Blackfriars Library.

36. GT to FvH, 10 July 1902, PP, BL, Add. MSS 44928.21-22.

37. Diary of MDP, 14 June 1902, PP, BL, Add. MSS 52372.

38. GT to MDP, 29 June 1902, published in *AL*, 2: 14.

39. See pp. 215-35 above.

40. GT to FvH, 16 September 1902, PP, BL, Add. MSS 44928.28.

41. GT to Bremond, 18 September 1902, FB, BN, NAF.

42. GT to Bremond, 25 September 1902, FB, BN, NAF.

43. See *AL*, 2: 388-403.

44. *O&W*, p. 102, from Augustine, *De doctrina Christiana*, bk. 1, chap. 34, GT's translation, "cleave": "cling."

45. *O&W*, pp. 102-3.

46. See FvH to GT, 31 October, 17 November 1902, PP, BL, Add. MSS 44928.41, 43.

47. FvH to GT, 8 September 1902, PP, BL, Add. MSS 44928.26-27. Wobbermin, like Troeltsch, came out of the Ritschlian school, but unlike

Troeltsch remained within that school. Troeltsch, *Die Absolutheit des Christentums und die Religionsgeschichte* Tübingen & Leipzig: J.C.B. Mohr & Paul Siebeck, 1902), p. ix, acknowledged his debt to Wobbermin for presenting objections that he hoped his book would at least in part answer. James Luther Adams, introduction to the English translation, *The Absoluteness of Christianity and the History of Religions*, trans. David Reid (Richmond: John Knox Press, 1971), p. 17, points out Troeltsch's dependence on Nicholas of Cusa for his position on the relationship of Christianity to other religions, a position with which GT largely agreed—if, in fact, GT did not borrow it from Troeltsch or from Falckenberg's presentation of Nicholas. See GT to FvH, 17 November 1902, PP, BL, Add. MSS 44928.43.

48. GT to MDP, 10 October 1902, PP, BL, Add. MSS 52367.

49. GT to FvH, 14 October 1902, PP, BL, Add. MSS 44928.38.

50. See pp. 237–38 above.

51. GT to FvH, 14 October 1902, PP, BL, Add. MSS 44928.38.

52. See GT to FvH, 16 September, 14 October 1902, PP, BL, Add. MSS 44928.30, 38.

53. See GT to FvH, 14 October 1902, PP, BL, Add. MSS 44928.38.

54. Johannes Weiss, *Jesus' Proclamation of the Kingdom of God*, trans. and ed. Richard Hyde Hiers and David Larrimore Holland (Philadelphia: Fortress Press, 1971), p. 133.

55. See Weiss's comments on his position relative to his father's in his introduction to the 2d ed. of *Die Predigt Jesu vom Reiche Gottes* (Göttingen: Vandenhoeck & Ruprecht, 1900), the edition that GT probably read. See FvH to GT, 8 September 1902, PP, BL, Add. MSS 44928.25–27.

56. See diary of FvH, 10 November 1902, HP, SAUL; and Loisy, *Mémoires*, 2: 154.

57. GT to FvH, 17 November 1902, PP, BL, Add. MSS 44928.42–43. GT thought the publication of *Études évangeliques* (Paris: Picard, 1902) "a more daring venture at the present juncture" in view of the recent political developments in Rome concerning the institution of the Biblical Commission. See Barmann, *Von Hügel*, pp. 79–93. On the development, composition of, and controversy surrounding *L'Évangile et l'Église*, see Loisy, *Mémoires*, 2: passim; and Barmann, *Von Hügel*, pp. 94–118.

58. See, e.g., Percy Gardner's review, *Hibbert Journal* 1 (April 1903): 604; and his further critique, "M. Alfred Loisy's Type of Catholicism," *Hibbert Journal* 3 (October 1904): 126–38. Overall, Gardner was delighted with *L'Évangile et l'Église*, but he found in Loisy not only an anti-Protestant animus that precluded a fair treatment of Harnack but also a false criterion on which to judge what does and what does not belong to history. He accused Loisy of the same charge that Loisy brought against Harnack—that he was unhistorical. How could Loisy subject scripture to historical criticism while exempting doctrine, seeing that "in the construction of history and in the construction of doctrine the spirit of the Church proceeded in just the same way"? (p. 134).

59. GT to Bremond, 18 November 1902, FB, BN, NAF. This remark was provoked not only by GT's own recent brawl with censors, but more immediately by one involving his confrere Herbert Lucas, who a year earlier had given up his chair of scripture at St. Bueno's and converted to the liberal camp. Only recently he had had one article censured and followed that

with a pamphlet in defense of Loisy. Of this pamphlet GT wrote to FvH: "[Lucas] has sent a pamphlet, in defence of Loisy, up to the censors and is, *pro more suo* riding at full gallop into the jaws of ecclesiastical death." 11 November 1902, PP, BL, Add. MSS 44928.43. *Pro more suo:* "in his usual manner."

60. FvH to GT, 26 November 1902, PP, BL, Add. MSS 44928.45–47, edited and published in *vH&T*, pp. 108–10. Don Brizio Casciola (1871–1957) was an Italian priest of liberal leanings, educated under Umberto Fracassini, later a close friend of Tommaso Gallarati-Scotti and Antonio Fogazzaro. FvH had met him in Rome as early as the winter of 1894–95 and thereafter maintained correspondence with him. GT also later corresponded with him. Casciola's papers are preserved in the library of the Istituto Teologico Salesiano in Messina in the care of Ferdinando Aronica. On Fawkes, see chap. 4, n. 131.

61. GT to Loisy, 20 November 1902, FL, BL, NAF 15662, published in *AL*, 2: 394. *Oculi omnium in te sperant:* "The eyes of all look to you in hope." Ps. 145: 15. GT's letters to Loisy show deference and a desire to impress—perhaps an indication of inferiority feelings on GT's part with regard to critical scholarship. It is ironic, then, that he should not get the title of Loisy's book correct.

62. Alfred Loisy, *The Gospel and the Church*, trans. Christopher Home (London: Isbister & Co., 1903), p. 166.

63. Ibid., pp. 170–71.

64. See chap. 6, n. 23.

65. GT, "Religion and Ethics," *Month* 101 (February 1903): 135–36, reprinted in the 3d ed. (1904) of *FM*, 2: 313–50.

66. Ibid., *Month* version, p. 136.

67. Ibid.

68. GT to FvH, 4 December 1902, PP, BL, Add. MSS 44928.49–50, published in part in *vH&T*, pp. 113–14, and *AL*, 2: 181. Cf. Johann Gottlieb Fichte, *The Vocation of Man*, trans. and ed. Roderick M. Chisholm (Indianapolis: Bobbs-Merrill Co., 1956), pp. 83–154. GT emphasized "development" here to indicate that he was using the word in Loisy's sense of "change." See pp. 264–65 above.

69. On this whole problem, see Francis M. O'Connor, S.J., "The Concept of Revelation in the Writings of George Tyrrell" (Ph.D. diss., Institut Catholique, Paris, 1963), and extracts from this: "George Tyrrell and Dogma," *Downside Review* 85 (January, April 1967): 16–34, 160–82. O'Connor implies that GT faced the dilemma between the "old" and "new" theories of development only with the publication of his two "Semper Eadem" articles in January 1904 and September 1905. The sources under discussion, however, show that he faced this dilemma as early as autumn 1902.

70. GT subsequently admitted the unworkableness of such a criterion and returned to a no-development stance. See O'Connor's studies cited in n. 69 above.

71. See chap. 3, n. 86.

72. FvH to GT, 4 December 1902, PP, BL, Add. MSS 44928.52–53, published in FvH, *Selected Letters*, pp. 113–15, and in part in *vH&T*, pp. 111–13.

73. GT to FvH, 17 November 1902, PP, BL, Add. MSS 44928.42–43. See also GT to Bremond, 18 November 1902, FB, BN, NAF.

74. See FvH to Edmund Bishop, 16 June 1908, published in Nigel Abercrombie, "Friedrich von Hügel's Letters to Edmund Bishop," *Dublin Review* 227 (October 1953): 425; and Barmann, *Von Hügel*, pp. 95–96, n. 6.

75. FvH to GT, 26 November 1902,

PP, BL, Add. MSS 44928.46–47, published in *vH&T*, pp. 109–10. FvH was referring to Fawkes's review of *L'Évangile et l'Église*, which had appeared in a recent issue of the *Edinburgh Review*. Fawkes later interviewed Loisy. Apparently that interview removed certain misapprehensions and converted Fawkes to Loisy's defense. See Loisy, *Mémoires*, 2: 235, 425–27; and GT to Loisy, 12 July 1903, 12 February 1908, FL, BN, NAF 15662. Fawkes remained publicly allied to Loisy, whereas FvH found it necessary to distinguish himself from Loisy as the latter fell under ecclesiastical censure. To the end of his life, FvH corresponded with Loisy, considered him a close friend, and never for a moment questioned his talent as a biblical critic, and, when he referred to Loisy in public lectures, he did so always affirmingly. But FvH was caught in the painful dilemma of trying to remain loyal to his friends without jeopardizing a greater good for the church. In an undated letter of advice from early 1922 to Algar Labouchere Thorold, writer and translator of spiritual works and, at that time, first press attaché at the British Embassy in Paris, FvH expressed the tension he felt regarding Loisy: "I do not think it would do for you to get to know L[oisy]. now. I certainly would not attempt to do so myself. For it is one thing to stick to an old friend, *qua* friend and not *qua* thinker, for fear of doing him great further harm; it is quite another thing to start an acquaintance with this same man, who cannot possibly be damaged by its not taking place. The excommunication question of course adds a further grave reason." Published in Bedoyère, *Baron von Hügel*, p. 319. References to FvH's attitude toward ex-priests occur throughout his and GT's correspond-

ence but one in particular is worth quoting. On 16 June 1905 GT wrote to Lilley about including ex-Romanists in an association of Anglican and Roman Catholic sympathizers: "For the cooperation of the best foreign R.C. liberals I am afraid the Baron's sympathy is *conditio sine qua non*; and I know that it is impossible to move him from his conviction as to the unwisdom of traffic between Liberal Romanists and Ex-Romanists. I am sure it is purely a question of politics with him & that he has full belief in the personal sincerity & goodness of those who leave our ranks. For myself politics is a small consideration & one of my best friends is an ex-priest; but the Baron's position is more prominent & delicate in many ways." LP, SAUL, MS 30804; see also n. 190 below. In 1909 Fawkes returned to Anglicanism and spent the rest of his life in a small country parish. See Vidler, *A Variety of Catholic Modernists*, pp. 157–60.

76. GT to FvH, 5 December 1902, PP, BL, Add. MSS 44928.59. See GT to FvH, 4 December 1902, PP, BL, Add. MSS 44928.51.

77. GT to FvH, 4 December 1902, fol. 50.

78. GT to MDP, 18 December 1902, PP, BL, Add. MSS 52367.

79. GT to Bremond, 29 December 1902, FB, BN, NAF; cf. GT to FvH, 11 January 1903, PP, BL, Add. MSS 44928.64–65. *Lampades nostrae extinguuntur:* "Our lamps have gone out," Matt. 25:1–13. *Date nobis de oleo vestro:* "Give us some of your oil," Matt. 25:7. In mentioning the demythologizing of hell, GT was perhaps referring to the treatment of the question of heaven and hell as reward and punishment after death in Joseph Turmel, "L'Eschatologie à la fin du IVᵉ siècle," *Revue d'histoire et de littérature religieuses* 5 (1900):

97–127, 200–32, 289–321, reprinted as a book under the same title in 1900 by Protat Frères, Paris. It is not certain when GT began reading Turmel, but he mentioned him in a letter to FvH of 11 January 1903, PP, BL, Add. MSS 44928.64, as if he had already finished the book. Turmel's turbulent ecclesiastical career ended with excommunication on 6 November 1930. See Vidler, A Variety of Catholic Modernists, pp. 56–62. "So long Thy power hath blessed me" and "angel-faces" are references to Newman's hymn, "Lead, Kindly Light," composed on a return voyage from Rome in the summer of 1833 when Newman's ship was becalmed for a week in the Straits of Bonifacio. See Ward, Life of Newman, 1: 55.

80. GT to Waller, 27 December 1902, WP, BL, Add. MSS 43680.122.

81. There are only eleven extant pieces of correspondence between 1 January and 15 March 1903. From 1 February until 15 March, when GT announced the appearance of CF, he wrote only two letters to FvH and two notes to MDP. Even if more letters should come to light, their number would not vitiate the point.

82. FvH to GT, 8 January 1903, PP, BL, Add. MSS 44928.61.

83. Loisy, Mémoires, 2: 177. Cardinal Mariano Rampolla del Tindaro (1849–1913) was Leo XIII's secretary of state.

84. See Alfred Loisy, My Duel with the Vatican, trans. Richard Wilson Boynton (New York: Greenwood Press, 1968), p. 229; see also Loisy, Mémoires, 2: 177–78; and Poulat, La Crise moderniste, pp. 125–60.

85. GT to FvH, 11 January 1903, PP, BL, Add. MSS 44928.62–63. Eduard von Hartmann (1842–1906), strongly influenced by Fechner, Lotze, and Schopenhauer, developed a philosophy of the unconscious in a work

by that title, Philosophie des Unbewussten (1869). Attempts to determine how GT came in contact with Hartmann's thought have led to nothing conclusive. But Loisy noticed a similarity between Hartmann and GT. In June 1904 Loisy discovered with astonishment and satisfaction Hartmann's trenchant critique of liberal Protestantism of the 1870–75 era in La Religion de l'avenir. "The principal idea," Loisy wrote in his journal of 3 June, "is that all forms of Christianity are really dead and cannot be improved except by radical change, and that from the ground up. At bottom, he thinks about Catholicism the same way I do, and the same way Hilaire Bourdon (Tyrrell) does. We are no longer Christians; we believe neither in the infallibility of the pope nor in his kingdom of heaven." Loisy, Mémoires, 2: 395. GT, of course, would take exception to this assessment.

86. GT to FvH, 11 January 1903, PP, BL, Add. MSS 44928.64–65.

87. Ibid., fols. 63–64. Jules Touzard (1867–1938), a Sulpician, had been a student of Loisy at the Institut Catholique, later became professor of Old Testament at the Séminaire Saint-Sulpice in Paris, and in 1906 assumed the chair Loisy had occupied at the Institut Catholique. Touzard was publicly prudent but did not escape a thunderbolt from Rome—"un foudre très mouillée" (Loisy, Mémoires, 2: 68)—because of his position on the origin of the Pentateuch.

88. See Loisy, Mémoires, 2: 194, and Poulat, La Crise moderniste, pp. 136–42.

89. GT to FvH, 26 January 1903, PP, BL, Add. MSS 44928.66–69. GT was referring to the warning FvH had sent from Rome in December 1901. Batiffol and Mignot had also been in Rome at that time and were meeting with FvH to discuss

Loisy's case. Pierre Batiffol (1861-1929), then rector of the Institut Catholique of Toulouse and editor of its publication, *Bulletin de littérature ecclésiastique* (the same journal that published Franon's attack on GT), was also a critical historian. He was finding it difficult to serve two masters, to be true to both Loisy and orthodoxy. In public he opted for the latter and expressed himself against Loisy. Batiffol called on FvH in Rome three times in quick succession and talked incessantly in a nervous effort to justify his attitude toward Loisy. This prompted FvH's remark to GT about Batiffol: "Alas, *he is a man not to be trusted:* pray take my word for it, and look out." FvH to GT, 18-20 December 1901, PP, BL, Add. MSS 44927.173. FvH was afraid that Batiffol would also compromise GT's position. On the occasion of Loisy's condemnation, Batiffol published an article critical of Loisy: "L'Évangile et l'Église," *Bulletin de littérature ecclesiastique* (Toulouse), 3d ser. 5 (20 January 1903): 3-15; see Loisy, *Mémoires,* 2: 200. *Principiell* should be *prinzipiell:* "on principle." On "Eppur si muove!" see chap. 4, n. 84. This phrase has several variations. GT used them all. "Ginx's Baby" is a reference to Edward Jenkins's satire, *Ginx's Baby: His Birth and Other Misfortunes* (London: Strahan & Co., 1870), on the struggles of rival sectarians over the education of a derelict child.

90. GT to Loisy, 27 January 1903, published in *GTL,* p. 83.
91. Loisy, *Mémoires,* 2: 395.
92. GT to MDP, 1 February 1903, PP, BL, Add. MSS 52367. *Mors et vita . . . :* "Life and death were locked in awesome combat," sequence of the mass for Easter Sunday.
93. "L'Abbe Loisy," *Pilot* 7 (31 January 1903): 113-14, signed "From our French correspondent."

94. GT to Bremond, 1 February 1903, FB, BN, NAF.
95. GT to FvH, 2 February 1903, PP, BL, Add. MSS 44928.71. *Entweder-Oder:* "either/or."
96. FvH to GT, 11 February 1903, PP, BL, Add. MSS 44928.73.
97. See the extract from FvH's letter to Loisy in Loisy, *Mémoires,* 2: 201.
98. "The Biblical Commission," *Tablet* 101 (7 February 1903): 213-14, signed "From our own correspondent." See diary of FvH, 8 February 1903, HP, SAUL.
99. FvH to GT, 11 February 1903, PP, BL, Add. MSS 44928.73. *Hic et nunc:* "here and now." Astonishingly, in a letter to Loisy of 8 February 1903, FvH suggested that Loisy write another book justifying his views but retracting nothing: "Fathers Tyrrell and L[ucas]. and I, and—I see it—also Mgr. Mignot, and all of us acting independently of each other, have thought of a publication by you of a brochure . . . which would retract nothing, but would explain with a calm, firm, and amiable dignity various points ill understood by many a sincere soul." Quoted in Loisy, *Mémoires,* 2: 218, published in Bedoyère, *Baron von Hügel,* p. 149. The originals of FvH's letters to Loisy have not been consulted for this study. They are preserved at the Bibliothèque nationale in Paris, Nouvelles acquisitions françaises, Fonds Loisy, vols. 15655-57. It is doubtful that it was FvH's suggestion that convinced Loisy to write an apologia. He was quite capable of that move on his own. But in any case, *Autour d'un petit livre* appeared in October 1903 and provoked a Roman condemnation.
100. GT to FvH, 14 February 1903, PP, BL, Add. MSS 44928.75-76.
101. FvH to GT, 24 February 1903, PP, BL, Add. MSS 44928.78-79.
102. GT to FvH, 28 February 1903, PP, BL, Add. MSS 44928.80-81. Doubtless GT was referring to Mgr.

Thomas Dunn, a member of Cardinal Vaughan's personal staff from 1894 to 1903.

103. Rudolf Sohm, *Kirchenrecht*, Systematisches Handbuch der deutschen Rechtswissenschaft, no. 8, 2 vols. (Leipzig: Duncker & Humblot, 1892-1923). GT of course read only vol. 1, *Die geschichtlichen Grundlagen*, a large book of over seven hundred pages. Vol. 2, *Katholisches Kirchenrecht*, did not appear until 1923.

104. GT to FvH, 28 February 1903, PP, BL, Add. MSS 44928.81. C.T.S.: the Catholic Truth Society; James Britten was its director.

105. Diary of MDP, 19 February 1903, PP, BL, Add. MSS 52373. *Coûte que coûte*: "Cost what it may."

106. GT to MDP, 6 March 1903, PP, BL, Add. MSS 52367. "An adamant harder . . .": Ezek. 3:9. *Spiritum rectum . . .*: "A steadfast spirit renew within me," Ps. 51:12, New American Bible translation.

107. GT to Waller, 15 March 1903, WP, BL, Add. MSS 43680.135. William Pollard & Co. of Exeter was the printer for *RFL*. Eugène Franon, in his review of June 1903 (see pp. 236-37 above), identified Pollard as the publisher. This confusion along with the simple fact that Pollard's was the only name attached to "Engels" might have prompted some unwanted inquiries.

108. GT to Bremond, 16 March 1903, FB, BN, NAF. Bremond's wish to visit GT in Richmond was denied by his provincial superior. GT and Bremond did not meet until the following December in London. Marcelle Tinayre (1872-1948), a French novelist, published the popular *La Maison du péché* in 1902.

109. GT to Waller, 19 March 1903, BL, WP, Add. MSS 43680.140. See also letter of 18 March 1903, fol. 137.

110. GT to Waller, 26 March 1903, WP, BL, Add. MSS 43680.141-42.

111. GT to Semeria, 29 March 1903, Semeria Papers, Provincial Archives of the Italian Barnabites. Semeria's letters to GT, like most letters to GT, are not extant.

112. Ibid.

113. Ibid. Christ's confession is recorded in Matt. 24:36 and Mark 13:32.

114. FvH to GT, 3 April 1903, PP, BL, Add. MSS 44928.84.

115. FvH to Blondel, 19 March 1904, published in part in Marlé, *La Crise moderniste*, p. 218.

116. The best treatment of this matter can be found in Christoph Theobald, "L'Entrée de l'histoire dans l'univers religieux et théologique au moment de la crise moderniste," in Jean Greisch, Karl Neufeld, and Christoph Theobald, *La Crise contemporaine du modernisme à la crise des herméneutiques*, Théologie historique, no. 24 (Paris: Beauchesne, 1973), pp. 7-85, esp. pp. 21-73; and Roger Aubert, "La Position de Loisy au moment de sa controverse avec M. Blondel," in *Journées d'Études Blondel-Bergson-Maritain-Loisy*, Centre d'Archives Maurice Blondel, no. 4 (Louvain: Institut supérieur de philosophie, 1977), pp. 75-90. The most extensive treatment is Marlé's, *La Crise moderniste*, pp. 70-254. See also Loisy, *Mémoires*, 2: 222-25, 391-94; Bedoyère, *Baron von Hügel*, pp. 146-47, 164-67; and for some interesting details on Bremond's part in the controversy, see E. Goichot, "En marge de la crise moderniste: La Correspondance Bremond-von Hügel, II—Les Années critique (1900-1907)," *Revue des sciences religieuses* 49 (July 1975): 222-24. For a terse treatment, see Barmann, *Von Hügel*, pp. 120-23.

117. GT to FvH, 8 April 1903, PP, BL, Add. MSS 44928.85-88, published in part in *AL*, 2: 187-88. Not long afterward GT would decide that the criterion he mentioned in the first paragraph quoted in the text was not so workable after all. See

remarks on this on pp. 266-69 above, and nn. 69 and 70 above.

118. FvH to GT, 15 April 1903, PP, BL, Add. MSS 44928.91.

119. GT to MDP, 21 June 1903, PP, BL, Add. MSS 52367. The joint publication was *The Soul's Orbit*, compiled, with additions, by MDP. The notes referred to were possibly those used by MDP to compose chap. 6, "He Was Subject to Them." On the composition of this book, see *AL*, 2: 83; and Loome, "Bibliography of Tyrrell," p. 290. "Caird's conception" can be found in vol. 2 of Edward Caird, *The Evolution of Religion*, Gifford Lectures, 1890-91, 1891-92, 2 vols. (Glasgow: James Maclehose & Sons, 1893).

120. See GT to Waller, 19 April 1903, WP, BL, Add. MSS 43680.147.

121. *AL*, 2: 188. The disguise worked, at least for the *Dictionary of National Biography*, 2d supp. 3: 543, where *CF* is described as "a translation . . . of an essay of a strongly liberal character, which he [GT] *had written in French* under the pseudonym Hilaire Bourdon," my italics.

122. See diary of MDP, 19 February 1903, PP, BL, Add. MSS 52372.

123. *CF*, pp. 12-13; all citations are to the 1910 ed.

124. *CF*, p. 13.

125. *CF*, p. 15. Carl Weizsäcker (1822-1919), liberal Protestant historian of the apostolic age.

126. *CF*, p. 17. GT's abbreviated reference is to Vincent of Lerins's famous "rule of faith"—*Quod ubique, quod semper, quod ab omnibus creditum est:* "What has been believed everywhere, always, and by all," *Commonitorium*, 2, par. 3. But GT applied the rule to what the theologians of the ascendancy were teaching rather than to what the church as a whole believed. In appendix 3 GT explained, "That the Holy Ghost 'dictated' such Scriptures is plainly a metaphor. No se-

rious man supposed that the picture of a dove whispering in the prophet's ear is to be taken for history. Yet the 'verbalism' of St. Augustine and other patristic interpreters implied a perfectly equivalent conception of the matter." *CF*, pp. 162-63. What inspiration meant for Augustine and the earlier councils, GT asserted, has been incorporated into present teaching without criticism and without consciousness of the development of the notion since that time. Adolf Jülicher (1857-1938), liberal Protestant New Testament scholar and church historian.

127. *CF*, pp. 17-18.

128. *CF*, pp. 19-20.

129. *CF*, p. 24.

130. *CF*, pp. 27-28.

131. *CF*, pp. 28-29.

132. *CF*, pp. 31-32.

133. *CF*, pp. 33-34.

134. *CF*, p. 43.

135. *CF*, pp. 43-44.

136. *CF*, pp. 45-46.

137. *CF*, p. 47.

138. *CF*, p. 48. GT quotes here James 2:19.

139. *CF*, pp. 57, 60. GT quotes here John 16:7.

140. *CF*, p. 61.

141. *CF*, p. 64.

142. *CF*, p. 65.

143. See pp. 216-25 above.

144. *CF*, p. 66.

145. *CF*, pp. 71-72.

146. *CF*, p. 74.

147. *CF*, pp. 79-80.

148. *CF*, p. 85.

149. *CF*, pp. 89-90. "*Spiritus est . . .*: "It is the spirit that gives life; the flesh is useless," John 6:63, New American Bible translation.

150. *CF*, pp. 92-93.

151. *CF*, pp. 93-94. These ideas, GT noted, are taken from Gustav Class, *Untersuchungen zur Phaenomonologie und Ontologie des menschlichen Geistes* (Leipzig: A. Deichert, 1896). This is the first mention of

Class. Later we learn that he was another of the baron's discoveries. See GT to MDP, 21 June 1903, PP, BL, Add. MSS 52367.

152. *CF*, pp. 98–99. *Securus judicat orbis terrarum:* "The world judges with assurance," i.e., there is wisdom in the multitude. These words of Augustine (*Contra epistolam Parmeniani*, 3.4.24) by which he disallowed the Donatist appeal to antiquity, were cited by Dr. Nicholas Wiseman in "The Anglican Claim of Apostolic Succession," *Dublin Review* 7 (August 1839): 139–80. Newman was thunderstruck by these words. He attested that they "absolutely pulverized" his theory of the Via Media and sent him on the road to Rome. See Newman, *Apologia pro vita sua*, p. 99. GT was following Newman here.

153. *CF*, p. 100.

154. *CF*, p. 101.

155. *CF*, p. 103.

156. *CF*, p. 138.

157. *CF*, p. 140.

158. *CF*, p. 145.

159. GT, *A Much-Abused Letter* (London: Longmans, Green & Co., 1906) was published with an introduction, pp. 1–35; notes, pp. 91–100; and epilogue, pp. 101–4. *A Letter to a University Professor*, undated, was printed no later than December 1903, since GT posted several copies to Lilley on 4 January 1904 and reported to him on 15 January that Bremond was already working on a French translation. GT to Lilley, 4, 15 January 1904, LP, SAUL, MSS 30769, 30770. The 1905 date of composition proposed by Crehan, *Father Thurston*, p. 62, requires correction.

160. The passages were published in questionable translation and out of context in the *Corriere della Sera* (Milan) of 1 January 1906, but their substance was accurate enough. The author was identified only as an English Jesuit. In the introduction of the 1906 edition of *A Much-Abused Letter*, GT supplied a retranslation with notes and an account of the correspondence that ensued between himself and Jesuit authorities in Rome.

161. Diary of FvH, 28 May 1903, HP, SAUL.

162. GT to Lilley, 14 June 1903, LP, SAUL, MS 30764. On the conversion of "Engels" to *LO*, see pp. 238–45 above.

163. GT to Bremond, 18 June 1903, FB, BN, NAF.

164. Exactly how much GT trusted himself to discuss with Thurston subsequent to the move to Richmond will remain uncertain until the Tyrrell-Thurston correspondence in the care of Fr. Joseph Crehan, S.J., Farm Street, London, is released for the scrutiny of scholars. Meanwhile, some idea can be gathered from the chapter on "Thurston and Tyrrell" in Crehan's *Father Thurston*.

165. GT to Waller, 20 June 1903, WP, BL, Add. MSS 43680.158.

166. GT to MDP, 21 June 1903, PP, BL, Add. MSS 52367.

167. GT to Waller, 20 June 1903, WP, BL, Add. MSS 43680.158. "H.E.": His Eminence Cardinal Vaughan, who died on Friday, 19 June 1903.

168. FvH to GT, 22 June 1903, PP, BL, Add. MSS 44928.101.

169. Ibid., fol. 102. See, *CF*, pp. 78–79, 94–105.

170. Ibid. See *CF*, pp. 16–26, 53–58, 161–70.

171. Ibid., fols. 102–3. The page numbers quoted by FvH convert to pp. 38, 78, and 103 in the 1910 ed.

172. GT to FvH, 27 June 1903, PP, BL, Add. MSS 44928.105. In subsequent editions the passage was corrected to read, "We can see clearly that theological intellectualism is perishing rapidly before pragmatism; before the co-ordination of the

understanding with the whole commonwealth of our spiritual faculties; of the brain, with the heart and affections; of knowledge, with life and action." GT's "slip," however, seems to have been more than a matter of carelessness. However much he strove to maintain equal emphasis on all the spiritual faculties, his reaction to the evils of intellectualism led him to overemphasize the affective faculty. This overemphasis is noticeable as early as "The Relation of Theology to Devotion." See pp. 91-97 above.

173. FvH to GT, 22 June 1903, PP, BL, Add. MSS 44928.103. See *CF*, pp. 136-38.

174. GT to FvH, 27 June 1903, PP, BL, Add. MSS 44928.105. As mentioned before, GT's position here was strongly influenced by Troeltsch's *Die Absolutheit des Christentums*, with its emphasis on the value of the individual. See Troeltsch, *Absoluteness of Christianity*, p. 17; also pp. 26, 121, from which GT perhaps borrowed the Pole Star metaphor.

175. FvH to GT, 22 June 1903, PP, BL, Add. MSS 44928.103. Page 187 is page 166 in the 1910 ed.

176. GT to FvH, 27 June 1903, PP, BL, Add. MSS 44928.106. The "Synthetic paper" was probably GT's response to FvH's "Experience and Transcendence," read at a meeting of the Synthetic Society on 28 May 1903. FvH recorded in his diary for 28 April 1903, HP, SAUL: "Read . . . Fr. Tyrrell's papers for 'Synthetic.'" Marcel Hébert's "La Dernière idole," *Revue de métaphysique et de morale* 10 (July 1902): 397-408, a radical and destructive criticism of Aquinas's proofs for the existence of God, argued that the ancient belief in the transcendent God must yield to the affirmation of the immanent Divine. Rivière, *Modernisme dans l'Église*, p. 149, called this article "a declara-

tion of apostasy." Indeed it was a final response to Cardinal Richard's invitation to Hébert to retract his *Souvenirs d'Assise* (Paris: Éditions original, 1899). Before the year was out Hébert had left the priesthood and the church. FvH had met Hébert in April 1896, when the latter was director of the École Fénelon of Paris. In July 1901 Richard denounced *Souvenirs d'Assise* for its propositions on the church, Christ's resurrection, and the idea of God. The following winter in Rome, FvH extended himself in negotiations with Cardinal José Vives y Tuto over the cases of both Hébert and Loisy. It was a very difficult situation. FvH liked Hébert personally, but he was not sympathetic with his ideas and he thought that too close an association of them with Loisy could only hurt Loisy. Consequently FvH was anxious that officials keep the cases separate while not, in that discrimination, prejudging one over the other. See diary of FvH, 23 February, 9 March 1902, HP, SAUL: also FvH to Hébert, 17 July 1901, 22 January, 24 February 1902, and FvH to MDP, 29 April 1902, in FvH, *Selected Letters*, pp. 100-9; Loisy, *Mémoires*, 2: 48 ff., 128-40; and Vidler, *A Variety of Catholic Modernists*, pp. 63-75.

177. FvH to GT, 22 June 1903, PP, BL, Add. MSS 44928.103-4.

178. Ibid., fol. 104.

179. Ibid. The identity of Goodrich remains obscure.

180. FvH to GT, 26 June 1903, PP, BL, Add. MSS 44928.109. See also FvH to GT, 7 July 1903, PP, BL, Add. MSS 44928.110-111. The Synthetic Society paper was no doubt his "Experience and Transcendence," delivered on 28 May 1903. See n. 176 above.

181. GT to Lilley, 14, 23 June 1903, LP, SAUL, MSS 30764, 30765.

182. GT to Lilley, 25 June 1903, LP, SAUL, MSS 30766.
183. GT to FvH, 27 June 1903, PP, BL, Add. MSS 44928.106-7. See also GT's much later explanation to Thurston of 30 November 1906, published in Crehan, *Father Thurston*, pp. 63-64. FvH had asked Barry to review Loisy's *L'Évangile et l'Église* for the *Pilot*. Barry did: *Pilot* 6 (20 December 1902): 532. The review mirrors Barry's quandry. In 1906 Barry converted to Anglicanism. See his autobiography, *Memories and Opinions*.
184. GT to FvH, 27 June 1903, PP, BL, Add. MSS 44928.108.
185. See pp. 270-73, 246-71 above.
186. GT to FvH, 27 June 1903, PP, BL, Add. MSS 44928.107-8. Cf. GT to Casciola, 15 August 1903, Casciola Papers, Istituto Teologico Salesiano.
187. GT to Casciola, 11 July 1903, Istituto Teologico Salesiano. See GT to FvH, 27 June 1903, PP, BL, Add. MSS 44928.107.
188. GT to Loisy, 12 July 1903, FL, BN, NAF 15662.
189. GT to Casciola, 15 August 1903, Istituto Teologico Salesiano.
190. Ibid. *Qui nimis probat . . . :* "He who proves too much proves nothing." "*Semper, ubique,* in *omnibus*" refers to the Vincentian canon; see n. 126 above. In this letter GT responded to a proposal—apparently it was Casciola's—to form a *progreto d'unione* among sympathizers. This seems to be the first mention of such a propsoal in GT's writings. GT reacted with pros and cons. The latter were (1) "that in dispersion we cannot be killed by a single blow," and (2) "a progressive party, unlike a statical and conservative party, is hard to unite because the members move at different rates, and stand at different stages (e.g. the minority at the Vatican council); the unity is one of tendency and direction, not of po-

sition; and unless all recognise this and exercise that same mutual tolerance which all profess to admire, disintegration sets in at once." On the other hand, such a party was "one of my very frequent dreams." He then suggested criteria for membership—one of which was that it exclude the overly liberal as well as the overly conservative—and a method of intercommunication that would be difficult to suppress. He promised to discuss the matter with FvH, who would be visiting him in Richmond from 18 August to 3 September. See diary of FvH for those dates, HP, SAUL. GT's dream was never realized, but it did lead to meetings and much correspondence in England between Roman Catholic modernists and sympathetic Anglicans, and got so far as an agenda of articles for the first volume of a projected series titled "New Tracts for New Times." The principal organizer and editor was A. L. Lilley. GT's idea for the tracts was analogous to that of the Tractarian Movement, but "Tractarianism *à rebours* for the Protestantising of Romanism . . . as Newman & Co.'s scheme made for the Romanising of Protestantism." GT to Lilley, 25 March 1905, LP, SAUL, MS 30796. To outline the program, GT executed an article along the lines of his "The Abbé Loisy: Criticism and Catholicism," *Church Quarterly Review* 58 (April 1904): 180-95, a combined review of *Harnack and Loisy* by T. A. Lacey, *L'Évangile et l'Église* and *Autour d'un petit livre* by Alfred Loisy, and *Les Religions d'autorité et la religion de l'esprit* by Auguste Sabatier. He called it "A Plea for Candour." Three years later the project ground to a halt, so GT wrote to Lilley on 9 June 1907, LP, SAUL, MS 30811, "If your tract-book is really dead might I have back the art. 'Conscience & Authority' [sic] to dish up" for *Il Rinnovamento*. Apparently Lilley had given GT's article a new title. In any case, "A Plea for Candour" was published as "Per la sincerità," *Rinnovamento* 2 (July 1907): 1–18. GT's letters to Lilley for those three years (June 1904 to June 1907) are filled with discussion of the tracts idea. Numerous references to correspondence and meetings about the "New Tracts" occur also in FvH's diaries: 12 June 1905; 16, 18, 19, 22, 25 June, 17 September 1906, HP SAUL; see also FvH to MDP, 3 January 1905, 19 June 1906, PP, BL, Add. MSS 45361. For what became of the Anglican interest in Roman Catholic modernism, see Vidler, *Modernist Movement*, pp. 216–69.

191. Diary of FvH, 20 August 1903, HP, SAUL.

192. Transcribed in FvH to GT, 10–12 November 1903, PP, BL, Add. MSS 44928.125–28.

193. The preface of *CCR* is dated 29 June 1909, two weeks prior to GT's death. MDP wrote the introduction and prepared the book for press with assistance from FvH, who asked that his name not appear in the introduction and advised that MDP should rather say too little than too much: "After all, it will be a *very great* point gained if you and I remain uncensured, or without their attempting to get us to subscribe to *Lamentabili* and *Pascendi*, with the alternative of suspension from the Sacraments." FvH to MDP, 14 September 1909, PP, BL, Add. MSS 45361, published in FvH, *Selected Letters*, p. 169.

194. *CCR*, pp. 274–75, all citations are to the 1910 ed.

195. *CCR*, pp. 275–76.

196. *CCR*, pp. 277–78.

197. *CCR*, pp. 278–79.

198. *CCR*, pp. 280–81.

199. *CCR*, p. 282.

200. It is a medical fact that stress will aggravate almost any pathological condition. The symptoms mentioned in GT's letters over a period of more than eight years indicate that he was quite possibly suffering from high blood pressure. Over a period of years this condition, if left untreated, will cause kidney failure. The kind of stress to which GT was subjected would doubtless contribute to high blood pressure and therefore aggravate his condition. See also chap. 6, nn. 95 and 117.

201. Transcribed in GT to Henry Clutton, Katherine Clutton Papers, Magdalen College. *Ad meipsum foedo . . .* : "To myself near moral ruin from a loathsome love of the Society." An expurgated version appears in *AL*, 2:285.

202. GT to FvH, 27 June 1903, PP, BL, Add. MSS 44928.105.

EPILOGUE

1. The five condemned works were *La Religion d'Israël, Études évangeliques, L'Évangile et l'Église, Autour d'un petit livre*, and *Le Quatrième Évangile*. See Loisy, *Mémoires*, 2: 283, 299–300.

2. [GT], "L'Affaire Loisy," *Pilot* 9 (2 January 1904): 10–11. See GT to FvH, 17 December 1903, PP, BL, Add. MSS 44928.135–36.

3. GT to Luis Martin, 8 February 1904, copy, PP, BL, Add. MSS 52368/A, published in *AL*, 2: 228–30.

4. Martin to GT, 15 February 1904, PP, BL, Add. MSS 52368/B.

5. GT to Martin, 23 February 1904, copy, PP, BL, Add. MSS 52368/A, published in *AL*, 2: 232–33.

6. Martin to GT, 24 April 1904, PP, BL, Add. MSS 52368/D. GT's letter to Martin of 9 April 1904 is missing.

7. GT, "Beati excommunicati," PP, BL, Add. MSS 52369. GT never published this MS. It is included as

an appendix to Kilfoyle, "Doctrinal Authority in the Writings of George Tyrrell."

8. GT, "Beati excommunicati," pp. 9-10.

9. GT, "L'Excommunication salutaire," *Grande Revue* 44 (10 October 1907): 661-72. See n. 7 above.

10. See GT to FvH, 25 May 1904, PP, BL, Add. MSS 44928.196.

11. GT to Martin, 11-26 June 1904, published in *AL*, 2: 458-99. GT sent this letter to Martin on 2 September 1905 with a covering letter, copy, PP, BL, Add. MSS 52368/I, published in *AL*, 2: 499.

12. GT to FvH, 3 July 1904, PP, BL, Add. MSS 44928.204.

13. Diary of MDP, 12 August 1905, PP, BL, Add. MSS 52373.

14. GT to Richard Sykes, 6 August 1905, copy, PP, BL, Add. MSS 52368/E, published in *AL*, 2: 236-37. *Ne scandalum gravius eveniat:* "Lest a greater scandal arise."

15. GT to Martin, 6 August 1905, copy, PP, BL, Add. MSS 52368/F, published in *AL*, 2: 238.

16. Martin to GT, 22 August 1905, PP, BL, Add. MSS 52368/H.

17. Martin to GT, 12 October 1905, PP, BL, Add. MSS 52368/K.

18. GT's letter to Martin of 14 November 1905 is missing. See *AL*, 2: 242.

19. Martin to GT, 25 November 1905, PP, BL, Add. MSS 52368/N, summarized in *AL*, 2: 243-44.

20. GT to Martin, 31 December 1905, copy, PP, BL, Add. MSS 52368/O, published in *AL*, 2: 245-49.

21. Martin to GT, 7 January 1906, PP, BL, Add. MSS 52368/P.

22. "Lettera confidenziale ad un amico professore di anthropologia," *Corriere della Sera* (Milan), 1 January 1906, afternoon ed., p. 3.

23. GT to Martin, 10 January 1906, copy, PP, BL, Add. MSS 52368/Q, published in *AL*, 2: 250. *Liberavi animam meam:* "I have freed my soul."

24. GT to Martin, 13 January 1906, copy, PP, BL, Add. MSS 52368/R, published in *AL*, 2: 250-51.

25. Martin to GT, 20 January 1906, PP, BL, Add. MSS 52368/S.

26. GT to Martin, 24 January 1906, including GT's statement for the press, copies, PP, BL, Add. MSS 52368/T, published in *AL*, 2: 501-2, 252.

27. Martin to GT, 1 February 1906, PP, BL, Add. MSS 52368/U.

28. Sykes to GT, 7 February 1906, PP, BL, Add. MSS 52368/X.

29. GT to Martin, 19 February 1906, copy, BL, Add. MSS 52368/Z.

30. GT to [Sykes?], 19 February 1906, copy, PP, BL, Add. MSS 52368/Y. *Tot verbis:* "in so many words." "*Gravis sui:* grounds for dismissal must be a matter that is "grave of itself."

31. GT, "Jesuit Secession: Rev. George Tyrrell Explains the Cause of His Separation," *Daily Chronicle* (London), 23 February 1906, p. 7.

32. Reprinted in a review of *Lex Credendi: A Sequel to Lex Orandi* by GT, *Month* 107 (May 1906): 552.

33. Ibid.

34. *LC*, p. 3; all citations are to the 1907 ed.

35. *LC*, pp. 8, 10-11, 49.

36. *LC*, pp. 59, 81.

37. *LC*, pp. 84-85.

38. *LC*, p. 247.

39. GT to MDP, 15 February 1906, published in *AL*, 2: 264. *Nemo tam . . . :* "No one so knows the passion of Christ with his or her heart as the one who has suffered similar pains."

40. GT to MDP, 9 March 1906, PP, BL, Add. MSS 52367. Franz von Hummelauer (1842-1914), a Jesuit exegete, had written extensively on paleogeology and the history of ancient Oriental peoples. In 1903 he was appointed a consultor of the Pontifical Biblical Commission, but he soon came under attack and

in 1908 withdrew from biblical research altogether. Geremia Bonomelli (1831-1914), bishop of Cremona, an advocate of separation of church and state and an opponent of the Papal States, had composed a pastoral letter on church-state relations in Lent of 1906. Pius X attacked it and ordered Bonomelli to appear before the Holy Office of the Inquisition on 8 March for a formal retraction. On Père Rose, see pp. 258-59 above. The Jesuit organ *Études* of 5 March 1906 attacked GT personally. Incensed, GT sent the editor a caustic reply and reminded him that French law required him to print it. It appeared in *Études* 107 (5 April 1906): 94-95. "Batiffol's Bulletin" is the *Bulletin de littérature ecclésiastique* (Toulouse), edited by Pierre Batiffol. More scurrilously GT wrote to Houtin, 13 March 1906, Fonds Houtin, BN, NAF 15743: "Truly we live in a reign of terror; & there is not the least doubt that these simultaneous symptoms are the result of a mot d'ordre of Pio X, inspired proximately by M. del Val; more remotely by M<u>dme</u> M. del Val; & ultimately by her confessor." "Ruthless" is the word that comes to mind to describe Pius X's role in the antimodernist campaign as documented by Erika Weinzierl, "Der Antimodernismus Pius' X," in *Der Modernismus*, ed. Erika Weinzierl (Graz: Styria, 1974), pp. 235-55. More compelling evidence for a *mot d'ordre* is offered in GT to MDP, 12 June 1908, PP, BL, Add. MSS 52367: "Also the Card. Archbp. of Milan told West that he moved against me only at Martin's request. That fits in admirably with the view that Martin sought a reason to dismiss me. I am sure the 'indiscretion' of the *Corriere* was also managed by him. He was an out-&-out double-dealer." Austin West was the Roman correspond-

ent for the *Monthly Register* and the *Daily Chronicle* and a friend of MDP and FvH.

41. GT to Cardinal Domenico Ferrata, 7 April 1906, published in *AL*, 2: 503. Whether GT's impression that the general could recall him coincided with that of the authorities will probably never be known for certain, as considerable confusion arose over whether GT was "expelled" (as he thought) or simply "released" (as GT thought the general wanted him to think). See pp. 320-24 above, and pp. 329-31 below. The still-closed Vatican and Jesuit archives in Rome could perhaps clarify this if they disclosed the nature of the specific exemptions granted to the Jesuit general for GT's case (see p. 321 and n. 16 above) and if they mentioned anything about a *mot d'ordre* from the pope. See GT to MDP, 9 March 1906, 12 June 1906, PP, BL, Add. MSS 52367; and GT to Houtin, 7, 13 March 1906, Fonds Houtin, BN, NAF 15743. If such an order were given, GT's argument would stand at least morally, if not legally. The normal legislation governing expelled religious, at any rate, provided foundation for GT's impression. Edward Fine, S.J., *Juris regularis tum communis tum particularis quo regitur Societas Jesu declaratio* (Prati: Libreria Ciachetti, Filii, 1909), p. 276, n. 2, indicates that the "expelled" religious is not freed from his vows and that his institute should annually recall him and, if he had mended his ways and if there were no grave disadvantages, was bound to readmit him. This interpretation was provided by the decree *Auctus admodum* of 4 November 1892 of the Sacred Congregation of Bishops and Regulars. However, Henricus Ramiere, S.J., *Compendium Instituti Societatis Jesu*, 3d ed., rev. Julius Besson, S.J., (Toulouse: A. Loubens & A. Trinchant, 1896), p.

333, n. 2, indicates that the Jesuit general asked for and was granted permission to continue to follow the procedures for expulsion layed down in the Jesuit Constitutions. In that case, if GT were "expelled" rather than "released," he would not be freed from his vows and would have been bound to reform and then apply for readmission to the Society, or else he would have had to find a benevolent bishop, provide an ecclesiastical patrimony, and then petition the Holy See for absolution from his suspension. But the Society would have had no obligation either to seek him out or even to readmit him after repentance if he did apply. But if GT were "released," it does not seem that he would have had an obligation to reform and apply for readmission. In either case, it does not seem that the general would have had authority unilaterally to recall him. GT prepared for public disclosure a lengthy autobiographical fragment, begun at Easter 1906 and completed 19 August 1906, edited and published in *AL*, 2: 271–81. On GT's relation to Cardinal Désiré Mercier over the incardination and/or *celebret* question and over GT's *Medievalism*, see the well-researched article by Robrecht Boudens, "George Tyrrell and Cardinal Mercier: A Contribution to the History of Modernism," *Église et théologie* 1 (October 1970): 313–51. Boudens cites important correspondence from the archives of the archdiocese of Malines, FM [doss. Tyrrell], between Mercier and GT, Mother Mary Stanislaus, Shane Leslie, Bishop John Cuthbert Hedley of Newport, and Merry del Val.

42. GT to Ferrata, 4 May 1906, published in *AL*, 2: 504.

43. Ferrata to Mercier, 18 June 1906, published in *AL*, 2: 504.

44. GT to Ferrata, 4 July 1906, privately printed, copy no. 11, Petre

Papers, University Library, Cambridge, general catalog no. 7.14.150[8], 4 pp., published in part in *AL*, 2: 302–3, published in full in French in Goût, *L'Affaire Tyrrell*, pp. 156–61.

45. Ibid., pp. 1, 4 in printed copy.

46. GT to Merry del Val, 20 July 1906, published in *AL*, 2: 505–6.

47. See GT to Bourne, 6 November 1906, and GT to Sykes, 6 November 1906, published in *AL*, 2: 309.

48. Gerard to Sykes, 2 December 1906, EPSJ Archives, published in *AL*, 2: 310.

49. GT to Dora Williams, 2 December 1906, published in *GTL*, p. 180.

50. GT to C. J. Longman, 13 June 1907, published in *AL*, 2: 318. GT's chapter, "Theologism," e.g., was a reply to Jules Lebreton's review, "La foi et la théologie d'après M. Tyrrell," *Revue pratique d'apologétique* 4 (1 February 1907): 542–50.

51. See *AL*, 2: 310–11. The move to Storrington was William Tyrrell's idea.

52. GT to MDP, 4 January 1907, PP, BL, Add. MSS 52367, edited and published in *AL*, 2: 312–13.

53. GT to MDP, 15 January 1907, published in *AL*, 2: 313.

54. *TSC*, p. ix.

55. See GT to FvH, 13 July 1907, PP, BL, Add. MSS 44930.44.

56. GT to Fr. Xavier de la Fourvière, 20 July 1907, published in *AL*, 2: 323.

57. [GT], "The So-Called Syllabus," *Church Times* 58 (2 August 1907): 133.

58. See GT to FvH, 31 July 1907, PP, BL, Add. MSS 44928.48.

59. GT to Xavier, 30 August 1907, published in *AL*, 2: 324. The letters of Father Xavier to GT are missing, as are most letters to GT, but they are referred to in *AL*, 2: 323–24.

60. GT to MDP, 30 August 1907, published in *AL*, 2: 325. GT read too much into the *Times*'s report. It stated only this: "The *Giornale d'I-*

talia, of Rome, says that Father George Tyrrell has been granted permission to celebrate Mass, he having forwarded to the Roman authorities a declaration that he will never publish anything without the consent of ecclesiastical authorities." *Times* (London), 30 August 1907, p. 8.

61. *Daily Chronicle* (London), 31 August 1907, p. 3. See GT, "Per la Sincerità," *Rinnovamento* 2 (July 1907): 1-18; and *AL*, 200-3. See also chap. 7, n. 190.

62. GT, letter to the editor, *Daily Chronicle* (London), 2 September 1907, p. 4. GT sent ten similar letters to English, French, and Italian newspapers. See Laubacher, *Dogma and Development,* pp. xxviii-xxix.

63. GT to Ferrata, 31 August 1907, published in *AL*, 2: 326-27. A year earlier GT outlined his stance on the censorship issue in an important letter to Wilfrid Ward of 27 August 1906, WFP, SAUL: "As to my decision it is quite irrevocable; but I think if you knew *all* the circumstances you would be satisfied that it was the lesser evil. To accept suspension is my best chance of escaping excommunication—tho' as things are going that may follow. That the censorship would have been more or less nominal is not to the point. It would cost me little or nothing to have my correspondence supervised as it has been for 25 years. It is simply a question of principle. Is the Church's authority over a priest so absolute that he has no private self left? Is he simply a 'minor' or an idiot or a slave? The monk freely, by his vow, becomes a 'minor' in canon law; he is incapable of a contract; he freely emasculates himself & as such he has no private life or private correspondence; his superior has a right to read every letter he sends *or receives.* But now, under Jesuit influence, the whole Church is governed like the Society; bishops are superiors; priests are religious. This is the very intoxication of authority; & true respect for authority forbids us to take such claims seriously. Were I to yield, they would try the same trick on us all, priests first & then laymen. As regards *private* correspondence the secular priest & layman are *exactly* on a footing. Would *you* submit yr. correspondence to censorship? Would the Duke of Norfolk? Having made the claim in my case they cannot retract it without loss of dignity, & so the *impasse* is final. But they will think twice before they try the trick again. There is no doubt that the whole thing is a miserable intrigue on the part of Rudolf Meyer S.J. & two or three of his fanatical collegues [*sic*] of the Merry del Val set. The late General would never have played so low for all his intransigence; but he used to say that Meyer simply lost his reason where I was in question—& now Meyer has his fling. I can't pretend not to feel the privations most deeply; but against the great religious loss there is some moral gain in being dissociated from the Roman clerical world with all its paltriness, intrigue, delation, envy, hatred, & malice. One feels cleaner & purer. Still I would fain hope for a day in which one might enlist again without sacrifice of principle; but what is there to hope from organised ignorance?"

64. "Il Caso Tyrrell," *Corrispondenza Romana* 113 (23 September 1907). In an earlier bulletin the editor, Giovanni Grandi, "Per il P. Tyrrel [*sic*]," *Corrispondenza Romana* 100 (9 September 1907), suggested that GT himself was to blame for rumors reported in certain journals that even his private correspondence was to be censored. "The truth is quite different," Grandi

wrote, "and Fr. Tyrrel [sic] is the first to know it. The Holy See requires that his private correspondence should not be employed to evade his obligations, acknowledged by him, concerning the ecclesiastical supervision of his writings intended for publication. It is easy to understand the value of and reason for such a demand. When all sincere Christian believers asked how a priest could have published that 'Letter to a Professor of Anthropology,' which is radically anti-Christian, Fr. Tyrrel and his friends answered that the priest had not published anything; that he had only replied with a private letter to a private letter from a professor; that the latter had given it to some acquaintances to read, and they, in their enthusiasm, requested copies for their private use; that for this purpose they had printed a few copies to serve as manuscripts for themselves alone; that purely by accident a third indiscreet party had seen it and published it on his own account. Evidently, with this system, one can write any kind of article or opusculum, supply the heading, 'Dear friend, I hereby answer your most welcome letter,' end up with 'Greetings from your affectionate N. N.,' thus turning it into private correspondence that will arouse the enthusiasm of friends and especially of a third indiscreet party who will publish it. This is the 'private correspondence' to which Rome alluded, demanding not to be ridiculed by documents which would nullify the promise to submit to ecclesiastical supervision the writings which Fr. Tyrrel would declare are destined for publication."

65. GT, letter to the editor, *Daily Chronicle* (London), 25 September 1907, p. 4.

66. If GT kept a copy of this letter of

11 October 1906 to Ferrata, it is missing but is referred to in *AL*, 2: 330.

67. Pius X, *Pascendi dominici gregis*, *Acta Sanctae Sedis* 40 (1907): 593-650.

68. See diary of FvH, 18-21 September 1907, HP, SAUL; and Barmann, p. 198.

69. GT, letter to the editor, *Giornale d'Italia*, 26 September 1907; GT, "The Pope and Modernism," *Times* (London), 30 September 1907, p. 4, and 1 October 1907, p. 5. The copious literature on the reaction to *Pascendi* points out repeatedly that the encyclical caricatured modernist views by tearing them out of context and lumping them together with complete disregard for wide variation and disagreement among modernists themselves. Still one finds in recent literature such unnuanced statements as this: In the area of biblical and historical criticism Tyrrell "developed Modernist views which were condemned by Pope Pius X in 1907." William J. Schoenl, "George Tyrrell and the English Liberal Catholic Crisis, 1900-01," *Downside Review* 92 (July 1974): 184.

70. FvH to GT, 30 September 1907, PP, BL, Add. MSS 44930.54-55, published in part in *vH&T*, p. 161.

71. GT, "The Pope and Modernism," pt. 2, p. 5. *Rabies theologorum:* "the ravings of theologians."

72. Ibid.

73. See pp. 319-20 above, and nn. 7 and 9 above.

74. Peter Amigo to GT, 22 October 1907, is missing but is referred to in *AL*, 2: 341. See *AL*, 2: 341-45; and GT to FvH, 23 October 1907, PP, BL, Add. MSS 44930.72.

75. GT to Augustin Leger, 24 December 1907, published in *AL*, 2: 339-40. *Scandalum pusillorum:* "scandal of the little ones." J. Augustin Leger had been a disciple of Blondel at the Collège Stanislas in

the 1890's, lectured at Laval University in Montréal in the early 1900s, then spent several years in England before returning to France. He was one of the original members of Le Sillon, which Pius X condemned in 1910. GT was referring in this letter to recent church-state affairs in France involving Mgr. Carlo Montagnini, the papal chargé d'affaires, and editorialized by Mgr. Umberto Benigni in La Corrispondenza Romana. Montagnini had been intimately involved with negotiations over the law of separation and the associations cultuelles and paved the way for Rome to appoint bishops to French sees without regard for French preferences. On 11 December 1906 the French government expelled Montagnini, seized his files, and appointed a commission to examine them. In succeeding months certain memorandums and correspondences from these files appeared in the French press and in the Times (London). They did not flatter Rome. See Maurice Larkin, Church and State after the Dreyfus Affair: The Separation Issue in France (New York: Barnes & Noble, 1973), pp. 146–69 and passim. Monsignor Benigni, the éminence grise behind Pius X during the antimodernist campaign, was the force behind La Corrispondenza Romana (1906–9), subsequently renamed Correspondence de Rome (1909–12). On him, see Émile Poulat, Catholicism, démocratie et socialisme (Paris: Casterman, 1977).

76. Pius X, speech of 17 April 1907, published in Civiltà cattolica 2 (1907): 358–59, quoted in Michele Ranchetti, The Catholic Modernists, trans. Isabel Quigly (London: Oxford University Press), pp. 195–96.

77. Ernesto Buonaiuti was its principal author. See FvH to GT, 19 April 1909, PP, BL, Add. MSS 44931.100.

78. The Programme of Modernism: A

Reply to the Encyclical of Pius X, "Pascendi dominici gregis," trans. by A. Leslie Lilley [GT] (London: T. Fisher Unwin, 1908), p. xxiv.

79. See GT to Lilley, 2 December 1907, LP, SAUL, MS 30854.

80. GT, "The Home and Foreign Review," Rinnovamento 3 (January 1908): 81–94, a review of The History of Freedom and Other Essays by Lord Acton.

81. Cardinal Désiré Joseph Mercier, "The Lenten Pastoral," published in GT, Medievalism, p. 9. Medievalism contains the complete pastoral in both French and English.

82. Ibid.

83. Ibid., pp. 187–88.

84. See FvH to GT, 15 September 1908, PP, BL, Add. MSS 44931.48.

85. FvH to GT, 22 September 1908, PP, BL, Add. MSS 44931.51.

86. FvH to GT, 27 June 1908, PP, BL, Add. MSS 44931.27–28, published in FvH, Selected Letters, pp. 152–53.

87. GT to FvH, 27 June 1908, PP, BL, Add. MSS 44931.30.

88. FvH to GT, 25 March 1908, PP, BL, Add. MSS 44931.7, published in part in vH&T, p. 168. See FvH, "The Abbé Loisy," Tablet 111 (7 March 1908): 378–79. The book in question was Loisy's Les Évangiles synoptiques. L. P. Jacks and G. Dawes Hicks were editor and subeditor of the Hibbert Journal.

89. GT to MDP, 1 April 1908, PP, BL, Add. MSS 52367. On 5 August 1907 FvH joined his wife and daughter Gertrud for several weeks' vacation at Levico in Tyrol. During this time he received a number of Italian friends and discussed strategy in the face of Lamentabili. From 27 to 29 August the Rinnovamento group met at nearby Molveno, the baron closing the meeting with "a little parting speech" on "the necessity of sincere, thorough critical work; of deep self-renouncing Xtian life; & of careful charity & magnanimity to'rds our opponents."

Diary of FvH, 5–29 August 1907, HP, SAUL.

90. GT to FvH, 6 April 1908, PP, BL, Add. MSS 44931.11, published in part in *vH&T*, p. 169.
91. FvH to GT, 16 April 1908, PP, BL, Add. MSS 44931.13–14, published in FvH, *Selected Letters*, pp. 148–50.
92. GT to MDP, 24 April 1908, PP, BL, Add. MSS 52367.
93. Ibid.
94. Houtin to Loisy, April 1908, published in Loisy, *Mémoires*, 3: 29, excerpts translated in Barmann, *Von Hügel*, p. 215.
95. GT to FvH, 24 August 1908, PP, BL, Add. MSS 44931.36–37.
96. GT to FvH, 18 October 1908, PP, BL, Add. MSS 44931.52. GT was slightly misled here. On 30 September 1908 Merry del Val had signed a letter to the French bishops ordering them to "adhere strictly" to a circular of 10 October 1907, according to the *désire vivement* of the Holy Father. But that letter fell short of absolutely forbidding clerics to attend state universities. They could attend in case of strict necessity and then only with the explicit permission of their bishop, who was to remind them of the grave dangers to which the study of history and philosophy and related disciplines would expose their faith. See *Acta Sanctae Sedis* 41 (1908): 41–42, 772–73.
97. See GT to FvH, 27 October 1908, PP, BL, Add. MSS 44931.59.
98. FvH to GT, 26 October 1908, PP, BL, Add. MSS 44931.55.
99. GT to Rev. Thomas McClelland, 28 November 1907, published in *AL*, 2: 373, where MDP referred to him as J. MacClelland. *Crockford's Clerical Directory* for 1917 lists him as Thomas McClelland. He was rector of Little Torrington at Exmouth, 1894–1908.
100. GT to Rev. W. Carr, 10 February 1905, published in *AL*, 2: 377; GT

to MDP, 30 April 1905, 8 May 1905, published in *AL*, 2: 368, 369.
101. GT to Arnold Harris Mathew, regionary Old Catholic bishop for England, 7 November 1906, 15 December 1907, EPSJ Archives.
102. See GT to James Penderel-Brodhurst, 17 February 1909, published in *AL*, 2: 385–87.
103. Twenty-three years later the Church of England recognized the Old Catholics in an accord signed on 2 July 1931 at Bonn.
104. GT to FvH, 4 December 1908, PP, BL, Add. MSS 44931.66–67; see FvH to GT, 3 December 1908, PP, BL, Add. MSS 44931.62–64.
105. FvH to GT, 7 December 1908, PP, BL, Add. MSS 44931.68–70.
106. See FvH to GT, 9 December 1908, PP, BL, Add. MSS 44931.73.
107. See FvH, "Father Tyrrell: Some Memorials of the Last Twelve Years of His Life," *Hibbert Journal* 8 (January 1910): 248. FvH was not the only one to notice a change in GT's bearing. On 10 March, just out of sickbed, GT lunched with Wilfrid Scawen Blunt, the diplomat, traveler, political gadfly, and poet. Blunt recorded in his diary for that day an interesting observation: "Tyrrell to-day was in his most attractive, least aggressive mood." W. S. Blunt, *My Diaries: Being a Personal Narrative of Events, 1888–1914* (reprint, New York: Alfred A. Knopf, 1932), p. 650. Fourteen letters from GT to Blunt were among the Blunt Papers at the estate of Lord Lytton in Somerset. In 1964 the letters were loaned to a member of the Lytton family and have not been seen since.
108. GT to FvH, 6 March 1909, PP, BL, Add. MSS 44931.82.
109. FvH, "Father Tyrrell," p. 248.
110. GT to FvH, 7 April 1909, PP, BL, Add. MSS 44931.89–90.
111. GT to FvH, 22 January 1909, PP, BL, Add. MSS 44931.80–81. Concerning Theophil Steinmann's *Die*

geistige Offenbarung Gottes in der geschichtlichen Person Jesu (1903), GT remarked, "I hope in my book to suggest a better Christological way, but am at present paralysed by the difficulty of any undertaking."

112. GT to FvH, 28 March 1909, PP, BL, Add. MSS 44931.87. *Mulierculae:* literally, "little women," but a term of contempt. The lecture was an abbreviated form of the text published in *EFI,* pp. 245-77. GT delivered this lecture at least once more—at Exeter College, Oxford, 12 June 1909.

113. "Hakluyt Egerton" [Arthur Boutwood], *Father Tyrrell's Modernism* (London: Kegan Paul, Trench, Trübner & Co., 1909). Athelstan Riley was then vice-president of the Church Union. The lecture with detailed notes and background was published by Loome, "'Revelation as Experience.'"

114. GT, "Revelation as Experience," p. 130; all citations are to Loome's published version.

115. Ibid., pp. 132, 135-36.

116. Ibid., p. 136; see also p. 148, n. 5.

117. Ibid., p. 143.

118. Ibid., p. 144.

119. Ibid.

120. Ibid., p. 146.

121. Albert A. Cock, *A Critical Examination of von Hügel's Philosophy of Religion* (London: Hugh Rees [1953]), p. 3. In a footnote here Cock recalled: "On this occasion Tyrrell doubted whether the uniqueness of the Christian revelation was any longer tenable." Loome, "'Revelation as Experience,'" p. 129, n. 34, rightly observes that GT's text does not warrant this conclusion, but that perhaps GT had said something to this effect during the discussion following the lecture or during their postmeeting long walk—or perhaps Cock was simply mistaken.

122. W. R. Inge, "The Meaning of Modernism," *Quarterly Review* 210 (April 1909): 571-603.

123. *CCR,* p. 44. GT to FvH, 9 April 1909, PP, BL, Add. MSS 44931.91, published in part in *AL,* 2: 398, indicates that GT had just reread Albert Schweitzer's *Von Reimarus zu Wrede* (1906) and Johannes Weiss's *Die Predigt Jesu vom Reiche Gottes* (1892) and *Christus: Die Anfänge des Dogmas* (1909), and that these had helped clarify for him the position toward liberal Protestantism that he took in *CCR.* See also Richard Ballard's generally fine article, "George Tyrrell and the Apocalyptic Vision of Christ," *Theology* 78 (September 1975): 459-67. Ballard catches well GT's argument for the necessity of apocalyptic in the expression of faith. Joseph Fitzer, "Tyrrell and LeRoy: Their Case Reopened," *Communio Viatorum* 18 (Winter 1975): 201-24, on the other hand, completely obscures GT's point. Fitzer's understanding and critique of GT's treatment of apostolic faith and the resurrection appearances are also quite unsound.

124. *CCR,* p. 77.

125. W. R. Inge, "Tyrrell's Last Book," *Hibbert Journal* 8 (January 1910): 438, a review of *Christianity at the Cross-Roads* by GT.

126. FvH to Lilley, 13 July 1909, LP, SAUL, MS 30556. The Southwark diocese secular priest was Charles Dessoulavy. A corresponding German report appears in FvH to Joseph Sauer, 19 July 1909. FvH's twenty-four letters to Sauer (1902–22) are in private hands at Freiburg im Breisgau.

127. MDP [and FvH], obituary notice for GT, *Daily Mail* (London), 16 July 1909 p. 9; MDP [and FvH], obituary notice for GT, *Times* (London), 16 July 1909, p. 13. The *Times* letter is published in *AL,* 2: 434-35.

128. FvH to Edmund Bishop, 16 July

1909, published in *Dublin Review* 227 (October 1953): 429. The manuscript letters of FvH to Bishop are among the Bishop Papers, Downside Abbey.

129. Evidence of Merry del Val's involvement in this refusal is given in Barmann, *Von Hügel*, pp. 229–32; and in *AL*, 2: 437–40.

130. *AL*, 2: 442.

131. *AL*, 2: 443–46. *Credo in communionem sanctorum:* "I believe in the communion of the saints."

132. *AL*, 2: 445, 434.

133. See Barmann, *Von Hügel*, p. 230.

134. John Cuthbert Hedley to Amigo, 12 August 1909, copy, Francis Bourne Papers, AAW, 124/5, quoted in Barmann, *Von Hügel*, p. 231.

135. Amigo to Bourne, 13 August 1909, Bourne Papers, AAW, 124/5, quoted in Barmann, *Von Hügel*, pp. 231–32.

136. See Barmann, *Von Hügel*, pp. 232–33, n. 4.

137. Bourne to Merry del Val, 15 August 1909, copy, Bourne Papers, AAW, 124/5, quoted in Barmann, *Von Hügel*, p. 232.

138. FvH to MDP, 14 September 1909, PP, BL, Add. MSS 45361.

139. *Acta Sanctae Sedis* 5 (1913): 276.

Selected Bibliography

The following works were particularly helpful in compiling this bibliography: Lawrence F. Barmann, *Baron Friedrich von Hügel and the Modernist Crisis in England* (Cambridge: At the University Press, 1972); James A. Laubacher, *Dogma and the Development of Dogma in the Writings of George Tyrrell (1861-1909)* (Louvain: Catholic University, 1939); and three works by Thomas Michael Loome: "A Bibliography of the Published Writings of George Tyrrell (1861-1909)," *Heythrop Journal* 10 (July 1969): 280-314; "A Bibliography of the Printed Works of George Tyrrell: Supplement," *Heythrop Journal* 11 (April 1970): 161-69; and *Liberal Catholicism, Reform Catholicism, Modernism: A Contribution to a New Orientation in Modernist Research*, Tübinger theologische Studien, vol. 14 (Mainz: Matthias-Grünewald-Verlag, 1979). The latter work contains, in addition to a bibliography of bibliographies, the fullest available description of archival sources and secondary sources on modernism published up to 1973. Nadia Lahutsky, Hans Rollmann, John Root, Francesco Turvasi, and Mary Jo Weaver have updated and corrected Loome's bibliography in *Current Research in Roman Catholic Modernism*, ed. Ronald Burke and George Gilmore (Mobile: Spring Hill College Press, 1980), pp. 34-85. The following bibliography attempts to update Loome's with respect to works concerning George Tyrrell. Limitations of space necessitated the listing of only the most pertinent works. Consequently many ancillary works cited in the notes will not be found below. The order of Tyrrell's printed works is generally Loome's. Among the secondary sources, works by the same author are listed chronologically.

434

Archives and Manuscript Collections

Albi (France). EUDOXE-IRÉNÉE MIGNOT PAPERS: In the care of Chanoine Marcel Bécamel. Among the papers are three surviving letters of GT from early 1902 concerning Mignot's essay, "La Méthode de la théologie" (1901). FvH's letters to Mignot are also at Albi, but the present writer consulted photocopies of them at University Library, St. Andrews, Scotland.

Bath, Somersetshire, Downside Abbey. EDMUND BISHOP PAPERS: Two letters from Robert Dell to Bishop from late 1909 concerning GT; a collection of important documents concerning St. George Mivart: fourteen letters from Mivart to Bishop (1897–1900), drafts of two replies from Bishop, one letter from Cardinal Vaughan (1900) with a draft of Bishop's reply, and one letter from Frank Rooke Ley (1900). Twenty-two letters from FvH to Bishop (1897–1913) were published by Nigel Abercrombie in the *Dublin Review* 227 (January, April, July, October 1953): 68–73, 179–89, 285–98, 419–38. Among various annotated books is Bishop's copy of M. D. Petre, *Autobiography and Life of George Tyrrell*. HUGH EDMUND FORD PAPERS: One letter from GT (6 March 1905) on biblical inspiration.

Cambridge, King's College Library. GT's breviary.

———, Trinity College. FREDERICK W. H. MYERS PAPERS: One letter from GT of 16 January 1901 lamenting the death of Henry Sidgwick, 4/128. HENRY SIDGWICK PAPERS: One letter of 13 July 1900 from GT to the bedridden Sidgwick, offering his "wretched prayers," c.95/174.

———, University Library, Anderson Room. MAUDE DOMINICA PETRE PAPERS: Five volumes of newspaper clippings concerning GT and the modernist controversy, most of them published after GT's death, compiled by MDP. Also an offprint of GT's essay, "A Chapter in Christian Ethics" (1903), rejected by the *Month*, and a copy of GT's printed letter of 4 July 1906 to Cardinal Ferrata, general library catalog no. 7.14.150[8]; see *Correspondence* below.

Freiburg in Breisgau, Faculty of Theology Library, University of Freiburg. JOSEPH SAUER PAPERS: A collection of modernist works including inscribed presentation copies from Bremond, Houtin, FvH, Loisy, Sabatier, and GT. A large number of folders containing offprints and newspaper clippings. Among these are one folder on GT and one on FvH and Bremond. Sauer's diaries and correspondence remain in private hands. Among the correspondence are fourteen letters from Bremond (1904–8), twenty-four from FvH (1902–22), four from Loisy (1903–6), and two from GT (1904, 1907).

London, Archives of the Archdiocese of Westminster. FRANCIS BOURNE PAPERS: A file of seven items on the condemnation of "modernism" and GT's excommunication (Bo. Roman Letters, VII/111): three letters from Cardinal Merry del Val to Bourne (two dated 17 October, one dated 12 December 1907); a draft of Bourne's reply (7 December

1907); two issues of *Corrispondenza Romana* ("Documentazioni Tyrelliane [*sic*]," no. 131, 16 October 1907, and "Il Modernismo e il Card. Newman," no. 155, 5 November 1907); and a copy of GT's printed "Letter to the Roman Catholic Bishop of Southwark," dated 27 October 1907 and headed in bold print, "Not for publication." A file of five letters from 1909 regarding difficulties consequent upon GT's funeral (Bo. 124/5): one from John Baptist Cahill, bishop of Portsmouth, to Bourne (n.d.); one from John Cuthbert Hedley, bishop of Newport, to Peter E. Amigo, bishop of Southwark (12 August); two from Amigo to Bourne (13, 15 August); and one to Bourne from Basil W. Maturin, the only Roman Catholic priest to attend GT's funeral other than Henri Bremond (7 September). A file of twenty letters, most of them from May and November 1909, the last from 10 March 1911, concerning charges of "modernism" against Wonersh Seminary for southern England (Bo. 4/11/1-20); correspondents include Amigo, Manuel J. Bidwell (chancellor of the Westminster archdiocese), Bourne, Joseph Butt (auxiliary bishop and vice-rector of the Beda College, Rome), Cahill, Dom Bede Camm of Maredsous Benedictine Abbey, and Denis Sheil of the Birmingham Oratory and Merry del Val's closest friend. JAMES MOYES PAPERS: Among these are a few letters of interest from Fr. David Fleming, O.F.M. (secretary of the Pontifical Biblical Commission and one of Merry del Val's informers in England), Merry del Val, and Vaughan. HERBERT VAUGHAN PAPERS: A file of correspondence with Merry del Val (V. 1/14) from 1896 to 1903 on such questions as the validity of Anglican orders, the conversion of English heretics, liberalism, Americanism, St. George Mivart, public criticism of the hierarchy, Wilfrid Ward, and GT. A file on Vaughan's decision in early 1902 to refuse the *imprimatur* for GT's *Oil and Wine* (V. 1/12/1-14): five letters from GT to Vaughan with drafts of six replies (1901-2); one letter to Vaughan from GT's provincial superior, Reginald Colley; reports of the three censors for *O&W;* and a clipping of an editorial from *Church Review and Church News.*

————, British Library, Additional Manuscripts. MAUDE DOMINICA PETRE PAPERS: Four groups of documents: (1) Both sides of the GT-FvH correspondence (1897-1909), Add. MSS 44927-31, 667 folios. (2) Letters of FvH to MDP covering the years 1899-1922, Add. MSS 45361-62. (3) Letters to MDP from numerous correspondents, Add. MSS 45744-45. (4) Sixteen volumes of miscellaneous manuscripts concerning GT arranged as follows: Vol. 1 (Add. MSS 52367): ninety-nine letters or fragments of letters from GT to MDP (8 July 1898 to 12 June 1908), constituting less than half of the original number. Vol. 2 (Add. MSS 52368): correspondence of GT with his Jesuit superiors in London and Rome (1900-1908); miscellaneous correspondence including three letters to GT from Archbishop Mignot (1902), one to GT from Laberthonnière (1904), and one to GT from A. L. Lilley (1908); correspondence and newspaper clippings relating to GT's death and burial, including MDP's journal for 13-14 July 1909 concerning GT's death agony. Vol. 3 (Add. MSS 52369): two manuscript essays in GT's hand:

"Revelation as Experience" and "Beati excommunicati." Vol. 4 (Add. MSS 52370): typescript of two letters from GT to FvH (28 March, 6 April 1908). Vol. 5 (Add. MSS 52371): the original manuscript in GT's hand of his last book, *Christianity at the Cross-Roads*. Vols. 6–13 (Add. MSS 52372-79): the manuscript diaries of MDP (1900-1942). Vol. 14 (Add. MSS 52380): letters to MDP from or relating to Henri Bremond (1900-1935). Vol. 15 (Add. MSS 52381): general correspondence of MDP for the years 1909–41 and correspondence of her literary executor, James Ovington Walker (1912-54). Vol. 16 (Add. MSS 52382A-D): four sketches by the artist, Leslie Canter, as illustrations for MDP's life of GT (1912). ALFRED RAYNEY WALLER PAPERS: Two folio volumes of letters from GT (24 October 1898 to 24 December 1908), a copy in GT's hand of a poem composed by him, and two letters from MDP to Waller (1909-10) (Add. MSS 43680-81).

———, Archives of the English Province of the Society of Jesus. Correspondence and documents concerning GT have been compiled from the files of three provincials who held office during GT's later years: John Gerard, provincial from 1897 to 1901, then editor of the *Month* until his death in 1912; Reginald Colley, provincial from 1901 to 1904; and Richard Sykes, provincial from 1904 to 1910. The papers concerning GT fall into four groups: (1) On the question of Vaughan's *imprimatur* for *Oil and Wine* (1900-1902): one letter from Gerard to GT, three from Gerard to Colley, twenty-one from GT to Colley with copies of six replies from Colley, three from GT to Vaughan, two from Vaughan to Colley, and one from Colley to Vaughan; several miscellaneous letters including three from M. S. Dalton to Colley and one from A. G. Knight to GT. (2) Letters subsequent to GT's dismissal from the Society of Jesus (November to December 1906): one letter from Sykes to Gerard with extracts from two letters of GT to Sykes and Gerard's reply; two letters from GT to Gerard with the draft of a reply to Gerard. (3) A typescript of forty-five letters of GT to the Old Catholic bishop Arnold Harris Mathew (1906-9). The location of the original letters is unknown. (4) A small packet of GT's sermon notes plus manuscripts of various essays from *Nova et Vetera*.

———, Heythrop College Library, GEORGE TYRRELL PAPERS: Five essays in manuscript by GT: "The 'Tabula Aurea' of Peter of Bergamo," dated February 1896, published in the *Heythrop Journal* 10 (July 1969): 275-79; "On Beauty" and "The Sublime," both from May 1899, published in the *Heythrop Journal* 11 (April 1970): 148-60; "Quid mihi et tibi?" and "How Do You Know?" both unpublished, preserved in the *Blandyke Papers* for April 1895 and May 1896 respectively.

———. WILFRID MEYNELL PAPERS: In the care of Mrs. Murray Sowerby, Meynell's daughter, the following letters and cards of GT: one note, three cards, and the fragment of one letter to Wilfrid Meynell; four notes and two postcards to J. G. Snead-Cox, editor of the *Tablet*; and an unpublished letter to the editor of the *Tablet* by GT, dated 20 October 1907.

———. HERBERT HENRY CHARLES THURSTON PAPERS: In the possession of Fr. Joseph H. Crehan, S.J. This important source is not open for researchers, so the complete content is still undisclosed. It does contain a collection of letters from FvH and GT to Thurston. To date, Crehan has published two installments of the GT letters in the *Month*, n.s. 40 (October 1968): 178–85, 2d n.s. 3 (April 1971): 111–15, 119.

Messina (Italy), Istituto Teologico Salesiano. DON BRIZIO CASCIOLA PAPERS: Two letters and one card from GT (1903–6) in English; eight letters of FvH (1899–1923) in either French or English.

Milan, Ambrosiana. TOMMASO GALLARATI-SCOTTI PAPERS: Nine letters from GT; fifty-four letters from FvH.

Oxford, Blackfriars Library. MARC-ANDRÉ RAFFALOVICH PAPERS: Forty-six letters from GT to Raffalovich (July 1898 to June 1909). Two other letters in GT's hand: a five-page draft, undated, to "G. H.," and a letter, undated, to "Thursby" (apparently a former Roman Catholic priest).

————, Bodleian Library. IDA ASHWORTH TAYLOR PAPERS: Six letters from GT to Ida Taylor (1902–9), MS Eng. Lett. c. 1, fol. 305; c. 2, fols. 223–32; one letter to Taylor from FvH (26 March 1907), MS Eng. Lett. c. 2, fols. 98–101.

————, Magdalen College. KATHERINE (Kitty) CLUTTON PAPERS: In the care of Dr. Arthur W. Adams, dean of divinity at Magdalen College. Among them are two groups of letters by GT: thirty-five to Katherine Clutton (15 June 1904 to 17 June 1909) and nine to her brother, Henry Clutton, a Roman Catholic priest (6 August 1902 to 7 October 1908). An unpublished essay by GT, "Rome's Opportunity," thirty-one-page typescript from the winter of 1901–2. A three-page account by Norah Shelley of GT's death and burial. A large number of letters, mostly concerning GT, from various correspondents, among whom are Arthur Francis Bell, A. L. Lilley, Maude Petre, and Norah Shelley.

Paris, Bibliothèque nationale. HENRI BREMOND PAPERS: The GT-Bremond correspondence, consisting of 115 cards and letters from GT to Bremond for the years 1898 to 1909. As of July 1980 the collection had been neither foliated nor assigned an acquisition number, but it is available in Nouvelles acquisitions françaises, Fonds Bremond. WILLIAM GIBSON (*second Lord Ashbourne*) PAPERS: Nouvelle acquisitions françaises, Fonds Gibson 16318, including letters from Mgr. Louis Duchesne, Georges Fonsegrive, Hyacinthe Loyson, Alfred Loisy, but none from GT. ALBERT HOUTIN PAPERS: A large collection of letters to Houtin, arranged alphabetically by author, in fifty folio volumes (Nouvelles acquisitions françaises, Fonds Houtin, 15688–737). Among the correspondents are Robert Dell (15697), Alfred Fawkes (15701), W. R. Hammersley (15708), Bernard Holland (15710), FvH (15711), Hugo Koch (15712), A. L. Lilley (15717), MDP (15727), Joseph Sauer (15732), and Norah Shelley (15732). Material concerning GT is grouped as a separate volume (15743): twenty-eight letters from GT to Houtin (1903–9), one letter from GT to Hyacinthe Loyson (5 October

1907), and one from GT to M. Perdrian, a former French priest (15 October 1908?); a draft of a biographical study of GT by Houtin. LU-CIEN LABERTHONNIÈRE PAPERS: Currently inaccessible. Among them are fourteen letters from GT (1903–7). FvH's letters to Laberthonnière are probably also in this collection, as thirty-six letters from Laberthonnière to FvH are preserved among the Hügel Papers at University Library, St. Andrews. ALFRED FIRMIN LOISY PAPERS (Nouvelles acquisitions françaises, Fonds Loisy): Fifteen letters from GT (15662) for the years 1902–9 and both sides of the FvH-Loisy correspondence (15655–57, 15632–33). There are sixteen other folio volumes of correspondence arranged alphabetically by author (15646–61). Among these are letters from William Barry (15649), J. E. Dillon (15652), Rudolf Eucken (15652), Alfred Fawkes (15653), A. L. Lilley (15658), MDP (15660), and Joseph Sauer (15661).

————, Archives of Saint-Sulpice. LOUIS VENARD PAPERS: Currently inaccessible. Among them are two important letters from GT to Venard (15 January, 29 March 1905) concerning GT's book *Lex Orandi* and his views on the 1904 Blondel-von Hügel-Loisy controversy concerning history and dogma.

Philadelphia, University of Pennsylvania, Henry Charles Lea Memorial Library. HENRY CHARLES LEA PAPERS: Nineteen letters of Arnold Harris Mathew to Lea with drafts of Lea's replies (1906–9) concerned mainly with the publication in 1907 of the third and revised edition of Lea's polemical *History of Sacerdotal Celibacy in the Christian Church.* The correspondence is important for understanding the role played by GT in urging the publication of the book and his relationship with Mathew.

Rome, Provincial Archives of the Italian Barnabites. GIOVANNI SEMERIA PAPERS: Sixty letters from FvH covering the years 1895–1921 and five letters from GT covering the years 1900–1905.

St. Andrews (Scotland), University Library. FRIEDRICH VON HÜGEL LIBRARY AND PAPERS: Five groups of materials: (1) *FvH's personal library* of several thousand books, periodicals, tracts, and offprints, many of them inscribed by their authors and heavily annotated by FvH. (2) *Letters to FvH,* numbering well over a thousand from ninety-two correspondents, including Edmund Bishop, Charles Dessoulavy, Rudolf Eucken, A. L. Lilley, Joseph Sauer, Ernst Troeltsch, and Wilfrid Ward. GT's letters to FvH became separated from this collection in the mid-1930s and are now among the Petre Papers in the British Library. (3) *Copies of letters from FvH to various correspondents,* whether in microfilm, photocopy, or typescript. They include sixty-four letters to Henri Bremond, twenty-three letters to Archbishop Mignot, and letters to Maurice Blondel and Rudolf Eucken, among others. Letters from other important correspondents are preserved at St. Andrews in their own collections (e.g., A. L. Lilley, Norman Kemp Smith, James Ward, and G. W. Young). (4) *Baron von Hügel's diaries,* forty-three volumes from 1877 to 1924, but lacking the volumes for

1880-83 and 1901. (5) *Miscellaneous manuscripts* written by FvH, including a lengthy biographical note on Padre Giovanni Semeria. ALFRED LESLIE LILLEY PAPERS: A great number of letters to Lilley. Most important are the 118 letters of GT (14 June 1903 to 21 June 1909) and the seventy letters of FvH (6 April 1903 to 6 January 1925). Other correspondents include Henri Bremond, Katherine Clutton, Robert Dell, Alfred Fawkes, Henry Scott Holland, Albert Houtin, W. R. Inge, Alfred Firmin Loisy, Paul Sabatier, and Norah Shelley. The seven letters of Norah Shelley (1909-11) are especially enlightening on GT's personal life during his last years. Included among these is a letter to Shelley from Edward Lawless, a former Jesuit priest and intimate friend of GT, one of the most touching testimonials written after GT's death. CHARLES EDWARD OSBORNE PAPERS: Ten letters and cards from GT (10 April 1906 to 9 October 1908), MSS 37018/9-18. FRANK ROOKE LEY PAPERS: A packet of correspondence and documents concerning the last years of the Roman Catholic liberal journal the *Weekly Register* and its short-lived successor the *Monthly Register*. His papers cover the years 1899 to 1902 and include a confidential memorandum on the *Weekly Register* by Rooke Ley and a "Report of the Financial Position and Journalistic Prospects of the 'Weekly Register'" by A. H. Pollen (summer 1901); five letters of Cardinal Vaughan (four to Rooke Ley, one to H.I.D. Ryder), with copies of six replies (four from Rooke Ley, two from Ryder); letters to Rooke Ley from Edmund Bishop, James Britten, Giovanni Genocchi, St. George Mivart, and Wilfrid Ward, among others; copies of letters from Henri Bremond and Lord Halifax. Rooke Ley also preserved a substantial number of letters from GT, which now seem to be lost. JAMES WARD PAPERS: Thirteen letters and cards to Ward from FvH (1902-21). They are especially enlightening on the development of FvH's religious philosophy. WILFRID WARD FAMILY PAPERS: An extensive collection of important documents, among which is GT's unpublished manuscript essay, "Who Are the Reactionaries?" composed in late April or May 1900, and the following letters or cards from GT to various recipients: sixty-two letters and six cards to Ward (1893-1909) with two typed transcriptions (sixty-seven entries); one letter and a card from 1906 and another letter, undated but probably also from 1906, to Mrs. Wilfrid Ward; four letters (1900-1906) to Mrs. Bellamy Storer; copies of two letters and one card (1903-7) to William Gibson. There are also important documents concerning GT's article "Semper Eadem" in the *Month* for January 1904; an autograph letter of 5 December 1903 from GT to Fr. John Gerard, editor of the *Month,* and a packet containing five letters from Ward to Gerard and Ward's unpublished reply to "Semper Eadem." There are also numerous important papers concerning FvH: 203 letters and cards from FvH to Ward (1881-1916), six letters from FvH to Mrs. Ward (1890, 1916-18), five copies or drafts of letters from Ward to FvH, and a copy in Mrs. Ward's hand of a letter of FvH to Cardinal Vaughan (27 September

1896). Finally of note are numerous drafts or copies of letters from Ward to various recipients and letters to him from several hundred correspondents, among whom are Bishop Peter Amigo, William Barry, Cardinal Francis Bourne, Henri Bremond, Robert Dell, Alfred Fawkes, William Gibson (Lord Ashbourne), Lord Halifax, Cardinal Désiré Joseph Mercier, Maude Petre, Cardinal Vaughan, and William J. (Willie) Williams. For a full description of these papers, see Mary Jo Weaver, "A Working Catalogue of the Ward Family Papers," *Recusant History* 15 (May 1979): 43–71. G. W. YOUNG PAPERS: A collection of letters from various correspondents: one from GT, twenty-one from FvH, other letters from Katherine Clutton, H. C. Corrance, A. L. Lilley, and Joseph Rickaby, S. J.

St. Paul, Minnesota, Archives of the Archdiocese of St. Paul and Minneapolis. JOHN IRELAND PAPERS: Three files of miscellaneous papers and letters in the process of being sorted. Correspondents are mostly church officials, among whom are Cardinals Pietro Gasparri, Rafael Merry del Val, Mariano Rampolla del Tindaro, and Serafino Vannutelli, but not GT. The letters of Merry del Val are of particular interest. Two letters (25 September, 28 December 1907) discuss *Pascendi*, and one of 14 February 1907 thanks Ireland for answering a "really infamous" article in the January issue of the *North American Review*, signed "A Catholic Priest." Those who know, said Merry del Val, "strongly suspect that the so-called 'Catholic priest' is no other than Father Tyrrel [*sic*] himself, or that in any case he has inspired the article . . . that unfortunate priest." The style, however, is unlike GT's. See "Three Years and a Half of Pius X," *North American Review* 184 (4 January 1907): 35–45; and Ireland's reply, "The Pontificate of Pius X," *North American Review* 184 (1 February 1907): 233–45. GT's letters to Ireland are still missing. They were perhaps among many other Ireland papers thought to have been destroyed.

San Francisco, University of San Francisco, Richard A. Gleeson Library, Special Collections. This library now holds Thomas Michael Loome's enormous collection of modernist materials, many of which are listed here in their separate archival collections. ELKIN MATHEWS PAPERS: One letter of 13 May 1909 from GT to Mathews, who apparently was acting on behalf of the ill Joseph P. Thorp in some agreement drafted by Thorp; one card of 28 May 1909 indicating change of address. Mathews was the publisher of GT's book of poetry, *Versions and Perversions of Heine & Others* (1909).

Somerset, the Lytton Estate. WILFRID SCAWEN BLUNT PAPERS: A great number of letters from various correspondents. Fourteen letters from GT were loaned to a member of the Lytton family in 1964 and have not been seen since. The papers are currently at the Fitzwilliam Museum, Cambridge, but will soon be returned to Viscount Knebworth of Sussex.

York, Borthwick Institute of Historical Research attached to the University of York. CHARLES LINDLEY WOOD, SECOND VISCOUNT HALIFAX

PAPERS: Among Lord Halifax's "General Church Papers, 1861-1933," are eleven letters of GT to Halifax (1897-1902); thirteen letters of FvH to Halifax (1895-1911); typescript copies of five letters of GT to Wilfrid Ward (1899-1901), which Ward had copied for Halifax in January 1910, along with a covering letter of 16 January 1910 from Ward. Also of interest are letters from various correspondents including Archbishop John Ireland, Cardinal Vaughan, and Wilfrid Ward.

Addendum: For one reason or another, the personal papers of certain other figures important to GT cannot now be located. In the following list, the designation "destroyed" does not necessarily refer to all the papers of the person in question, but at least to those pertinent to GT. PETER E. AMIGO PAPERS, Archives of the Diocese of Southwark, Archbishop's House, London: Mgr. John McGettrick in a letter to Gary Lease, 19 July 1979: "I regret to say that a few years ago many of Archbishop Amigo's papers were destroyed in a fire. Among them were some if not all of those connected with Tyrrell. As for the rest, I am afraid they have still not been sorted and consequently I could not place them at your disposal." WILLIAM BARRY PAPERS: If still extant, they are almost certainly in private hands, but many letters to various correspondents survive in separate collections. WILFRID SCAWEN BLUNT PAPERS: Although most of Blunt's papers are intact (see above under "Somerset"), fourteen letters from GT to Blunt are missing. ERNESTO BUONAIUTI PAPERS: Destroyed. ALBERT A. COCK PAPERS: Destroyed. ROBERT DELL PAPERS: GT's letters to Dell have been lost or destroyed since the late 1930s. MDP was their last known holder. There is no trace of letters to Dell from Alfred Loisy or FvH, but many important letters from Dell to various correspondents survive in separate collections. CHARLES DESSOULAVY PAPERS: No one has yet discovered his papers, but GT to FvH, 11 June 1905, BL, Add. MSS 44929.30, indicates that GT was "copiously corresponding" with Dessoulavy. XAVIER DE LA FOUVIÈRE PAPERS: Still undiscovered. CHARLES GORE PAPERS: George Prestige, *Life of Charles Gore* (London: William Heinemann, 1935), p. 265, reports that "Tyrrell sent immense letters about his aims, his difficulties and some of his friends," but the whereabouts of Gore's papers is unknown. According to Prestige they were in the Dr. Williams Library, London, but the present librarian denies this. EDUARD HERZOG PAPERS: Preserved in the archives of the Christkatholische Kirche der Schweiz, Bern, Herzog's papers remain inaccessible because they are not organized. GT and Arnold Harris Mathew were in correspondence with him. LAURENCE HOUSMAN PAPERS: The collection at County Library, Street, Somerset, does not contain the letters of GT to Housman. Loome made an exhaustive search and suspects the letters have been destroyed. JOHN IRELAND PAPERS: The letters of GT to Ireland, so far as may be known, are not among any of the known deposits of Ireland papers, many of which are thought to have been destroyed. RAFAEL MERRY DEL VAL PAPERS: Lorenzo Bedeschi, in a letter of 10 March 1976 to Gary Lease, reports that a mysterious fire in the study of Cardinal Nicolo Canali, who had been Merry del Val's devoted secretary and passionate promoter of his canonization, destroyed all of Merry del Val's unpublished papers in Canali's possession. The fire occurred in 1961, shortly after Canali's death. See Gary Lease, "Merry del Val and Tyrrell's Condemnation," in *Proceedings of the Roman Catholic Modernism Working Group of the American Academy of Religion*, ed. Ronald Burke and George Gilmore (Mobile: Spring Hill College Duplicating Service, 1979), pp. 29, 54 n. 20. Other researchers have turned up very little of interest in the Vatican archives and various other archives in Rome. GEORGE ERNEST NEWSOM PAPERS: The letters of GT and FvH to Newsom are no longer among the papers in the possession of Newsom's son, G. H. Newsom, Esq., of Devizes, Wiltshire. NORAH SHELLEY PAPERS: Shelley probably destroyed her personal papers before her death in 1933. JOSEPH P. THORP PAPERS: Thorp's wife informed Alec Vidler that "'an enemy' had long ago destroyed Tyrrell's letters." Vidler, *A Variety of Catholic Modernists* (Cambridge: At the University Press, 1970), pp. 169–70. ERNST TROELTSCH PAPERS: Destroyed in Berlin during the last months of World War II. WILLIAM J. (Willy) WILLIAMS PAPERS: Most of Williams's papers have disappeared. The most significant extant letters are the twenty-four undated letters from Williams to Wilfrid Ward in the Ward Family Papers at University Library, St. Andrews.

THE PRINTED WORKS OF GEORGE TYRRELL

Monographs

1897

Nova et Vetera: Informal Meditations for Times of Spiritual Dryness. London: Longmans, Green & Co., 1897.

Notes on the Catholic Doctrine of Purity. Roehampton: Manresa Press, 1897.

1898

Hard Sayings: A Selection of Meditations and Studies. London: Longmans, Green & Co., 1898.

1899

External Religion: Its Use and Abuse. London: Sands & Co., 1899, 1906.[4]

1901

The Faith of the Millions: A Selection of Past Essays. 2 vols. London: Longmans, Green & Co., 1901. The third edition (1904) deletes chap. 20, "An Apostle of Naturalism," and introduces two others, "Religion and Ethics" and "Vita Nuova," both published in the *Month* in 1903.

1902

A Handful of Myrrh: Devotional Conferences. London: Catholic Truth Society, 1902. Published anonymously.

"A. R. Waller," [GT]. *The Civilizing of the Matafanus: An Essay in Religious Development.* London: R. Brimley Johnson, 1902. The work is GT's, but his friend Waller edited the work for publication and published it under his own name, according to GT's wishes. It was written no later than the first half of 1900.

"Dr. Ernest Engels" [GT]. *Religion as a Factor of Life.* Exeter: William Pollard & Co. [1902]. William Pollard & Co. was technically not the publisher but the printer. The publisher's name was not included.

Oil and Wine. N.p. [1902]. Reprint, London: Longmans, Green & Co., 1907. The book was first printed without title page and "for private circulation only" in 1902 by Manresa Press, Roehampton. GT's introduction is dated Easter 1900. The preface to the 1907 edition notes that the book was first published in April 1906 by Sydney Mayle (Priory Press) of Hampstead.

1903

"Hilaire Bourdon" [GT]. *The Church and the Future (L'Église et L'Avenir).* Abridged and rearranged. N.p.: The Author, 1903. Reprinted as GT, *The Church and the Future*, preface by Maude D. Petre (Hampstead: Priory Press, 1910).

Lex Orandi; or, Prayer and Creed. London: Longmans, Green & Co., 1903.

1904

A Letter to a University Professor. N.p. [1903–4]. Reprinted as *A Much-Abused Letter.* London: Longmans, Green & Co., 1906. The "letter" was written near the end of 1903 and printed about the same time. The 1903 printing was anonymous, but the 1906 publication bore GT's name.

The Soul's Orbit; or, Man's Journey to God. Compiled with additions by M. D. Petre. London: Longmans, Green & Co., 1904. The book was published under MDP's name, but GT was its principal author: "Roughly we may call him sole or chief author of Chapters I, II, III, IV, V, IX, XI, XIV; and part-author of Chapters VI, VII, VIII, XIII; with the remaining chapters he had comparatively little to do." *AL*, 2: 83.

1905

Another handful of Myrrh: Devotional Conferences. London: Catholic Truth Society, 1905. Published anonymously.

1906

Lex Credendi: A Sequel to Lex Orandi. London: Longmans, Green & Co., 1906, 1907[2].

1907

Through Scylla and Charybdis; or, The Old Theology and the New. London: Longmans, Green & Co., 1907.

1908

Medievalism: A Reply to Cardinal Mercier. London: Longmans, Green & Co., 1908.

1909

Christianity at the Cross-Roads. London: Longmans, Green & Co., 1909. Left in handwritten manuscript at GT's death, it was prepared for publication by MDP with assistance from FvH.

1912

Autobiography and Life of George Tyrrell. 2 vols. London: Edward Arnold, 1912. Vol. 1: *Autobiography of George Tyrrell, 1861–1884,* arranged, with supplements, by M. D. Petre. Vol. 2: *Life of George Tyrrell from 1884 to 1909,* by M. D. Petre.

1914

Essays on Faith and Immortality. Arranged by M. D. Petre. London: Edward Arnold, 1914.

Translations

1901

Hemmer, Hippolyte. *A Letter to a Christian Lady on the Liberty of the Children of God.* London: Catholic Truth Society, 1901. Translator anonymous.

1902

Mignot, Eudoxe-Irénée, "The Method of Theology," *Weekly Register* 105 (10, 17, 24 January 1902): 34–36, 64–65, 97–99. Reprinted as *The Method of Theology.* London: Catholic Truth Society, 1902. Translator anonymous.

1907

What We Want: An Open Letter to Pius X from a Group of Priests. Translated from the Italian, together with the papal discourse of Pius X on the occasion of the conferring of the cardinal's hat on those recently promoted to the purple, April 17, 1907, which called forth the Letter, by A. Leslie Lilley. London: John Murray, 1907. A translation of *A Pio X. Quello che vogliamo: Lettera aperta di un gruppo di sacerdoti* (Milan: The Author, 1907). FvH in his diary for 27 August 1907 stated that the author was Don Luigi Piastrelli. The English translation appeared with a preface by Lilley. GT did much of the translation but did not want his name to appear.

1908

The Programme of Modernism: A Reply to the Encyclical of Pius X, "Pascendi dominici gregis." Translated from the Italian with an introduction by A. Leslie Lilley. London: T. Fisher Unwin, 1908. A translation of *Il Programma dei modernisti: Risposta all'enciclica di Pio X "Pascendi dominici gregis"* (Rome: Società internazionale scientifico-religiosa, 1908). FvH to GT, 28 November 1907, Petre Papers, BL, Add. MSS 44930.106 indicates that the principal author was Ernesto Buonaiuti. GT's correspondence with Lilley confirms that GT was the principal translator and author of the introduction.

Prefaces and Introductions

1898

Hatzfeld, Adolphe. *Saint Augustine.* London: Duckworth & Co., 1898. Notes by GT.

Joly, Henri. *The Psychology of the Saints.* London: Duckworth & Co., 1898. Notes by GT.

Kurth, Godefroid. *Saint Clotilda.* London: Duckworth & Co., 1898. Notes by GT.

de Broglie, Emmanuel. *Saint Vincent de Paul.* London: Duckworth & Co., 1898.

1899

Joly, Henri. *Saint Ignatius of Loyola.* London: Duckworth & Co., 1899.

Sepet, Marius. *Saint Louis.* London: Duckworth & Co., 1899.

de Broglie, Jacques Victor Albert. *Saint Ambrose.* London: Duckworth & Co., 1899.

1900

Ignatius of Loyola. *The Testament of Ignatius Loyola.* Translated by E. M. Rix. London: Sands & Co., 1900.

Largent, Augustine. *Saint Jerome.* London: Duckworth & Co., 1900.

"Peregrinus" [M. S. Dalton]. *Meditations on the Psalms of the Little Office.* London: Sands & Co., 1900.

de Margerie, Amédée. *Saint Francis de Sales.* Translated by Margaret Maitland. London: Duckworth & Co., 1900.

1902

Juliana of Norwich. *XVI Revelations of Divine Love Shewed to Mother Juliana of Norwich 1373.* London: Kegan Paul, Trench, Trübner & Co., 1902.

1903

Petre, Maude D. *Where Saints Have Trod: Some Studies in Asceticism.* London: Catholic Truth Society, 1903.

Thomas à Kempis. *Of the Imitation of Christ.* London: Unit Library, 1903.

Harting, Johanna H. *Catholic London Missions from the Reformation to the Year 1850*. London: Sands & Co., 1903.

1905

Thompson, Francis. *Health and Holiness: A Study of the Relations between Brother Ass, the Body, and His Rider, the Soul*. London: Burns Oates & Washbourne, 1905.

1907

McGinley, A. A. *The Profit of Love: Studies in Altruism*. London: Longmans, Green & Co., 1907.

Bremond, Henri. *The Mystery of Newman*. London: Williams & Norgate, 1907.

1908

Loisy, Alfred. *The Gospel and the Church*. Translated by Christopher Home. London: Sir Isaac Pitman & Sons, 1908.

1909

Tyrrell, George. *Zwischen Scylla und Charybdis: Oder die alte und die neue Theologie*. Jena: Eugen Diederichs, 1909.

Reviews

1886

"A Symposium on Immortality." *Month* 56 (February 1886): 195–205. Review of *Immortality: A Clerical Symposium; or, What Are the Foundations of the Belief in the Immortality of Man?* (London: Nisbet, 1885).

1891

Month 73 (November 1891): 431–35. Unsigned. Review of Franz Schmid, S.J., *Quaestiones selectae ex theologia dogmatica* (Paderborn: Ferdinandi Schöningh, 1891).

1893

"The Oxford School and Modern Religious Thought." *Month* 79 (December 1893): 560–58; 80 (January 1894): 59–68. Review of Wilfrid P. Ward, *William George Ward and the Oxford Movement* (London: Macmillan & Co., 1889), and *William George Ward and the Catholic Revival* (London: Macmillan & Co., 1893).

1894

"Witnesses to the Unseen: The Wish to Believe." *Month* 81 (June 1894): 222–33. Review of Wilfrid P. Ward, *Witnesses to the Unseen and Other Essays* (London: Macmillan & Co., 1893).

1895

"Mr. Balfour and the Foundations of Belief." *Month* 83 (April 1895): 457–72; 84 (May 1895): 16–32. Review of Arthur James Balfour, *The Foundations of Belief: Being Notes Introductory to the Study of Theology* (London: Longmans, Green & Co., 1894).

"The New Sociology." *Month* 84 (August 1895): 502–22. Review of Benjamin Kidd, *Social Evolution* (London: Macmillan & Co., 1894).

"An Apostle of Naturalism." *Month* 85 (October, November 1895): 215–28, 358–73. Reprinted in *FM*, 2: 158–214, but omitted in the 3d ed. (1904). Review of Samuel Laing, *Modern Science and Modern Thought* (London: Chapman & Hall, 1885), *Problems of the Future and Essays* (London: Chapman & Hall, 1889), and *Human Origins* (London: Chapman & Hall, 1892).

"The Hypostatic Union." *Month* 85 (December 1895): 588–90. Review of J. B. Terrien, S.J., *S. Thomae Aquinatis . . . doctrina sincera de unione hypostatica Verbi Dei cum humilitate amplissime declarata.* Paris: Lethielleux, 1894.

1896

"The Ethics of Suppression in Biography." *Month* 88 (November 1896): 360–67. Review of Edmund Sheridan Purcell, *Life of Cardinal Manning, Archbishop of Westminster* (London: Macmillan & Co., 1896).

1897

"A Life of de Lamennais." *Month* 89 (January 1897): 19–27. Reprinted in *FM*, 2: 80–95. Review of William Gibson, *The Abbé de Lamennais and the Liberal Catholic Movement in France* (London: Longmans, Green & Co., 1896).

"Socialism and Catholicism." *Month* 89 (March 1897): 280–88. Review of Edward Soderini, *Socialism and Catholicism* (London: Longmans, Green & Co., 1896).

Month 90 (September 1897): 329–30. Unsigned. Review of Henri Joly, *Psychologie des saints* (Paris: Lecoffre, 1897).

"What Is Mysticism?" *Month* 90 (December 1897): 601–11. Reprinted in *FM*, 1: 253–72. Review of Henri Joly, *Psychologie des saints* (Paris: Lecoffre, 1897).

1898

"Wiseman: His Aims and Methods." *Month* 91 (February 1898): 142–50. Reprinted in *FM*, 1: 22–39. Review of Wilfrid P. Ward, *The Life and Times of Cardinal Wiseman*, 2 vols. (London: Longmans, Green & Co., 1897).

"Sabatier on the Vitality of Dogmas." *Month* 91 (June 1898): 592–602. Reprinted in *FM*, 1: 115–35. Review of Auguste Sabatier, *The Vitality of Christian Dogmas and Their Power of Evolution: A Study in Religious Philosophy* (London: A. & C. Black, 1898).

"Through Art to Faith." *Month* 92 (July 1898): 23–35. Reprinted in *FM*, 2: 111–35. Review of Jorris Karl Huysmans, *En Route* (London: Kegan Paul, 1896), and *The Cathedral* (London: Kegan Paul, 1898).
"The Making of Religion." *Month* 92 (September, October 1898): 225–40, 347–63. Reprinted in *FM*, 2: 215–76. Review of Andrew Lang, *The Making of Religion* (London: Longmans, Green & Co., 1898).

1899
"Two Estimates of Catholic Life." *Month* 93 (May 1899): 449–58. Reprinted in *FM*, 2: 61–79. Review of Mrs. Humphry Ward, *Helbeck of Bannisdale* (London: Smith, Elder, 1898), and Mrs. Wilfrid Ward, *One Poor Scruple* (London: Longmans, Green & Co., 1899).
"Authority and Evolution: The Life of Catholic Dogma." *Month* 93 (May 1899): 493–504. Reprinted with slight modification in *FM*, 1: 136–57. Review of André de la Barre, S.J., *La Vie du dogme catholique: Autorité, évolution* (Paris: Lethielleux, 1898).
"Zoophily Again." *Weekly Register* 100 (16 September 1899): 381–83. Review of La Marquise de Rambures, *L'Église et la pitié envers les animaux, textes originaux* (Paris: Lecoffre, 1899).

1900
"Coventry Patmore." *Month* 96 (December 1900): 561–73. Reprinted as "Poet and Mystic" in *FM*, 2: 40–60. Review of Basil Champneys, *Coventry Patmore* (London: George Bell & Sons, 1900).

1901
"The Trinity at Trinity." *Month* 97 (February 1901): 127–38. Reprinted as "Idealism in Straits" in *FM*, 2: 348–69. Review of Charles F. d'Arcy, *Idealism and Theology: A Study of Presuppositions* (London: Hodder & Stoughton, 1899).
"A Useful Booklet." *Weekly Register* 103 (3 May 1901): 564. Unsigned. Review of Maude D. Petre, *The Temptation of Doubt* (London: Catholic Truth Society, 1901).
Four unsigned articles in the *Weekly Register* (1901), later the *Monthly Register* (1902). The first is almost certainly by GT, the second certainly by him, the third probably by him, and the fourth almost certainly by MDP, perhaps with GT's assistance: (1) "Up-to-Date Catechism." *Weekly Register* 103 (24 May 1901): 646–47. (2) "Catechism at Rome." *Weekly Register* 104 (30 August 1901): 262–63. Review of Don Brizio Casciola, *Illustrazioni morali sopra alcuni punti della dottrina cristiana* (Rome, 1901). (3) "The Catechism." *Weekly Register* 105 (7, 14, 21 February 1902): 160–61, 193–94, 224–25. Review of Bishop James Bellord, *Religious Education and Its Failures* (Notre Dame, Ind.: Ave Maria Press, 1901). (4) "Concerning Catechism and Catechists." *Monthly Register* 1 (May 1902): 53–54.
"L'Inquiétude religieuse." *Month* 98 (August 1901): 214–18. Unsigned. Review of Henri Bremond, S.J., *L'Inquiétude religieuse: Aubes et lendemains de conversions* (Paris: Perrin & Co., 1901).

"A Prose Poet of Childhood." *Month* 98 (September 1901): 245–52. Review of *A Prose Poet of Childhood*, selections from Jean Paul Richter by K. B. Sharman (Hampstead: Sydney C. Mayle, 1901).

Month 98 (September 1901): 437–40. Unsigned. Review of Hall Caine, *The Eternal City* (London: William Heinemann, 1901).

"A Victim for Her People." *Weekly Register* 104 (13 September 1901): 329–30. Unsigned, but GT is probable. Review of J. R. Huysmans, *Sainte Lydwine de Schiedam* (Paris: P.V. Stock, 1901).

Weekly Register 104 (20 September 1901): 362–63. Unsigned, but GT is probable. Review of Hall Caine, *The Eternal City* (London: William Heinemann, 1901).

1902

"Principles of Western Civilization." *Month* 99 (April 1902): 412–18. Review of Benjamin Kidd, *Principles of Western Civilization* (London: Macmillan & Co., 1902).

Monthly Review 1 (April 1902): 39–40. Unsigned. Review of Edmund G. Gardner, *Desiderio: An Episode of the Renaissance.* London: J. M. Dent, 1902.

"Un Noviciat De Vie Chrétienne Dans Le Monde." *Monthly Register* 1 (May 1902): 55–57. Unsigned. Review of Hedwig Zamoyska, *Ideals in Practice: With Some Account of Women's Work in Poland*, trans. Lady Margaret Domville, preface by Miss Mallock (London: Art & Book Co., 1903).

Monthly Register 1 (July 1902): 118–19. Unsigned. Review of Maude D. Petre, *Devotional Essays* (London: Catholic Truth Society, 1902).

"The Bible-Question in France." *Monthly Register* 1 (October 1902): 277–78. Unsigned. Review of Albert Houtin, *La Question biblique chez les Catholiques de France au XIXᵉ siècle* (Paris: Picard, 1902).

"An Eirenicon." *Monthly Register* 1 (November 1902): 319–20. Unsigned. Review of W. R. Carson, *An Eucharistic Eirenicon*, introd. Rt. Hon. Viscount Halifax (London: Longmans, Green & Co., 1902).

1903

"Religion for Childhood and Manhood." *Month* 101 (January 1903): 100–101. Unsigned. Review of Henri Bremond, *L'Enfant et le vie* Paris: Perrin & Co., 1903), and *Ames religieuses* (Paris: Victor Rétaux, 1902).

Month 101 (June 1903): 655–57. Unsigned, but GT is probable. Review of Charles E. Osborne, *The Life of Father Dolling* (London: Edward Arnold, 1903).

"Religious Philosophy." *Pilot* 8 (1 August 1903): 111. Unsigned. Review of Lucien Laberthonnière, *Essais de philosophie religieuse* (Paris: Lethielleux, 1903).

"Post Mortem." *Month* 102 (October 1903): 367–78. Review of Frederick W. H. Meyers, *Human Personality and Its Survival of Bodily Death* (London: Longmans, Green & Co., 1903).

"Religion and Work." *Month* 102 (December 1903): 561–71. Review of Rudolf Eucken, *Gesammelte Aufsätze zur Philosophie und Lebensanschauung* (Leipzig: Dürr'sche Buchhandlung, 1903), and Hedwig Zamoyska, *Ideals in Practice: With Some Account of Women's Work in Poland*, trans. Lady Margaret Domville, preface by Miss Mallock (London: Art & Book Co., 1903).

1904

"Semper Eadem." *Month* 103 (January 1904): 1–17. Reprinted as "Semper Eadem I" in *TSC*, pp. 106–32. Review of Wilfrid Ward, *Problems and Persons* (London: Longmans, Green & Co., 1903).

"The Abbé Loisy: Criticism and Catholicism." *Church Quarterly Review* 58 (April 1904): 180–95. Unsigned. Review of T. A. Lacey, *Harnack and Loisy* (London: Longmans, Green & Co., 1904); Alfred Loisy, *L'Évangile et l'Église* (Paris: Picard, 1902), and *Autour d'un petit livre* (Paris: Picard, 1903); and Auguste Sabatier, *Les Religions d'autorité et le religion de l'esprit* (Paris: Fischbacher, 1904).

1905

"Consensus Fidelium." *New York Review* 1 (August–September 1905): 133–38. Reprinted as "The Corporate Mind" in *TSC*, pp. 254–63. Review of Hippolyte Delehaye, S.J., *Les Legendes hagiographiques* (Brussels: Bureau des Bollandistes, 1905).

"The Limits of the Theory of Development." *Catholic World* 81 (September 1905): 730–44. Reprinted as "Semper Eadem II" in *TSC*, pp. 133–54. Review of Wilfrid Ward, *Problems and Persons* (London: Longmans, Green & Co., 1903).

"The Rights and Limits of Theology." *Quarterly Review* 203 (October 1905): 461–91. Unsigned. Reprinted with emendations in *TSC*, pp. 200–241. Review of William James, *The Varieties of Religious Experience* (London: Longmans, Green & Co., 1902); Albert Réville, *Histoire du dogme de la divinité de Jésus-Christ* (Paris: Alcan, 1869); Auguste Sabatier, *Les Religions d'autorité et la religion de l'esprit* (Paris: Fischbacher, 1904); Paul Wernle, *Die Anfänge unserer Religion* (Tübingen: J. C. B. Mohr, 1901); and Andrew White, *A History of the Warfare of Science with Theology in Christendom* (New York: Appleton, 1903).

1906

"Newman through French Spectacles': A Reply." *Tablet* 106 (4 August 1906): 163–65. Signed "Francophil." Review of Henri Bremond, *Newman: Le Développement du dogme chrétien* (Paris: Bloud & Gay, 1905).

1907

"Chesterton among the Critics." *Nation* 1 (15 June 1907): 608. Signed "G.T." Review of *The Book of Job*, introd. G. K. Chesterton (London: Wellwood, 1907).

"Was Job a Heretic?" *Nation* 1 (29 June 1907): 672. Signed "G.T." Review of Francis Coutts, *The Heresy of Job*, with the inventions of William Blake (London: John Lane, 1907).

Hibbert Journal 5 (July 1907): 917–21. Review of R. J. Campbell, *The New Theology* (London: Chapman & Hall, 1907).

1908

"The Home and Foreign Review." *Rinnovamento* 3 (January 1908): 81–94. Review of Lord John Emerich Edward Dalberg-Acton, *The History of Freedom and Other Essays* (London: Macmillan & Co., 1907).

Hibbert Journal 6 (January 1908): 435–42. Review of Henri Bergson, *L'Évolution créatrice* (Paris: Alcan, 1907).

Hibbert Journal 6 (April 1908): 707. Review of "William Scott Palmer" [Mary Emily Dowson], *The Church and Modern Men* (London: Longmans, Green & Co., 1907).

"The Mystical Element of Religion." *Nation* 4 (19 December 1908): 475–76. Unsigned. Review of Friedrich von Hügel, *The Mystical Element of Religion as Studied in Saint Catherine of Genoa and Her Friends* (London: J. M. Dent, 1908).

"Mysticism and Religion." *Guardian*, 30 December 1908, p. 2184. Unsigned. Review of ibid.

1909

Hibbert Journal 7 (April 1909): 687–89. Review of ibid.

"Philosophy of Religion." *Catholic World* 88 (April 1909): 103–7. Unsigned, and attributable to GT only with reservations. Review of ibid.

"The Mystical Element of Religion." *Quarterly Review* 211 (July 1909): 101–26. Review of ibid.; Edward Grubb, *Authority and the Light Within* (London: Clarke, 1908); and Caroline Stephen, *Light Arising: Thoughts on Central Radiance* (Cambridge: Heffer, 1908).

"The Free Catholic Church." *Nation* 5 (10 July 1909): 536–37. Review of J. M. Lloyd-Thomas, *The Free Catholic Church* (London: Williams & Norgate, 1907).

Essays (Including Letters to Editors)

1889

"The Contents of a Pre-Adamite Skull." *Month* 67 (September 1889): 56–73.

"Cramming and Other Causes of Mental Dyspepsia." *Month* 67 (November 1889): 410–19. Unsigned.

1891

"Among the Korahites." *Month* 72 (May 1891): 81–93.

"Aquinas resuscitatus." *American Catholic Quarterly Review* 16 (October 1891): 673–90. Unsigned.

1892

"A Long-Expected Visitor." *Month* 74 (January 1892): 61-70.
"A Lesson from the Skies, on Universal Benevolence." *March* 76 (November 1892): 387-97.

1895

"Who Made the Sacraments?" *Month* 83 (January 1895): 120-30.
"Zoolatry." *Month* 85 (September 1895): 1-12.
"Jesuit Zoophily: A Reply." *Contemporary Review* 68 (November 1895): 708-15.

1896

"The 'Tabula Aurea' of Peter de Bergamo," *Blandyke Papers* 68 (February 1896). Reprinted in *Heythrop Journal* 10 (July 1969): 275-79.
"A Change of Tactics." *Month* 86 (February 1896): 215-27. Reprinted as "A More Excellent Way" in *FM*, 1: 1-21.
"Lippo: The Man and the Artist." *Month* 88 (December 1896): 465-72. Reprinted in *FM*, 2: 96-110.

1897

"The Clergy and the Social Problem." *American Catholic Quarterly Review* 22 (January 1897): 151-59.
"Keeping up Appearances." *Month* 89 (February 1897): 132-41. Signed "Digamma."
"Round *versus* Russell." *Month* 89 (April 1897): 358-70.
"The Old Faith and the New Woman." *American Catholic Quarterly Review* 22 (July 1897): 630-45. Reprinted as "A Great Mystery" in HS, pp. 241-60.
"The Prospects of Reunion." *Month* 90 (July 1897): 1-15. Reprinted in *FM*, 1: 40-67.
"The Religious State and Modern Society." *American Ecclesiastical Review* 17 (July 1897): 1-20. Reprinted as "The Way of the Counsels" in *HS*, pp. 261-94.
"Ecclesiastical Development." *Month* 90 (October 1897): 380-90.

1898

"Sacerdotalism in the Catholic Church." *American Ecclesiastical Review* 18 (April 1898): 350-64.
"'Liberal' Catholicism." *Month* 91 (May 1898): 449-57. Reprinted in *FM*, 1: 68-84.
"The Church and Scholasticism." *American Catholic Quarterly Review* 23 (July 1898): 550-61. Reprinted as "The Use of Scholasticism" in *FM*, 1: 205-27.

1899

"Rationalism in Religion." *Month* 93 (January 1899): 1-16. Reprinted in *FM*, 1: 85-114.

"Books That Have Influenced Me: 'Alice's Adventures in Wonderland,' 'Through the Looking Glass.'" *Weekly Register* 99 (27 May 1899): 666–67. Reprinted in *GTL*, pp. 291–97.

"A Problem in Apologetic." *Month* 93 (June 1899): 617–26. Reprinted as "Adaptability as a Proof of Religion" in *FM*, 2: 277–96.

"Our Duty to Fallible Decision." *Weekly Register* 100 (1 July 1899): 5–7.

"A Point of Apologetic." *Month* 94 (August, September 1899): 113–27, 249–60. Reprinted as "Adaptability as a Proof of Religion" in *FM*, 2: 296–347.

"The True and the False Mysticism." *American Ecclesiastical Review* 21 (October, November, December 1899): 389–403, 472–89, 607–17. Reprinted in *FM*, 1: 273–344.

"The Relation of Theology to Devotion." *Month* 94 (November 1899): 461–73. Reprinted in *FM*, 1: 228–52, and as "Lex Orandi, Lex Credendi" in *TSC*, pp. 85–105.

"A Perverted Devotion." *Weekly Register* 100 (16 December 1899): 797–800. Reprinted in *EFI*, pp. 158–71.

1900

"A Light from the Past." *Month* 95 (January, March 1900): 12–23, 250–58. Reprinted as "Juliana of Norwich" in *FM*, 2: 1–39.

"Cardinal Mazzella." *Weekly Register* 101 (30 March 1900): 393. Unsigned.

Letter to the Editor. *Weekly Register* 101 (1 June 1900): 686. Reprinted in *AL*, 2: 128–29.

"The Mind of the Church." *Month* 96 (August, September 1900): 125–42, 233–40. Reprinted in *FM*, 1: 158–204.

"M. Blondel's Dilemma." *Pilot* 2 (27 October 1900): 534. Signed "E.F.G."

"Tracts for the Million." *Month* 96 (November 1900): 449–60. Reprinted in *FM*, 2: 136–57.

1901

"Dogma and Dogmatism." *Catholic World* 72 (January 1901): 468–77. Signed "E.F.G."

Letter to the Editor: "The Anglo-Roman Pastoral." *Pilot* 3 (2 March 1901): 282. Signed "A Conservative Catholic."

Letter to the Editor: "Inquiry and Belief." *Weekly Register* 103 (26 April 1901): 536. Signed "S.T.D."

"The Recent Anglo-Roman Pastoral." *Nineteenth Century* 49 (May 1901): 736–54. Although published under Lord Halifax's signature, the article was by GT except for the introduction and conclusion.

"Lord Halifax Demurs." *Weekly Register* 103 (3 May 1901): 549–50. Unsigned.

Letter to the Editor. *Weekly Register* 103 (17 May 1901): 630. Signed "S.T.L."

Letter to the Editor. *Weekly Register* 103 (24 May 1901): 662–63. Signed "S.T.L."

Letter to the Editor. *Weekly Register* 103 (7 June 1901): 726-27. Signed "S.T.L."

Letter to the Editor: "The Anglo-Roman Pastoral." *Pilot* 4 (6 July 1901): 23-24. Signed "E.F.G." Reprinted in *Weekly Register* 104 (16 August 1901): 198.

"Docens Discendo." *Weekly Register* 104 (19 July 1901): 68-69. Unsigned.

"Jesuits and Their Critics." *Weekly Register* 104 (2 August 1901): 133-34. Unsigned.

"Traits of the Controversial Spirit." *Weekly Register* 104 (18, 25 October, 1, 8, 15 November 1901): 477-78, 509-10, 541-42, 572-74, 604-5. Unsigned. Attribution of these five articles to GT is only tentative.

1902

"The Pontifical Commission on Scripture." *Pilot* 5 (11 January 1902): 40-41. Unsigned.

Letters to the Editor: "The Method of Theology." *Weekly Register* 105 (24 January, 14 February 1902): 116, 211. Signed "Theologian."

"An Outsider's View of Religious Development." *Weekly Register* 105 (7 March 1902): 285-86. Unsigned. Attribution to GT is very tentative.

"A Tribute to Father Dolling. By a Roman Catholic Friend." *Pilot* 5 (7 June 1902): 600. Unsigned.

"A Plea for Gossip." *Month* 100 (September 1902): 225-31.

"The Limitations of Newman." *Monthly Register* 1 (October 1902): 264-65. Unsigned.

"Mysteries a Necessity of Life." *Month* 100 (November, December 1902): 449-59, 568-80. Reprinted in *TSC*, pp. 155-90.

1903

"Christianity and the Natural Virtues." *International Journal of Ethics* 13 (January 1903): 286-97.

"Religion and Ethics." *Month* 101 (February 1903): 130-45. Reprinted in *FM* (3d ed., 1904), 2: 313-50.

"A Chapter in Christian Ethics." Refused by the *Month*. Distributed privately by GT. One offprint preserved in University Library, Cambridge.

"Vita Nuova." *Month* 102 (July 1903): 23-38. Reprinted in *FM* (3d ed., 1904), 2: 351-80.

1904

"L'Affaire Loisy." *Pilot* 9 (2 January 1904): 10-11. Signed "From a Correspondent."

Letter to the Editor: "The Case of M. Loisy." *Pilot* 9 (30 January 1904): 116. Signed "The Writer of 'L'Affaire Loisy.'"

Letter to the Editor. *Tablet* 103 (30 January 1904): 77. A condensation of a longer letter printed in *AL*, 2: 221-23.

1905

"Anglican Liberalism. By an outsider." Unpublished, dated 1905. Quoted extensively in *AL*, 2: 366-68.

"The Dogmatic Reading of History." *New York Review* 1 (October-November 1905): 269-76. Reprinted as "Prophetic History" in *TSC*, pp. 242-53, with a note to explain its relationship to *LO*.

"The Spirit of Christ." *Dolphin* 8 (October, November, December 1905): 385-98, 519-45, 657-70. Reprinted with emendations as chaps. 1-14, pt. 1 of *LC*, pp. 1-81.

"Hope as a Factor of Religion." *Catholic World* 82 (November 1905): 193-98.

"Notre attitude en face du Pragmatisme." *Annales de philosophie chrétienne* ser. 4, 1 (December 1905): 225-32. Reprinted as "Pragmatism" in *TSC*, pp. 191-99.

1906

"Lettera confidenziale ad un amico professore di antropologia." *Corriere della Sera* (Milan), 1 January 1906, afternoon ed., p. 3. Excerpts from *A Letter to a University Professor* published in Italian and without GT's permission.

"The Language of Devotion." *Canadian Month* 2 (January 1906): 14-16.

"The Prayer of Christ." *Catholic World* 82 (January, March 1906): 446-58, 796-806; 83 (April 1906): 54-64. Reprinted as pt. 2 of *LC*, pp. 82-132.

Letter to the Editor: "Father Tyrrell's Reply." *American Ecclesiastical Review* 34 (February 1906): 199-200.

Letter to the Editor: "Les Concordats et les libertés gallicanes." *Demain*, 16 February 1906, pp. 9-10. Signed "Hippolyte Lefevre."

Letter to the Editor: "Jesuit Secession: Rev. George Tyrrell Explains the Cause of His Separation." *Daily Chronicle*, 23 February 1906, p. 7. *Tablet* 108 (24 February 1906): 286.

Letter to the Editor. *Études* 107 (5 April 1906): 94-95.

Letter to the Editor: "La Valeur critique de l'histoire religieuse." *Demain*, 27 April 1906, p. 8.

Letter to the Editor: "Une Réponse du P. Tyrrell." *Demain*, 1 June 1906, p. 11.

Letter to the Editor. *Demain*, 27 July 1906, p. 12.

1907

"Da Dio o dagli uomini?" *Rinnovamento* 1 (April 1907): 393-414. Reprinted as "From Heaven, or of Men?" with a lengthy introduction in *TSC*, pp. 360-86.

Letter to the Editor: "Personal." *Church Times* 57 (5 April 1907): 436.

Letter to the Editor: "The Views of 'Ernst [*sic*] Engels.'" *Tablet* 109 (6 April 1907): 537. Signed "George Tyrrell (Ernst Engels)."

Letter to the Editor: "The Rev. G. Tyrrell: A Correction." *Tablet* 109 (6 April 1907): 537.

Letter to the Editor: "An Exoneration." *Church Times* 57 (19 April 1907): 496.

"Per la sincerità." *Rinnovamento* 2 (July 1907): 1-18.

"Théologisme: Réponse à M. Lebreton." *Revue pratique d'apologétique* 4 (15 July 1907): 499-526. Reprinted as "'Theologism': A Reply" in *TSC*, pp. 308-54.

"Autour de Newman." *Demain*, 19 July 1907, p. 605.

Letter to the Editor: "The So-Called Syllabus." *Church Times* 58 (2 August 1907): 133. Signed "A Roman Catholic."

"Scholastica o filosofia dell'azione? Sussiste il dilemma?" *Rinnovamento* 2 (September-December 1907): 386-93 [pagination defective].

Letters to Editors concerning the *celebret* question (see *AL*, 2: 322-31; Raoul Goût, *L'Affaire Tyrrell* [Paris: Émile Nourry, 1909], pp. 179-86): (1) *Daily Chronicle*, 2 September 1907, p. 4. (2) *Giornale d'Italia*, 6 September 1907. (3) *Daily Chronicle*, 25 September 1907, p. 4. (4) *Giornale d'Italia*, 27 September 1907. (5) *Siècle*, 28 September 1907. (6) *Daily Chronicle*, 29 September 1907. (7) *Giornale d'Italia*, 29 September 1907. (8) *Temps*, 29 September 1907. (9) *L'Univers*, 9 October 1907. (10) *L'Univers*, 27 October 1907. (11)-(14) *Tablet* 110 (28 September, 5, 12, 19 October 1907): 487, 541, 575-76, 615. These four numbers of the *Tablet* also supply useful documentation of the affair, including (1) extracts in English translation of documents published in Mgr. Umberto Benigni's *Corrispondenza Romana*, (2) GT's letter to the *Daily Chronicle* of 25 September 1907, (3) GT's letter dated 31 August 1907 to the *Giornale d'Italia* of 6 September 1907, (4) GT's letter to the *Westminster Gazette* of 25 September 1907, and (5) GT's letter to the *Church Times* of 27 July 1906.

Letter to the Editor: "Fiera risposta del Padre Tyrrell all'Enciclica di Pio X." *Giornale d'Italia*, 26 September 1907, p. 1.

"The Pope and Modernism." *Times* (London), 30 September 1907, p. 4: 1 October 1907, p. 5.

"L'Excommunication salutaire." *Grande Revue* 44 (10 October 1907): 661-72. Never published in English, the original MS, dated 18 May 1904, is preserved in the Petre Papers at the British Library, Add. MSS 52369.

Letter to the Editor: "The Vatican and Father Tyrrell." *Times* (London), 2 November 1907, p. 10.

"The Condemnation of Newman." *Guardian*, 20 November 1907, pp. 1896-97; 27 November 1907, p. 1957.

Letter to the Editor: "Cardinal Newman and the Late Encyclical." *Times* (London), 2 December 1907, p. 8.

Letter to the Editor: "The Condemnation of Newman." *Guardian*, 11 December 1907, p. 2060.

Response to the Question: "Assistons-nous à une dissolution ou à une évolution de l'idée religieuse et du sentiment religieux?" In *La Question religieuse—Enquête internationale*, edited by Frédéric Charpin, pp. 196-99. Paris: Sociéte du Mercure de France, 1908.

1908

"The Prospects of Modernism." *Hibbert Journal* 6 (January 1908): 241–55. Reprinted in *Living Age* 208 (15 February 1908): 387–95.

"Il primato spirituale di Roma." *Nova et Vetera* 1 (10 January 1908): 4–8.

Letter to the Editor: "Modernism as a Gnosis." *Church Times* 59 (17 January 1908): 68.

Letter to the Editor: "Modernism." *Church Times* 59 (31 January 1908): 128.

"Il potere giuridico della Chiesa." *Nova et Vetera* 1 (10 March 1908): 141–48.

Letter to the Editor. *Giornale d'Italia*, 30 March 1908. Published in a shortened version in *La Croix*, 3 April 1908.

Letter to the Editor. *Annales de philosophie chrétienne*, ser. 4, 6 (April 1908): 88–89. Although signed "G. Tyrrell," the letter was in fact written by Henri Bremond and revised before publication by Lucien Laberthonnière. The original letter in Bremond's hand with extensive modifications by Laberthonnière is preserved among the Laberthonnière Papers at the Bibliothèque nationale in Paris.

"In Aid of Ex-Priests." *L'Exode. Organe du mouvement: Hors de Rome* 2 (10 April 1908): 2. Unsigned.

"Teologia aprioristica." *Nova et Vetera* 1 (25 April 1908): 249–53.

"Parusia e socialismo." *Nova et Vetera* 1 (10 May 1908): 281–85. Reprinted as "The Parusia and Socialism" in *EFI*, pp. 239–44.

"'Scientia inflat' o il pragmatismo di S. Paolo." *Nova et Vetera* 1 (25 May 1908): 320–26.

"Mediaevalism and Modernism." *Harvard Theological Review* 1 (July 1908): 304–24.

"Il sacerdozio-affare." *Nova et Vetera* 2 (10–25 August 1908): 65–73.

"Sono necessarie le Chiese?" *Rinnovamento* 4 (September-December 1908): 280–96. This essay had been delivered as a lecture on 10 November 1908 to the Phratry, a society of laymen of the Church of England. Johannes Jacobus Stam, *George Tyrrell: 1861–1909* (Utrecht: H. Honig, 1938), p. 195, reported that the paper was printed in the original English for private circulation only, but to date no copies have come to light.

"The Eucharistic Congress." *Guardian*, 16 September 1908, p. 1522. Unsigned.

"The Eucharist and the Papacy." *Guardian*, 16 December 1908, p. 2105.

Letter to the Editor: "The Society of St. Thomas of Canterbury." *Guardian*, 30 December 1908, p. 2189. Signed "One Who Knows."

1909

"In difesa dei modernisti." *Rinnovamento* 5 (February 1909): 169–79.

A comment on a paper by R. B. Haldane (February 1900). In *Papers Read Before the Synthetic Society, 1896–1908, and Written Comments Thereon Circulated among the Members of the Society*. Presented to the members of the Synthetic Society by the Rt. Hon. Arthur James Balfour. For private circulation. London: Spottiswoode & Co., 1909.

A comment on "The Finite God," a paper by J. Ellis McTaggart (19 March 1903). In ibid., pp. 404-7.

A comment on "Analogy and Agnosticism," a paper by J. S. Smith (30 April 1903). In ibid., pp. 421-24.

Letter to the Editor. *Church Times* 61 (26 March 1909): 430. Signed "C.F.G.T." ["Catholic Father George Tyrrell"?]. Assignment to GT is tentative.

Letter to the Editor: "What Is Continuity?" *Church Times* 61 (2 April 1909): 444. Signed "Romanus."

"Appeal to the English." *L'Exode. Organe du mouvement: Hors de Rome* [mid-April 1909?]. This periodical is rare. Attempts to locate a copy have been unsuccessful.

"The Dearth of Clergy." *Contemporary Review* 95 (May 1909): 574-88.

"Divine Fecundity." *Quest* 1 (October 1909): 13-28. An abbreviated form of an essay published in full in *EFI*, pp. 245-77.

"The Point at Issue." In *Jesus or Christ? Hibbert Journal Supplement for 1909*, pp. 5-16. London: Williams & Norgate, 1909.

1911

"Loi et conscience: Essai inédit." *Revue moderniste internationale* 2 (March 1911): 107-11. Reprinted as "Does Holiness Enlighten?" in *EFI*, pp. 28-32, and dated there by MDP as 1904-06.

"La Foi salutaire: Essai inédit." *Revue moderniste internationale* 2 (May 1911): 226-29. Reprinted as "Saving Faith" in *EFI*, pp. 235-38, and dated there by MDP as 1904.

"La Double vie de l'homme: Essai inédit." *Revue moderniste internationale* 2 (June 1911): 278-79. Reprinted as "The Soul's Centre" in *EFI*, pp. 228-30, and dated there by MDP as 1904.

1912

"Sul farisaismo." In *Il Papa e il modernismo di Giorgio Tyrrell*, preface by Arnoldo Cervesato, pp. 233-39. Rome: Enrico Voghera, 1912. A collection of GT's articles in *Rinnovamento* and *Nova et Vetera*, with the exception of this one essay, which seems not to have appeared before 1912 and for which no English original has been located.

Recent Publications

"The 'Tabula Aurea' of Peter de Bergamo." *Heythrop Journal* 10 (July 1969): 275-79. This essay, in Tyrrell's hand and signed by him, is preserved in the *Blandyke Papers* 68 (February 1896) at Heythrop College, London.

"On Beauty." *Heythrop Journal* 11 (April 1970): 148-57.

"The Sublime." *Heythrop Journal* 11 (April 1970): 157-60. Copies of this and "On Beauty" are preserved at Heythrop College in an exercise book belonging to the late Fr. V. Wilkin. Both essays were written by

GT, perhaps in May 1899, and later copied by Father Wilkin in his exercise book.

"'Revelation as Experience': An Unpublished Lecture of George Tyrrell." Edited with notes and historical introduction by Thomas Michael Loome. *Heythrop Journal* 12 (April 1971): 117–49. Originally composed as a lecture, it was delivered by GT at King's College, London, on 26 March 1909. The original MS, in Tyrrell's hand, is entitled, "Revelation as Experience: A Reply to Hakluyt Egerton." It is preserved in the Petre Papers at the British Library, Add. MSS 52369.

Poems

"What Is Love?" *Nation* 4 (28 November 1908): 346. A translation of a poem by "Friedrich Halm" [Eligius Franz Joseph, Freiherr von Muench-Bellinghausen], signed "G.T." Reprinted in *Versions and Perversions of Heine & Others* (London: Elkin Mathews, 1909), under the German title, "Mein Hertz [*sic*] ich will dich fragen."

Versions and Perversions of Heine & Others. London: Elkin Mathews, 1909. Dedicated to "W.S.B." [Wilfrid Scawen Blunt]. Most of the poems are translations from the French, Italian, and German; the rest are original.

"It Cannot Be That the Son of So Many Tears Should Be Lost." In *Letters and Notices of the English Province of the Society of Jesus* 56 (May 1948): 121.

"Emitte lucem tuam." In *Letters and Notices of the English Province of the Society of Jesus* 57 (January 1949): 3. Dedicated "to W.R. on his ordination day." Fr. William Roche (1856–1945) was ordained on 22 September 1889. He was "perhaps the best-loved of all his Jesuit friends." *AL*, 2: 33.

Correspondence

Letter to Charles E. Osborne, containing GT's recollections of his friend, Robert Dolling. In Charles E. Osborne, *The Life of Father Dolling*, pp. 19–22. London: Edward Arnold, 1903.

"To His Eminence Cardinal Ferrata, Prefect of the S. Congregation of Bishops & Regulars." Dated 4 July 1906. One hundred fifty copies printed for private circulation by William Pollard & Co., Exeter. Four pages, unpaginated. Copy at University Library, Cambridge, general catalog no. 7.14.150^8, with the following inscriptions in GT's hand: "No. 11" and "Confidential" on the first page, and at the bottom of the fourth page, "Boutre. Vinon. Var.," Bremond's home from which GT posted this copy.

"A Letter to the Roman Catholic Bishop of Southwark." Dated 27 October 1907 and printed for private circulation ("not for publication"). Copy preserved in the archives of the archdiocese of Westminster.

"Father Tyrrell. The Career of a Brave and Patient Fighter. An Unpublished Letter." *Daily Graphic*, 24 July 1909, p. 11. Text of a letter by GT from 19 November 1907 on the effect of his excommunication on the modernist movement.

"Father Tyrrell and the Old Catholics." *Guardian*, 28 July 1909, p. 1185. Texts of two private letters dated 28 November 1907 and 17 February 1909. Names of the addressees not included. Later reprinted in *Revue internationale de théologie* 17 (December 1909): 814-16.

Letter to Eduard Herzog, Old Catholic Bishop of Bern, 4 November 1908. In Eduard Herzog, "George Tyrrell," *Revue internationale de théologie* 17 (December 1909): 754-64. Reprinted under the title "The Late Father Tyrrell and the Old Catholics," *Guardian* 20 October 1909, p. 1664.

Letters to Ernesto Buonaiuti. *Revue moderniste internationale* 1 (1910): 22-27, 63-65, 101-3, 145-46. Reprinted in Ernesto Buonaiuti, *Le Modernisme catholique*, pp. 129-30, 133-36, 143-49. Paris: Rieder, 1927.

Three letters to Albert Houtin, 1908. In Albert Houtin, *Autour d'un prêtre marié: Histoire d'une polémique*, pp. 209-13. Paris: Chez l'auteur, 1910.

Letters to various recipients. In M. D. Petre, *Autobiography and Life of George Tyrrell*, 2 vols., passim. London: Edward Arnold, 1912.

George Tyrrell's Letters. Selected and edited by M. D. Petre. London: T. Fisher Unwin, 1920.

Letters to Alfred Loisy. In Alfred Loisy, *Mémoires pour servir à l'histoire religieuse de notre temps*, 3 vols., passim. Paris: Émile Nourry, 1930-31.

Letters to Maude Dominica Petre. In M. D. Petre, *My Way of Faith*, pp. 274-85. London: J. M. Dent & Sons, 1937.

Letters to Herbert Thurston, S.J. In Joseph Crehan, S.J., *Father Thurston: A Memoir with a Bibliography of His Writings*, pp. 48-72. London: Sheed & Ward, 1952. In Crehan, "More Tyrrell Letters—I," *Month*, n.s. 40 (October 1968): 178-85; "Tyrrell in His Workshop," *Month*, 2d n.s. 3 (April 1971): 111-15, 119.

Letters to Baron Friedrich von Hügel. In numerous secondary sources. Among the more accessible are Friedrich von Hügel, *Selected Letters 1896-1924*, edited with a memoir by Bernard Holland (London: J. M. Dent & Sons, 1926); M. D. Petre, *Von Hügel and Tyrrell: The Story of a Friendship* (London: J. M. Dent & Sons, 1937); and Michael de la Bedoyère, *The Life of Baron von Hügel* (London: J. M. Dent & Sons, 1951).

Letters to Wilfrid Ward. In Maisie Ward, *The Wilfrid Wards and the Transition*, 2 vols. passim. London: Sheed & Ward, 1934-37. In *Letters from a "Modernist": The Letters of George Tyrrell to Wilfrid Ward, 1893-1908*. Edited by Mary Jo Weaver. Shepherdstown, W. Va.: Patmos Press, 1981.

Letters to various recipients: to Alfred Loisy (27 January 1904) and an unidentified recipient (a Mr. Hunnybun) (17 October 1902). In *Search* 6 (March, April 1968): 436-39, 480.

Letters to André Raffalovich (1898–1909). In Thomas Michael Loome, "Tyrrell's Letters to André Raffalovich," *Month*, 2d n.s. 1 (February, March 1970): 95–101, 138–49.

Lettres de George Tyrrell à Henri Bremond. Translated and edited by Anne Louis-David. Preface by Maurice Nédoncelle. Paris: Aubier Montaigne, 1971.

Works Criticized and Revised

Petre, M. D. "Devotion and Devotions." *Weekly Register* 104 (22, 29 November, 6 December 1901): 635–36, 669–70, 701–2.

———. *Devotional Essays.* London: Catholic Truth Society, 1902.

von Hügel, Friedrich. "Official Authority and Living Religion" (1904). In Friedrich von Hügel, *Essays and Addresses*, 2d ser., pp. 3–23. London: J. M. Dent & Sons, 1926.

Williams, W. J. *Newman, Pascal, Loisy and the Catholic Church.* London: Francis Griffiths, 1906.

von Hügel, Friedrich. *The Mystical Element of Religion as Studied in Saint Catherine of Genoa and Her Friends*, 2 vols. London: J. M. Dent & Sons, 1908.

SELECTED SECONDARY SOURCES

Monographs

Abercrombie, Nigel. *The Life and Work of Edmund Bishop.* Foreword by David Knowles. London: Longmans, Green & Co., 1959.

Arnold, Matthew. *The Complete Prose Works of Matthew Arnold.* Edited by R. H. Super. Vol. 6: *Dissent and Dogma: Literature and Dogma.* Ann Arbor: University of Michigan Press, 1968.

Barmann, Lawrence F. *Baron Friedrich von Hügel and the Modernist Crisis in England.* Cambridge: At the University Press, 1972.

Barry, William Francis. *Memories and Opinions.* London: G. P. Putnam's Sons, 1926.

Bedoyère, Michael de la. *The Life of Baron von Hügel.* London: J. M. Dent & Sons, 1951.

Belfield, John H. "The 'Theological' Method of George Tyrrell: A Study of the Modernist Crisis in the Light of George Tyrrell's Thought." Ph.D. dissertation, Catholic University of America, Washington, D.C., 1963.

Bella, Julius I. "George Tyrrell's Conception of the Relation between Religion and Theology." Ph.D. dissertation, Yale University School of Philosophy, New Haven, 1939.

Bergson, Henri Louis. *Essai sur les données immediates de la conscience.* Paris: Félix Alcan, 1889.

———. *Matière et mémoire.* Paris: Félix Alcan, 1896.

————. *L'Évolution créatrice.* Paris: Félix Alcan, 1907.

————. *Time and Free Will: An Essay on the Immediate Data of Consciousness.* Translated by F. L. Pogson. London: George Allen & Co., 1910; 8th printing, London: George Allen & Unwin, 1971.

————. *Creative Evolution.* Translated by Arthur Mitchell. London: Macmillan & Co., 1911.

————. *Matter and Memory.* Translated by N. M. Paul and W. S. Palmer. 2d ed. London: George Allen & Co., 1912.

————. *The Two Sources of Morality and Religion.* Translated by R. Ashley Audra and Cloudesley Brereton, with the assistance of Horsfall Carter. New York: Henry Holt & Co., 1935.

Bessmer, Julius. *Philosophie und Theologie des Modernismus.* Freiburg: Herdersche Verlagshandlung, 1912.

Blondel, Maurice. *L'Action: Essai d'une critique de la vie et d'une science de la pratique.* Paris: F. Alcan, 1893; reprint, Paris: Presses Universitaires de France, 1950.

————. *Études blondéliennes.* Edited by Jacques Paliard. 3 vols. Paris: Presses Universitaires de France, 1951–54.

————. *Premiers écrits.* Paris: Presses Universitaires de France, 1956.

————. *The Letter on Apologetics and History and Dogma.* Translated with an introduction by Alexander Dru and Illtyd Trethowan. New York: Holt, Rinehart, and Winston, 1964.

————, and Bremond, Henri. *Henri Bremond et Maurice Blondel: Correspondance.* Edited with an introduction by André Blanchet. 3 vols. Paris: Aubier Montaigne, 1970–71.

————, and Laberthonnière, Lucien. *Correspondance philosophique: Maurice Blondel, Lucien Laberthonnière.* Edited by Claude Tresmontant. Paris: Éditions du Seuil, 1961.

————, and Valensin, Auguste. *Correspondance, 1899–1947.* Edited by Henri de Lubac. 3 vols. Paris: Aubier, 1957–65.

Blunt, Wilfrid Scawen. *My Diaries: Being a Personal Narrative of Events, 1888–1914.* Foreword by Lady Gregory. Reprint. New York: Alfred A. Knopf, 1932.

Boland, André. *La Crise moderniste hier et aujourd'hui.* Paris: Éditions Beauchesne, 1980.

Bouillard, Henri. *Blondel and Christianity.* Translated by James M. Somerville. Washington, D.C.: Corpus Books, 1969.

[Boutwood, Arthur A.] "Hakluyt Egerton." *Father Tyrrell's Modernism: An Expository Criticism of "Through Scylla and Charybdis" in an Open Letter to Mr. Athelstan Riley.* London: Kegan Paul, Trench, Trübner & Co., 1909.

Bremond, Henri. *L'Inquiétude religieuse.* Paris: Perrin & Co., 1901.

————. *The Mystery of Newman.* Translated by H. C. Corrance. Introduction by Rev. George Tyrrell. London: Williams & Norgate, 1907.

[————] "Sylvain Leblanc." *Un clerc qui n'a pas trahi: Alfred Loisy d'après ses mémoires.* Paris: Émile Nourry, 1931; critical ed.: *Une oeuvre clandestine d'Henri Bremond.* Uomini e dottrine, no. 18. Introduction by Émile Poulat. Rome: Edizioni di storia e letteratura, 1972.

————, and Blondel, Maurice. *Henri Bremond et Maurice Blondel: Correspondance.* Edited with an introduction by André Blanchet. 3 vols. Paris: Aubier Montaigne, 1970–71.

Brüngel, Ferdinand. "Die Religionsphilosophie des Modernisten George Tyrrell (1861–1909)." Ph.D. dissertation, Ludwig-Maximilian University, Munich, 1968.

Brunetière, Ferdinand. *La Science et la religion.* Rev. ed. Paris: Perrin, 1916.

Buonaiuti, Ernesto. *Le Modernisme Catholique.* Translated by René Monot. Paris: Rieder, 1927.

Burke, Ronald, and Gilmore, George, eds. *Current Research in Roman Catholic Modernism.* Proceedings of the Roman Catholic Modernism Working Group of the American Academy of Religion. Mobile: Spring Hill College Press, 1980.

————, and ————, eds. *Proceedings of the Roman Catholic Modernism Working Group of the American Academy of Religion* (Mobile: Spring Hill College Duplicating Service, 1979).

Catalogues of the English Province of the Society of Jesus. Roehampton: Manresa Press, 1879–1909.

Class, Gustav. *Untersuchungen zur Phaenomonologie und Ontologie des menschlichen Geistes.* Leipzig: A. Deichert. 1896.

Colin, P.; Houssaye, J.; Breton, S.; et al. *Le Modernisme.* Paris: Éditions Beauchesne, 1980.

Continho, Lucio de Veige. *Tradition et histoire dans la controverse moderniste.* Rome: Gregorian University, 1954.

Crehan, S.J., Joseph H. *Father Thurston: A Memoir with a Bibliography of His Writings.* London: Sheed & Ward, 1952.

Daly, Gabriel. *Transcendence and Immanence: A Study in Catholic Modernism and Integralism.* Oxford: Clarendon Press, 1980.

Delmont, Monsignor. *Modernisme et modernistes.* Paris: P. Lethielleux, 1909.

Desjardins, Paul. *Catholicisme et critique: Reflexions d'un profane sur l'affaire Loisy.* Paris: Cahiers de la Quinzaine, 1905.

Dilthey, Wilhelm. *Einleitung in die Geisteswissenschaften.* Leipzig: Duncker & Humblot, 1883.

Dimnet, Ernest. *La Pensée catholique dans l'Angleterre contemporaine.* Paris: V. Lecoffre, 1906.

Döllinger, Johan Joseph Ignaz von. *A History of the Church.* Translated by Edward Cox. 4 vols. in 2. London: Dolman, 1840–42.

————. *The Church and the Churches.* Translated by William B. MacCabe. London: Hurst & Blackett, 1862.

[————] "Janus." *The Pope and the Council.* Authorized translation from the German. 2d ed. London: Rivingtons, 1869.

————. *Prophecies and the Prophetic Spirit in the Christian Era.* Translated by Alfred Plummer. London: Rivingtons, 1873.

————. *The First Age of Christianity and the Church.* Translated by Henry Nutcombe Oxenham. 2 vols. London: Allen, 1877.

————. *Briefe und Erklärungen . . . über die vaticanischen Dekreten, 1869–1887.* Edited by F. H. Reusch. Munich: O. Beck, 1890.

Dolling, Robert. *Ten Years in a Portsmouth Slum.* 6th ed. London: S. C. Brown, Langham & Co., 1903.

Duhm, Bernhard. *Das Geheimnis in der Religion.* Lecture given on 11 February 1896. Freiburg: J.C.B. Mohr, 1896.

Egerton, Hakluyt, pseud. See Boutwood, Arthur A.

Eucken, Rudolf. *Die Lebensanschauungen der grossen Denker: Eine Entwickelungsgeschichte des Lebensproblems der Menschheit von Plato bis zur Gegenwart.* Leipzig: Veit & Co., 1890.

————. *Der Kampf um einen geistigen Lebensinhalt: Neue Grundlegung einer Weltanschauung.* Leipzig: Veit & Co., 1896.

————. *Der Wahrheitsgehalt der Religion.* Leipzig: Veit & Co., 1901.

————. *The Problem of Human Life: As Viewed by the Great Thinkers from Plato to the Present Time.* Translated by Williston S. Hough and W. R. Boyce Gibson. London: T. Fisher Unwin, 1911.

————. *The Life of the Spirit.* Translated by F. L. Pogson. Crown Theological Library, vol. 26. London: Williams & Norgate, 1913.

Falckenberg, Richard. *Grundzüge der Philosophie des Nicolaus Cusanus, mit besonderer Berücksichtigung der Lehre vom Erkennen.* Breslau: W. Koebner, 1880.

Faupel, Bruno. *Die Religionsphilosophie George Tyrrells.* Freiburger theologische Studien, vol. 99. Freiburg: Herder, 1976.

Fawkes, Alfred. *Studies in Modernism.* London: Smith, Elder, & Co., 1913.

Fechner, Gustav Theodor. *Die drei Motive und Gründe des Glaubens.* Leipzig: Breitkopf & Härtel, 1863.

Fichte, Johann Gottlieb. *The Vocation of Man.* Translated and edited with an introduction by Roderick M. Chisholm. Indianapolis: Bobbs-Merrill Co., 1956.

Gallarati-Scotti, Tommaso. *The Life of Antonio Fogazzaro.* Translated by Mary Prichard Agnetti. London: Hodder & Stoughton, 1922.

Gibson, William. *The Abbé de Lamennais and the Liberal Catholic Movement in France.* London: Longmans, Green & Co., 1896.

Gisler, Anton. *Der Modernismus.* 4th ed. Einsiedeln: Benziger & Co., 1913.

Goetz, Joseph W. "Analogy and Symbol: A Study in the Theology of George Tyrrell." Ph.D. dissertation, King's College, Cambridge University, 1969.

Goût, Raoul. *L'Affaire Tyrrell: Un épisode de la crise catholique.* Paris: Émile Nourry, 1909.

Grandi, Giovanni, ed. *Corrispondenza Romana* (Rome), 1907–12. Renamed *Correspondance de Rome* from October 1909. Reprint. 6 vols. in 3. Milan: Feltrinelli Reprint, 1971.

Greisch, Jean; Neufeld, Karl; and Theobald, Christoph. *La Crise contemporaine du modernisme à la crise des herméneutiques.* Théologie historique, no. 24. Paris: Beauchesne, 1973.

Gruber, Jacob W. *A Conscience in Conflict: The Life of St. George Jackson Mivart.* New York: Columbia University Press, 1960.

Harnack, Adolf von. *What Is Christianity?* Translated by Thomas Bailey Saunders. Introduction by Rudolf Bultmann. New York: Harper Torchbooks, 1957.

Hatch, Edwin. *The Influence of Greek Ideas and Usages upon the Christian Church.* The Hibbert Lectures, 1888. Edited by A. M. Fairbairn. 7th ed. London: Williams & Norgate, 1898.

Healey, S.J., Charles J. "The Invisible Church and the Visible Church in the Writings of George Tyrrell." Ph.D. dissertation, Gregorian University, Rome, 1970.

Hébert, Marcel. *Souvenirs d'Assise.* Paris: Éditions original, 1899.

————. *L'Évolution de la foi catholique.* Paris: Félix Alcan, 1905.

Heiler, Friedrich. *Alfred Loisy (1857-1940): Der Vater des katholischen Modernismus.* Munich: Erasmus-Verlag, 1947.

d'Hendecourt, Marie-Madeleine. *Essai sur la philosophie du Père Laberthonnière.* Paris: Librairie philosophique J. Vrin, 1947.

Hermann, E. *Eucken and Bergson: Their Significance for Christian Thought.* 5th ed. London: James Clarke & Co., 1913.

Hodges, H. A. *Wilhelm Dilthey: An Introduction.* London: Kegan Paul, Trench, Trübner & Co., 1944.

Hogan, J. B. *Clerical Studies.* Boston: Marlier & Co., 1898.

Hogarth, Henry. *Henri Bremond: The Life and Work of a Devout Humanist.* London: SPCK, 1950.

Holmes, J. Derek, and Murray, Robert. *Newman: On the Inspiration of Scripture.* London: Geoffrey Chapman, 1967.

Houtin, Albert. *La Question biblique chez les Catholiques de France au XIXe siècle.* Paris: Alphonse Picard & Sons, 1902.

————. *L'Américanisme.* Paris: Librairie Émile Nourry, 1904.

————. *La Question biblique au XXe siècle.* 2d ed. Paris: Émile Nourry, 1906.

————. *Histoire du modernisme catholique.* Paris: Chez l'auteur, 1913.

————. *Un Prêtre symboliste: Marcel Hébert (1851-1916).* Paris: F. Rieder & Co., 1925.

————. *The Life of a Priest: My Own Experience, 1867-1912.* Translated by Winifred Stephens Whale. London: Watts & Co., 1927.

————, and Sartiaux, Félix. *Alfred Loisy: Sa vie, son oeuvre.* Edited by Émile Poulat. Paris. Éditions du Centre National de la Recherche Scientifique, 1960.

von Hügel, Friedrich. *The Papal Commission and the Pentateuch.* London: Longmans, Green & Co., 1906.

————. *The Mystical Element of Religion as Studied in Saint Catherine of Genoa and Her Friends.* 2 vols. London: J. M. Dent & Co., 1908.

————. *Selected Letters, 1896-1924.* Edited with a memoir by Bernard Holland. London: J. M. Dent & Sons, 1927.

James, William. *The Will to Believe and Other Essays in Popular Philosophy.* New York: Longmans & Co., 1897.

Janet, Pierre Marie Félix. *État mental des hystérique: Les Stigmates mentaux.* Preface by Jean Martin Charcot. 2 vols. Paris: Reuff, 1892-94.

Joly, Henri. *Psychologie des saints.* 2d ed. Paris: Librairie Victor Lecoffre, 1897.

——. *The Psychology of the Saints.* Preface by George Tyrrell. London: Duckworth, 1898.

Jones, Sir Henry. *A Critical Account of the Philosophy of Lotze: The Doctrine of Thought.* Glasgow: Maclehose & Sons, 1895.

Jordan, L. H. *Modernism in Italy.* London: Henry Frowde, 1909.

Juliana of Norwich. *XVI Revelations of Divine Love Shewed to Mother Juliana of Norwich 1373.* Preface by George Tyrrell. London: Kegan Paul, Trench, Trübner & Co., 1902.

Kelly, S.J., Eugene Daniel. "Wilfrid Ward's Position in the Modernist Movement." M.A. thesis, St. Louis University, St. Louis, Mo., 1951.

Kerlin, Michael J. "Historical Religion in the Thought of Friedrich von Hügel and George Tyrrell." Ph.D. dissertation, Lasallianum, Rome, 1966.

Kilfoyle, Daniel. "The Conception of Doctrinal Authority in the Writings of George Tyrrell." Ph.D. dissertation, Union Theological Seminary, New York, 1970.

Die Kirche und der liberale Katholizismus: Gemeinsames Hirtenschreiben des Cardinal-Erzbischofs unter der Bischöfe der Kirchenprovinz Westminster. Frankfurter Zeitgemässe Broschüren 20.5 (February 1901). Hamm i. W.: Verlag von Breer & Thiemann, 1901.

Klein, Felix. *Americanism: A Phantom Heresy.* Atchison, Kans.: Aquin Book Shop, 1951.

Kübel, Johannes. *Geschichte des katholischen Modernismus.* Tübingen: J.C.B. Mohr, 1909.

Laberthonnière, Lucien. *Essais de philosophie religieuse.* Paris: P. Lethielleux, 1903.

——. *Le Réalisme chrétien précéde de Essais de philosophie religieuse.* Preface by Claude Tresmontant. Paris: Éditions du Seuil, 1969.

——, and Blondel, Maurice. *Correspondance philosophique: Maurice Blondel, Lucien Laberthonnière.* Edited by Claude Tresmontant. Paris: Éditions du Seuil, 1961.

Lacey, T. A. *Harnack and Loisy.* Introduction by Lord Halifax. London: Longmans, Green & Co., 1904.

——. *The Historic Christ.* London: Longmans, Green & Co., 1905.

Lagrange, Marie-Joseph. *M. Loisy et le modernisme, à propos des "Memoires."* Jurisy (Seine-et-Oise): Éditions du cerf, 1932.

Laubacher, James A. *Dogma and the Development of Dogma in the Writings of George Tyrrell (1861-1909).* Louvain: Catholic University, 1939.

Lebreton, Jules. *The Encyclical and Modernist Theology.* Translated by Alban Goodier, S.J. London: Catholic Truth Society, 1908.

Lecanuet, Édouard. *L'Église de France sous la troisième Republique.* Vol. 4: *La Vie de l'Église sous Léon XIII.* Paris: J. de Gigord, 1930.

Lejeune, Paul. *Introduction à la vie mystique.* Paris: P. Lethielleux, 1899.

468 GEORGE TYRRELL: IN SEARCH OF CATHOLICISM

Leo XIII, Pope. *Allocutiones, epistolae, constitutiones, alique acta praeci-pua.* 7 Vols. Vol. 5: *1891–94;* vol. 6: *1894–97;* vol. 7: *1897–1900.* Bruges: Desclée, de Brouwer & Co., 1887–1906.

LeRoy, Edouard. *Dogme et critique.* Paris: Librairie Bloud & Co., 1907.

————. *Une Philosophie nouvelle: Henri Bergson.* Paris: Félix Alcan, 1912.

Letters to His Holiness Pope Pius X by a "Modernist." Chicago: Open Court Publishing Co., 1910.

Lilley, Alfred Leslie, trans. *What We Want: An Open Letter to Pius X from a Group of Priests.* London: John Murray, 1907. GT did much of the translation but did not want his name to appear.

————. *Modernism: A Record and Review.* London: Sir Isaac Pitman & Sons, 1909.

————, trans. and ed. *The Programme of Modernism: A Reply to the Encyclical of Pius X, "Pascendi Dominici Gregis."* London: T. Fisher Unwin, 1908. GT's correspondence with Lilley confirms that GT was the principal translator of the book and author of the introduction.

Loisy, Alfred Firmin. *Études bibliques.* Amiens: Rousseau-Leroy, 1894. 2d ed. Paris: Picard, 1901. 3d ed., 1903.

————. *Les Évangiles synoptiques.* Vol. 1: Amien: Rousseau-Leroy, 1894; vol. 2: Amien: Jourdain-Rousseau, 1896.

————. *La Religion d'Israël.* Paris: Letouzey & Co., 1901.

————. *Études évangéliques.* Paris: Alphonse Picard & Sons, 1902.

————. *L'Évangile et l'Église.* Paris: Alphonse Picard & Sons, 1902.

————. *Autour d'un petit livre.* Paris: Alphonse Picard & Sons, 1903.

————. *The Gospel and the Church.* Translated by Christopher Home. London: Isbister & Co., 1903.

————. *Le Quatrième Évangile.* Paris: Alphonse Picard & Sons, 1903.

————. *Quelques lettres sur des questions actuelles et sur des événements récents.* Ceffonds: Chez l'auteur, 1908.

————. *Simples réflexions sur le décret du saint-office Lamentabili sane exitu et sur l'encyclique Pascendi dominici gregis.* Ceffonds: Chez l'auteur, 1908.

————. *Choses passées.* Paris: Émile Nourry, 1913.

————. *Mémoires pour servir à l'histoire religieuse de notre temps.* 3 vols. Paris: Émile Nourry, 1930–31.

————. *George Tyrrell et Henri Bremond.* Paris: Émile Nourry, 1936.

————. *The Birth of the Christian Religion.* Authorized translation by L. P. Jacks. London: George Allen & Unwin, 1948.

Loome, Thomas Michael. *Liberal Catholicism, Reform Catholicism, Modernism: A Contribution to a New Orientation in Modernist Research.* Tübinger theologische Studien, vol. 14. Mainz: Matthias-Grünewald-Verlag, 1979.

Lotze, Rudolf Hermann. *Grundzüge der Religionsphilosophie: Diktate aus den Vorlesungen.* 2d ed. Leipzig: G. Hirzel, 1888–1891.

Louis-David, Anne, trans. and ed. *Lettres de George Tyrrell à Henri Bremond.* Paris: Aubier Montaigne, 1971.

McCool, Gerald A. *Catholic Theology in the Nineteenth Century: The Quest for a Unitary Method*. New York: Seabury Press, 1977.

MacDougall, Hugh A. *The Acton-Newman Relations: The Dilemma of Christian Liberalism*. New York: Fordham University Press, 1962.

Madiran, Jean. *L'Intégrisme: Histoire d'une histoire*. Paris: Nouvelles Éditions Latines, 1964.

Major, H. D. *English Modernism: Its Origins, Methods, Aims*. Cambridge: Harvard University Press, 1927.

Marlé, René. *Au coeur de la crise moderniste*. Paris: Aubier Montaigne, 1960.

Mathew, Arnold Harris. *An Episcopal Odyssey: An Open Letter to . . . Randall Thomas Davidson, D.D., Lord Archbishop of Canterbury*. London: Kingsdown [1915].

May, J. Lewis. *Father Tyrrell and the Modernist Movement*. London: Burns Oates & Washbourne, 1938.

Meehan, Joseph F. "Dogmatic Relativism in the Theology of George Tyrrell." Ph.D. dissertation, Gregorian University, Rome, 1953.

Mehok, Charles J. "The Ecclesiology of George Tyrrell." Ph.D. dissertation, Catholic University of America, Washington, D.C., 1970.

Mercier, Désiré Joseph. *Modernism*. Translated by M. Lindsay. London: Burns & Oates, 1910.

Michelitsch, Anton. *Der biblisch-dogmatische "Syllabus" Pius' X. samt der Enzyklika gegen den Modernismus und dem Motu proprio vom 18. November 1907 erklärt*. 2d ed. Graz: Styria, 1908.

Mozley, J. K. *Some Tendencies in British Theology: From the Publication of Lux Mundi to the Present Day*. London: SPCK, 1951.

Münsterberg, Hugo. *Psychology and Life*. Westminster: A. Constable, 1899.

———. *Grundzüge der Psychologie*. 2 vols. Leipzig: J.A. Barth, 1900.

Murray, Robert, and Holmes, J. Derek. *Newman: On the Inspiration of Scripture*. London: Geoffrey Chapman, 1967.

Nédoncelle, Maurice. *La Philosophie religieuse en Grande-Bretagne de 1850 à nos jours*. Paris: Librairie Bloud & Gay, 1934.

———. *Le Pensée religieuse de Friedrich von Hügel*. Paris: J. Vrin, 1935.

Nelson, Claude, and Pittenger, Norman, eds. *Pilgrim of Rome: An Introduction to the Life and Work of Ernesto Buonaiuti*. Digswell Place: James Nisbet & Co., 1969.

Newman, John Henry. *Letter to the Duke of Norfolk*. London: B. M. Pickering, 1875.

———. *An Essay in Aid of a Grammar of Assent*. London: Longmans, Green & Co., 1895.

———. *Oxford University Sermons*. London: Longmans, Green & Co., 1909.

———. *Essays, Critical and Historical*. 2 vols. New impression. London: Longmans, Green & Co., 1919.

———. *An Essay on the Development of Christian Doctrine*. Edited with a preface and introduction by Charles Frederick Harrold. London: Longmans, Green & Co., 1949.

———. *Apologia pro vita sua*. Edited by David J. DeLaura. New York: W. W. Norton & Co., 1968.

Nouvelle, A. *L'Authenticité du Quatrième Évangile et la thèse de M. Loisy*. Paris: Librairie Bloud & Co., 1907.

O'Connor, Francis M. "The Concept of Revelation in the Writings of George Tyrrell." Ph.D. dissertation, Institut Catholique, Paris, 1963.

O'Grady, John Francis. "The Doctrine of Nature and Grace in the Writings of George Tyrrell." Ph.D. dissertation, Pontifical University of St. Thomas Aquinas in Urbe, Rome, 1969.

Oldmeadow, Ernest. *Francis Cardinal Bourne*. 2 vols. London: Burns Oates & Washbourne, 1940-44.

Ollé-Laprune, Léon. *De la certitude morale*. Paris: E. Belin, 1880.

———. *Ce qu'on va chercher à Rome*. Paris: A. Colin, 1895.

Osborne, Charles E. *The Life of Father Dolling*. London: Edward Arnold, 1903.

Paggiaro, Luigi. *Il Modernismo, a cinquant'anni della sua condanna*. Padova: Presbyterium, 1957.

Paliard, Jacques ed. *Études blondeliennes*. 3 vols. Paris: Presses Universitaires de France, 1951-54.

Papers Read before the Synthetic Society, 1896-1908. Presented to the members of the Synthetic Society by the Rt. Hon. Arthur James Balfour, August 1909. For private circulation. London: Spottiswoode & Co., 1909.

Perrin, Marie-Thérèse. *Laberthonnière et ses amis*. Theologie historique, vol. 33. Paris: Éditions Beauchesne, 1975.

Petre, Maude D. *The Soul's Orbit, or Man's Journey to God*. London: Longmans, Green & Co., 1904.

———. *Catholicism and Independence: Being Studies in Spiritual Liberty*. London: Longmans, Green & Co., 1907.

———. *Autobiography and Life of George Tyrrell*. 2 vols. London: Edward Arnold, 1912.

———. *Modernism: Its Failure and Its Fruits*. London: T. C. & E. C. Jack, 1918.

———. *My Way of Faith*. London: J. M. Dent & Sons, 1937.

———. *Von Hügel and Tyrrell: The Story of a Friendship*. London: J. M. Dent & Sons, 1937.

———. *Alfred Loisy: His Religious Significance*. Cambridge: At the University Press, 1944.

———, ed. *George Tyrrell's Letters*. London: T. Fisher Unwin, 1920.

Poulat, Émile. *Histoire, dogme et critique dans la crise moderniste*. Paris: Casterman, 1962.

———. *Intégrisme et catholicisme intégral*. Paris: Casterman, 1969.

———. *Catholicisme, démocratie et socialisme: Le mouvement catholique et Mgr. Benigni de la naissance du socialisme à la victoire du fascisme.* Paris: Casterman, 1977.

————, ed. *Alfred Loisy: Sa vie et son oeuvre,* by Albert Houtin and Felix Sartiaux. Paris: Éditions du Centre National de la Recherche Scientifique, 1960.

Pryzywara, Erich. *Religionsphilosophie katholischer Theologie.* Munich: R. Oldenbourg, 1927.

Quin, Malcolm. *Memoirs of a Positivist.* London: G. Allen & Unwin, 1924.

Ranchetti, Michele. *The Catholic Modernists: A Study of the Religious Reform Movement, 1864–1907.* Translated by Isabel Quigly. London: Oxford University Press, 1969.

Ratté, John. *Three Modernists: Alfred Loisy, George Tyrrell, William L. Sullivan.* London: Sheed & Ward, 1968.

Rawlinson, G. C. *Recent French Tendencies from Renan to Claudel: A Study in French Religion.* London: Robert Scott, 1917.

Récéjac, Jérôme-Eduoard. *Essais sur les fondements de la connaissance mystique.* Paris: Félix Alcan, 1896.

Rickaby, S.J., Joseph. *The Modernist.* London: Catholic Truth Society, 1908.

Rivière, Jean. *Le Modernisme dans l'Église.* Paris: Librairie Letouzey & Co., 1929.

Robson, W. W., ed. *Essays and Poems Presented to Lord David Cecil.* London: Constable, 1970.

Rodé, François. *Le Miracle dans la controverse moderniste.* Paris: Beauchesne, 1965.

Roe, W. G. *Lamennais and England: The Reception of Lamennais' Religious Ideas in England in the Nineteenth Century.* London: Oxford University Press, 1966.

Rolando, Daniele. *Christianesimo e religione dell'avvenire nel pensiero di George Tyrrell.* Florence: Le Monnier, 1978.

Rose, O.P., Vincent. *Études sur les Évangiles.* Paris: H. Welter, 1902.

Sabatier, Charles Paul Marie. *Modernism.* The Jowett Lectures for 1908. Translated by C. A. Miles. London: T. Fisher Unwin, 1908.

Sabatier, Louis Auguste. *The Vitality of Christian Dogmas and Their Power of Evolution: A Study of Religious Philosophy.* Translated by Mrs. Emmanuel Christen. Preface by W. H. Freemantle. London: Adam & Charles Black, 1898.

————. *Outlines of a Philosophy of Religion Based on Psychology and History.* Translated by T. A. Seed. London: Hodder & Stoughton, 1900.

————. *The Religions of Authority and the Religion of the Spirit.* Memoir by Jean Réville. London: Williams & Norgate, 1904.

Saint-Jean, R. *L'Apologétique philosophique: Blondel, 1893–1913.* Paris: Aubier, 1966.

Saintyves, P. *La Réforme intellectuelle du clergé et la liberté d'enseignement.* Paris: Émile Nourry, 1904.

Sartiaux, Félix. *Joseph Turmel, prêtre, historien des dogmes.* Paris: Les Éditions Rieder, 1931.

————, and Houtin, Albert. *Alfred Loisy: Sa vie, son oeuvre.* Edited by Émile Poulat. Paris: Éditions du Centre National de la Recherche Scientifique, 1960.

Schmidt, Martin, and Schwaiger, Georg, eds. *Kirchen und Liberalismus im 19. Jahrhundert.* Studien zur Theologie und Geistesgeschichte des Neunzehnten Jahrhunderts, vol. 19. Göttingen: Vandenhoeck & Ruprecht, 1976.

Schnitzer, Joseph. *Der katholische Modernismus.* Berlin: Protestantischer Schriftenvertrieb, 1912.

Schopenhauer, Arthur. *The World as Will and Representation.* Translated by E.F.J. Payne. 2 vols. New York: Dover Publications, 1966.

Schwaiger, Georg, and Schmidt, Martin, eds. *Aufbruch ins 20. Jahrhundert: Zum Streit um Reformkatholizismus und Modernismus.* Studien zur Theologie und Geistesgeschichte des Neunzehnten Jahrhunderts, vol. 23. Göttingen: Vandenhoeck & Ruprecht, 1976.

Schweitzer, Albert. *The Quest of the Historical Jesus: A Critical Study of Its Progress from Reimarus to Wrede.* Translated by W. Montgomery from the 1st German ed., *Von Reimarus zu Wrede* (1906). New York: Macmillan Co., 1969.

Sciuto, Francesco. *Alle origini del modernismo Italiano.* Catania: Centro di studi sull'antico Cristianesimo, University of Catania, 1966.

Scoppola, Pietro. *Crisi modernista e rinnovamento cattolico in Italia.* Bologna: Il Mulino, 1961.

Smith, S.J., Sydney F. *The Oath against Modernism.* London: Catholic Truth Society, 1911.

Sohm, Rudolf. *Kirchenrecht.* Vol. 1: *Die geschichtlichen Grundlagen.* Systematisches Handbuch der deutschen Rechtswissenschaft, div. 8, vol. 1. Leipzig: Duncker & Humblot, 1892.

————. *Outlines of Church History.* Translated by May Sinclair. London: Macmillan & Co., 1913.

Stam, Johannes Jacobus. *George Tyrrell: 1861-1909.* Utrecht: H. Honig, 1938.

Steinmann, Jean. *Friedrich von Hügel: Sa vie, son oeuvre et ses amités.* Paris: Aubier, 1962.

Steinmann, Theophil. *Die geistige Offenbarung Gottes in der geschichtlichen Person Jesu.* Göttingen: Vandenhoeck & Ruprecht, 1903.

Sullivan, William Laurence. *Under Orders.* Boston: Beacon Press, 1966.

Sutcliffe, Edmund. *Bibliography of the English Province of the Society of Jesus, 1773-1953.* London: Manresa Press, 1957.

Talbot, Edward Stuart. *The Church's Stress: Words on Some Present Questions of Thought and Action Spoken to the Clergy of the Diocese of Southwark at His Primary Visitation in the Cathedral Church of St. Saviour.* London: Macmillan & Co., 1907.

Thorp, Joseph Peter. *Friends and Adventures.* London: Jonathan Cape, 1931.

Tresmontant, Claude, ed. *Correspondance philosophique: Maurice Blondel, Lucien Laberthonnière.* Paris: Éditions du Seuil, 1961.

Trevor, Meriol. *Prophets and Guardians: Renewal and Tradition in the Church.* London: Hollis & Carter, 1969.

Trippen, Norbert. *Theologie und Lehramt im Konflikt: Die kirchlichen Massnahmen gegen den Modernismus im Jahre 1907 und ihre Auswirkungen in Deutschland.* Freiburg: Herder, 1977.

Troeltsch, Ernst. *Die Absolutheit des Christentums und die Religionsgeschichte.* Tübingen and Leipzig: J.C.B. Mohr and Paul Siebeck, 1902.

———. *Christian Thought: Its History and Application.* Translated by various hands. Edited with an introduction and index by Friedrich von Hügel. London: University Press, 1923.

———. *The Social Teaching of the Christian Churches.* Translated by Olive Wyon. Introduction by H. Richard Niebuhr. 2 vols. New York: Harper Torchbooks, 1960.

Troiani, Sebastiano. "L'experienze religiosa nel pensiero di George Tyrrell." Ph.D. dissertation, Pontifical International Institute of St. Anselm, Rome, 1972.

Vaughan, Herbert. *Letters of Herbert Cardinal Vaughan to Lady Herbert of Lea, 1867-1903.* Edited by Shane Leslie. Introduction by James Brodrick, S.J. London: Burns & Oates, 1942.

Vidler, Alec R. *The Modernist Movement in the Roman Church: Its Origin and Outcome.* Cambridge: At the University Press, 1934.

———. *A Century of Social Catholicism, 1820-1920.* London: SPCK, 1964.

———. *A Variety of Catholic Modernists.* Cambridge: At the University Press, 1970.

Viollet, Paul. *L'Infallibilité du Pape et la Syllabus.* Paris: P. Lethielleux, 1904.

Walgrave, Jan Hendrick. *Newman: Le Développement du dogme.* Tournai: Casterman, 1957.

———. *Newman the Theologian: The Nature of Belief and Doctrine as Exemplified in His Life and Works.* Translated by A. V. Littledale. London: G. Chapman, 1960.

Ward, Maisie. *The Wilfrid Wards and the Transition.* 2 vols. London: Sheed & Ward, 1934-37.

———. *Unfinished Business.* London: Sheed & Ward, 1964.

Ward, Wilfrid. *The Wish to Believe: A Discussion Concerning the Temper of Mind in Which a Reasonable Man Should Undertake Religious Inquiry.* London: Kegan Paul, Trench & Co., 1885.

———. *William George Ward and the Catholic Revival.* London: Macmillan & Co., 1893.

———. *Witnesses to the Unseen and Other Essays.* London: Macmillan & Co., 1893.

———. *The Life and Times of Cardinal Wiseman.* 2 vols. London: Longmans, Green & Co., 1897.

———. *Problems and Persons.* London: Longmans, Green & Co., 1903.

———. *Ten Personal Studies.* London: Longmans, Green & Co., 1908.

———. *Last Lectures*. Introductory study by Mrs. Wilfrid Ward. London: Longmans, Green & Co., 1918.

Weaver, Mary Jo, ed. *Letters from a "Modernist": The Letters of George Tyrrell to Wilfrid Ward, 1893–1908*. Shepherdstown, W. Va.: Patmos Press, 1981.

Weill, Georges. *Histoire du Catholicisme Libéral en France, 1829–1908*. Paris: Félix Alcan, 1909.

Weinzierl, Erika, ed. *Der Modernismus: Beiträge zu seiner Erforschung*. Graz: Styria, 1974.

Weiss, Johannes. *Die Predigt Jesu vom Reiche Gottes*. Göttingen: Vandenhoeck & Ruprecht, 1892.

———. *Christus: Die Anfänge des Dogmas*. Tübingen: J.C.B. Mohr, 1909.

Wells, David F. *The Prophetic Theology of George Tyrrell*. Chico, Calif.: Scholars Press, 1981.

Wernle, Paul. *Die Anfänge unserer Religion*. Tübingen: J.C.B. Mohr, 1901.

Williams, William John. *Newman, Pascal, Loisy and the Catholic Church*. London: Francis Griffiths, 1906.

Windelband, Wilhelm. *Geschichte der Philosophie*. 2d ed. Tübingen: J.C.B. Mohr, 1900.

———. *Präludien: Aufsätze und Reden zur Einleitung in die Philosophie*. 2d ed. Tübingen: J.C.B. Mohr, 1903.

Wobbermin, Georg. *Theologie und Metaphysik: Das Verhältnis der Theologie zur modernen Erkenntnistheorie und Psychologie*. Berlin: A. Duncker, 1901.

Zamoyska, Hedwig. *Sur le travail*. Paris: P. Lethielleux, 1902.

Articles

"L'Abbé Loisy." *Pilot* 7 (31 January 1903): 113–14. Signed "From our French correspondent."

Abercrombie, Nigel. "Edmund Bishop and St. George Mivart." *Month* 193 (March 1952): 176–80.

———. "Friedrich von Hügel's Letters to Edmund Bishop." *Dublin Review* 227 (January, April, July, October 1953): 68–78, 179–89, 285–98, 419–38.

Addis, W. E. "The Pope's Encyclical and the Crisis in the Roman Church." *Contemporary Review* 92 (January-June 1907): 585–96.

Angot des Rotours, Baron J. "La Religion intérieure d'après un Jesuite anglais." *Quinzaine* 6 (16 July 1900): 141–57.

Aubert, Roger. "Deux documents antimodernistes inédits." *Ephémérides Theologicae Lovanienses* 37 (May-September 1961): 557–79.

———. "Recent Literature on the Modernist Movement." *Concilium*, no. 17 (1966), pp. 91–108.

———. "Henri Bremond et la crise moderniste." *Revue d'histoire ecclésiastique* 72 (April-June 1977) 332–48.

————. "La Position de Loisy au moment de sa controverse avec M. Blondel." In *Journées d'Études Blondel-Bergson-Maritain-Loisy*, pp. 75–90. Centre d'Archives Maurice Blondel, no. 4. Louvain: Institut supérieur de philosophie, 1977.

Bainvel, Jean. "Le Dernier livre de George Tyrrell." *Études* 123 (20 June 1910): 737–75.

Ballard, Richard. "George Tyrrell and the Apocalyptic Vision of Christ." *Theology* 78 (September 1975): 459–67.

Barry, William. Review of *L'Évangile et l'Église*, by Alfred Loisy. *Pilot* 6 (20 December 1902): 532.

Batiffol, Pierre. "L'Évangile et l'Église." *Bulletin de littérature ecclésiastique* (Toulouse), 3d ser. 5 (20 January 1903): 3–15.

————. "Notre campagne contre le P. Tyrrell." *Revue de théologie et des questions religieuses* 6 (September 1909): 389–402.

Bécamel, M. "Lettres de Loisy à Mgr. Mignot: A propos de la crise moderniste." *Bulletin de littérature ecclésiastique* (Toulouse) 67 (January, April, July, October 1966): 3–44, 81–114, 170–94, 257–86.

————. "Autres lettres de Loisy à Mgr. Mignot." *Bulletin de littérature ecclésiastique* (Toulouse) 69 (October 1968): 241–68.

Bella, Julius I. "Father Tyrrell's Dogmas." *Church History* 8 (December 1939): 316–41.

Bernard-Maitre, Henri. "Lettres d'Henri Bremond à Alfred Loisy." *Bulletin de littérature ecclésiastique* (Toulouse) 69 (January, July, October 1968): 3–24, 161–84, 269–89; 70 (January 1969): 44–56.

"The Biblical Commission." *Tablet* 101 (7 February 1903): 213–14. Signed "From our own correspondent."

Blondel, Maurice. "Lettre sur les exigences de la pensée contemporaine en matière d'apologétique et sur la méthode de la philosophie dans l'étude du problème religieux." *Annales de philosophie chrétienne* 131 (January 1896):337–53, 467–82, 599–616; 132 (July 1896):131–47, 255–67, 337–59.

————. "L'Illusion idéaliste." *Revue de metaphysique et de morale* 6 (November 1898: 726–46.

————. "À propos de la certitude religieuse: Réponse à Ed. Péchegut." *Revue du clergé français* 29 (15 February 1902): 643–59.

————. "Histoire et dogme: Les Lacunes philosophiques de l'exégèse moderne." *Quinzaine* 56 (16 January; 1, 16 February 1904): 145–67, 349–73, 433–58.

————. "De la valeur historique de dogme." *Bulletin de littérature ecclésiastique* (Toulouse), 3d ser. 7 (January 1905): 61–71.

————. "Le Point de départ de la recherche philosophique." *Annales de philosophie chrétienne* 151 (January 1906): 337–60; 152 (June 1906): 225–50.

[————] "La Notion et le rôle du miracle." *Annales de philosophie chrétienne* 154 (July 1907): 337–62. Signed "Bernard de Sailly."

Boudens, Robrecht. "George Tyrrell and Cardinal Mercier: A Contribution to the History of Modernism." *Église et théologie* 1 (October 1970): 313–51.

Bremond, Henri. "Father Tyrrell as an Apologist." *New York Review* 1 (June-July 1905): 762-70.

———. "La Méthode apologétique du Père Tyrrell." *Demain*, 4 May 1906, pp. 2-16.

Burke, Ronald. "An Orthodox Modernist with a Modern View of Truth." *Journal of Religion* 57 (April 1977): 124-43.

———. "Loisy's Faith: Landshift in Catholic Thought." *Journal of Religion* 60 (April 1980): 138-64.

———. "Revising the Study of Modernism." *Journal of Ecumenical Studies* 17 (Fall 1980): 670-76.

Caird, Edward. "Christianity and the Historical Christ." *New World* 6 (March 1897): 1-13.

Chapman, Ronald. "The Thought of George Tyrrell." In *Essays and Poems Presented to Lord David Cecil*, edited by W. W. Robson, pp. 140-68. London: Constable, 1970.

Clifford, Cornelius. "Modernism, Father George Tyrrell, and Miss M. D. Petre." *Review of Religion* 3 (January 1938): 159-65.

Clutton, K. M. "The Death of George Tyrrell." *Modern Churchman* 22 (March 1933): 678-86.

Colombo, Giuseppe. "Esperienza e rivelazione nel pensiero di G. Tyrrell." *La Scuola Cattolica* 106 (1978): 544-68.

Corrance, Henry C. Review of *Christianity at the Cross-Roads*, by George Tyrrell. *Revue moderniste internationale* 1 (June 1910): 311-26.

Crean, John. "Modernism: The Philosophical Issue." *Continuum* 3 (Summer 1965): 145-51.

Crehan, S.J., Joseph H. "More Tyrrell Letters—I." *Month*, n.s. 40 (October 1968): 178-85.

———. "Tyrrell in His Workshop." *Month*, 2d n.s. 3 (April 1971): 111-15, 119.

———. "What Influenced and Finally Killed George Tyrrell." *Catholic Medical Quarterly* 26 (April 1974): 75-85.

Daly, Gabriel. "Some Reflections on the Character of George Tyrrell." *Heythrop Journal* 10 (July 1969): 256-74.

———. "Tyrrell's 'Medievalism.'" *Month*, n.s. 42 (July-August 1969): 15-22.

Dell, Robert. "A Liberal Catholic View of the Case of Dr. Mivart." *Nineteenth Century* 47 (April 1900): 669-84.

———. "A Convert's Experiences of the Catholic Church." *Contemporary Review* 77 (June 1900): 817-34.

———. "Mr. Wilfrid Ward's Apologetics." *Nineteenth Century* 48 (July 1900): 127-36.

———. "The Movement for Reform within the Catholic Church." *Contemporary Review* 78 (November 1900): 693-709.

———. "The Crisis in the Catholic Church." *Fortnightly Review*, n.s. 455 (1 November 1904): 846-60.

———. "George Tyrrell." *Cornhill Magazine*, n.s. 27 (November 1909): 665-75.

Dillon, E. J. "The Papal Encyclical on the Bible." *Contemporary Review* 65 (April 1894): 576-608.

————. "Intellectual Liberty and Contemporary Catholicism." *Contemporary Review* 66 (August 1894): 280–304.

————. "Theological Book-Keeping by Double Entry." *Contemporary Review* 66 (September 1894): 351–73.

[————]. "Liberal Catholicism." *Contemporary Review* 72 (December 1897): 854–66. Signed "Romanus."

[————]. "Catholicism *versus* Ultramontanism." *Contemporary Review* 82 (December 1902): 776–807. Signed "Voces Catholicae."

[————]. "The Abbé Loisy and the Catholic Reform Movement." *Contemporary Review* 83 (March 1903): 385–412. Signed "Voces Catholicae."

[————]. "Professor Loisy and the Teaching Church." *Contemporary Review* 85 (February 1904): 224–44. Signed "Voces Catholicae."

Dilthey, Wilhelm. "Das natürliche System der Geisteswissenschaften im 17. Jahrhundert." *Archiv für Geschichte der Philosophie* 5 (1892): 480–502; 6(1893): 60–127, 225–56, 347–79, 509–45.

Dimnet, Ernest. "Une Meilleure voie." Review of *The Faith of the Millions,* by George Tyrrell. *Revue du clergé français* 31 (1, 5 June; 1 July 1902): 5–23, 129–49, 351–72.

Dru, Alexander. "The Importance of Maurice Blondel." *Downside Review* 80 (April 1962): 118–29.

————. "Modernism and the Present Position of the Church." *Downside Review* 82 (April 1964): 103–10.

Dupuy, O.P., B. D. "Newman's Influence in France." In *Rediscovery of Newman: An Oxford Symposium,* edited by John Coulson and A. M. Allchin, pp. 147–73. London: Sheed & Ward, 1967.

Emonet, Benoît. "Cas de conscience de M. Loisy." *Études* 98 (March 1904): 737–58.

Erasmi, Ernst. Introduction to *Das Christentum am Scheideweg,* the German translation of *Christianity at the Cross-Roads,* by George Tyrrell. Munich: Ernst Reinhart Verlag, 1959.

Fawkes, Alfred. "Modernism: A Retrospect and a Prospect." *Hibbert Journal* 8 (October 1909): 67–82.

————. "Father George Tyrrell." *Nation* 5 (24 July 1909): 601–2.

Fitzer, Joseph. "Tyrrell and LeRoy: Their Case Reopened." *Communio Viatorum* 18 (Winter 1975): 201–24.

Franon, Eugène. "Un Nouveau manifeste catholique d'agnosticisme." *Bulletin de littérature ecclésiastique* (Toulouse), 3d ser. 5 (June 1903): 157–66.

————. "Un Scolastique anti-intellectualiste." *Bulletin de littérature ecclésiastique* (Toulouse), 3d ser. 7 (June 1905): 165–73.

————. "La Philosophie religieuse du P. Tyrrell." *Bulletin de littérature ecclésiastique* (Toulouse), 23 (1906-7): 34–49.

Gardner, Percy. Review of *L'Évangile et l'Église,* by Alfred Loisy. *Hibbert Journal* 1 (April 1903): 602–6.

————. "M. Alfred Loisy's Type of Catholicism." *Hibbert Journal* 3 (October 1904): 126–38.

————. "Discussions: M. Loisy's Type of Catholicism—II." *Hibbert Journal* 3 (April 1905); 601-2.

Gardner, Ralph. "Two Jesuits." *Modern Churchman* 42 (December 1952): 350-59.

Gerard, John. "The Papal Encyclical: From a Catholic's Point of View." *Hibbert Journal* 6 (January 1908): 256-63.

"Giorgio Tyrrell: Necrologia." *Rinnovamento* 6 (1909): 139-44.

Goetz, Joseph W. "Father Tyrrell and the Catholic Crisis." *New Blackfriars* 50 (August 1969): 589-98.

Grandi, Giovanni. "Per il P. Tyrrel [*sic*]." *Corrispondenza Romana* 100 (9 September 1907).

————. "Il Caso Tyrrell." *Corrispondenza Romana* 113 (23 September 1907).

Grandmaison, Léonce de. Review of *L'Évangile et l'Église*, by Alfred Loisy. *Études* 94 (20 January 1903): 145-74.

————. "Pie X, Pape." *Études* 117 (5 November 1908): 291-307.

————. "Le Roman du modernisme." *Études* 142 (5 January 1915): 90-103.

————. "L'École catholique de Tübingen et les origines du modernisme." *Recherches de science religieuse* 9 (November-December 1919): 387-409.

Grasso, Domenico. "La conversione e l'apostasia di George Tyrrell." *Gregorianum* 38 (1957): 446-80, 593-629.

Halifax, Viscount. "The Recent Anglo-Roman Pastoral." *Nineteenth Century* 291 (May 1901): 736-54. Except for the introduction and conclusion, this article was by Tyrrell.

Hanbury, O.S.B., Michael. "Von Hügel's Vocation." *Pax* 41 (Autumn-Winter 1951): 126-34.

————. "Von Hügel and Tyrrell." *Month*, 1st n.s. 32 (December 1964): 323-26.

————. "Von Hügel Today: A Forerunner of Vatican II." *Tablet* 219 (20 November 1965): 1291-93.

Hartrett, Thomas P. "A Modernist Ecclesiology: The Relationship of Church and Doctrine in the Writings of George Tyrrell." *Dunwoodie Review* 11 (May 1971): 125-69.

Headlam, Arthur C. "The Modernist Christology." *Church Quarterly Review* 93 (January 1922): 201-32.

Healy, S.J., Charles J. "Tyrrell on the Church." *Downside Review* 91 (January 1973): 35-50.

————. "Aspects of Tyrrell's Spirituality." *Downside Review* 95 (April 1977): 133-48.

————. "Maude Petre: Her Life and Significance." *Recusant History* 15 (May 1979): 23-42.

Hébert Marcel. "La Dernière idole." *Revue de métaphysique et de morale* 10 (July 1902): 397-408.

Holmes, J. Derek. "Cardinal Raphael Merry del Val—An Uncompromising Ultramontane: Gleanings from His Correspondence with England." *Catholic Historical Review* 60 (April 1974): 55-64.

Holmes, Edmond. "Tyrrell on 'The Church'." *Hibbert Journal* 24 (January 1926): 322–33.

von Hügel, Friedrich. "The Papal Encyclical and Mr. Gore." *Spectator,* 19 May 1894, pp. 684–85.

———. "The Roman Catholic View of Inspiration." *Spectator,* 2 June 1894, p. 750.

———. "The Church and the Bible: The Two Stages of Their Inter-Relation." *Dublin Review* 115 (October 1894): 313–41; 116 (April 1895): 306–37; 117 (October 1895): 275–304.

———. "Professor Eucken on the Struggle for Spiritual Life." *Spectator,* 14 November 1896, pp. 679–81.

———. "The Case of the Abbé Loisy." *Pilot* 9 (9 January 1904): 30–31.

———. "The Case of M. Loisy." *Pilot* 9 (23 January 1904): 94.

———. "Discussions: M. Loisy's Type of Catholicism." *Hibbert Journal* 3 (April 1905): 599–600.

———. "Experience and Transcendence." *Dublin Review* 138 (April 1906): 357–79.

———. "L'Abate Loisy e il problema dei Vangeli Sinottici." *Rinnovamento* 3 (January-June 1908): 209–34; 4 (July-December 1908): 1–44; 5 (January-June 1909): 229–72, 396–423.

———. "The Abbé Loisy." *Tablet* 111 (7 March 1908): 378–79.

———. Review of *Les Évangiles synoptiques,* by Alfred Loisy. *Hibbert Journal* 6 (July 1908): 926–30.

———. Obituary notice for George Tyrrell. *Times* (London), 16 July 1909, p. 13. *Daily Mail,* 16 July 1909, p. 9. Written in conjunction with Maude Petre but not signed by von Hügel.

———. Letter on the circumstances of George Tyrrell's death. *Daily Graphic,* 31 July 1909, p. 12. Originally published in the *Corriere della Sera* (Milan), then retranslated by von Hügel for the *Daily Graphic.*

———. "The Death-Bed of Father Tyrrell." *Tablet* 114 (31 July 1909): 182.

———. "The Late Father Tyrrell and the Faith." *Tablet* 114 (6 November 1909): 738.

———. "Father Tyrrell: Some Memorials of the Last Twelve Years of His Life." *Hibbert Journal* 8 (January 1910): 233–52.

———. "The Religious Philosophy of Rudolf Eucken." *Hibbert Journal* 10 (April 1912): 660–77.

———. "Father Tyrrell." *Tablet* 120 (30 November 1912): 866–67.

Hulshof, Jan. "The Modernist Crisis: Alfred Loisy and George Tyrrell." *Concilium* 113 (1978): 28–39.

Hurley, Michael. "George Tyrrell: Some Post-Vatican II Impressions." *Heythrop Journal* 10 (July 1969): 243–55.

Inge, W. R. "The Meaning of Modernism." *Quarterly Review* 210 (April 1909): 571–603.

———. "Tyrrell's Last Book." Review of *Christianity at the Cross-Roads,* by George Tyrrell. *Hibbert Journal* 8 (January 1910): 434–38.

———. "Two Catholic Modernists." In *Our Present Discontents,* by W. R. Inge, chap. 8. London: Putnam, 1938.

James, William. "The Philosophy of Bergson." *Hibbert Journal* 7 (April 1909): 562-77.

Jenkins, R.G.F. "Tyrrell's Dublin Days." *Month*, n.s. 42 (July 1969): 8-15.

Kelly, James J. "The Modernist Controversy in England: The Correspondence between Friedrich von Hügel and Percy Gardner." *Downside Review* 99 (January 1981): 40-58.

Kübel, Johannes. "George Tyrrells letztes Buch." *Die Christliche Welt* 23 (23 September 1909): 919-24.

――――. "George Tyrrell." *Deutsches Christentum: Neue Folge der Bremer Beiträge* 4 (1910): 113-23.

――――. "Aus dem letzten Buch George Tyrrells (Auszug aus 'Medievalism')." *Jahrbuch für die evangelische-lutherische Landeskirche Bayerns* (1910), pp. 69-78.

Laberthonnière, Lucien. "Le Problème religieux." *Annales de philosophie chrétienne* n.s. 33 (February-March 1897): 497-511.

――――. "Le Dogmatisme moral." *Annales de philosophie chrétienne* n.s. 38 (August-September 1898): 531-62; n.s. 39 (October-November 1898): 27-45, 146-71.

――――. "Pour le dogmatisme moral." *Annales de philosophie chrétienne*, n.s. 41 (January 1900): 398-425.

――――. "La Question de méthode en apologétique." *Annales de philosophie chrétienne*, 4th ser. 2 (August 1906): 500-515.

――――. "Dogme et théologie." *Annales de philosophie chrétienne*, 4th ser. 4 (September 1907): 561-601; 5 (October 1907): 10-65; 5 (February 1908): 479-521; 7 (October 1908): 5-79; 9 (December 1909): 279-313 (incomplete).

Lease, Gary, "Merry del Val and Tyrrell's Condemnation." *Proceedings of the Roman Catholic Modernism Working Group of the American Academy of Religion*, edited by Ronald Burke and George Gilmore, pp. 25-63. Mobile: Spring Hill College Duplicating Service, 1979.

Lebreton, S.J., Jules. "'Lex Orandi,' par le P. Tyrrell." *Études* 106 (5 March 1906): 693-95.

――――. "Autour de Newman." *Revue pratique d'apologétique* 3 (15 January 1907): 488-504.

――――. "La Foi et la théologie d'après M. Tyrrell." *Revue pratique d'apologétique* 3 (1 February 1907): 542-50.

――――. "Catholicisme: Réponse à M. Tyrrell." *Revue pratique d'apologétique* 4 (15 July 1907): 527-48.

――――. "L'Encyclique et la théologie moderniste." *Études* 113 (20 November 1907): 497-524.

――――. "Origine et développement du christianisme d'après Fr. Heiler et George Tyrrell." *Recherches de science religieuse* 28 (October 1938): 482-96.

Leo XIII, Pope. "Providentissimus Deus." *Acta Sanctae Sedis* 26 (1893): 269-92.

――――. "Litterae Apostolicae 'Gravissime Nos,' quibus Constitutiones Societatis Jesu de doctrina S. Thomae Aquinatis profitenda confirmantur." In *Allocutiones, epistolae, constitutiones, alique acta praecipua*, vol. 5: 1891–94, pp. 133–43. Bruges: Desclée, de Brouwer & Co., 1887–1906.

——. "Ad Anglos regnum Christi in fidei unitate quaerentes." *Acta Sanctae Sedis* 27 (1895): 583–93.

——. "Testem benevolentiae" (22 January 1899). *Acta Sanctae Sedis* 31 (1899): 470–79.

——. "Depuis le jour" (8 September 1899). *Acta Sanctae Sedis* 32 (1899–1900): 193–213.

LeRoy, Edouard. "Qu'est-ce qu'un dogme?" *Quinzaine* 63 (16 April 1905): 495–526.

——. "Essai sur la notion du miracle." *Annales de philosophie chrétienne*, 4th ser. 3 (October-December 1906): 5–33, 166–91, 225–59.

"Lettres Romaines." *Annales de philosophie chrétienne*, 3d ser. 3 (January-March 1904): 349–59, 473–88, 601–20.

"Liberalism Again." *Church Review* 41 (7 November 1901): 711.

Lilley, Alfred Leslie. "Biblical Criticism in France, II." *Guardian*, 25 February 1903, pp. 267–68.

——. "L'Affaire Loisy." *Commonwealth* 8 (March 1903): 73–76.

——. "A Roman Catholic Protest against the Recent Vatican Policy." *Commonwealth* 11 (July 1906): 216–20.

——. "The Religion of George Tyrrell." *Commonwealth* 14 (December 1909): 361–64.

Lloyd Thomas, J. M. Review of *Christianity at the Cross-Roads*, by George Tyrrell. *Christian Commonwealth* 29 (1 December 1909): 153–54.

Loisy, Alfred Firmin. "La Question biblique et l'inspiration des Écritures." *L'Enseignement biblique* 12 (1893): 1–16.

[——]. "Le Devéloppement chrétien d'après le cardinal Newman." *Revue du clergé français* 16 (1 December 1898): 5–20. Signed "A. Firmin."

[——]. "L'Évangile selon Saint Jean." *Revue du clergé français* 20 (1 November 1899): 484–506. Signed "Isidore Després."

[——]. "Les Preuves et l'économie de la révélation." *Revue du clergé français* 21 (15 March 1900): 126–53. Signed "A. Firmin."

[——]. "L'Idée de la révélation." *Revue du clergé français* 21 (1 January 1900): 250–71. Signed "A. Firmin."

[——]. "La Lettre de Leon XIII au clergé de France et les études d'Écriture Sainte." *Revue du clergé français* 23 (1 June 1900): 5–17. Signed "Isidore Després."

——. "Chronique bibliographique." Review of *Through Scylla and Charybdis* and *Christianity at the Cross-Roads*, by George Tyrrell. *Revue d'histoire et de littérature religieuses*, n.s. 2, no. 6 (1911): 608–11.

Loome, Thomas Michael. "A Bibliography of the Published Writings of George Tyrrell (1861–1909)." *Heythrop Journal* 10 (July 1969): 280–314.

——. "Tyrrell's Letters to André Raffalovich." *Month*, 2d n.s. 1 (February, March 1970): 95–101, 138–49.

————. "A Bibliography of the Printed Works of George Tyrrell: Supplement." *Heythrop Journal* 11 (April 1970): 161–69.

————. "'Revelation as Experience': An Unpublished Lecture of George Tyrrell." *Heythrop Journal* 12 (April 1971): 117–49.

————. "The Meanings of Modernism." *Tablet* 225 (5 June 1971): 544–47.

Luzzi, Giovanni. "The Roman Catholic Church in Italy at the Present Hour." *Hibbert Journal* 9 (January 1911): 307–23.

Macpherson, Duncan. "Von Hügel on George Tyrrell." *Month*, 2d n.s. 4 (December 1971): 178–80.

Major, H.D.A. "Father Tyrrell." In *Great Christians*, edited by R. S. Forman, pp. 553–74, London: Ivor Nicholson & Watson, 1934.

Martin, Luis. "Epistola ad Patres et Fratres Societatis Jesu de aliquibus nostrorum temporum periculis cavendis." In *Epistolae praepositorum Generalium ad Patres et Fratres Societatis Jesu*, vol. 4, pp. 268–332. Brussels: Sumptis Provinciae Belgicae S.J., 1908.

Mercier, Désiré Joseph Cardinal. "The Lenten Pastoral." In *Medievalism: A Reply to Cardinal Mercier*, by George Tyrrell, pp. 1–21. London: Longmans, Green & Co., 1908.

Mignot, E. I. "La Méthode de la théologie." *Bulletin de littérature ecclésiastique* (Toulouse), 3d ser. 3 (1901): 253–74.

Mivart, St. George. "Modern Catholics and Scientific Freedom." *Nineteenth Century* 18 (July 1885): 30–47.

————. "The Catholic Church and Biblical Criticism." *Nineteenth Century* 22 (July 1887): 31–51.

————. "Happiness in Hell." *Nineteenth Century* 32 (December 1892): 899–919.

————. "The Happiness in Hell: A Rejoinder." *Nineteenth Century* 33 (February 1893): 320–38.

————. "Last Words on the Happiness in Hell." *Nineteenth Century* 33 (April 1893): 637–51.

————. "The Index and My Articles on Hell." *Nineteenth Century* 34 (December 1893): 979–90.

————. "The Roman Catholic Church and the Dreyfus Case." *Times* (London), 17 October 1899, pp. 13–14. See also *Times* (London), 22 November 1899, p. 14.

————. "The Continuity of Catholicism." *Nineteenth Century* 47 (January 1900): 51–72.

————. "Some Recent Catholic Apologists." *Fortnightly Review*, n.s. 67 (1 January 1900): 24–44.

————. "Scripture and Roman Catholicism." *Nineteenth Century* 47 (March 1900): 425–42.

Moyes, James. "Modernism and the Papal Encyclical." *Nineteenth Century* 62 (December 1907): 865–78.

————. Letter to the Editor: "The Abbé Loisy." *Tablet* 3 (14 March 1908): 416–17.

Newman, John Henry. "On the Introduction of Rationalistic Principles into Religion." In *Essays, Critical and Historical*, pp. 30–101. New impression. London: Longmans, Green & Co., 1919.

Newsom, G. E. "George Tyrrell." *Church Quarterly Review* 69 (October 1909): 114-45.

O'Brien, Gerald. "Anti-Modernism: The Integralist Campaign." *Continuum* 3 (Summer 1965): 187-200.

O'Connor, S.J., Francis M. "Tyrrell's Crossroads." *Heythrop Journal* 5 (April 1964): 188-91.

————. "Tyrrell: The Nature of Revelation." *Continuum* 3 (Summer 1965): 168-77.

————. "George Tyrrell and Dogma." *Downside Review* 85 (January, April 1967): 16-34, 160-82.

O'Grady, John F. "Did Modernism Die?" *Month*, n.s. 39 (May 1968): 265-73.

Padberg, John. "The Modernist Crisis Half a Century Later." *Proceedings of the Catholic Theological Society of America* 20 (1965): 51-66.

Petre, Maude D. Obituary notice for George Tyrrell. *Times* (London), 16 July 1909, p. 13. *Daily Mail*, 16 July 1909, p. 9. Written in conjunction with Friedrich von Hügel but not signed by him.

————. "Friedrich von Hügel: Personal Thoughts and Reminiscences." *Hibbert Journal* 24 (October 1925): 77-87.

————. "George Tyrrell and Friedrich von Hügel in Their Relation to Catholic Modernism." *Modern Churchman* 17 (June 1927): 143-54.

————. "Von Hügel and the Great Quest." *Modern Churchman* 21 (December 1931): 475-83.

————. "Alfred Loisy (1857-1940)." *Theology* 41 (September 1940): 132-40.

————. "A Religious Movement of the First Years of Our Century." *Horizon* 6 (November 1942): 328-40.

Pius X, Pope. "Lamentabili." *Acta Sanctae Sedis* 40 (1907): 470-78.

————. "Pascendi dominici gregis." *Acta Sanctae Sedis* 40 (1907): 593-60.

Poulat, Émile. "Bibliographie Alfred Loisy." In *Alfred Loisy: Sa vie, son oeuvre*, by Albert Houtin and Félix Sartiaux, pp. 303-24. Paris: Éditions du Centre National de la Recherche Scientifique, 1960.

Provencher, Normand. "Une Tentative de renouvellement de l'herméneutique biblique: Le Modernisme d'Alfred Loisy." *Église et Théologie* 9 (1976): 341-66.

Reardon, B.M.G. "Von Hügel and the Modernist Movement." *Ampleforth Journal* 74 (Autumn 1969): 376-85.

————. "The Modernist Movement in Retrospect." *Ampleforth Journal* 75 (Summer 1970): 213-21.

————. "Newman and the Catholic Modernist Movement." *Church Quarterly* 4 (July 1971): 50-60.

Rickaby, Joseph. "The Church and Liberal Catholicism." *Month* 97 (April 1901): 337-46.

Rivière, Jean. "La Crise moderniste devant l'opinion d'aujourd'hui." *Revue des sciences religieuses* 20 (January-April 1940): 140-57.

————. "Qui rédigea l'encyclique 'Pascendi'?" *Bulletin de littérature ecclésiastique* (Toulouse) 47 (April-September 1946): 146-61.

Rollmann, Hans. "Troeltsch, von Hügel, and Modernism." *Downside Review* 96 (January 1978): 35–60.

―――. "Holtzmann, von Hügel, and Modernism." *Downside Review* 97 (April, July 1979): 128–43, 221–44.

Root, John D. "English Catholic Modernism and Science: The Case of George Tyrrell." *Heythrop Journal* 18 (July 1977): 271–88.

―――. "George Tyrrell and the Synthetic Society." *Downside Review* 98 (January 1980): 42–59.

Roure, Lucien. "Scolastique et modernistes." *Études* 114 (5 February; 20 March 1908): 289–307, 767–89.

Sabatier, Paul. "De la situation religieuse de l'Église catholique romaine en France, à l'heure actuelle." *Hibbert Journal* 9 (October 1910): 1–14.

Salter, S.J., John M. "Father Tyrrell's View of Revealed Truth." *Catholic World* 89 (April 1909): 27–40.

Schoenl, William J. "George Tyrrell and the English Liberal Catholic Crisis, 1900–01." *Downside Review* 92 (July 1974): 171–84.

Schroeder, Oskar. "Einleitung: George Tyrrells religiöse Entwicklung." In *Das Christentum am Scheideweg*, by George Tyrrell, pp. 9–40. Munich: Ernst Reinhart Verlag, 1959.

―――. "George Tyrrell, der führende Kopf des Modernismus." *Werkhefte: Zeitschrift für Probleme der Gesellschaft und des Katholizismus* 20 (1966): 280–91, 311–27, 356–63, 394–404.

Seitz, Anton. "Tyrrells Modernismus: Eine Rechtfertigung der Enzyklika Pius' X." *Jahrbuch für Philosophie und spekulative Theologie* 25 (1911): 121–46.

Semeria, Giovanni, "Un metodo e un modello d'apologia cristiana: A proposito d'un libro del P. Tyrrell." *Studi religiosi* 4 (November-December 1904): 561–78.

Siegfried, F. P. "Lex Orandi Again." *Ecclesiastical Review* 30 (April 1904): 363–71.

Smith, Sydney R. "What Is Modernism?" *Month* 111 (March 1908): 284–301.

―――. "Newman's Relation to Modernism." *Month* 120 (July 1912): 1–15.

Smith, Warren Sylvester. "George Tyrrell and the Modernists." *Christian Century* 80 (17 April 1963): 490–92.

Snape, H. S. "Two Jesuits and the Church: Teilhard and Tyrrell." *Modern Churchman*, n.s. 5 (July 1962): 255–60.

Spens, W. "Leaders of Theological Thought: George Tyrrell." *Expository Times* 40 (1929): 263–68.

Stirnimann, H. "Zur Enzyklika 'Pascendi': Eigenart und Gültigkeit." *Freiburger Zeitschrift für Philosophie und Theologie* 8 (1961): 254–74.

Swete, H. B. "'Modernism' and the Church." *Guardian*, 29 January 1908, pp. 175–76.

Taille, Maurice de la. "Sur l'Encyclique 'Pascendi.'" *Études* 113 (5 December 1907): 645–69.

Theobald, Christoph. "L'Entrée de l'histoire dans l'univers religieux et théologique au moment de la crise moderniste." In *La Crise contem-*

poraine du modernisme à la crise des herméneutiques, by Jean Greisch, Karl Neufeld, and Christoph Theobald, pp. 7–85. Théologie historique, no. 24. Paris: Beauchesne, 1973.

Thomas, S.J., Alfred. "George Tyrrell: From Student Days." *Heythrop Journal* 11 (April 1970): 170–72.

Thurston, Herbert. "Old Unhappy Far-Off Things." Review of *Father Tyrrell and the Modernist Movement*, by J. Lewis May. *Month* 160 (July 1932): 80–82.

Toohey, S.J., J. H. "Newman and Modernism." *Tablet* 111 (1908): 7–9, 47–48, 86–88, 122–25.

Trevor, Meriol. "George Tyrrell: A Rejoinder." *Month*, 2d n.s. 1 (April 1970): 199.

Troeltsch, Ernst. "Geschichte und Metaphysik: Erwiderung auf Kaftans Angriff gegen die Selbständigkeit der Religion." *Zeitschrift für Theologie und Kirche* 8.1 (1898): 1–69.

———. "Die wissenschaftliche Lage und ihre Anforderungen an die Theologie." *Sammlung gemeinverständlicher Vorträge und Schriften aus dem Gebeit der Theologie und Religionsphilosophie*, no. 20. Tübingen: J.C.B. Mohr, 1900.

Turmel, Joseph. "L'Eschatologie à la fin du IVᵉ siècle." *Revue d'histoire et de littérature religieuses* 5, no. 2 (1900): 97–127, 200–232, 289–321.

Vaughan, Cardinal Herbert and the Bishops of the Province of Westminster. "The Church and Liberal Catholicism: Joint Pastoral." *Tablet* 97 (5, 12 January 1901): 8–12, 50–52.

Virgoulay, René. "Note d'exégèse blondélienne de l'Action à la Lettre de 1896." *Recherches de science religieuse* 57 (April-June 1969): 205–19.

———. "La Méthode d'immanence et l'Encyclique Pascendi." *Recherches de science religieuse* 58 (July-September 1970): 429–54.

Ward, Wilfrid. "The Wish to Believe." *Nineteenth Century* 11 (February 1882): 195–216.

———. "New Wine in Old Bottles." *Nineteenth Century* 27 (June 1890): 942–56.

———. "The Scholastic Movement and Catholic Philosophy." *Dublin Review*, 3d ser. 50 (April 1891): 255–71.

———. "The Rigidity of Rome." *Nineteenth Century* 38 (November 1895): 786–804.

———. "Liberalism and Intransigeance." *Nineteenth Century* 47 (June 1900): 960–73.

———. "Newman and Sabatier." *Fortnightly Review*, n.s. 69 (1 January 1901): 808–22.

———. "Cardinal Newman." *Weekly Register* 103 (16 February 1901): 196–98.

———. "Doctores Ecclesiae." *Pilot* 3 (22 June 1901): 774–76.

———. "The Time-Spirit of the Nineteenth Century." *Edinburgh Review* 194 (July-September 1901): 92–131.

———. "The Pope and France." *Nineteenth Century* 61 (January 1907): 27–41.

————. "Two Views of Cardinal Newman." *Dublin Review* 141 (July 1907): 1-15.

————. "The Encyclical 'Pascendi.'" *Dublin Review* 142 (January 1908): 1-10.

Weaver, Mary Jo. "Wilfrid Ward, George Tyrrell, and the Meanings of Modernism." *Downside Review* 96 (January 1978): 21-34.

————. "A Working Catalogue of the Ward Family Papers." *Recusant History* 15 (May 1979): 43-71.

————. "George Tyrrell and the Joint Pastoral Letter." *Downside Review* 99 (January 1981): 18-39.

Weinzierl, Erika. "Der Antimodernismus Pius' X." In *Der Modernismus: Beiträge zu seiner Erforschung*, edited by Erika Weinzierl, pp. 235-55. Graz: Styria, 1974.

Wells, David F. "The Pope as Antichrist: The Substance of George Tyrrell's Polemic." *Harvard Theological Review* 65 (April 1972): 271-83.

————. "George Tyrrell: Precursor of Process Theology." *Scottish Journal of Theology* 26 (February 1973): 71-84.

Young, Ivan R. "Aspects of the Problem and Tragedy of De Lamennais and Fr. Tyrrell." *Theology* 34 (June 1937): 362-72.

Index

Abbott, J. H. R., chap. 6, n. 17
Acton. *See* Dalberg-Acton
Altkatholicizmus. *See* Old Catholics
Amette, Archbishop Léon Adolphe, 342–43
Amigo, Bishop Peter Emmanuel, 182–83, 345, chap. 5, n. 66; letter to Bourne, 359–60; reprisals after GT's death/burial, 356–61; & the Tyrrell case, 331–32, 337–38
Anglican orders question, 152–53
Angot des Rotours, Baron J., 196–97, chap. 6, n. 46
Apologetics, 74–76, chap. 3, n. 83; *See also* GT, apologetic for Roman Catholicism; Blondel (various subentries)
Aquaviva, Very Rev. Claudio, & Jesuitism, 137–38, 156, chap. 4, n. 78; and the Ratio Studiorum, chap. 5, n. 73
Arnold, Matthew, *Literature and Dogma*, chap. 3, n. 48; GT, influence on, chap. 3, nn. 48, 115
Augustine, 24, 198–99, 201, 204, 261, 262, chap. 6, n. 36, chap. 7, nn. 126, 152
d'Azeglio, Taparelli, 29

Balfour, Arthur James, 1st Earl of Balfour, 39–40, 73
Ball, Miss, 8
Ballard, Richard, epil. n. 123
Barry, William Francis, 307–9, chap. 4, n. 87, chap. 7, n. 183
Batiffol, Pierre, 275, 328, chap. 7, n. 89
Baum, Gregory, 75–76

Beatrice, Portinari, (Dante's inspiration), chap. 3, n. 122
Becker, Ernest, chap. 3, n. 49
Bell, James, 5
Benigni, Mgr. Umberto, 337, epil. n. 75
Benson, Charles W., 9–10, 12–13
Bergson, Henri, 133, 195–96, 210–12, 219, chap. 6, n. 80; on the intellect and conceptual knowledge, the inadequacy of, 202–3; on intuition, its role, 202–3; WORKS: *Essais sur les données immediates de la conscience*, 195, 202, 203, 209–12; *L'Évolution créatrice*, 201–2; *Matière et mémoire*, 194–95, 202–3
Bickell, Gustav, 53
van den Biesen, Christian, 307–8
Bishop, Edmund, advice to von Hügel in the modernist crisis, 359; comments on Tyrrell's *Autobiography and Life*, 113–14, chap. 4, n. 5; response to *Medievalism*, 341–42
Blondel, Maurice, 72–85, 92–93, 96, 121, 133, 188, 307–9, chap. 3, nn. 54, 74, 75, 77, 80; anti-intellectualism, accused of, chap. 3, nn. 77, 80; & apologetics, shift in, 75–77, chap. 3, nn. 74, 75, 77, 80; & Bremond 73–74, 308; Eucken, assessment of, chap. 3, nn. 91, 92; immanentism, accused of, 197, chap. 3, nn. 75, 80; & James, chap. 3, n. 115; & Leo XIII's letter to the French clergy, chap. 6, n. 39; & "the logic of action," 74–77, 197–98, chap. 3, n. 77;

& "method of immanence," 75-77, chap. 3, nn. 75, 80; Loisy's Christology, controversy with FvH on, 281-85, 307-10; & proofs for God, chap. 3, nn. 77, 80; Schleiermacher, relation to, chap. 3, n. 74; scholasticism, criticism of, chap. 3, n. 80; scholasticism, relation to, chap. 3, n. 77. LETTER TO: Bremond, chap. 3, n. 91. WORKS: "À propos de la certitude religieuse," 199, 204; L'Action, 74-75, 79, 133, 195-200, chap. 3, nn. 75, 77, 208; "Letter on Apologetics," 75-77, chap. 3, nn. 80, 87; "L'Illusion idéaliste," 83-84, chap. 3, n. 112, Matière et mémoire, chap. 6, n. 34

Blunt, Wilfrid Scawen, epil. n. 107

Boedder, Bernard, chap. 2, n. 23; & Blondel, 72-73

Bonomelli, Geremia, 327-28, epil. n. 40

Bouden, Henri-Marie, 23

Bourdon, Hilaire. See GT, pseudonyms

Bourne, Cardinal Francis, 358-60; approval, then disapproval of Lex Orandi, 240-42; refused GT Catholic burial, 356-57; & reprisals after GT's death/burial, 357-59. LETTER TO: Merry del Val, 359-60

Boutwood, Arthur (pseud. Hakluyt Egerton), 349-51

Bremond, Henri, 47, 60-61, 72-73, 79, 83-92, 99-102, 109, 110, 126, 138, 308, chap. 3, n. 48, chap. 4, n. 88, chap. 5, n. 10; & the modernist crisis, 276, chap. 3, n. 118, chap. 7, n. 159; & Newman, 72-73, 276; & the Society of Jesus, disaffection from, 84-92, 120-21, 169-70, 319-20, chap. 5, n. 10; & GT, 120-21, 169-70, 328, chap. 3, n. 120, chap. 5, nn. 10, 32; & GT's death/burial, 356-59; works on Newman, chap. 3, n. 70; suspension, 358

Bright's Disease. See GT, illness

Britten, James, 139, 279, chap. 7, n. 104. LETTER TO: W. P. Ward, 163

de Broglie, Jacques-Victor-Albert, chap. 6, n. 36

Brunetière, Ferdinand, 73-74, chap. 6, n. 36

Brunschvicg, Leon, chap. 3, n. 75

Buonaiuti, Ernesto, 345

Butler, Cuthbert, 307

Butler, Bishop Joseph, Analogy of Religion, 12, chap. 1, n. 25

Caird, Edward, chap. 3, n. 54, chap. 7, n. 118

Carr, W., 346

Casciola, Brizio, 264, 307-8, 310-11, chap. 7, n. 60

Castelein, André, 97

Catherine of Genoa, Saint, 80-82. See also FvH, & Catherine of Genoa, Saint. WORKS: The Mystical Element of Religion

Chamney, Arthur (GT's uncle), chap. 1, n. 38

Chamney, Mary (GT's mother), 4-6, 11, chap. 1, n. 38

Chamney, Robert (GT's uncle), 8

Champneys, Basil, 96-97, 134

Chapman, Ronald, chap. 1, nn. 2, 7

Charbonnel, Victor, chap. 4, n. 87

Charnley, Alexander, 101, 242, chap. 5, n. 20

Christie, Albany, 20-21

Civiltà Cattolica, 89-90, 101-3, chap. 2, n. 63

Clarke, Richard, 32, 100, chap. 1, n. 9

Clarke, Robert Francis, chap. 3, n. 163

Class, Gustav, chap. 7, n. 151

Clutton, Henry, 316, chap. 7, n. 31

Clutton, Katherine (Kitty), 182

Cock, Albert A., 351-52, epil. n. 121

Colley, Reginald, 148-51, 274-75; death, chap. 5, n. 32; letters to GT, 174, 177-79, 180-81; Oil and Wine affair, 167-83, chap. 5, n. 20

Comte, Auguste, 63

Corrispondenza Romana & the Tyrrell case, 334

Coupé, Charles, chap. 2, n. 23

Crehan, Joseph H., chap. 2, nn. 9, 10, 18, 19, 23, 30, chap. 3, n. 212, chap. 7, n. 159; on GT's excommunication, chap. 6, n. 95; on GT's insignificance, chap. 6, n. 95; & the Thurston papers, chap. 7, n. 164; & "What Killed George Tyrrell," chap. 6, nn. 95, 114, 117

Dalberg-Acton, John Emerich Edward, 1st Baron Acton, 160, 246, chap. 4, n. 142

Dalton, M. S., chap. 4, n. 127
Daly, Gabriel, 4
David. See Louis-David, Anne
Dell, Robert Edward, chap. 3, n. 183, chap. 4, n. 131; "A Liberal Catholic View of the Case of Dr. Mivart," 103–8; & the Mivart case 105–9; & the *Weekly Register*, 152, chap. 3, n. 183
Després, Isidore. See Loisy, pseudonyms of
Dessoulavy, Charles, epil. n. 126
Development of doctrine. See Newman, & development of doctrine; GT, on development of doctrine
Dilthey, Wilhelm, 274–75, chap. 6, n. 58
Dimnet, Ernest, 43, chap. 3, n. 2
Döllinger, Johann Joseph Ignaz von, 57, 160, chap. 4, n. 132
Dolling, Robert, & the *Oil and Wine* affair, 167–69, 180–81; & GT's conversion, 16–20. LETTER TO: GT, 181
Douais, Bishop Célestin, 259
Dreyfus, Alfred, 100
Duschesne, Louis, 53, 121, 307–8
Duhm, Bernhard, chap. 6, n. 58
Dunn, Mgr. Thomas, 278–79, chap. 7, n. 102

Eck, Samuel, 274
E.F.G. See GT, pseudonyms
Egerton, Hakluyt. See Boutwood, Arthur
Ehrhard, Albert, 79–80
Engels, Ernest. See GT, pseudonyms
Erastianism, 54–57, 58–59, 60–62, 68–70. See also GT, on Erastianism
Études, 87–88, GT, attack on, epil., n. 40
Eucken, Rudolf, 96, 133, 188, 195–96, 198–201, 306; Blondel's *L'Action*, espousal of, 79; & FvH, chap. 3, n. 96; influence of Lotze on, chap. 3, n. 104; influence of Schleiermacher on, chap. 3, n. 104; Newman, compared to, chap. 3, n. 91. LETTERS TO: FvH, 238, chap. 3, n. 96. WORKS: *Der Kampf um einen geistigen Lebensinhalt*, 200, 271; *Der Wahrheitsgehalt der Religion*, 79, 271, 273
Eyre, William, 26

Falckenberg, Richard, 261
Farm Street, 32, 37, 108, 111

Fawkes, Alfred, 264, 270, 284, 307, 342, 347–48
Fechner, Gustav, chap. 6, n. 80, chap. 7, n. 85
Fénelon de Salignac de la Mothe, François, 51–52
Ferrari, Archbishop Andrea Carlo, 339
Ferrata, Cardinal Domenico, & GT's secularization 328–29, 333–35. LETTER TO: Mercier, 329
Féval, Paul Henri Corentin, 20, 24, 91
Fichte, Johann Gottlieb, 73, 79, chap. 3, n. 74, chap. 6, n. 80
Firmin. See Loisy, pseudonyms of
Fitzer, Joseph, epil., n. 123
Fogazzaro, Antonio, chap. 7, n. 60
Fonsegrive, Georges, 109, chap. 4, n. 9, chap. 6, n. 46
Fontaine, Julien, 259, chap. 6, n. 87
de la Fourvière, Xavier, MDP, action against, 360; & GT, 331–34, 346, 355–56
Fracassini, Umberto, chap. 7, n. 60
Franon, Eugène, 236–37, 241, chap. 6, n. 136, chap. 7, n. 107
Franzelin, Cardinal Johannes Baptist, 100, 103, 288, chap. 3, n. 163

Gallarati-Scotti, Tommaso, 343, chap. 7, n. 60
Gallwey, Peter, 164, chap. 4, n. 161, chap. 6, n. 95
Gardner, Percy, 274, 290
le Gaudier, Antoine, 87
Gayraud, Hippolyte, 273–74, 275–76
Gelli, Sostene. See GT, pseudonyms
Genocchi, Giovanni, 307
Gentili, Antonio, chap. 4, n. 45
Gerard, John, 49, 101, 102, 105, 107, 111, 134, 139, 148–49, 173–74, chap. 3, nn. 175, 212; & the *Oil and Wine* affair, 179–81, chap. 5, n. 20. LETTERS TO: Colley, 173–74, 180–81, chap. 3, n. 212
Gibson, William, 49
Gildea, William, 178, chap. 5, n. 43
Goetz, Joseph W., chap. 2, n. 13
Goldstein, Julius, 237–38
Gore, Bishop Charles, 142, chap. 4, n. 88
Goût, Raoul, chap. 2, n. 6
Grandi, Giovanni, epil., n. 64
Grey, Stephen. See GT, pseudonyms
Gunkel, Hermann, 263, 288

Halifax. See Wood.
Harnack, Adolf von, 123, 127, 206, 250–53, 263–70, 288, 290, 307–8, 353–54
von Hartmann, Eduard, chap. 7, n. 85
Hatch, Edwin, 204–8, 290, chap. 4, n. 33
Healey, Charles J., chap. 6, n. 17
Hébert, Marcel, 239, 306, chap. 7, n. 176
Hedley, John Cuthbert, 359, epil., n. 41
Hegel, Georg Wilhelm Friedrich, 73, 79, 288, chap. 3, n. 74
Heron, Mrs., née Melinda Tyrrell (GT's aunt), 7
Holtzmann, Heinrich J., 237, 288–89, 307
Holy Office of the Inquisition, & Lamentabili, 332–33
Houtin, Albert, 194, 307, chap. 6, n. 36; La Question biblique, 254–56. LETTER TO: Loisy, 345–46
von Hügel, Baron Friedrich, Blondel, controversy with, 282–83, 307–8; & Bremond, 86–88; centrist position in the church, 51–52, 80, 121, 277–78, chap. 7, n. 75; & Catherine of Genoa, Saint, 80–83, chap. 4, n. 67; Christianity at the Cross-Roads, the publication of, 359; & Eucken, chap. 3, n. 96; formational influences on, 51–54; Gertrud (daughter), effect on, 79, 270, chap. 3, n. 87; & Halifax, chap. 4, n. 120; & Hébert, 239, chap. 7, n. 176; & historical criticism, 52–53, 80, 264–65, 282–85; & Huvelin, 52. INFLUENCES ON FvH: Blondel, 83, 198–99; Eucken, 79, 199–200; Fénelon, 51–52; Liberal Protestant tradition, 53, 79–80, 82–83, 269–70; Lotze, chap. 3, n. 104; Newman, 52; Nicholas of Cusa, chap. 6, n. 194; & the joint pastoral, 147–48, 162–64; & Loisy, 239, 269–70, 274–78, 282–85, 347, chap. 4, n. 101, chap. 7, nn. 89, 99, 176; Loisy, distinguishing himself from, 342–45, chap. 7, n. 75; & Loisy's L'Evangile et l'Église, condemnation of, 275–79; Loisy's opinion of, 80, 277, chap. 3, n. 101; & the Mivart case, 101–4, 107; & the mystical element of religion, 53, 72–73, 80–81, 87, 189, 192–93, chap. 3, n. 110, chap. 4, n. 67; & "New Tracts for New Times," chap. 7, n. 190; & orthodoxy, concern for, 269–70, 304–9, 341–45, chap. 3, n. 110, chap. 7, n. 75, &

MDP, 199–201, & the Rinnovamento group, 343–46, epil., n. 89; Schleiermacher's influence on, chap. 3, n. 104; & GT's death/burial, 354–60; GT, first meeting with, 43, 51; GT, friendship with, 43, 50–51, 53–54, 269–71, 306–8, 344–45, chap. 3, no. 110 (see also GT, FvH [various subentries]; INFLUENCE OF: FvH); GT, growing concern about, 238–39, 269–71, 303–9, 341, 346–49; & GT's Religion as a Factor of Life, 237–40; & GT's troubles over External Religion, 151; on ex-priests, 342–44, 347–48, chap. 6, n. 22, chap. 7, n. 75; on Lamentabili, 332–33, epil., n. 89; on Pascendi and GT's response, 335; on Roman authorities, 121, chap. 4, n. 28; on Schleiermacher, chap. 3, n. 104; on Scholasticism, 199; on science and progress, 103; on science and the spiritual life, 80–81; on the Society of Jesus, 87, 199; on GT's Medievalism, 341–42; on GT's writings, 96–97, 126, 162, 199, 303–9, 341–42, 348–49, chap. 3, n. 10; on ultramontanes, 121; on W. P. Ward, 103–4, 108–9; & modernists, differentiates himself from, 53, 269–70, 304, chap. 7, n. 75. LETTERS FROM: GT. See GT, LETTERS TO: FvH. LETTERS TO: Bishop, 356–57; Delehaye, chap. 3, n. 18; Eucken, chap. 3, n. 96; Lilley, 355–56; Loisy, chap. 7, n. 99; Newman, 52; Newsom, chap. 3, n. 10; MDP, 360, chap. 7, n. 193; Ryder, 52; Thorold, chap. 7, n. 75; GT, 51, 77–78, 79, 80–81, 83, 84–85, 86, 96, 107, 109, 115, 121, 126, 151, 162, 163–64, 192–93, 195, 199, 200–201, 205, 239, 241, 264–65, 269–70, 273, 277, 278, 282, 284–85, 304–8, 335, 341–48, chap. 3, nn. 110, 195, chap. 6, nn. 22, 58, chap. 7, n. 89; W. P. Ward, 103, 108–9, 147, 163. WORKS: "The Historical Method and the Documents of the Hexateuch," 80; The Mystical Element of Religion, 83, 314, 343, chap. 3, n. 110, chap. 4, n. 67; von Hügel, Gertrud, 77–79, 269
von Hummelauer, Franz, 328, epil., n. 40
Humphrey, William, 101, 164, chap. 4, n. 161

Hutton, Richard Holt, chap. 4, n. 46
Huvelin, Henri, 52, chap. 6, n. 46
Huxley, T. H., 39, 102, chap. 2, n. 32

Ignatius of Loyola, 102, 106, 137
Index of Forbidden Books, 100, 123, 237, 360, chap. 3, n. 2
Inge, William Ralph, 352–53, 354
International Scientific Congress for Catholics, 80, chap. 3, n. 101

James, William: & Blondel, chap. 3, n. 115; influence on GT, chap. 3, n. 115, chap. 6, n. 17; *The Will to Believe*, chap. 3, n. 115, chap. 6, n. 17
Janet, Pierre, 133, 209, chap. 4, n. 67
Jessop, Augustus, chap. 2, n. 49
"Joint Pastoral": 110, 132, 143–46, 152–65, chap. 3, n. 202; controversy in the press on, chap. 4, n. 128; English bishops' dissent over, chap. 4, n. 92; Germany, its notice in, chap. 4, n. 92; papal approbation of, 144–45, 153–56, chap. 4, n. 127
Joly, Henri, chap. 3, n. 87, chap. 4, n. 67
Jones, James, 21
Juliana of Norwich, 102, 191, 216–17, 222, chap. 3, n. 171
Jülicher, Adolf, 288

Kant, Immanuel, 73, 77, 193, 288, chap. 3, n. 74, chap. 6, n. 80
Kegan Paul, Charles, 83, chap. 3, n. 109, chap. 6, n. 128
Kelly, Anne, 11–12
Kerr, Henry, 21–22
Kidd, Benjamin, 257–58, chap. 3, n. 54; *Social Evolution*, 40–42
Kilfoyle, Daniel, chap. 3, n. 145
Kleutgen, Josef, 29
Knight, A. G., 168, chap. 5, n. 5

Laberthonnière, Lucien, 72–73, 77, 79–80, 83–85, 92–93, 96, 121, chap. 3, n. 54; "Le Dogmatisme moral," 73, 77, 83; "Le Problème religieux," 77, 79–80
Lacordaire, Jean Baptiste Henri, 24
Laing, Samuel, 42
de Lamennais, Félicité, 49–50
Lamentabili sane exitu, 332–33
Lamy, Albert, chap. 6, n. 90
Latitudinarianism. *See* Erastianism

Laubacher, James A., chap. 4, n. 25, chap. 5, n. 11
Lease, Gary, chap. 3, n. 56
Lebreton, Jules, 241
Leger, Augustin, 337–38, epil., n. 75
Lejeune, Paul, 193
Leo XIII, Pope, 57, 152; & Blondel's "Letter on Apologetics," 75; & the "Joint Pastoral," approbation of, 144–45, 154, 155; WORKS: *Ad Anglos*, chap. 2, nn. 51, 52, 63; *Aeterni Patris*, 25, 30, 32; *Gravissime Nos*, 30; Letter to the French clergy, chap. 6, n. 39
Lescher, Wilfrid, 164, chap. 4, n. 161
Le Sillon, epil., n. 75
Leslie, Shane, epil., n. 41
Liberal Catholicism, 144, 301–2. *See also* "Joint Pastoral"
Liberalism, 100–1, 164–65, chap. 4, n. 93. *See also* GT: & "amended Gallicanism"; liberalism & conservatism; & mediating liberalism; & W. P. Ward's liberalism. *See also* W. P. Ward: liberalism; WORKS: "Liberalism and Intransigeance"
Liberatore, Matteo, 29
Liddon, Henry P., 17
Lilley, Alfred Leslie, 31, 250–51, 303, 308, 339, chap. 2, n. 4
Loisy, Alfred Firmin, 80, 96, 121, 147–48, 188–89, 195–96, 204, 239, 249–52, 254, 259, 263–67, 272–79, 307–8, 311–12, chap. 3, n. 209, chap. 6, nn. 36, 38, chap. 7, n. 85; bibliography on, chap. 6, n. 36; character, development of, 121, chap. 3, n. 101; & Christology, 282–85; condemnation of, 147–48, 273–74, 274–79, 319–20, 342–44, chap. 4, n. 101, chap. 6, nn. 38, 39, epil., n. 1; & development of doctrine, 252–53, 265–66, 268–69; *Études évangéliques*, 264–65; excommunication of, 343–44; (his) faith, the question of, 254; Harnack, critique of, 250–53, 263–66; FvH, view of, 80, 276–77, chap. 3, n. 101; *L'Évangile et Église*, 263–66, 273–74; condemnation of, 275–79; pseudonyms of: Firmin, chap. 6, n. 36; Isidore Després, chap. 6, n. 39; significance of, 250–52, chap. 4, n. 102
Lonergan, Bernard, chap. 3, n. 83
Loome, Thomas Michael: FvH, the key

to understanding, 52; Loisy, answers to his view of, chap. 7, n. 20; Trevor, Meriol, refutation of, chap. 5, n. 28; Tyrrell bibliography, chap. 4, n. 12

Lotze, Rudolf Hermann, 79, 81, 83, chap. 6, n. 80, chap. 7, n. 85; *Microcosmus*, 83; *Outlines of the Philosophy of Religion*, 83; Schleiermacher's influence on, chap. 3, n. 104

Louis-David, Anne, chap. 4, n. 46

Lucas, Herbert, 274, 278, chap. 7, nn. 59, 99

Lynch, Miss, & GT's conversion, 15–16, chap. 1, n. 38

McClelland, Thomas, epil., n. 99

McTaggart, James, chap. 6, n. 148

M, Father (Thomas Rigby?), 24–25, 25–26, chap. 1, nn. 52, 53

Mabillon, Jean, 51–52

Magee, Archbishop William, 138, chap. 4, n. 80

Mallock, William Hurrell, 127, chap. 4, n. 48

Manning, Cardinal Henry Edward, 161, 162, chap. 3, n. 109

Maréchal, Joseph, chap. 3, n. 83

Martin, Very Rev. Luis (GT's superior general), 37, 99–101, 105, 106–7, 150–52, 172, 172–73, 173–74; & GT, correspondence with, on release from the Society of Jesus, 319–25; GT, criticism of, 172–73; & GT's dismissal from the Society of Jesus, 319–25, 327–28, epil., nn. 40, 41. LETTERS TO: Gerard, 101; GT, 100–1, 320–25

Mathew, Bishop Arnold Harris, chap. 4, n. 142, epil., n. 101

Maturin, William, 16–17

Mazzella, Cardinal Camillo, 37, chap. 2, n. 27

Mercier, Désiré Joseph, GT, attack on, 340–41; & GT's secularization 328–29, epil., n. 41

Merry del Val, Cardinal Rafael, 68–69, 100, chap. 3, n. 169, chap. 4, n. 93; *External Religion*, reaction to, 68–69; FvH, reprisals against, 184–85; the "Joint Pastoral," offer to author, 144–45; & the Mivart affair, 99–101; "modernists," campaign against, 68, 319, 358–60, epil., nn. 40, 129; Newman's

condemnation, suggestion of, chap. 3, n. 72; MDP, reprisals against, 358–60; research on, state of current, chap. 3, n. 56; & the Tyrrell case, 329–31, epil., nn. 41, 63, 64; GT, refusal of catholic burial for, epil., n. 129. LETTERS TO: French bishops, epil., n. 96; Vaughan, 99–101, 144–45, chap. 3, n. 169

Meyer, Rudolf, 107–8, 150, 172–73, chap. 3, n. 197, epil., n. 63. LETTERS TO: Colley, 172–73; Gerard, 107–8, chap. 3, n. 197

Meyers, Mrs., 5–7

Mignot, Bishop Eudoxe-Irénée, 80, 137–38, 273–74, 307–8, chap. 7, n. 89; "modernists," relationship with, 273–74, 277, chap. 3, n. 102, chap. 7, nn. 89, 99. LETTER TO: FvH, 80

Mivart, St. George Jackson, 99–105, 106–7, 120–21; "The Continuity of Catholicism," 99–100; "Happiness in Hell," 100–1; "Some Recent Catholic Apologists," 99–100

Montagnini, Carlo, 338, epil., n. 75

Montalembert, Charles Forbes, comte de, *Monks of the West*, 16

Monthly Register (formerly *Weekly Register*), chap. 4, n. 25

Moore, Sebastian, chap. 3, n. 49

Morris, John, 23–26

Moyes, James, 123–24, 178, 333

Münsterberg, Hugo, 188, 203–4, chap. 6, nn. 80, 83

Mumford, James, *The Catholic Scripturist*, 20–21

Murri, Romolo, 237

Neo-Platonism, 81–82

Neo-scholasticism & Italian Jesuits, 29; & the Jesuit-Dominican controversy, 29–31; & papal policy, 30

Newman, Cardinal John Henry, 109–11, 121, 127, 154–55, 255–56, chap. 3, nn. 70, 72, chap. 4, n. 15, chap. 7, n. 152; & apologetics, shift in, 73–74; condemnation, the question of, 123–24, chap. 3, n. 72, chap. 4, n. 33; development of doctrine, 95–96, 123–24, 127, 252–53, 311–12; & the French apologists, 73–74, chap. 3, n. 72; FvH, influence on, 52, 73; Loisy, influence

on, 276, chap. 3, n. 72; the "modernists," centrality to, chap. 3, nn, 72,
91; GT, influence on, 73, 91-93, chap.
2, n. 35, chap. 7, n. 152; ultramontanes, criticism of, chap. 4, n. 19; via
media, 110-11, chap. 7, n. 152; the
will in religious certitude, 73-74.
WORKS: An Essay on the Development of Christian Doctrine, 122-23,
chap. 4, n. 33; Apologia, 106, chap. 4,
n. 124; Grammar of Assent, 31, 52,
73-74; Loss and Gain, 52
Newsom, George Ernest, "George Tyrrell," memorial, chap. 3, n. 10
Nicholas of Cusa, 239, chap. 6, n. 194,
chap. 7, n. 47

O'Connor, Francis M., chap. 7, n. 69
Old Catholics, 346-49, chap. 4, n. 142
Ollé-Laprune, Léon, 73, chap. 6, nn. 36,
46
van Ortroy, François, chap. 3, n. 195

Palmieri, Dominico, 29
Pascendi dominici gregis, 335-40; reaction to, epil., n. 69
Patmore, Coventry, 133-34, chap. 4, n.
68
Paul, Charles Kegan. See Kegan Paul
Perraud, Cardinal Adolphus Louis, 75
Petre, Maude Dominica, 26-27, 69, 85-
86, 88, 92, 132-33, 136-39, 147, 163-64,
193-94, 199-201, 247, 259-60, 279-80,
303-4, 331-34, chap. 3, nn. 171, 175,
209, chap. 4, nn. 13, 31, chap. 6, n. 95;
Autobiography and Life, publication
of, 360; & Bremond, 85-86; "A Change
of Tactics," assessment of, chap. 2, n.
50; Christianity at the Cross-Roads,
collaborated with publishing, 359;
diary, 200, 206-9, 321-22; FvH's influence on, 199-200; independent thinker,
206-13, chap. 6, n. 95; oath against
modernism, refusal to take, 360; reprisals against, 358-60; GT, tutoring of,
on Eucken, 199-202; & GT's death/
burial, 354-60; GT's papers, executrix
of, 208-9, chap. 3, n. 99
Pius IX, Pope, anti-liberal campaign,
114, 145
Pius X, Pope, 68, anti-modernist campaign, 328-30, 338-40, 342-44, 345-46,

epil., nn. 40, 75; Bonomelli's position
on separation of church & state, at-
tack on, epil., n. 40; Loisy, condemna-
tion of, 319; oath against "modern-
ism," 360; "Pascendi dominici gregis,"
335-40; GT, opposed to, 37
Podmore, Frank, chap. 6, n. 113
Polanyi, Michael, chap. 2, n. 35
Pollard, William, chap. 7, n. 107
Pontifical Biblical Commission, 277
Porter, George, 21
Poulat, Émile, chap. 6, n. 36
Powell, Mrs. Jack Sweetman-Powell,
née Adela Petre, 356, 360
Pringle-Pattison, Andrew Seth, 94-95,
chap. 3, n. 142
Purbrick, Edward J., 24, chap. 1, n. 38

Quinzaine, 115
Quarterly Review, 103-4

Raffalovich, André, 42-43, 258-59, chap.
2, n. 46, chap. 5, n. 28
Rahner, Karl, 313-14, chap. 3, n. 83
Rampolla del Tindaro, Cardinal Mari-
ano, 273-74
Rassegna Nazionale, 150-51
Rashdall, Hastings, chap. 6, n. 146
Rathmines School, 9-10, 12
Ratio studiorum, 185-86, chap. 4, n. 78,
chap. 5, n. 73
Rawlinson, Gerald Christopher, 347
Récéjac, Jérôme-Édouard, chap. 6, n.
22; Fondements de la connaissance
mystique, 192-94, 203-4
Renan, Ernest, 309; influence on Loisy,
chap. 3, n. 72
Richard de la Vergne, Cardinal François
Marie: condemnation of Hébert's Sou-
venirs d'Assise, chap. 7, n. 176; con-
demnation of Loisy, 259, 273-76, 278-
79, chap. 4, n. 101
Rickaby, Joseph, 26, 156, chap. 1, n. 56
Rigby, Thomas, 25, 30-31, chap. 1, n. 51
Riley, Athelstan, epil., n. 113
Rinnovamento, 339, 343-44
Riotta, Francesco Paolo, 21
Ritschl, Albrecht, 263, chap. 6, n. 17
Rodriguez, Alfonso, & Jesuitism, 156-57,
chap. 4, n. 135
Rooke Ley, Frank, 120-21, 148, 152, 154,
161-62, chap. 4, n. 25

Roothaan, Joannes Philippus, 87
Rose, Vincent, 258–59, 328
des Rotours, Baron J. Angot, 196–97, chap. 6, n. 45
Rottmanner, Odilo, 307
Row, Charles Adolphus, 33
Ryder, Henry Ignatius Dudley, 52, 162

Sabatier, Auguste, 59, 194–95, chap. 6, n. 36; *The Vitality of Christian Dogmas*, 59
Sacred Congregation of the Index, 100, 360
Salimei, Francesco, 335
Sauer, Joseph, 238, 312–13. LETTERS TO: FvH, 238, 312–13
Schell, Herman, 53
Schelling, Friedrich Wilhelm Joseph von, 73, 79, chap. 3, n. 74
Schillebeeckx, Edward, 313–14
Schleiermacher, Friedrich Daniel Ernst, 73, chap. 3, nn. 62, 74, 77, 104
Schobel, Victor J., 162
Schoenl, William J., epil., n. 69
Scholasticism, 24–27, 73. *See also* GT, & neo-scholasticism; on scholasticism
Schopenhauer, Arthur, 288, chap. 6, n. 80, chap. 7, n. 85
Schweitzer, Albert, 353–54
Scott Holland, Henry, 142, chap. 4, n. 88
Scotti. *See* Gallarati-Scotti
Semeria, Giovanni, 96, 126, 151, 253–54, 281, 307–8, chap. 4, n. 46; FvH, friendship with, 151, chap. 3, n. 100; GT, friendship with, 126–27, 253–54
Semmelroth, Otto, 313
Seth. *See* Pringle-Pattison
Sheil, Denis, letter from Merry del Val, chap. 3, n. 56
Shelley, Norah, and family, 328, 330, 345, 348
Sidgreaves, Walter, 25
de Smedt, Charles, 52
Smith, Sydney, 101, 132–33, chap. 2, n. 52, chap. 4, nn. 71, 131; "Leo XIII's Letter to the English People," chap. 2, n. 52
Society of Jesus & the Thomist-Suarezian controversy, 29–31
Sohm, Rudolph, 279–81, 288, 290; *Kirchenrecht*, 279–81, 299
Sordi, Serafino, 29

Spalding, Bishop John, 150–51
Spencer, Herbert, 102
Spinoza, Baruch, 73, chap. 3, n. 74, chap. 6, n. 80
Stam, Johannes Jacobus, chap. 4, n. 13
Stanislaus, Mother Mary, 328, epil., n. 41
S.T.L. *See* GT, pseudonyms
Suárez, Francisco, 25, 29–30
Suarezianism, 29–31
Suarezian-Thomist controversy, 29–31
Sweetman-Powell, Mrs. Jack, née Adela Petre, 356, 360
Synthetic Society, 176–77, 303, chap. 3, n. 142

T, Father (Joseph Rickaby), 26, chap. 1, n. 56
Terrien, J. B., 38, chap. 2, n. 30
Tertullian, 97–98
Thomas Aquinas, 194–95, 198–99, 204, chap. 3, n. 110; *Summa contra gentiles*, 40; theism, 24, 29–31, 39–40
Thomas à Kempis, 204
Thomist-Suarezian controversy, 29–32, 36–40
Thorp, Joseph, chap. 2, n. 23
Thurston, Herbert, 32; 34–35, 38, 46, 101, 303, chap. 2, nn. 9, 30
Tinayre, Marcelle, 280
Touzard, Jules, 275–76, chap. 7, n. 87
Trevor, Meriol, chap. 5, n. 28
Troeltsch, Ernst, 79, 275, 282, 301, 307–8, chap. 6, n. 58, chap. 7, n. 47; *Die Absolutheit des Christentums*, 275, 301, chap. 7, nn. 47, 174
Turinaz, Bishop Charles-François, 255–56, chap. 7, n. 22
Turmel, Joseph, 274–75, 307–8, chap. 7, n. 79
Tyrrell, George, Altkatholicizmus (*see* GT, & Old Catholics); (his) "amended Gallicanism," 160–62, chap. 4, n. 143; & Anglicanism, rejection of, 346; & Anglo-Catholicism, 9–10, 13–14, 16–20, 50–51; & anonymous publications, 113–16; (his) apologetic for Roman Catholicism, 43–48, 68–72, 105–7, 116, 127–28, 134–36, 143–44, 182–87, 246–317; (his) apologetic for Roman Catholicism, the genesis of, 29, 48, 113, 115–16, 154, 205–7, 238, 249–87; (his) apologetic for Roman Catholicism,

Protestantizing influences on, 72–73, 87, 194, 205–7 (see also GT, influence of varii); (his) apologetic for Roman Catholicism, the shift in, 77, 92–93, 143; (his) apologetic for Roman Catholicism, the Thomistic element in, 78; (his) apologetics, seeds of, 12–13; apologia, 169, 171–72, 175, 180–82; & Augustinian will-tradition, 73, 78, 217; Autobiography and Life placed on the Index, 360; & biblical criticism, 34–35, 79, 80, 126, 131–32, 195–96, 248–66 (see also GT, on scripture; historical-biblical criticism, its effect on GT); & biblical interpretation, 42, 249–50 (see also GT, on scripture); birth, 4; & Blondel, defense of, 197–99; & Blondel's thought, 197 (see also GT, influence of: Blondel); & Bremond, 169, 321, 327–28, chap. 3, n. 120, chap. 7, n. 108; Bremond, his advice to, on leaving the Society of Jesus, chap. 5, n. 10; & Bright's Disease, 348–49, 354–55, chap. 6, nn. 95, 114, 117, 128; burial, 356–59, epil., n. 129; & the canonical problem of his release from the Society of Jesus, 320–24, 328–30, epil., n. 41; the celebret issue, 327–35, epil., n. 41; censors, reply to, 102–3; & (Roman) censors, 101, 102, 115, 167, 173, 179–81; & censorship, 214–15, chap. 6, n. 128; & (English) censorship, 101, 102, 167, 168–69, 171–82, 187, 238–40, chap. 5, n. 20; & censorship of correspondence, 329, 332–35, epil., nn. 62, 64; (his) Christian anthropology, 65–68; (his) Christology, 117–20, 124–25, 227, 232–33, 242–43, 261, 269, 281–82, 283–85, 352; & church authorities, conflict with, 97, 99–102, 104–8, 148–51, 167–82, 193 (see also GT, secularization effort; excommunication; Amigo; Bourne; Ferrata; Mercier, Merry del Val; Pius X); & the condemnation of Il Rinnovamento, 339; (his) conservatism and liberalism, 5–6, 155–56; conversion, 11–21; cyprus sojourn, 21; death, 354–56; death, premonition of, 208, 214; & Dell's apologia of Mivart, 105–7; democratic sympathies, 6, 8–9, 11, 17, 23, 160–62; departure from London,

132, 173–74, 176–77, chap. 3, n. 212; & Dolling, 16–20, 31; early amorality, 10; early conceptions of God, 6–7; early education, 6–7; early militant orthodoxy, 28, 34, 37–51, 106–7, 216, chap. 3, nn. 44, 109, 110; early scheming, 8, 17–18, 26; early unbelief, 10–11; early unorthodoxy, 8, 11–12; & ecclesiastical superiors, his relation to, 8, 23–24, 48, 85, 100–1, 121, 166–67, 255, 256, 328–30 (see also Amigo; Colley; Ferrata; Gerard; Martin; Merry del Val; Meyer; Pius X; Sykes; Vaughan); (his) ecclesiology 43–47, 63–68, 69–71, 117–20, 122–32, 156–64, 205–7, 229–34, 243–44, 247–49, 287–302; (his) elitism, 58–59, 62–63, 70, 90; & the English Province of the Society of Jesus, 87, 90–91, 105–6, 110, 121, 139, 173–74, 331, chap. 1, n. 38, chap. 3, nn. 158, 175, 212 (see also Colley; Gerard; Sykes); & esteem of others, 31, chap. 3, n. 158; Études, reply to attack by, epil., n. 40; & Evangelicalism, 6–12, chap. 1, n. 10; excommunication, 182–83, 246–47, 301–3, 336–38, 344, chap. 5, n. 66, chap. 6, n. 95; family, 4–5; & form criticism, 242–43; German, knowledge of, 34–35, 79, 111–12, 199–201, 253, chap. 2, n. 17, chap. 6, nn. 58, 80; & the German Idealist tradition, 73, 79, chap. 6, n. 80; & Grangegorman Church, 13–14, 16–17; Halifax, collaboration with, 152–56; & Hegelianism, chap. 3, n. 54; & historical criticism, 42, 77, 126, 131–32, 154, 163–64, 186, 227, 247–266; & historical method, 61, 72; historical-biblical criticism, effect on GT, 249–62, 263–67, 269–79; & homosexuality, 174–76, chap. 5, n. 28; FvH, collaboration on the Mystical Element of Religion with, 133, 331, chap. 3, n. 110; FvH, friendship with, 43, 50, 53, 87, 269–70, 343–44, 347–48 (see also FvH, [various subentries]; FvH, growing independence from, 239, 269–71, 341–55, 347–48; & G. von Hügel, chap. 3, n. 87; Ignatian principles, commitment to, 47, 87–91, 169–70, 176; illness, 172, 348–49, 354–55, chap. 5, nn. 23, 37, chap. 6, n. 94, chap. 7, n. 200; & the Index, 237, 360;

(his) immanentism, 194, 219–21, chap. 3, n. 114; imprudence, accused of, 173–74, chap. 3, n. 212; (his) inconsistencies, 29, 49; INFLUENCE OF: Acton, 246, chap. 4, n. 142; Arnold, 189–90, 351–52, chap. 3, nn. 48, 115; Bergson, 133, 202–3, 208–13, 219, 230, 266, 272, chap. 6, nn. 80, 99, 146, 155; Blondel, 74–79, 83–84, 89, 92–93, 127, 133, 188, 193–202, 243, 266, chap. 3, nn. 47, 76, 87, 115, 208, chap. 6, n. 141; Bremond, 60, 72, 85–92, 169–70; Caird, 260, 285; Dilthey, 266, chap. 6, n. 58; Döllinger, 246, chap. 4, n. 142; Duhm, 262, chap. 6, n. 58; Eucken, 79, 133, 188, 195, 200–2, 260–62, 266, 272, 274, chap. 3, n. 95; (his) father, 4–5; Fichte, 79, 262, 266, 268, chap. 3, n. 95, chap. 6, n. 80; Gunkel, 263, 266; Harnack, 245, 266, 267–68, 290, chap. 4, n. 33; Hatch, 205–7, 290, chap. 4, n. 33; Hegel, 201; Houtin, 254–56; FvH, 43, 51–52, 60, 72–87, 92, 96–97, 109–15, 121, 126, 133, 188–89, 192, 196–201, 203–4, 206, 239, 249, 260–75, 282–85, 306–7, 347–48, chap. 2, n. 17, chap. 3, n. 208, chap. 4, nn. 10, 46, 67, 117, chap. 6, nn. 58, 80; Hutton, chap. 4, n. 46; James, chap. 3, n. 115, chap. 6, n. 17; Janet, 133, 209–10, 212, chap. 4, n. 67, chap. 6, n. 113; Joly, chap. 4, n. 67; Juliana of Norwich, 191–92, 216–17, 222, chap. 3, n. 171; Kant, 194; Kegan Paul, chap. 3, n. 109; Laberthonnière, 77, 79–80, 194–97, 266, chap. 3, n. 115; Loisy, 126–27, 188, 193–96, 242–43, 249–54, 263–69, 273–78, 281–85, 311–12, chap. 3, n. 209, chap. 4, n. 46, chap. 6, n. 36, chap. 7, n. 61; Lotze, 79, 83, chap. 3, n. 95; Miss Lynch, 15, 20; (his) mother, 6, 11–12, 15, 18, 26–27 (see also Chamney, Mary; GT, & [his] parents); Münsterberg, 188, 203–4, chap. 6, n. 141; Newman, 14, 31, 73, 91–93, 351, chap. 2, n. 35, chap. 7, n. 152 (see also GT, & Newman; GT, Newman's theory of development, rejection of; Newman [various subentries]); non-rational factors, 23, 25; Patmore, chap. 4, n. 68; Rashdall, chap. 6, n. 146; Récéjac, 192–94, 204; Rigby, 30–31; Ritschl, 266, chap. 6, n.

17; A. Sabatier, 194, chap. 6, nn. 36, 169; Schopenhauer, chap. 6, n. 80; Schweitzer, epil., n. 123; Semeria, 253–54; Sohm, 279, 290, 299; Thomas Aquinas, 31, 189, 194–95, chap. 6, n. 54; Troeltsch, 79, 262, 275, 282, 301, chap. 6, n. 58, chap. 7, nn. 47, 174; J. Weiss, 263–68, 270–71, 311, epil., n. 123; Wernle, 253, 266, 290; Zamoyska, 204–6; INFLUENCES ON GT'S PHILOSOPHY OF RELIGION: 188–214, 219, 238; Arnold, 189–90; Bergson, 201–3, 208–13, 219, 238; Blondel, 188, 237; Eucken, 188; FvH, 188; Ignatius of Loyola, 192; Juliana of Norwich, 191–92; Loisy, 188; Münsterberg, 188, 237; Newman, 189; Récéjac, 192–93; Thomas Aquinas, 189; the "Joint Pastoral," its effect on GT, 164–65; "Joint Pastoral," reply to, 147–48, 152–65, chap. 3, n. 97, chap. 4, n. 131; (his) journal, 213, chap. 6, n. 114; & Kantianism, 39–40; & Kegan Paul, 83, chap. 3, n. 109, chap. 6, n. 128; & Lamennais, 49–50; Lamentabili, reply to, 332–33; last sacraments, his reception of, 354–56; last will and testament, 358; Leo XIII on Thomism, allied with, 37, 38, 46–47; (his) liberalism & conservatism, 5–6, 54–73, 92–93, 106, 109–11, 133, 268–69, 287–302, chap. 3, n. 48; Loisy, support of, 204, 319; Malta sojourn, 21–22, 27, 33; & Martin, 37, 99–101, 105, 106–8, 150–52 (see also Martin); Mass, importance of, 110; & mediating liberalism, 43–47, 48–113, 69–72, 102–4, 238 (see also GT & Ward, Wilfrid, [his] liberalism); & Merry del Val, 68–69, 100, 329–30; & the Mivart affair, 99–108, 120–21; "modernist" phase, 92–93, 99–100, 111–12, 319–60; modus vivendi, 88–91, 120–21; moral coercion, resentment of, 8–9, 26 (see also GT, secularization effort); Moses, identification with, 113–14, 116, 126, 193, 271, 302, 361, chap. 4, nn. 10, 15, 22; & (his) mother, 6, 11–12, 15, 18–19, 26–27; & mysticism 46, 82–83, 87, 192–93, 198, 229, 250, 260, 348, chap. 2, n. 57, chap. 3, n. 110; (his) natural inclinations, 3, 18; need to love & be loved, 11, 22; &

neo-scholasticism, 29–33, 78; & novelty, appeal of, 8–9, 13; & Newman, 14, 31, 52, 54, 62, 73, 127, 154, 155–56, 169, 189, 246, 268–69, 290, chap. 2, nn. 6, 35, chap. 4, n. 124, chap. 6, n. 46; Newman's theory of development, rejection of, 95, 243, 246, 283–84, 290–91, 311–12, chap. 3, n. 145; & the *Oil and Wine* affair, 167–82, 214–15; the *Oil and Wine* affair, its effect on GT, 181–82, chap. 5, n. 20, chap. 6, n. 128; & Old Catholics, 346–48, chap. 4, n. 142; on action, its primacy, 243–44, chap. 6, n. 59 (*see also* GT, influence of: Blondel); on Anglican orders, their validity, 43; on Anglicanism, 43, 50–51, 183, 186, 304, 346 (*see also* GT & Anglicanism, rejection of); on the apocalypticism of the gospels, 363–68, 292, 311; on the apostles, their role, 128–29; on apostolic succession, 299–300; on assent to noninfallible decisions, 157–58 (*see also* GT, on infallibility); on authority in the church, its limits, 147–48, 154–60, 290–96, 329–30, 332, 336–37, 351, epil., n. 63 (*see also* GT, on the church, its authority); on authority in religion, 37, 55–56, 62–71, 106–7, 153, 156–61, 298–99, chap. 2, n. 26; on authority in religion, abuse of, 55–56, 66–67, 94, 126–27, 153–65, 255, 290–91, 298, 301–2, 329–30, 332–33, 335–37, epil., n. 63; on bishops & synods, 128–29; on Blondel & Augustine, 198; on Blondel & Newman, 197; on Blondel & scholasticism, 78–80, 83–84, 197–99; on Calvinism, 45; on capitalism, 40–41; on character (*see* GT, on personality & freedom); on Christ, his human consciousness, 124–25, 281–83, 284–85, 294; on Christ, his humanity, 281–83, 284–85; on Christ, ipsissima verba, 130; on Christ, his teaching, 292–93; on Christianity as the ultimate religious expression, 301; on the church & scholasticism, 59–61, 70–71; on the church as essentially democratic, 299–300; on the church as sacrament of Christ's spirit, 313–15, 353; on church authorities, the role of, 243–44, 287–88, 325–26 (*see also* GT, on the church, its authority); on the church, the distinc-

tion between the existing and real, 88, (*see also*, GT, on the church, its nature; on the church of the future); on the church, its apostolicity, 353; on the church, its authority, 45, 85–89, 94–96, 118–20, 127–28, 153–65, 243–44, 255, 293–96, epil., n. 63 (*see also* GT, on authority in the church, its limits); on the church, its charismatic vs. institutional element, 293–94, 299–301, 304; on the church, its divinity, 294–95, 299–300; on the church, its doctrine, 70, 226–27, 243–45 (*see also* GT, on dogma [various subentries]); on the church, its mind, 63, 123–32, 147, 288, 298–99, chap. 4, n. 51; on the church, its nature, 230, 232–33, 294–96, 313–15; on the church, its politicism, 255–58, 295, 299–300, 312, chap. 7, n. 31; on the church, its reformability, 315; on the church, its relation to progress, 58–59, 70, 110, 118–20, 184–87, 257–58; on the church, its root evil, 184–87; on the church, its teaching office, 62, 94–96; on the church, its use of Latin, 60–61, 70–71; on the church of the future, 121–22, 312–15, 346–49; on church officials, 138–39, 150–51, 258–59, 275–76, 278–79, 297, 329–30, 333, 335–38; on church officials in Rome, 116–22, 150–52, 255–56, 274–76, 295, 338, 347; on church-state relations, 58–59, 70, chap. 2, n. 55; on the clergy-laity schism, 184–85; on clericalism, 184–86; on conceptualization, its anological nature, 221–22, 306 (*see also* GT, on dogma [various subentries]); on conformity in religion, 71–72, 118–20, 170–71, 298–99, 301–2; on conscience, 65–66, 67–68, 72, 223–24, 243–44; on the Counter-Reformation, 65–66; on Creed, 93–96, 235, 242–43, 258, 352, chap. 6, n. 173; on criticism, its necessity, 224; the Crucifixion, 65, 102; on the deposit of faith, 59–60, 63, 70–71, 92–93, 96, 116–20, 121, 123–32, 269, 296, 325–26; on development of doctrine/dogma, 59–64, 70, 92–93, 95–96, 116–20, 123–32, 161, 226–27, 243–45, 252–53, 268–69, 290–91, 311–12, chap. 3, nn. 41, 44, chap. 7, nn. 69, 70; on development of doctrine according to natural laws, 127–32, 290, 297–99; on development of doctrine and the role of the Holy Spirit, 119, 124–25, 127–32, 226–27, 242, 252–53, 269, 284, 296–99, 325–27, chap. 7, n. 126; on development of doctrine—the problem, 249–53, 263–69, 283–85, 290–91; on devotion, its relation to theology, 91–99, 124–25, 158–59, 243–44; on the discernment of Christ's spirit, 325–27; on the Divine Teacher fallacy, 155–61, 299; on doctrinal expression related to culture, 118–19; on doctrine (see GT, on dogma [& various subentries]); on dogma, 17–18, 194–95, 226–27; on dogma, its formulation, 61–62, 70–71, 95–96, 194–95, 225–27, 235, 242–43, 296–99, 350–52; on dogma, its limits, 55–56, 258; on dogma, its necessity, 54–55, 61–66, 70, 194–95, 258, 293; on dogma, its objective vs. symbolic character, 194–95, 233–34, 242–45, 296–98; on dogma, its ontology, 296–97; on dogma, its truth, 61–62, 70–71, 225–27, 242–43, 296–99, 351–52; on Ecclesia docens/ecclesia discens, 145–46, 154–61; on ecumenical councils, 128–29, 157; on ecumenism 152–54, 186–87, 237, 337; on Erastianism, 54–59, 61–62, 69–70; on the eschatological message of Jesus, 353 (see also Weiss, J.); on ethics, chap. 6, n. 23 (see also GT, on morality & religion, the difference between them; on morality, its role in religion); on the Eucharist, 232–33, 236; on experience in religion, 72, 350–52; on external religion, 13–15, 17–18, 63–69, 70–72, 81, 84–85, 229–34, 243–45, 314–15, 353; on faith & reason/understanding/science, 33–34, 38–43, 46–47, 54–55, 61–62, 67–68, 70, 92, 98–99, 233–36, 243–45, 259–60, 262, 266–67, 351–52; on faith, its nature, 154, 193–94; on feeling/affection/sentiment in religion, 15–16, 24, 97, 217–26, 242, 258, 293, 350–52, chap. 7, n. 172; on feeling as the mainspring of life, 218–19; on freedom & personality, 208–14, 266–67, 314, chap. 6, n. 155; on the future, its primacy, 258; on God & the Absolute, chap. 6, n. 146; on God's justice, 97–99; on God, the idea of, 24, 261, 306; on God's mercy, 97–99; on God's nature, 231, 351–52; on God's personality, 231, 306, chap. 6, n. 155; on God's personhood, 230, 351–52; on the gospels, their religious vs. historical value, 242–43, 292; on grace, 230–33; on habit & determinism vs. freedom, 207–13, 218–19, chap. 6, nn. 99, 155; on hell, 97–99; on historical-biblical criticism, 184, 288–91, 299–300; on the Holy Spirit & the church, 231, 244–45, 266–67, 293–99, 313–14, 325–27; on the Holy Spirit & development of doctrine, 118–19, 124–25, 127–32, 226–27, 242–43, 252–53, 268–69, 283–84, 296–99, 325–27, chap. 7, n. 126; on the Holy Spirit & revelation, 124–25, 127–32, 226–27, 242–43, 268–69, 283–84, 325–37, chap. 7, n. 126; on the Holy Spirit working outside the Catholic Church, 99; on ideas, their role in religion, 218–22, 222–27, 235, 243–45; on Ignatian discernment, 224–25; on the Incarnation, 64–66, 95, 281–82; on indefectibility, 66–67 (see also GT, on inerrancy; on infallibility); on individuality in religion, 222–27, 231–32, 233–34, 258, 298–99, 301–2, 327, chap. 7, n. 174; on inerrancy, 42, 287–91, 301–2, 304–5 (see also "GT: on infallibility"); on infallibility, 63, 126–30, 132, 153–64, 186–87, 289–91, 298, 329–30, 333, 336, 351; on inspiration of persons, 156–57, 159–61, 195–96, 225–27, 351; on inspiration of scripture, 42, 131–32, 195–96, 252, 288–89, chap. 7, n. 126; on institutional vs. charismatic element of the church, 293–95, 299–300, 304; on institutionalization of Christianity, 293–301 (see also GT, on religion as organization; on external religion; GT, WORKS: External Religion); on the integration of all faculties, 197–98, 200–205, 216–17, chap. 7, n. 172; on the intellect, its role, 189, 191–92, 217–36, 243–45; on intellectualism, 292–93, chap. 7, n. 172 (see also GT, on rationalism); on interiority in religion, 64–69, 71–72, 81, 84–85; on intuition, its role, 189, 202–3; on ipsissima verbi of Christ, 130; on Jesuit formation, 23, 87; on Jesuitism, 137–38, 154, 156, 159–60, 169, 179, 198,

255–56, epil., n. 63; on the Kingdom of God, 252–53, 257–58, 264–68, 292; on the Kingdom of God & the church, 265–66; on knowledge of God, 217–30, 235; on knowledge of God's will, 222–36; on knowledge of the real, 220–23, chap. 6, n. 146; on *La Civiltà Cattolica*, chap. 2, n. 63; on the laity, their role, 156–57, 184–85; on the laity-clergy schism, 184–85; on language in revelation & dogma, the inadequacy of, 62–63, 93–96, 350–52; on latitudinarianism (*see* GT, on Erastianism); on lex orandi, lex credendi, 94–96, 159, 243–45, 269; on Liberal Protestantism, 40, 43–44, 59–60, 82–83, 194, 244–45, 257, 263, 268–69, 296–97, 352–54, chap. 3, nn. 48, 54; on Loisy's condemnation, 319–20; on Loisy's theory of development of doctrine, 268–69, 311–12; on the Lord's Prayer, 326–27; on love of God, 24, 295–96, 301; on love of God & of neighbor, 189, 224, 227–36; on the mind of the church, 63, 121–32, 147, 288, 298–99, chap. 4, n. 51; on miracles, 281–82, 291–92, 299–300; on the "modernist's" position, 315, 335–37, 349, 352–54; on morality & religion, the difference between them, 226–29, 234–36, 266–67, 292–93, 351, 353, chap. 6, n. 58; on morality, its role in religion, 66–69, 72; on mystery, its necessity, 98–99, 262, 292, chap. 6, n. 58; on the natural & supernatural, 198, 210–11; on neo-Platonism, 81–82; on Newman's "condemnation," 155–56, chap. 3, n. 72; on obedience in religion, 65–68, 71–72, 297–302; on one, true religion, its possibility, 305–6; on orthodoxy & heterodoxy, 119–20, 161–62, 291–93, 301–2; on the papacy as office, 63, 71, 128–32; on papal absolutism, 155–60; on papal powers, their limits, 124, 128–32, 155–64, 290–92, 299–300, 325–26, 329–30; on *Pascendi*, 182–83, 335–39; on personality & freedom, 208–13, 266–67, 314, chap. 6, n. 155; on prayer, 67–69, 228–29, 245; on priests' involvement in social issues, chap. 2, n. 55; on progress, 118, 183–87, 256–58; on prophets, their role, 128, 135, 227, 229–30, 257, 302, chap.

4, n. 10; on "protectionism" as the root evil in the church, 184–87; on Protestantism (*see* GT, Protestantism, critique of); on the psychology of religion, 94–96, 208–13, 218–21, 235, chap. 3, n. 108; on rationalism, 54–55, 61–64, 82–83, 94–95, 97–99, 234–35, 250, 277–78, 292–93, 305–6, chap. 6, n. 169; on *reductio ad absurdum*, 121–22, 123, 139–40; on the relation of theology to devotion, 91–99, 124–25, 159, 243–44; on religion as organization, 229–36 (*see also* GT, on external religion; WORKS: *External Religion*); on religion as a social phenomenon, 224–26, 228, 229–36; on religion, its essence, 218–21, 223–26, 351–52, 353–54; on religion, its foundation, 217; on the Resurrection, 65; on revelation, 65, 67–68, 93–96, 116–20, 122–32, 158, 226–27, 234–35, 258, 350–52, chap. 3, n. 41, epil., n. 121; on revelation & the Holy Spirit, 124–25, 127–32, 226–27, 242–43, 269, 284, 325–27, chap. 7, n. 126; on religion, its role, 227–29 (*see also* GT, WORKS: *Religion as a Factor of Life*, exposition); on religion & morality's role, 66–69, 72; on revelation & theology, 93–96, 116–20 (*see also* GT, WORKS: "The Relation of Theology to Devotion"); on the Roman Catholic Church, its reformability, 315; on Roman Catholicism as the highest expression of Christianity, 301; on Roman Catholicism, the catholicity of, 55, 58–59, 70, 299–300, 304, 314–15; on Roman centralization, 102; on the Roman system, 127, 139–40, 183–87 (*see also* GT, on vaticanism); on Rome's hostility to biblical criticism, 252; on Rome's theologians, 123, 139–40, 148, 154, 157, 198, 255–56, 290–96, 312, 336–37; on the rule of faith, 287–89, 291, chap. 7, nn. 126, 190; on sacraments, 65–66, 230, 314; on saints as teachers in the church, 96, 229–30, 242–43, 300, 312, 326; on scholasticism, 25–26, 31–35, 60–62, 139–40, 197–98, 255–56, 258, 291; on science & religion 227, 234–36, (*see also* GT, on faith & reason); on scripture, 63–64, 67–68, 128–32, 198; on scripture & sacraments, 205–7, 232–33; on scripture, its literal interpretation, 119; on the seminary system, 23, 32–33, 38, 80, 142, 156, 170, 175–76, 184–86; on the *sense* of God, 82; on the sheep & shepherd metaphor, 154–61; on the Society of Jesus (*see* GT, & the Society of Jesus [various subentries]); on the spirit of Christ, 325–27, 351; on the spiritual life, its nature, 222–23; on the subconscious, 211–13, chap. 6, n. 113; on supernaturalism, 198; on symbols, 219–22, 242–43, 250, 296; on the teaching office of the church, 62, 94–96; on temporary religious orders, 88, 137; on the theologians, their role, 243–44; on theological language, its abuse, 94–95; on theology, its relation to devotion, 91–99, 124–25, 159, 243–44; on theology, its role, 91–96, 243–44; on Thomism vs. Suarezianism, 24–26, 30–38, 46–47, 78; on tradition, 54, 131–32; on traditional apologetics, 139–40, 275–76, 277–78, 287–96, 350–52; on truth & its test, 220–22, 225–26, 243–45; on ultramontanes, 101, 103, 116–22, 145–46, 147–48, 248–49, 305–6, 309; on the understanding, its role (*see* GT, on the intellect, its role); on the validity of non-Catholic religions, 301, 305–6; on Vaticanism, 13, 16–17, 126–27 (*see also* GT, on Romanism); on the virgin birth, its Christological interpretation, 242–43; on the will in religion, 67–68, 71–72, 188–92, 217–19, 221–36, 266–67; on the "wish to believe," chap. 3, n. 24; on women in the church, 185; on Word & Sacrament, 230, 232–33, 236; ordination, 27; & (his) parents, 4–5, chap. 1, n. 5 (*see also* M. Chamney; W. H. Tyrrell); peers, relation to, 8–9, 25, chap. 1, n. 54; (his) personality, 3–4, 5–6, 9–12, 20, 22, 48–49, 110, 114–15, 121–22, 166, 169, 189, 193–94, chap. 3, n. 212, chap. 6, n. 117; (his) personality, early influences on, 4–18, 20, 22; & MDP, friendship with, 193, 207, 259, 321, 331, chap. 3, n. 209, chap. 6, n. 95 (*see also* GT, letters to MDP; MDP [various subentries]); (his) philosophy of religion, 188, 196–99, 216–36, 243–45; (his) philosophy of religion, genesis of, 29, 133, 143, 154, 188,

217; & Pius X, 37 (*see also* Pius X); the poor, his love for, 17, 27; (his) popularity, 36, 177; (his) pragmatism, 233–36; & process theology, chap. 6, n. 157; professor of philosophy at Stonyhurst, 36–47, 85, chap. 2, n. 23 (*see also* GT, Stonyhurst, removal from); & a progressive party, chap. 7, n. 190; Protestantism, his accommodation to, 43–48, 184, 194–95; Protestantism, his critique of, 28–29, 41–48, 58–60, 62–66, 71, 82–83, 183–84, 293–94, 297, 304, chap. 2, nn. 55, 57, chap. 3, n. 44; & provincial superiors (*see* Colley; Gerard; Sykes); & pseudonymous publication, 181, 182, 213–15, 237–40, 246–47, 280–81, 302–3, chap. 4, nn. 7, 8, 12, 131; (his) rationalism, 13–14, 15–16, 17–18, 20–21, 24–26, 234–35, chap. 6, n. 169; at Richmond-in-Swaledale, 108, 111–13, 131–32, 170, 195, chap. 3, n. 100, chap. 4, n. 63, chap. 5, n. 14; & the Roman Catholic Church (*see* GT, on the church [various subentries]; on the Roman Catholic Church; on Roman Catholicism); the Roman Catholic Church, commitment to, 87, 102, 121, 183–84, 346–49, 354, 358; Roman Catholicism, conversion to, 11–21; Roman Catholicism, introduction to, 11–12; Roman officials, his relation to, 37, 46–47, 101–2, 115, 149, chap. 3, nn. 158, 195 (*see also* GT, church authorities, conflict with; on church officials in Rome; on Vaticanism); & Rudolf Meyer, 107, 150, 172–73, chap. 3, n. 197, epil., n. 63; & St. Beuno's Essay Society, 32; & St. Beuno's faculty, 46–47; St. Bueno's, studies at, 27, 31–36; at St. Helen's mission, 27; the scriptorium at Farm Street, assignment to & removal from, 37, 47, 88, 104–12 (*see also* GT, departure from London); secularization effort, 322–24, 327–35, epil., n. 41; self-disregard, 20, 26, 35, 88, 91, 113–14, 121–22, 138, 142–43, 170–71, 193, 246–47, 257, 271; self-portrait, 4–6, 20, 35, 50, 113–14; & Semeria, chap. 3, n. 100 (*see also* Semeria, Giovanni); sham, hatred of, 10, 14–21, 246–47; & the Shelley family, 328, 331, 346, 348; the Society of Jesus, his changing relationship with, 107-8, 115-16, 120-21, 132-33, 136-43, 148-51, 169-82, 279-80, 319-25; the Society of Jesus, conflict with authorities of, 8, 22-23, 36, 96-97, 99-108, 148-51, 166-82, 193 ((see also GT & the Society of Jesus [various subentries]; & Bourne; & Colley; & Gerard; & Martin; & Merry del Val; & Sykes; & Vaughan); the Society of Jesus, disaffection from, 25, 36, 87-92, 110, 246-47 (see also GT, the Oil and Wine affair); the Society of Jesus, dismissal from, 148-51, 246-47, 302-3, 319-25, 327-28, chap. 4, n. 117, epil., nn. 40, 41; Society of Jesus, his distinction between the existing and ideal, 88, 91; the Society of Jesus, earliest impressions of, 18-19, 20-23; the Society of Jesus, his judgment on, 20-23, 26, 36, 85-91, 96-97, 136-43, 148-49, 156, 169-71, 185-86, 320-22, chap. 5, n. 10, chap. 6, n. 95; the Society of Jesus, his vocation to, 13-15, 18-24; & the Spiritual Exercises of St. Ignatius, 87-88, 102, 136-37; Stonyhurst, removal from, 36-38, 47, 85-86; Stonyhurst, studies at, 30-31; at Storrington, 331-32, 335, 339, 346, 354-55, epil., n. 51; & Suarezianism, 25, 36-38; & (his) superior general (see GT, & Martin; see also Martin); & the Synthetic Society, 176-77, chap. 7, n. 176; Thomas Aquinas, his knowledge of, chap. 3, n. 110; Thomism, critique of, 24-26, 36-40, chap. 2, n. 25; & Thurston, 32, 34-35, 303, chap. 7, n. 164; & truth, passion for, 4; & Louy Tyrrell, 6, 18-19, chap. 1, n. 38 (see also Tyrrell, Louisa); & Willie Tyrrell, 4-5, 7-16 (see also Tyrrell, William); vagabond existence, 5; Vatican II, his principles reborn in, 360; & Vaughan, 37, 100, 149, 174, chap. 3, nn. 169, 212, chap. 6, n. 128; & W. P. Ward, friendship with, 56, 103-4, chap. 3, n. 207; & W. P. Ward's liberalism, 44, 47, 54-57, 64-65, 69-72, 104, 109-11; W. P. Ward's liberalism, departure from, 60-73, 104-5, 109-11, 238, 243-45, 246, 255, 268-69, 273-74, chap. 4, n. 146; writer for the Month, 49-64, 85, 101-1. LETTERS FROM: FvH. See FvH, LETTERS TO: GT. LETTERS TO: Abbott, chap. 6, n. 17; Bremond, 47, 82-83, 84, 86-91, 99-100, 101-2, 111, 120, 126, 138, 170, 172, 177, 179, 183, 195, 196, 213-14, 215, 216, 253, 255, 256, 260, 261, 264, 272-73, 276, 280, 303, chap. 3, n. 100, chap. 4, n. 46, chap. 6, nn. 58, 128; Carr, 346; Casciola, 310, 311-12, chap. 7, n. 190; H. Clutton, 316, chap. 7, n. 31; Colley, 150, 150-51, 167-68, 170-71, 171-72, 174-77, 180-81, 181-82; Dimnet, 43; Ferrata, 334; de la Fourvière, 333; Gerard, 139-43, chap. 3, n. 212; Goût, chap. 2, n. 6; Halifax, 153, 153-54, 241, chap. 4, n. 92; Houtin, epil., n. 40; FvH, 61, 78, 80, 82, 83, 87, 101, 102, 115, 120-21, 123, 126, 127, 137-38, 145, 151, 155, 156, 162, 164, 167, 171, 172, 178, 182, 188, 194-95, 195, 195-96, 196-97, 199, 200, 201, 203-4, 204, 205, 208-9, 238-39, 239, 239-40, 240, 250, 251, 252-53, 253, 254, 256, 259, 260, 262, 264, 268, 271, 274, 274-75, 275-76, 276, 278-79, 283-84, 305, 305-6, 306, 309-10, 310, 317, 321, 342, 344, 345, 347, 349, chap. 2, n. 63, chap. 4, nn. 8, 22, 31, 93, chap. 5, n. 20 chap. 6, nn. 23, 58, chap. 7, nn. 57, 59, epil., n. 111; Lilley, 31, 240, 241, 303, 308, 309, chap. 7, nn. 75, 190; Loisy, 249-50, 251, 265, 276, 310; McClelland, 346; Martin, 151, 320, 321, 322-23, 323, 324; Martin, the "great letter," 321-22, chap. 2, n. 6; Mathew, 346; Mazzella, 37; Merry del Val, 329; Meyer, 172; MDP, 49, 69, 88, 113, 132, 136, 136-37, 139, 147, 148-49, 149-50, 150, 163-64, 169, 172, 178, 181, 193, 194, 196, 200-1, 201, 203, 203-4, 204, 205, 206, 206-7, 208, 208-9, 209, 210, 211-12, 213, 214, 215, 253, 255, 257, 259, 262, 272, 276, 279-80, 285, 303-4, 327, 327-28, 331, 331-32, 333, 344, 345, chap. 2, n. 8, chap. 3, nn. 109, 115, chap. 4, nn. 117, 155, chap. 5, nn. 10, 32, chap. 6, nn. 23, 95, epil., n. 40; Raffalovich, 42-43, 196, 208; Rooke Ley, 120, 147-48, 152, 154, 161-62; Semeria, 126, 151, 281-82; Sykes, 321, 324; Thurston, 32, 34-35, 35, 38, 46, chap. 2, nn. 9, 28; Vaughan, 182; Waller, 115, 116, 116-17, 214-15, 215,

216, 238, 240, 249, 273, 280, 281, 303, chap. 6, n. 128; W. P. Ward, 56, 96, 101, 102, 103, 105, 107, 109–10, 111, 124–25, 126, 130, 131, 132, 155, 164, chap. 6, n. 169, epil., n. 63; Williams (Dora), 331; WORKS: "An Apostle of Naturalism," 41–42; "Aquinas Resuscitatus," 32; "Authority and Evolution, the Life of Catholic Dogma," 62–64, chap. 3, n. 47; Autobiography, 26–27, 114, 169, 360, chap. 5, n. 11; "Beati Excommunicati," 320–21, 337, epil., n. 7; "Catholicism Re-stated," chap. 5, n. 66 (see also The Church and the Future); "A Change of Tactics," 43–47, 49, 54, 69, chap. 2, n. 50; Christianity at the Cross-Roads, 313, 319, 349, 352–54, 360, chap. 7, n. 190; The Church and the Future ("Bourdon"), 92, 164–65, 182, 187, 204, 239, 246–317 (FvH's appraisal of, 304–8; its historical context and development, 246–87; its relation to Loisy, 273–74, 275–81; its relation to Religion as a Factor of Life, 239, 248; GT's attitude at time of composition of, 246–49, 272–79, chap. 3, n. 143; see also: GT, effect of historical-biblical criticism on); "The Church and Scholasticism," 60–61; "The Church and Its Future," 313–15; The Civilizing of the Matafanus, 110–11, 114–22, 124–25, 129–30, 164, 214; "The Clergy and the Social Problem," chap. 2, n. 55; "The Condemnation of Newman," chap. 3, n. 72; "The Contents of a Pre-Adamite Skull," 34; "Coventry Patmore," chap. 4, nn. 68, 70; "Cramming and Other Causes of Mental Dyspepsia," 33; "Da Dio o dagli uomini?" chap. 3, n. 10; "Divine Fecundity," 349; "Ecclesiastical Development," chap. 3, n. 44; "Ethical Preludes," chap. 6, n. 23 (see also Religion as a Factor of Life); External Religion, 64–69, 71–72, 81, 84–85, 150–51, 197, 199, chap. 3, n. 54 (influence of Blondel on, 83–85, 199; GT's troubles over, 150–51); The Faith of the Millions, 42–43, 44, 49, 92–93, 178, chap. 4, n. 117, chap. 5, n. 13; "From Heaven, or of Men?" chap. 3, n. 10; Hard Sayings, 43, 83, chap. 3, n. 54; "The Hypostatic Union," 38; "Jesuits and Their Critics," 169, chap. 5, n. 11; "Keeping Up Appearances," 50; "L'Affair Loisy," 319; Letter to the Church Times, 333; Letter to Ferrata, 329; Letter to the Giornale d' Italia (on Pascendi), 335–37; letter to the Pilot (on the "Joint Pastoral") 155–56; A Letter to a University Professor (see A Much-Abused Letter); letters to the Daily Chronicle (on his ecclesiastical status), 325, 334; letters on the "Joint Pastoral," chap. 4, n. 131; Lex Credendi, 92, 325–27; Lex Orandi, 92, 237–45, 325 (its relation to Religion as a Factor of Life, 238–40; its significance in GT's theological development, 243–45; reactions to, 241–42; receives imprimatur, 240–41); "Lex Orandi, Lex Credendi" (see "The Relation of Theology to Devotion"); "'Liberal' Catholicism," 58–59; "A Life of de Lamennais," 49–50; "The Limitations of Newman," 243; "Lord Halifax Demurs," 160–61; "M. Blondel's Dilemma," 197–99; Medievalism, 122, 319, 340–42; "The Mind of the Church," 123, 127–32, 141, 147, 157; "A More Excellent Way" (see "A Change of Tactics"); "Mr. Balfour and the Foundations of Belief," 39–40; A Much-Abused Letter, 302–3, chap. 7, nn. 159, 160 (& GT's dismissal from the Society of Jesus & excommunication, 302–3, 322–25, 330, epil., n. 64; its French translation by Bremond, chap. 7, n. 159); "Mysteries a Necessity of Life," 238, 262, chap. 6, n. 58; "The New Sociology," 40–41; "Non Tali Auxilio," 122–23, 127–32; Nova et Vetera, 17, 43, chap. 1, n. 34; Oil and Wine, 115, 123, 167–82, 194, 214–15, 261, chap. 5, n. 3; Oxford Conferences, first set (see External Religion); Oxford Conferences, second set (see Religion as a Factor of Life); "The Oxford School and Modern Religious Thought," 56; "Per la sincerità" (see "A Plea for Candour"); "A Perverted Devotion," 47, 90–91, 97–108, 110, 126, 152, chap. 2, n. 63, chap. 3, n. 171; "A Plea for Candour," 333, chap. 7, n. 190; "Plea for Greater Sincerity" (see "A Plea for Candour"); "The Pope and Modernism," 335–37; preface to *Mother Juliani*, 215, 216–17, 222, 233, chap. 6, n. 128; preface to *Saint Francis de Sales*, 190–91, chap. 6, n. 8; *The Programme of Modernism*, 338–39; "The Prospects of Reunion," 50–51, 54, 152, chap. 3, n. 10; *Psicologia della religioni*, 237; "Rationalism in Religion," 61–62; "Reflections on Catholicism," chap. 4, n. 81; "The Relation of Theology to Devotion," 90–97, 99, 122, 178–79, 224, chap. 3, n. 10, chap. 6, n. 58 (influenced by Juliana of Norwich, chap. 3, n. 171; its foundational place in GT's theology, 92–93; its similarity to Dilthey's thought, chap. 6, n. 58); "Religion and Ethics," 267–68; *Religion as a Factor of Life* ("Engels"), 39, 92, 188–241, 258, 260, 267, chap. 3, n. 108 (exposition of, 216–36; influenced by Bergson, 202–3, 208–14, 219; influenced by Blondel, 199, 220–22, 224, 237; influenced by Münsterberg, 237; influenced by Zamoyska, 214; its composition, 208–16; its publication, 214–16; its underlying focus on ethics, 206–7, 214, 218, 221, 232–36; reactions to, 236–39); "Revelation as Experience," 349–52; review of *Principles of Western Civilization* by Benjamin Kidd, 256–58; "Rome's Opportunity," 179, 182–87; "Round *versus* Russell," 50; "Sabatier on the Vitality of Dogmas," 59–60; "Semper Eadem," 111, 243; "Socialism and Catholicism," 50; "A Symposium on Immortality," 33–34; "The 'Tabula Aurea' of Peter de Bergamo," 38; *The Testament of Ignatius Loyola*, introduction, epilogue, and notes to, chap. 3, n. 171; *Through Scylla and Charybdis*, 92, 331–32, 349–50; "Tracts for the Million," 134–36, 148, chap. 3, n. 31, chap. 4, n. 70; "The True and the False Mysticism," chap. 2, n. 57; "Un Noviciat De Vie Chretienne Dans Le Monde," 204–6; "What Is Mysticism?" chap. 3, n. 87; "Who Are the Reactionaries?" 105–7, 126; "Wiseman: His Aims and Methods," 54–55

Tyrrell, Lizza (GT's cousin), 5
Tyrrell, Louisa (GT's older sister, Louy),

4–5, 5, 18–19, chap. 1, n. 38
Tyrrell, Melinda (GT's aunt, Mrs. Heron), 7
Tyrrell, William (GT's older brother, Willie), 4–5; influence on GT, 7–16; relation to mother, 10–11
Tyrrell, William George, 1st Baron Tyrrell (GT's cousin), 331, 355–56, 357–58, epil., n. 51
Tyrrell, William Henry (GT's father), 4–5
Tyrrell's life, historian's view of, 3–4
Tyrrell's writings, the nature of, 113–14, 247–49

Ultramontanism, 101–2, 145–46, 164–65, chap. 4, n. 19. *See also* GT, on ultramontanes
Urquhart, Hattie, 331

Vatican I, 57, 127, 145–46, 147–48, 156, 157, 158–59, 160–61, 163–65, chap. 4, n. 15
Vatican II, chap. 3, n. 83
Vaughan, Cardinal Herbert Alfred, 37, 100–1, 103, 149–50, 162, 174, 240, 279, 304, chap. 3, nn. 169, 212, chap. 4, n. 25, chap. 7, n. 167; & the "Joint Pastoral," 144–46, 162–63; & the Mivart case, 99–101, 103, 144–45, chap. 3, n. 163, chap. 4, n. 90; & the *Oil and Wine* affair, 177–83, 214–15. LETTERS TO: Colley, 179–80; Mivart, 100; GT, 179–80
Vidler, Alexander Roper, chap. 7, n. 20
Vigilance committees, 345
Vincent of Lerins, chap. 7, nn. 126, 190. *See also* GT, rule of faith
Volkelt, Johannes, 274
Voltaire, 288

Waller, Alfred Rayney, 115, 116–17, chap. 4, n. 22. *See also* GT, letters to Waller
Ward, James Hull, 142, chap. 4, n. 88
Ward, Maisie, 110
Ward, Wilfrid P., 35, 44, 47, 54–57, 80, 100–12, 123–26, 131–32, 147, 162–64, 246, 255, chap. 2, n. 51, chap. 4, n. 155; authority in the church, 56–57, 106–8, 108–10, 154–55; Bremond's *Mystery of Newman*, opinion of, chap. 3, n. 70; development of dogma, 56–57;

liberalism, 54–57, 92–93, 106–8, 108–10; FvH, relation to, 103–4, 108–9; & the "Joint Pastoral," 162–64; & the Mivart affair, 99–108, 108–10, 110–11; & Newman, 56, 154–55; on Newman, Blondel, & GT, chap. 3, n. 73; Protestantism, critique of, 56–57; LETTERS TO: FvH, 103–4; Josephine Ward, 177, chap. 5, n. 37. WORKS: *Cardinal Wiseman*, 54–57, 103–4; "Doctores Ecclesiae," 162–64, chap. 4, n. 155; "Liberalism and Intransigeance," 106–8, 108–10, 110–12; "New Wine in Old Bottles," 56–57; *Problems and Persons*, 110–11; "The Rigidity of Rome," 43–44, 47, chap. 2, nn. 49, 59; "Unchanging Dogma and Changeful Man," chap. 3, n. 149. *See also* GT, & W. P. Ward (several subentries)

Ward, William George ("Ideal"), 52, 56

Weaver, Mary Jo, chap. 3, n. 207

Weekly Register (later *Monthly Register*), chap. 4, n. 25

Weiss, Bernhard, 263

Weiss, Johannes, 263–66, 288–89, 311–12, 353–54; *Die Predigt Jesu vom Reiche Gottes*, 263–65, 311

Weiss, C. H., chap. 6, n. 80

Weizsäcker, Carl, 288

Wells, David F., chap. 6, n. 157

Wernle, Paul, 253–54, 290

West, Austin, epil., n. 40

White, José-Marie Blanco, chap. 4, n. 81

Wilberforce, Samuel, 17

Williams, Dora, 331, chap. 5, n. 63

Williams, William John (Willy), 182, 307–8, chap. 5, n. 63

Wiseman, Cardinal Nicholas, 54–56, chap. 7, n. 152

Wobbermin, Georg, 262, chap. 7, n. 47

Wood, Sir Charles Lindley, 4th Baronet and 2nd Viscount Halifax, 152–56, 160–64, chap. 4, n. 120

Wundt, Wilhelm, chap. 6, n. 80

Zamoyska, Countess Hedwig, 204–6; & Blondel, 205; & Ollé-Laprune, 205; *Sur le travail*, 204–5

A Note on the Type

The text of this book was set by phototypesetting
in Caledonia, designed by W. A. Dwiggins, the
eminent American graphic artist. A modern typeface
fashioned after the old Scotch Roman with excellent
weight of line making it one of the most readable
types of this decade. It has that simple, hard
working feet-on-the-ground quality that has made it
so popular today.

This book was composed by Techna Type, Inc.

Printed and bound by The Maple Press Company,
of York, Pennsylvania.

This edition was first published in August 1981.

Designed by Howard N. King